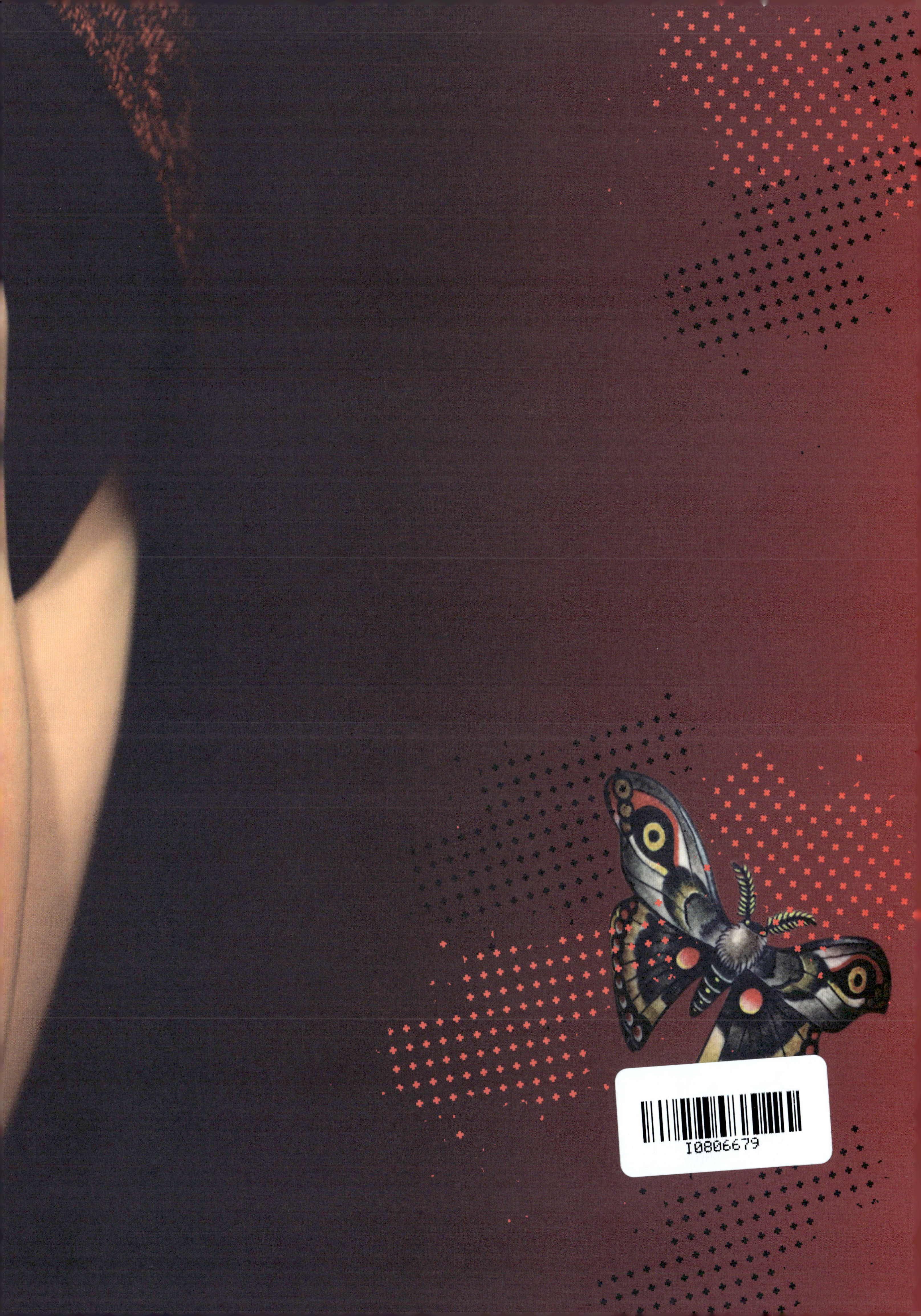

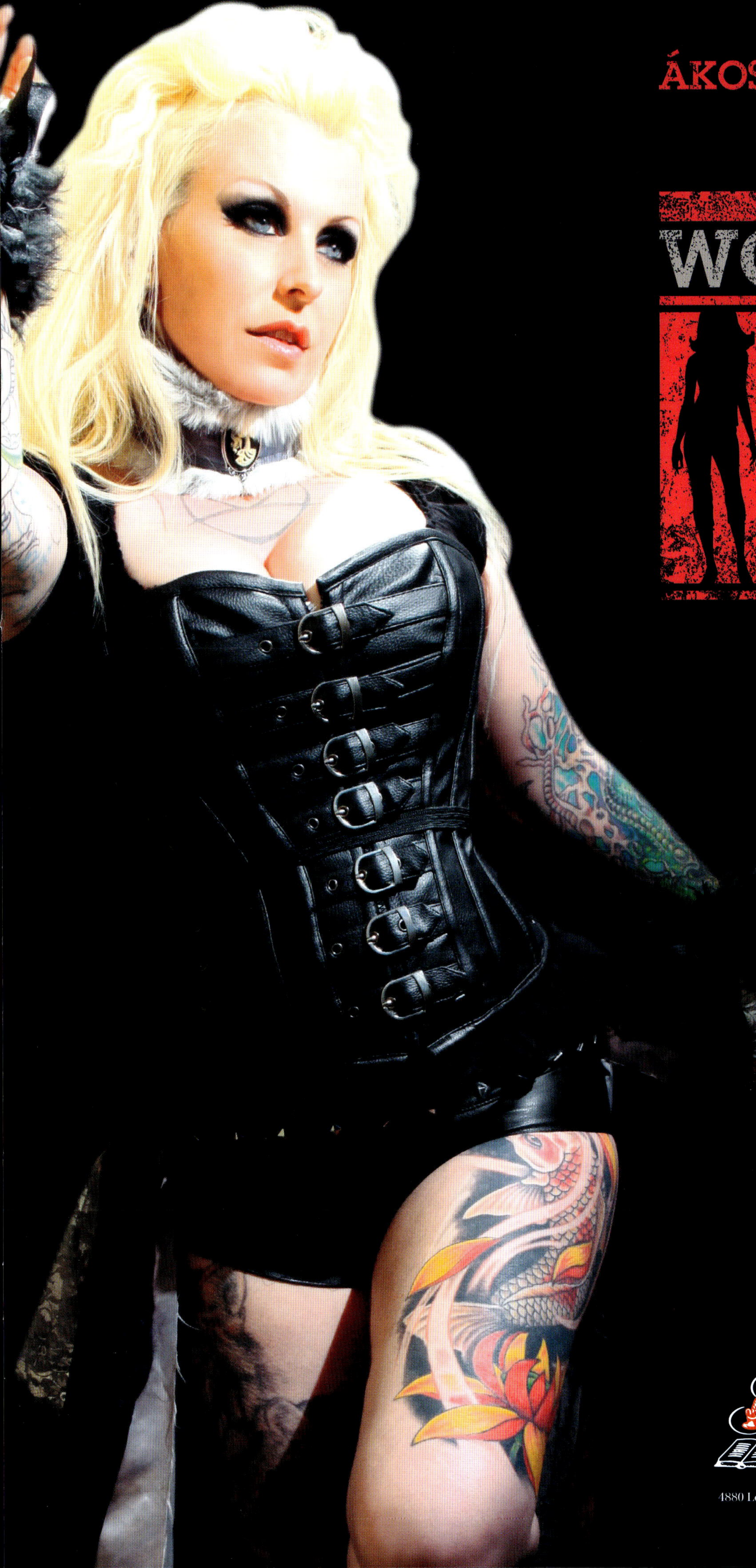

ÁKOS BÁNFALVI

THE WOMEN of INK

15 INTERNATIONAL TATTOO ARTISTS

Schiffer Publishing Ltd®
4880 Lower Valley Road • Atglen, PA 19310

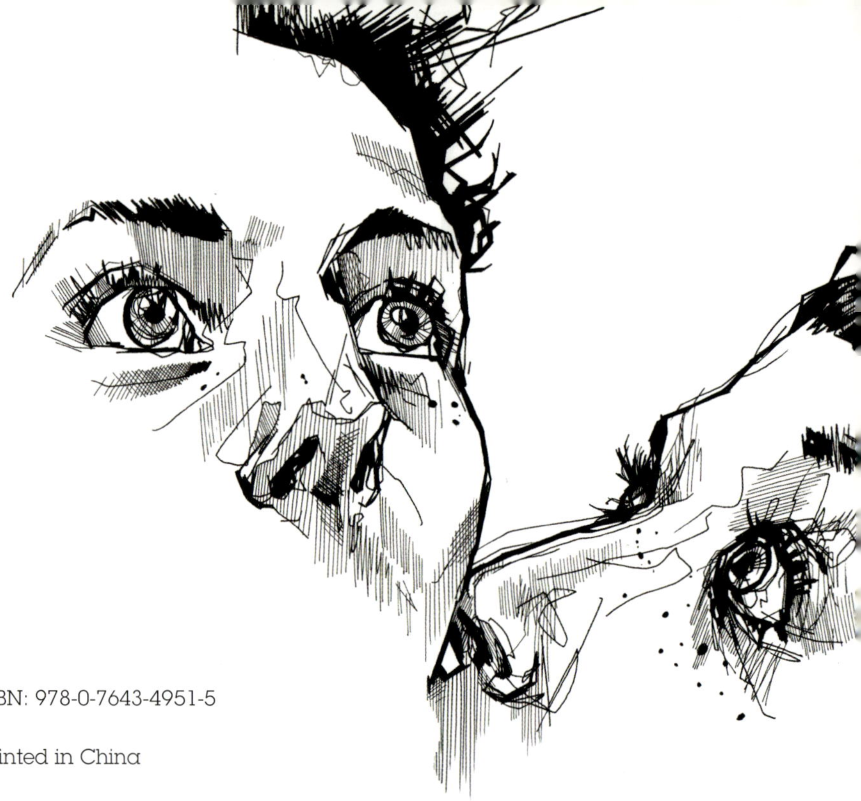

ÁKOS BÁNFALVI

Library of Congress Control Number: 2015944102

Designed by **DANIELLE D. FARMER**
Cover design by **JUSTIN WATKINSON**
Type set in Lubalin Graph/Bickham Script Pro/Velvenda Cooler/Zurich BT

ISBN: 978-0-7643-4951-5

Printed in China

Published by Schiffer Publishing, Ltd.
4880 Lower Valley Road
Atglen, PA 19310
Phone: (610) 593-1777; Fax: (610) 593-2002
E-mail: Info@schifferbooks.com

For our complete selection of fine books on this and related subjects, please visit our website at www.schifferbooks.com. You may also write for a free catalog.

This book may be purchased from the publisher. Please try your bookstore first.

We are always looking for people to write books on new and related subjects. If you have an idea for a book, please contact us at proposals@schifferbooks.com.

Schiffer Publishing's titles are available at special discounts for bulk purchases for sales promotions or premiums. Special editions, including personalized covers, corporate imprints, and excerpts can be created in large quantities for special needs. For more information, contact the publisher.

Front cover model: Moni Marino.
Back cover tattoo: Xu Yi Lili.

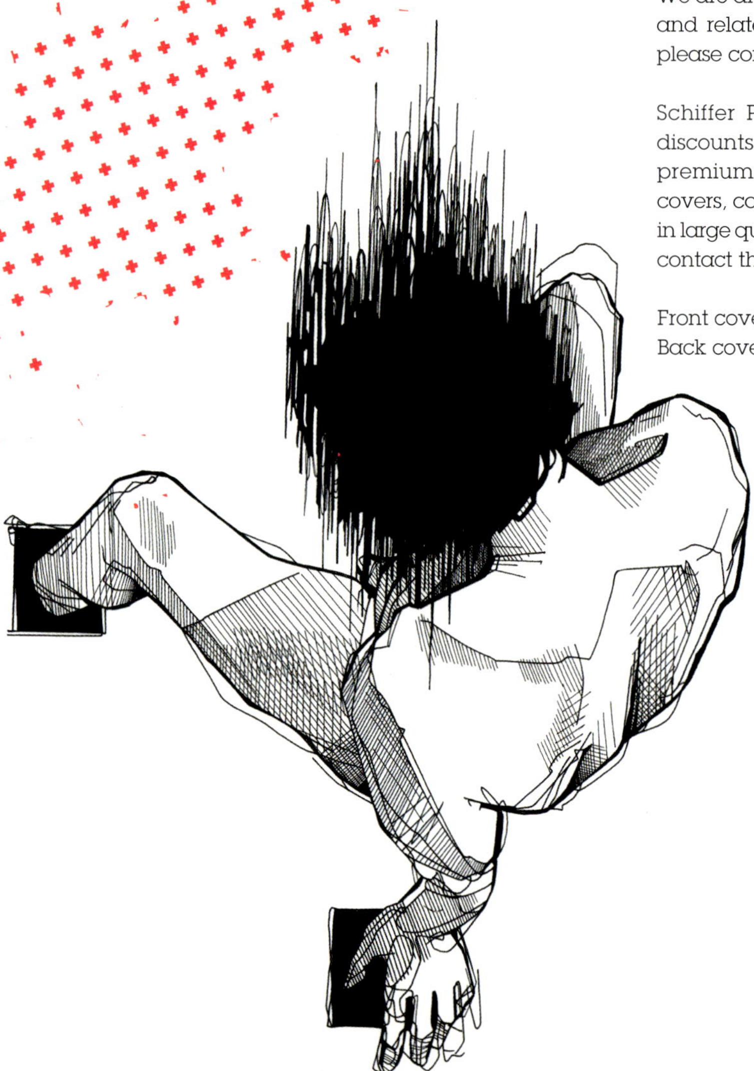

CONTENTS

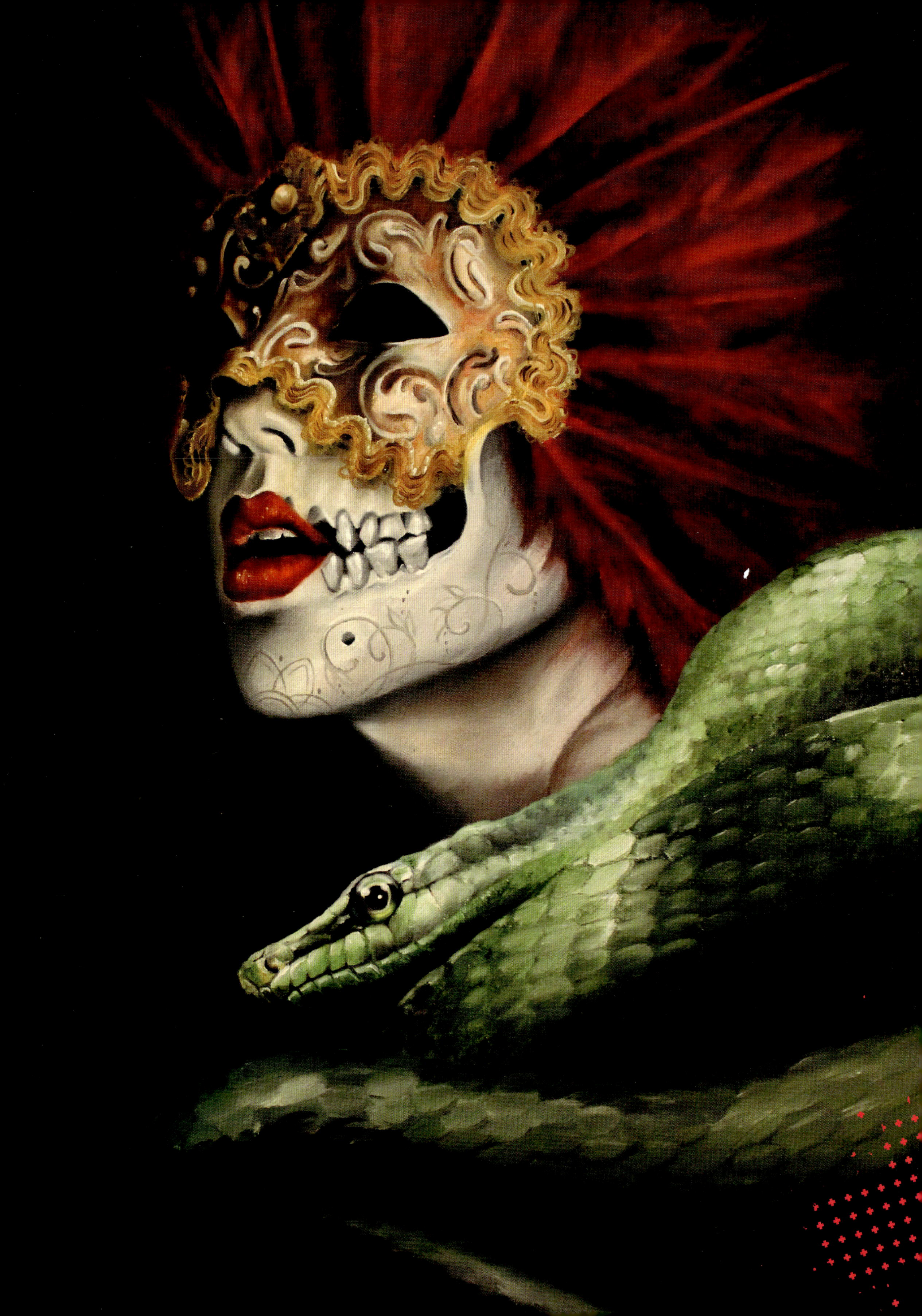

FOREWORD

A collection of some of the most talented female tattoo artists in the world, this book features interviews and the art of these accomplished ladies in the world of tattooing. These female tattoo masters have successfully earned their place in an industry that remains somewhat male dominated. It is often said that nothing can compare to a woman's touch. This book is a tribute to the ladies who grace our beloved industry and make it a little more beautiful. In a combination of talent, grace, passion, beauty, and artistic genius, we present women from all over the world whose tattoo artistry is extraordinary.

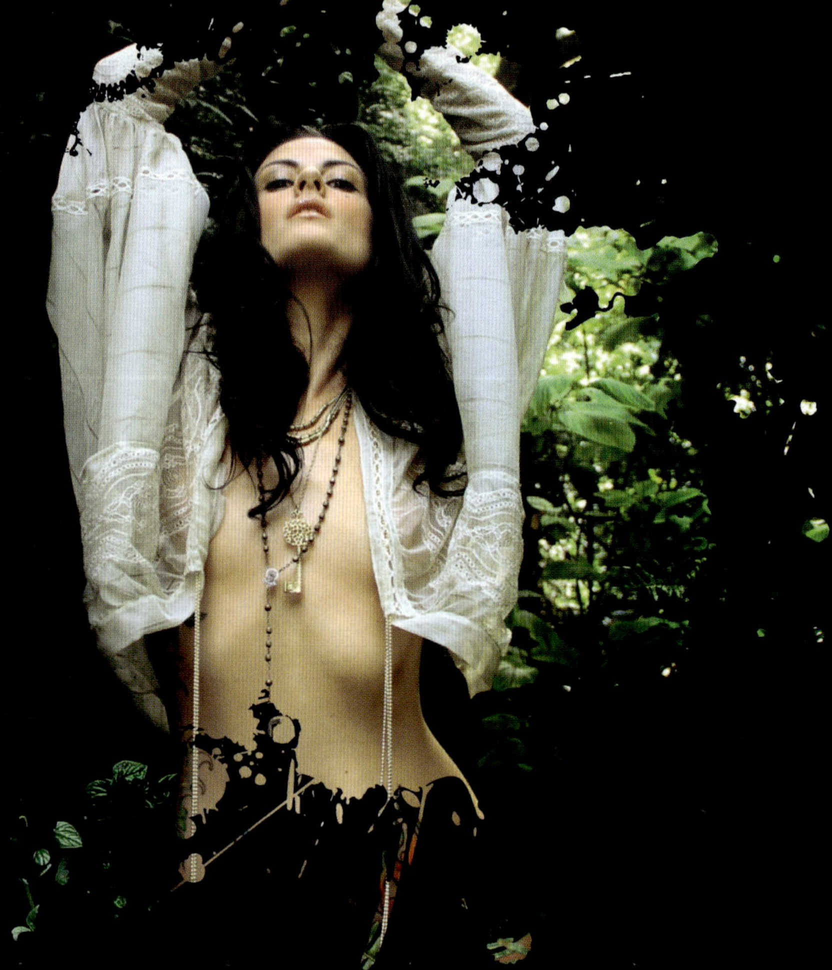

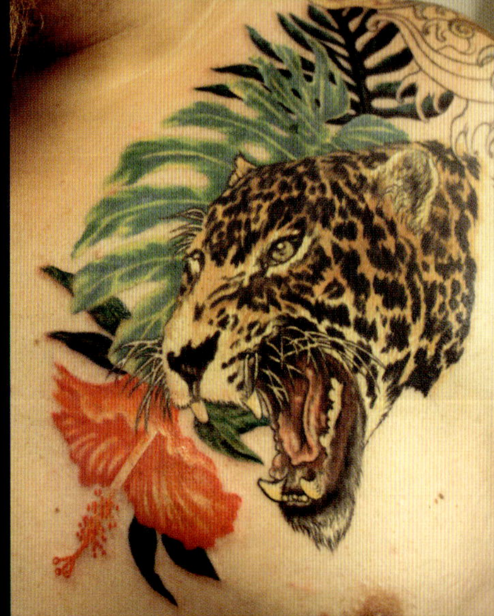

JULIE BECKER is a daydreamer and a reclusive adventure seeker, living outside the box. Before she learned how to tattoo, Julie designed a few small business logos, and painted anything she could: cars, walls, furniture, clothes, fabric. Her art background also included doing pencil portraits, silkscreening, hand painting, paint mixing, airbrushing, and make-up. These skills made the aspects of tattooing easier for her to learn.

Julie BECKER

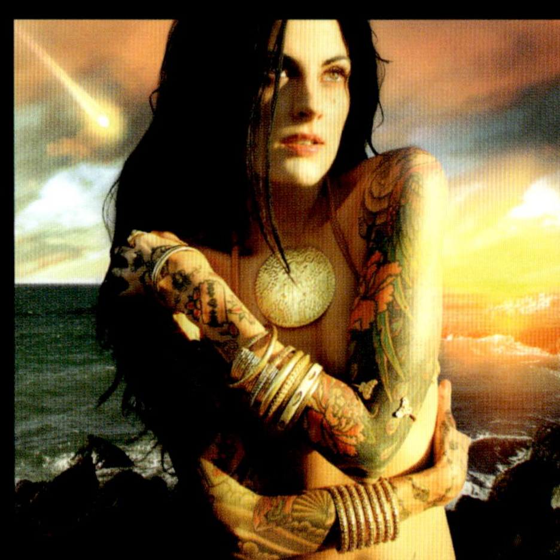

> "I only do what I feel spiritually aligned to do"

www.juliebeckertattoo.com
www.facebook.com/juliebeckerart
juliebeckertattoo.tumblr.com

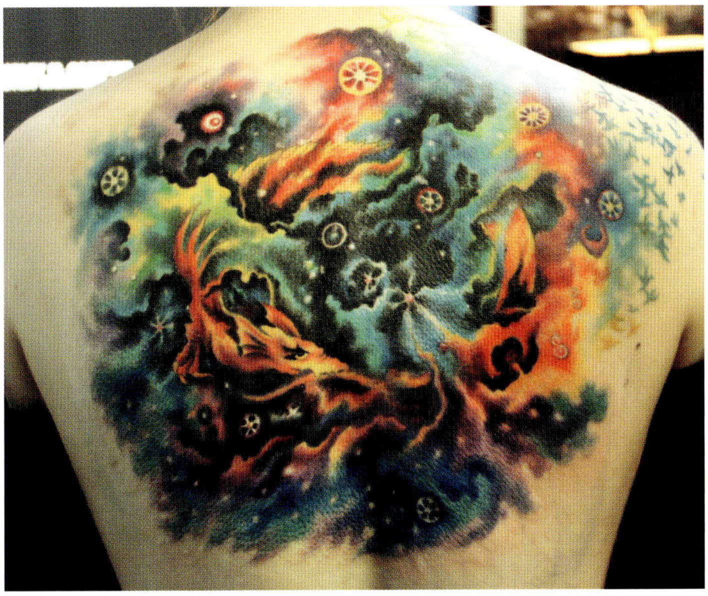

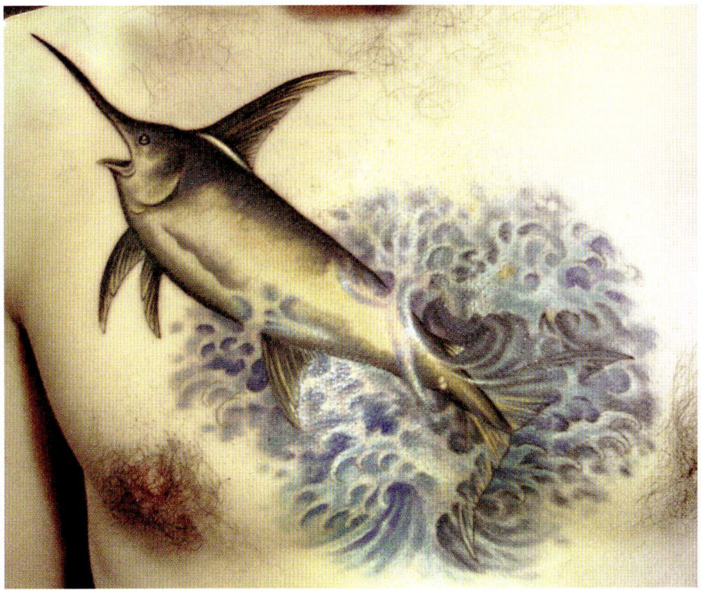

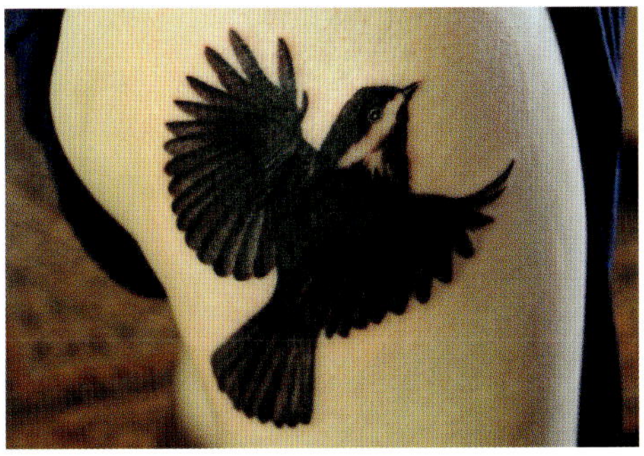

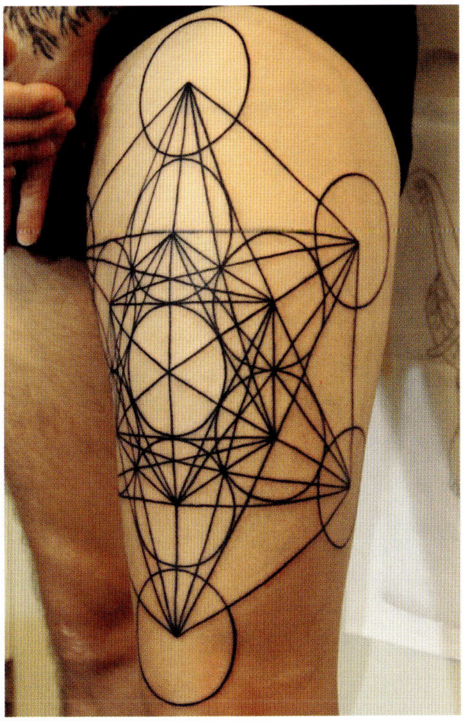

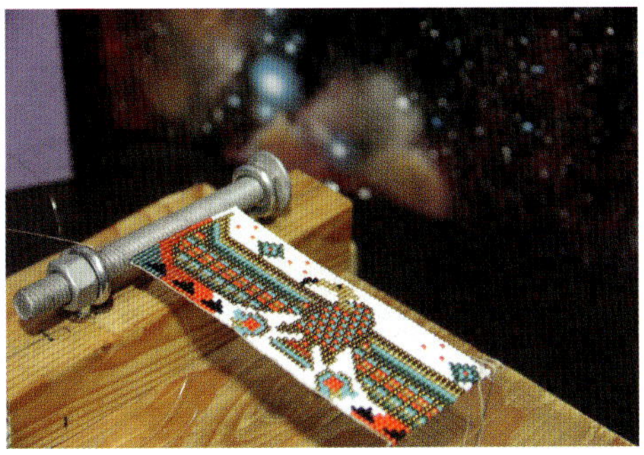

How long have you been a tattoo artist? Did you have a formal apprenticeship?

I did my first two tattoos in 1997 and then I did a formal apprenticeship with Kevin Quinn that lasted two years. I've been tattooing for eighteen years.

What's it like being a female artist in a primarily male workplace?

When I started tattooing I was nineteen, and I grew up with two brothers, so to me there was nothing unusual about being in a male dominated environment. There are guys you like and guys you don't, there are girls you like and girls you don't. What makes it easy to get along with someone, male or female, is your ability to be nice, and to give people the benefit of the doubt.

Do you feel that male customers treat you differently?

I suppose when I started tattooing in the late '90s it was still kind of a novelty to see a girl working in a tattoo shop who wasn't working the front counter. I did have my share of skeptics, but my objective isn't to care about other people projecting their insecurities onto me—my objective is to do a great tattoo.

Though the dynamics are constantly changing, there are obviously many fewer women tattoo artists in the industry than men. Has being a female ever presented challenges to you along the way? Do you feel you have had to work even harder than might have been necessary for a man, to achieve the success you have?

I have spent very little time in the past fourteen years alongside my peers. I have chosen to make tattoos in an environment that is suited to the pace of my consciousness. This allows me to have my energy focused on only the person I am tattooing, and why. I view success as being happy in my own skin, and I am. When I do visit tattoo shops, I am always drawn to groups of tattooers that hold the same "frequency" that I do. If I find that I'm not vibing with someone, I look at what our real conflicts are, and it generally has nothing to do with our genders.

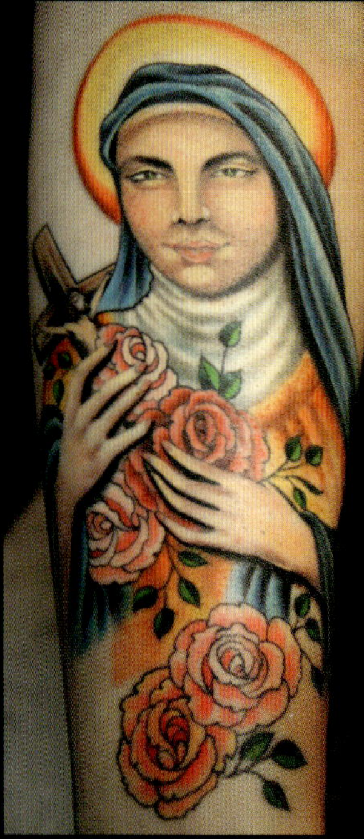
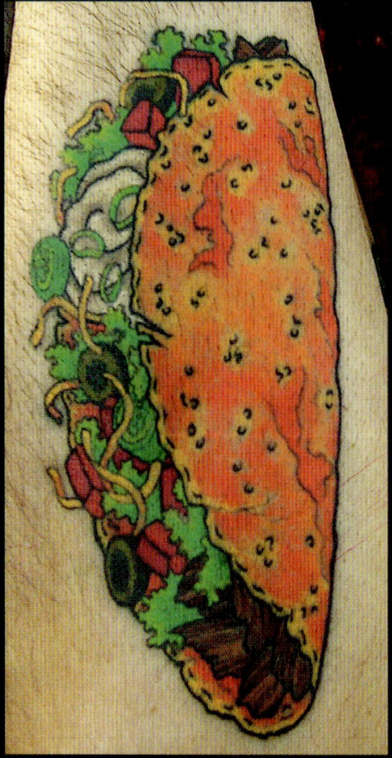
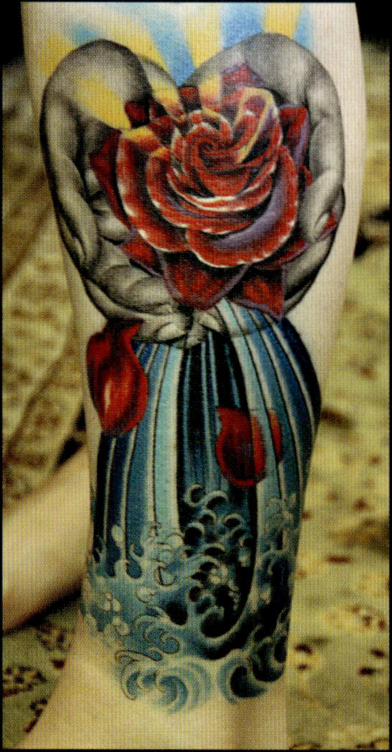
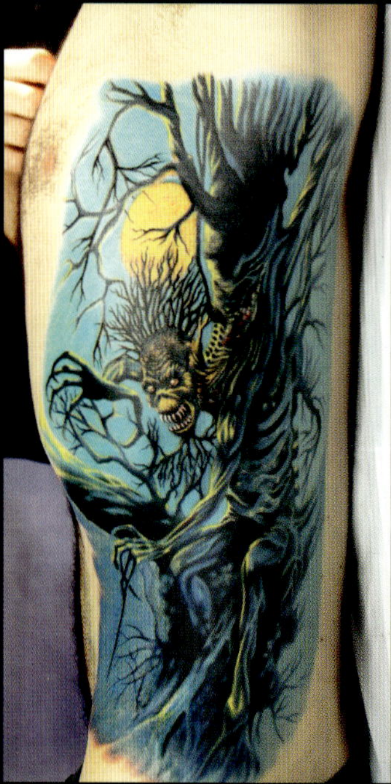
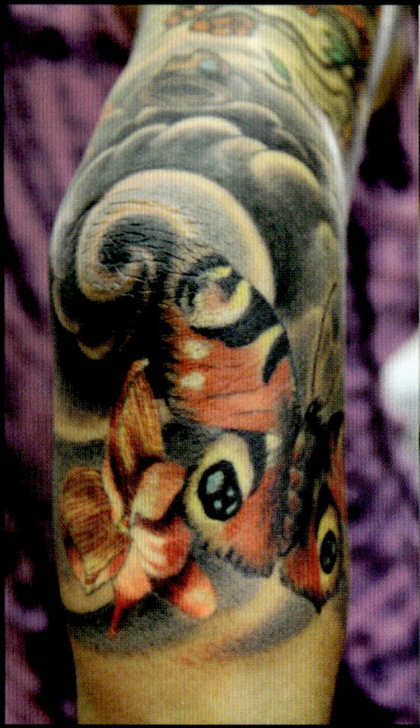
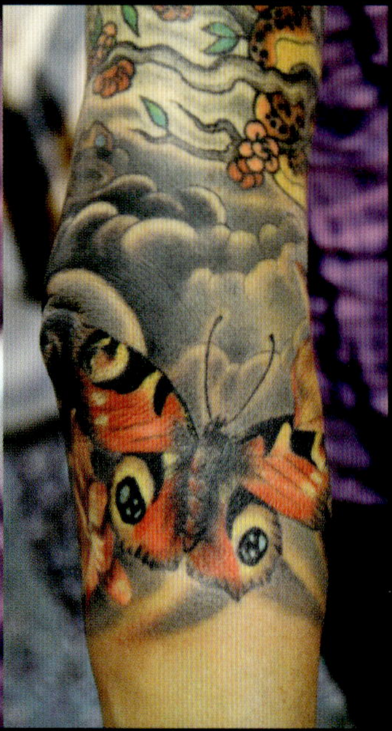
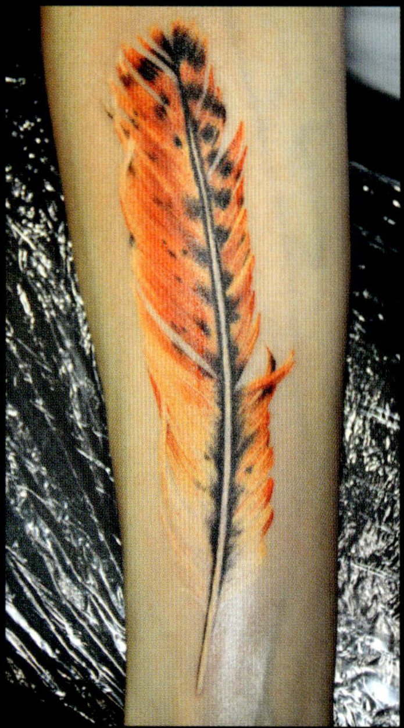
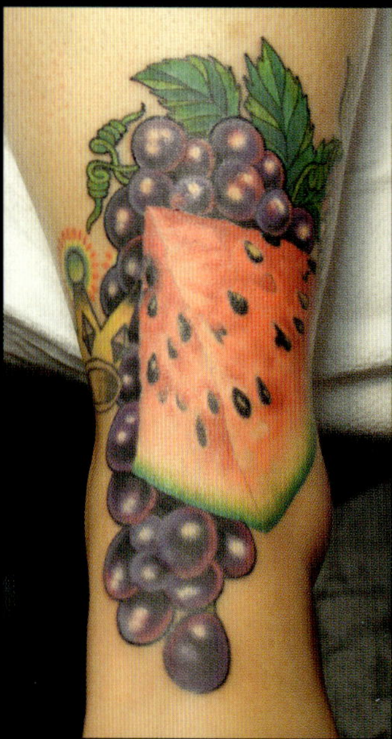
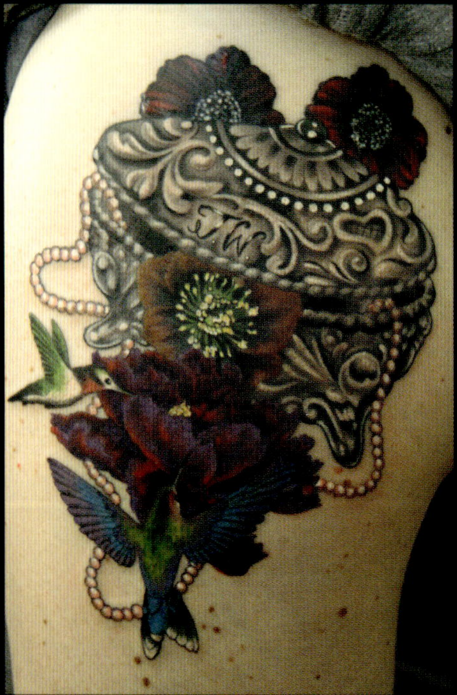
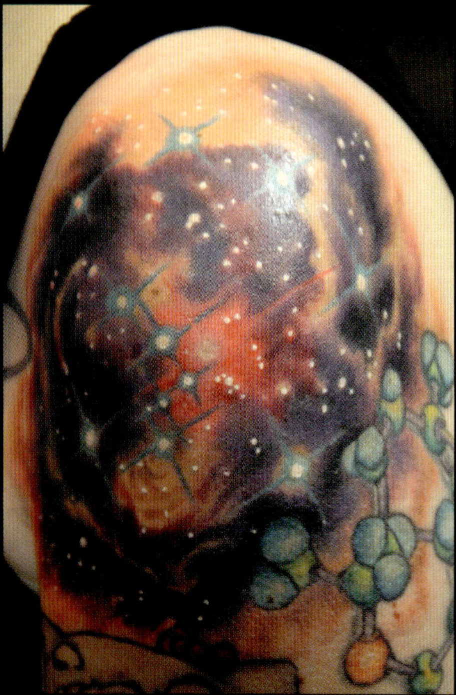
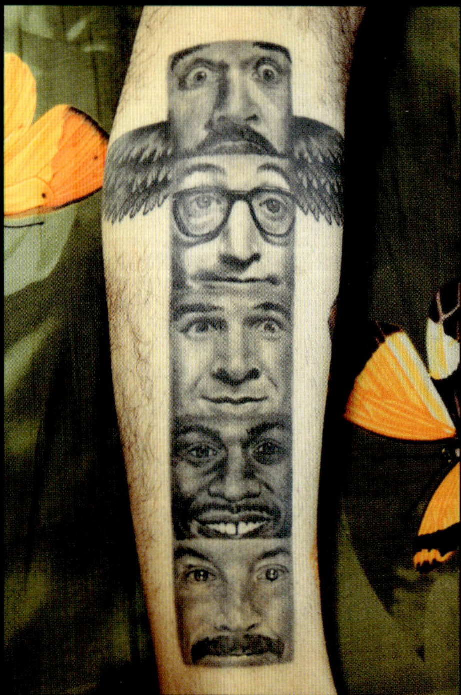

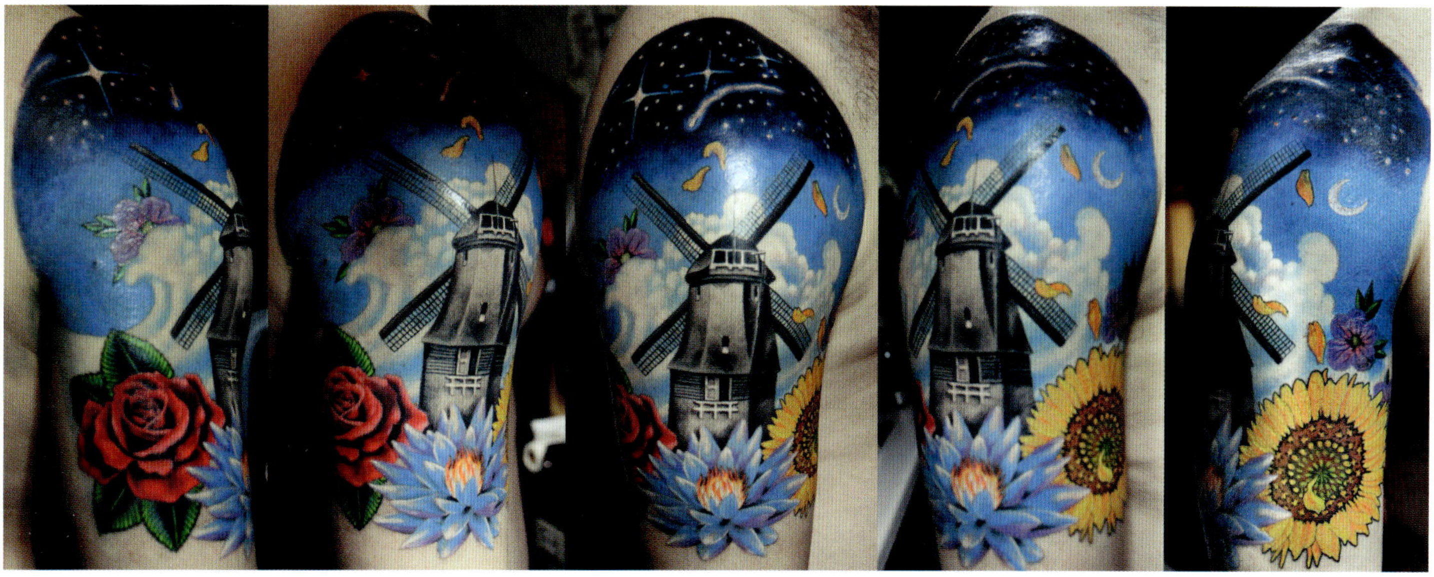

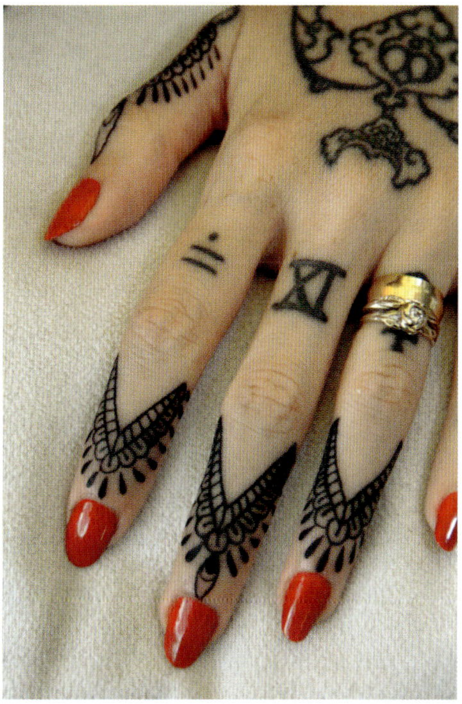

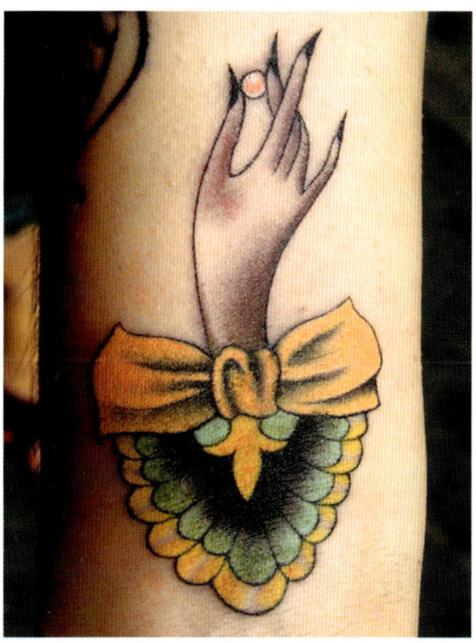

Tell me more about the shop you work at; what's it like working there, and what makes up a typical day?

I have created a private studio in a converted church, and my husband and I recently converted a 1974 Airstream to look like a spaceship. We travel around the US with it. I love to make tattoos in shops when I travel.

Do you see tattooing as a job or as a way to express your creative side?

For the most part, tattooing isn't what I consider work. Tattooing has been a religion of sorts for me. It is a way to clean your soul by setting it free.

What inspires you when you create your designs?

What inspires me are the client's ideas. For me the design process is very personal. I try to do a psychic reading for the client and channel the images from my third eye, while merging with the client's intent.

What do you enjoy most about tattooing, and what are some of the challenges?

What I enjoy the most is the connecting and the happiness. The challenge is to do what I do without being a part of the mainstream, to which I do not relate.

Art can be a great influence on someone's personality. What is the best lesson that you've learned from your art journey?

Art is truly subjective.

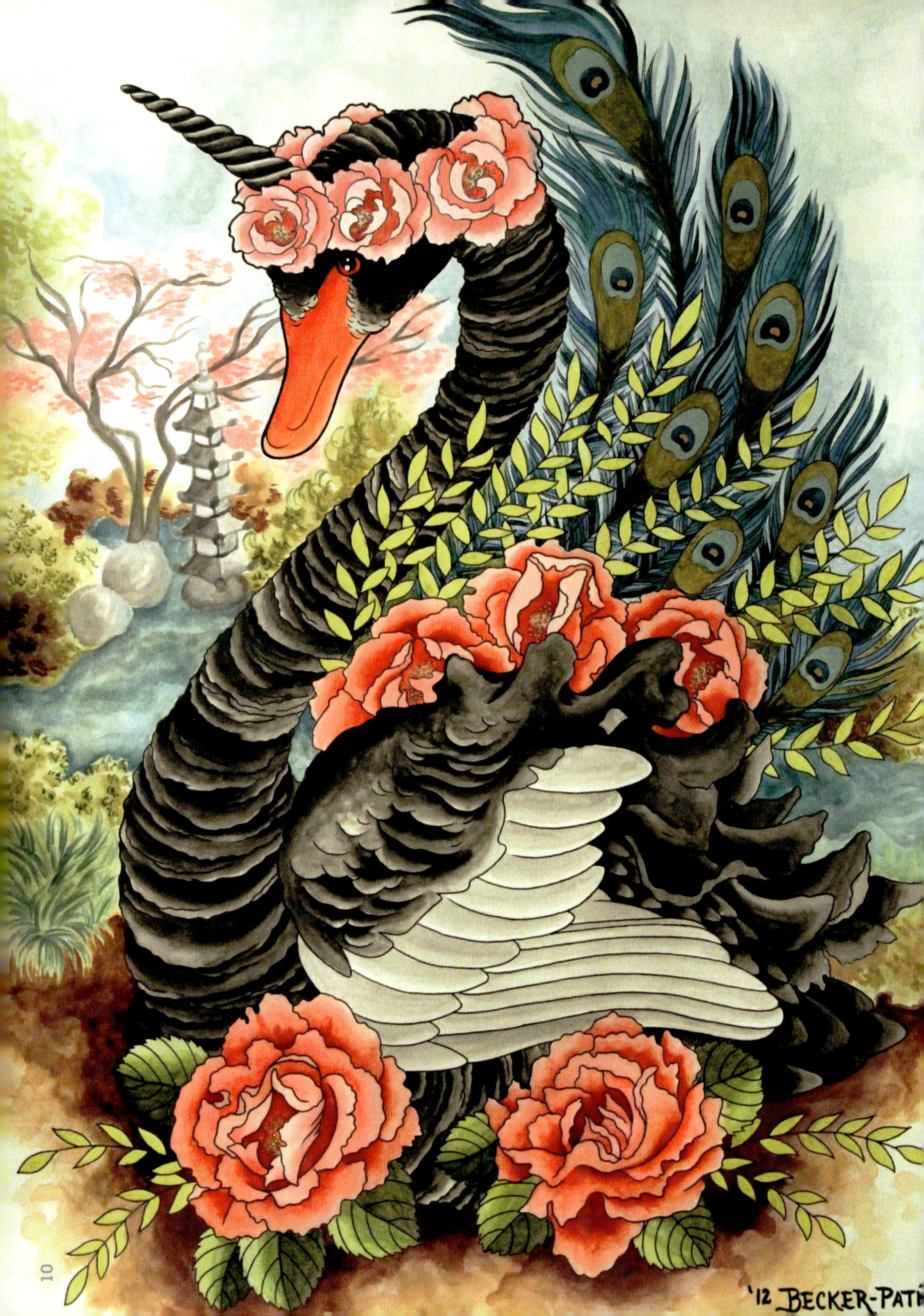
'12 BECKER-PATI

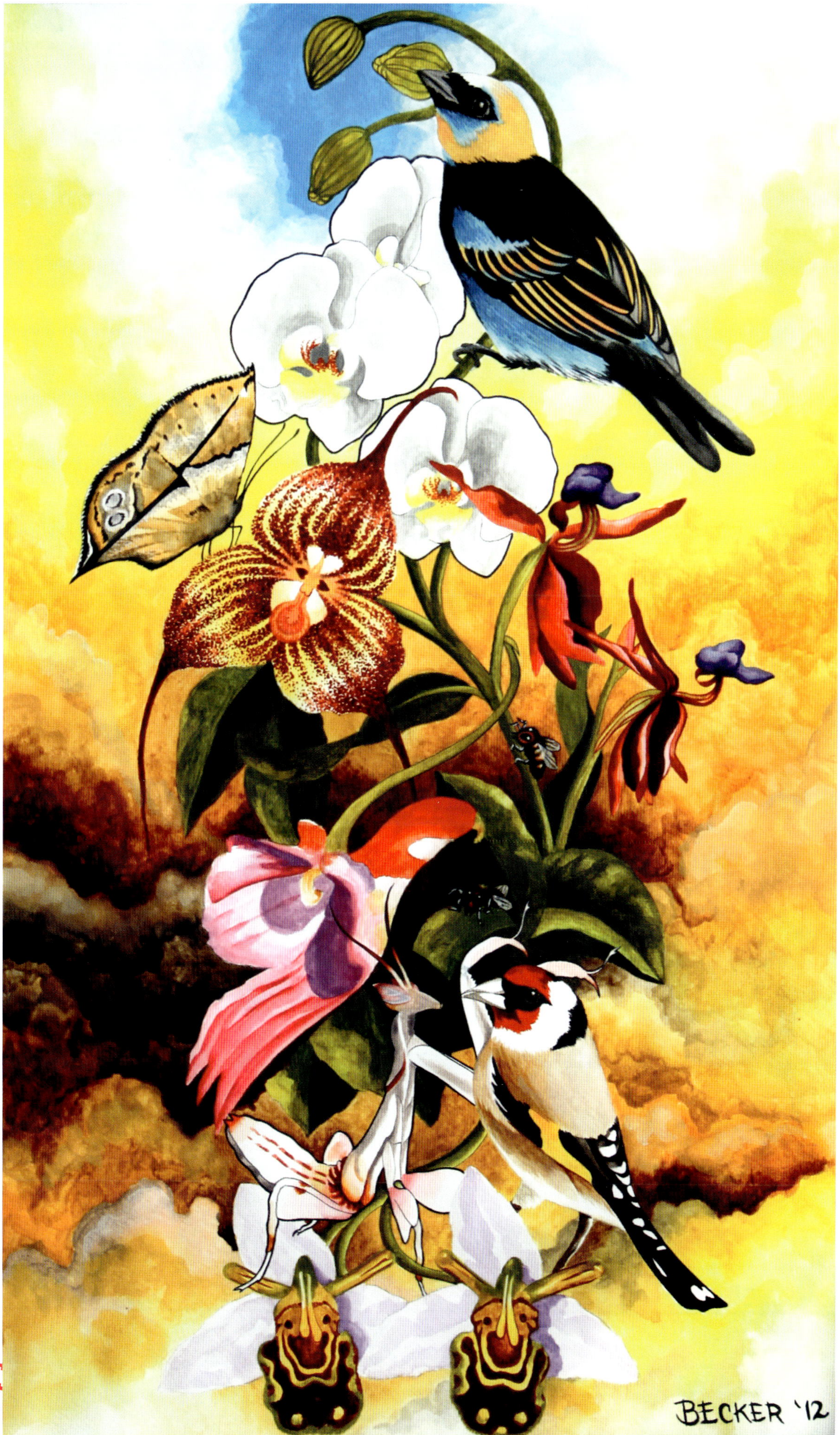
BECKER '12

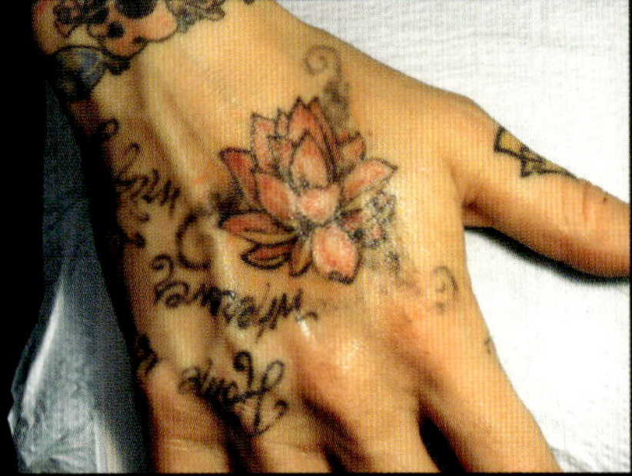
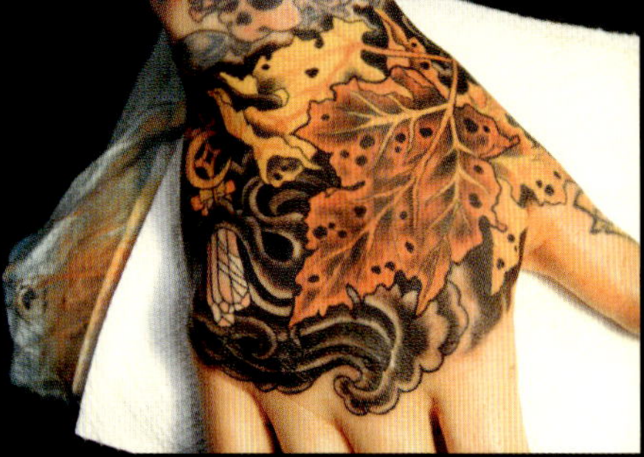
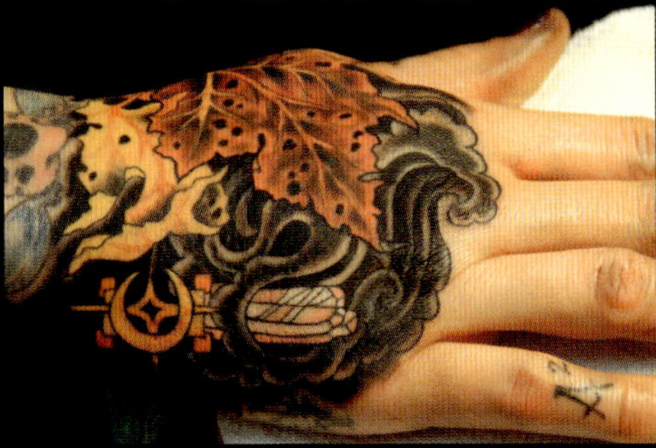
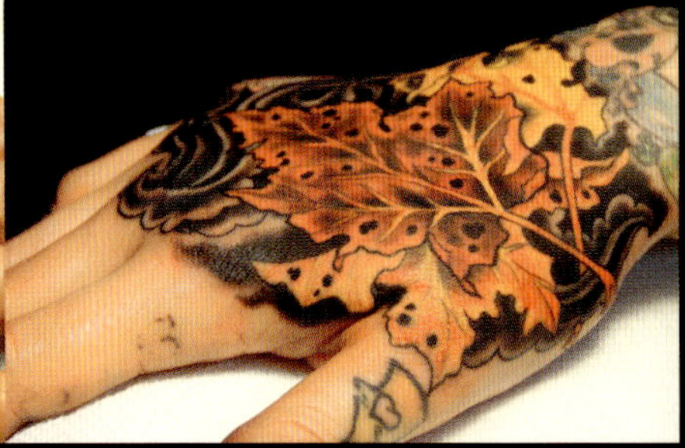
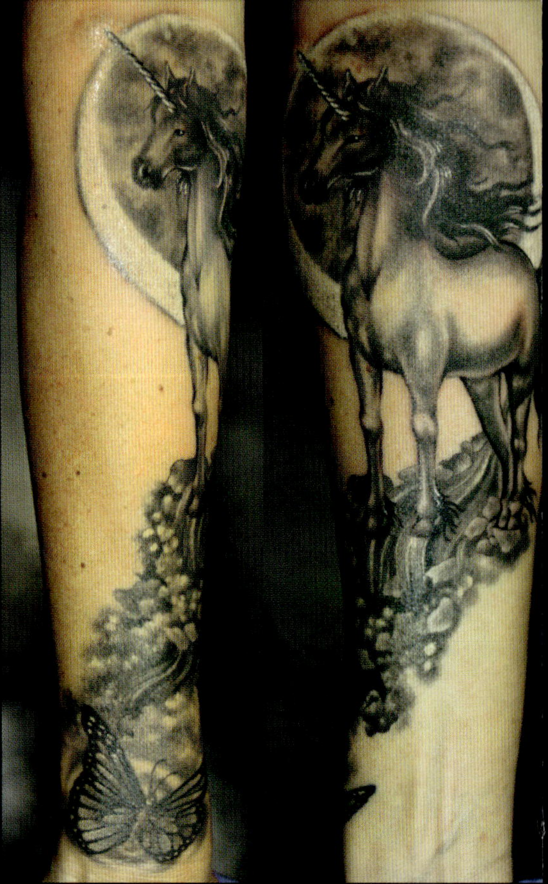
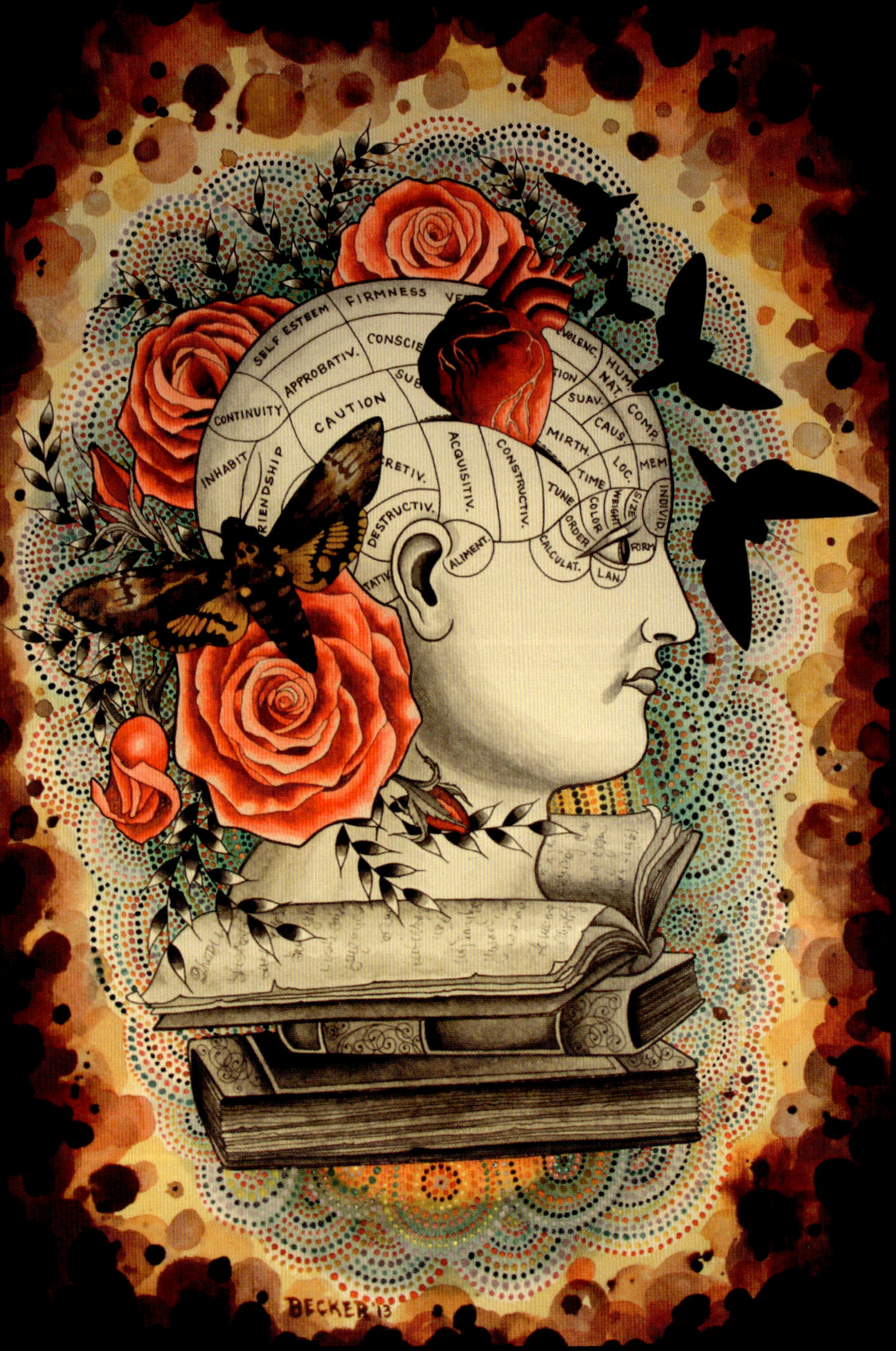
FIRMNESS
SELF ESTEEM
CONSCIE
APPROBATIV.
CONTINUITY
CAUTION
INHABIT
FRIENDSHIP
ACQUISITIV.
CONSTRUCTIV.
DESTRUCTIV.
ALIMENT.
MIRTH.
TIME
TUNE
COLOR
ORDER
CALCULAT.
LAN.
FORM
SIZE
WEIGHT
INDIVID
LOC.
MEM
CAUS.
COMP
SUAV.
HUM
NAT.
BECKER 13
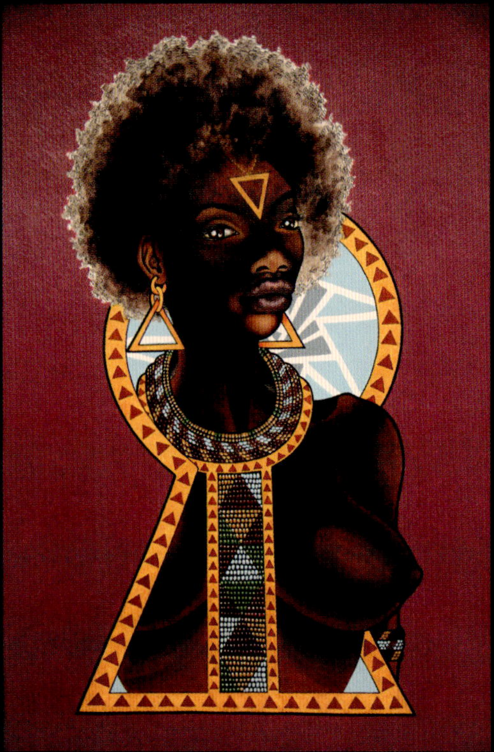
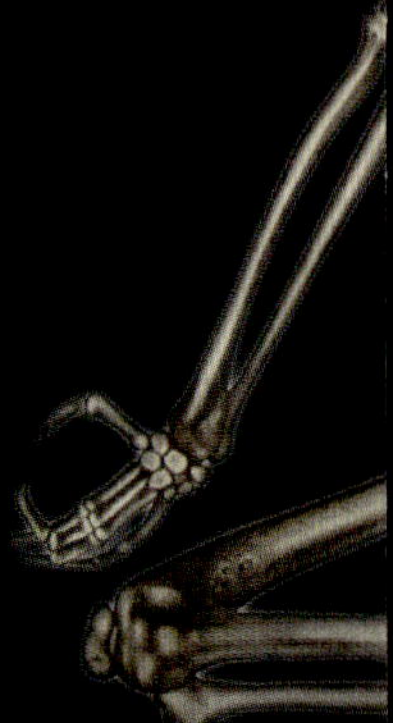

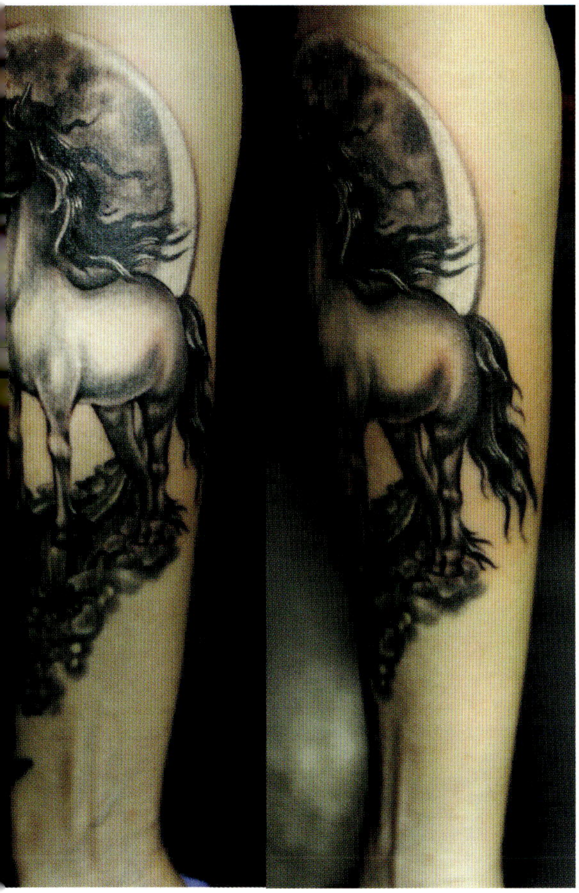

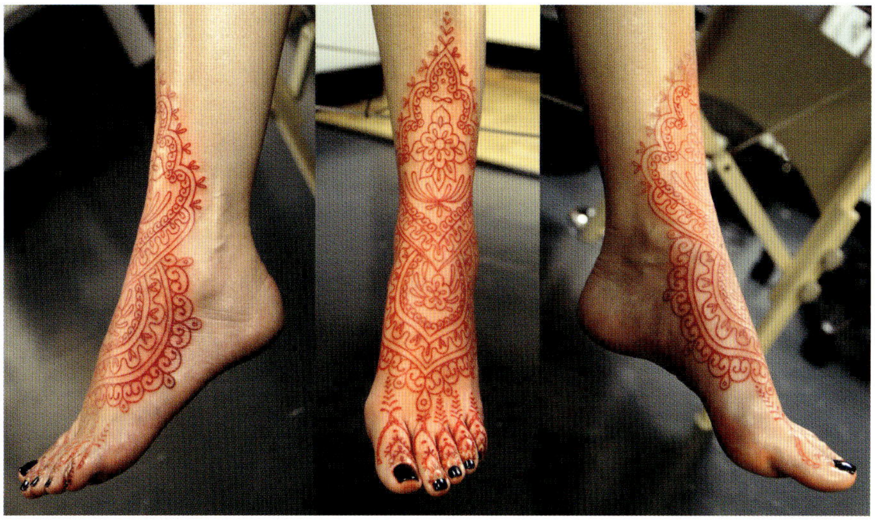

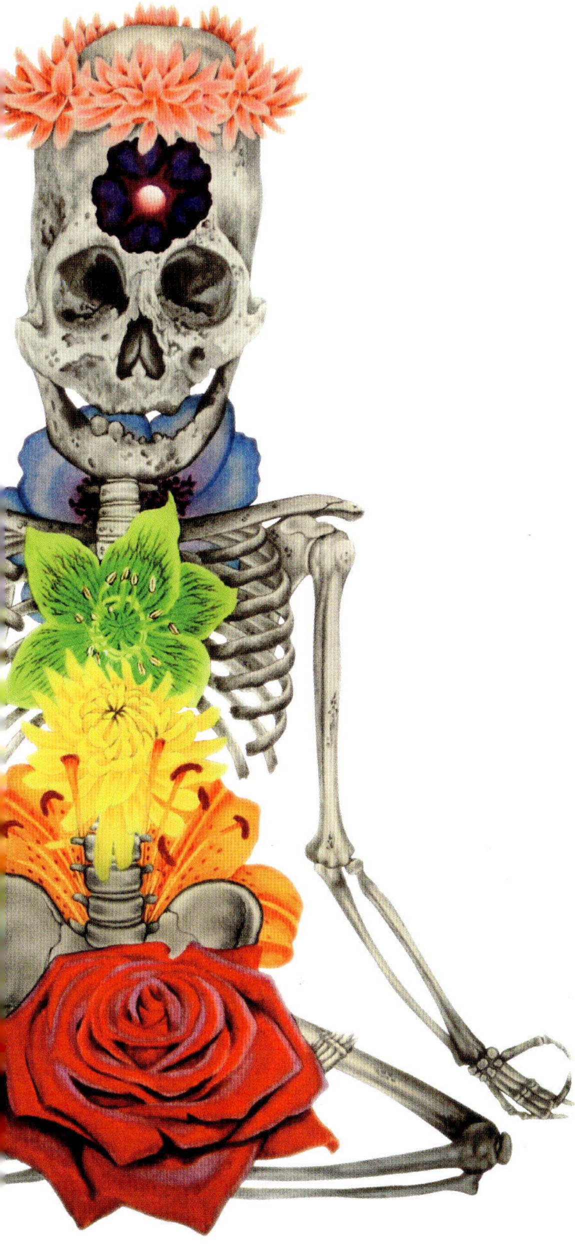

How did your style progress and develop to the point you are at now?

Avoiding industry contact, pushing my ideas on inexperienced clients, and developing my third eye.

Describe how your role models and any other sources of inspiration have affected your tattoo style.

I was taught to have integrity, which means I stand behind my tattoos. I know how the body ages and I have studied the styles that hold up best over time.

What's one of your favorite pieces that you've tattooed on someone else?

One of my favorites is a taco I tattooed on my husband.

What's one of your favorite pieces on your own body, and who did it?

My all-time favorite tattoo is still my Janis Joplin bracelet by Lyle Tuttle, reproduced on me by Jason Brown.

What is your favorite thing about being a tattoo artist?

Making people happy.

What is the most interesting tattoo you have been asked to do?

A pin-up of a woman holding her husband's severed penis...

Is there any subject or taboo you wouldn't ink on someone, even if it was their request or design?

Yes, lots of things, but not because I am the moral police; because I only do what I feel spiritually aligned to do.

Have you noticed a change in the types of images people have asked for over the years you've been tattooing?

It all goes in waves...cyclical waves.

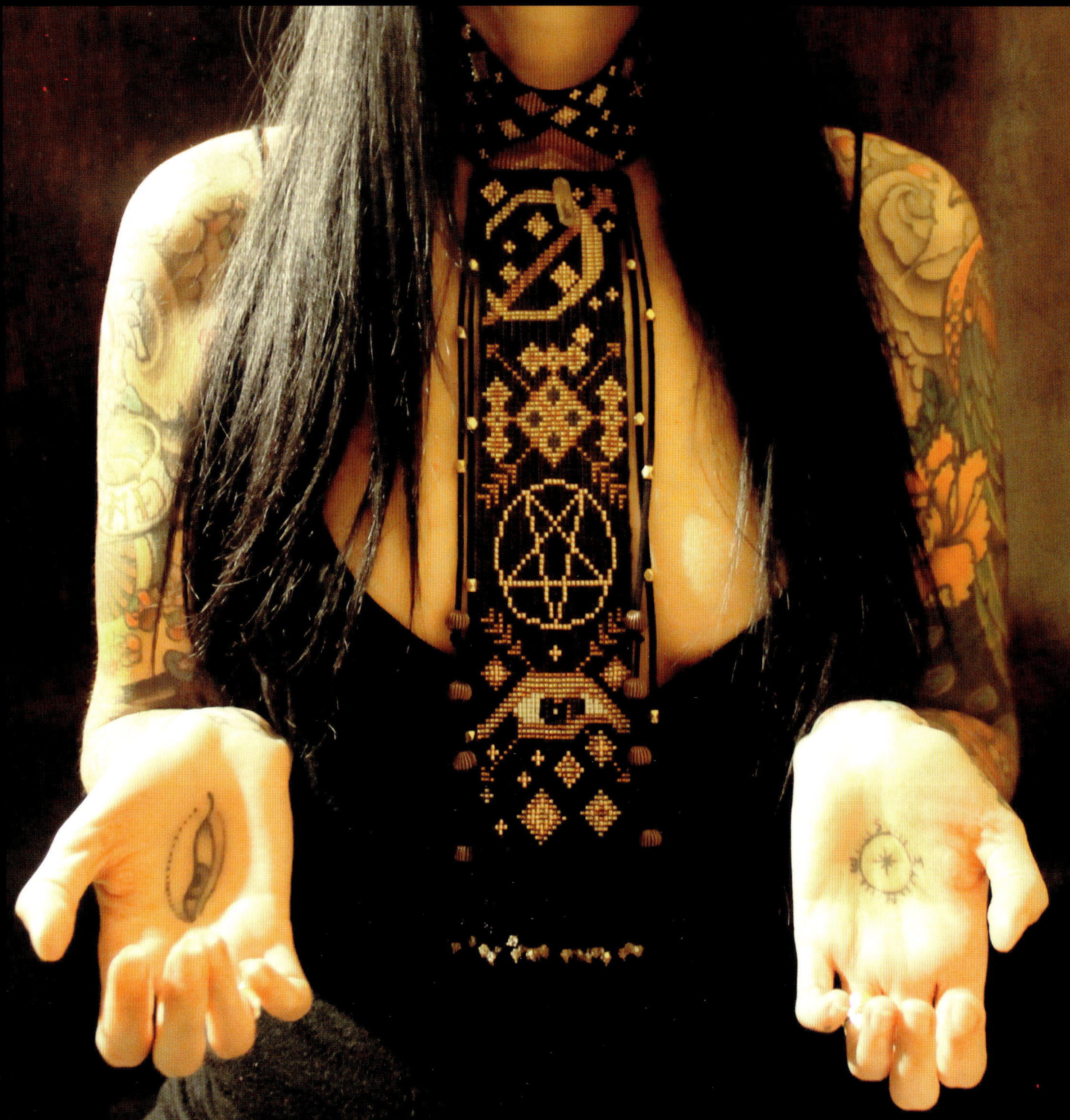

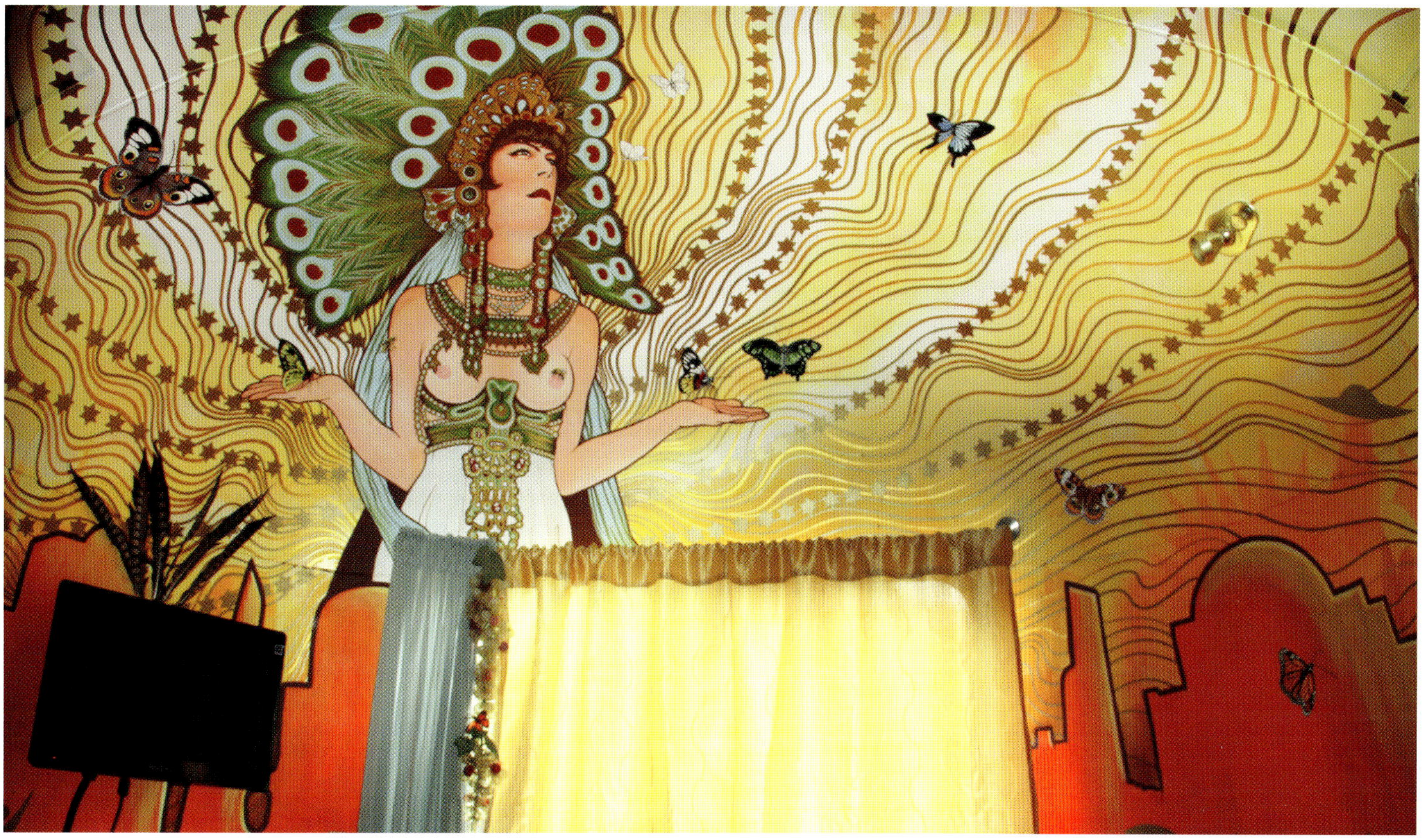

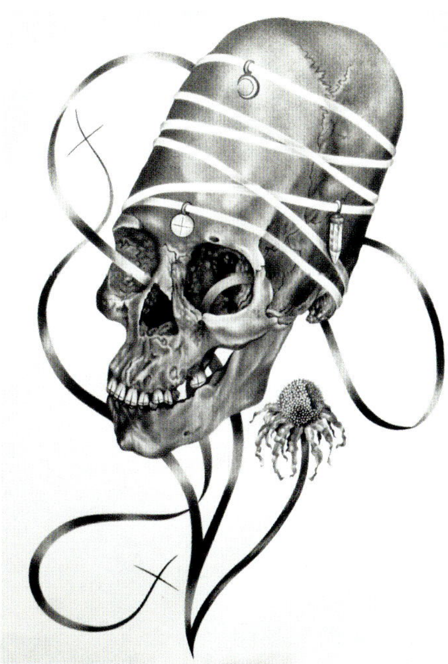

Tattoos seem very mainstream now. Do you think that's good or bad?

I think it is annoying; it has its negative and positive attributes for everyone I guess. I have noticed the infiltration of all these non-tattooer-owned businesses making money off the tattoo community, but that doesn't really concern me, because I have always danced to the beat of my own drum. I am not into corporate sponsorship.

Is there anything else you'd like to say?

I am moving in a direction of health, physical healing, and allowing myself to create in many areas of art and life to keep me inspired. I have never been interested in being a technical artist—I have always strived to communicate futuristic ideals of a utopian society with people who want to be groovy and leave their anger, guilt, and competitive nature in the past with other outmoded belief systems. I think spreading the beauty of nature and the human spirit is enough.

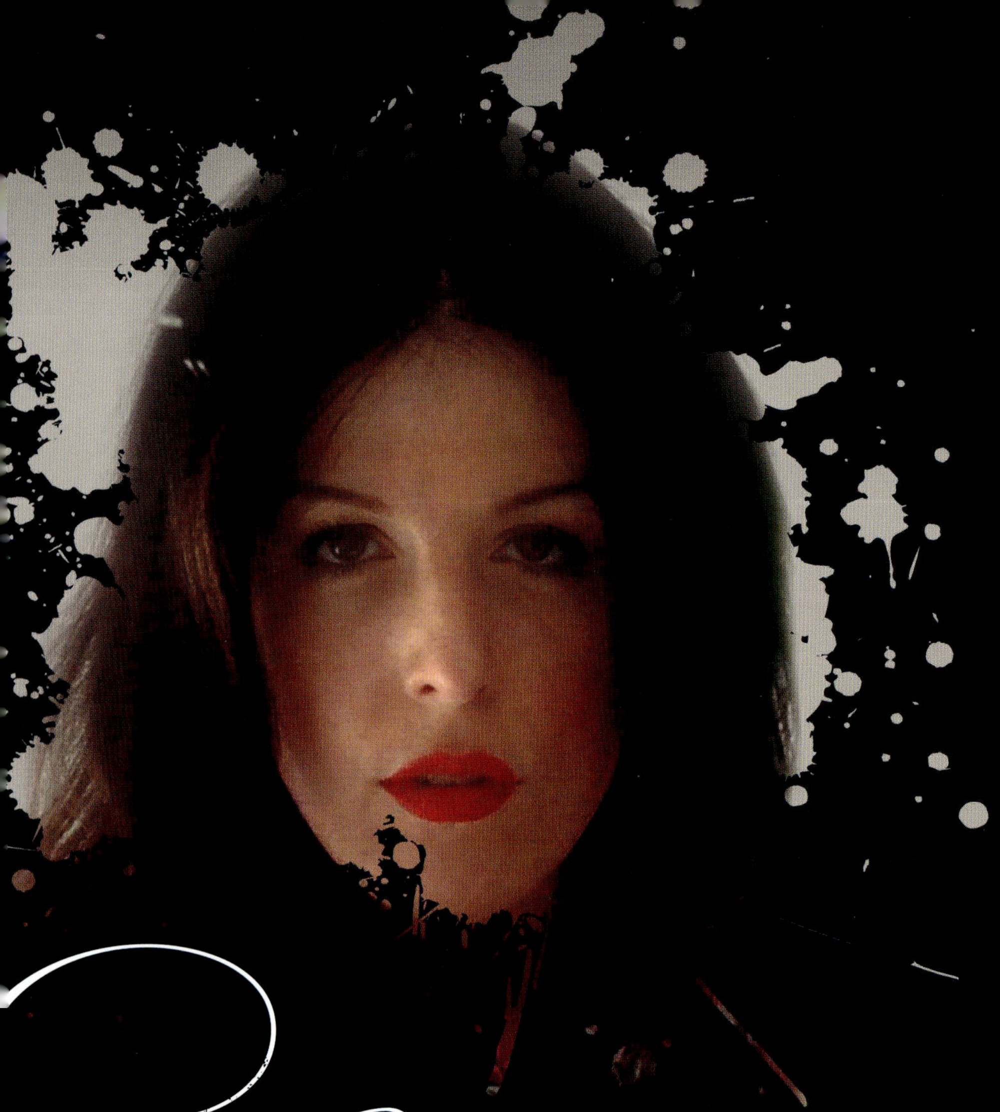

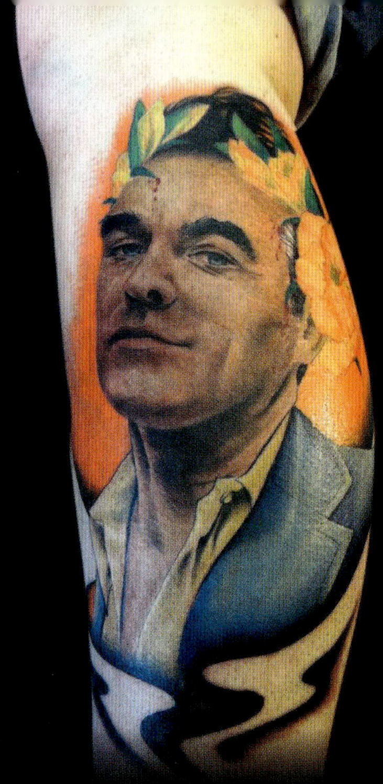

Chantale COADY

CHANTALE COADY wanted to become a tattoo artist the moment she walked into a tattoo studio to get her first tattoo at the age of fourteen. It created an excitement inside her that she'd never felt anywhere else. Chantale has been tattooing for six years now. It took her a very, very long time to finally get an apprenticeship, but she was willing to wait to do it the right way. That was very important to her.

"The majority of my clients are male and love me"

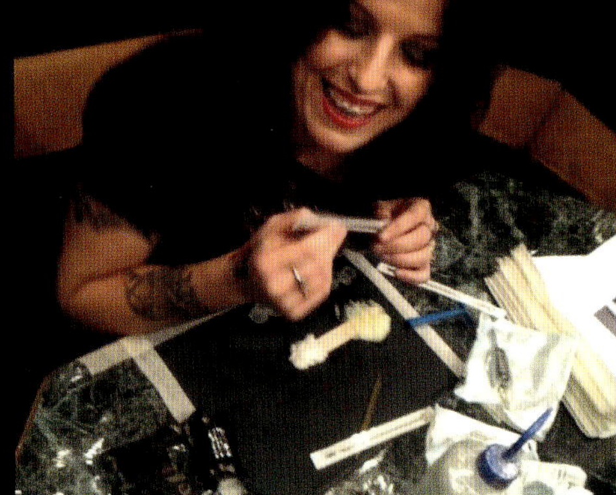

www.picturehousetattoostudio.com
www.facebook.com/chantale.coady
www.facebook.com/pages/Chantale-Coady/264617313581246
twitter.com/ChantaleCoady

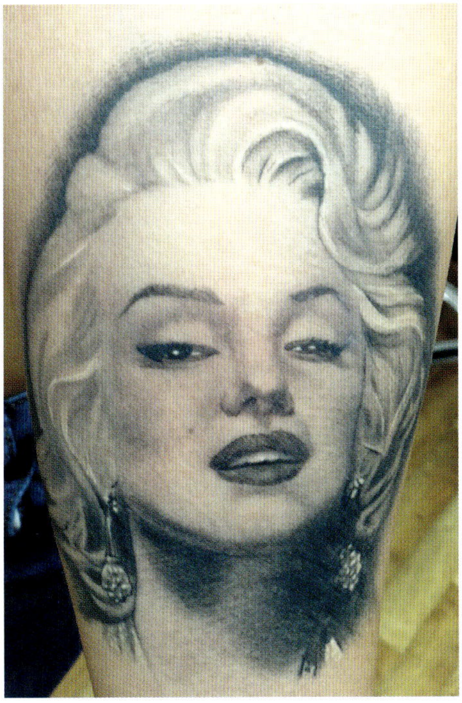

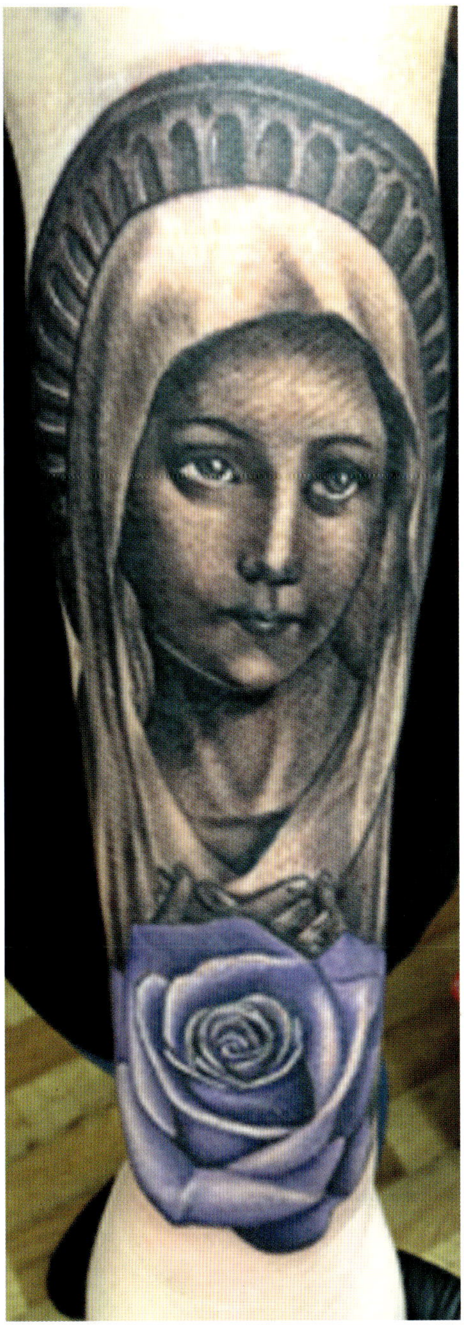

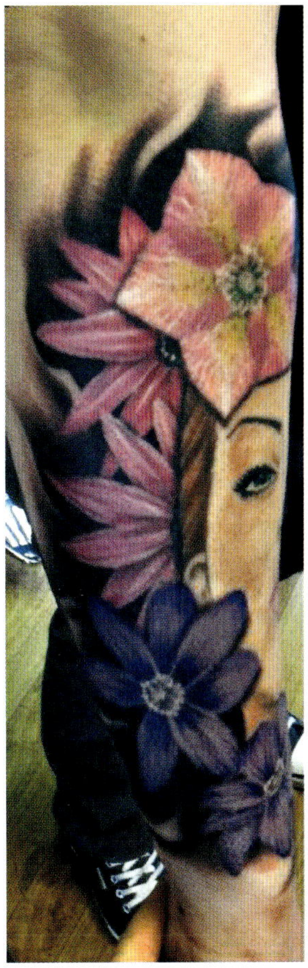

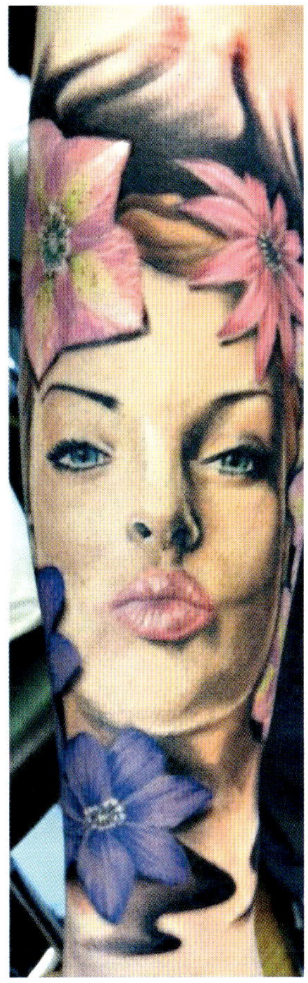

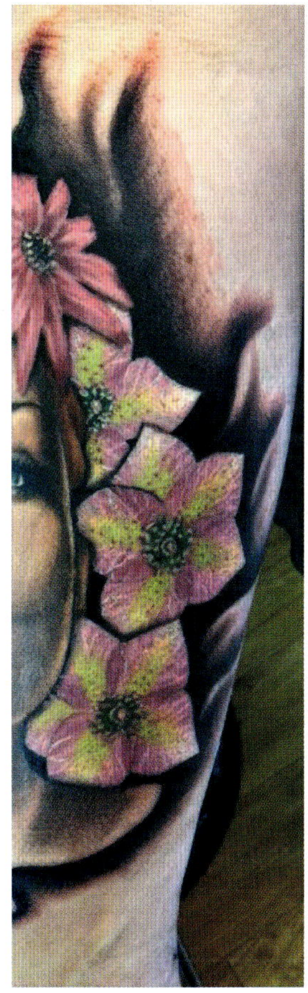

What did you do before you started tattooing?

I have done numerous jobs from shoveling donkey manure to working in IT for the Ministry of Defence. But when I finally got my apprenticeship I was assistant manager of a beachfront restaurant in Dee Why, Sydney, Australia, and doing my Diploma in Fine Arts.

Where did you learn to tattoo? Did you have a formal apprenticeship? If so, can you tell me about this time in your life and how it prepared you for all that you do now?

I had thought that I had scored myself a proper apprenticeship, but unfortunately that was not to be. I had been practicing on friends and family for three weeks when the owner walked in and said I was good enough to be tattooing customers and making money. I didn't feel I was ready, and burst into tears when I got home I was so scared. But I was more scared of the owner, so I sucked it up and did as I was told. But after a year there I grew some balls and left, and have never let anyone dictate to me what I can and can't do in this industry since.

I then moved on to a great studio in Sydney called Platinum Ink, where I worked with another girl called Jane Stuart. This was where I met Michael Schelen, who was to turn my world upside down. He guested with us for two weeks and I sat on his shoulder like a parrot watching everything, taking it all in, and asking hundreds of questions. He's an amazing black-and-gray artist and I consider him my mentor. I fell in love with his work and set myself a challenge from that moment to be as good as him.

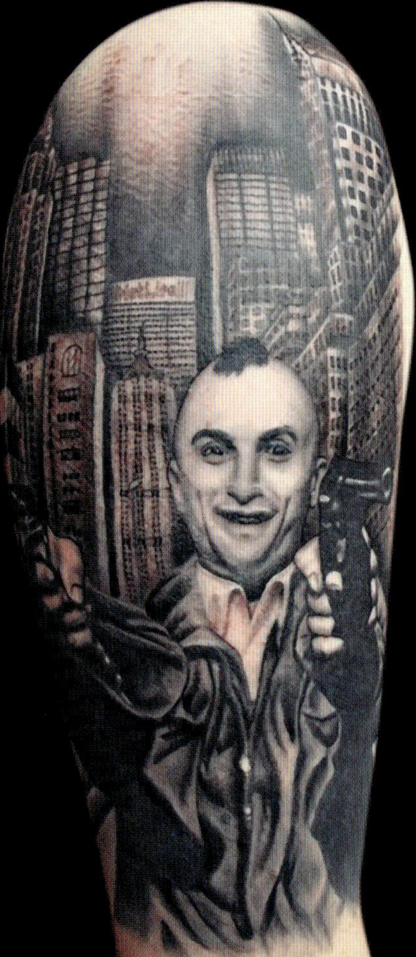
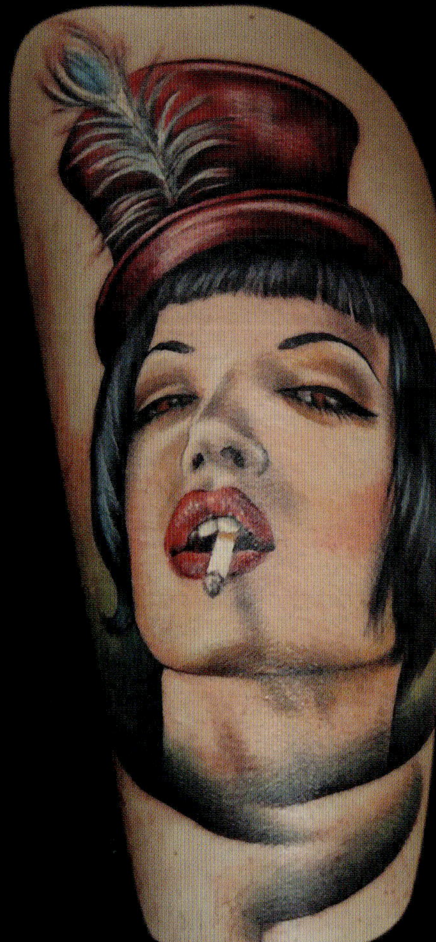
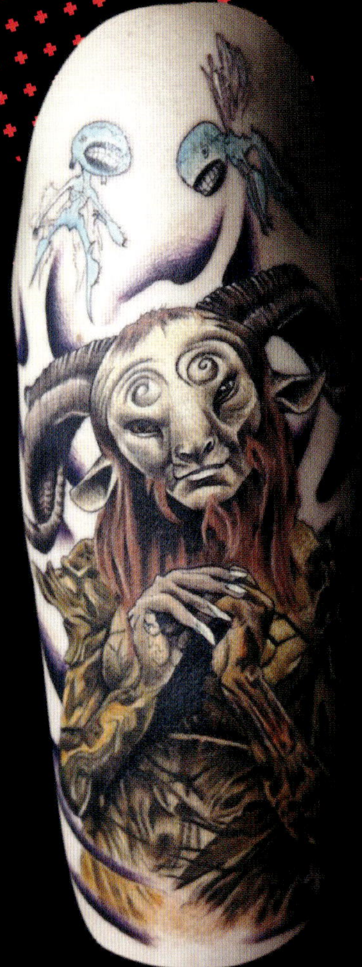
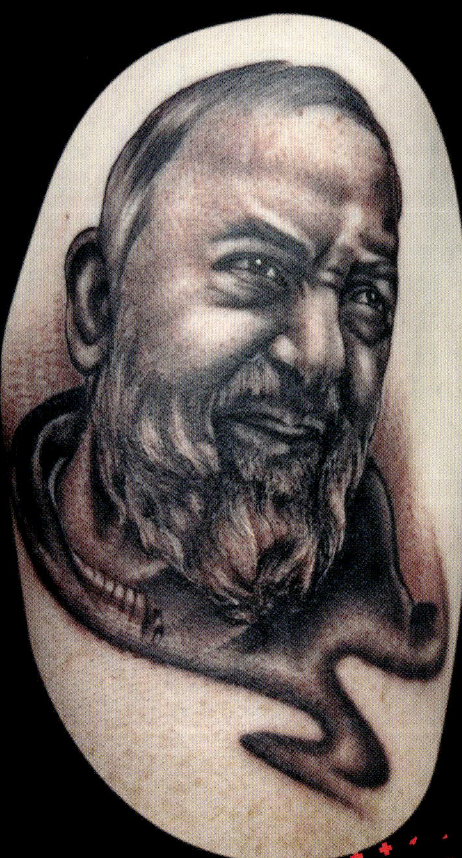
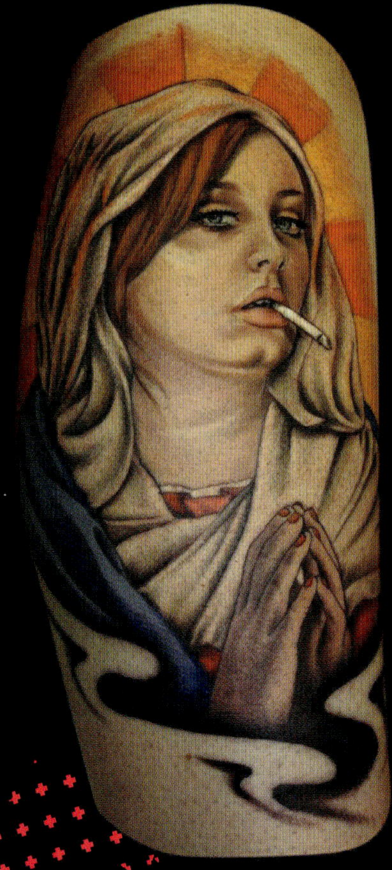
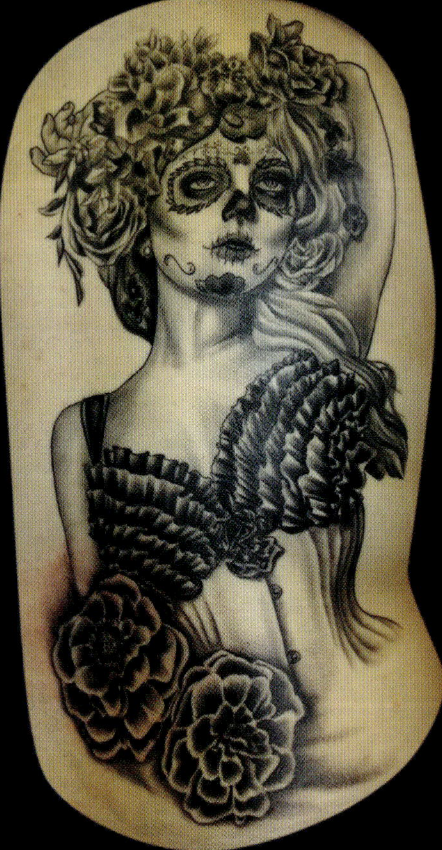

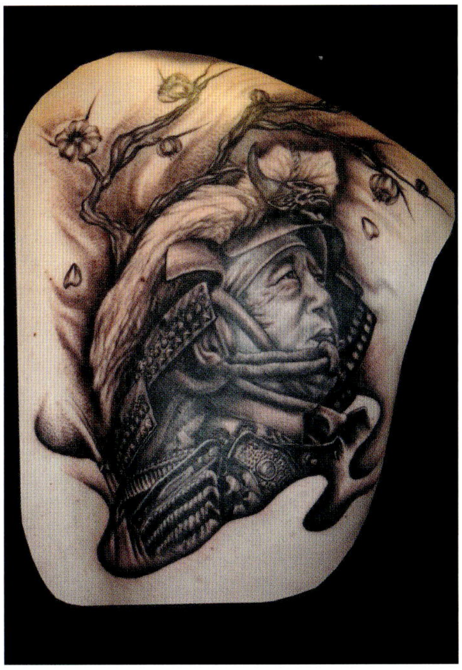

What's it like being a female artist in a primarily male workplace?

To be honest, I don't really have any issues with it. I'm lucky enough to have some of the best artists in the world as close friends and they are equally male and female and all treat me the same. I think the industry has moved past that now.

Do you feel that male customers treat you differently?

The majority of my clients are male and love me. I have no idea why 'cause I generally abuse the shit out of them. *(Laughs.)*

What did your family and friends think about you getting into the business?

They have all supported me one hundred percent.

Tell me about your shop.

I love my studio! It's called Picture House and is decorated like a vintage cinema. We even have old red-velvet cinema seats in the waiting area, and flat screen TVs, so that clients can watch movies while they get tattooed. I want it to be an experience when you get tattooed here, so that you leave wanting to tell people about it and not just show off your amazing new tattoo. I've got a team of amazing tattoo artists that all have different styles, too, so we cater for everyone, and most importantly, all my artists are fun and happy. I've been in too many studios where artists spend their time bitching and moaning about the industry and other artists and studios. I don't want to be around that.

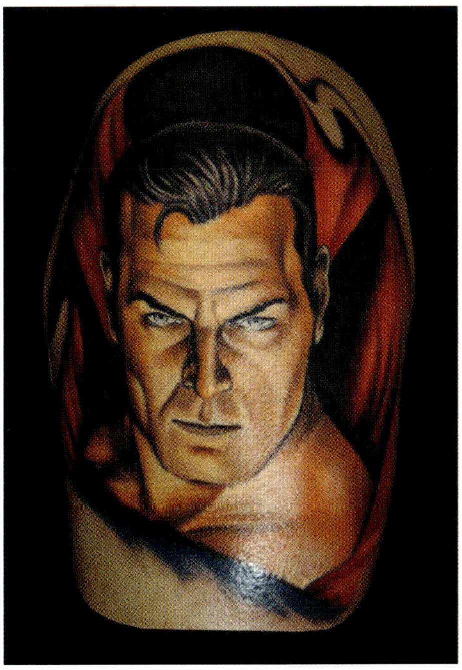

Describe how you go about creating a tattoo from concept to finished design. How do you try to put your own unique touch on your tattoos?

I probably work different to a lot of people; every time I'm on the Internet and see things I think would make good tattoos, I save them in a folder, then when I come in in the morning I look at what jobs I have in, and go through my folder and find things that relate. Then when my client comes in, I show them and go from there. As I do realism, I mostly work from real photos, then I tend to freehand all backgrounds straight onto the skin, as it makes everything flow together better.

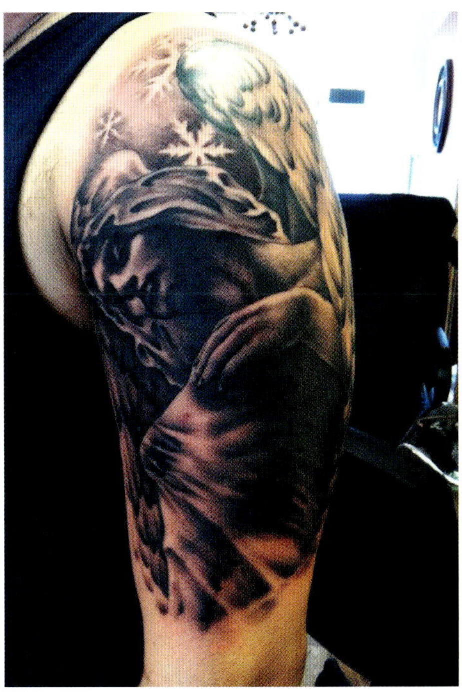

What was the first tattoo you ever did? Can you tell us about it?

It's a little daffodil that wraps around my ankle, it's not that bad actually, but I did carve a crater into it when trying to put the yellow in!

How would you describe your style? And which tattoo style do you like best?

Realism, and realism.

What's the hardest part about being a tattoo artist?

Coming up with ideas that haven't been done.

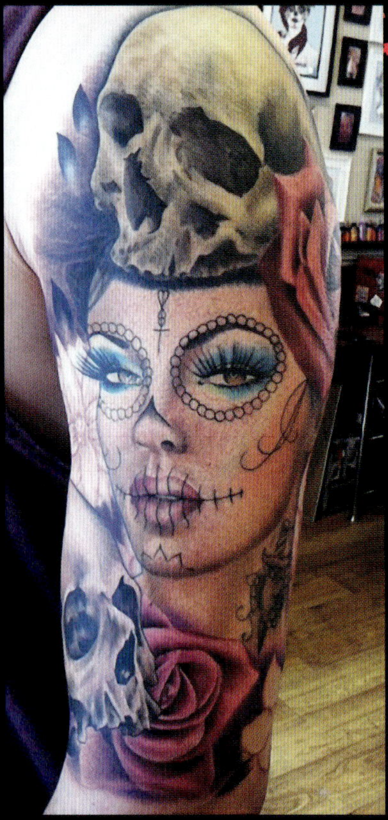
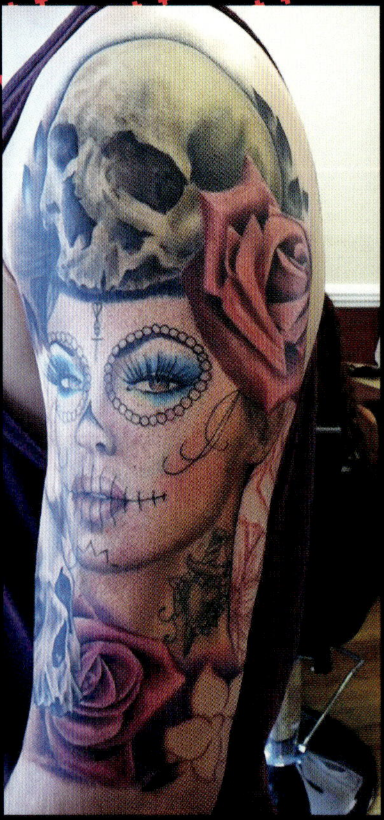
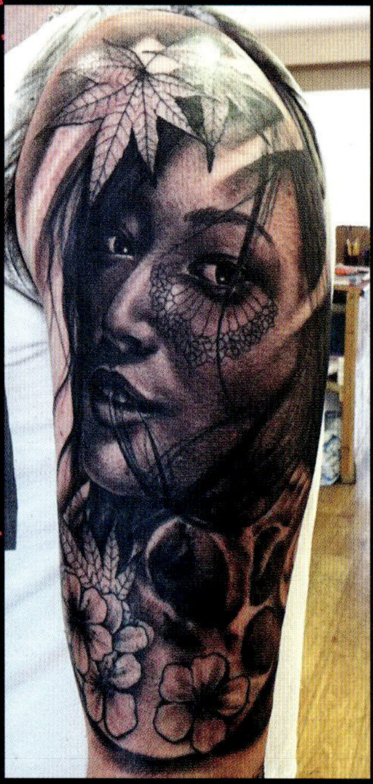
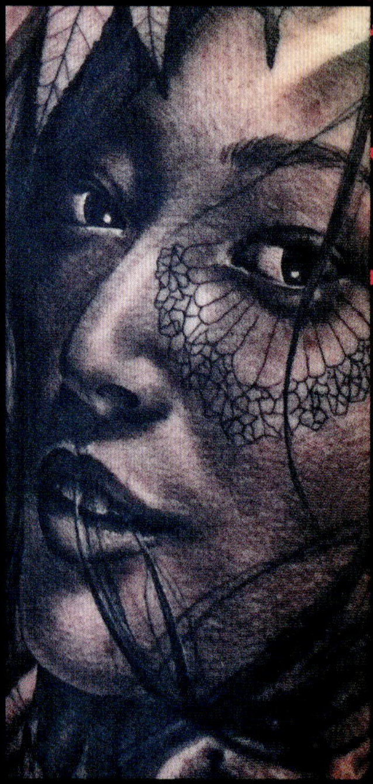
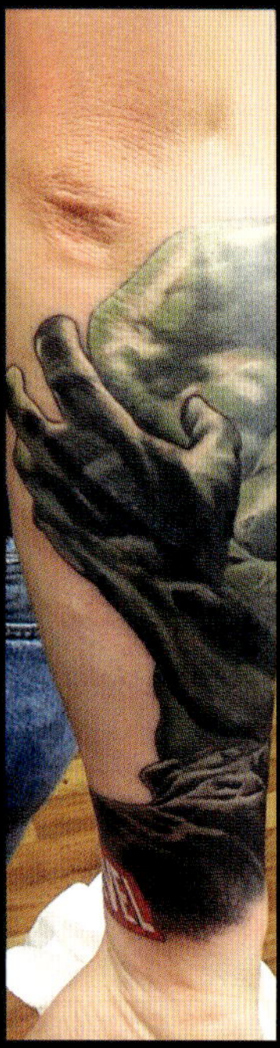
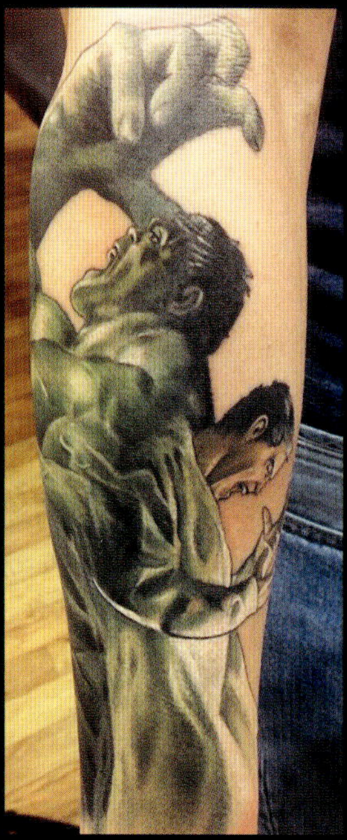
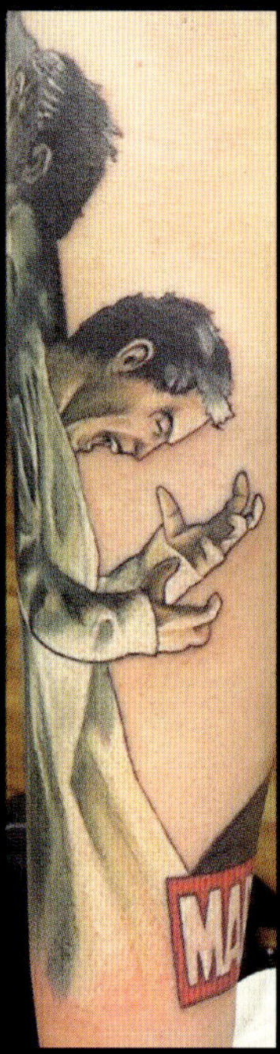
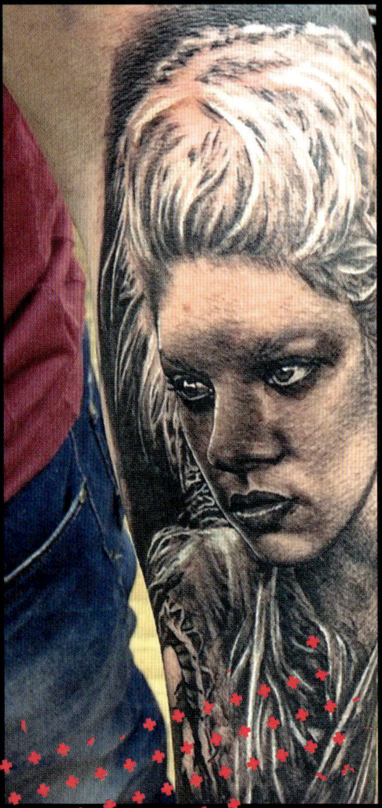
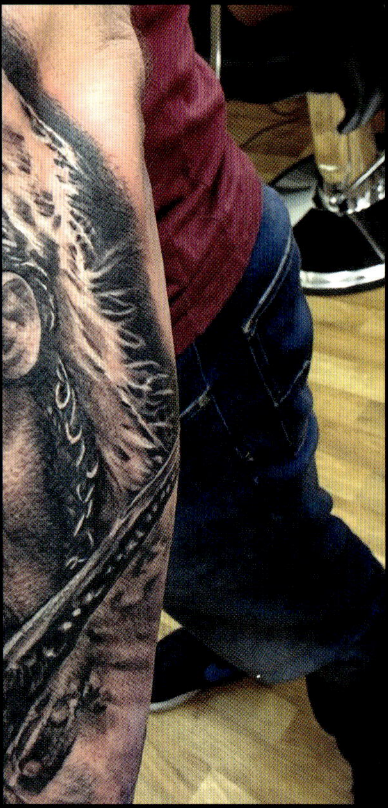
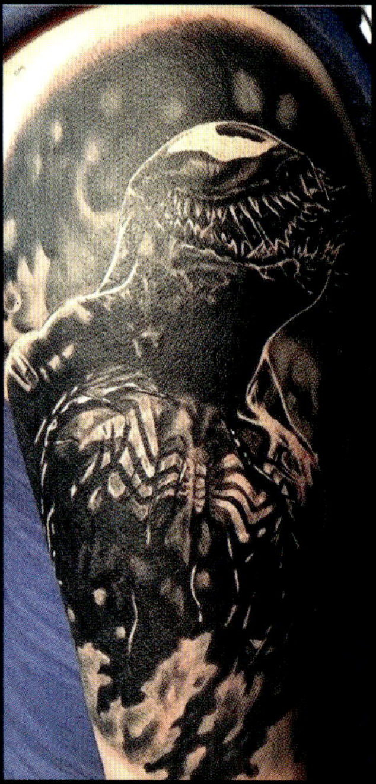
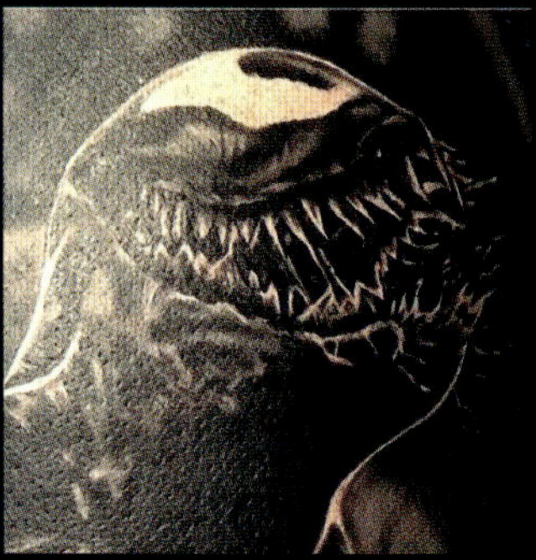
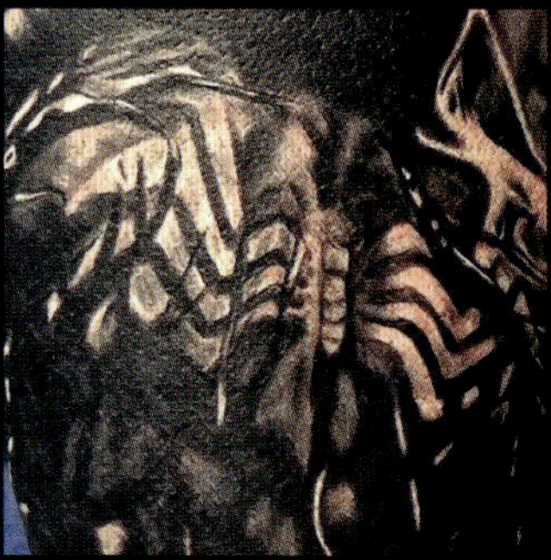

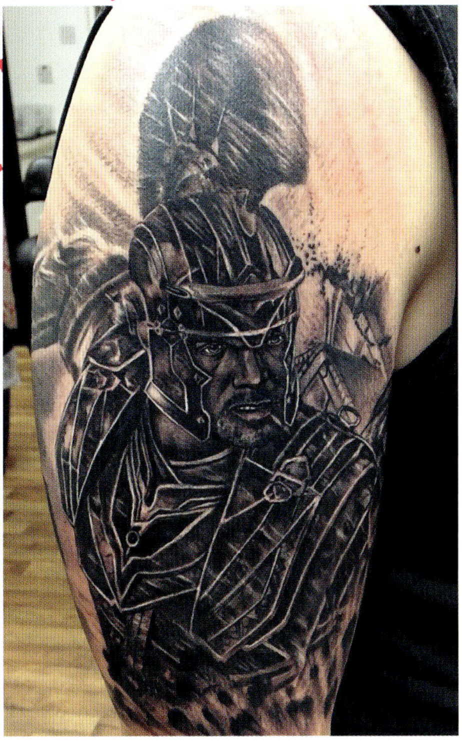

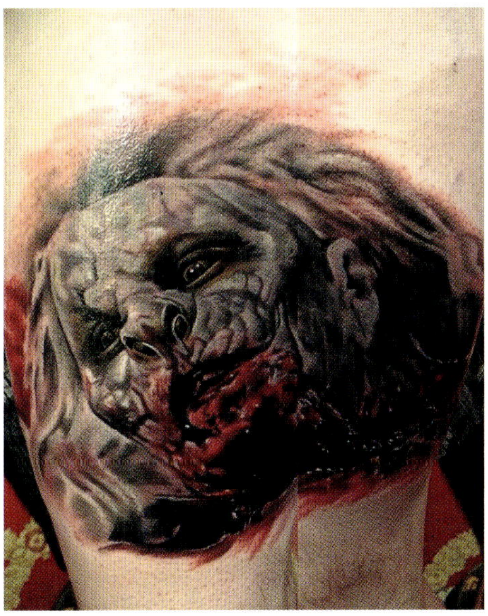

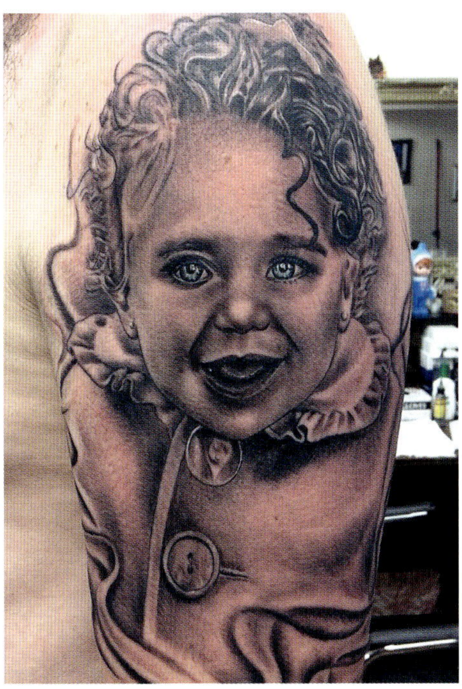

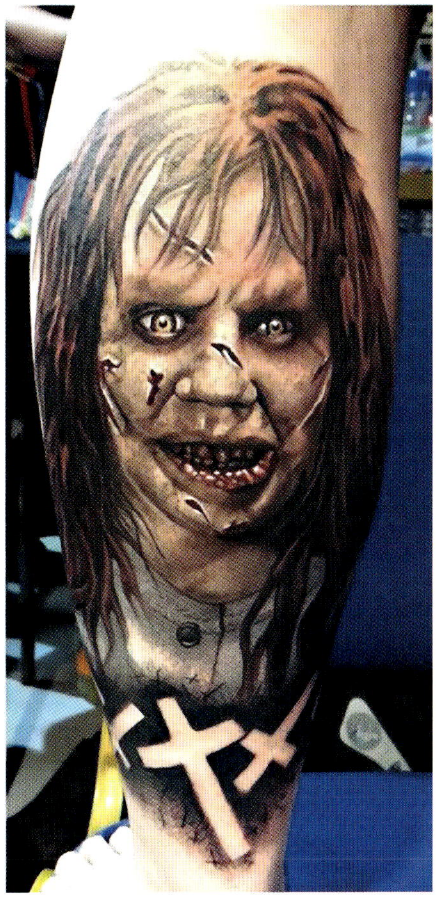

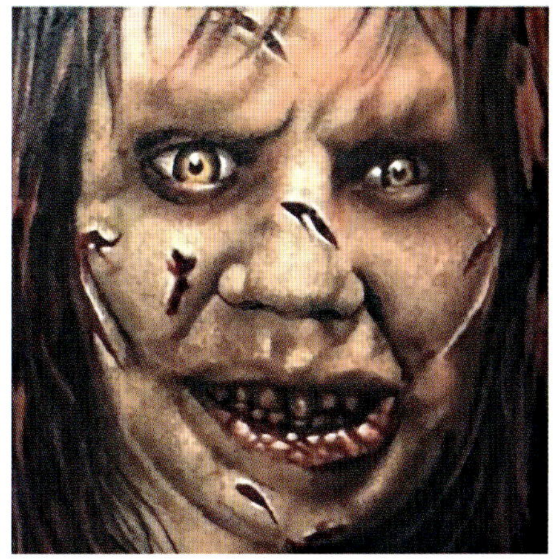

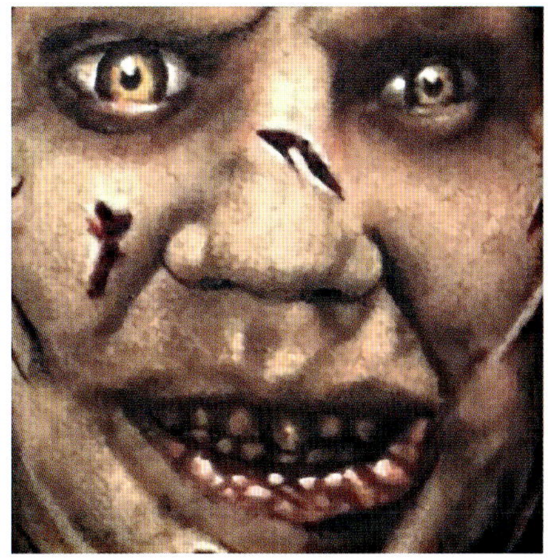

What's the most rewarding part about being a tattoo artist?

I don't let my clients look in the mirror until I've finished the tattoo, so for me, every day, it's watching their face when they look in the mirror at the finished piece.

What do you think a client should expect from you as a tattoo artist, and what do you, on the other hand, expect from a client to make a successful tattoo and a good collaboration?

Trust! My client should trust me to give them the best tattoo. And I expect my client to trust me, as they've come to me because they like what I do.

What criteria do you think that a tattoo convention should have to be really successful, both for you as a tattoo artist, but also for the visitors? Can you give some examples of conventions that meet these criteria well?

The best artists around, great entertainment, fair judging in competitions, private areas for artists, fair booth prices, and fair entry ticket prices. Some of my favorite conventions I have worked at are Tattoo Jam Liverpool and Tattoo Tea Party.

How would you describe the current status of tattoos among the general public in England?

There's scratchers opening up studios or setting up at home everywhere, due to crappy equipment being sold to anyone on

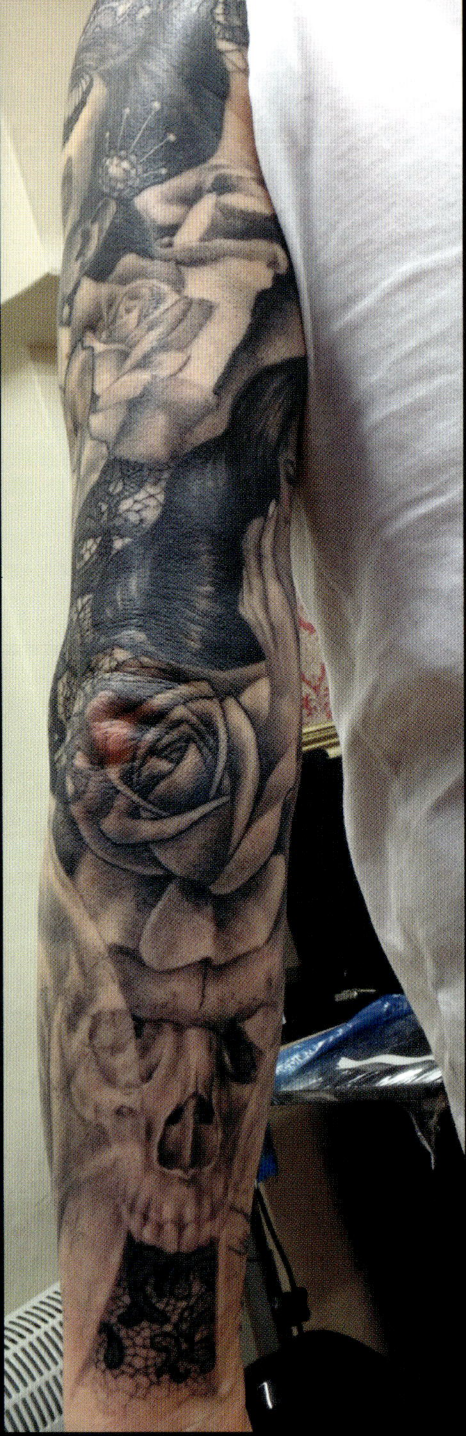
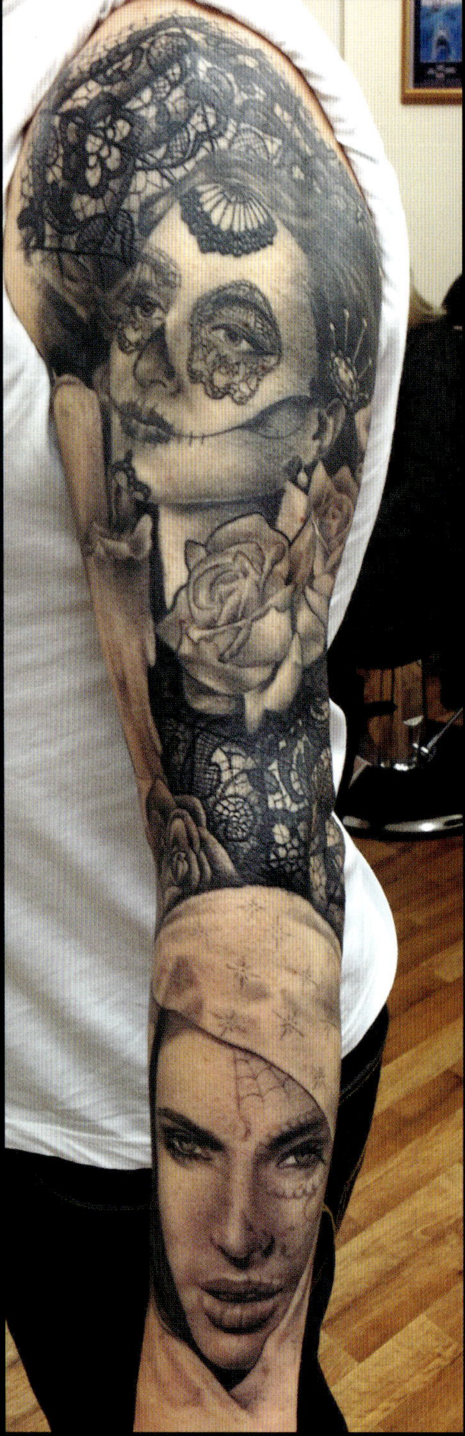
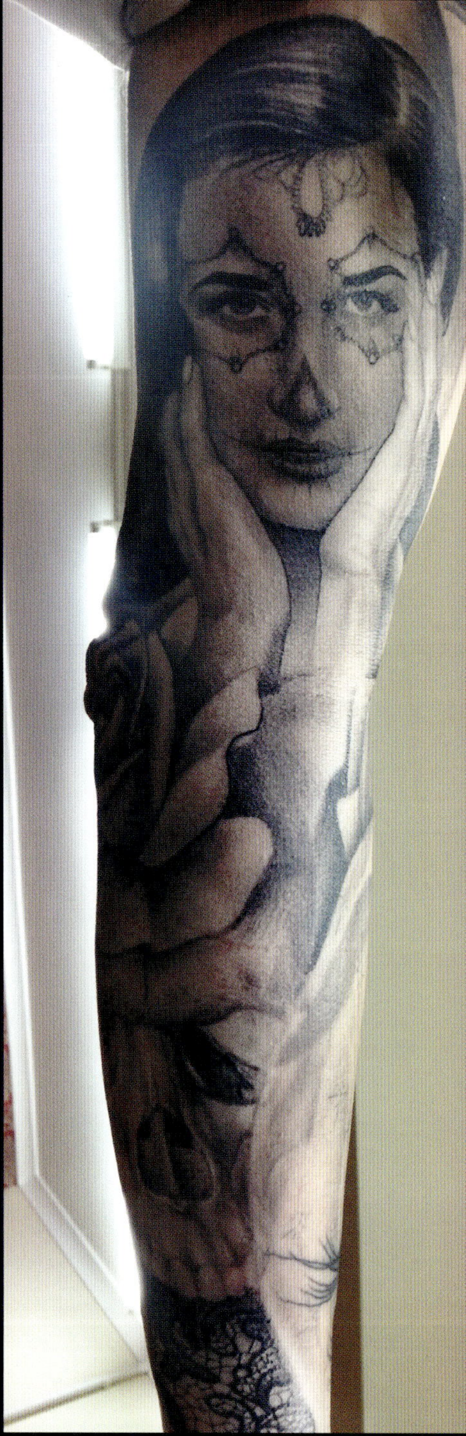
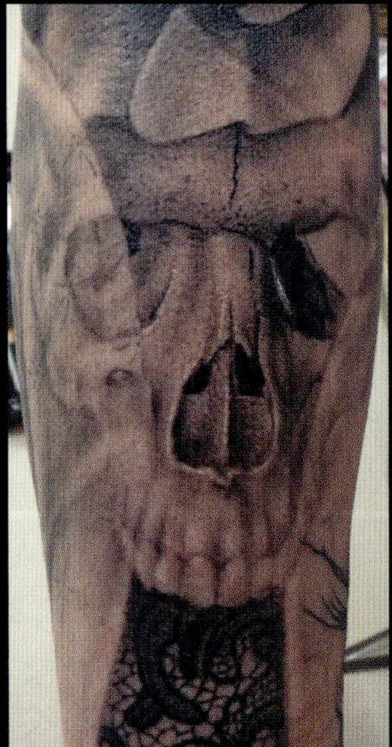
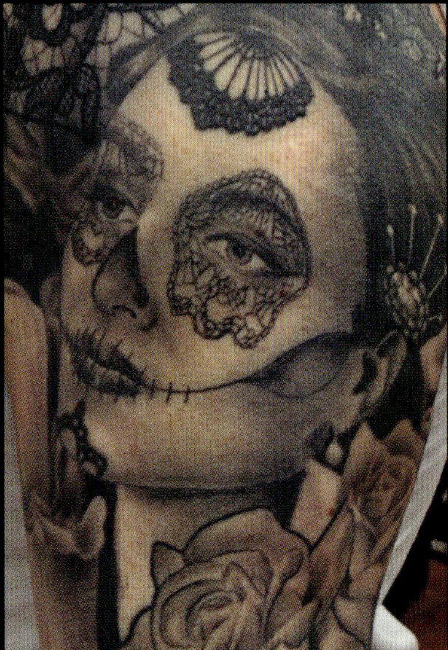
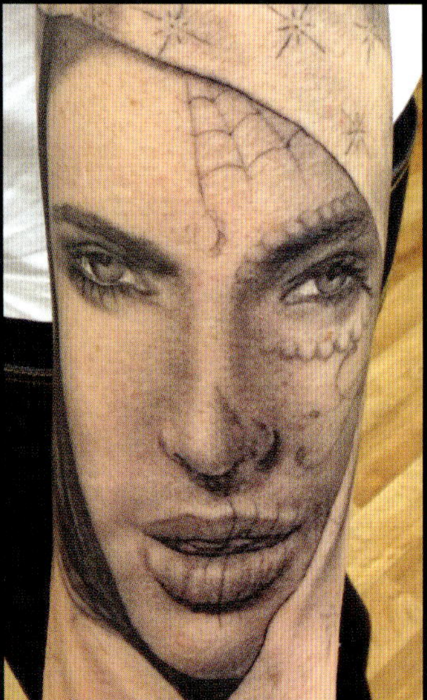
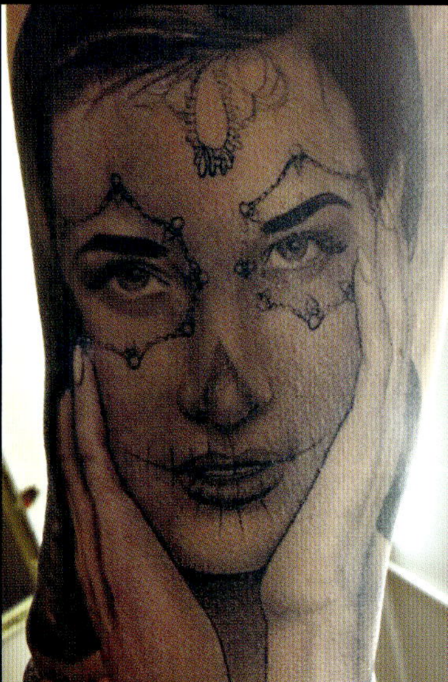

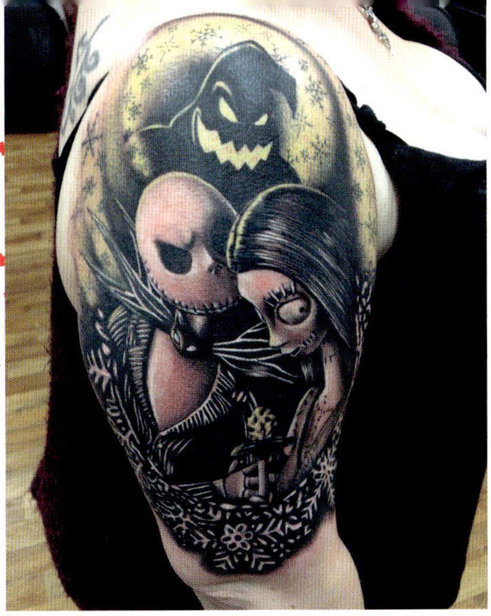

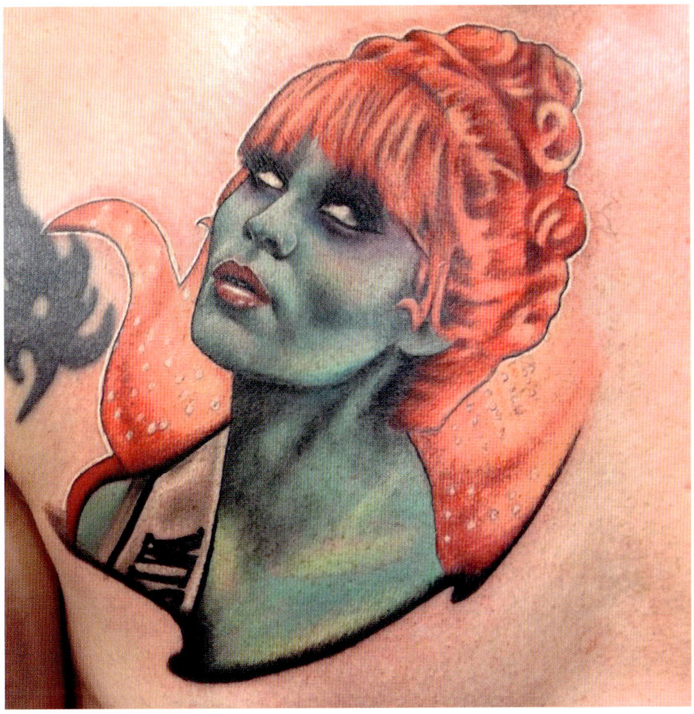

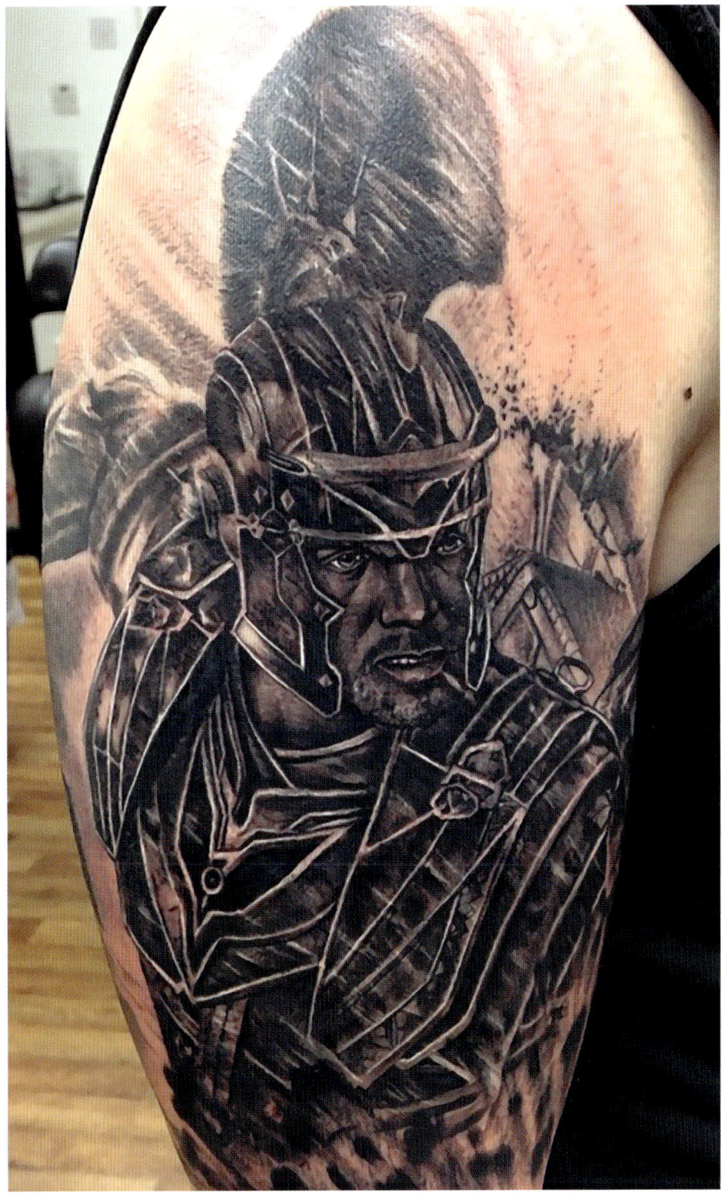

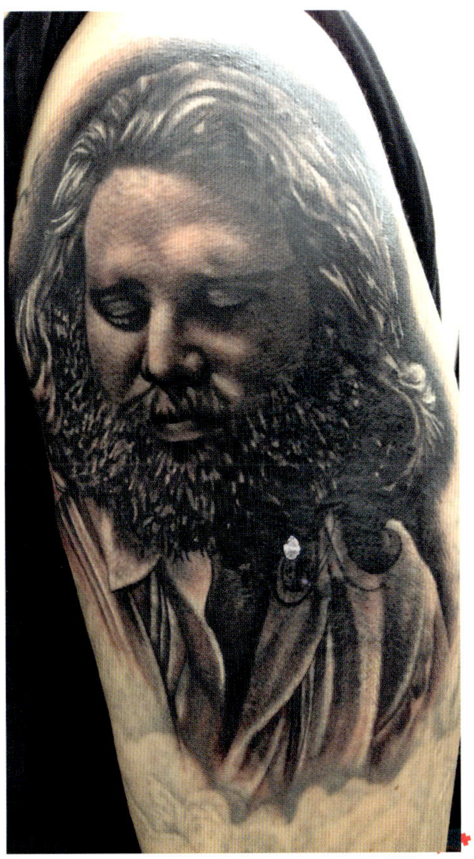

the Internet, and this brings a lot of people price comparing or coming to us for advice about fixing or covering crap done by these scratchers.

TV shows, Internet, and especially social networks like Facebook and Twitter have come to have an extremely wide influence in recent years. What positive and negative impacts do you think it has for the future development of the tattoo industry?

It's great in that it's connecting artists all over the world, and through this we're able to inspire each other with amazing work that gets posted. It's also good in that a lot more clients are able to research and find artists they want to get work by. It's also negative in that it's creating what I like to call rockstar tattooists who get into the industry for the money and status, because it's cool to be a tattooist. They're not getting into it for the art, and therefore have no respect.

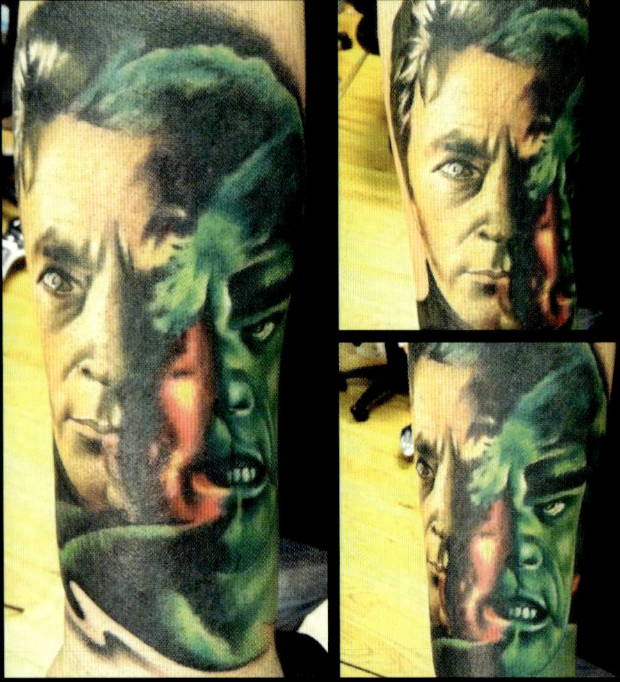
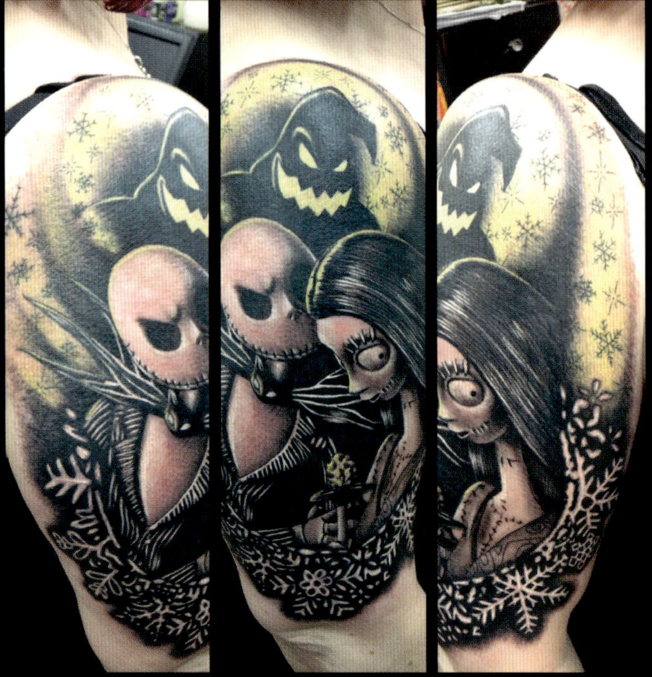
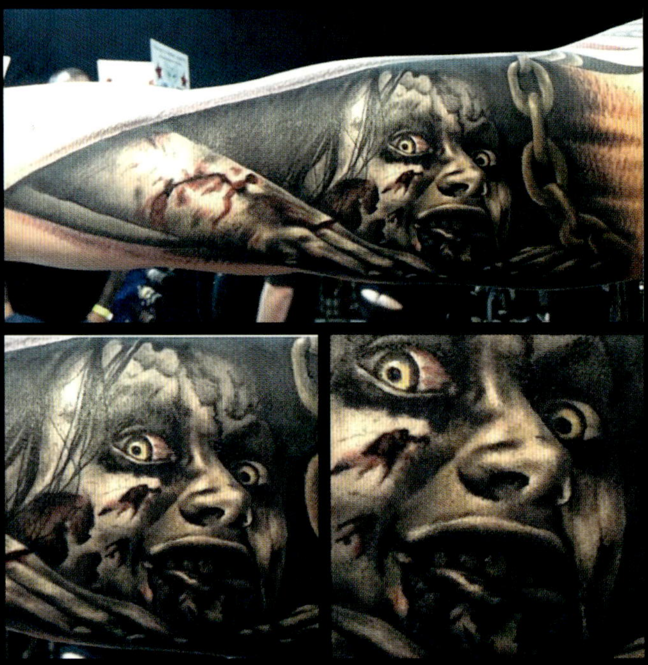
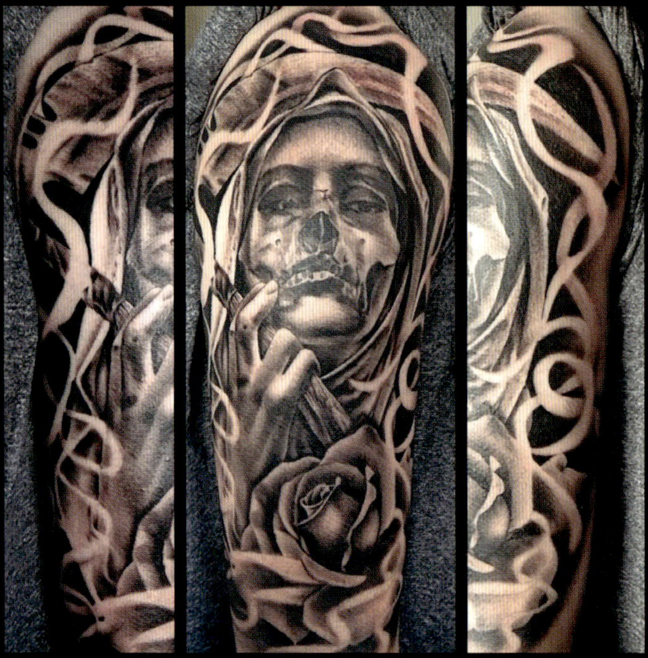
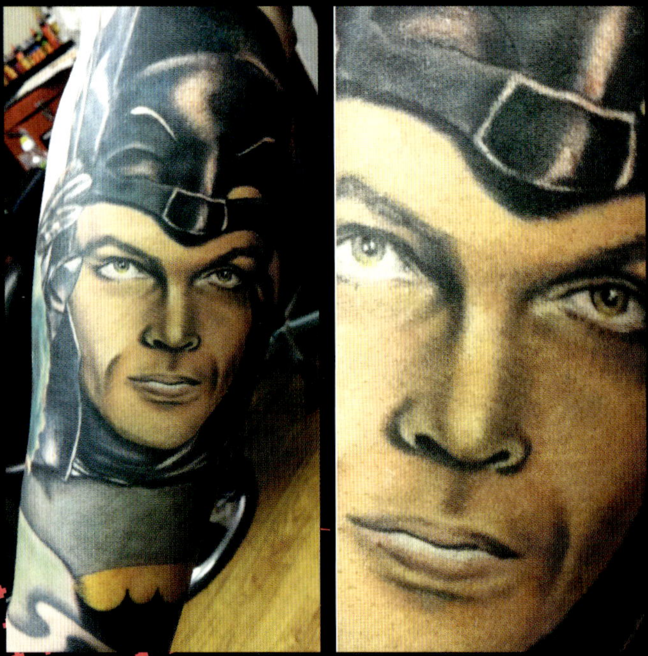
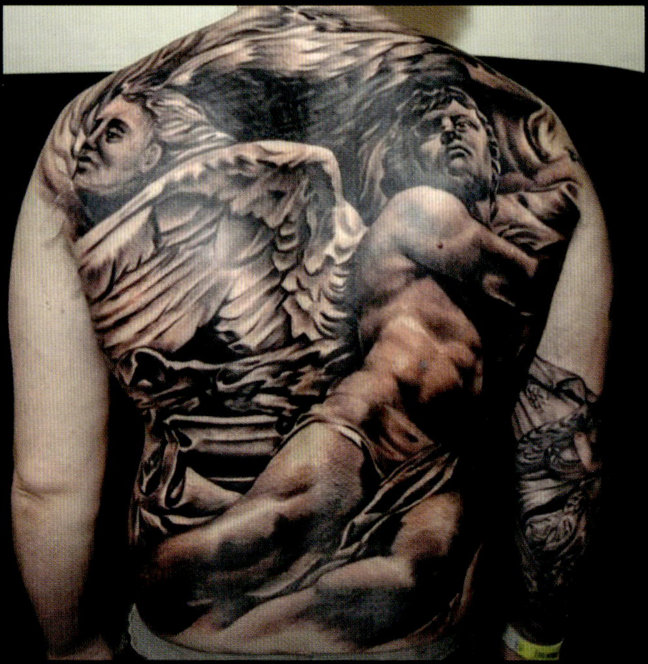

CHANTALE COADY

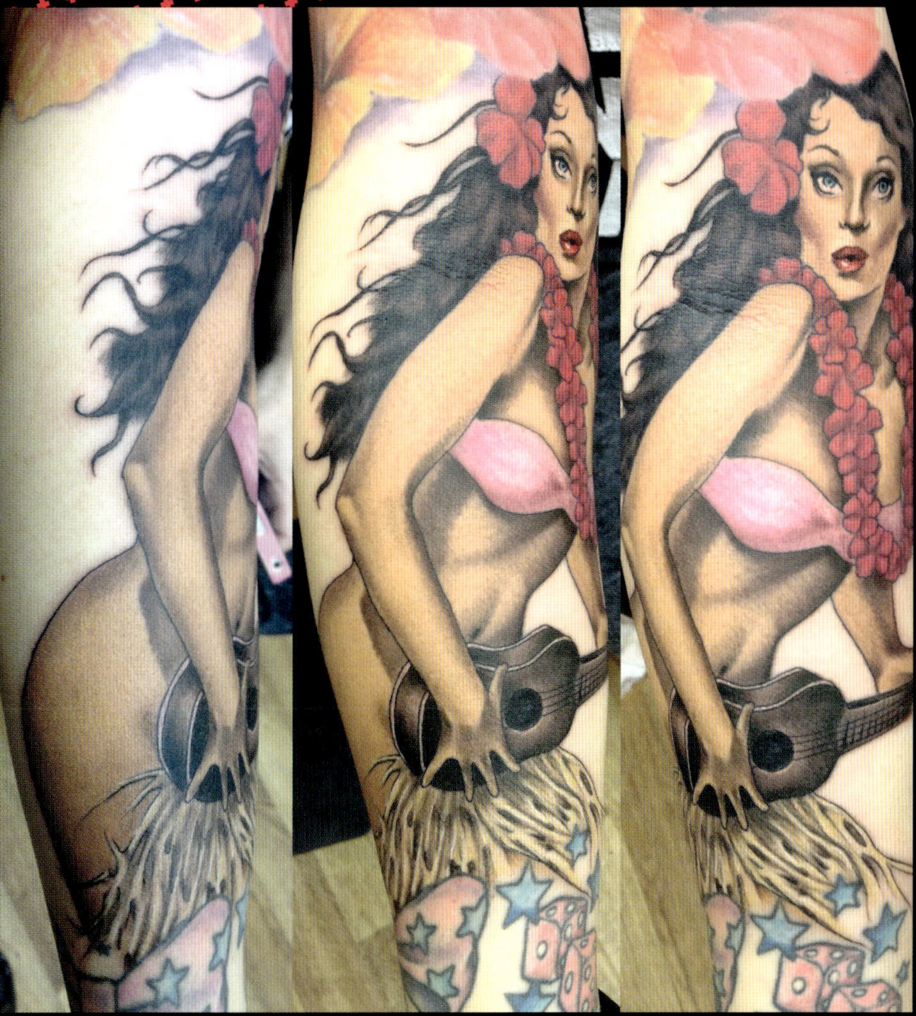

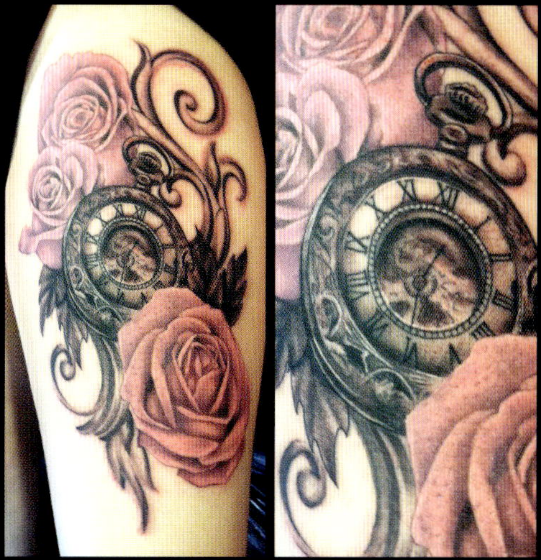

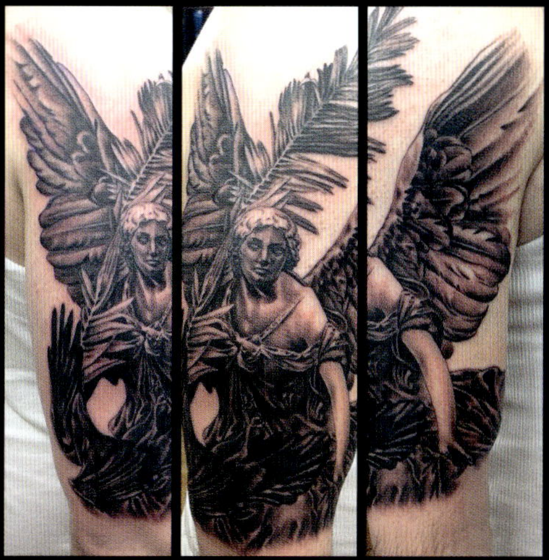

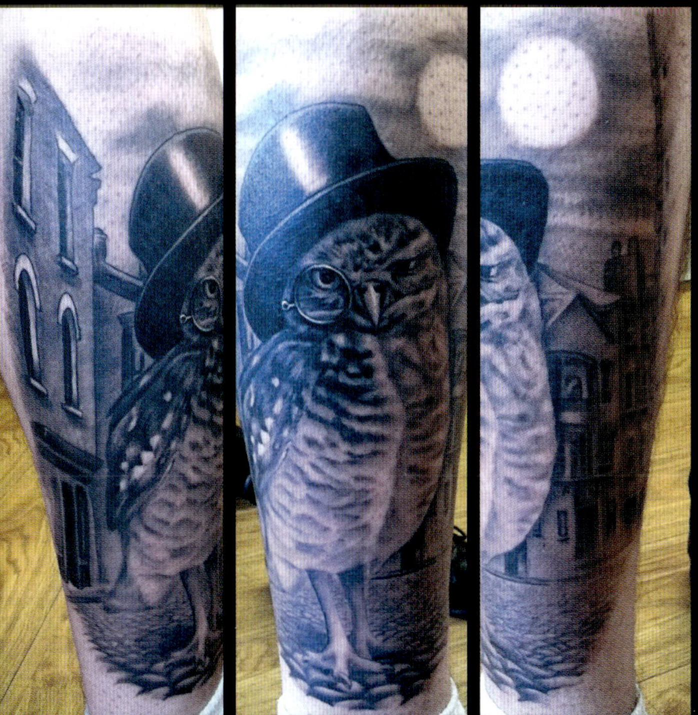

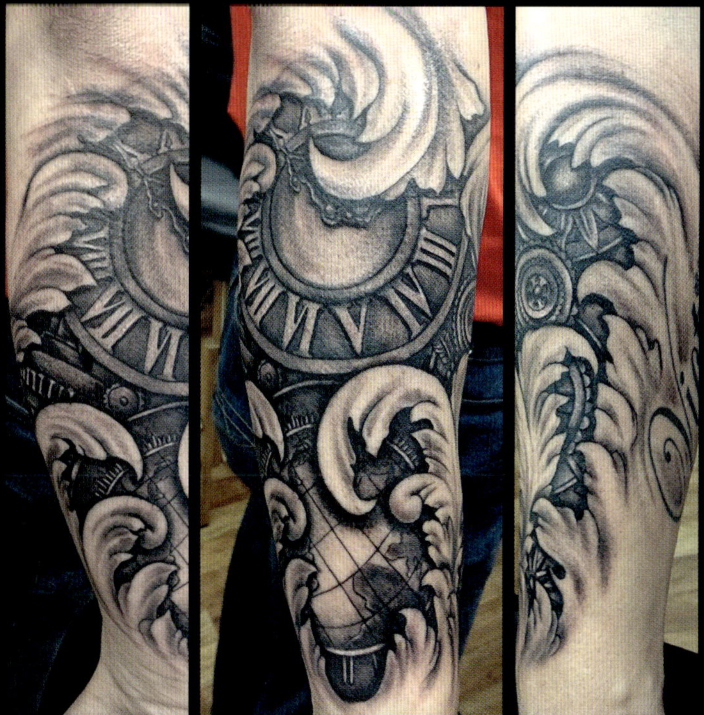

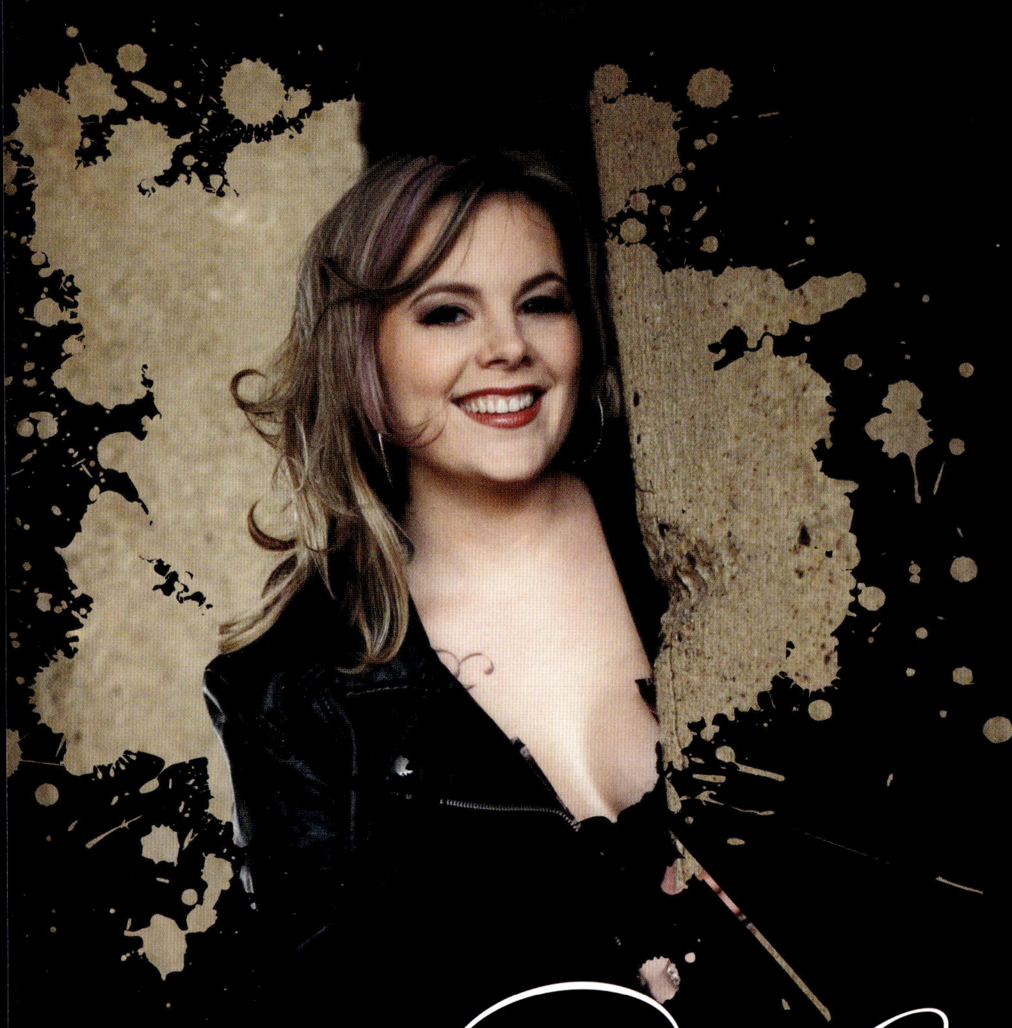

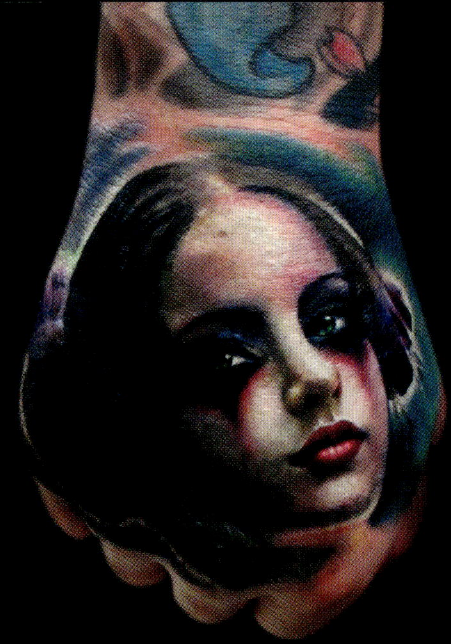

LIZ COOK always knew she wanted to be a professional artist. Her parents and family really wanted her to do something in life that Liz would be happy with, and art never felt like "work." It was always chill time. Growing up, she drew all the time. Liz had to be doing something otherwise she'd drive her mom crazy; when she wasn't drawing, Liz was making something...like making up codes, crocheting doll outfits, sewing mini pillows, making up board games, and even making her own tarot cards.

Liz COOK

"TV shows often present unrealistic tattoo situations that potential clients perceive as truth"

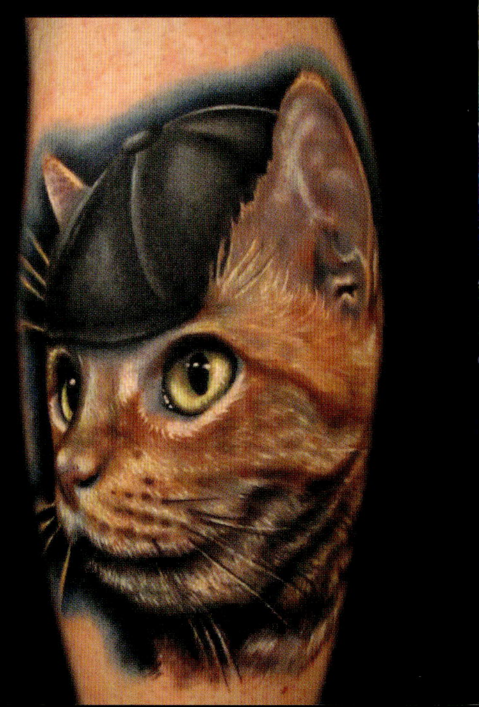

lizcooktattoo.com
www.facebook.com/lizcooktattoo
instagram.com/lizcooktattoo
lizcooktattoo.tumblr.com
twitter.com/LizCookTattoo
rebelmusetattoo.com

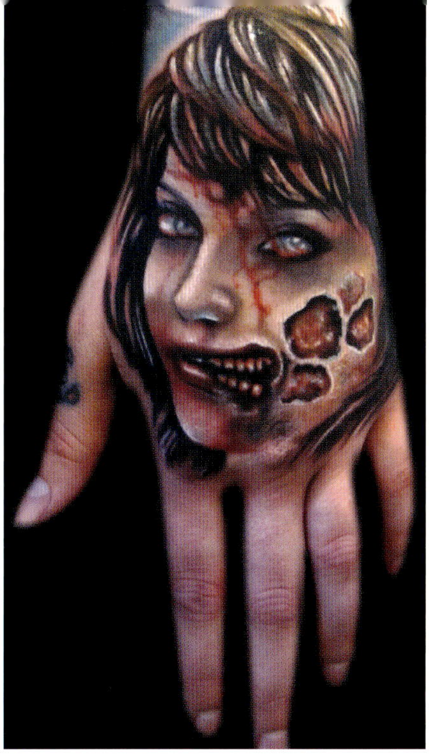

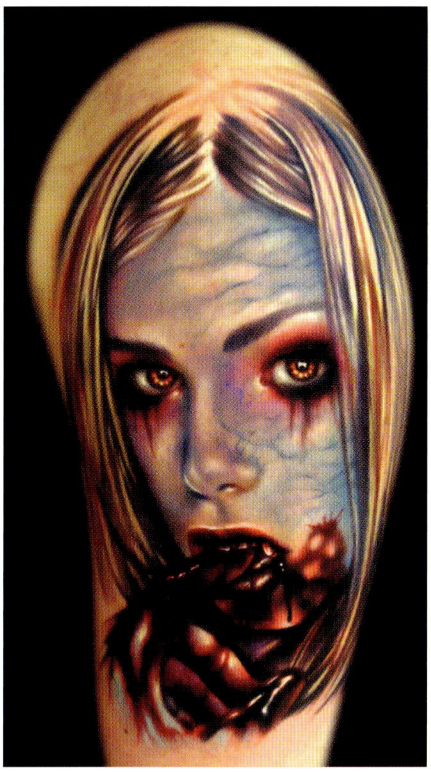

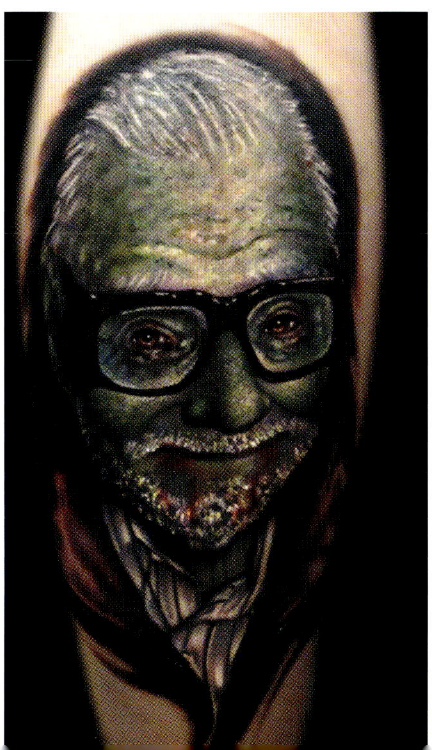

What did you do before you started tattooing?

The year before I started tattooing, I was a temporary receptionist for a variety of companies in Perth, Australia, while I was on a holiday working visa. The years before that, while I was going to university, I waitressed at a couple of restaurants, and was a swim instructor, a lifeguard, a clothing retail associate, and again a receptionist.

What was your initial exposure to the tattoo world, and when did you first add your own piece of ink to your skin? Was that a transformative time in your life?

Growing up, it wasn't really anything that was in my face every day. I remember playing with my best friends and sisters when we were little and drawing on each other with sharpened sticks to make pretend tattoos, and sometimes when we went to a kid restaurant there'd be the fake stick-on tattoos. I don't remember my parents ever saying, "Don't get tattoos," but we never really thought to ask. It never occurred to me that tattoos had any negative association with them.

I didn't actually see my first tattoo until my first serious boyfriend, who had a couple that were really good. I had no clue, though, that not every tattooer could pull off a good tattoo. When I did get my first, which happened to be right after me and my boyfriend split, I didn't know to research artists. This was in 2003, so it was kind of different back then. Unfortunately, the artist was so bad and really scarred me. I didn't even get another tattoo until I started tattooing. It was then that I realized how bad that guy really was. It certainly helped motivate me to make sure that I never did that to people.

What's it like being a female artist in a primarily male workplace?

Awesome! It makes it a lot easier to stand out. No, but really, I feel like it's easy to say that about a lot of professions, but I really try to not think of it that way and try to just do my thing. Especially these days with all the social media, your work really gets out there and people can see whether or not it's good before they even know you're a guy or gal.

Do you feel that male customers treat you differently?

No, not really any different than a guy would treat me in other situations. I can be pretty "dude-ish" at times which maybe makes them more comfortable. I definitely like to joke around and BS during sessions, but that's really with everyone.

What did your family and friends think about you getting into the business?

They loved it! Everyone got free tattoos! Also, my parents were really happy that I wasn't going to be a poor starving artist anymore. They were worried when I went to school for art because I didn't take any commercial or advertising art classes, just painting and drawing classes.

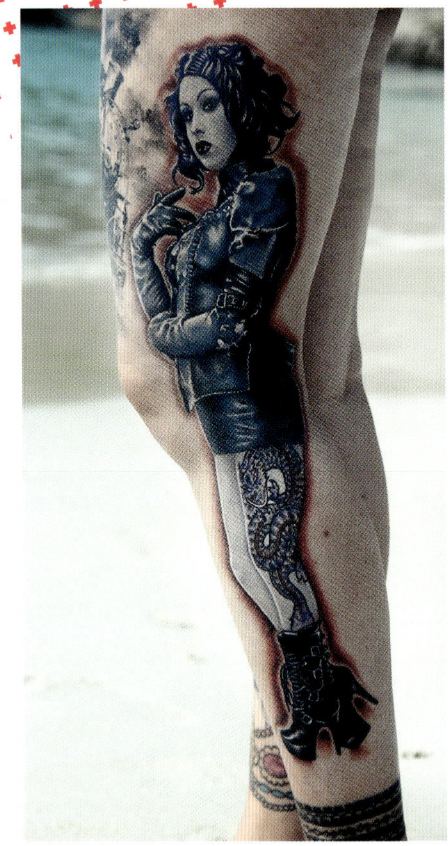

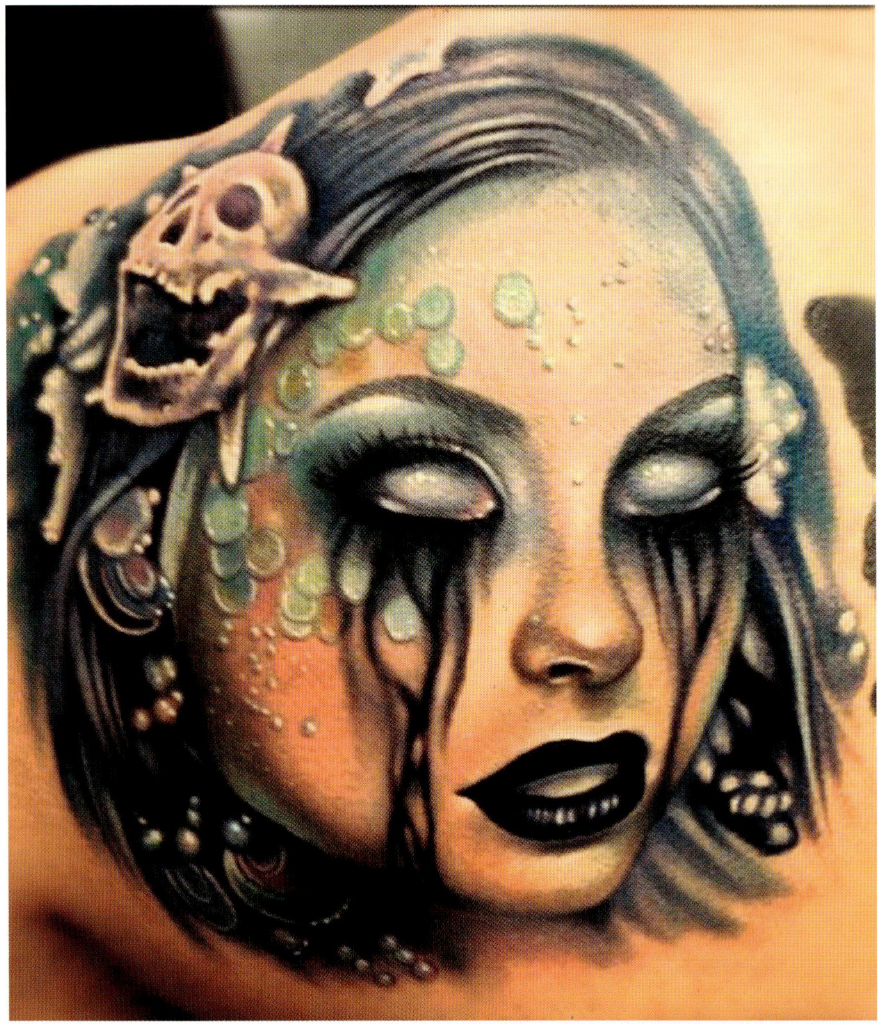

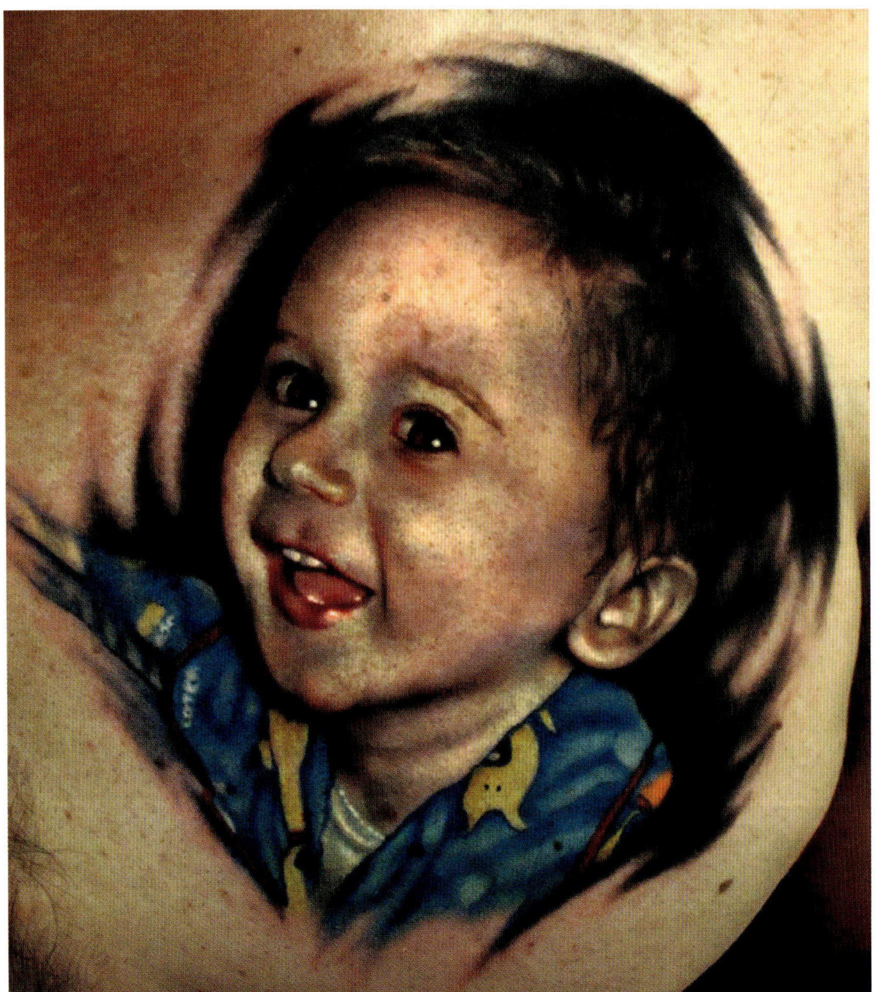

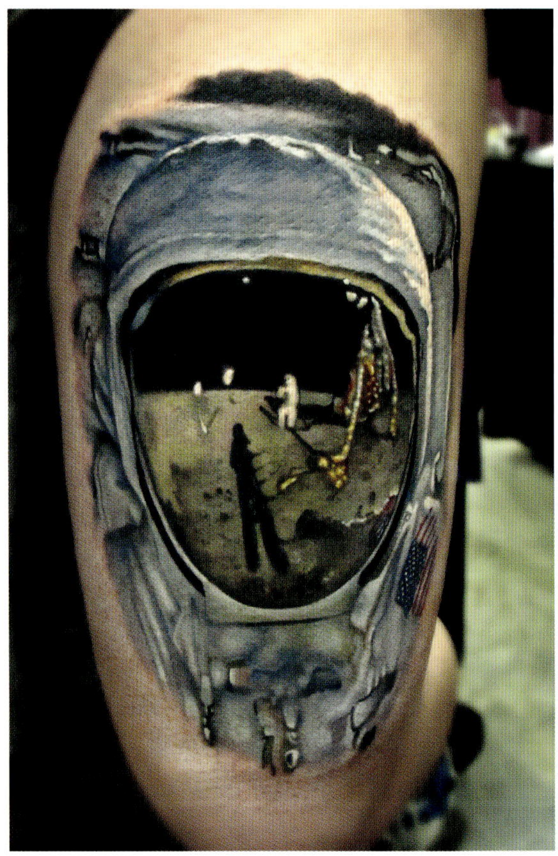

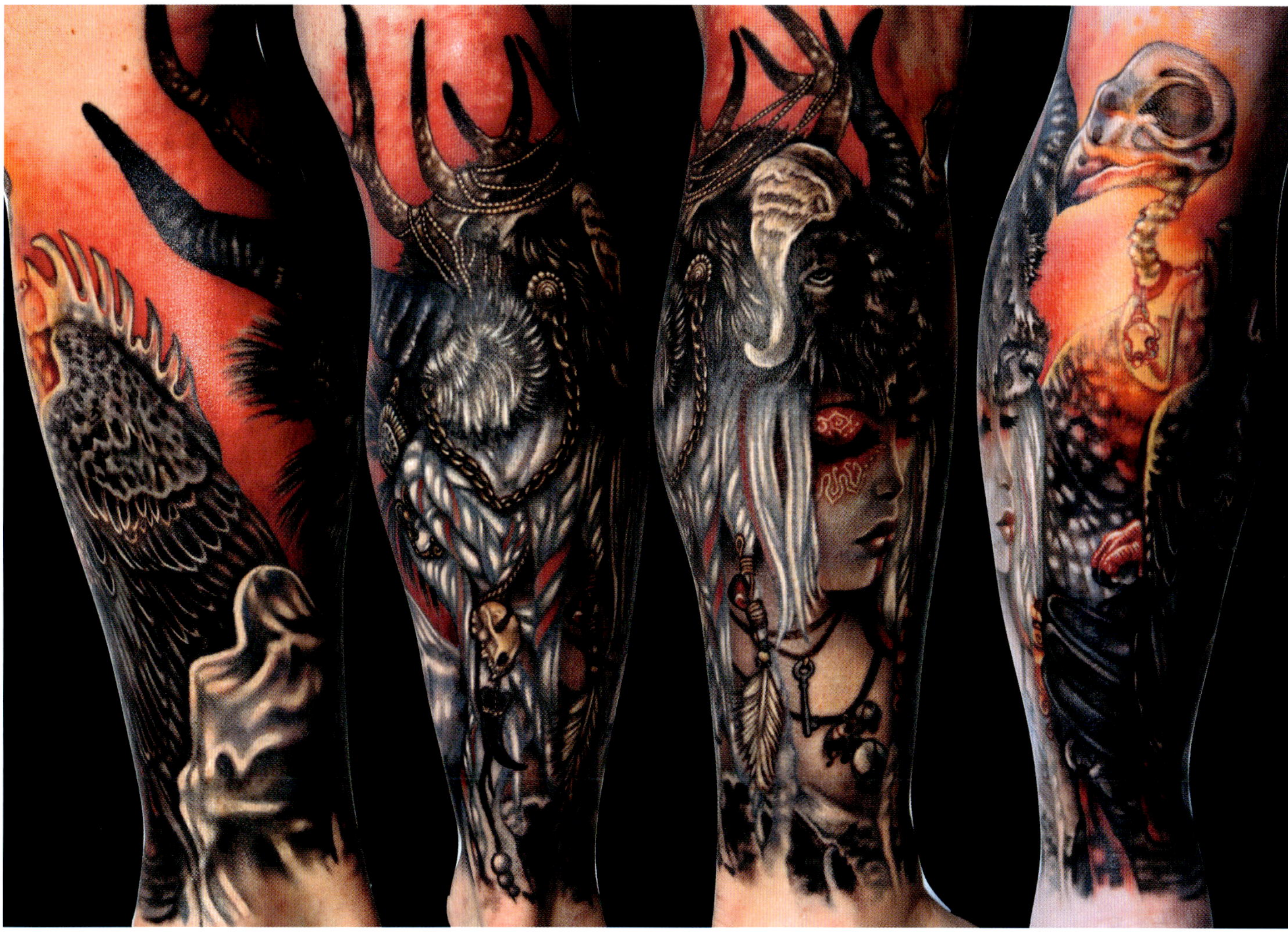

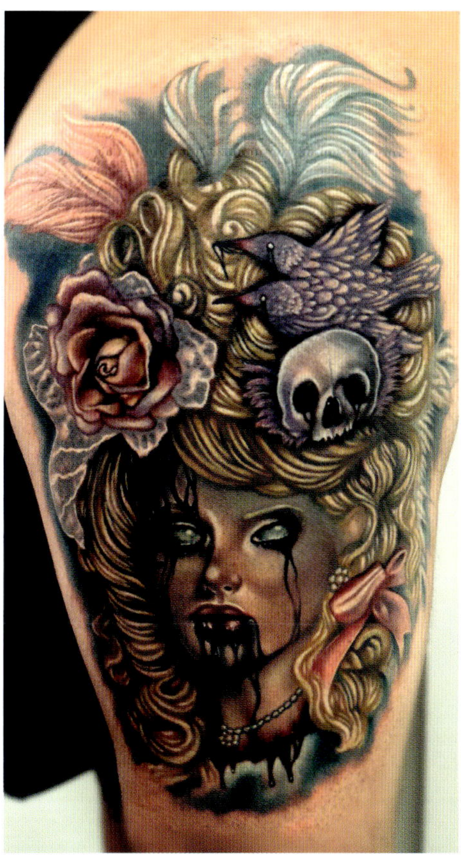

Tell me more about the shop you work at, Rebel Muse Tattoo; what's it like working there?

I own the shop with my husband, Cookie, and our business partner Dave Mushaney. It's really a chill shop where everybody does their own schedule and bookings. We're really fortunate to have an awesome team of people that are constantly pushing each other while still having fun, and we also are lucky enough to have a badass shop manager who keeps us all in check, Ellen Mushaney, Dave's lovely wife.

Describe how you go about creating a tattoo from concept to finished design. How do you try to put your own unique touch on your tattoos?

First, I really want to know the direction the client expects. Some people will say that I have the artistic freedom to do whatever, but when it comes down to it, they really don't mean that. So I try to get people to at least throw around a few ideas that can inspire. A few different ideas really lets me get into the client's head a little more, which will set the tone for the pieces and prevent me from just having to pull something out of thin air.

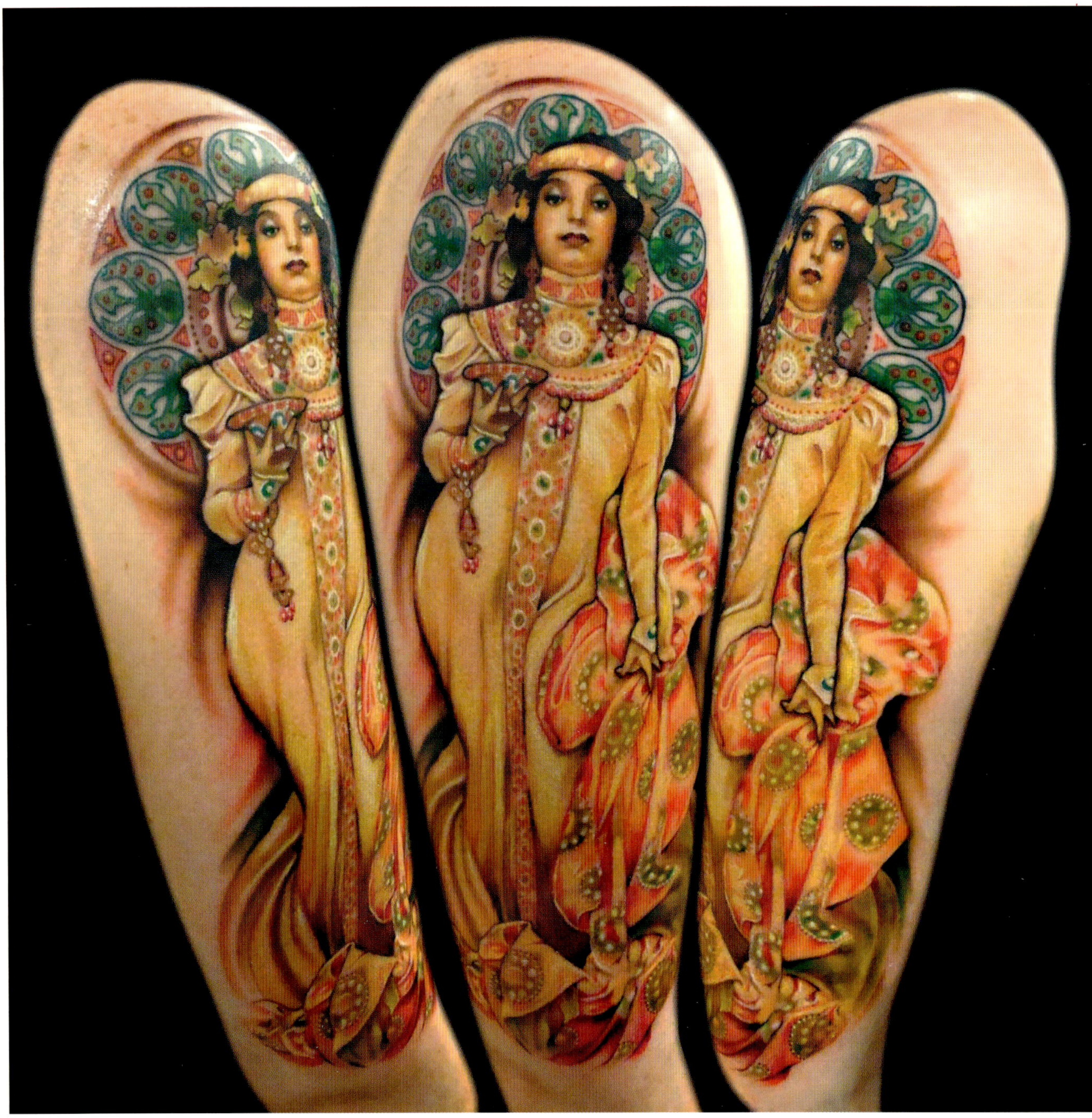

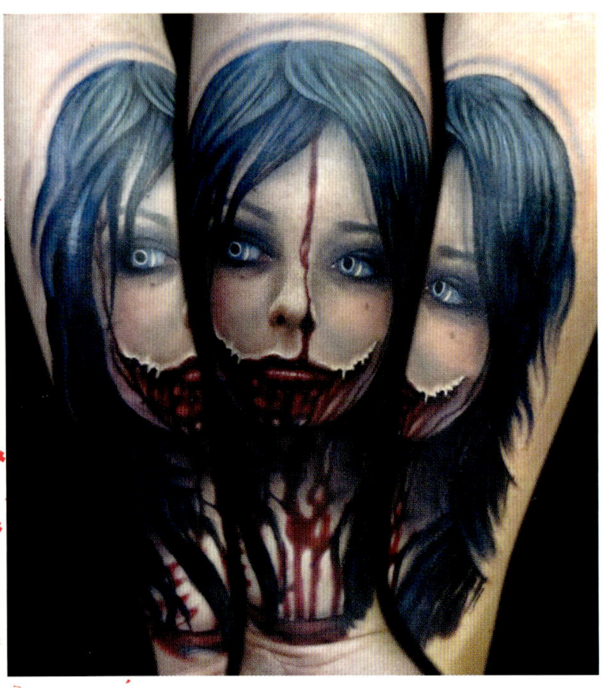

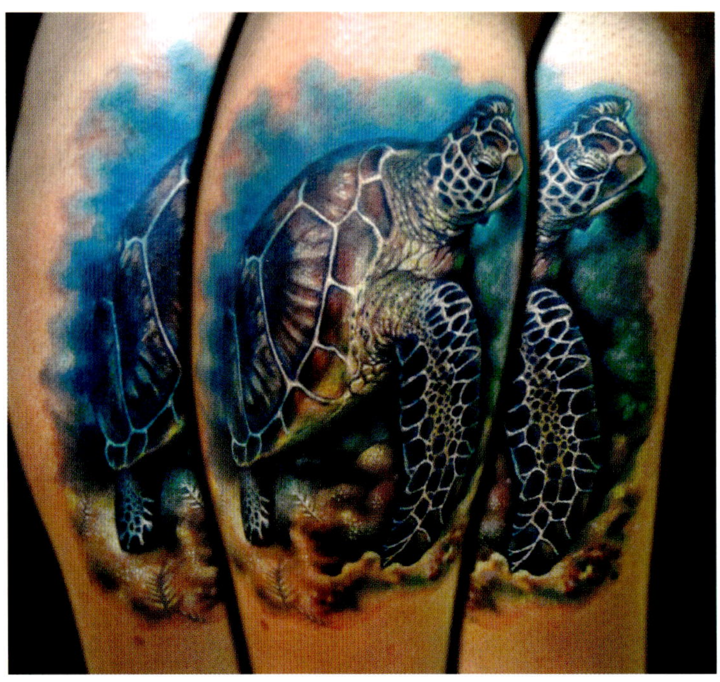

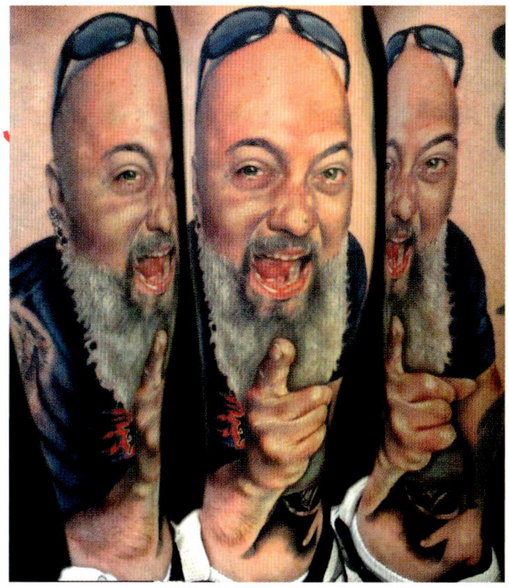

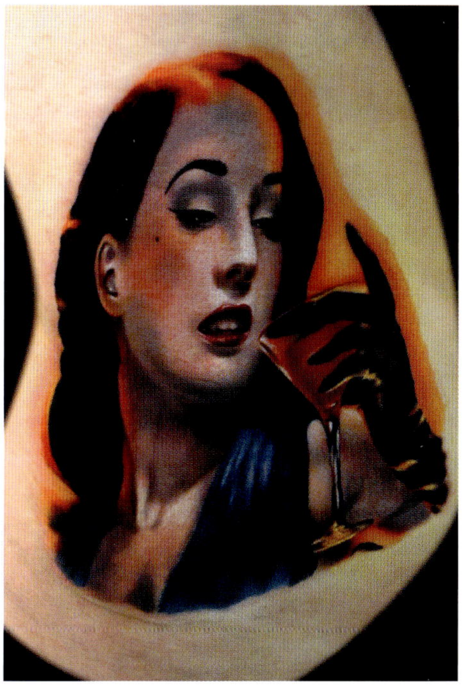

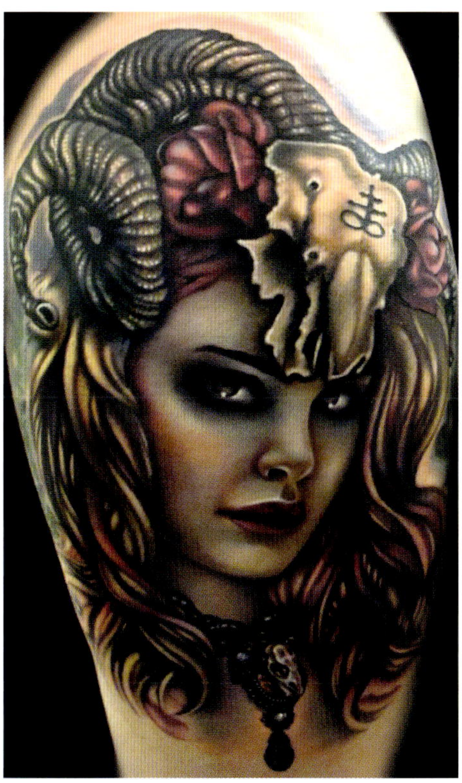

Then, lots of research. Sometimes it could be days of research spread out over months, depending on when the client is actually scheduled to come in. Sometimes it may be only a day, if it's something that I'm already super-familiar with. After that, the designing. Most of my pieces I design in Photoshop with photo manipulation, digital painting, and drawing, which could take anywhere from a couple of hours to a couple of days depending on the size. If it's a color piece, I work out a couple of directions I think it could go depending on the "color potential" of the client's skin; I mean what colors you can use in their skin that will heal closest to the perceived actual color tattooed. For example, someone who has lighter pale skin has a greater range of color potential than someone with olive or tan skin.

What was the first tattoo you ever did? Can you tell me about it?

The first tattoo I did, in order to get my apprenticeship, was on my husband. It was the line design of new school–ish geisha on his right pec. I totally didn't even know how to stretch that area properly, but I wanted to show them that I could do something big, and not just little lettering.

What is your favorite style of work to tattoo? What would your dream piece be to work on?

My favorite styles are portraits, realism, horror, pin-ups and black-and-gray. There's not just one piece that would be the dream piece…I'm constantly inspired so it's more like, "I haven't done this in a while," or "I haven't done this in this way yet." It's funny though, because there are a couple of things out there that you would think I've tattooed but I actually haven't yet. For instance, at the moment, I've never tattooed a compass, but I have a few people on my waitlist who want one. It always seems that if I start teeling like there's something I haven't done, within a few weeks I'll have at least three requests booked in for it.

Describe how your role models and any other sources of inspiration have affected your tattoo style.

Growing up, I was really into comic art, so some of my first sources of inspiration were Boris Vallejo, Julie Bell, J. Scott Campbell, Nei Ruffino, and Olivia de Berardinis. I loved their colors and techniques. I also fell in love with the work of Alphonse Mucha, and had a lot of exposure to all the awesome graphics in video games and their amount of detail. There's so much art that I feel I've been exposed to with school and traveling that it's hard to pinpoint just a few role models and sources that directly affect my work. When I first started tattooing, my teacher had Mike Devries's *Let's Be Realistic* and Guy Aitchison's *Reinventing the Tattoo*. I was so impressed by those books and I knew straight away, I wanted to do tattoos as amazing as theirs.

What's one of your favorite pieces that you've tattooed on someone else?

I love the Mike Kelly portrait that I did on my husband's leg. He's a great friend of ours and every time I look at it, the look on his face totally cracks me up.

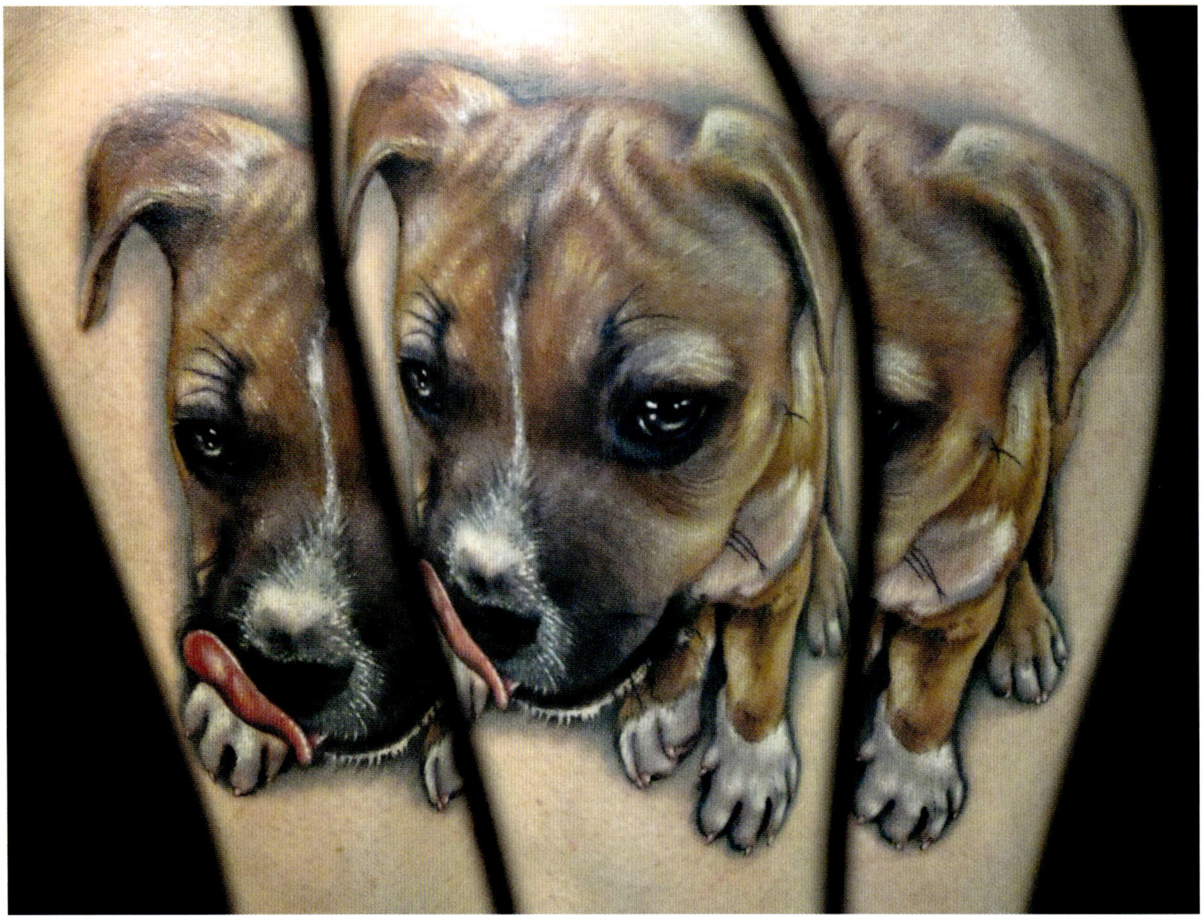

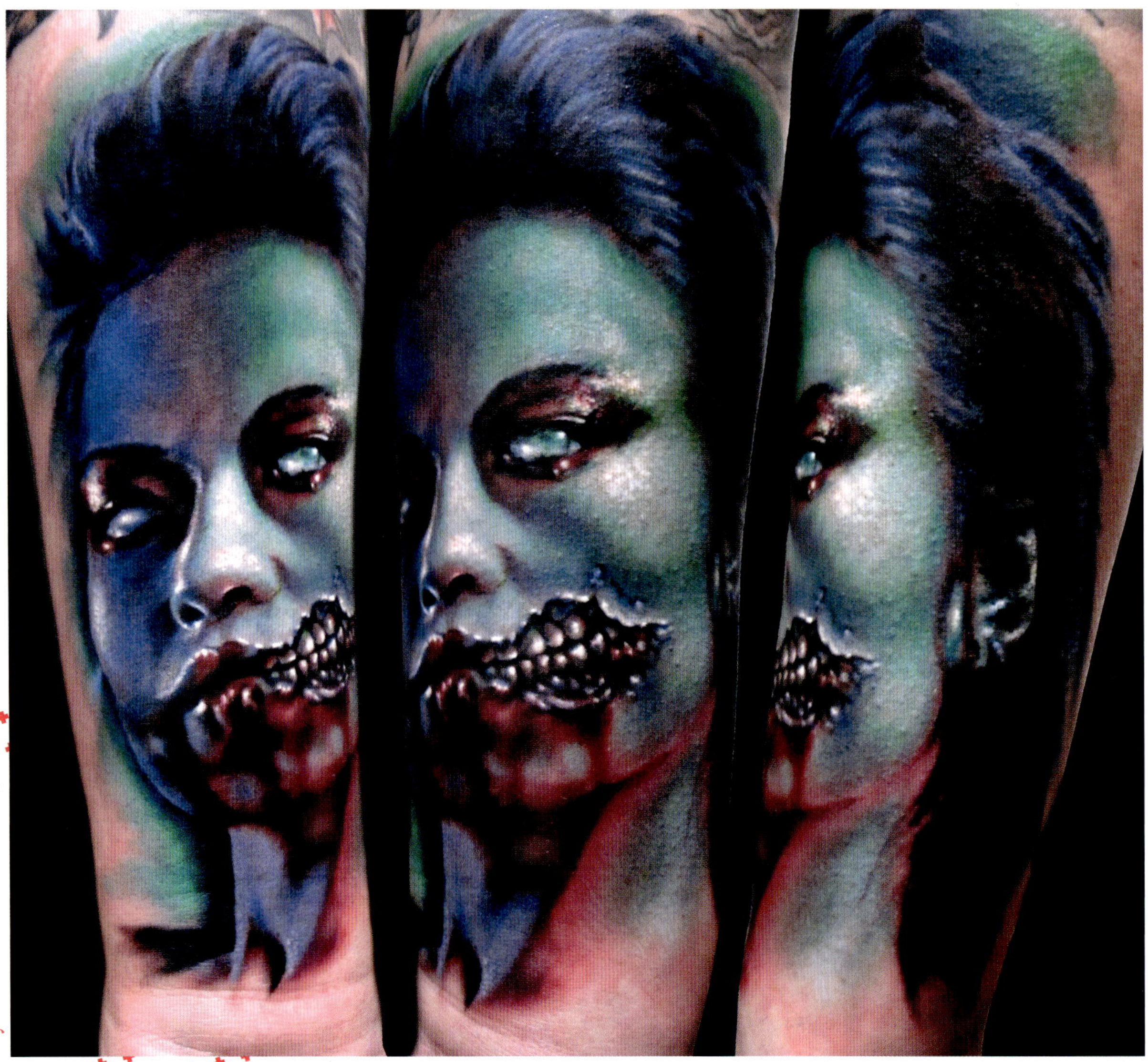

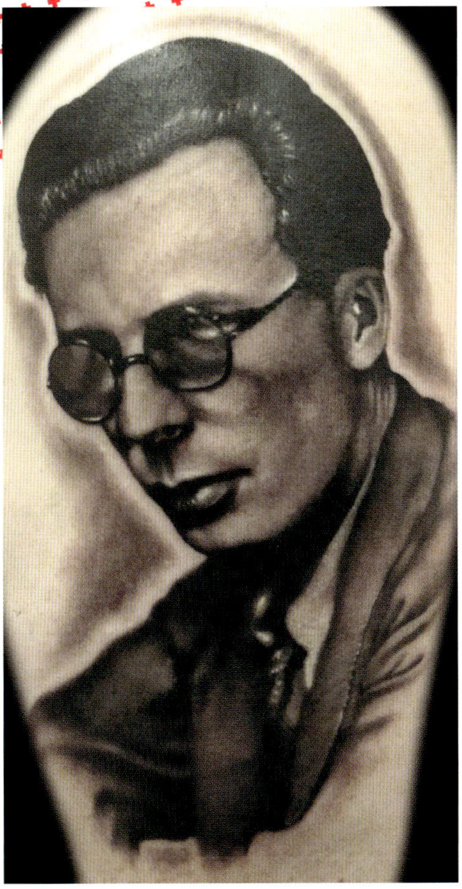

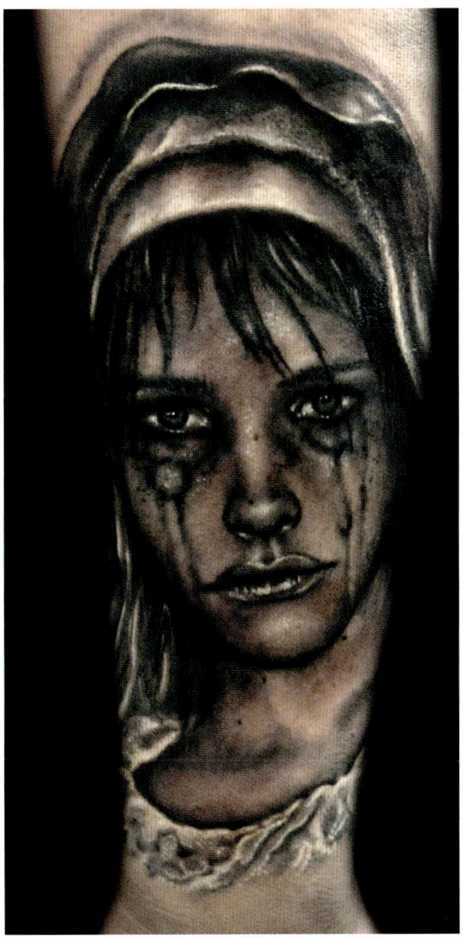

What's one of your favorite pieces on your own body, and who did it?

It's easier to say what I don't like! All my "big girl" tattoos are by amazing artists who put themselves into their work completely. I love my right lower arm that's by James "Calvin" Ellis from Perth, Australia. It makes me think of us doing our apprenticeships at the same time, and how so much has happened since.

What is your favorite thing about being a tattoo artist?

The freedom to be able to manipulate and manage your own schedule. I'm always trying to fit in everything, so this happens all the time.

Do you have a funny tattoo story?

There are so many! From amateur Internet porn stars to kids having to be chased out with baseball bats. Actually, one night at our shop, some of the guys were working really late into the night. One was getting ready to leave and remote-started his car. The cops that were in our area that night evidently found that suspicious. Because the doors were unlocked to the studio, they walked in. When the artist came around the corner into the lobby, the cops drew their guns on him like he was an intruder! Then one of the other artists working heard the commotion and came running into the lobby to help, and the cops pointed their guns at him too. Obviously after a bit of questioning, the cops realized they'd made a mistake. It's even funnier because the artists were the chillest guys out of everyone at the studio.

You have built up such a loyal clientele. What is your waiting list like right now and what is the best way for a collector to make an appointment with you?

My waitlist gets pretty crazy, but the best way to get in eventually (you may have to wait anywhere from six months to a couple of years) is to have a flexible schedule and be open to artist freedom with a basic concept in mind. The best and fastest way to get in touch with me is to fill out the online consultation form on my website, lizcooktattoo.com.

How would you describe the current status of tattoos among the general public in the US?

I think it's pretty accepted. I think the statistics are something like 23% of the country has tattoos. Most of them still are hidden or able to be covered, but sleeves and highly visible work are definitely becoming more and more popular in all age groups.

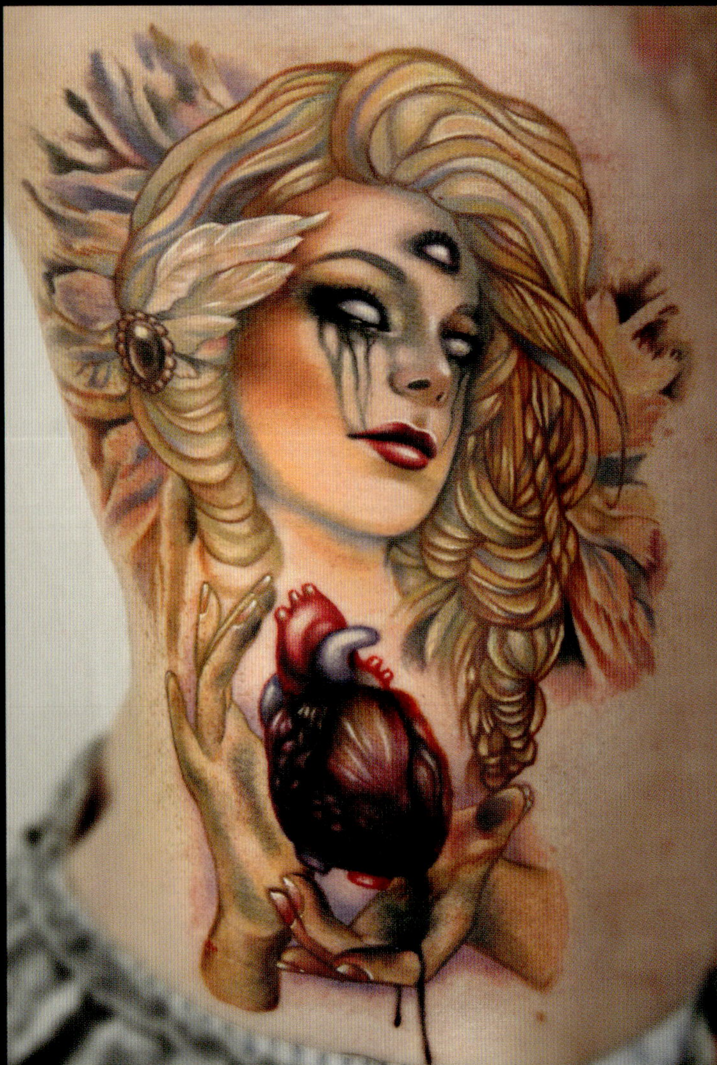

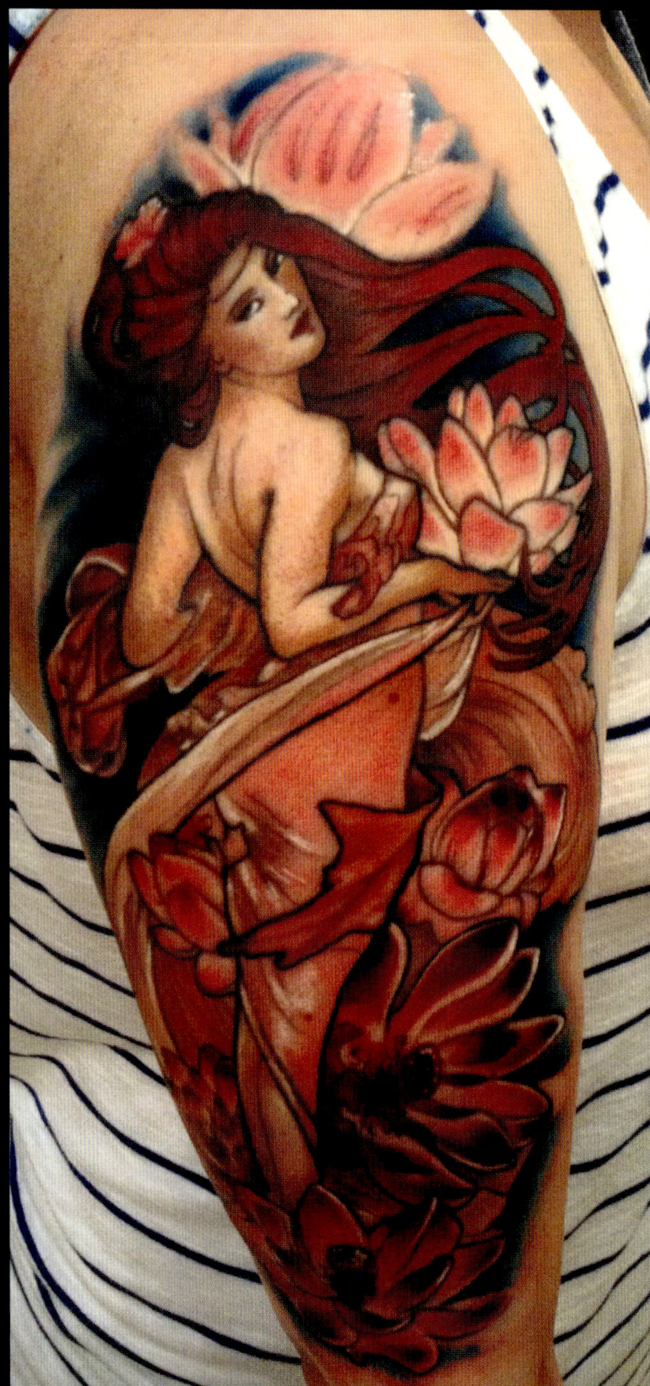

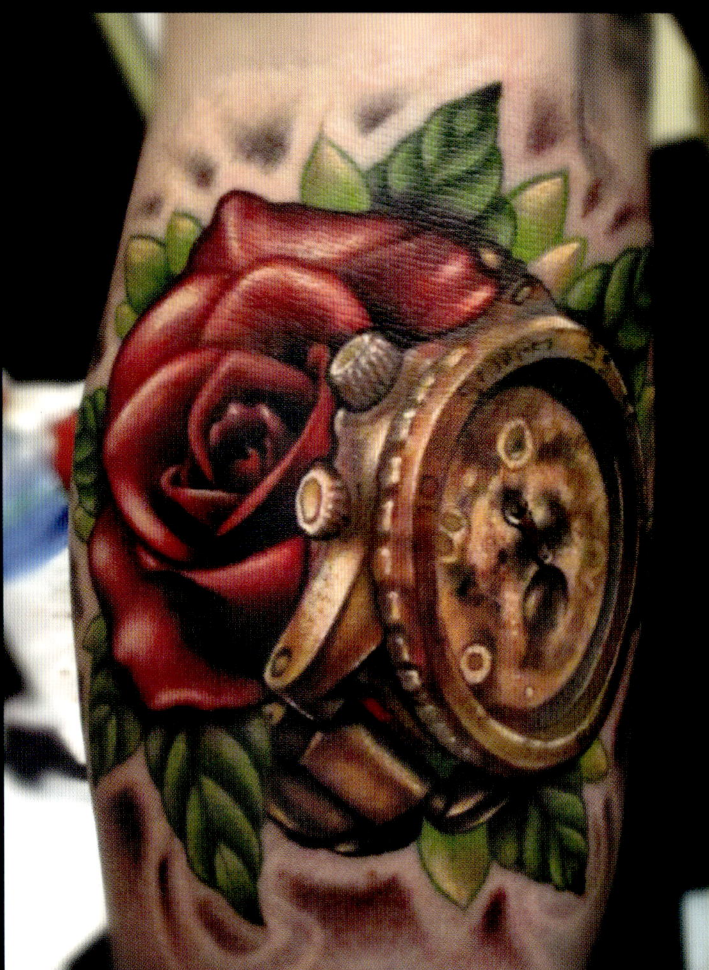

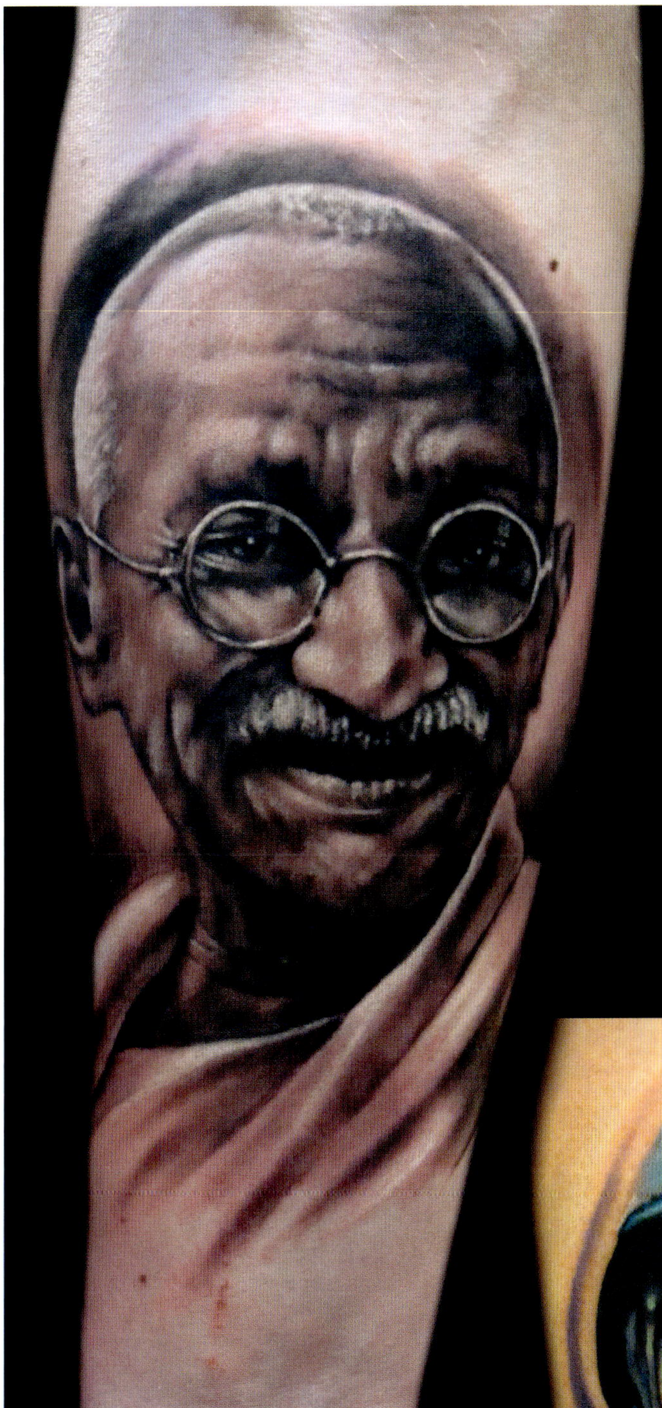

TV shows, Internet, and especially social networks like Facebook and Twitter have come to have an extremely wide influence in recent years. What positive and negative impacts do you think it has for the future development of the tattoo industry?

It's definitely a double-sided sword. On a good note, there's so much more exposure to tattoos, which brings acceptance, which leads to a more sustainable tattoo industry. The downside is that the TV shows often present unrealistic tattoo situations that potential clients perceive as truth, whether it's as simple as how long a tattoo actually takes to do, or even costs. It also glorifies and dramatizes a field that has so much behind-the-scenes work to maintain day to day business, that newbies to tattooing, as well as the general public, are seriously misled in terms of how much work is really required to be a good tattooer. We are made to look like we just "draw" on people all day…like it's as easy as doodling in a notebook in grade school. For the future, it now stands to reason that we must work even harder to change this perception of tattooing as easy, in order to get the authority as art/cosmetic service providers that would in any other field be considered more legitimate.

As for Facebook and Instagram, they certainly provide an excellent means of advertising and marketing more directly to a specific demographic unique to each individual tattooer, that is simple to personally control. The negative is that everyone has an opinion, whether or not it's true, and it does require personal policing of pages to get rid of spam and rude people who inevitably provide unsolicited negative comments. Also, it means that it's much harder for future and current artists to stand out, especially without having some understanding of marketing via social networks.

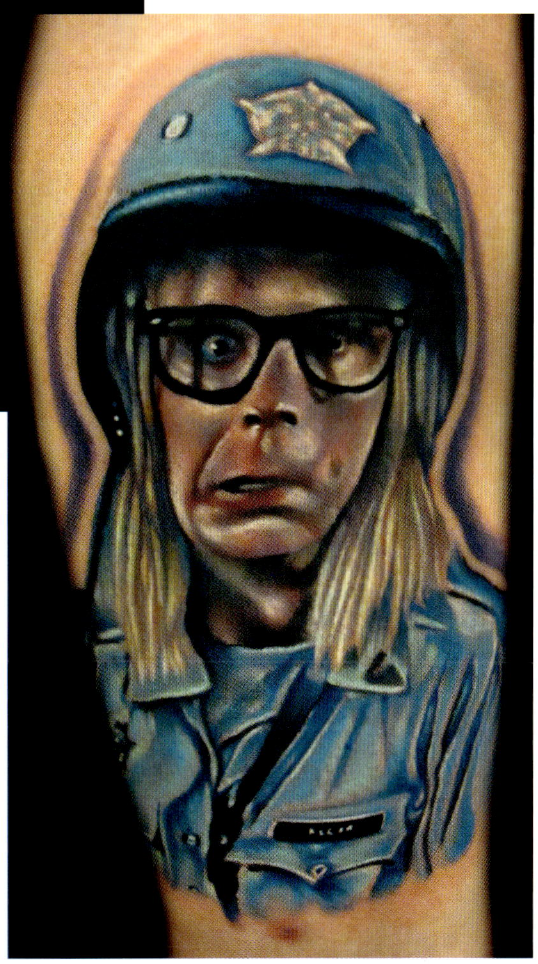

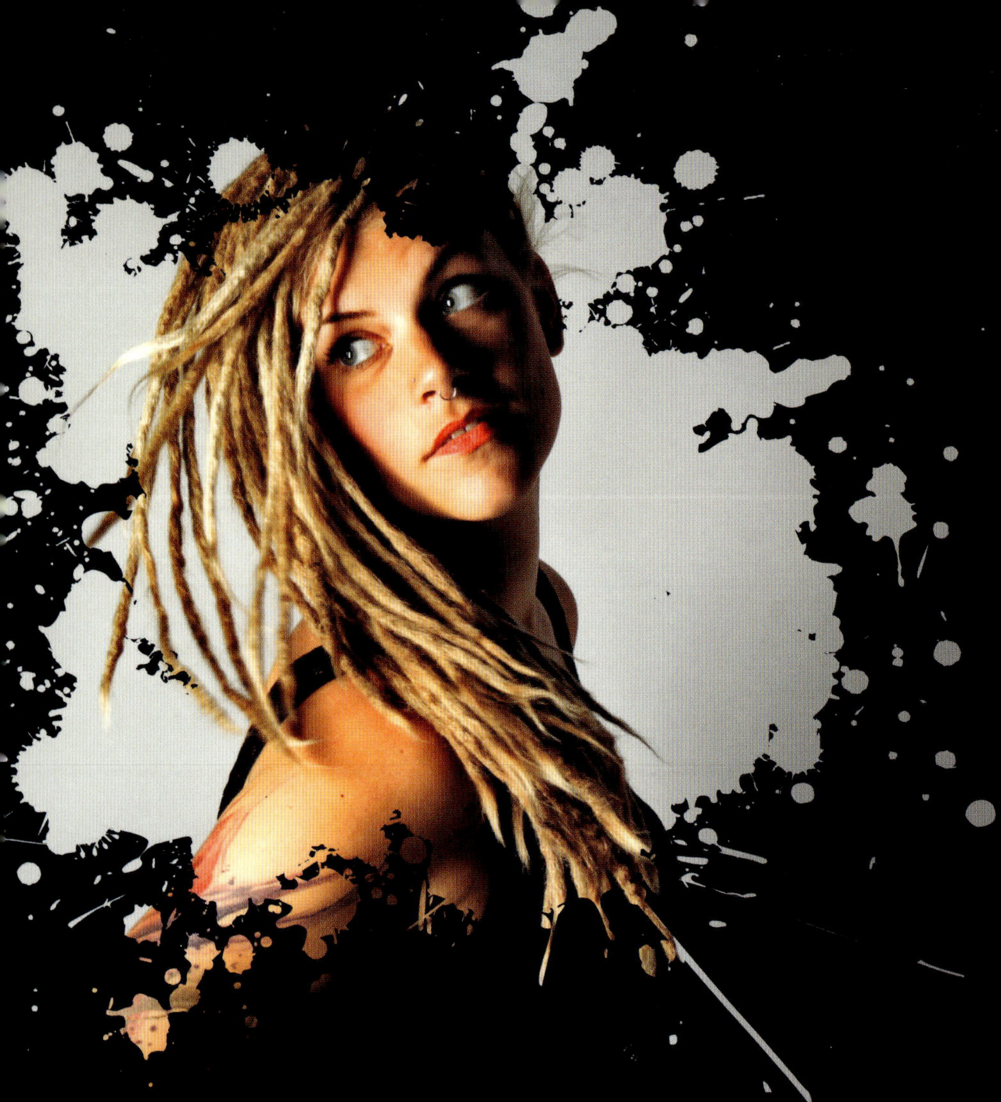

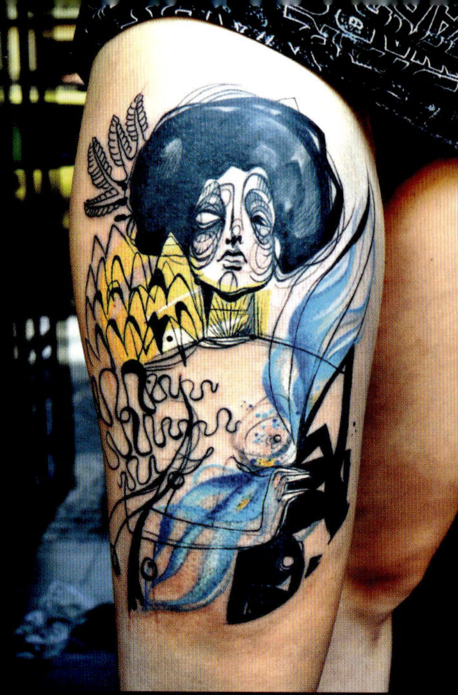

PETRA HLAVÁCKOVÁ was born in Brno, Czech Republic, and grew up in a village nearby. Being surrounded by nature and lots of animals influenced her way of thinking about life and the world. She studied illustration in high school and animation in university. She spent one semester in Spain, studying mainly drawing, painting, and graphic design. During that time Petra experimented with a tattoo machine, which she bought when she was seventeen.

Petra HLAVÁCKOVÁ

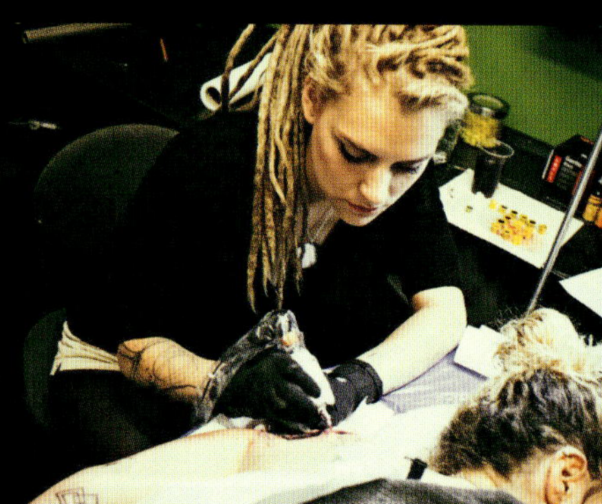

"Women who are tattoo artists are strong enough to get to the same position as men"

petratattoo.com
www.facebook.com/petratattoo
www.facebook.com/petrahlavackovaa

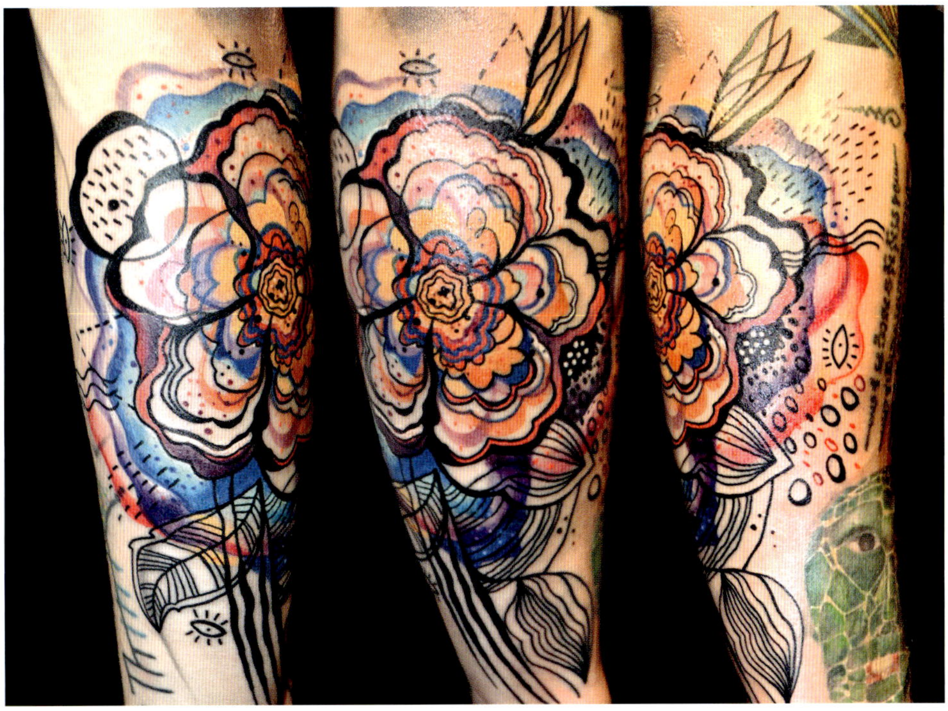

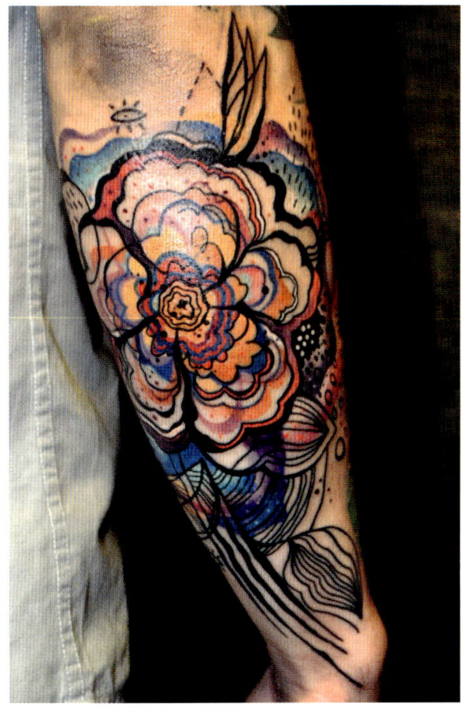

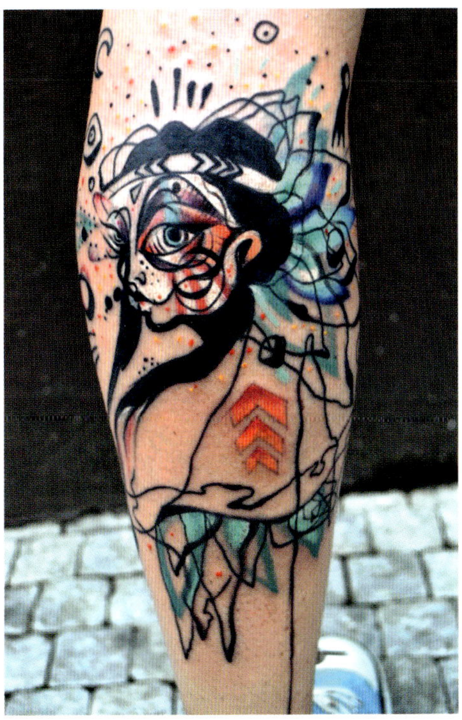

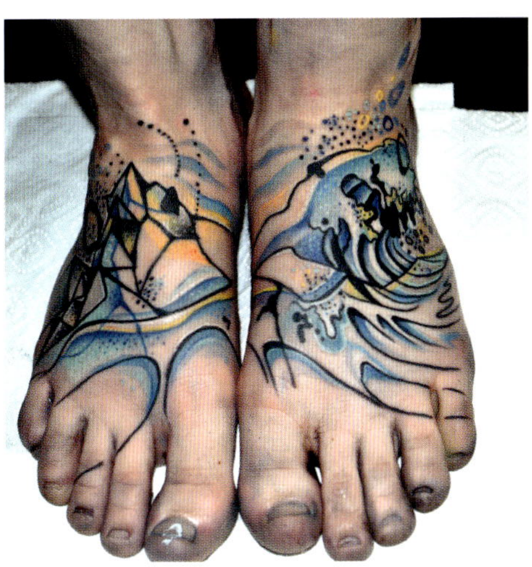

When you were a child, did you think you would grow up to become an artist, or work in the artistic field? Do you remember drawing and creating a lot as a child?

I don't remember if I had ever thought about doing something else. In fact I can't really do anything else, and expressing myself through art was the easiest way to exist. When they asked us what we wanted to be when we grew up, I never knew. I just knew "I wanna draw."

But I loved work in bars; that was my career before I started to draw on skin. I need to work with people, so that's why that was perfect work for me.

When I was small, I was drawing all the time, never really liked television, it made me scared, I would rather draw my own worlds. My parents saw that I loved drawing more than is normal for kids, and sent me to art school. They also supported me incredibly from the beginning, with tattooing.

When did you know that you wanted to be a tattoo artist, and what were the first steps you took to learn the craft?

I knew that I wanted to do tattooing or piercing even before I bought my own machine. It attracted me from the time I was fifteen, maybe earlier. I loved the atmosphere in tattoo shops. When we had lunch break in high school, I went to tattoo shops and stared at tattoo artist like they were gods, asking them stupid questions. I also stared at a few pictures in books or magazines and was hypnotized by tattoo colors, techniques, permanence…I was a kid and those places and people seemed to me little bit scary, magical, respectful.

One day I bought a tattoo machine and started training on my friends, who I appreciate so much now, because they believed in me in the beginning. They didn't pay me for that, we didn't have any money. Instead of that we had small or big celebrations after every tattoo, and they invited me out for beer and shots.

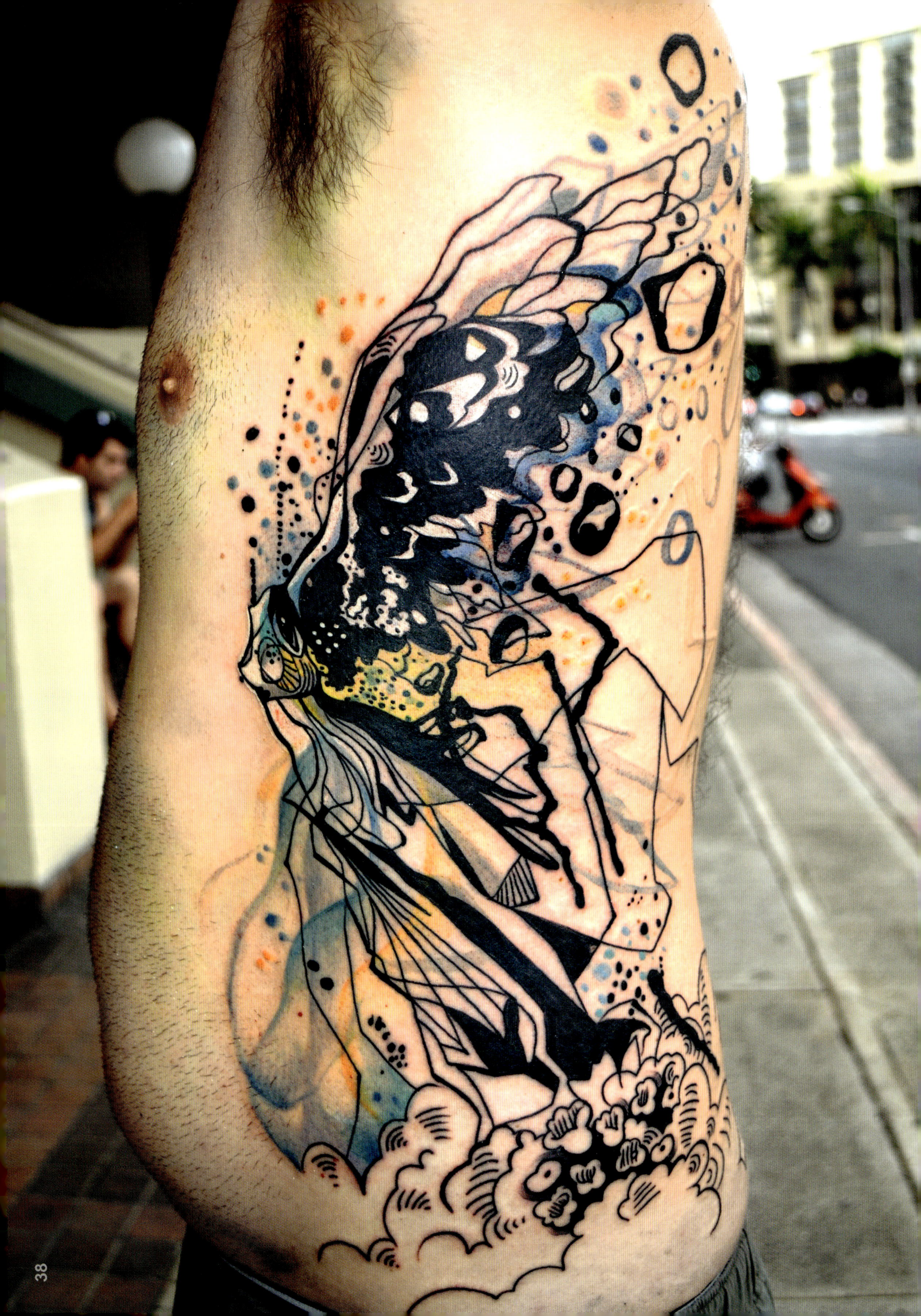

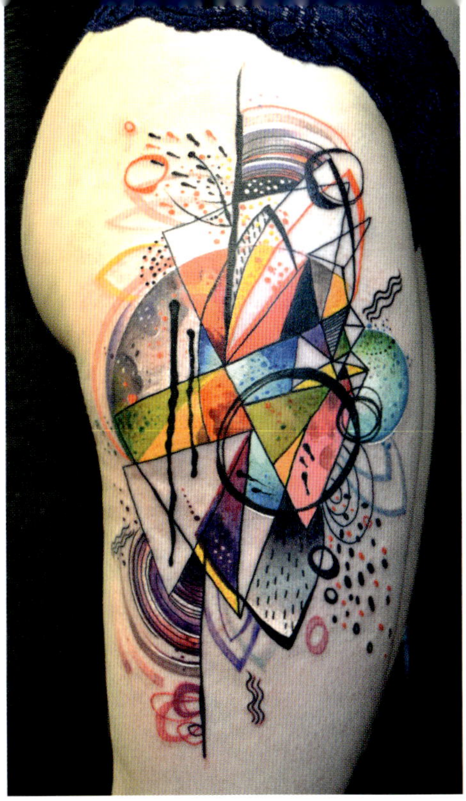

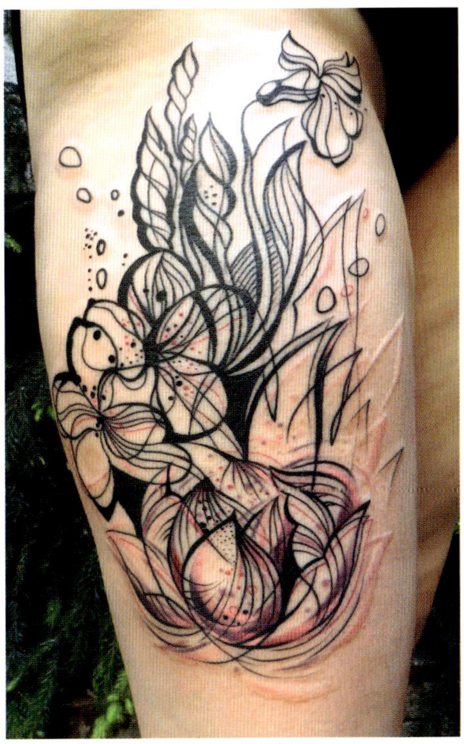

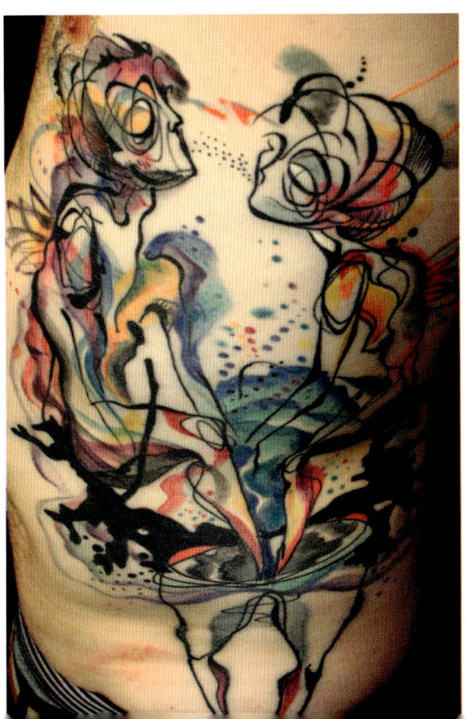

But it was really hard at the begining—nothing had function the way it should. I learned the craft properly after I came to Prague.

Do you feel that male customers treat you differently?

I don't think so. If somebody wouldn't feel comfortable about the fact that a woman is tattooing him, they just wouldn't come to get a tattoo from me.

More important than gender is that we find with the other person, the client, a common way; we connect our ideas together and see how the project is developing on his or her body. I believe that for that it doesn't matter if I'm a woman or a man.

Do you feel that female tattoo artists are treated fairly in the business? How do you feel things have changed for women in tattooing, as well as for yourself from when you started out?

I think women who are tattoo artists are strong enough to get to the same position as men. I personally don't know any tattoo artists who treat women artists differently. I think they are happy to have us in this craft; we both can offer some different view on what we doing, how, and why. It's good symbiosis.

Tell me more about the shop you work at; what's it like working there, and what makes up a typical day?

I work at Bobek Tattoo, which is based in downtown Prague. Peter Bobek started this shop, he hired Ernesto, then they took me on, and we found Jan. The typical day is a lot of people, a lot of coffee, good atmosphere. Lots of incredibly talented guest artists circulate through our place; because I keep moving, there is free space for them from time to time.

Describe how you go about creating a tattoo from concept to finished design. How do you try to put your own unique touch on your tattoos?

First I need to see from the client's e-mail some creative idea, something that is original and enthuses me. In that moment, some visions begin in my head. It makes me more creative when I see people are thinking about what they are getting, not just copying some other ideas. It makes me happy to work with people's personalities, with their influences in life, or with unusual topics. When it doesn't have any deeper meaning, then it's just work for me.

Then I want to meet and speak with my customers for consultations, to finalize my vision of the future image. For doing the actual designs I need to get lost for a whole weekend in my room. It's a kind of meditation during which I draw, listen to music, and drink coffee and tea.

The first day I just take all the ideas which I have and freely let them go on paper. I'm really not rationally controlling that part, because something is leading my hands. It's like automatic drawing, where there are no rules, just feelings.

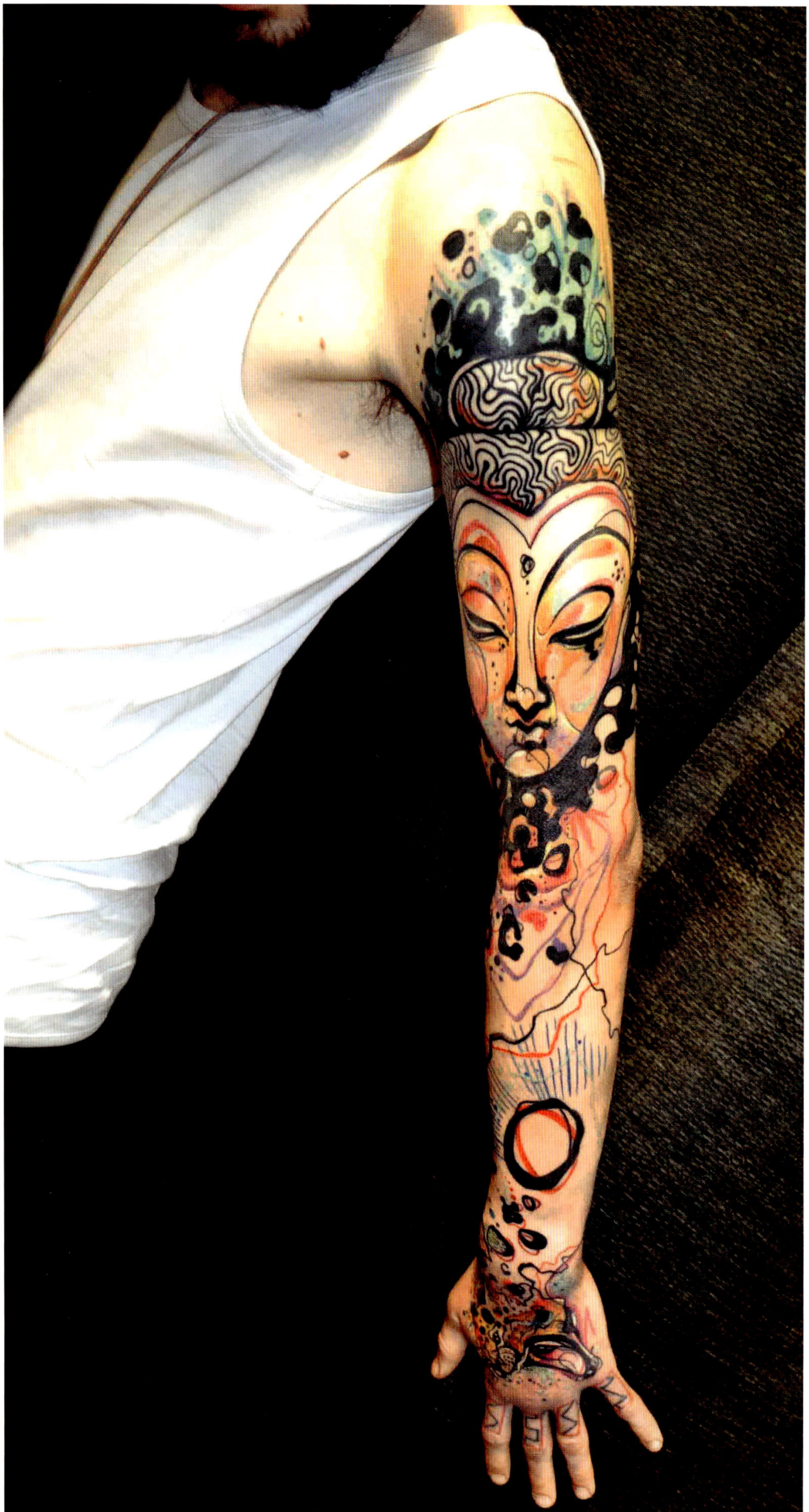

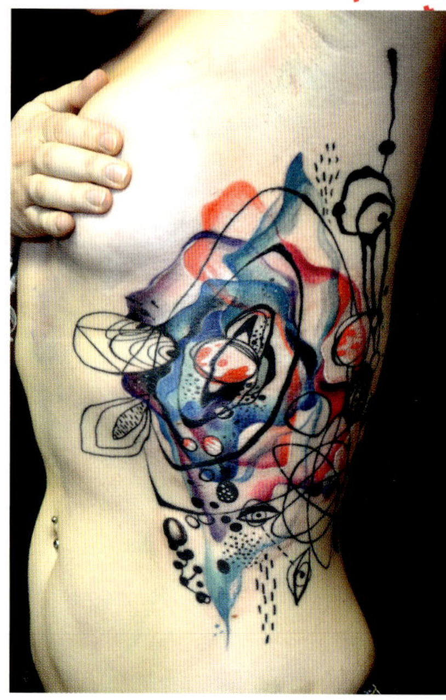

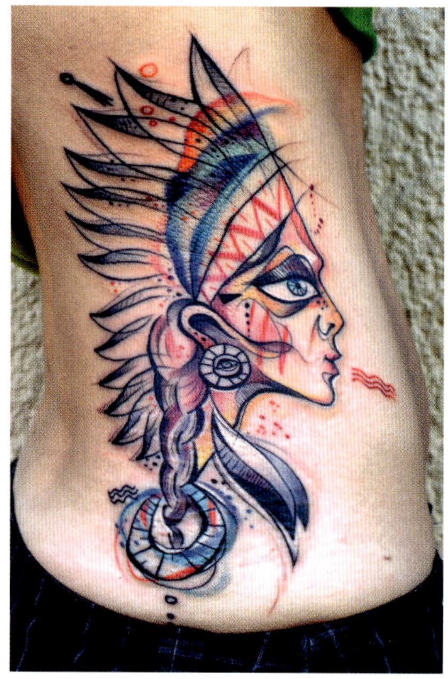

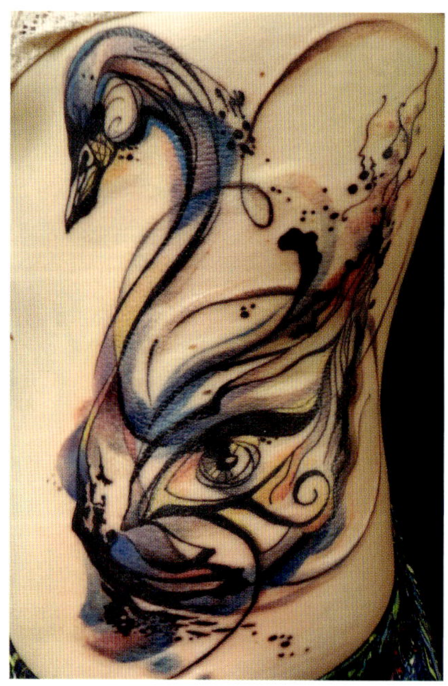

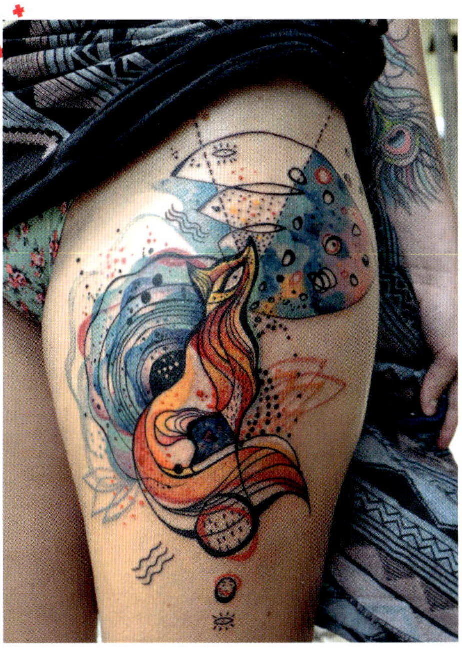

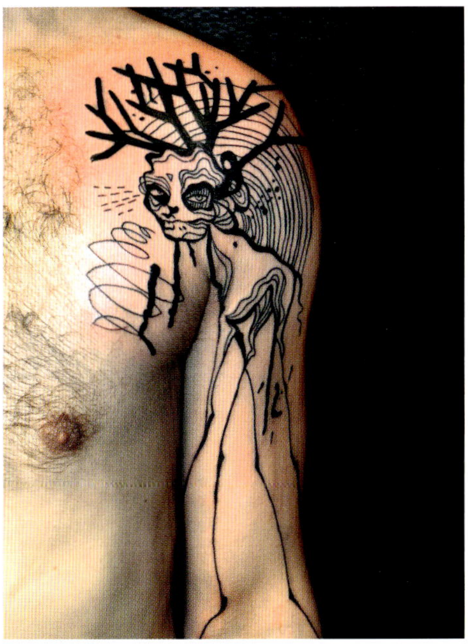

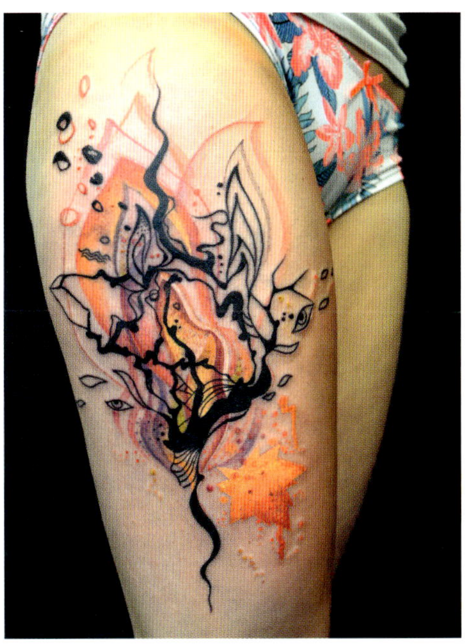

The next day I work on those drawings again, thinking about them and giving them a more understandable and cleaner form, if that's needed. Then I speak about the drawing with the client. I like to work freely with the body, not to be limited by centimeters. After I put some stenciling on their body, I draw a little bit more until we feel it's ready and the customer is satisfied.

What was the first tattoo you ever did? Have you always worked in the same general style?

My first tattoo was on my friend Matej. It was a small tattoo of a hurricane. I was scared, and if he wouldn't have pushed me into that, I would never have started tattooing. I worked a long time on tattoos which were not mine; I wasn't proud of them, but I had to train in technique, learn how to use the machine. After I started at Bobek Tattoo, I didn't do anything else, just drawing and tattooing, and I found the style that I wanted to work in. I knew that there was something inside, something that wants to be captured on paper and later on skin, so I was trying to find it through nonstop drawing.

You are an incredible artist. How did your professional tattoo art journey lead you in this direction?

I couldn't imagine that animation or illustration would be my job one day, because it's really reclusive work. I would get crazy from that quickly. I had the need to work with lot of people in some art field. When I started in art I didn't expect that tattooing could be my job one day, because I had huge respect for that field. After some time tattooing, though, I couldn't imagine doing anything else.

What's your tattoo style of choice and why?

I don't like how it seems like everything in the world has to be named, so I don't really have a name for it. It is just style, which arose during those years of drawing. It's still growing, and I don't know what I should I call it during this period either. I work like this because it's the most natural way for me to work right now.

Describe how your role models and any other sources of inspiration have affected your tattoo style.

Unconsciously, I reflect everything in my work, everybody and every moment, something less and something more. Reality is a big part of my inspiration. The rest I take from nature, art, the subconscious…

From artists, I found my inspiration in Czech painters who made art from some internal higher calling, mainly Karel Malich or Václav Boštík. A painter who works with spiritual topics and who I really appreciate is Alex Grey. I love David Lynch's animations and his paintings. Another very important painter and theorist for me is Kandinsky, and his thinking about influence of colors and shapes in painting.

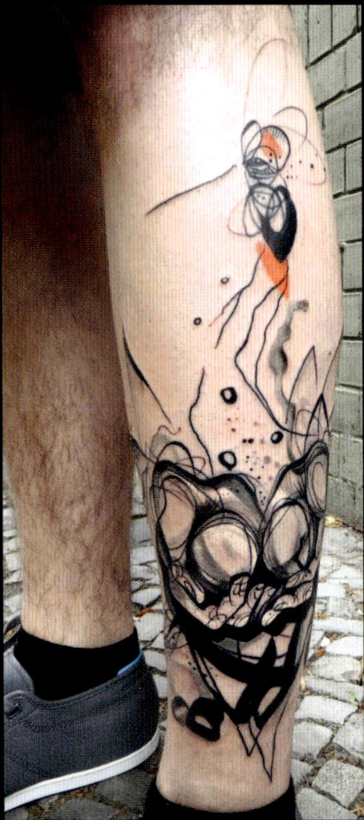
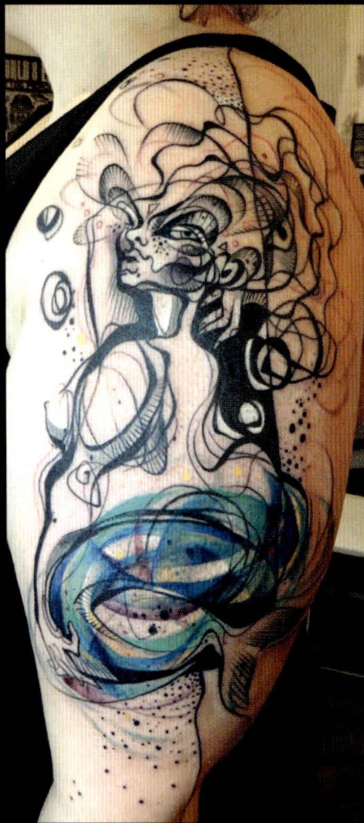
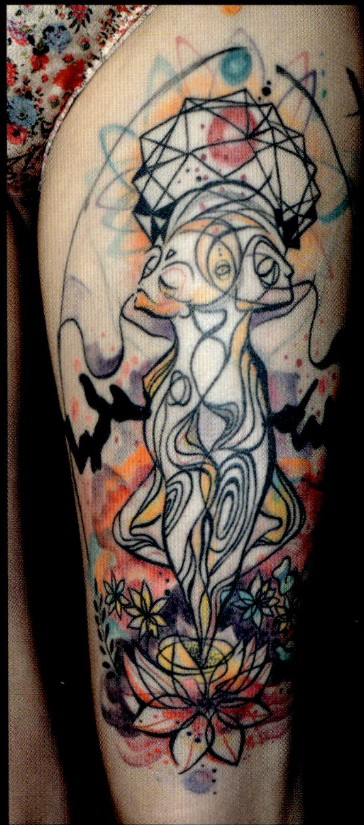
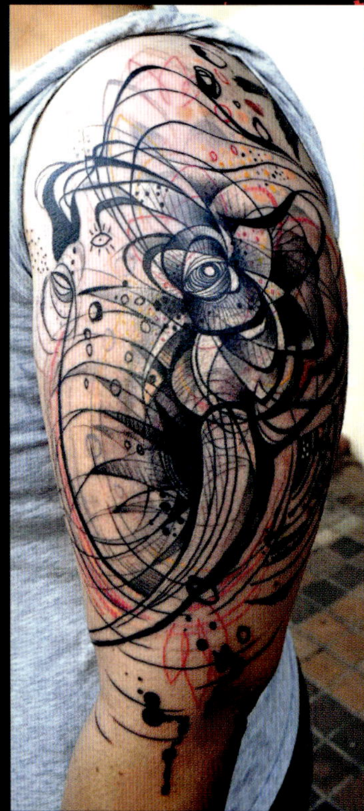
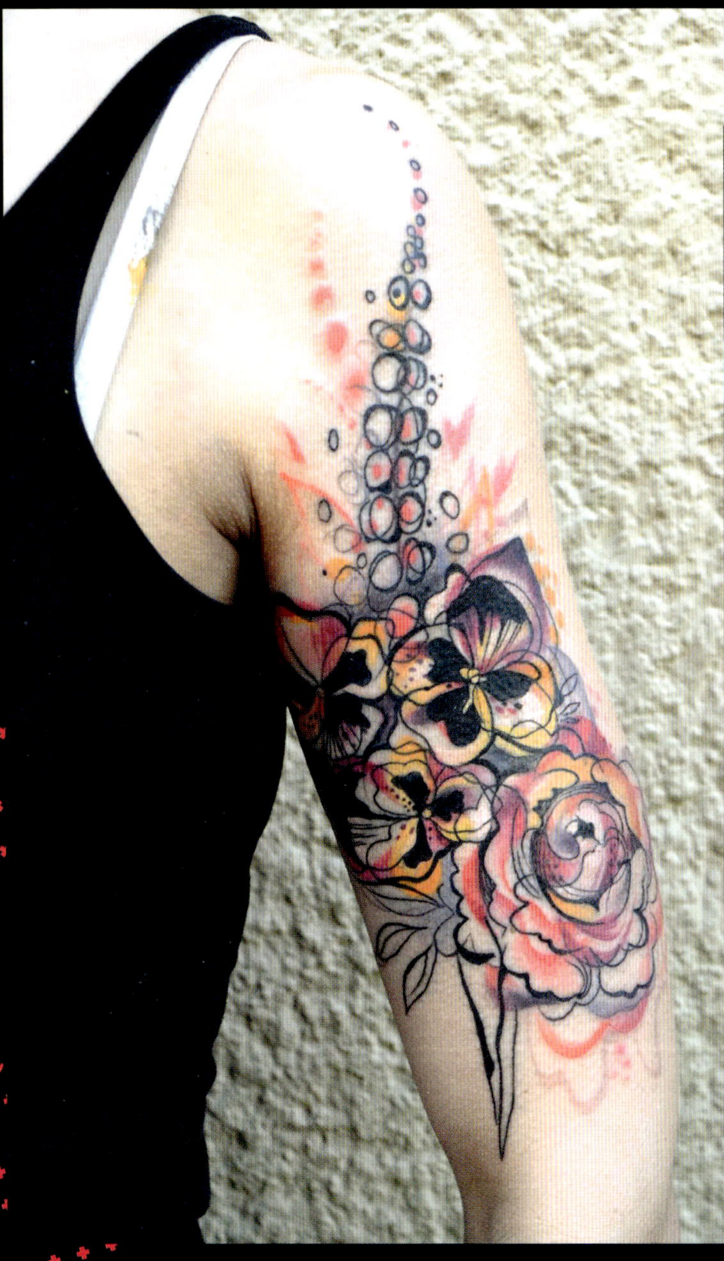
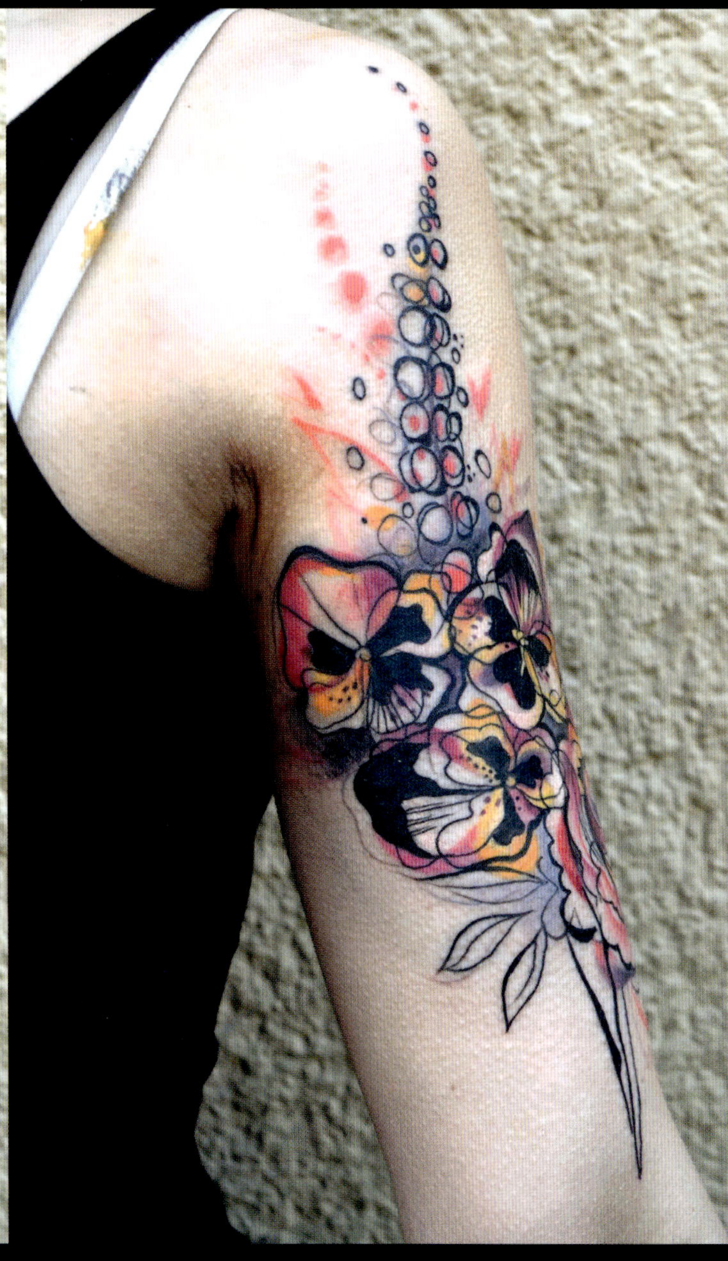

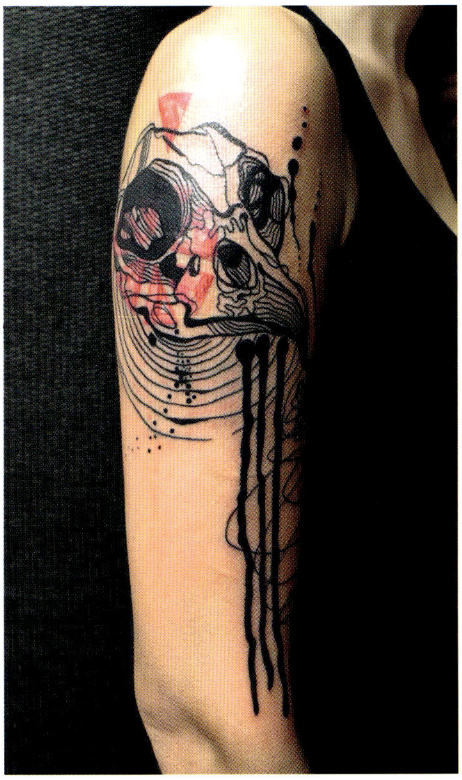

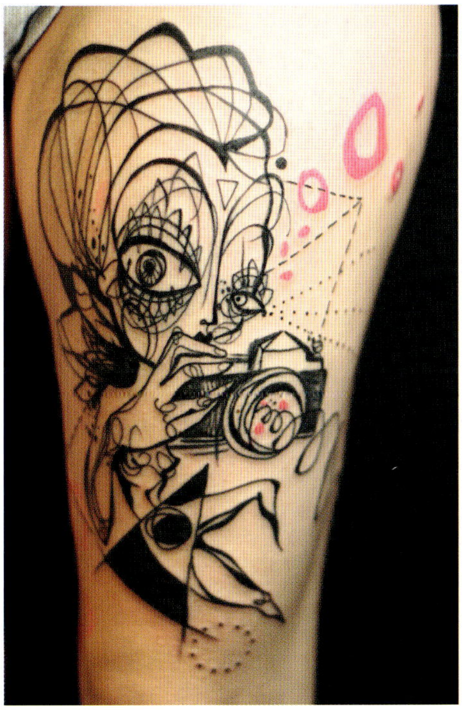

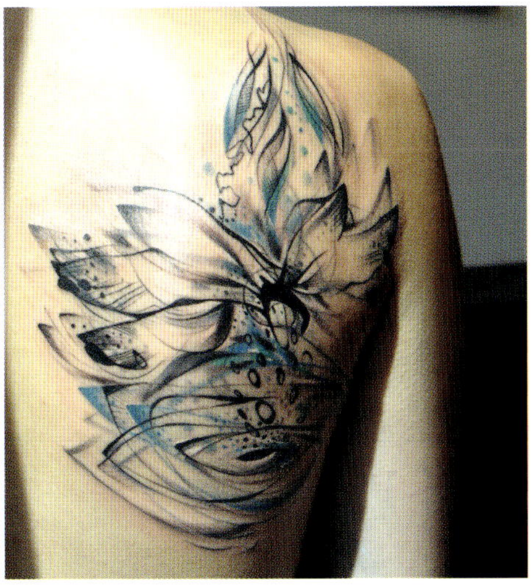

Music has also strongly influenced me. I love electronic projects from the north and that visual aesthetic, such as Oni Ayhun, The Knife, Iamamiwhoami, Sigur Ros. I've worked with dreams ever since I was small, and that's why surrealism is really close to my heart. I'm fascinated by art styles where coincidence plays an important role, such as Art Informel or Dadaism. I think it's important to free ourselves and work more freely with no rules. I'm also fascinated by shamans, native ceremonies, experiencing rituals...

What's one of your favorite pieces that you've tattooed on someone else?

I couldn't choose only one, since every new tattoo I make is my favorite, in the moment when it's fresh, new, and I'm seeing the happy owner of that new tattoo. But maybe my favorite is one I made for my mum. It's really small, but it symbolizes a lot for me, that I could make a tattoo for her.

What's one of your favorite pieces on your own body, and who did it?

I love all of them the same except for the one that's newest; I like it most. It's an abstract, on my upper belly, made by Musa.

What is your favorite thing about being a tattoo artist?

I enjoy the unlimited freedom—tattoo artists can be free in everything, in what they do, where they are, we can choose even the people we work with...It can be incredibly creative work, and it's not necessary to concentrate only on one field. I enjoy the option to travel, to take inspiration from all over the world, and see how it influences my creations. Different cultures, their aesthetics, and their people inconspicuously influence my tattoos.

What do you think makes tattoos special?

It's a totally unique way to express ourselves and reflect our self-transformation. Tattoos are special when they represent our state of mind or show our values. Besides aesthetic and identification functions, the tattoo can strive for a higher purpose, be a powerful tool. It influences a person's life, and tattoo artists should work with that.

Have you noticed a change in the types of images people have asked for over the years you've been tattooing?

I definitely do more freehands now, than at the beginning. Customers trust me more, which I really appreciate. The type of images changes very often, depending on what I want to do. I start to work on something that I'm interested in, and then it attracts people who feel same way. It also depends which part of the world I'm in.

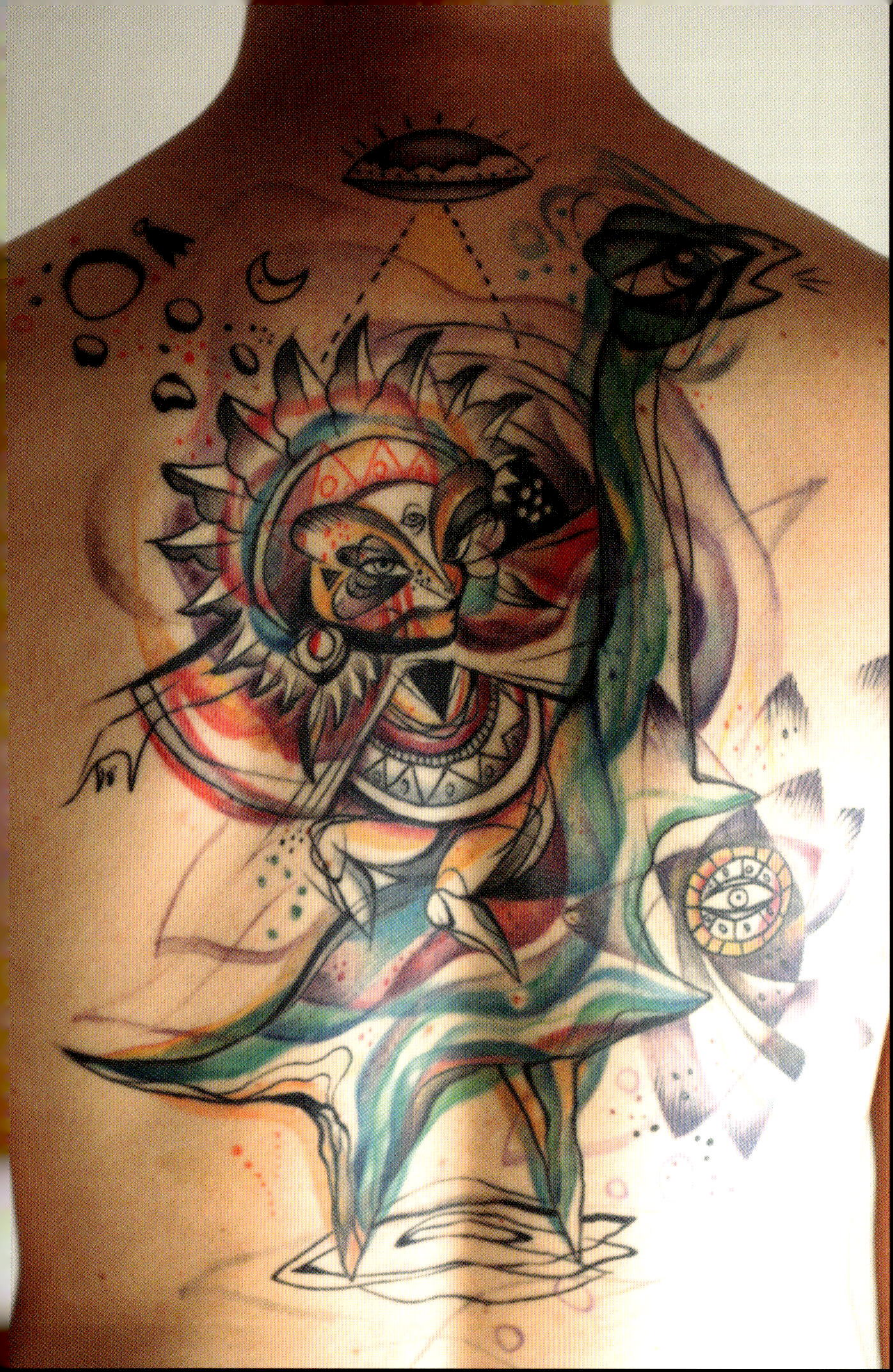
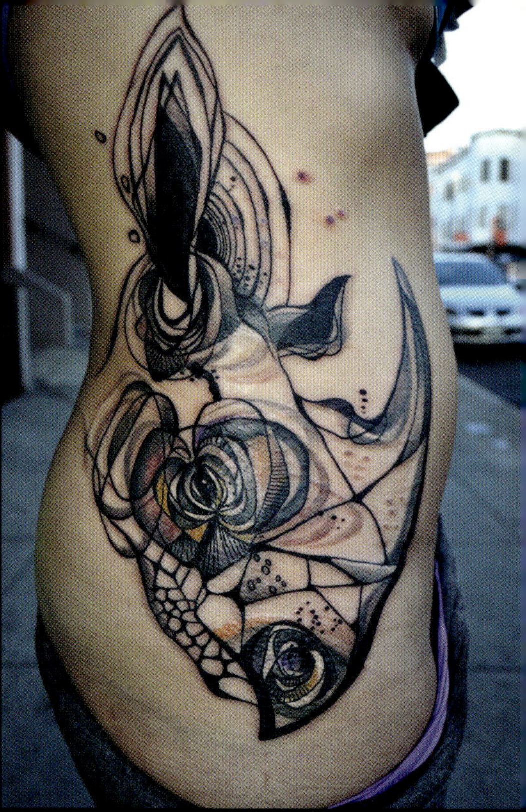
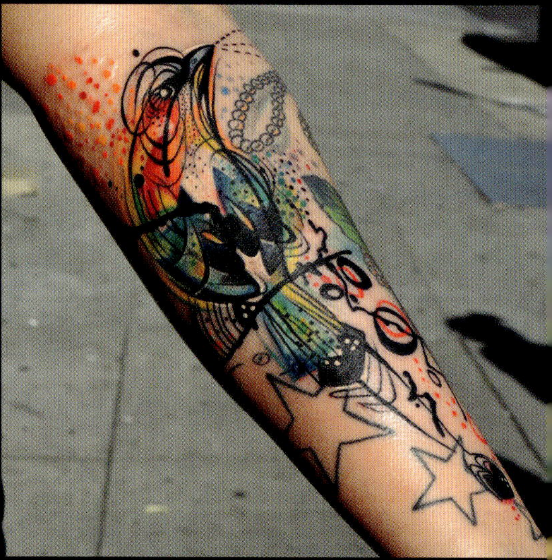
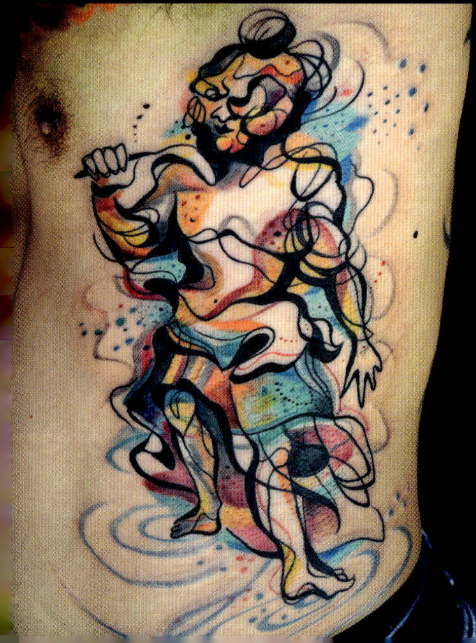
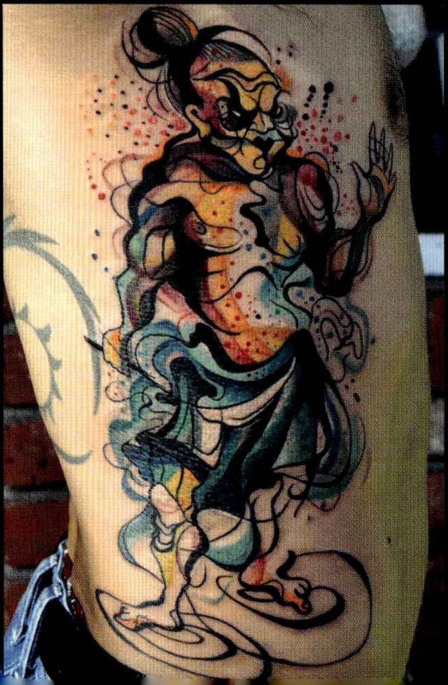
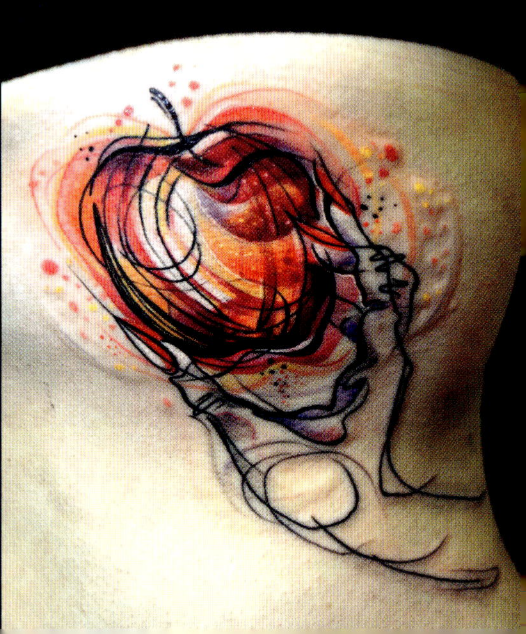

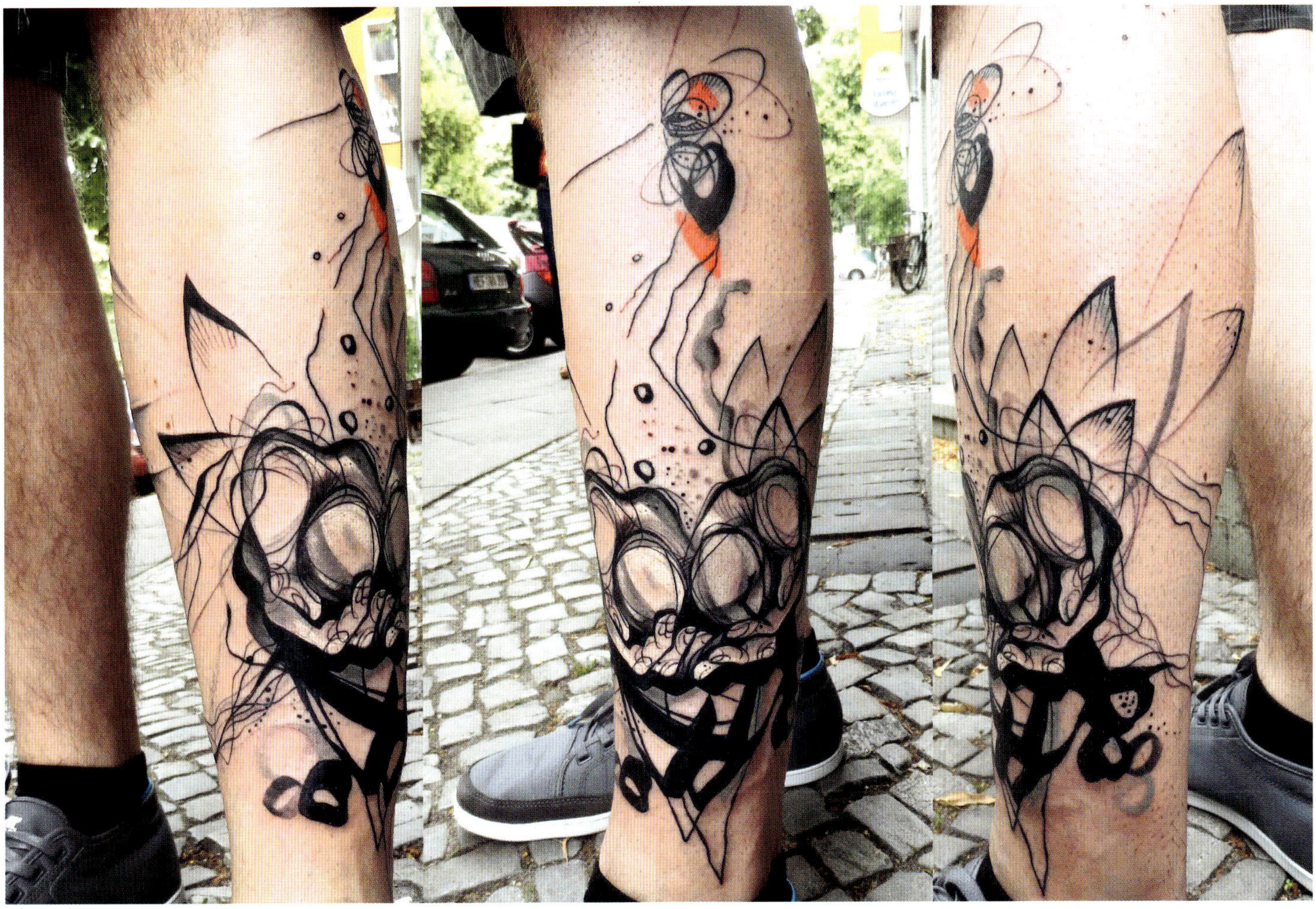

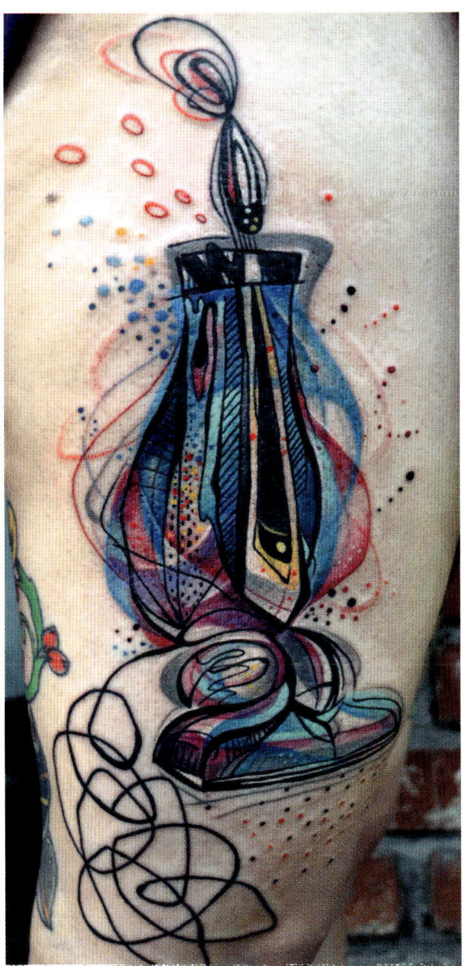

Tattoos seem very mainstream now. Do you think that's good or bad?

Yes, it's huge fashion now. It has positives and negatives. I'm happy when I see so many original tattoos on the streets of Berlin. You can see that people also think about what it should say, not just how it looks. I enjoy this fashion side of it when the tattoo is original and not superficial. On the other hand, there are so many bad copies of bad tattoos everywhere, from people not thinking about reasons, about why they are getting what. Maybe it's because this time period that we're in is so instant and easy for people, that it's too hard even to find a personal topic these days. But I don't want to judge; I'm sure this situation has a meaning for tattoo culture and its history.

Luckily, there are more and more original tattoo artists, who are going against the mainstream, pushing the borders of tattooing every day, and showing how many options tattooing can have.

Is there anything else you'd like to say?

I'm incredibly grateful to be meeting so many interesting, creative people every day, and grateful that I can do this dream work. People, don't be blind, live in every moment, everybody is an artist and we are all one.

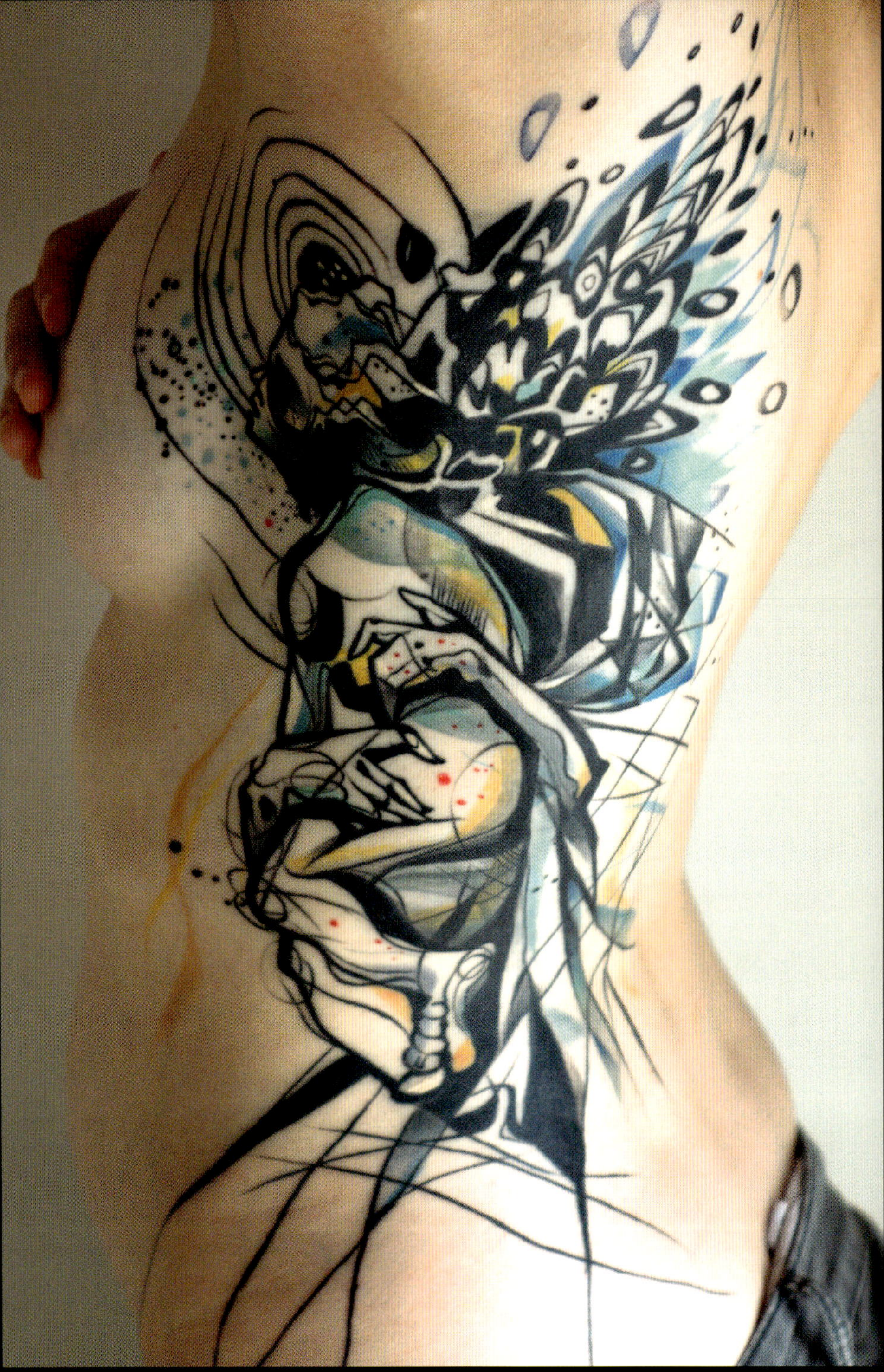

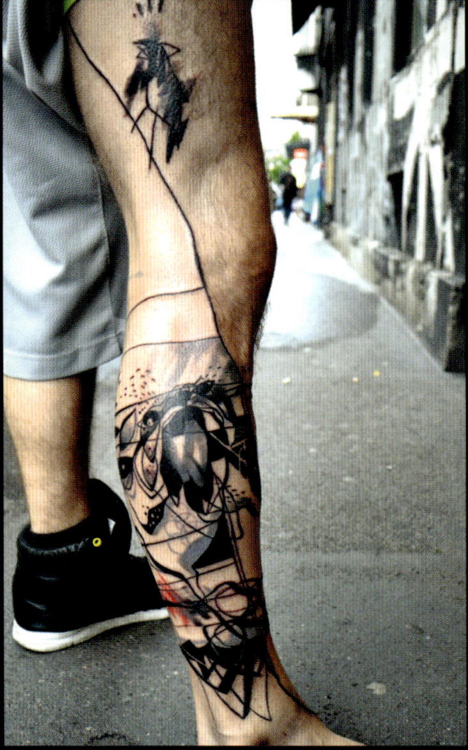

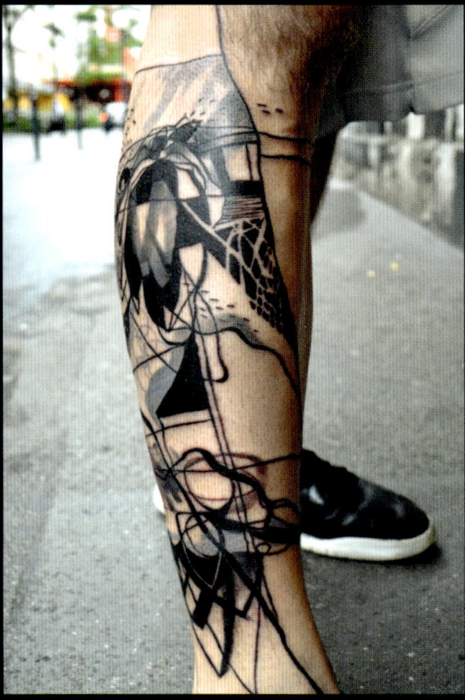

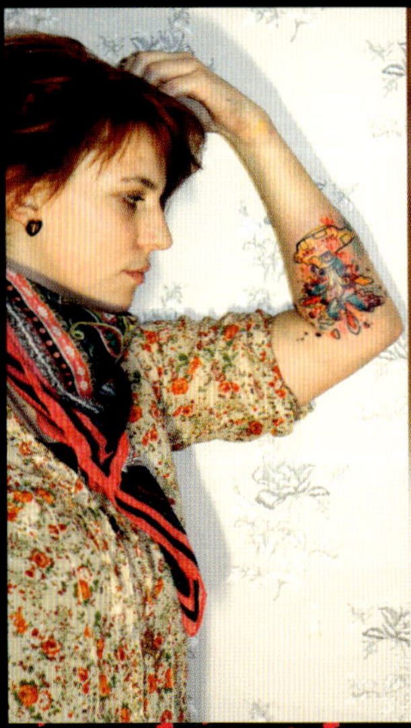

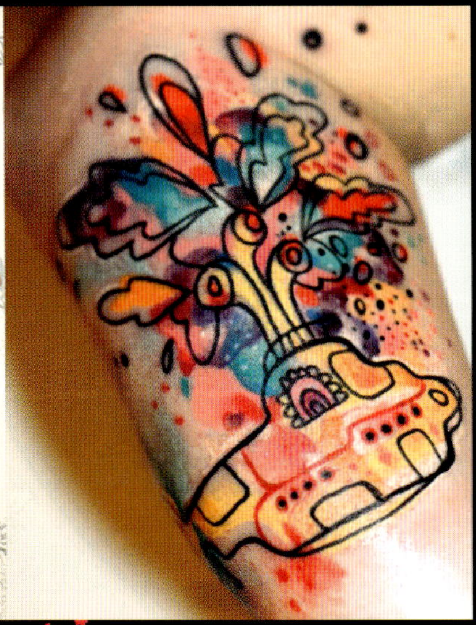

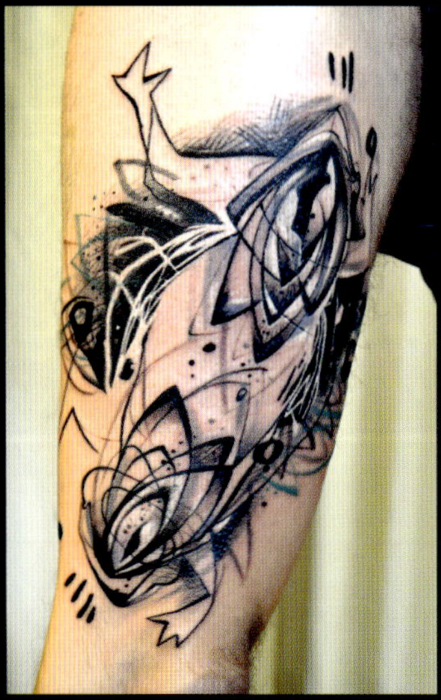

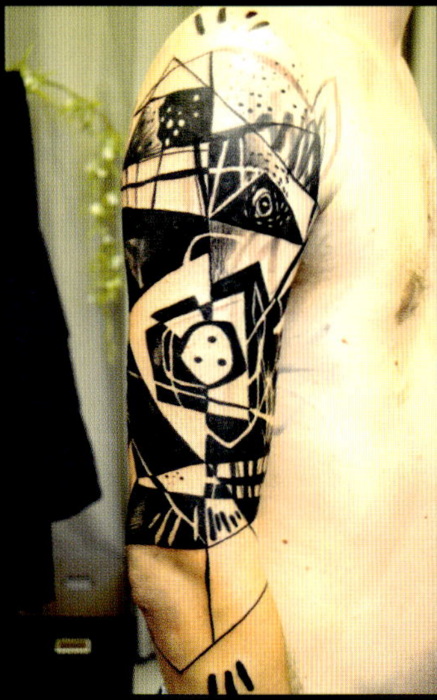

PETRA HLAVÁČKOVÁ

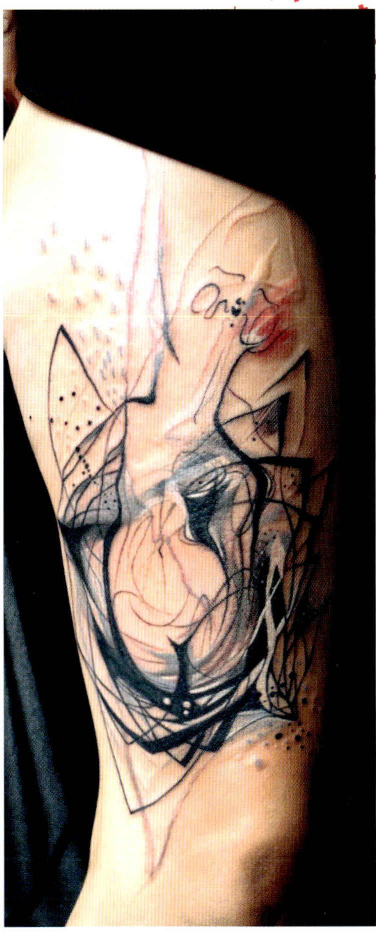

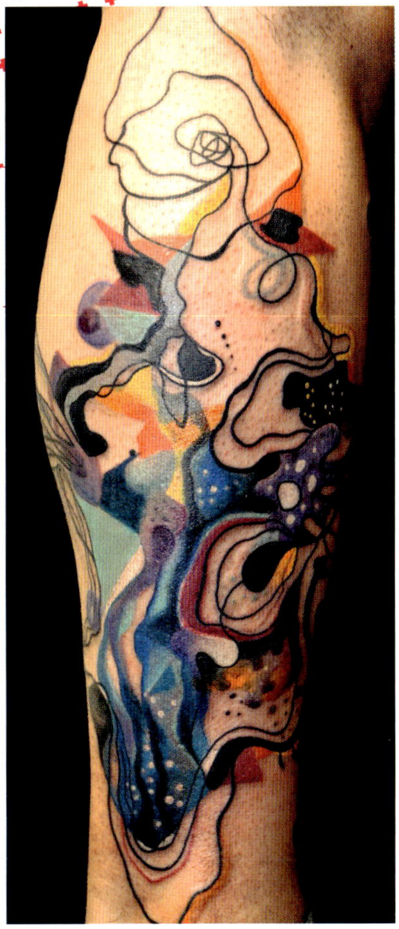

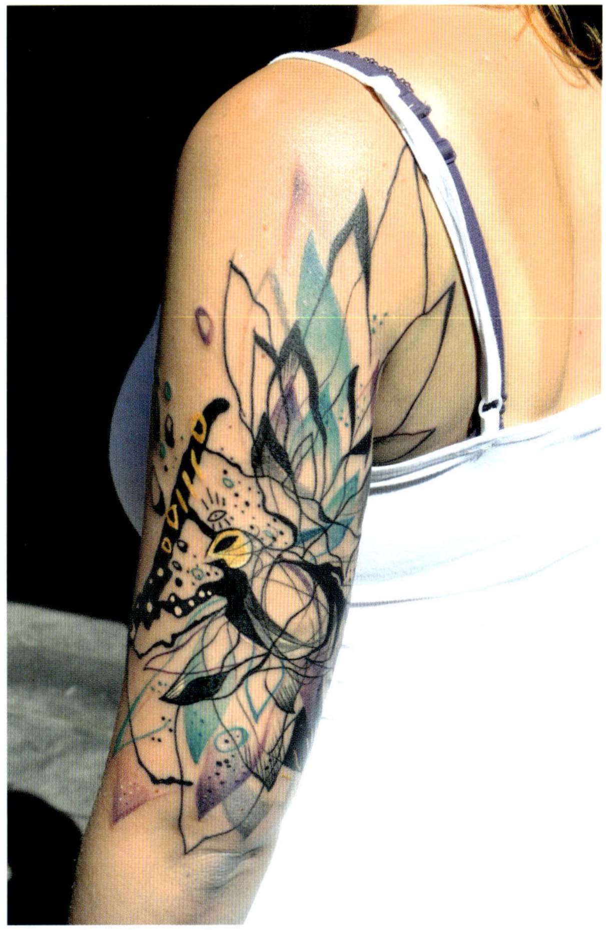

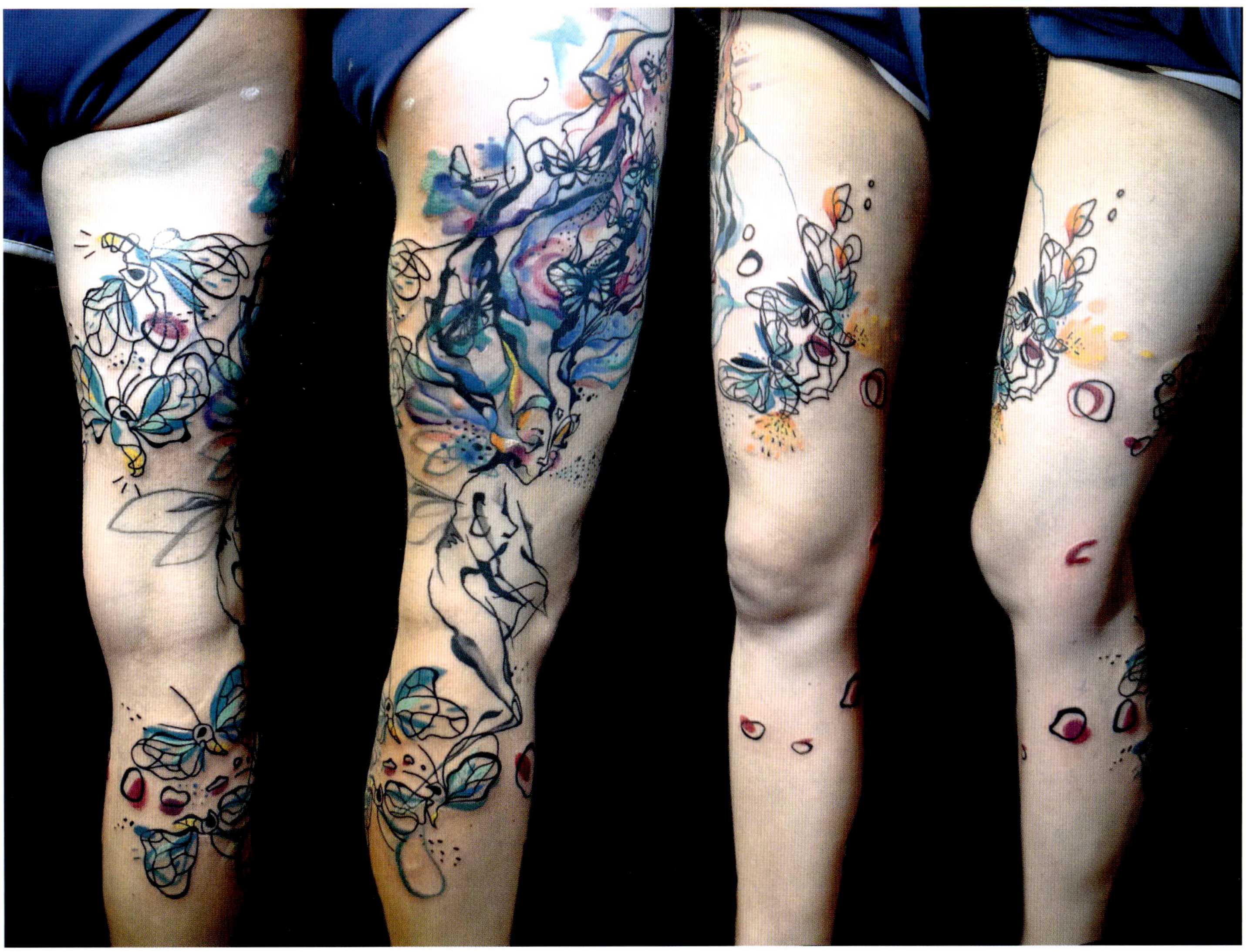

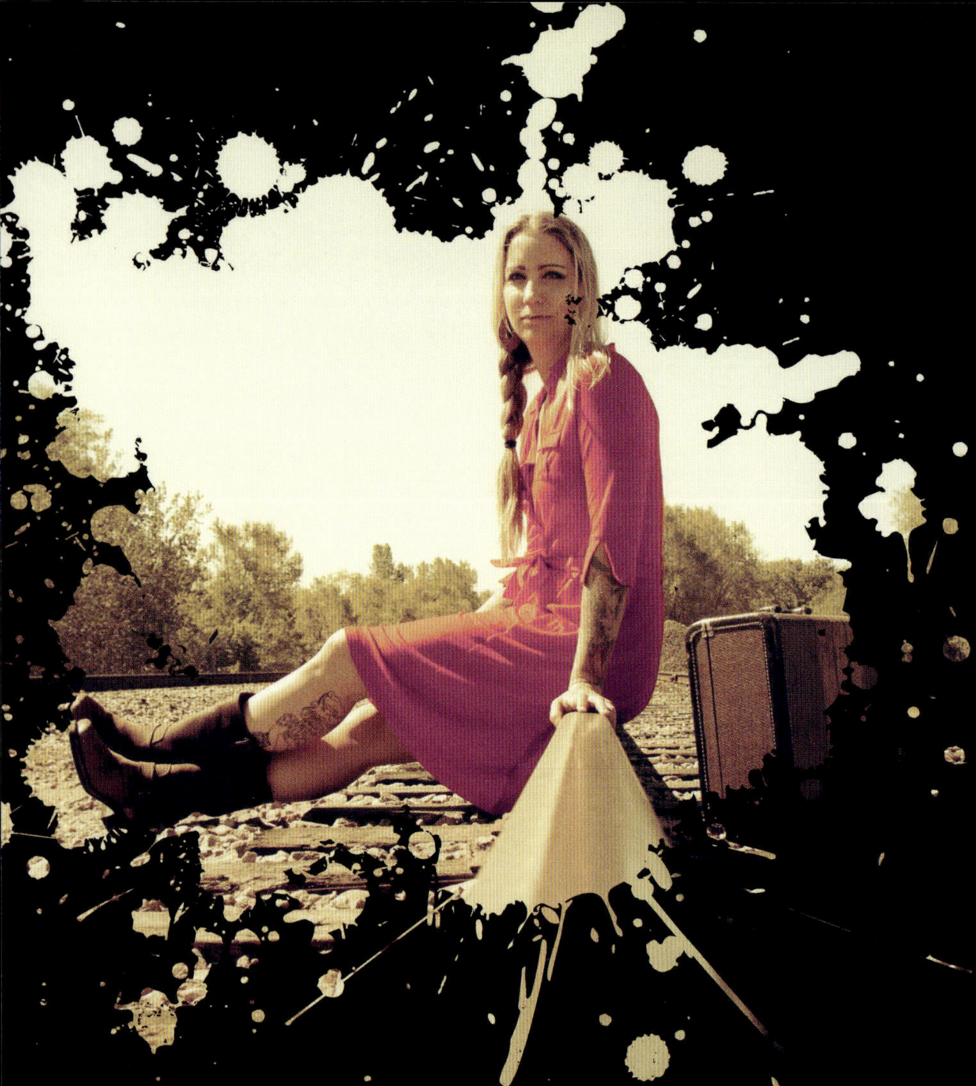

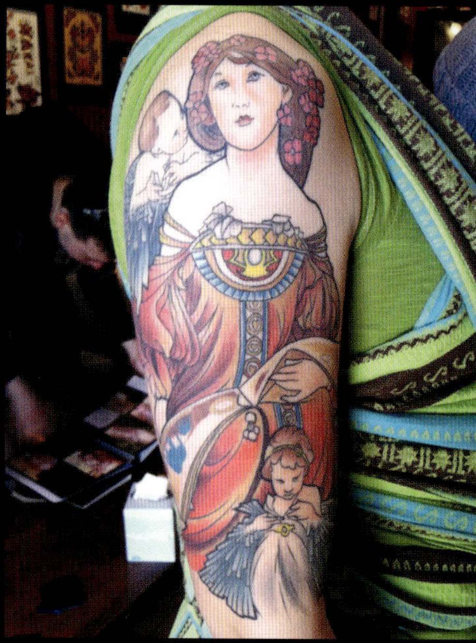

With more than nineteen years of experience, **MEGAN HOOGLAND** has made quite a name for herself as one of the top female tattoo artists in the US. The owner of Mecca Tattoo in Mankato, Minnesota, she works diligently on the convention circuit and has been featured in numerous magazines worldwide. Megan is a master in black-and-gray tattooing, and specializes in portrait tattooing and reproduction work—with a twist, making each piece that she works on her own.

Megan HOOGLAND

"I think sometimes being a female gave me attention I didn't deserve"

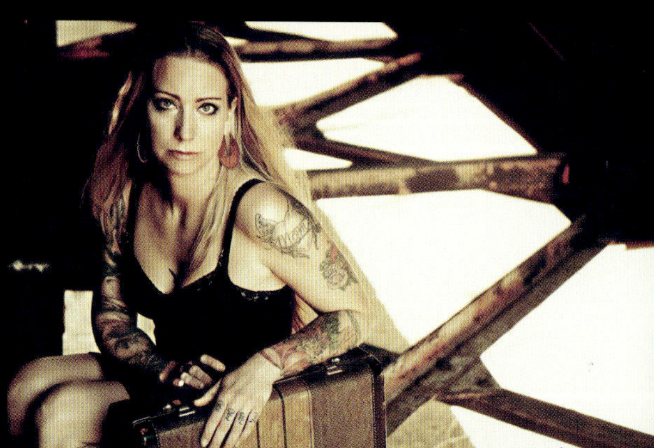

www.meganhoogland.com
shop.meganhoogland.com
www.facebook.com/meganhoogland
www.facebook.com/megan.hoogland.7
meccatattoo.com

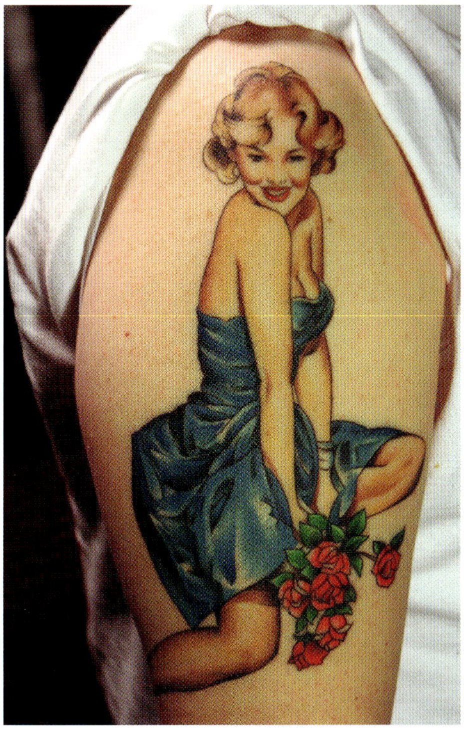

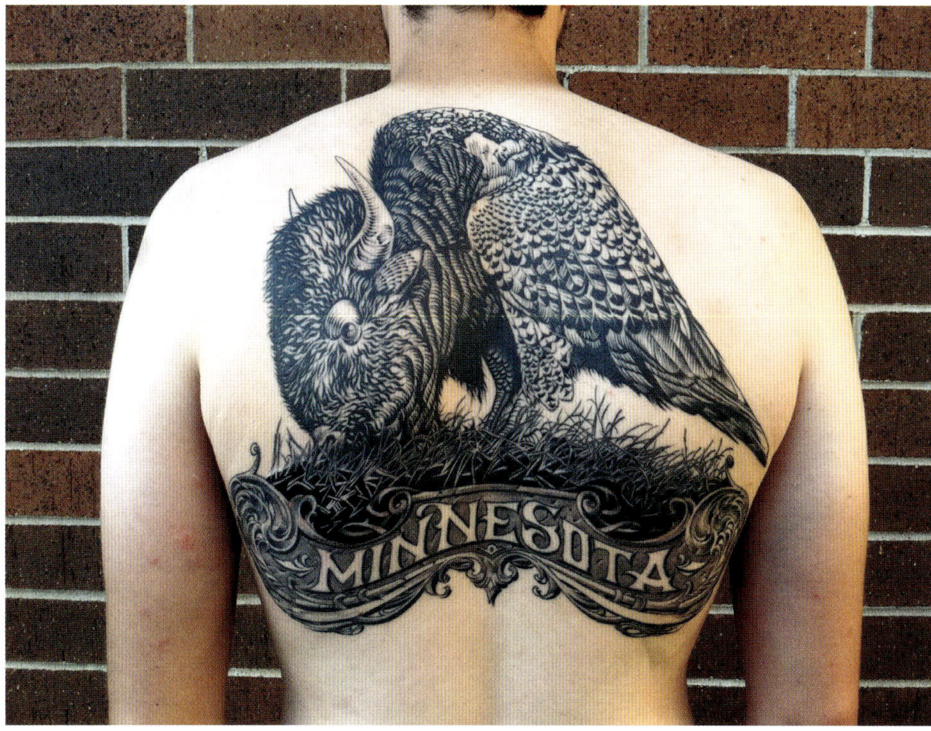

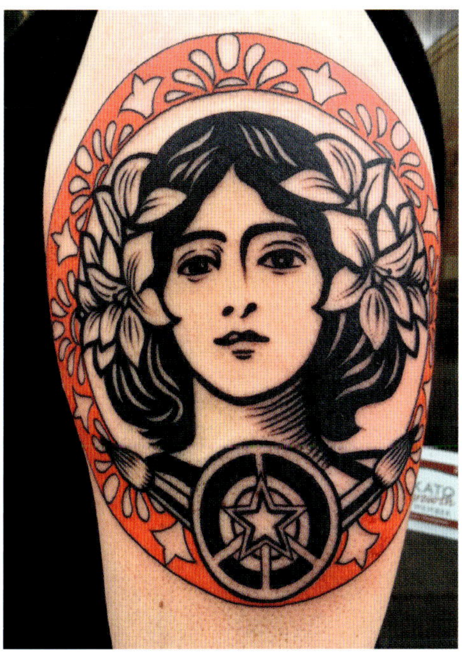

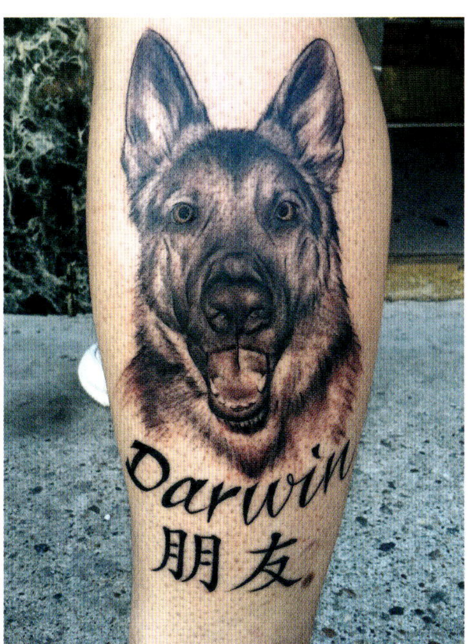

What did you do before you started tattooing?

Before I started tattooing, I was a waitress/bartender, and was going to school to be an EMT.

How long have you been a tattoo artist? Did you have a formal apprenticeship?

I've been tattooing for about nineteen years, and did have an apprenticeship that taught me the basics, but I learned most of what I know from traveling, doing guest spots and conventions around the world.

What's it like being a female artist in a primarily male workplace?

I don't really consider it being out of the ordinary; I think I've proved myself with my peers. I guess I'm also just used to it!

Do you feel that male customers treat you differently?

No, not at all.

Though the dynamics are constantly changing, there are obviously many fewer women tattoo artists in the industry than men. Has being a female ever presented challenges to you along the way? Do you feel you have had to work even harder to achieve the success you have than might have been necessary for a man?

I definitely had to work as hard as any male. I think sometimes being a female gave me attention I didn't deserve.

Tell me more about the shop you work at, Mecca Tattoo; what's it like working there, and what makes up a typical day?

Right now it's me and two other artists, Kelly and John. John has been the only male in the shop for the last year, and we just hired

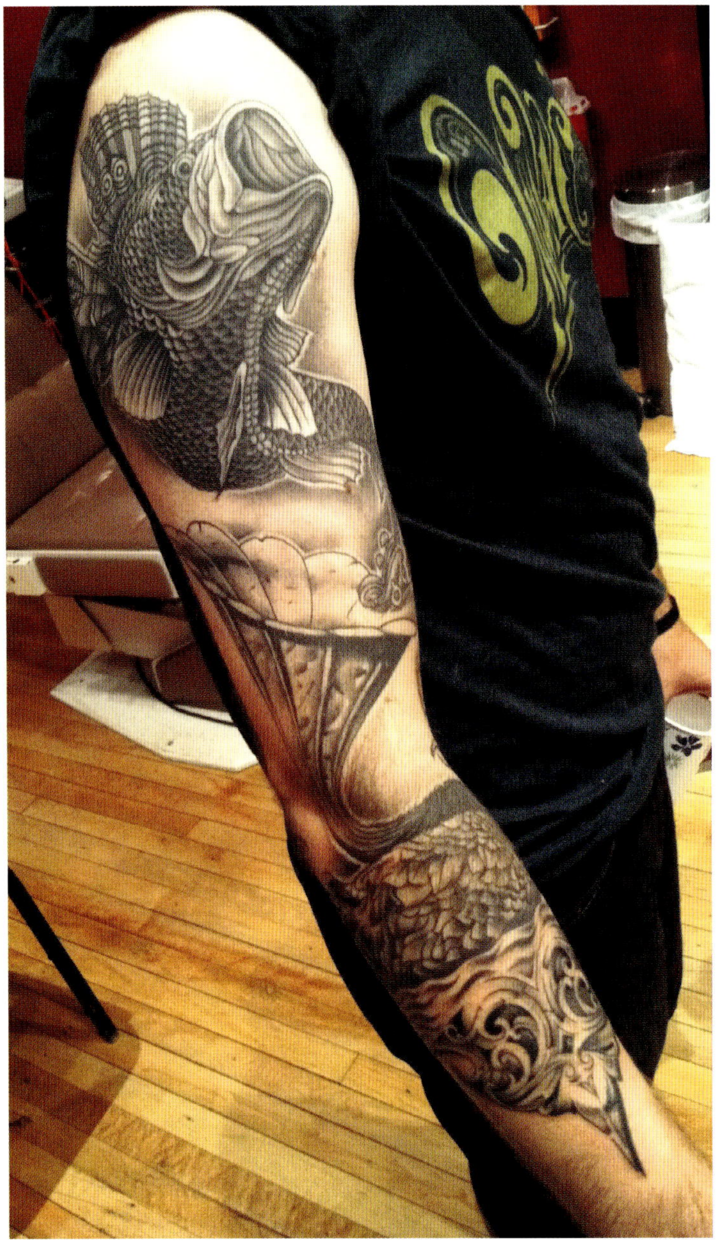

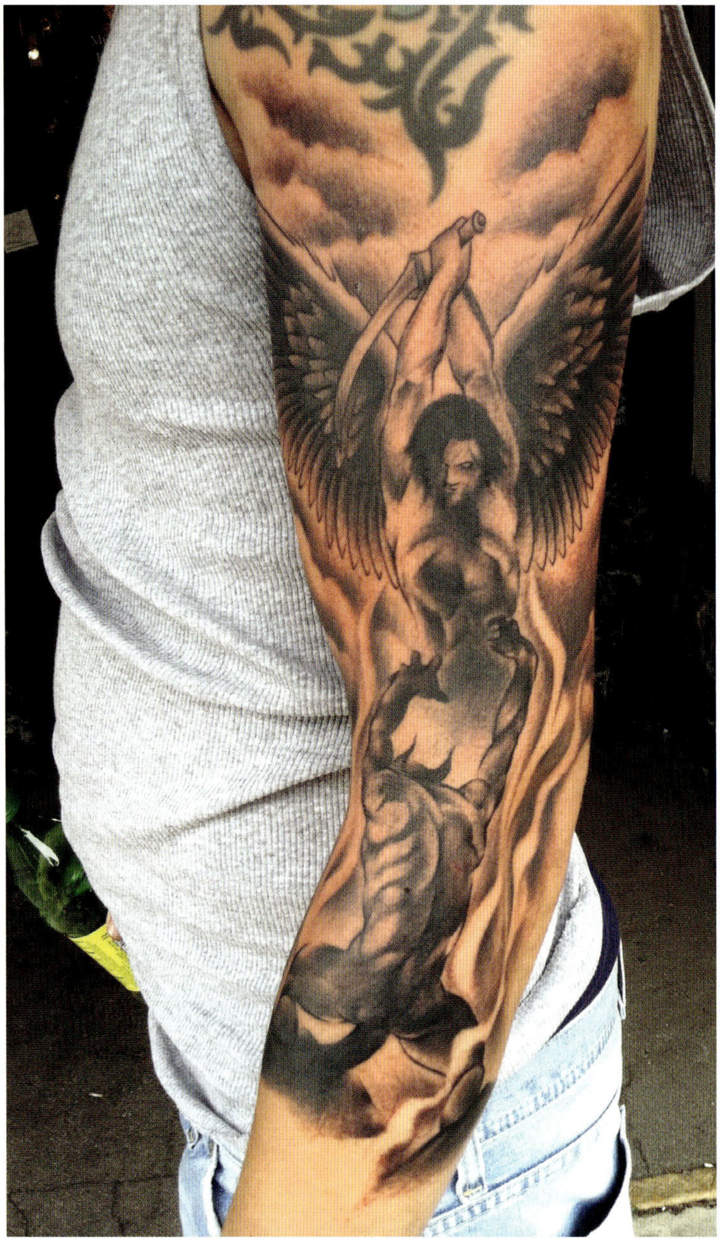

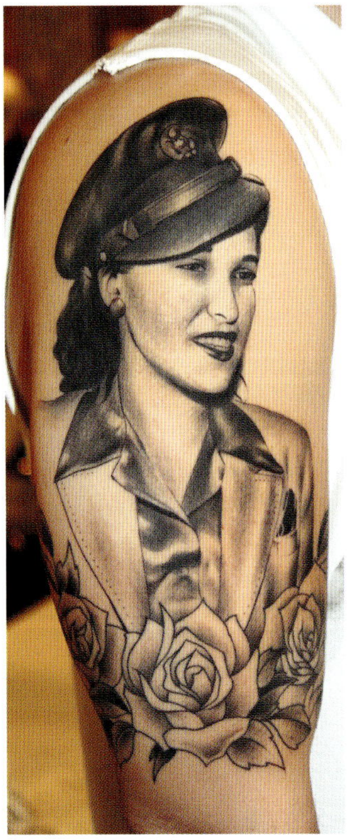

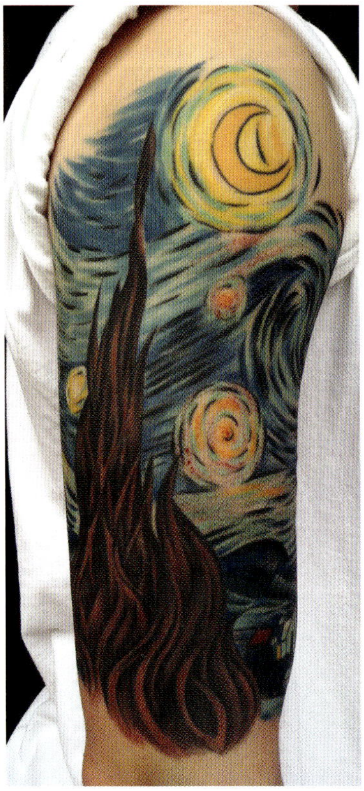

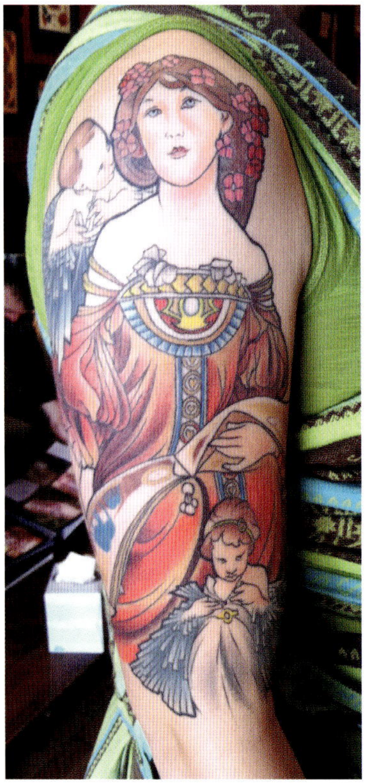

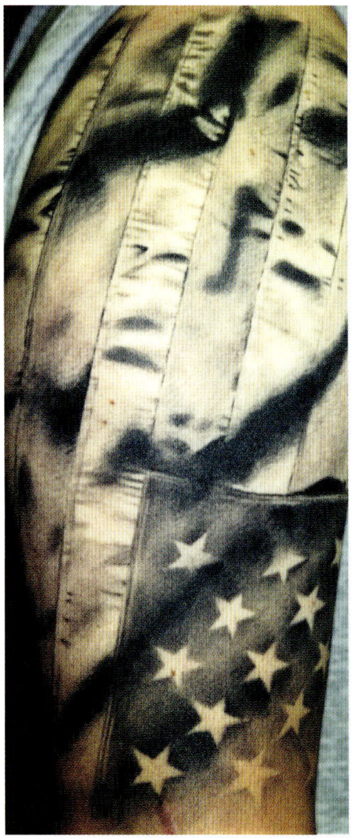

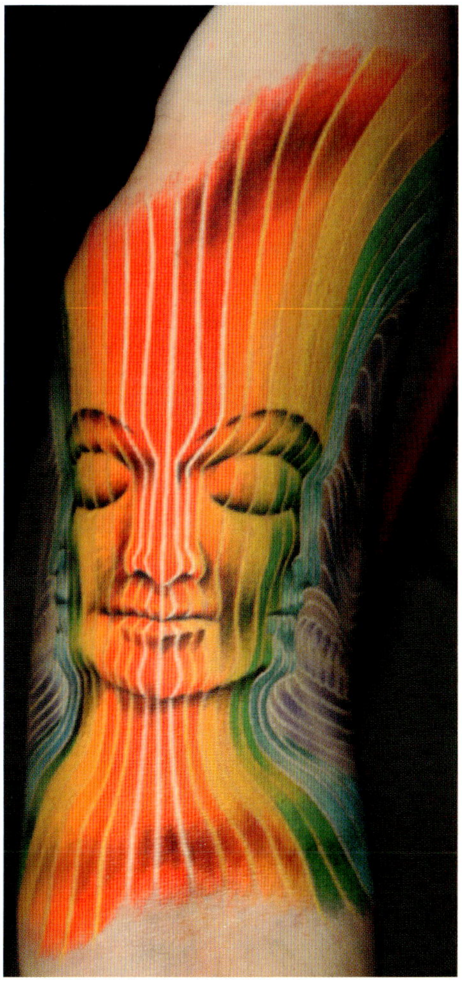

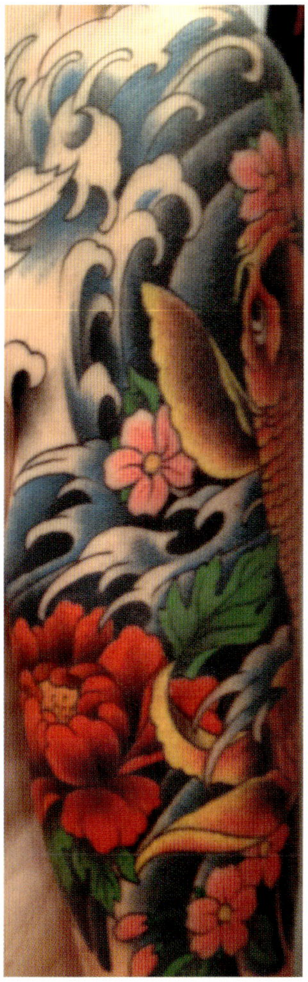

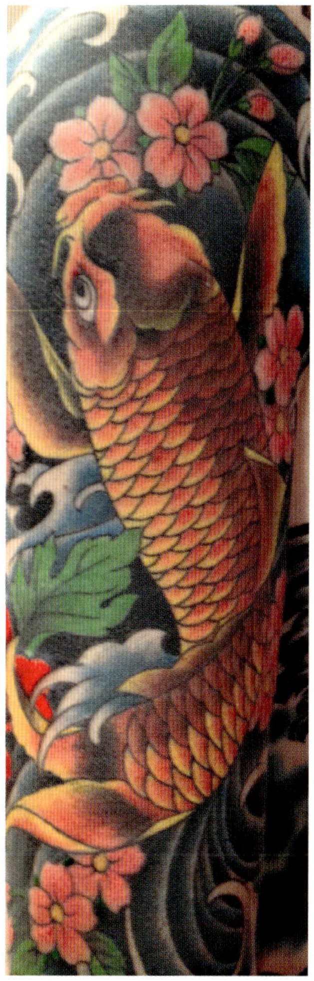

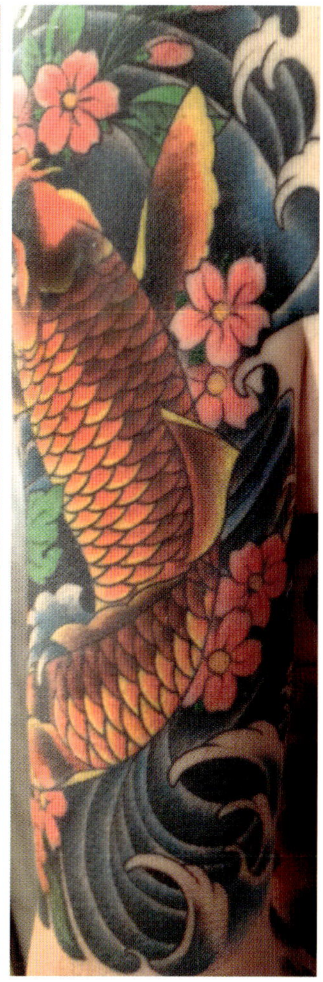

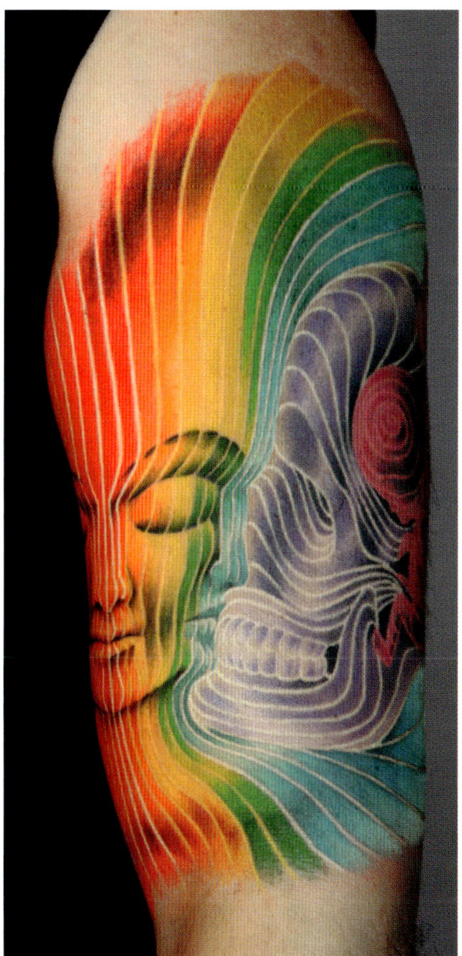

another male artist. But to me, gender doesn't matter. The quality of work and overall personality is what matters to us, to make the shop run smoothly.

Do you see tattooing as a job or as a way to express your creative side?

Both. There are definitely days it's a job, and other days it's my meditation.

What inspires you when you create your designs?

Just the customer ideas and my intuition.

What do you enjoy most about tattooing, and what are some of the challenges?

My customers, the atmosphere, doing awesome artwork, and how fast the industry is evolving.

Art can be a great influence on someone's personality. What is the best lesson that you've learned from your art journey?

Be humble and learn from others.

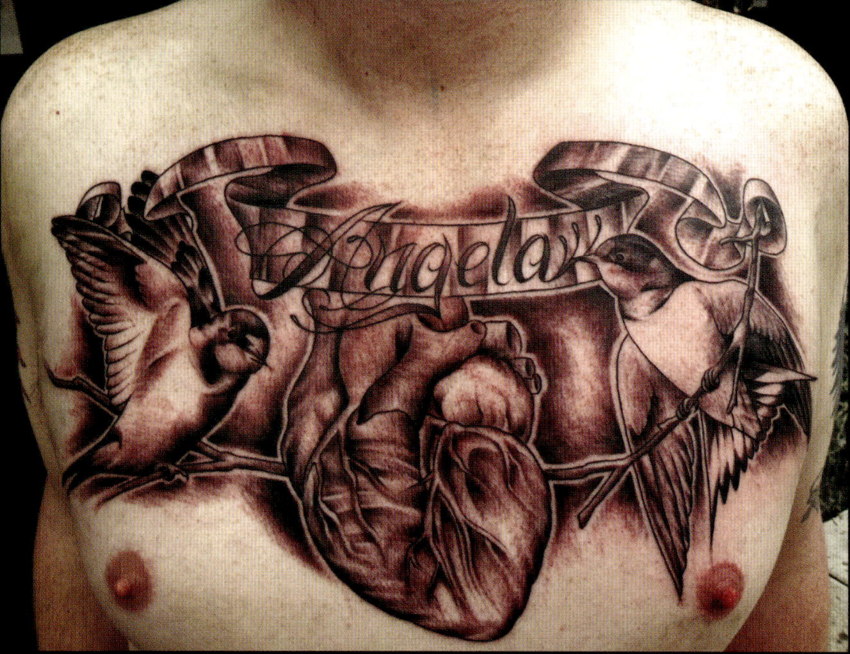
Angela

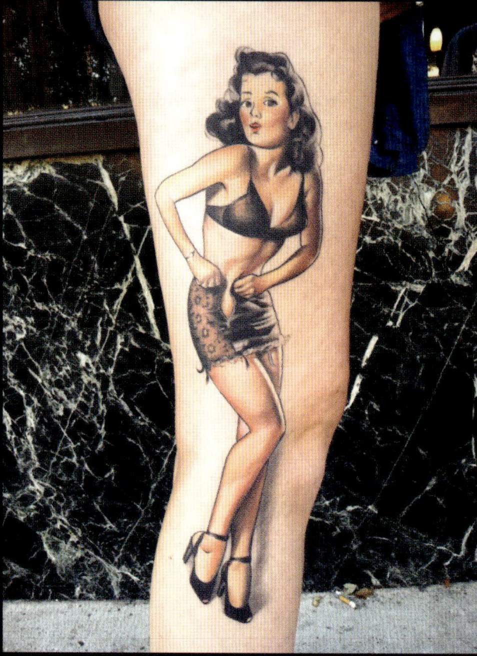

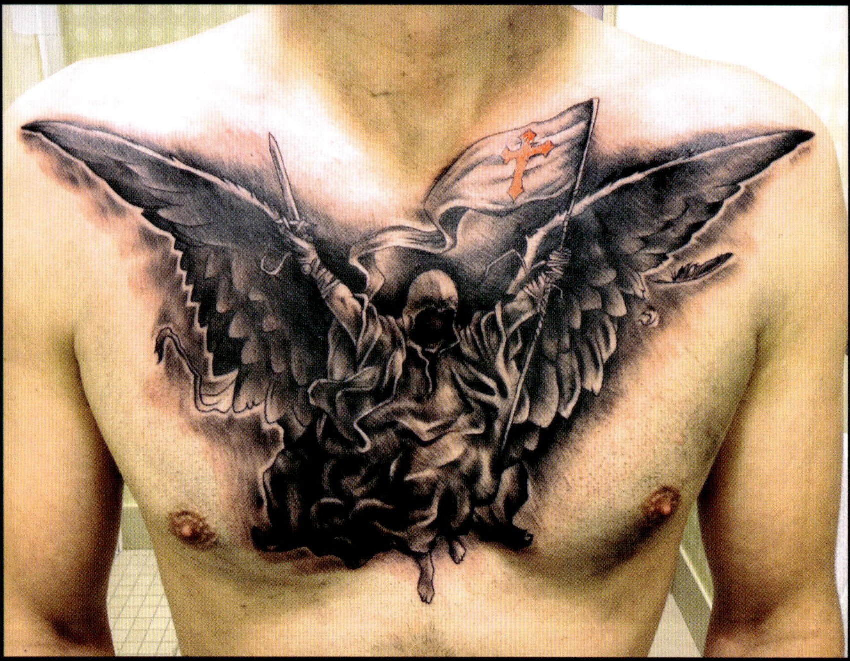

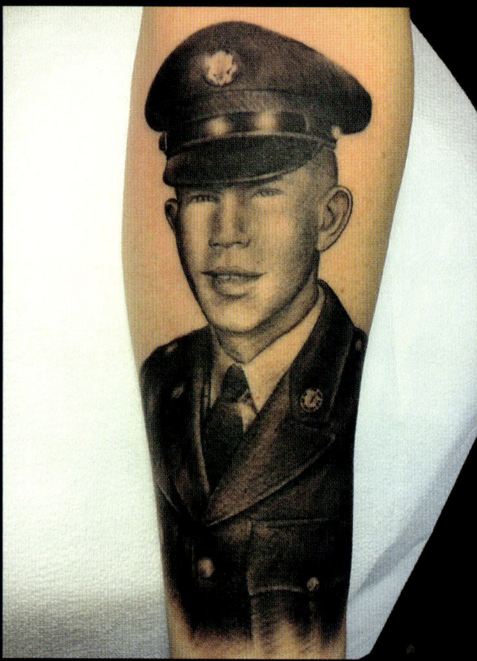

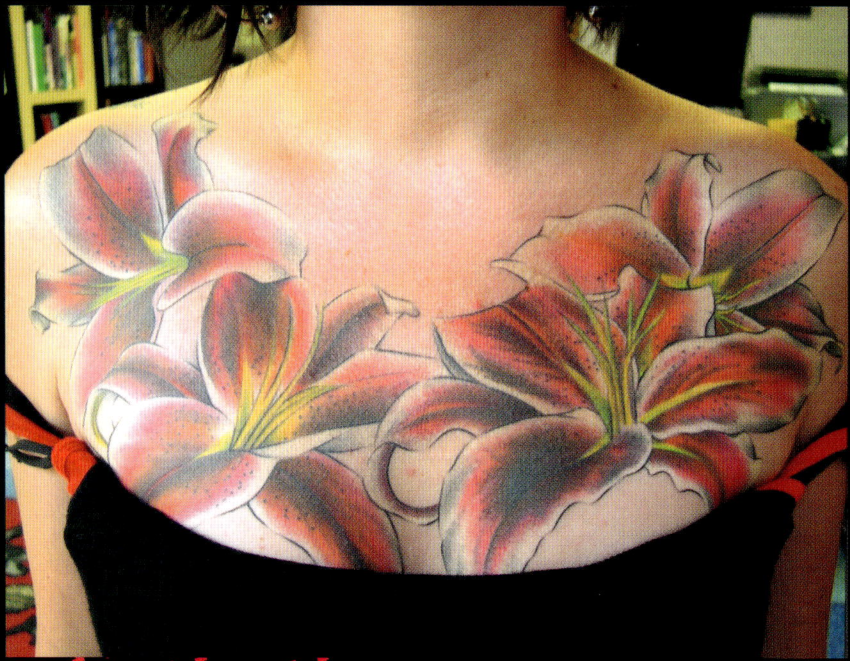

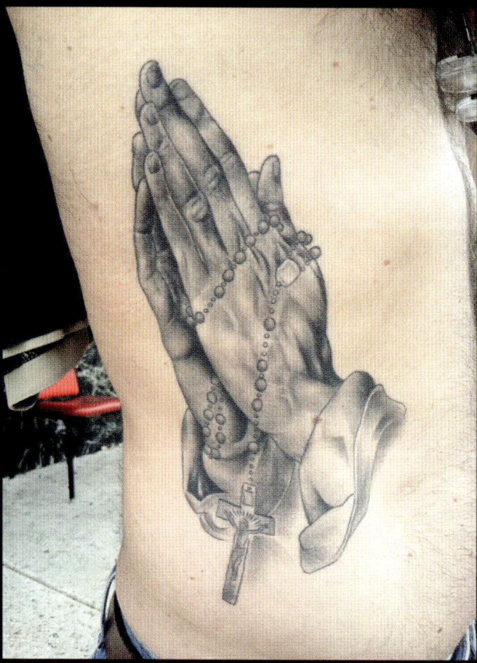

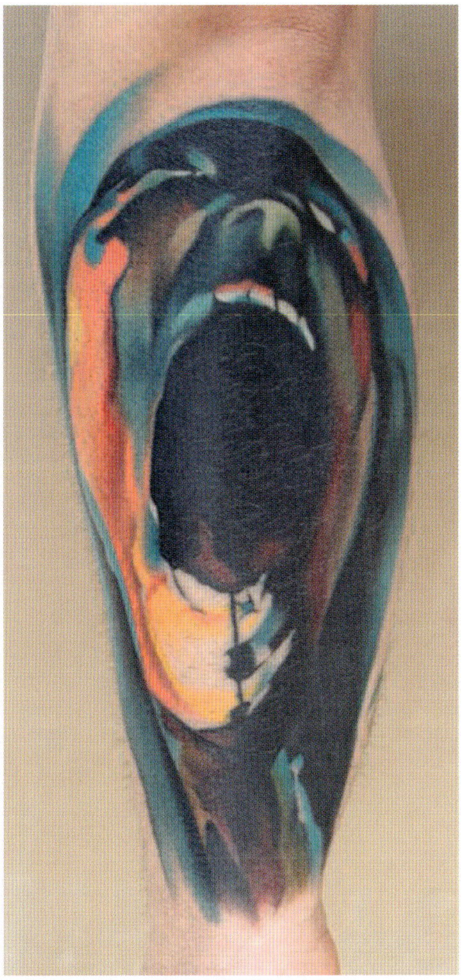

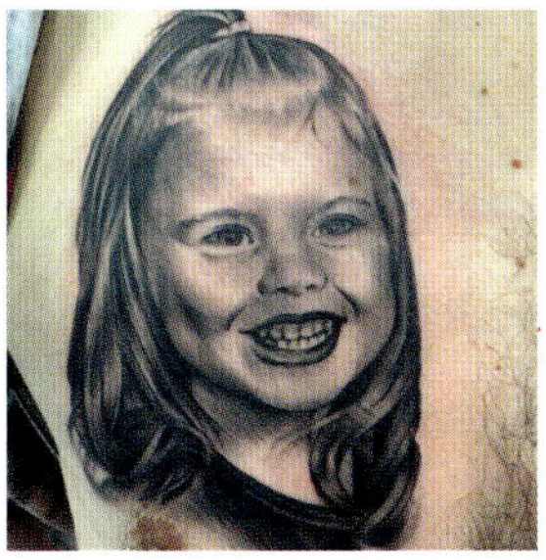

How did your style progress and develop to the point you are at now?

A lot of trial and error, and a lot of questions! If there was something I wanted to learn, I'd find someone who was good at it and watch them for hours.

Describe how your role models and any other sources of inspiration have affected your tattoo style.

I just try to incorporate anything that inspires me into what I do. I also do a lot of reproduction tattooing, and make sure to credit the artist.

What's one of your favorite pieces that you've tattooed on someone else?

The Aaron Horkey Minnesota back piece turned out pretty awesome.

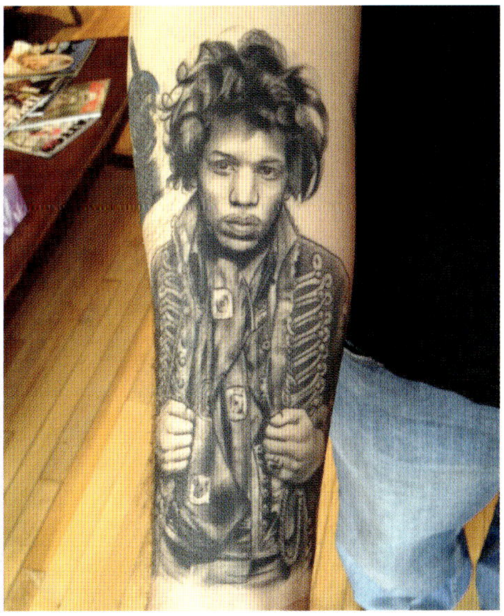

What's one of your favorite pieces on your own body, and who did it?

The rose on my hand, by BJ Betts.

What is your favorite thing about being a tattoo artist?

The freedom to travel and set my own rules and hours.

What is the most interesting tattoo you have been asked to do?

They're each unique in their own way.

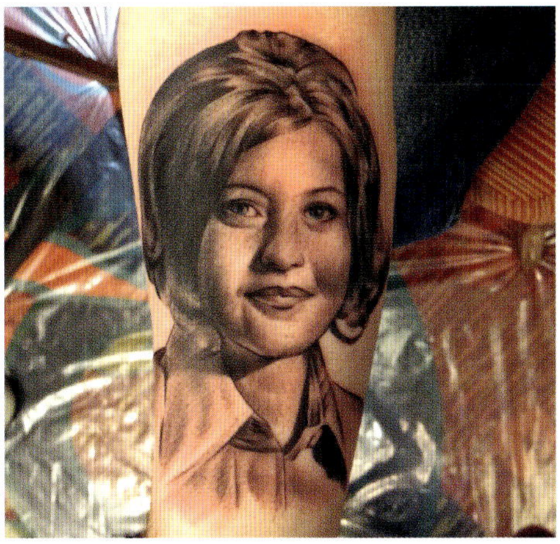

Is there any subject or taboo you wouldn't ink on someone, even if it was their request or design?

It would depend on the context.

Have you noticed a change in the types of images people have asked for over the years you've been tattooing?

Yes, people are much more open-minded now, mostly because technical ability in the industry as a whole has gotten better.

Tattoos seem very mainstream now. Do you think that's good or bad?

Both.

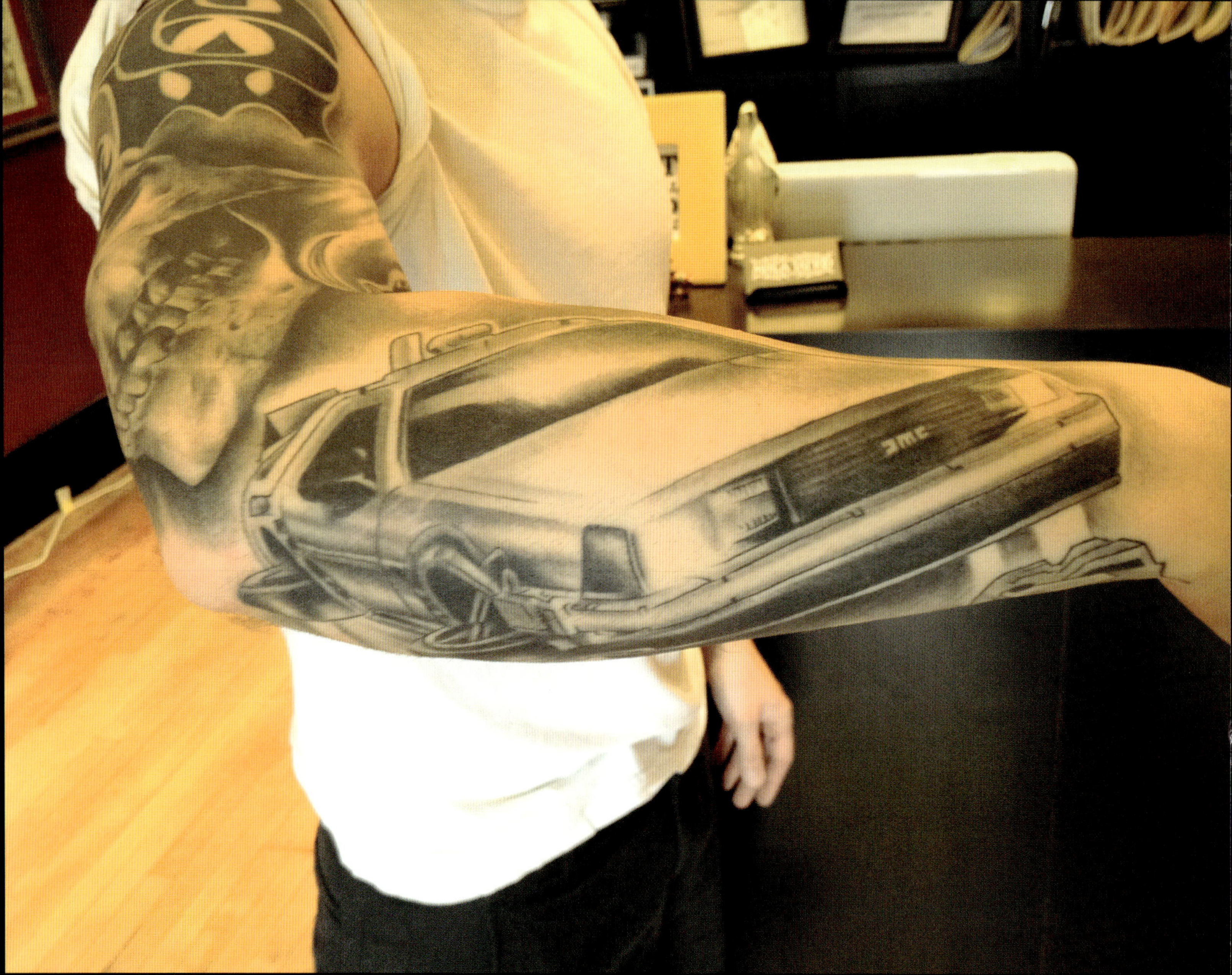
DMC

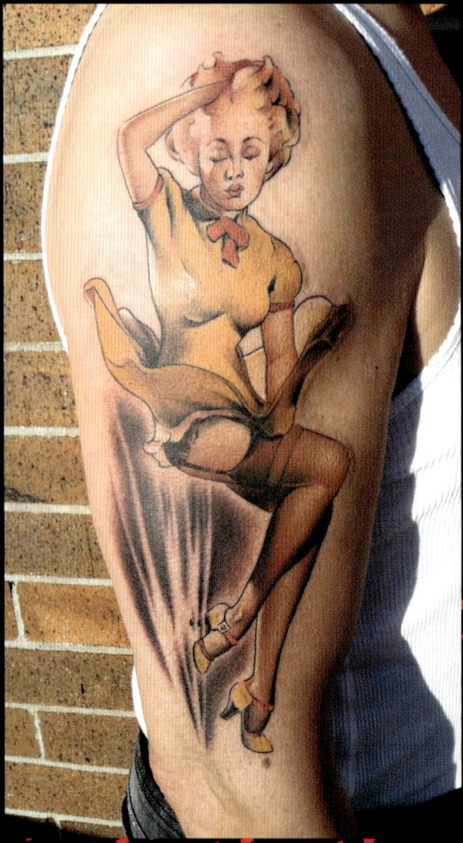

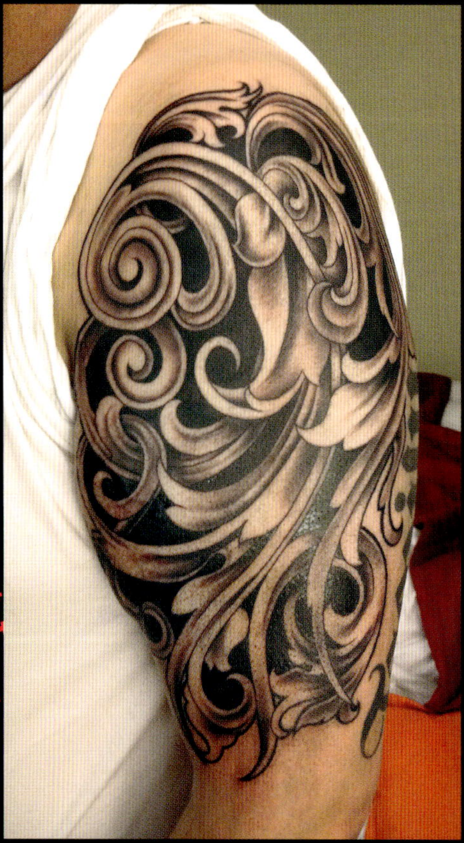

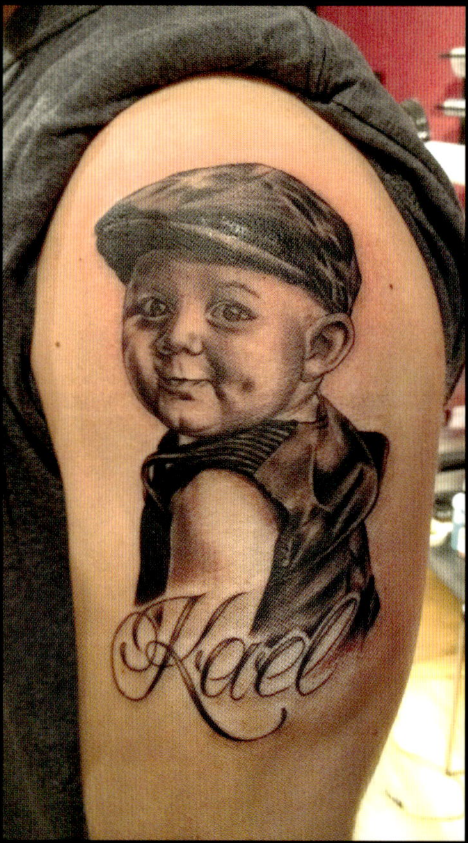
Kael

MEGAN HOOGLAND

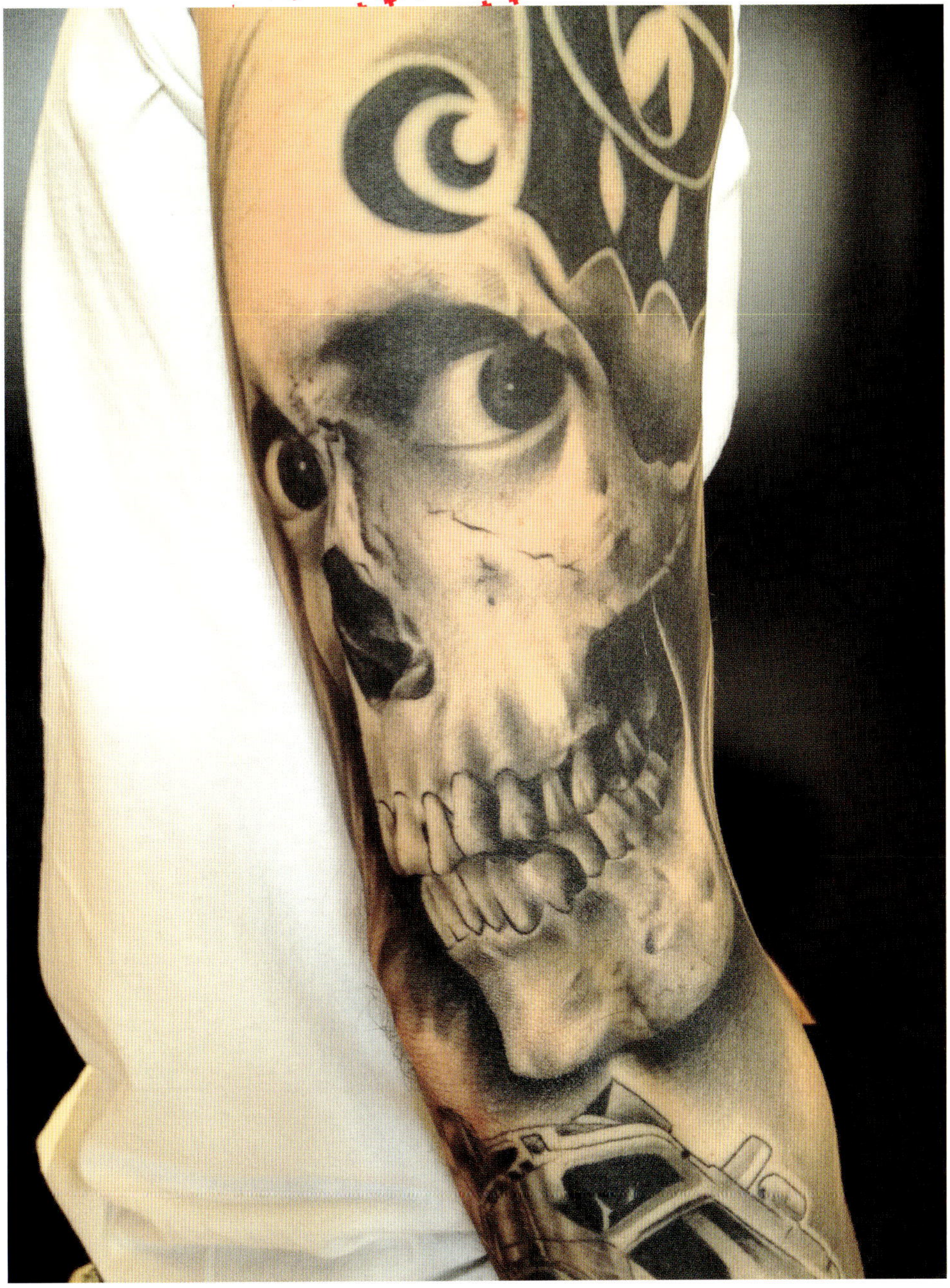
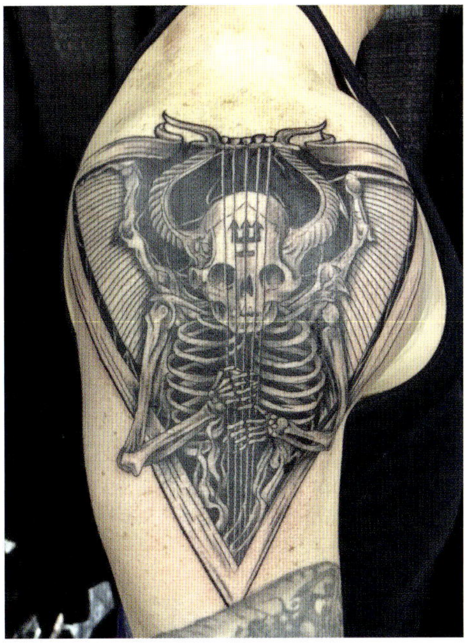
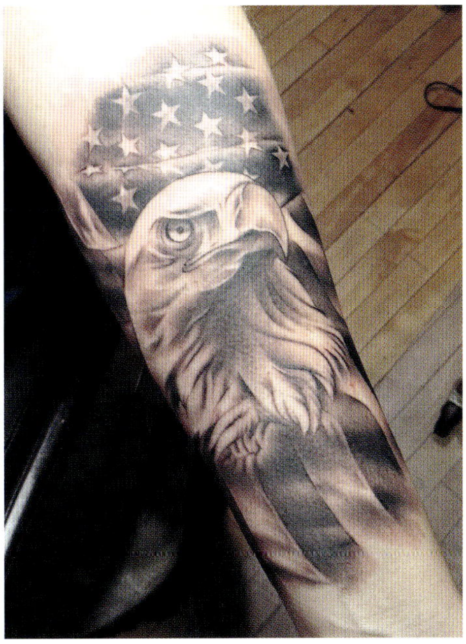
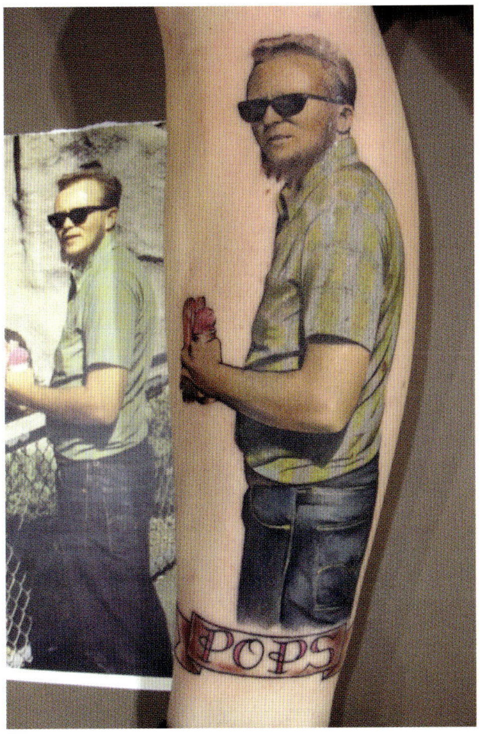

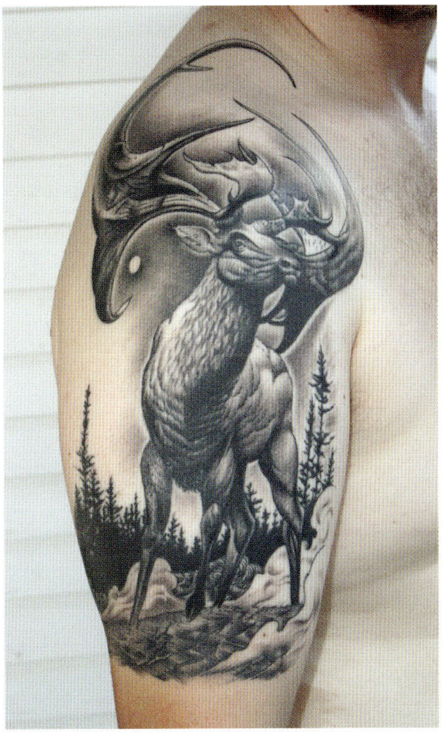
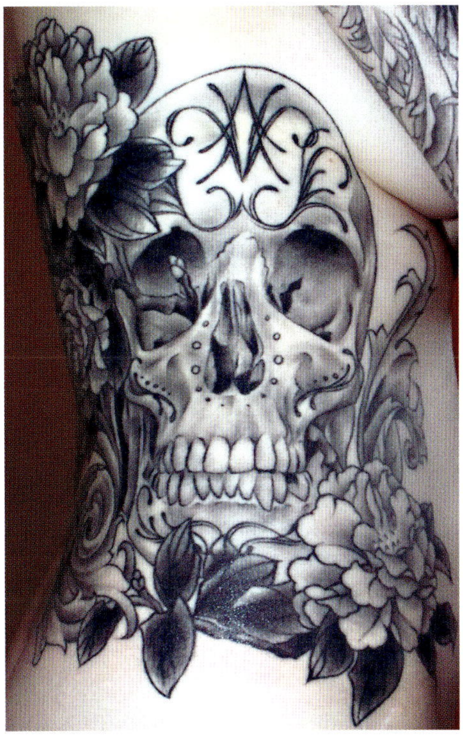

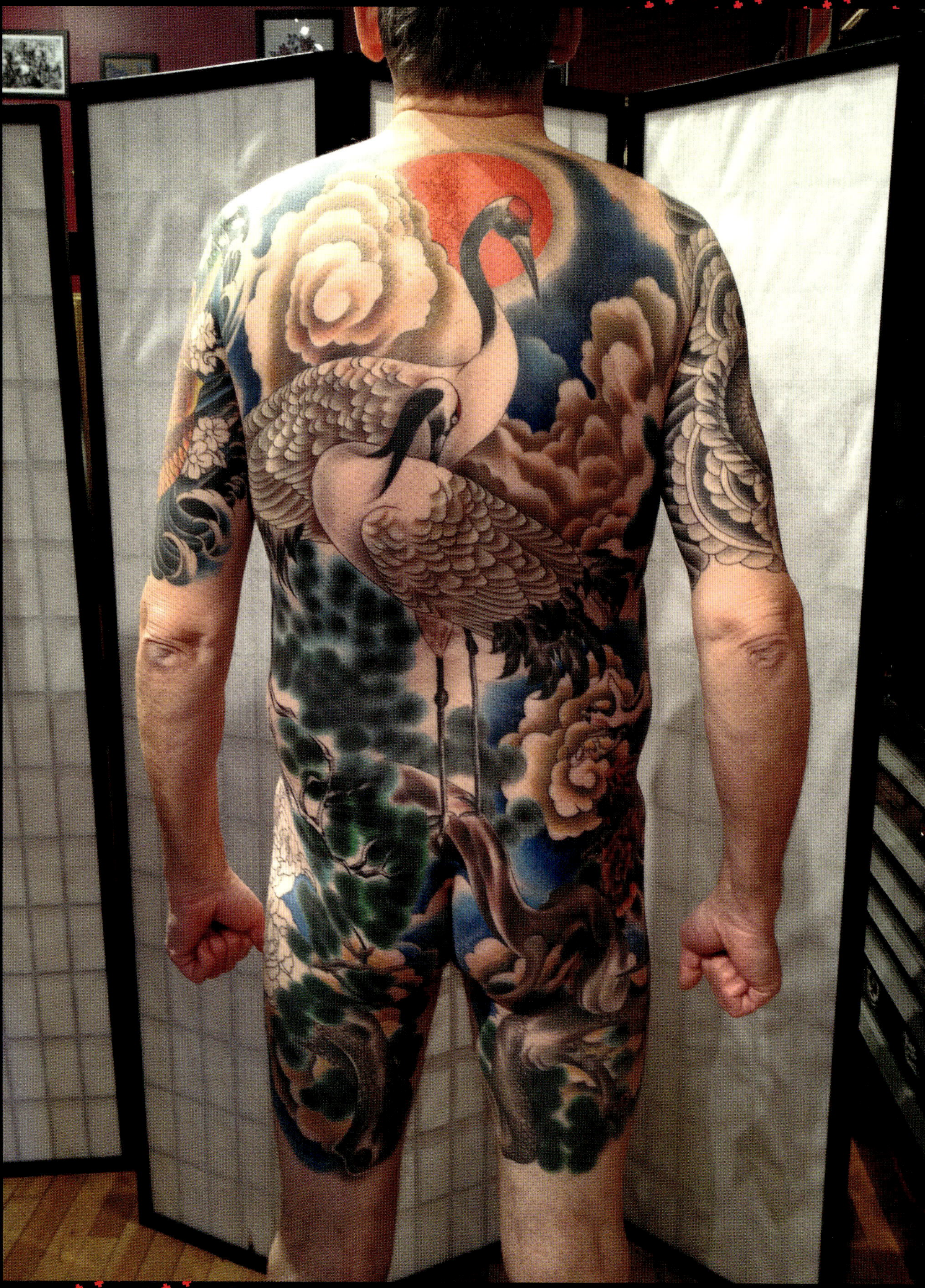

MEGAN HOOGLAND

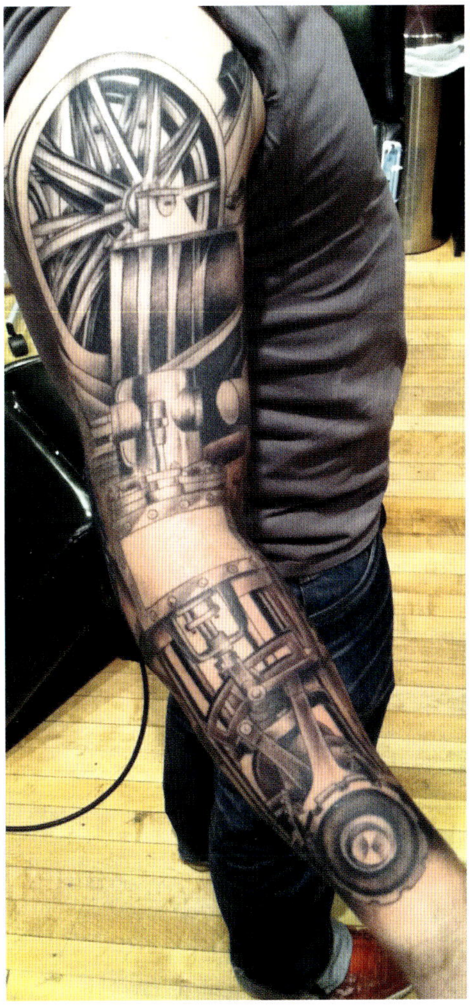

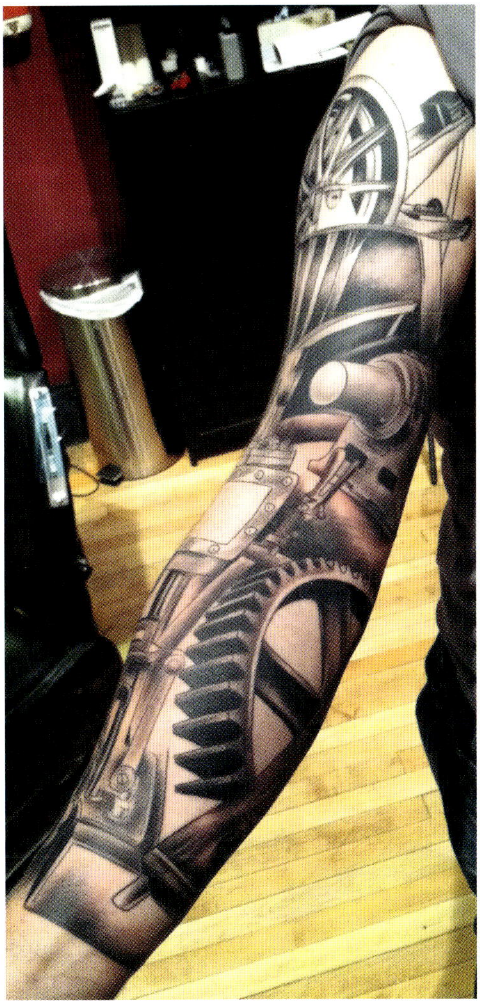

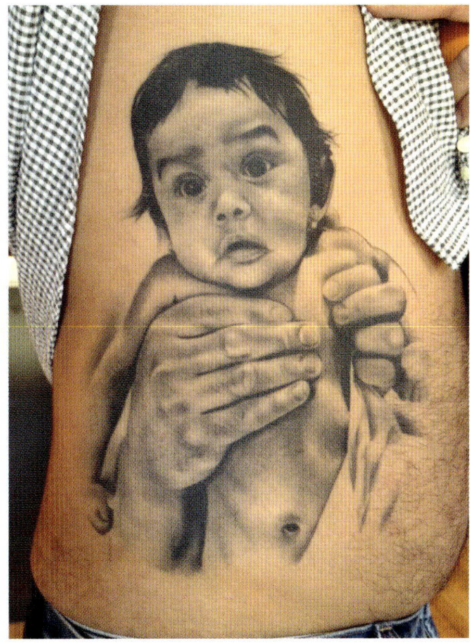

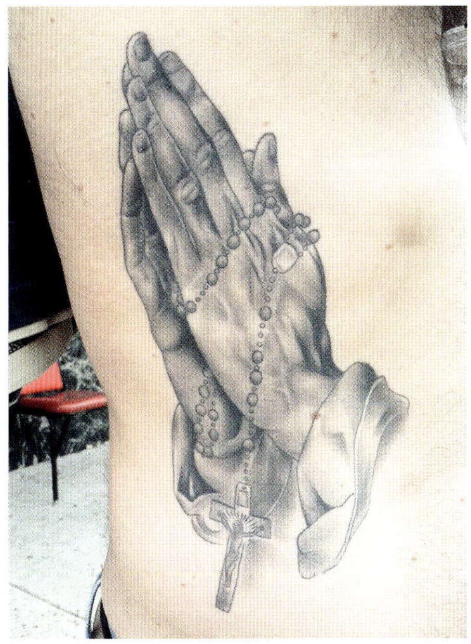

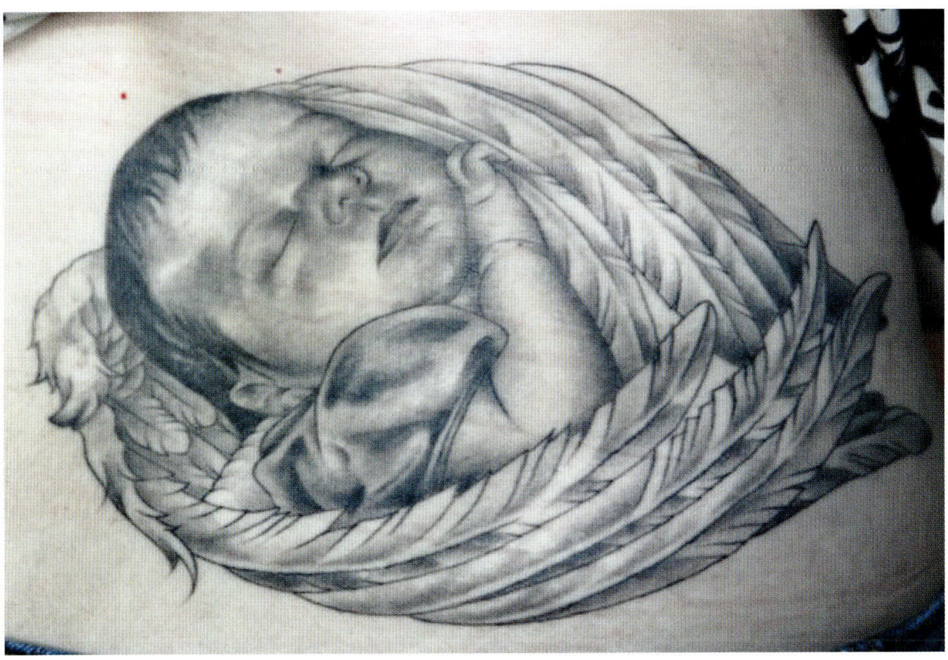

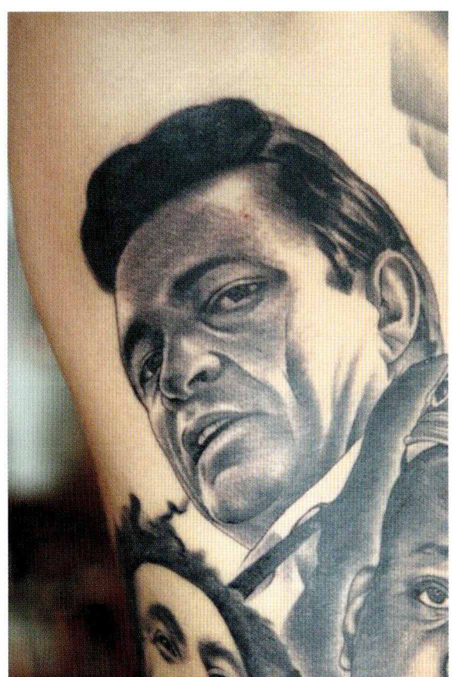

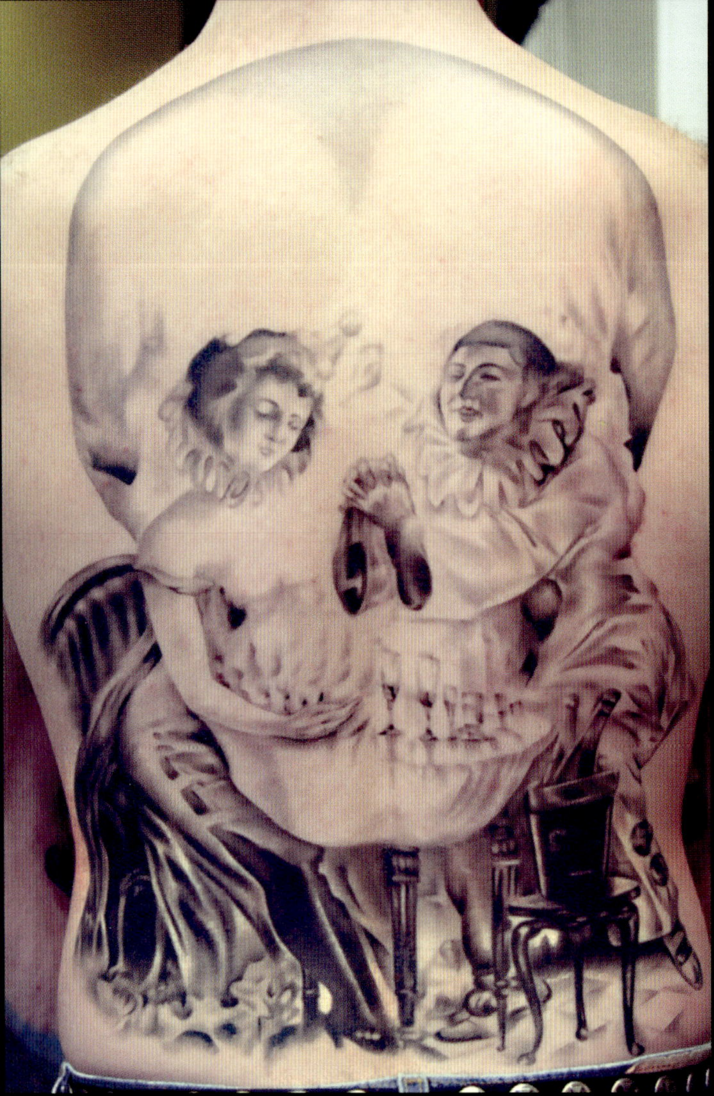
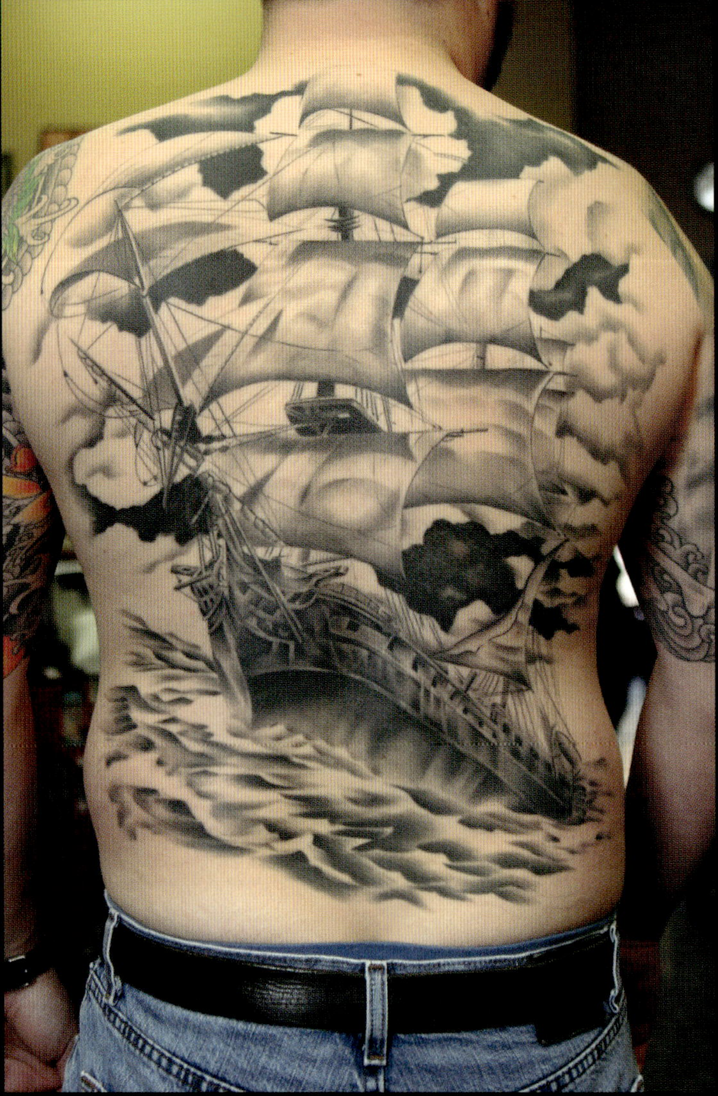
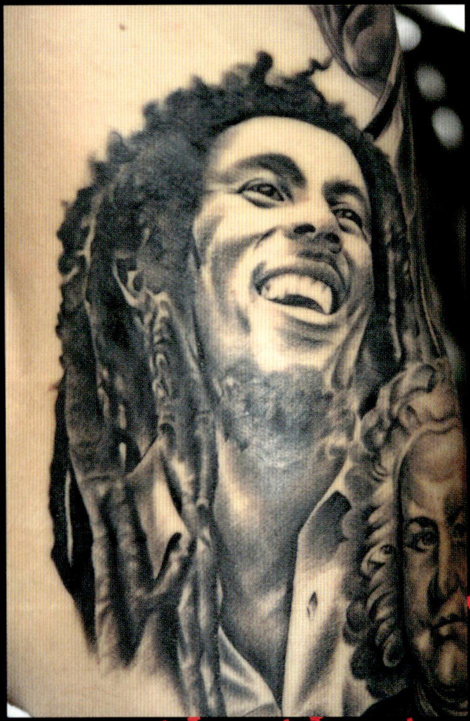
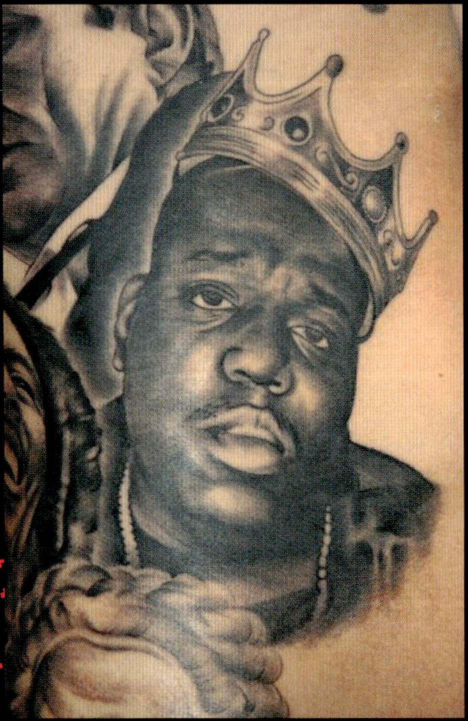
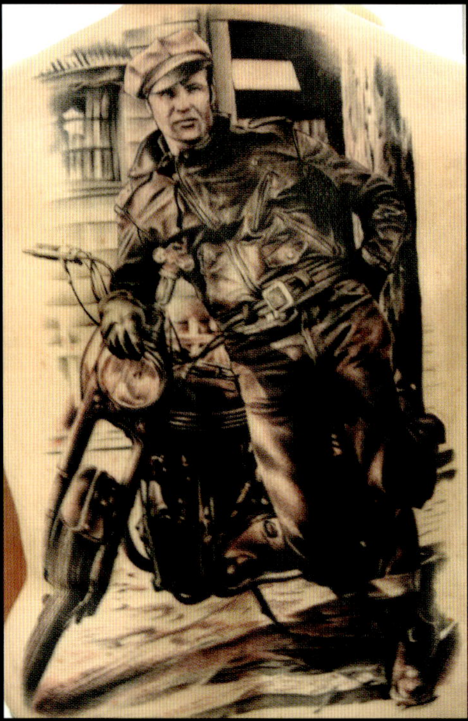

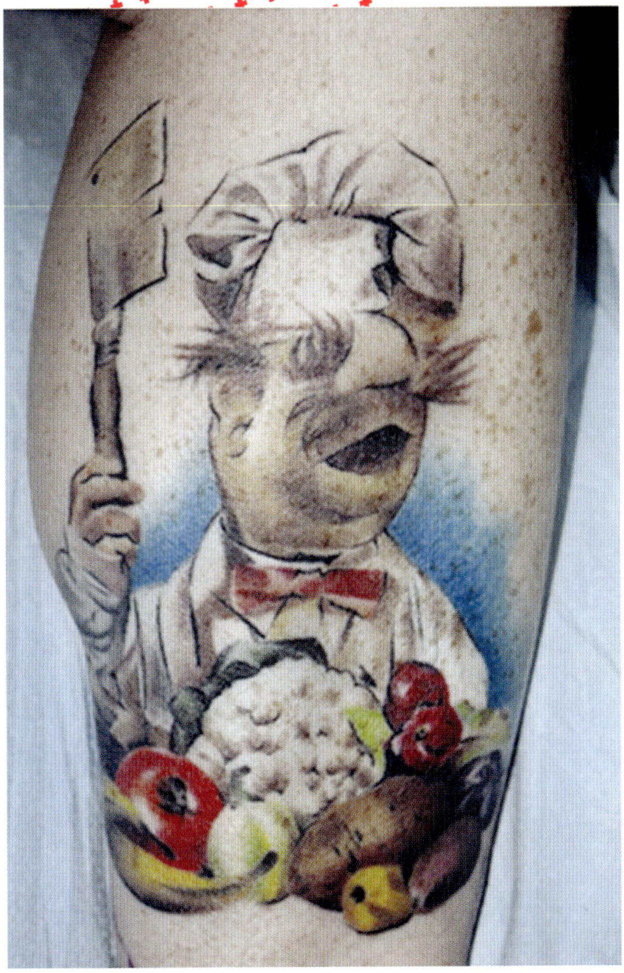

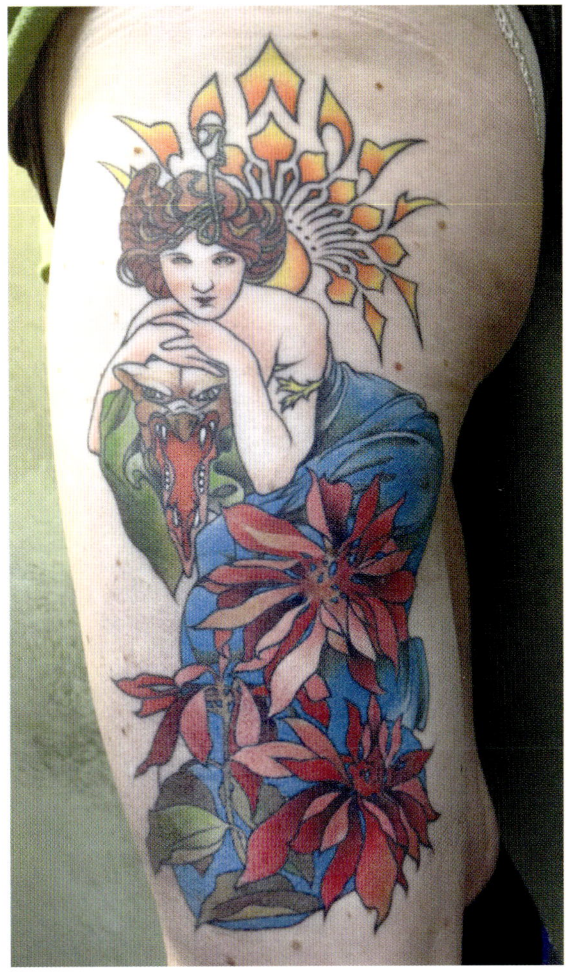

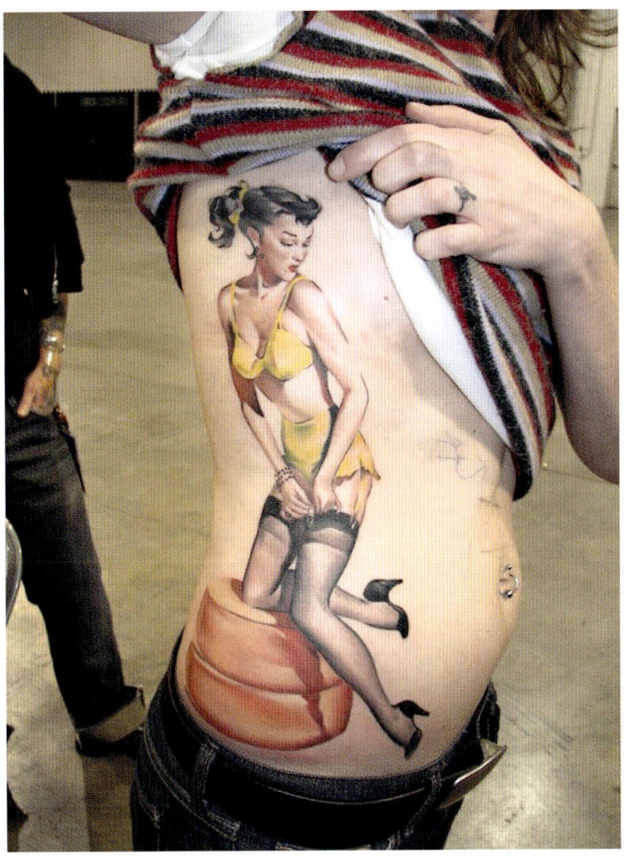

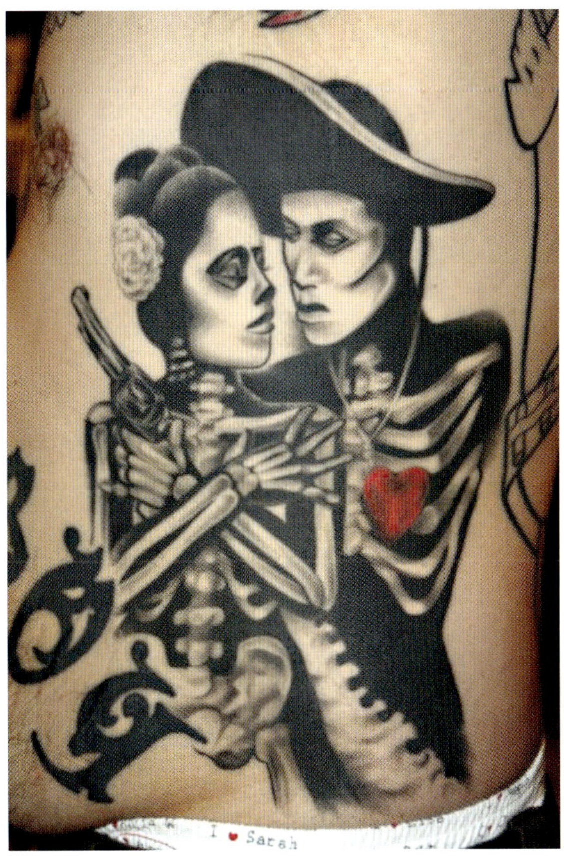
I ♥ Sarah

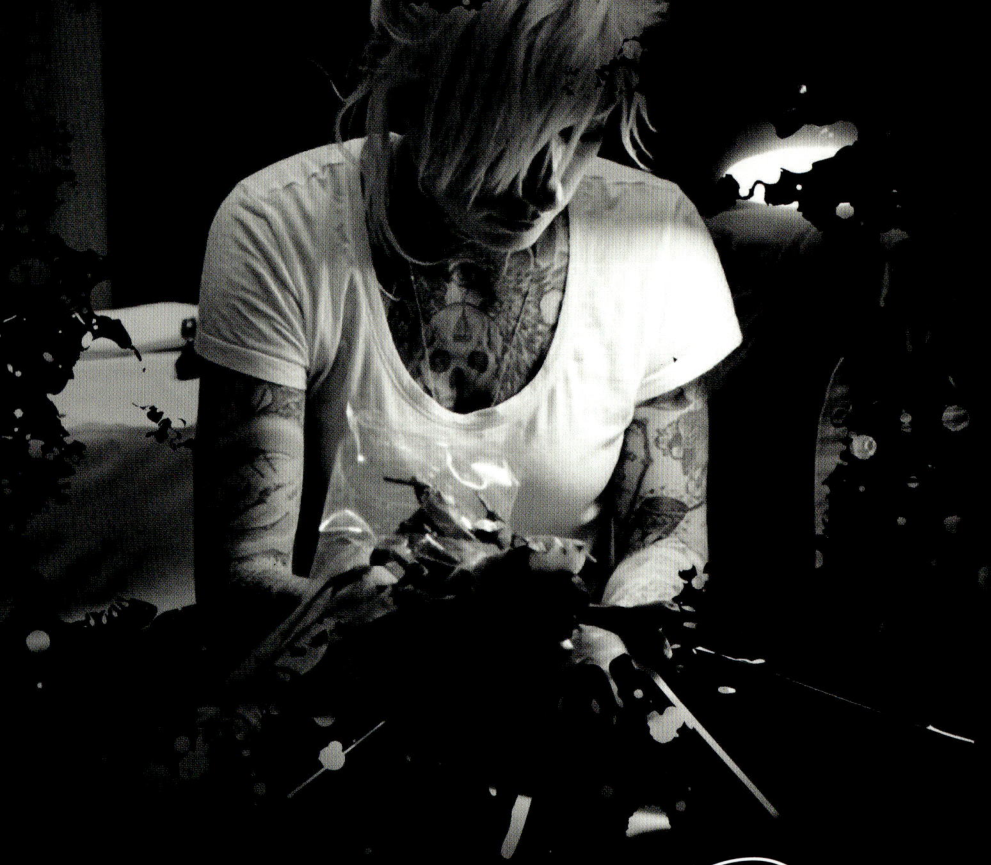

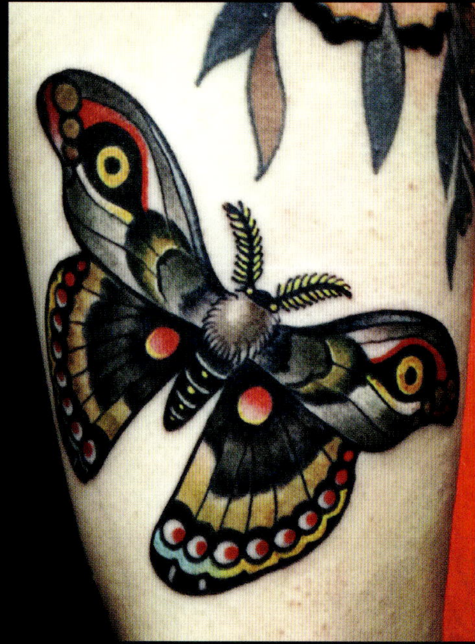

EVA HUBER is thirty-one years old, and has been tattooing for twelve years. Before tattooing, Eva worked doing whatever she could find: she worked as a nanny, prep cook and dishwasher, movie theater attendant, line cook, waitress, and finally as a retail associate—which she wasn't very fond of.

Eva HUBER

"People come and go, tattoos are forever"

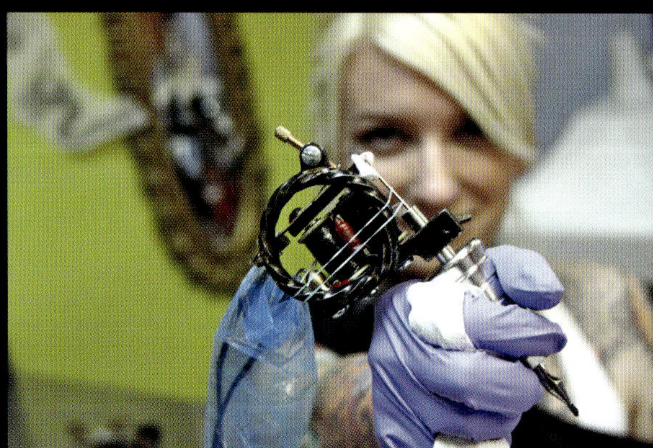

www.tattoosbyeva.com
twitter.com/Eva_Huber

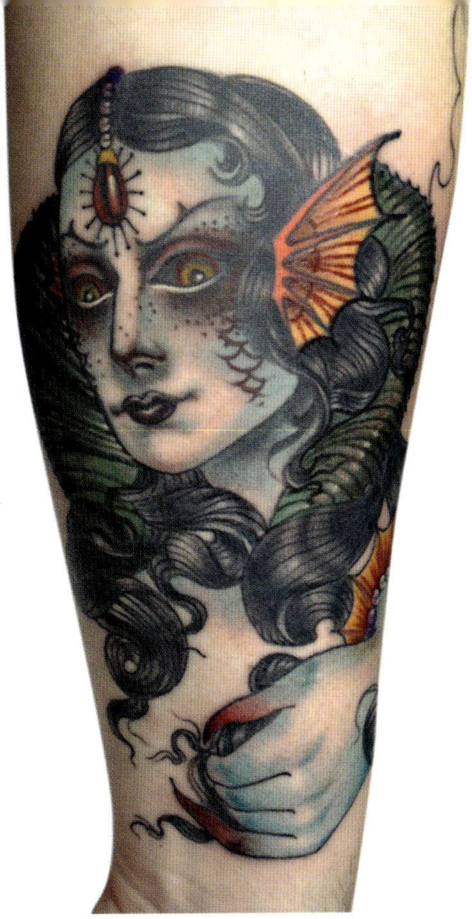

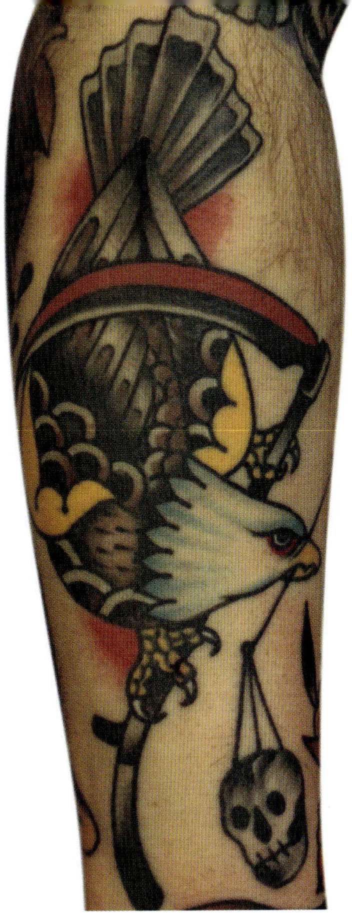

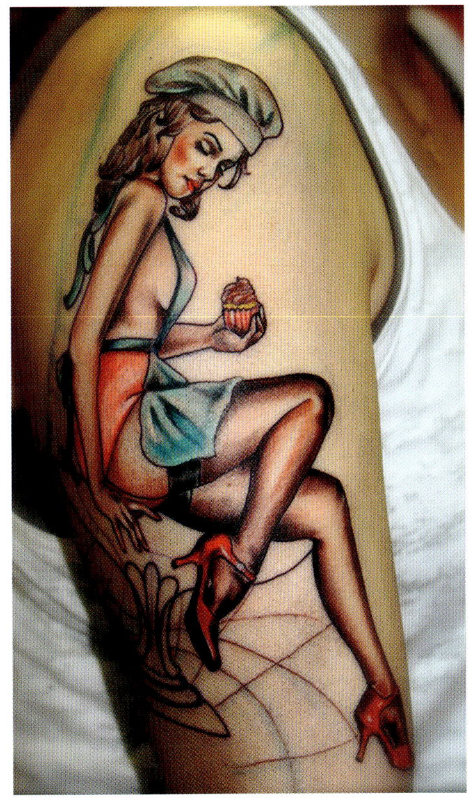

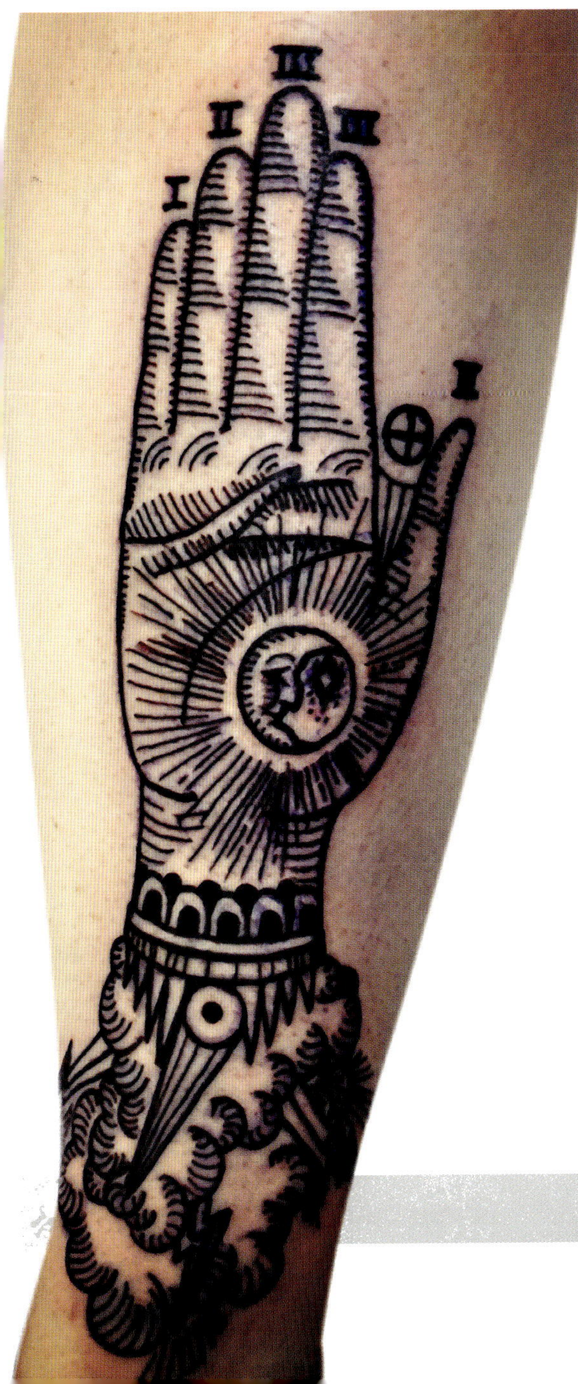

When you were a child, did you think you would grow up to become an artist, or work in the artistic field? Do you remember drawing and creating a lot as a child?

For as long as I can remember I have always been making a drawing or painting something, assembling things together…as I grew older, I began exploring photography, making jewelry, sewing clothes.

What was your initial exposure to the tattoo world and when did you first add your own piece of ink to your skin? Was that a transformative time in your life?

I first saw my uncle Norman with "True Love" tattooed across his knuckles…I couldn't have been much older than eight, nine years old. Then when I was maybe twelve or thirteen, one of my older sisters had me come into her bedroom, where she then in front of me hand-poked a cross onto her ankle with a sewing needle and India ink. Up until about age sixteen (which is when I got my first tattoo) I thought tattooed and pierced people were kind of freaks and I didn't really want anything to do with them.

Of course getting tattooed was transformative, it is each and every time that it happens, at least for me. Crossing that threshold from being on the same playing field with everyone and then a few hours later wearing an irremovable badge felt like a rite of passage. I was now separate from my peers and now joining the ranks of those who didn't listen to what others recommended, and truly making my own decision.

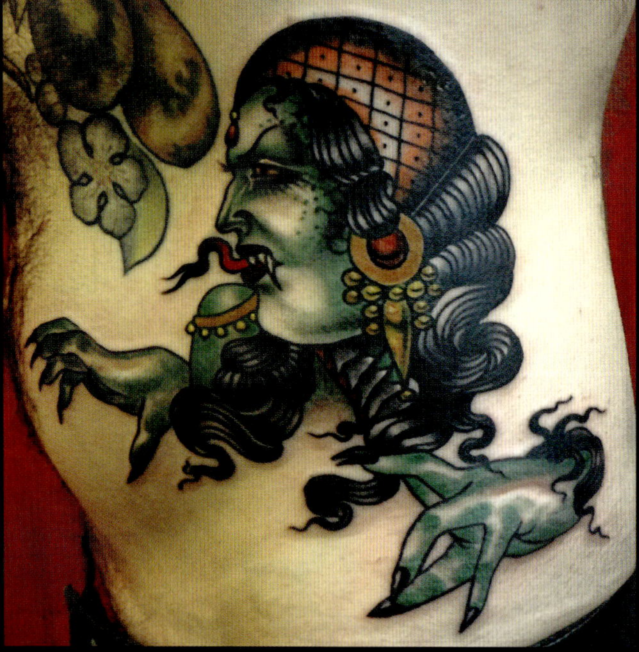
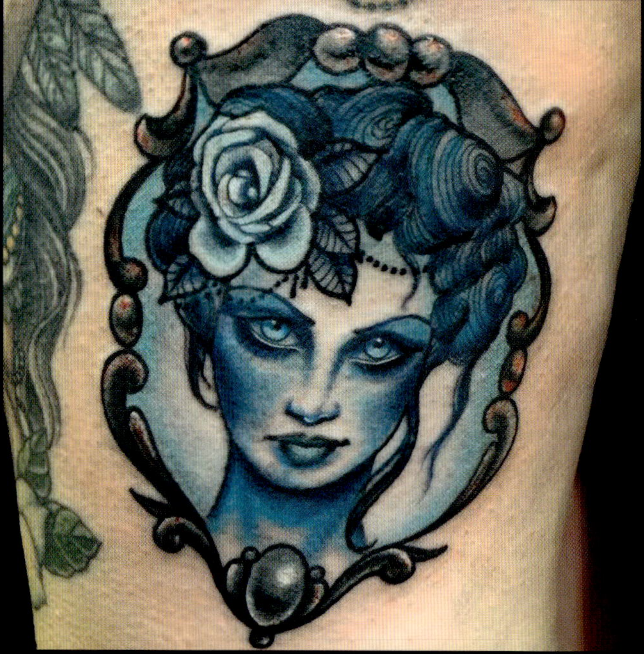
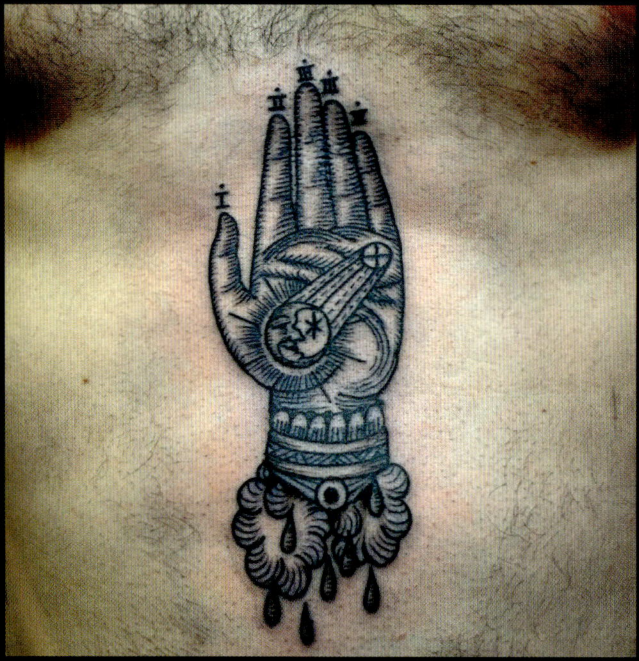
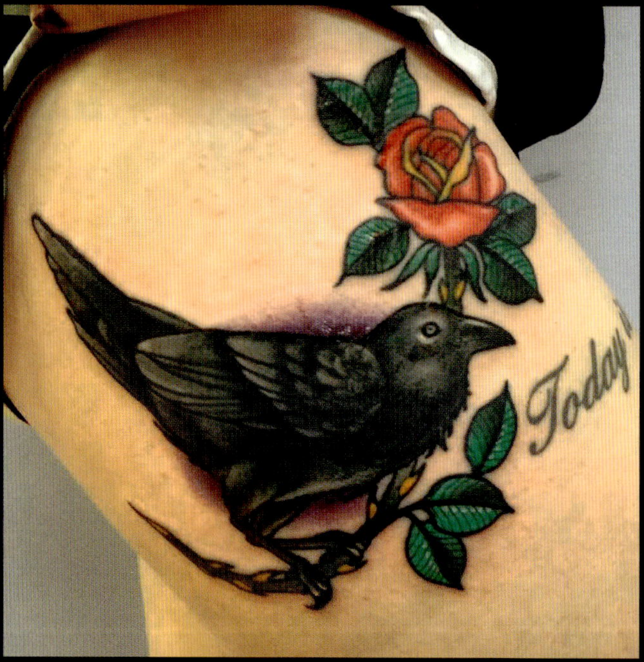
Today
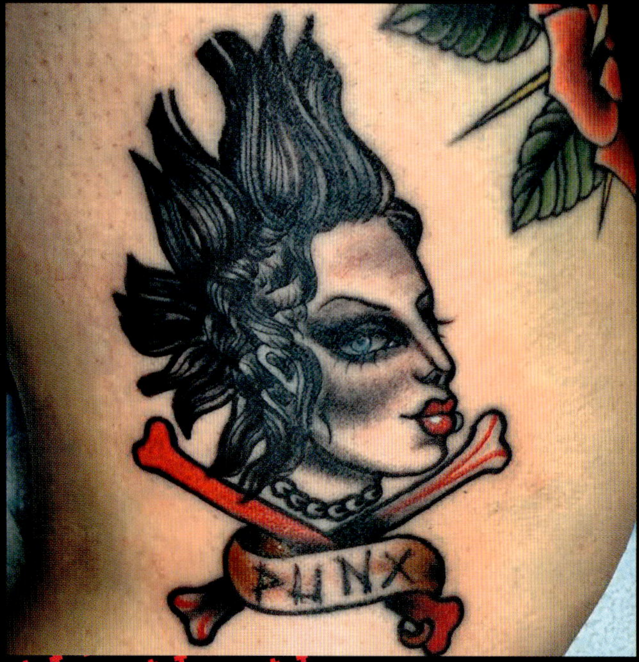
PUNX
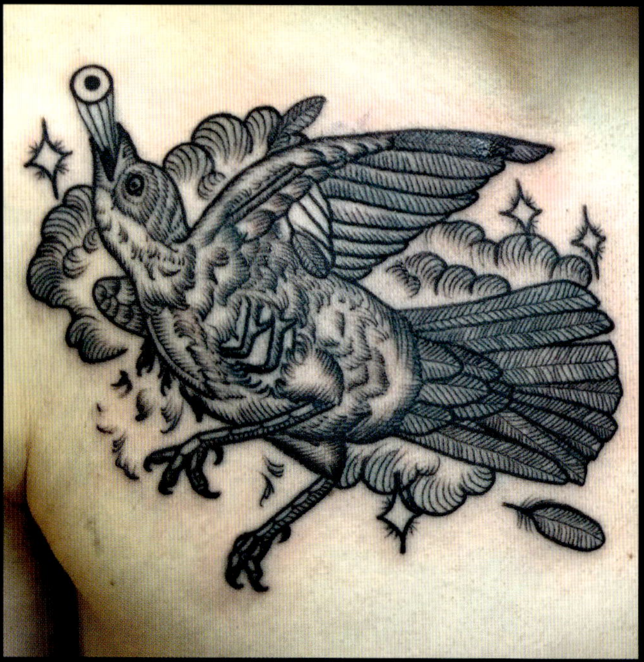

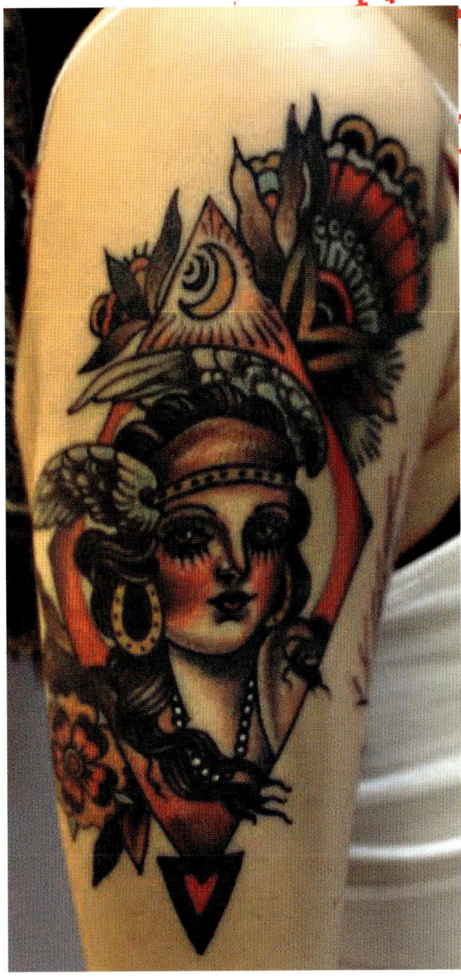

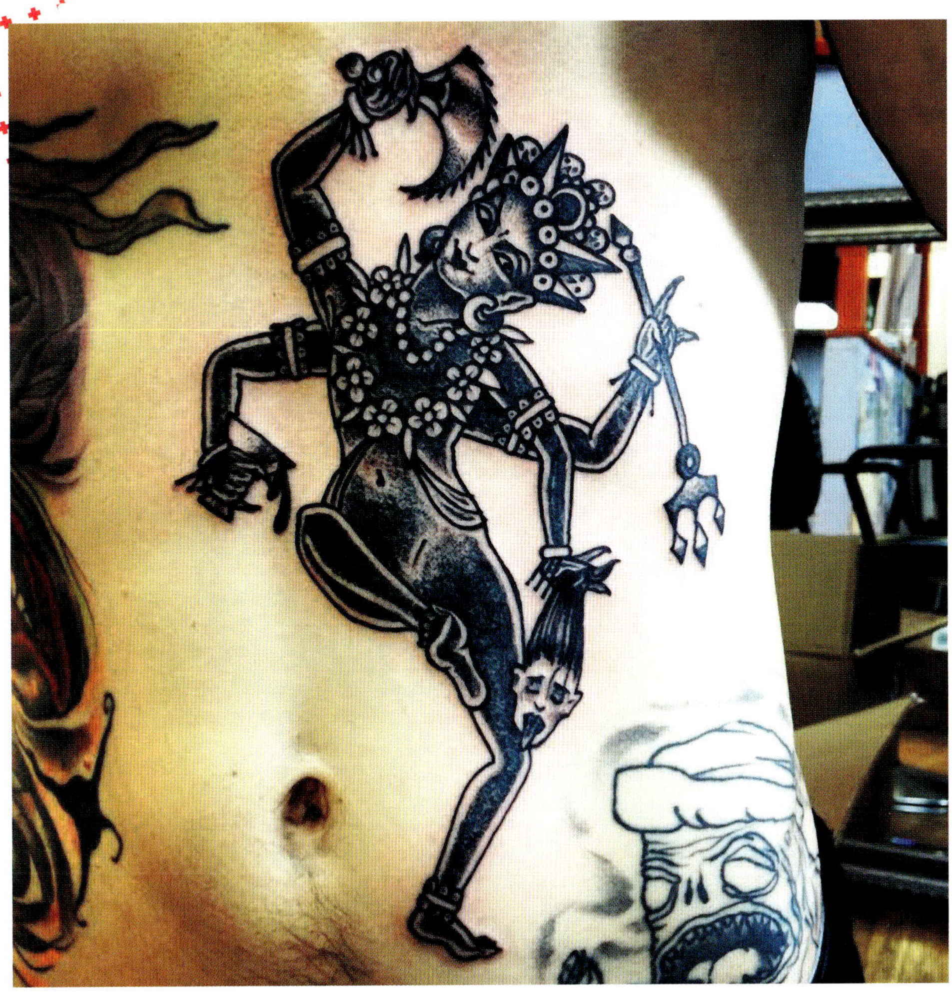

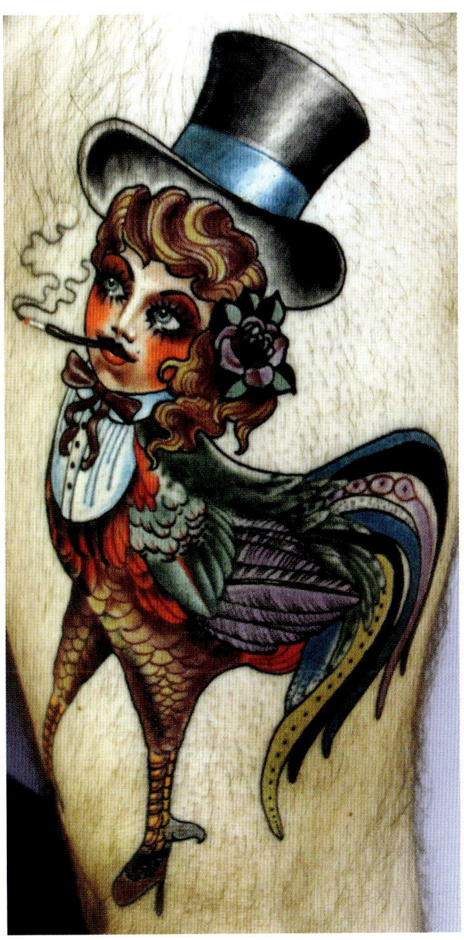

What's it like being a female artist in a primarily male workplace?

It's like any other job except way cooler, because you get to hang out with people who "get" and understand the passion of art and rebellion and embrace and live that life, the same as I do.

Do you feel that male customers treat you differently?

No. People only treat you differently if you command that type of attention and that is not what I'm after.

What did your family and friends think about you getting into the business?

They were very supportive and encouraging, and continue to be.

Tell me more about the shop you work at; what's it like working there?

At this moment in time I am without an actual "home base" shop, but I am traveling around the United States, having just traveled Europe making tattoos and art. Each shop is unique and filled with lovely human beings who are passionate about their tattooing. Today I'm writing to you from East Side Ink, in the Lower East Side of New York City. There is a fantastic group of individuals who work here and it's really in quite a gem of a location. NYC is always alive and full of energy...

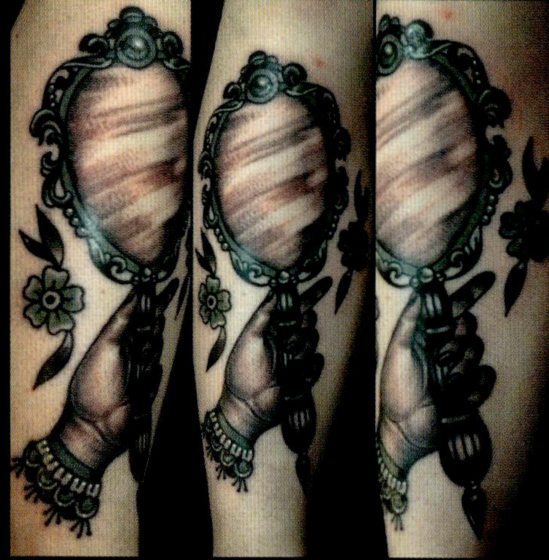

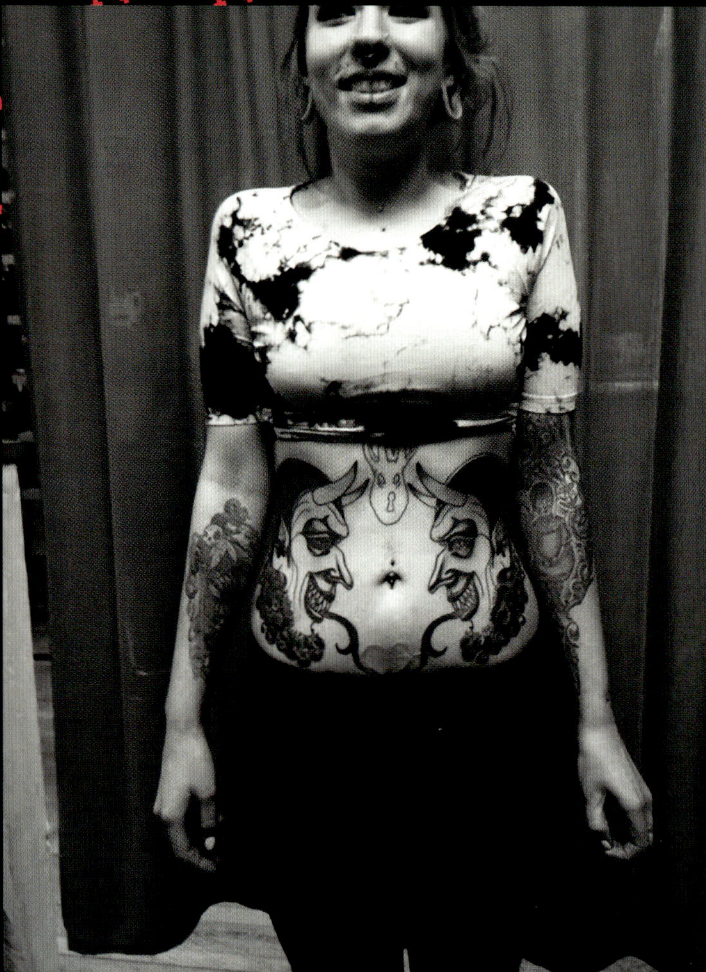

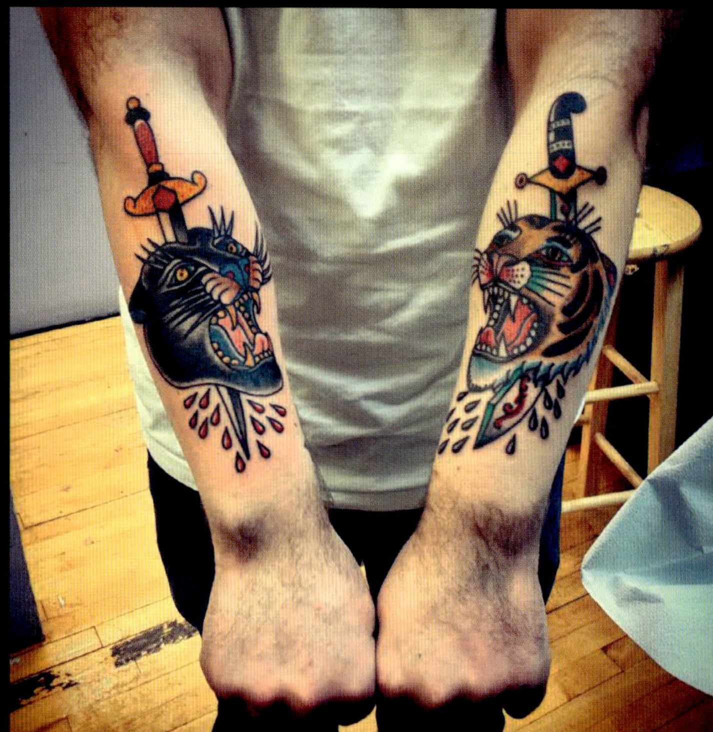

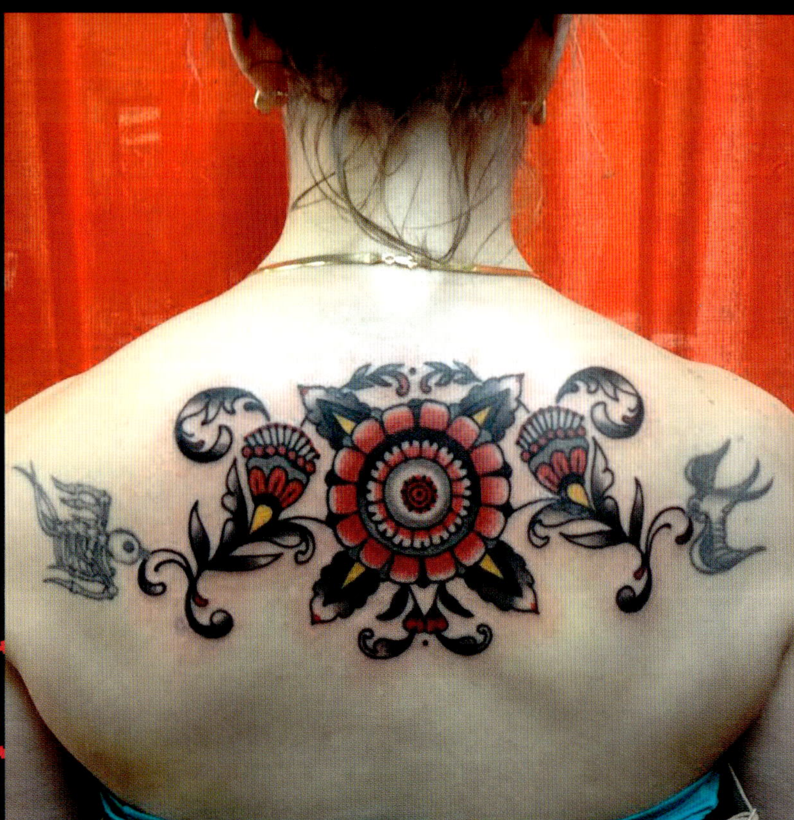

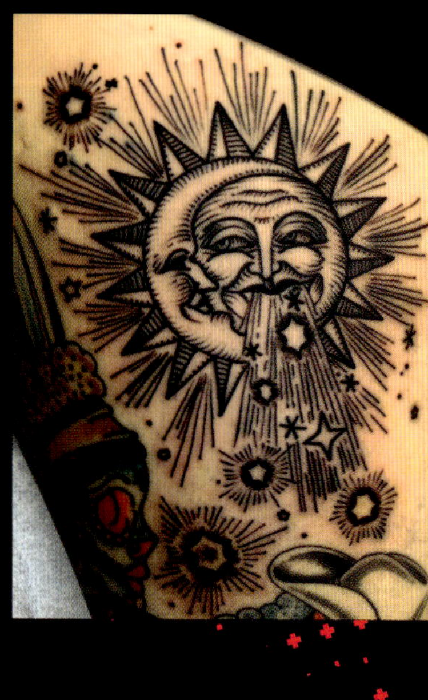

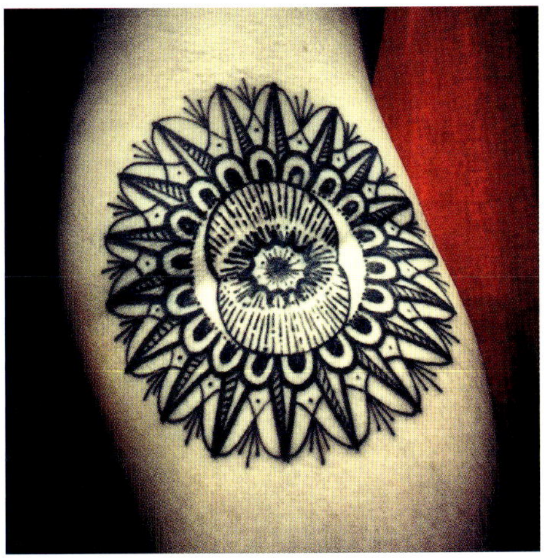

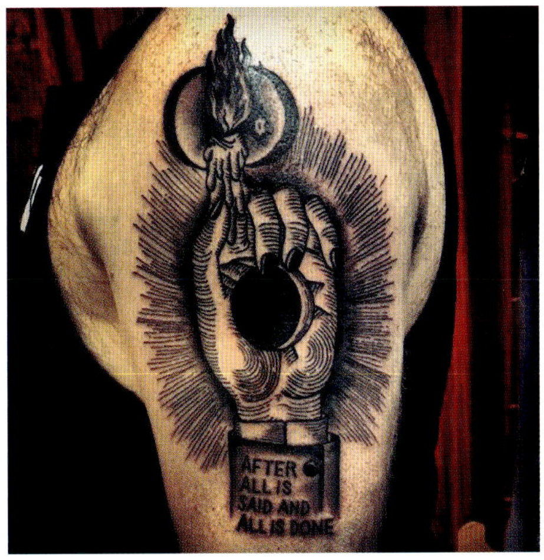

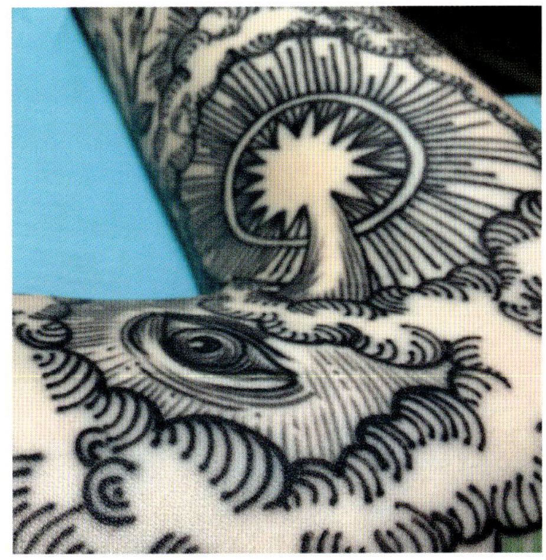

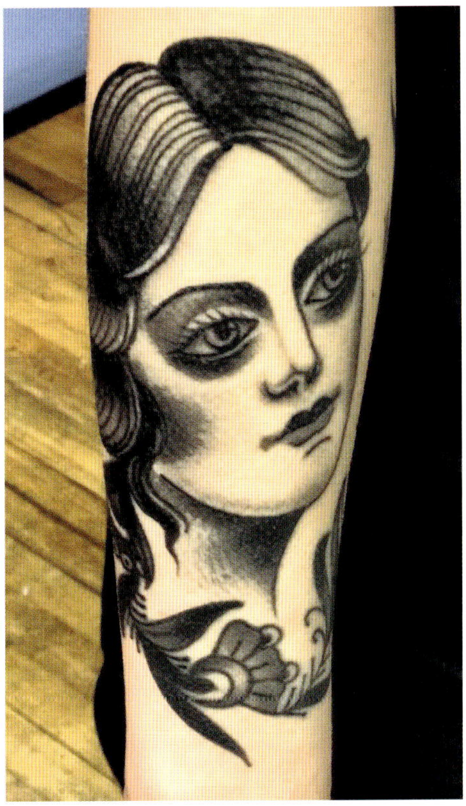

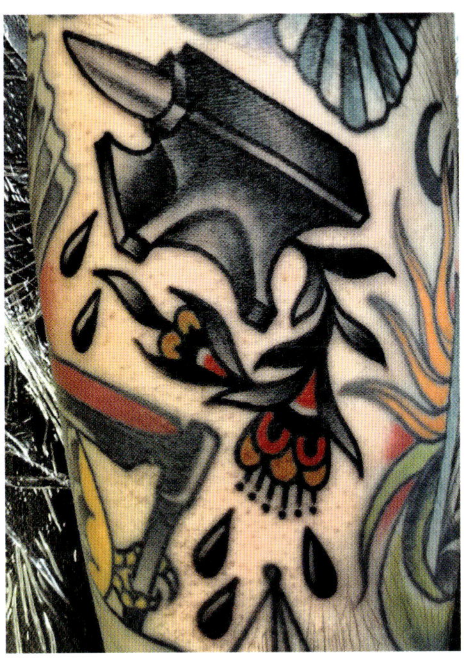

Describe how you go about creating a tattoo from concept to finished design. How do you try to put your own unique touch on your tattoos?

Typically I just hear or read what the person is looking to get and I draw it. Inevitably, whether I mean to or not, things come out looking like I did them, just because I did. Maybe that makes me sound like an asshole, but even when tracing a sailor Jerry rose, there are traces of my fingerprints in the design because it's coming from my physical body of language. When it comes to custom designs though, I can't really explain it. It's just something that happens, it's how I see things after studying the works of those before me and combining it with influence I am subjected to from a daily basis of existence.

What was the first tattoo you ever did? Can you tell me about it?

It was a tiny line on the leg of one of my mentor's friends. Totally was not expecting to tattoo that day, but he surprised me and just wanted me to get my toes into the pool and check out the temperature. The following week I outlined a fly on my mentor David's arm.

What is your favorite style of work to tattoo? What would your dream piece be to work on?

I really enjoy just about anything so long as the client isn't trying to micromanage me. Traditional folk art designs are always really a treat for me. A dream piece would probably be a sleeve of pork-chop tattoos of just weird imagery done in a traditionally influenced way. Lots of black and minimal color.

Describe how your role models and any other sources of inspiration have affected your tattoo style.

They always encourage me to want to do better, and keep pushing my own limits of understanding with art. They also help me to remember my place in tattooing, which is just being a channel for it, not trying to sit on an invisible throne that is meaningless.

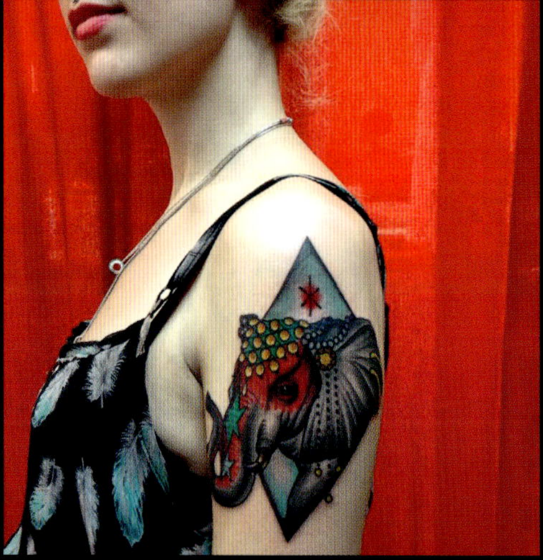
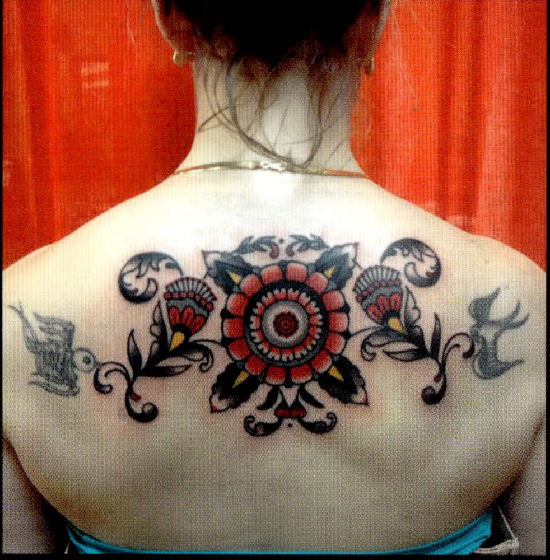
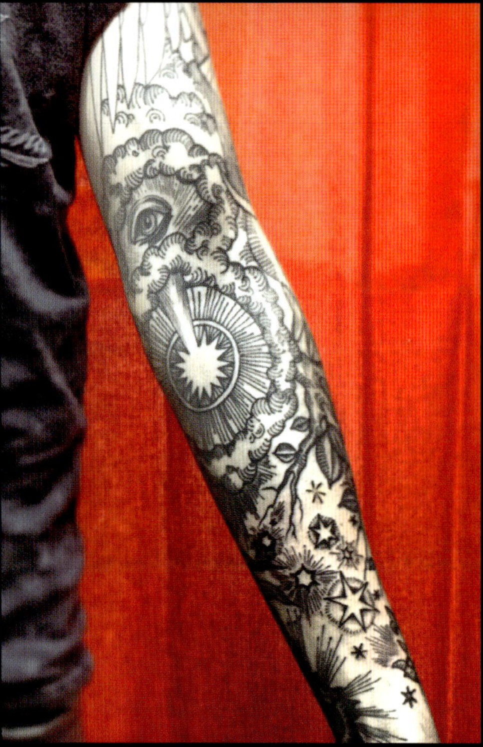
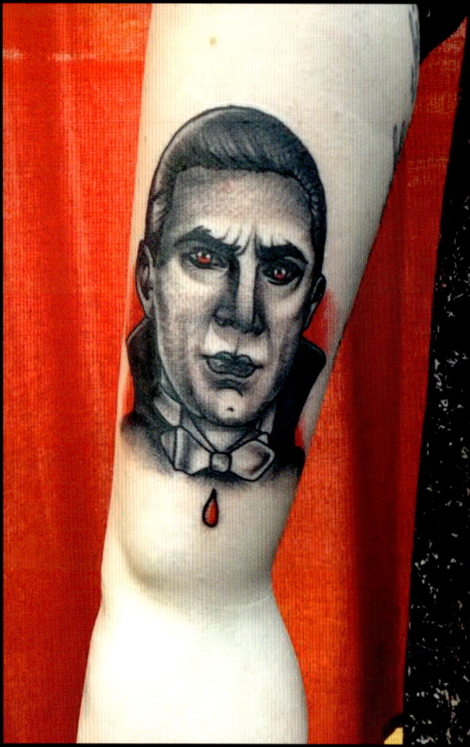
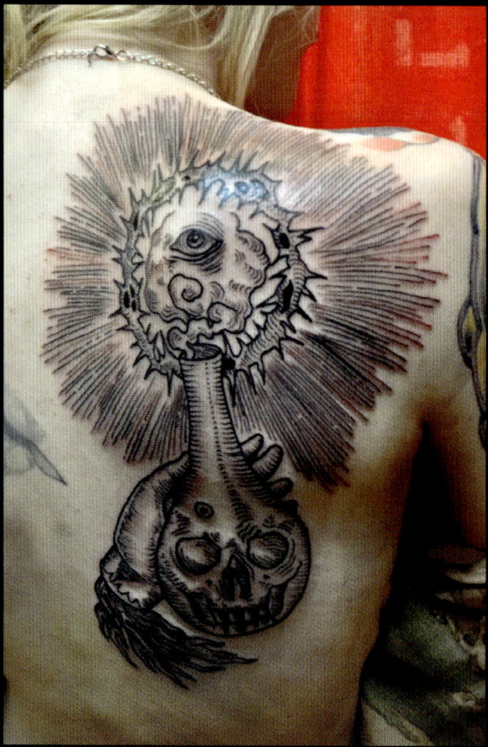
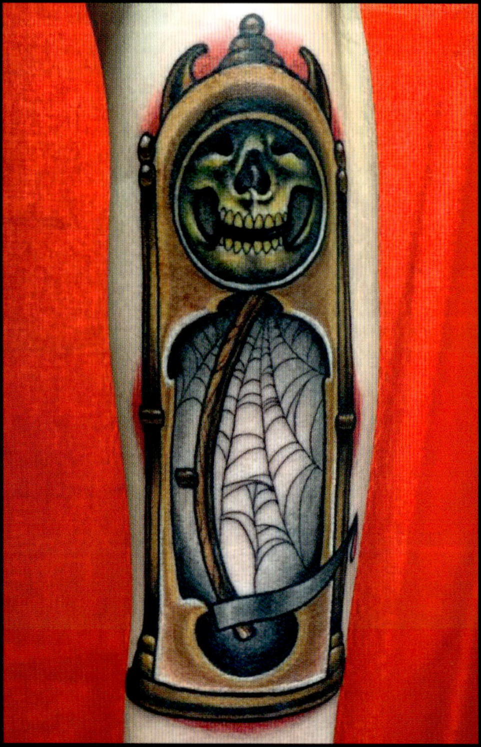
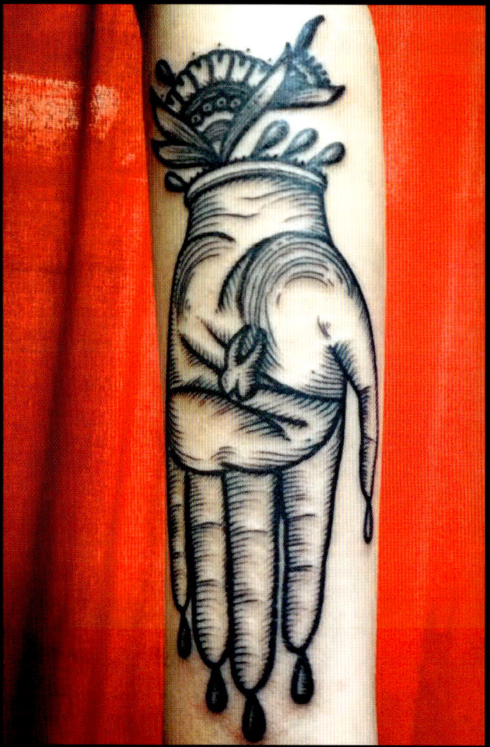

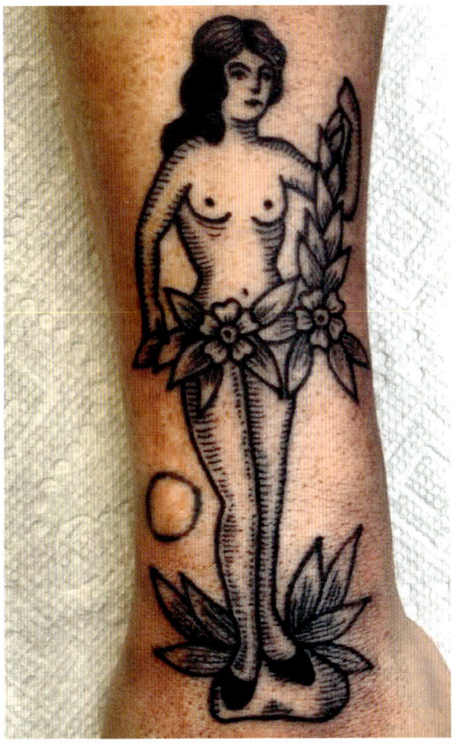
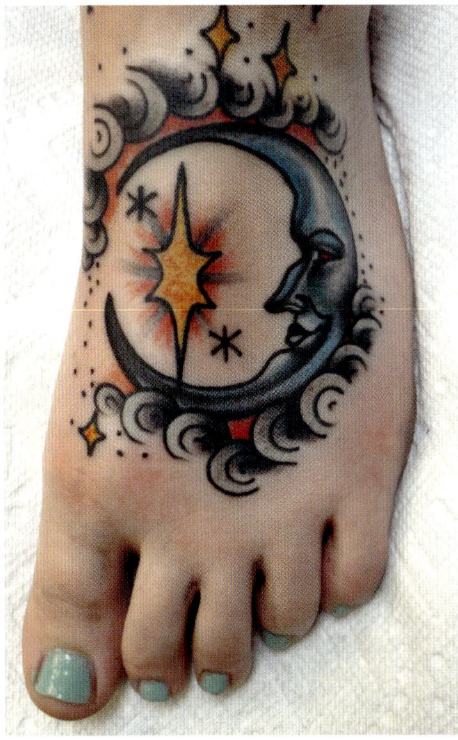
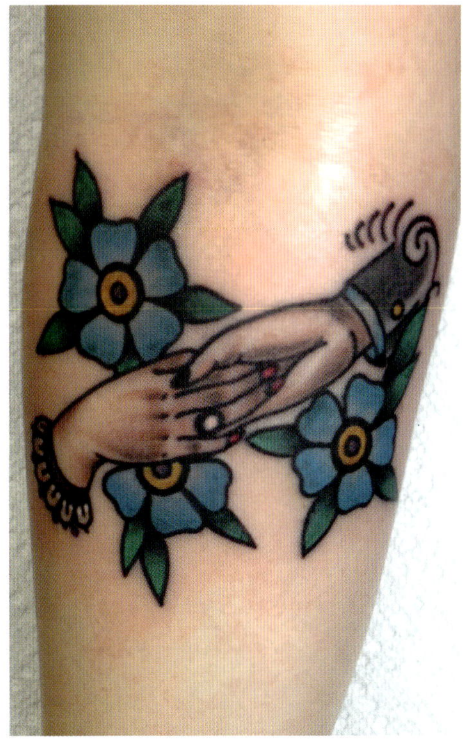
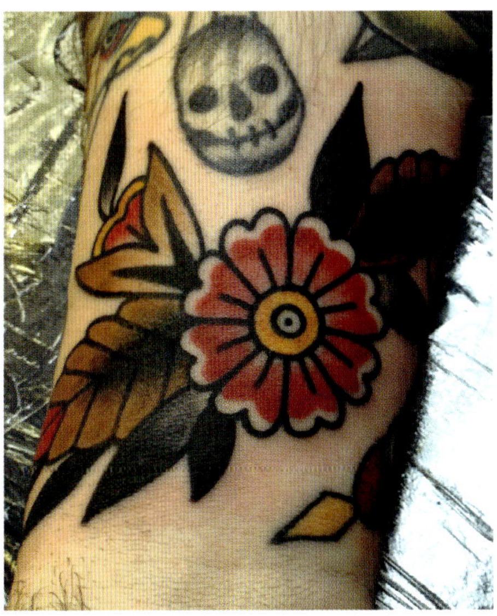
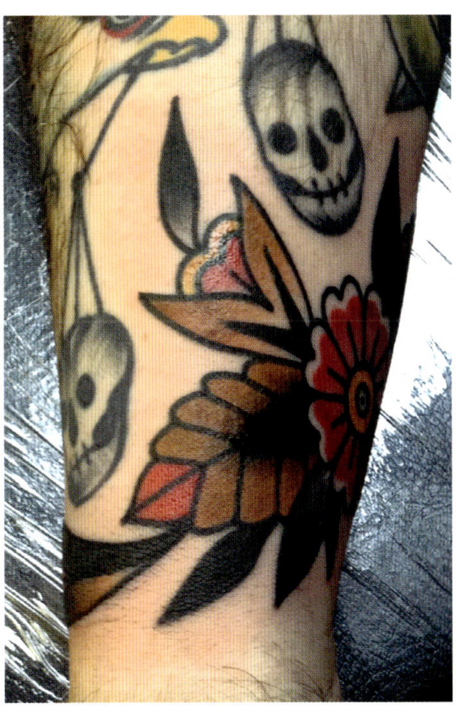

What's one of your favorite pieces on your own body, and who did it?

My fingers…done by Thomas Hooper.

What is your favorite thing about being a tattoo artist?

The freedoms that come with it. Traveling, being a weirdo and getting paid for it, connecting with other people to discuss and share ideas in art, good food.

You have built up such a loyal clientele. What is your waiting list like right now and what is the best way for a collector to make an appointment with you?

People can just check my Instagram (@eva_jean) or e-mail me (tattoosbyeva@gmail.com) because I'm traveling indefinitely and that's the best way to get hold of me, to find out where I am and will be.

How would you describe the current status of tattoos among the general public?

Extremely accessible and very popular.

TV shows, Internet, and especially social networks like Facebook and Twitter have come to have an extremely wide influence in recent years. What positive and negative impacts do you think it has for the future development of the tattoo industry?

People come and go, tattoos are forever.

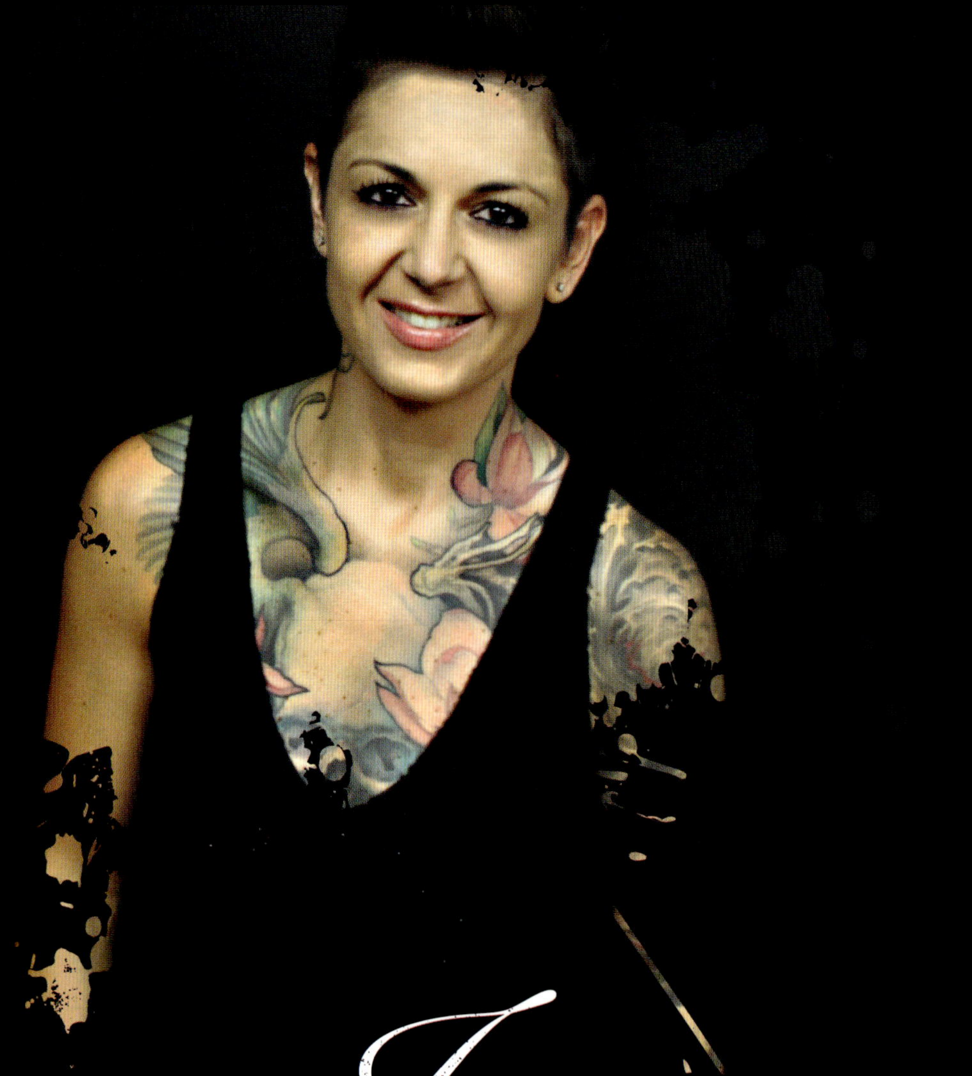

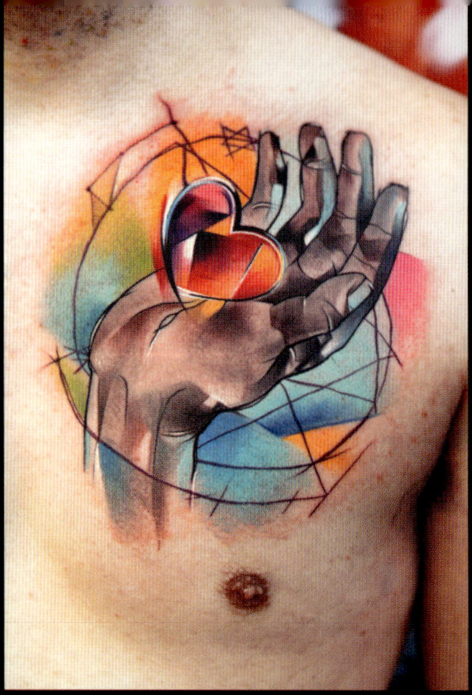

IVANA BELAKOVA was studying business and accounting in Slovakia. Just after she finished her studies her friend asked Ivana whether she would like to try to tattoo, since she wanted to open up her own shop. Ivana took this opportunity and started to practice on her family and friends right away. She has never had any other job besides this one.

Ivana TATTOO ART

"I have very nice customers who respect my work and me as an artist"

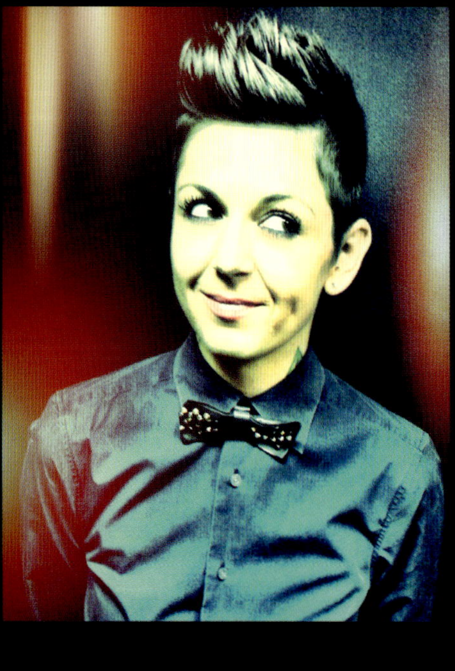

www.ivanatattooart.com
www.facebook.com/pages/Ivana-Tattoo-Art/208943449123095
instagram.com/ivanatattooart
ivanatattooart.tumblr.com

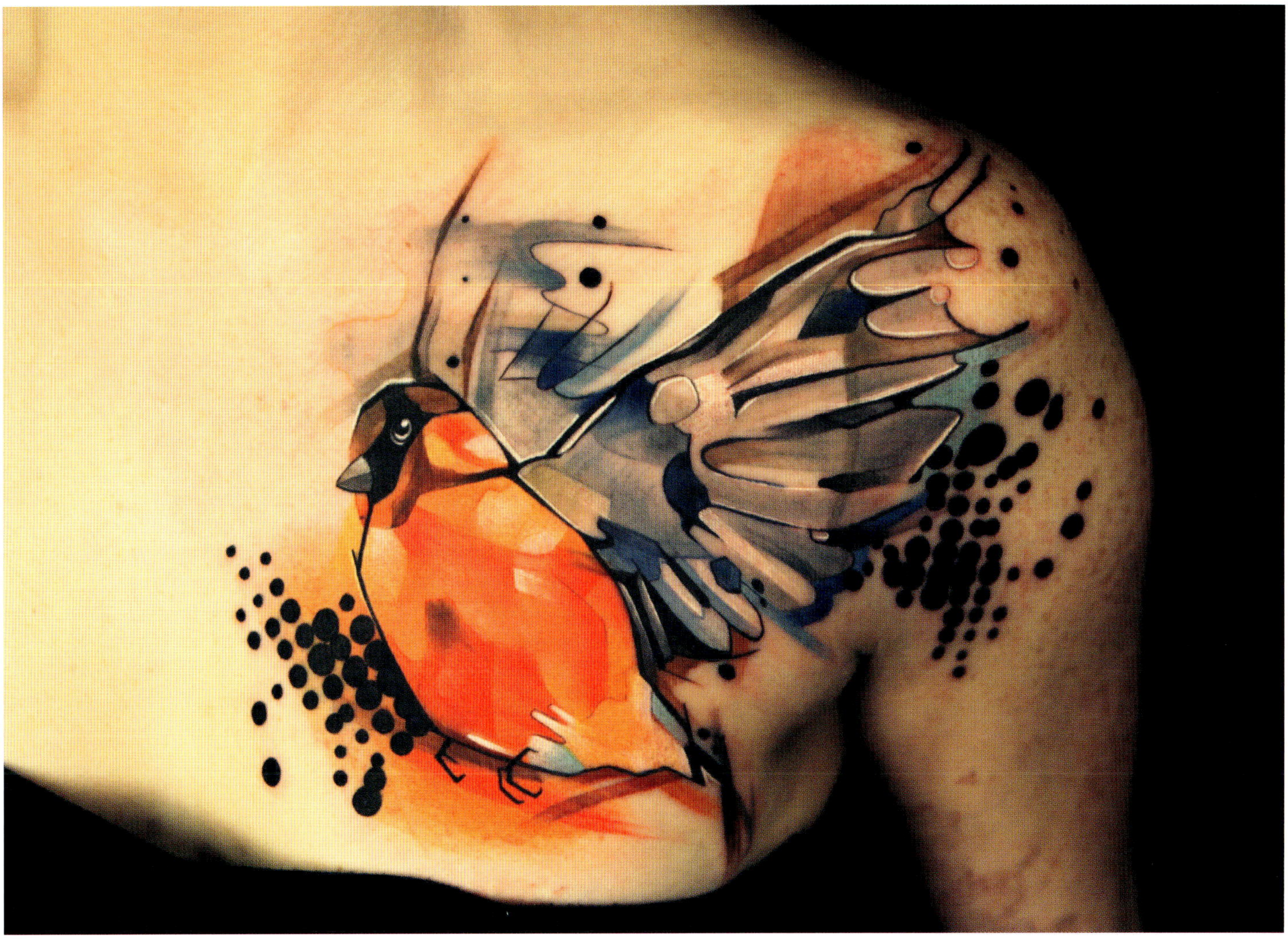

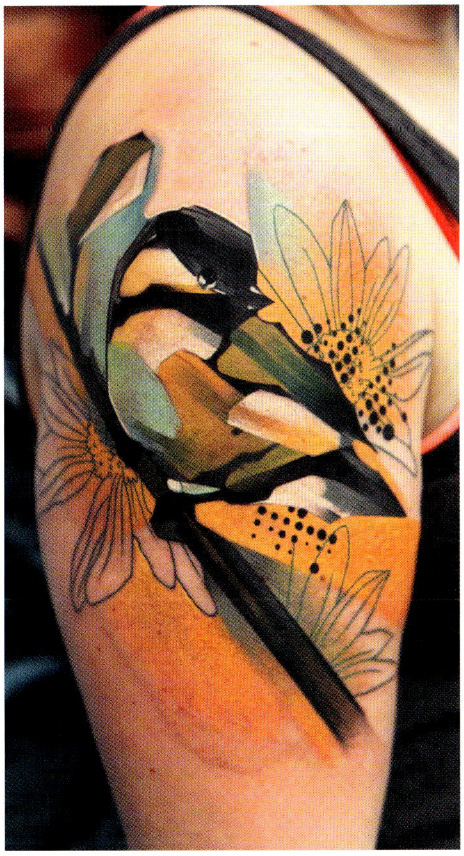

What made you want to become a tattoo artist and how long have you been tattooing?

Tattooing really came to me. I had no idea what I wanted to do for a job. After the first tattoo I did I got hooked up and I knew tattooing was something I wanted to do for my living. I've been tattooing for around thirteen years now.

Where did you learn to tattoo? Did you have a formal apprenticeship? If so, can you tell me about this time in your life and how it prepared you for all that you do now?

I am self taught and I never had any formal apprenticeship. I was very committed and dedicated from the beginning. All my spare time I spent tattooing or drawing, since I wanted to learn as much as I could. Practice makes perfect, and in my case it was really lots of hard work to get myself where I wanted to be! Yet, I am constantly learning and improvising.

My travels and working with all different artists push me forward too! Everyone I have worked with has taught me something. It wasn't necessarily tattooing technique itself; it may have been approach, attitude, commitment.

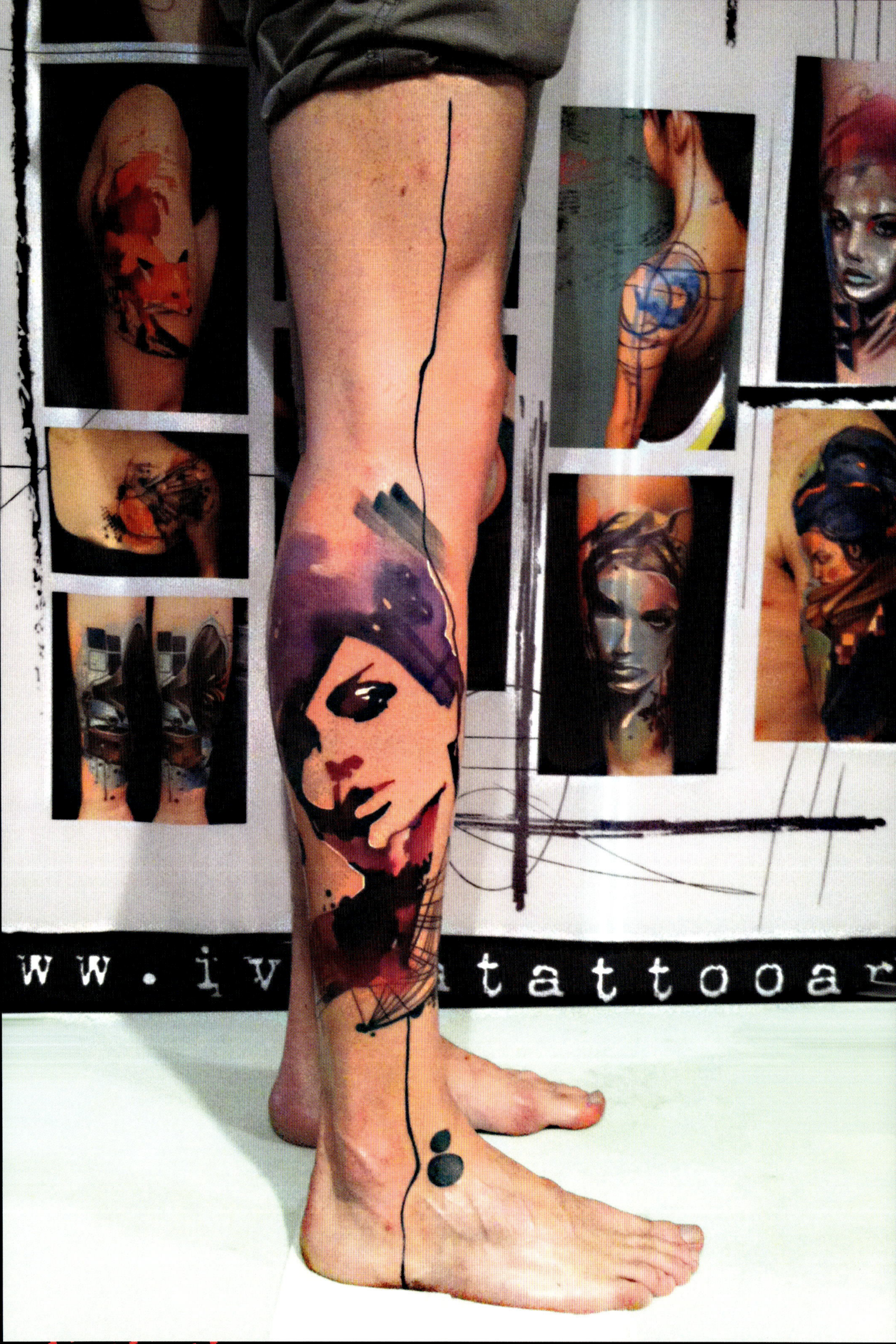

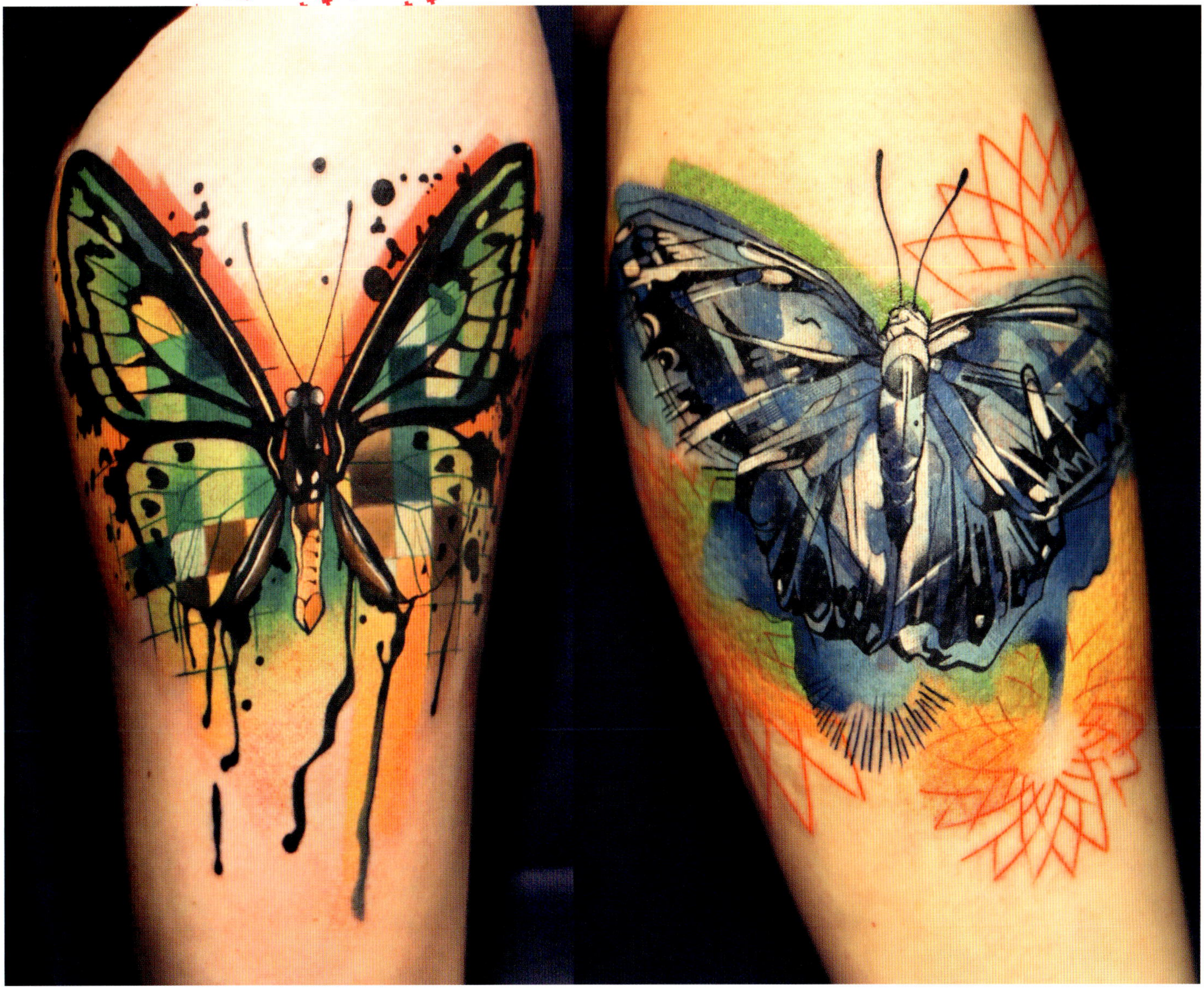

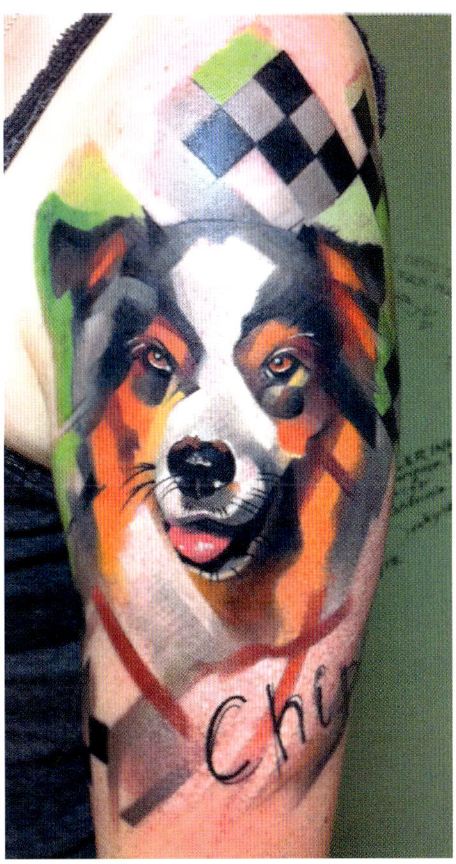

What's it like being a female artist in a primarily male workplace?

I don't see differences, to be honest. I do my thing; I do what I love the most.

Do you feel that male customers treat you differently?

No, I don't. I have very nice customers who respect my work and me as an artist.

What did your family and friends think about you getting into the business?

My friends and family fully supported me, although my parents thought I was nuts.

Tell me about your shop, please!

The shop I'm currently working at is the oldest tattoo shop in the US, in Long Beach, California. Part of it is kept as a museum. It's spacious, beautiful, with a great vibe. It used to be very famous many years ago; sailors came to get their tattoos done in here.

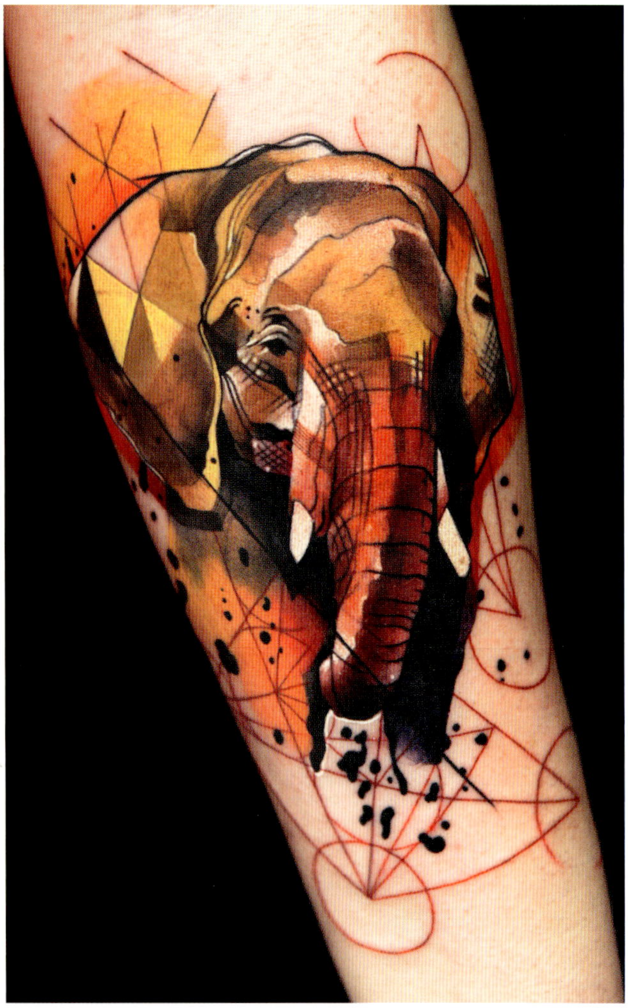

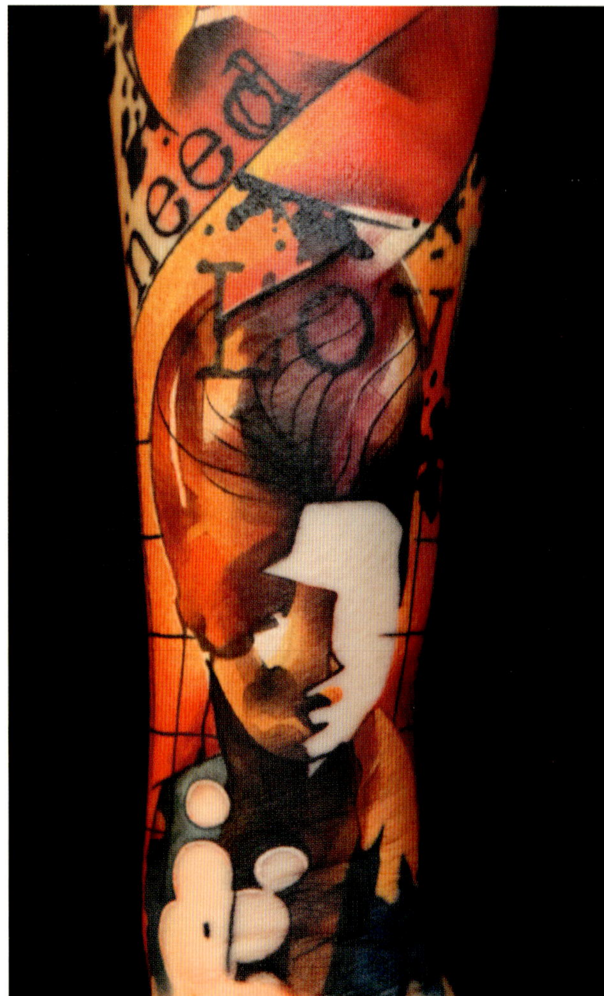
need

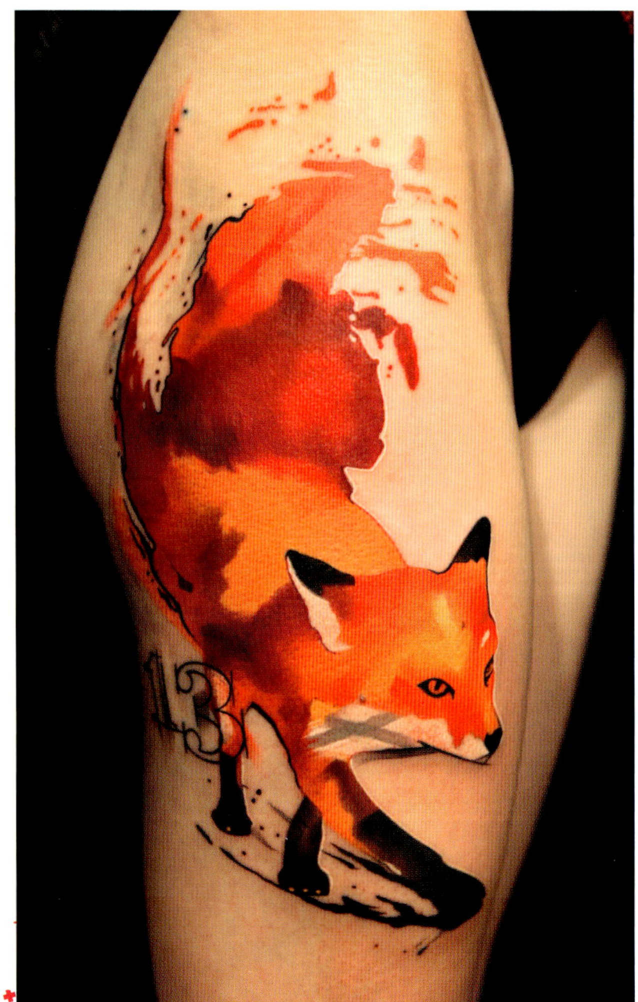
13

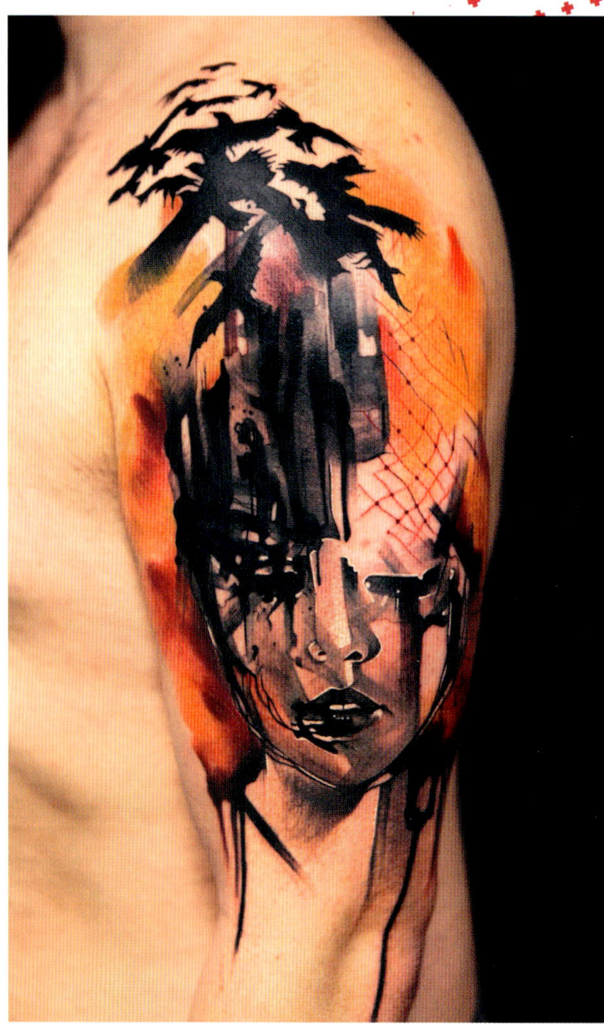

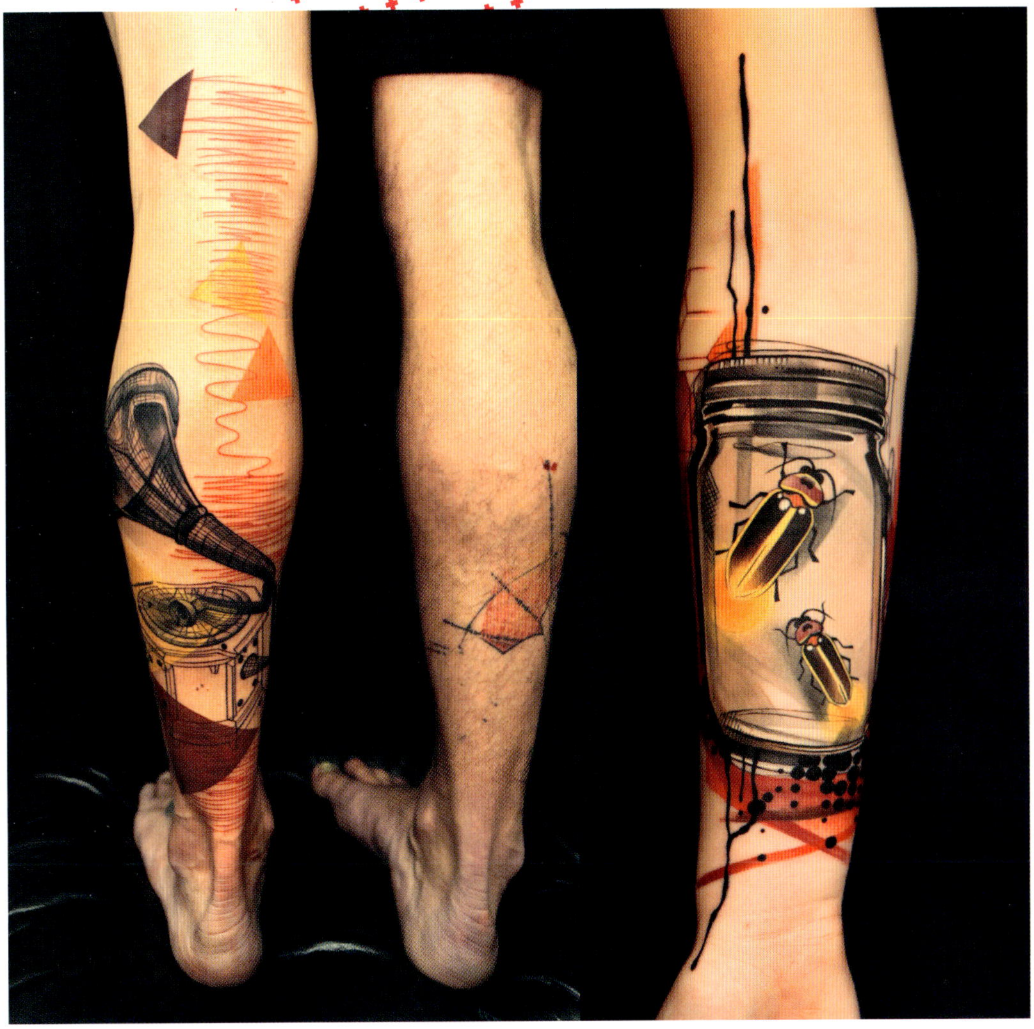

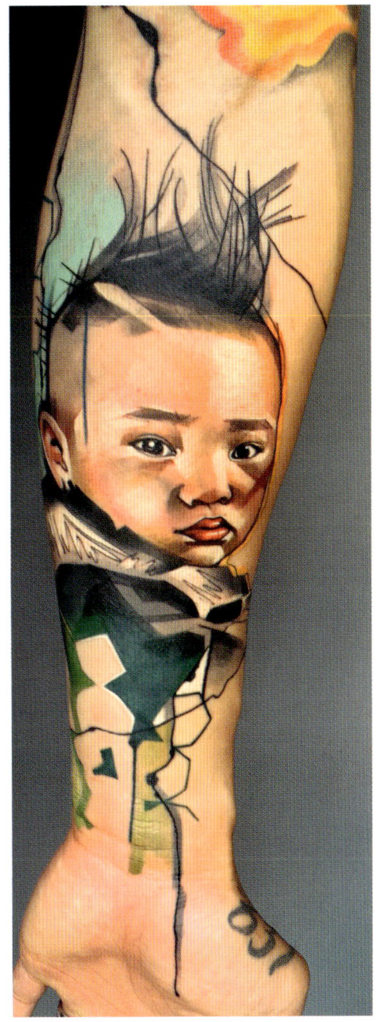

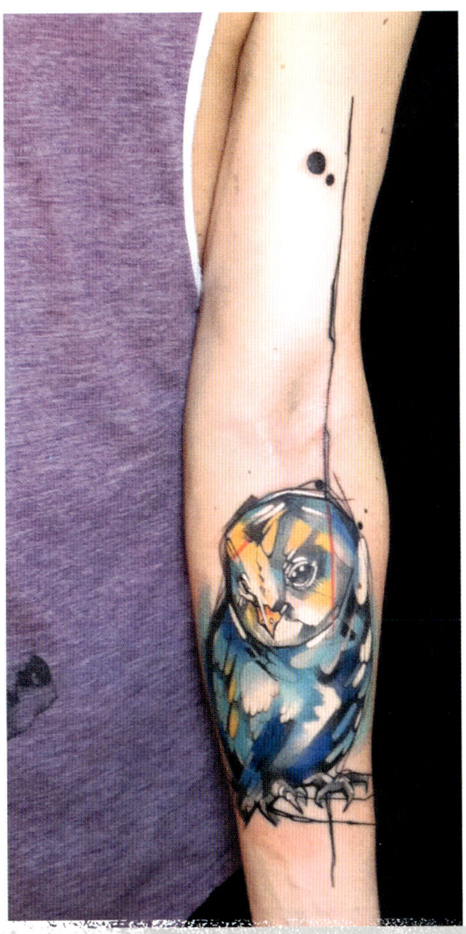

We have an array of artists with many different stylistic influences. So far this has been the best experience working at a shop.

Describe how you go about creating a tattoo from concept to finished design. How do you try to put your own unique touch on your tattoos?

First I need to know what my customers want. If I like the idea, I will do my search and look for some references. And that's really all I need.

I work from references. Final touches, compositions, etcetera. I make up in my head while I am tattooing. Every person has a different vibe for me and I get a better feel once I see my client. I am prepared for the day of an appointment only to a certain extent. I like to improvise and make it more custom for each of my customers.

What was the first tattoo you ever did? Can you tell me about it?

It was a little ornamental thing on the leg. It took me two hours to do that time, because I am very precise. Now it's about a fifteen-minute job for me.

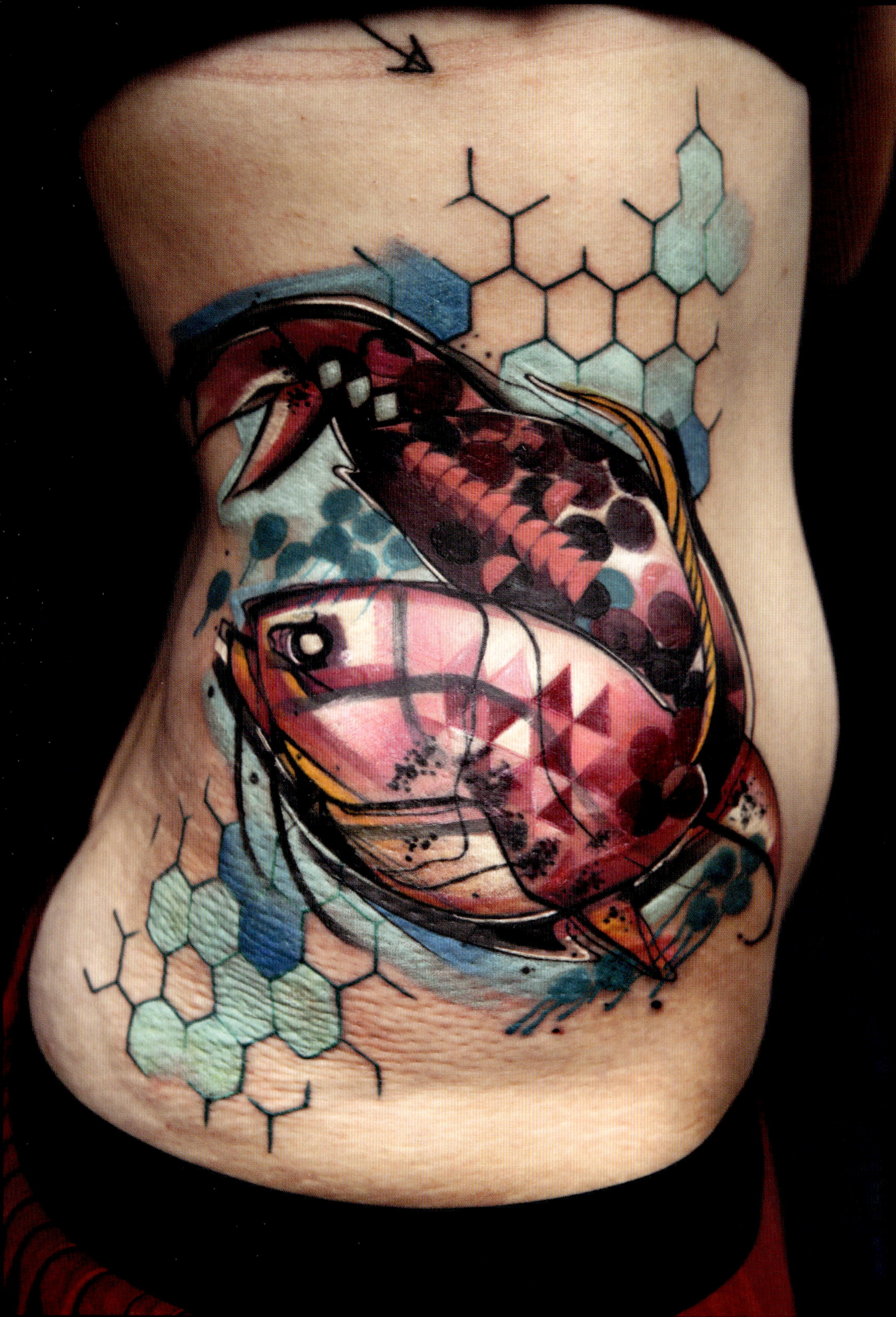

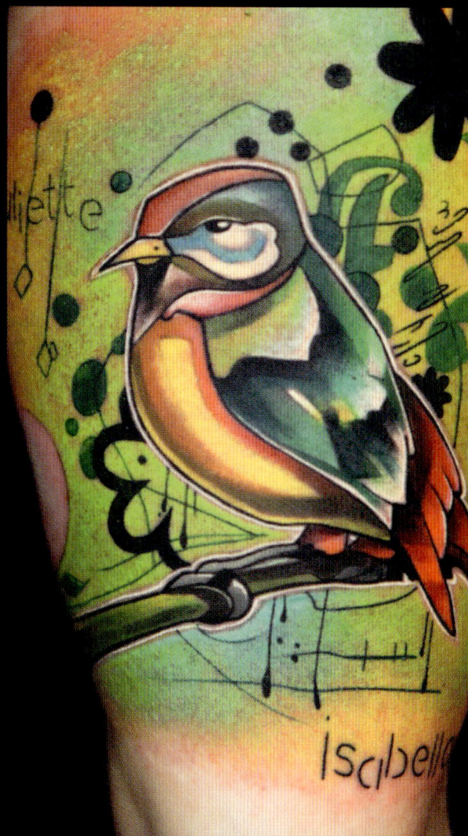

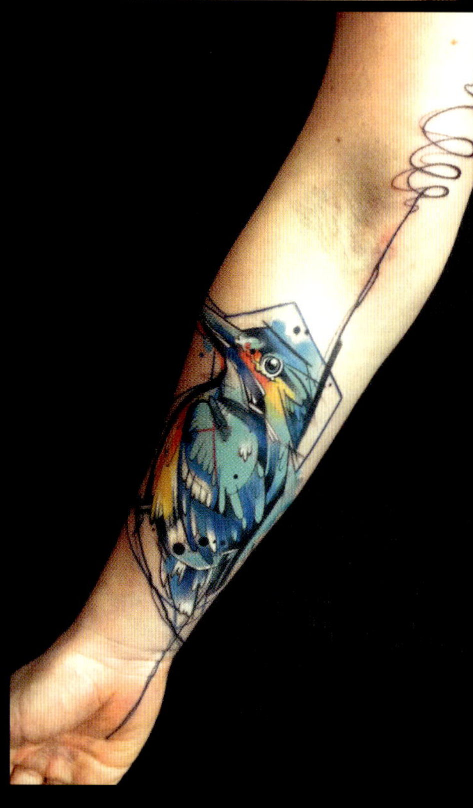

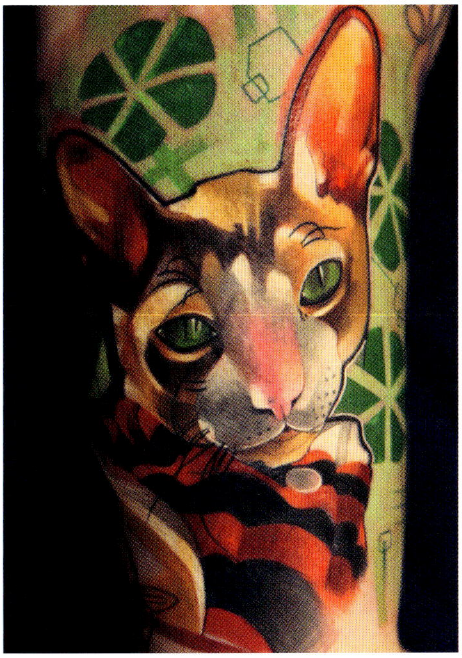

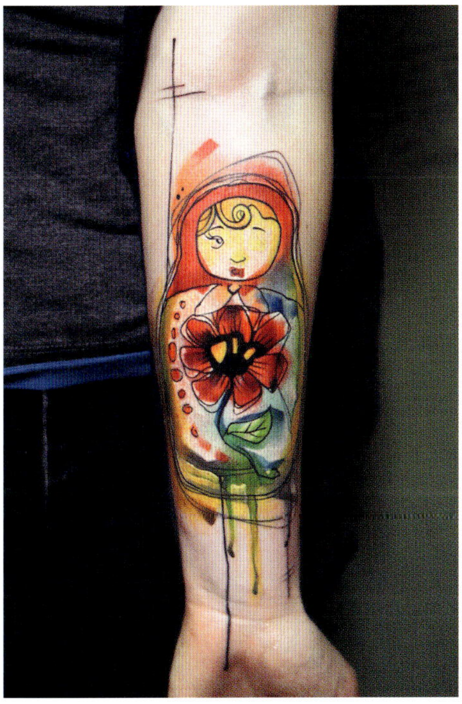

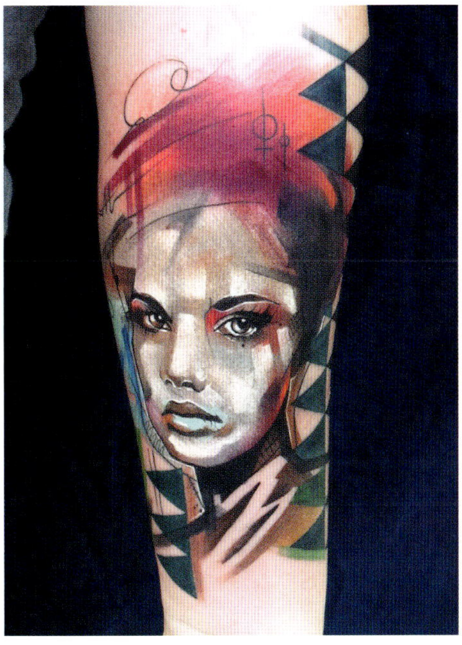

How would you describe your style? And which tattoo style do you like best?

I call my style funky color because I can't think of an exact description or name. I mix things and styles together, I guess. I play with graffiti, illustrations, paintings, drawings, realism, geometry, and somehow a mix of all these things looks good together. I really cannot pick one style I like the best, but naturally I lean toward modern funky-looking designs. Lots of freehand, abstract things. For me the overall feel of the tattoo is very important, and how it sits on the body. The actual idea is the most important. That's what I always appreciate the most!

Describe how your role models and any other sources of inspiration have affected your tattoo style.

My style is constantly evolving and changing, and I think that is a natural process. My style at the moment is not definite and never will be. My inspirations come from my surroundings; my travels, fashion, life crises, nature, and people. Everything that inspires me is a constant change that I don't ever set limits on.

Do you have a funny tattoo story?

I think that for every person I tattoo there's a funny story. I love joking with every client in the beginning and telling them I'm going to tattoo something completely different than what they came in for. The reactions are quite hilarious because some of them don't really understand my sense of humor, but it always ends in a good laugh.

What's the hardest part about being a tattoo artist?

For me the hardest part is understanding and dealing with my clients. As a tattoo artist, most the time you never meet or see your potential clients 'til the day of their appointment, so it's really hard to get a feel for who they are and what they want. Of course I have my own style, and what they want is what I do, but you want to make each piece unique to each client even though you only have a couple hours to do so.

Also, as a tattoo artist, your job never ends. I can't just come home from work and do nothing. I still have to prepare my stuff for the next day, deal with my e-mails, and with organizing things. Sometimes I feel pressured or stressed out because I want to constantly give my best and I do not always feel a hundred percent.

What's the most rewarding part about being a tattoo artist?

Freedom and what comes with it. Travels. It gives me satisfaction when I do some nice tattoo for my client. When I see them happy and proud of their piece.

I meet new interesting people constantly, and sometimes we become great friends.

Tattooing makes me happy; for me it's an outlet. It heals my soul when I feel down. I love pushing myself outside the box and

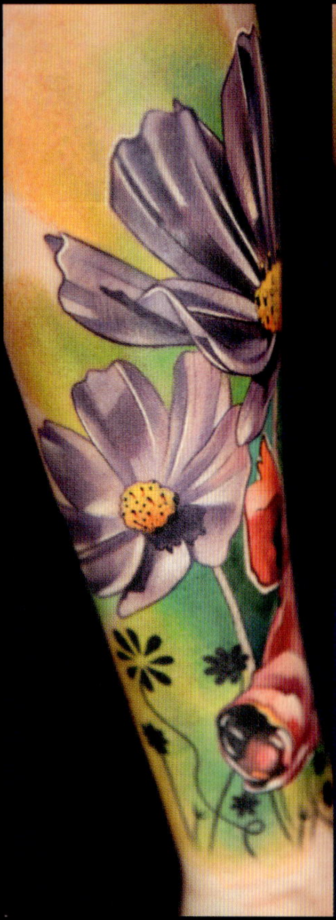
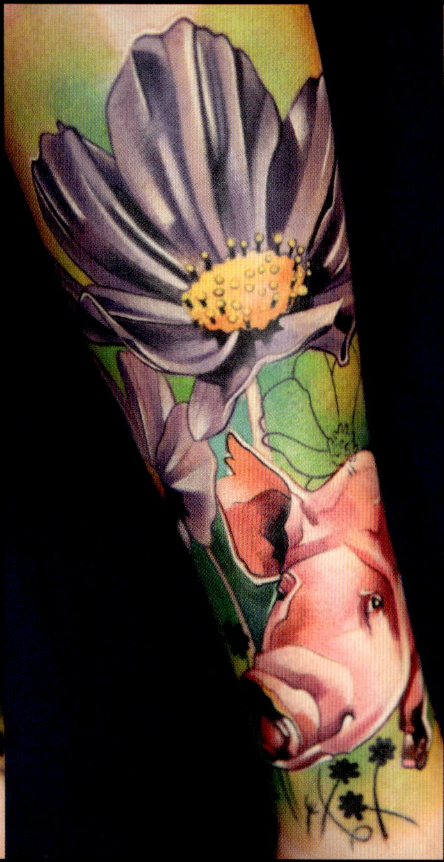
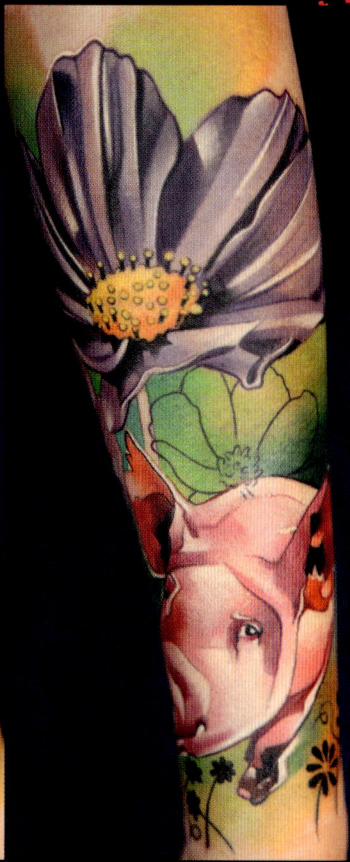
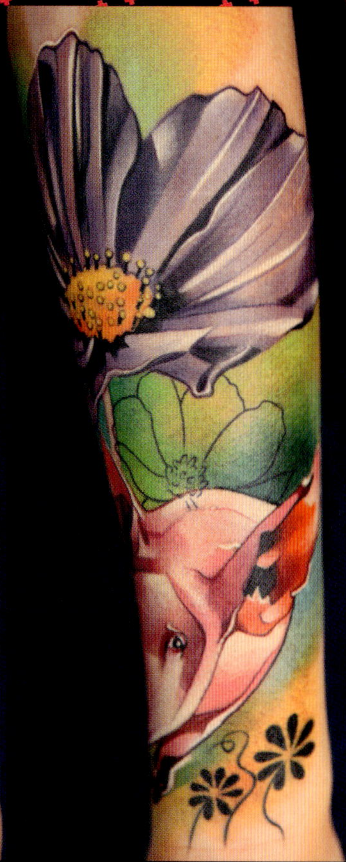
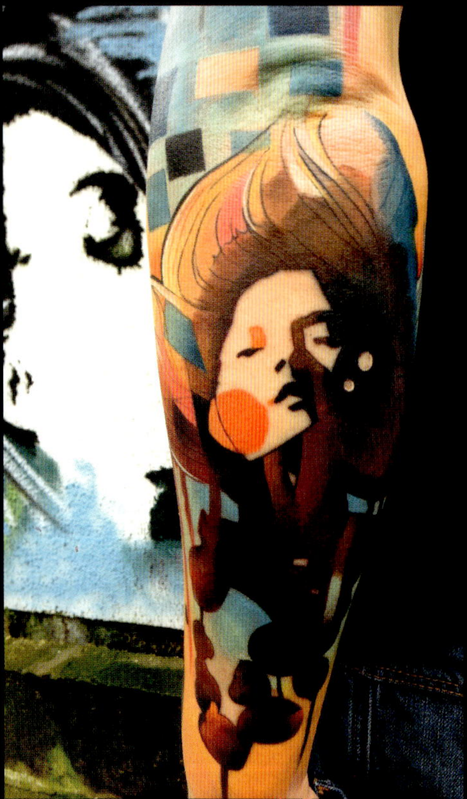
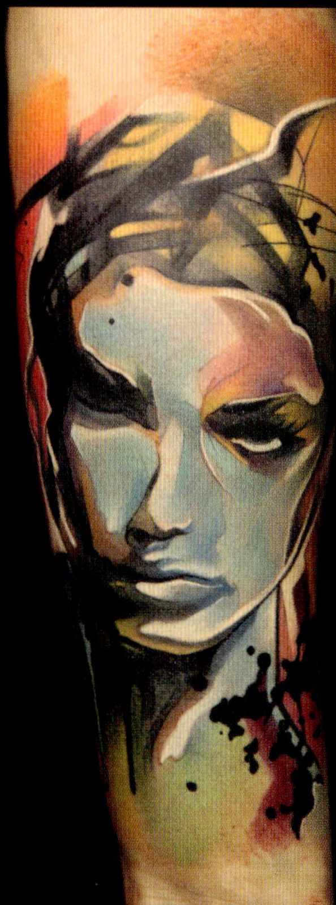
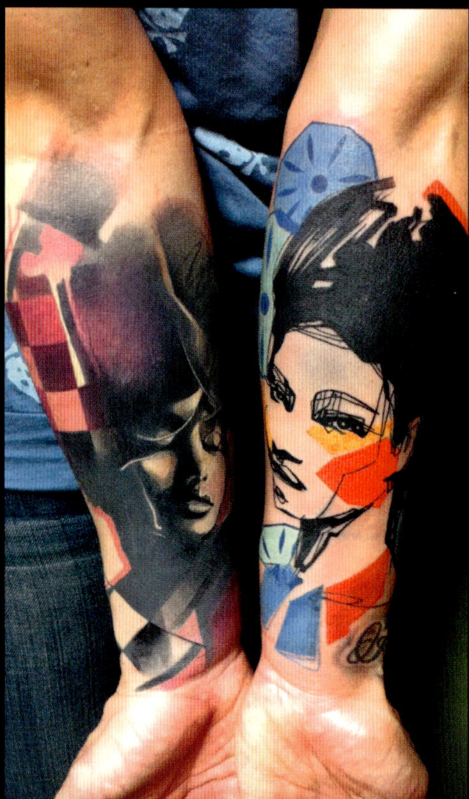

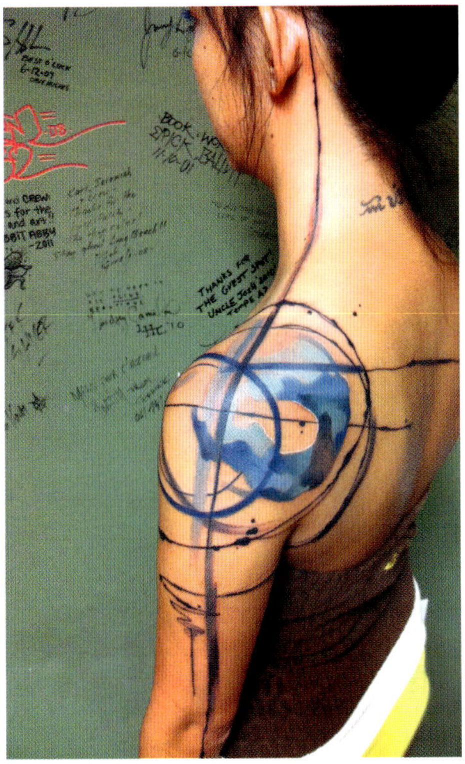

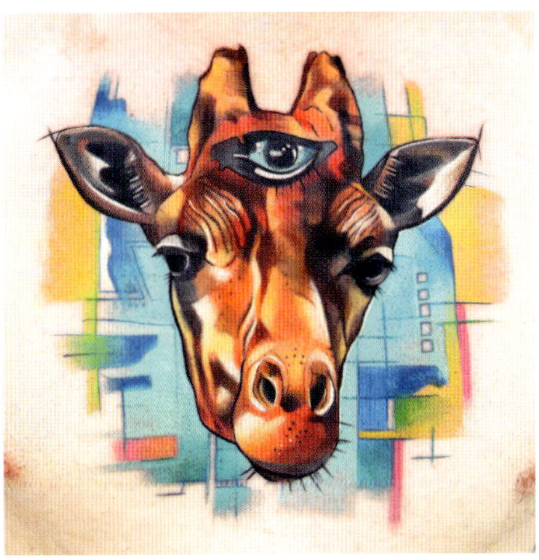

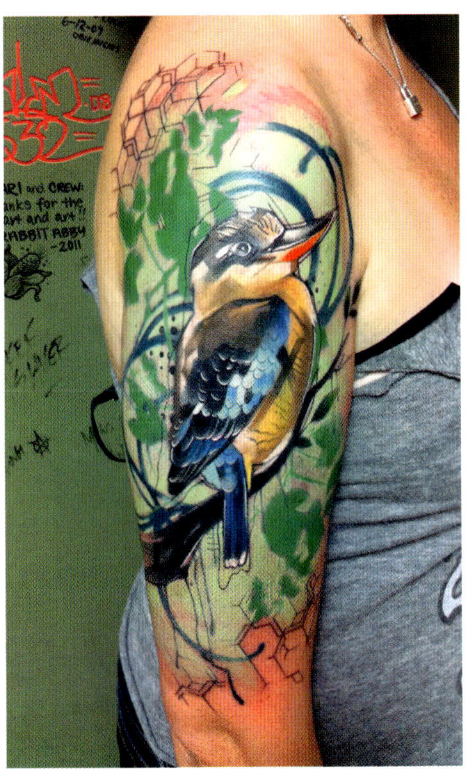

constantly challenging myself. When you do that you see incredible progress in your art, and that's why I tattoo.

What do you think a client should expect from you as a tattoo artist, and what do you, on the other hand, expect from a client to make a successful tattoo and a good collaboration?

Professionalism when it comes to being on time, being ready with the design, and taking care of their and my safety (hygiene). I expect my client to give me a creative freedom in what I do and also be committed to finish their existing piece. I expect them to come on time too, and to be open-minded as much as they can.

What criteria do you think that a tattoo convention should have to be really successful, both for you as a tattoo artist, but also for the visitors? Can you give some examples of conventions that meet these criteria well?

They should have a good program, a good choice of artists, entertainment, an art gallery, vendors, food and drinks, a high attendance. Most importantly, diversity; people come to see a collaboration of multiple artists around the world with different backgrounds.

For an artist, it's always helpful to have basic materials like paper towels, gloves, etcetera, so we don't have to carry them. I like the International London Tattoo Convention and Le Mondial Paris the best so far. There're also some other smaller shows I really enjoy, but those two are my favorites. The good thing about small shows is that it's very chill atmosphere and I get time to look around and talk to other artists more.

How would you describe the current status of tattoos among the general public?

As where I'm from (Slovakia), the younger generation of people are more open-minded; they are into bigger and more artistic pieces. People are less judgmental and more courageous. Older generations of people still don't understand it properly and they don't like tattoos. From what I've heard from my travels and clients, I think things are quite similar in a majority of other countries. People are getting more accepting as years go on, and hopefully generations to come will change the negativity associated with tattoos.

TV shows, Internet, and especially social networks like Facebook and Twitter have come to have an extremely wide influence in recent years. What positive and negative impacts do you think it has for the future development of the tattoo industry?

Thanks to social media we can have clients worldwide. We can travel anywhere and be booked out. We can get sponsors. People can see more of our work, and interact with us more. Social media is giving them more choice, as they see all this great artwork and they can find suitable artists for themselves more easily.

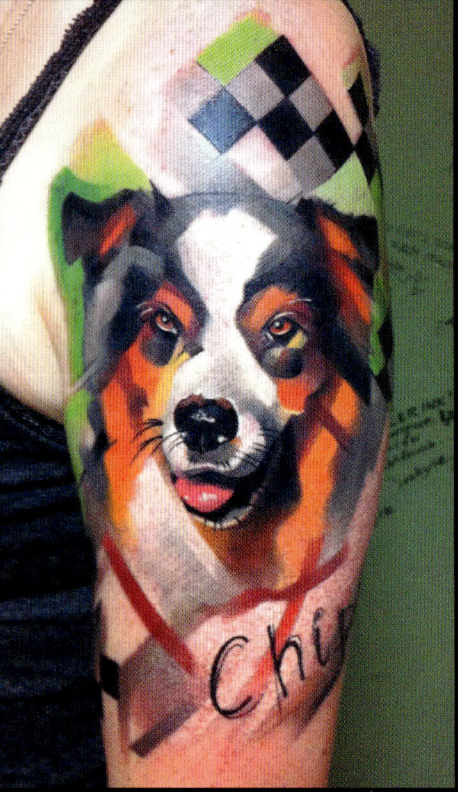
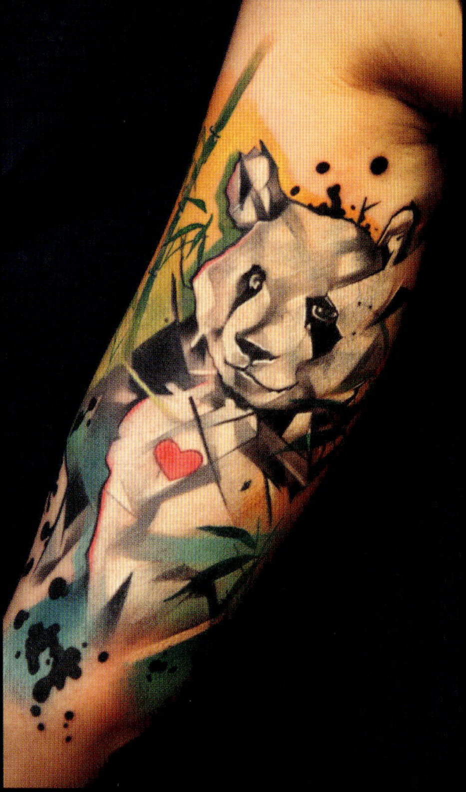
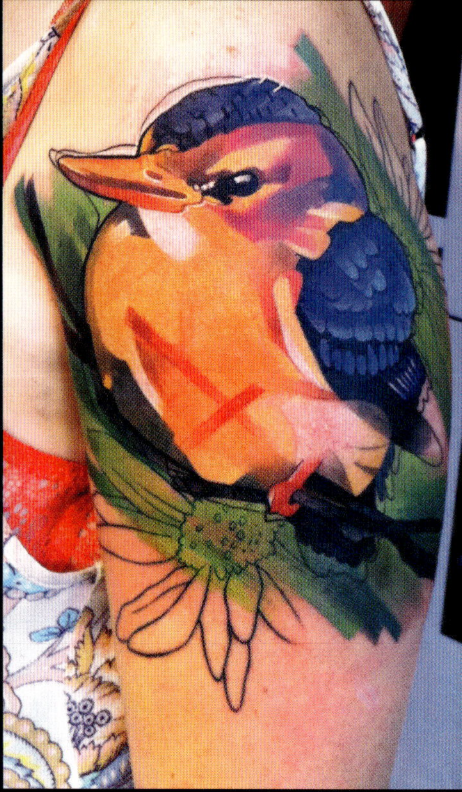
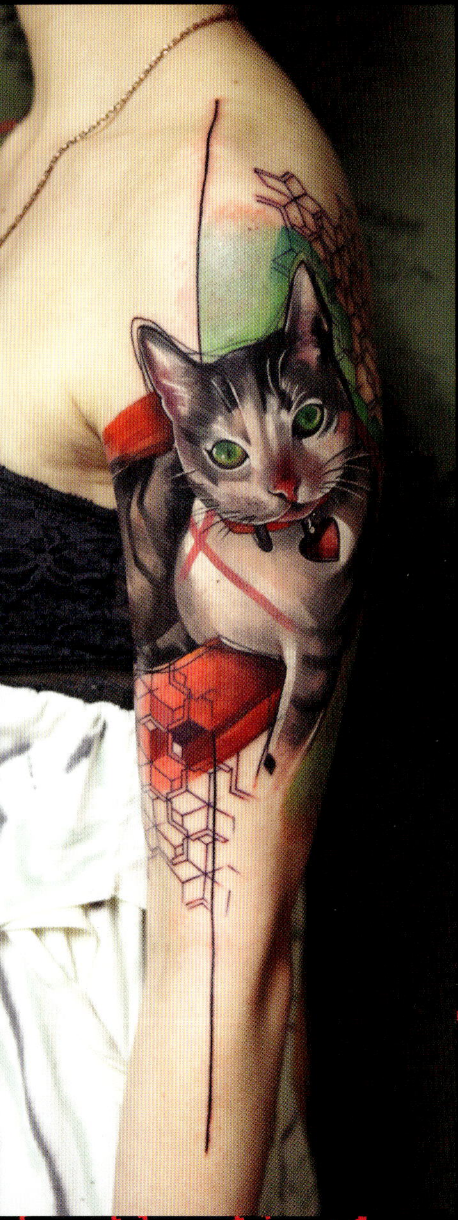
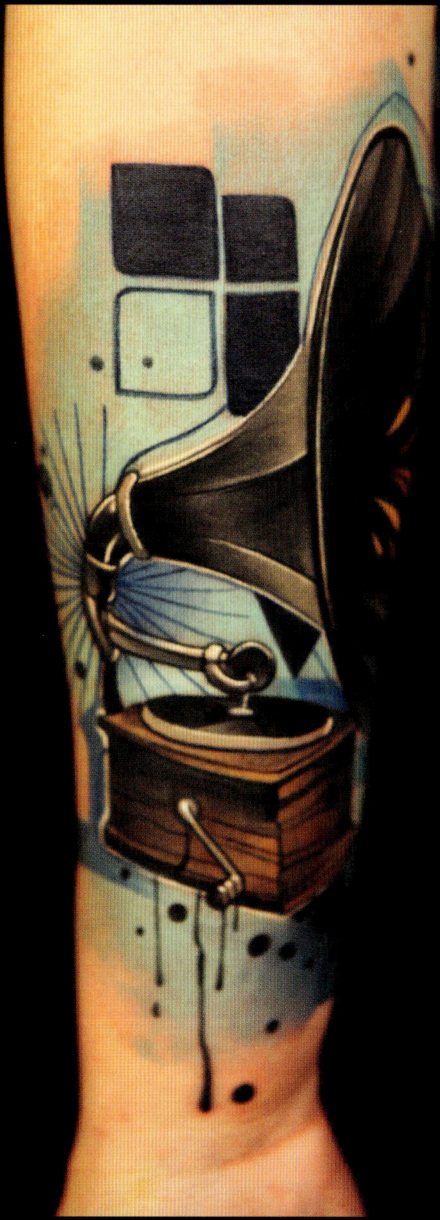
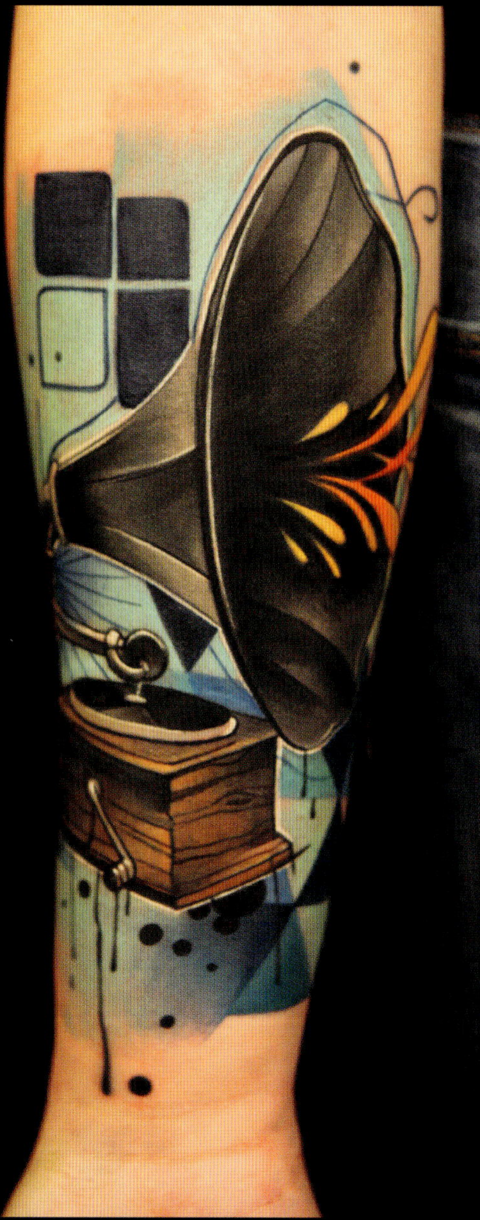

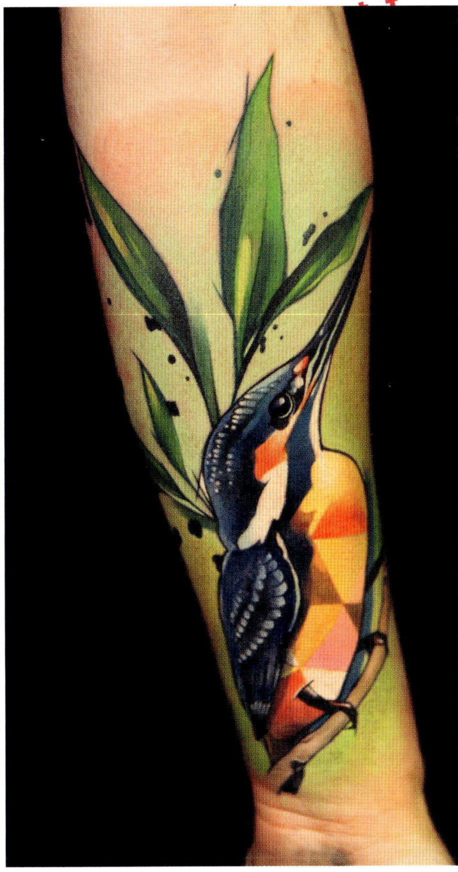

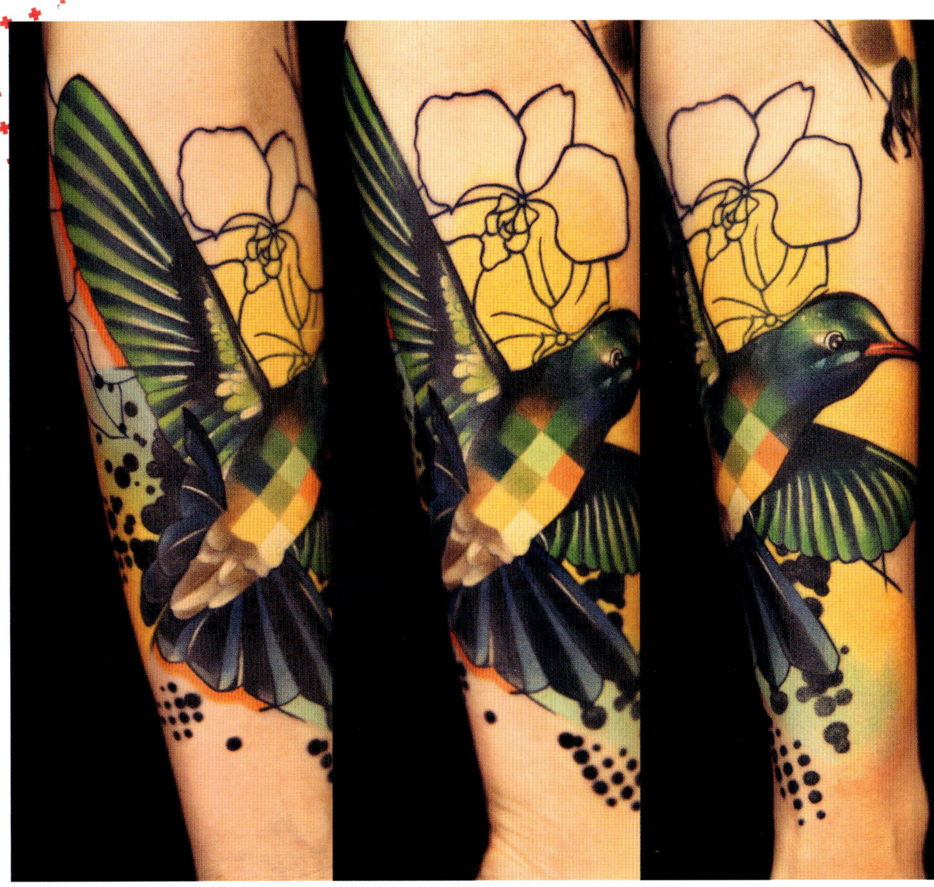

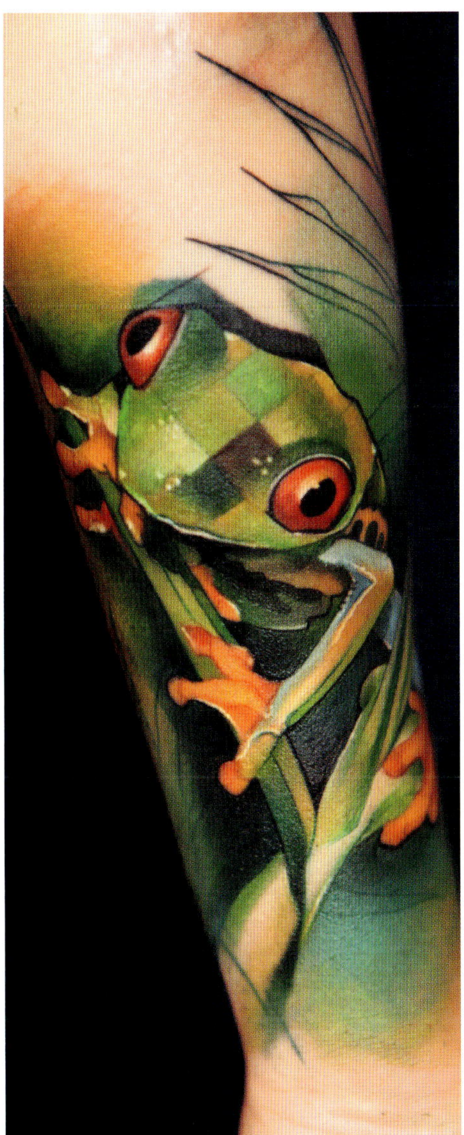

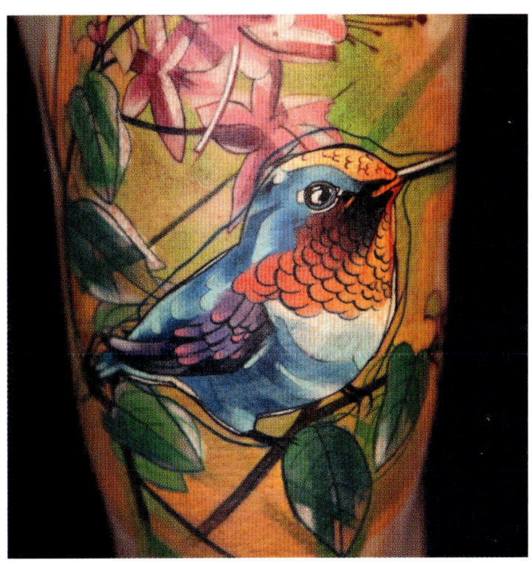

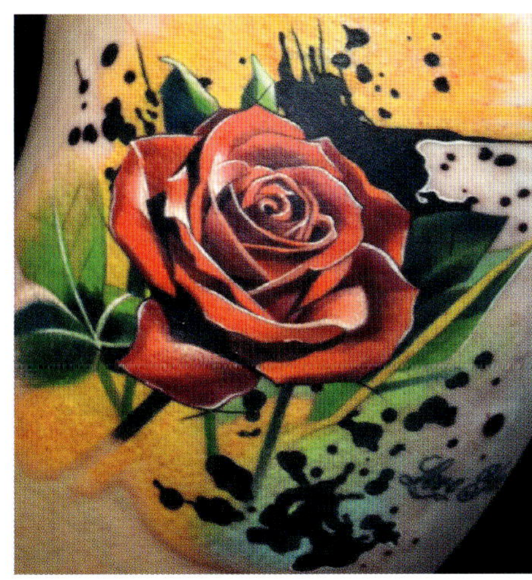

Another positive thing is that there's more competition among artists and also tattoo suppliers. This means we have to do our best, we have to constantly improve. It pushes us forward. With tattoo suppliers it works the same way I guess. They have to give us the best product and constantly develop something new that helps us to give our best in high quality.

As for the negatives: people have a different perception from how tattooing actually is. Watching all those TV shows, they think they can get exactly what they want and it will take five minutes. Also to a certain extent I disagree with the shows, as tattooing is not about the competition. For me it's about quality art and significance behind the tattoo. Lately I have noticed that lots of people think being a tattoo artist is cool and a rock-star job and they wanna become one too. Regardless of their abilities.

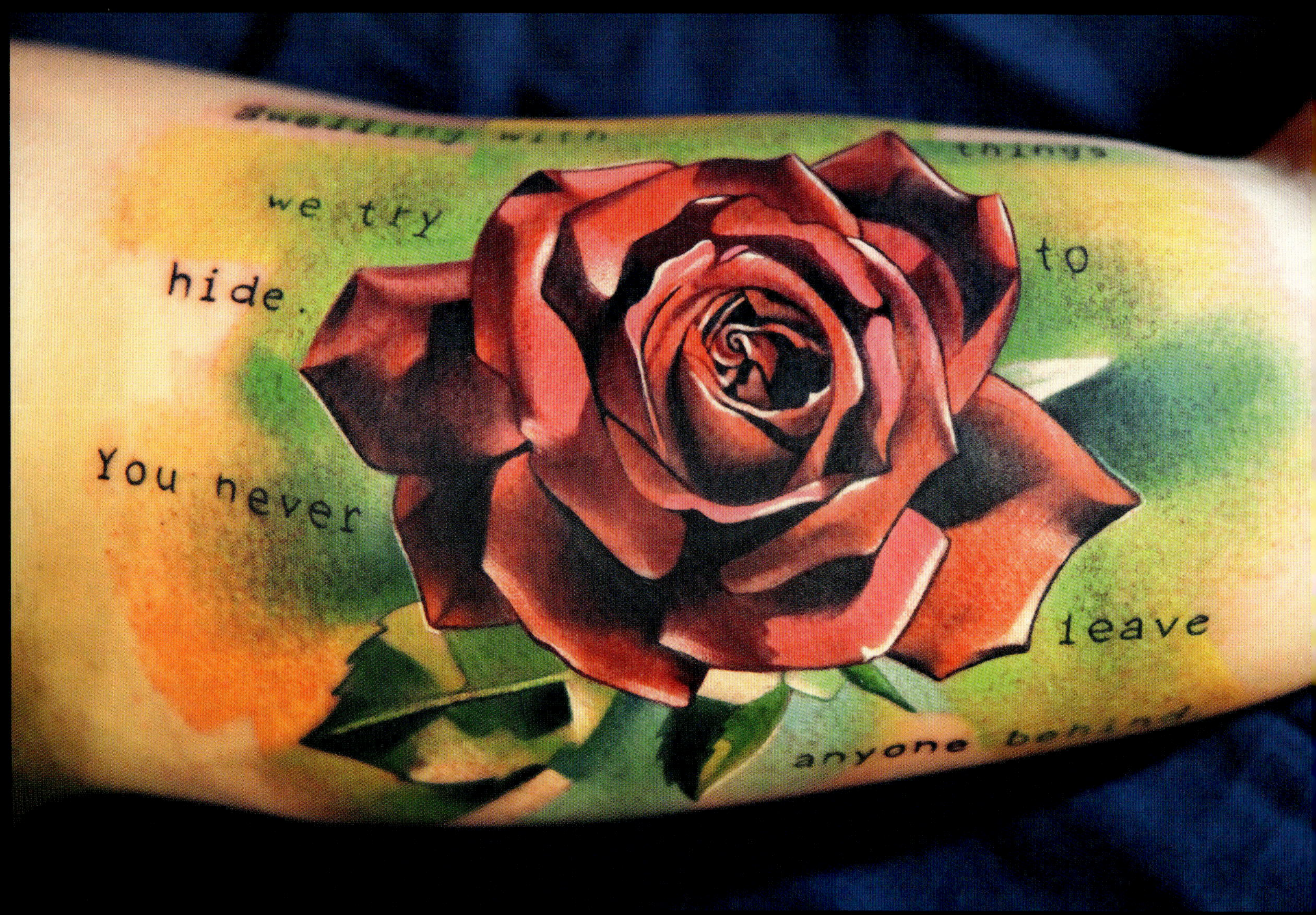
things
we try
hide.
to
You never
leave
anyone

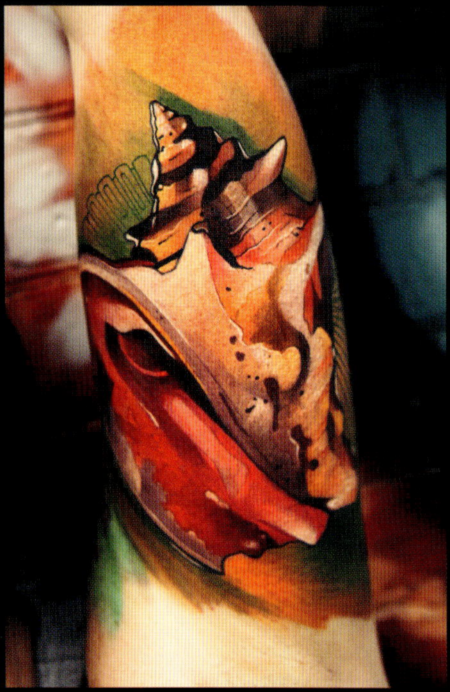

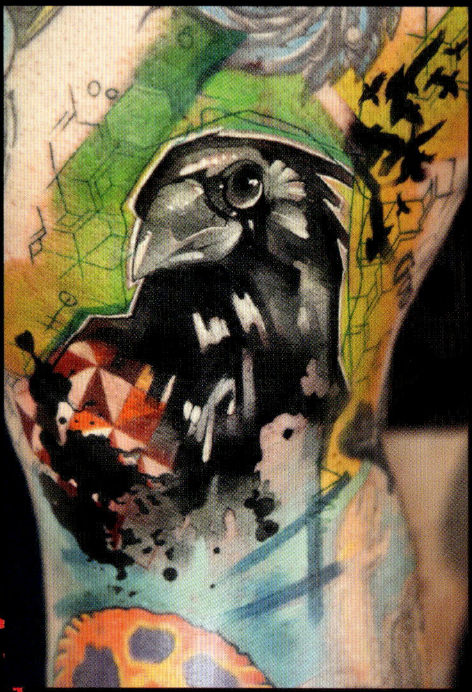

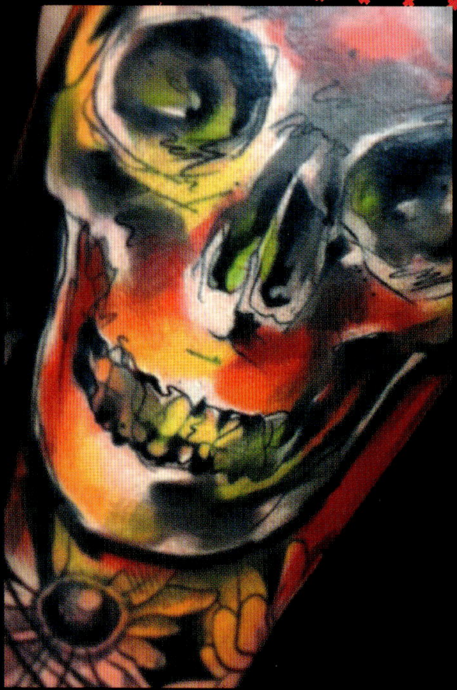

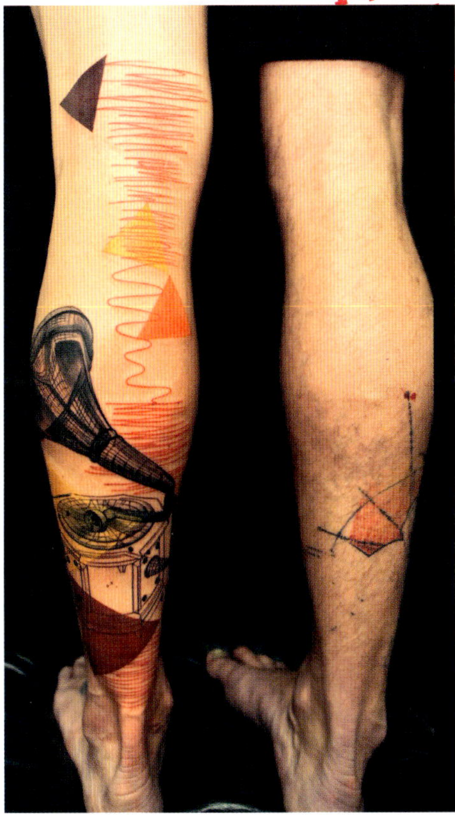

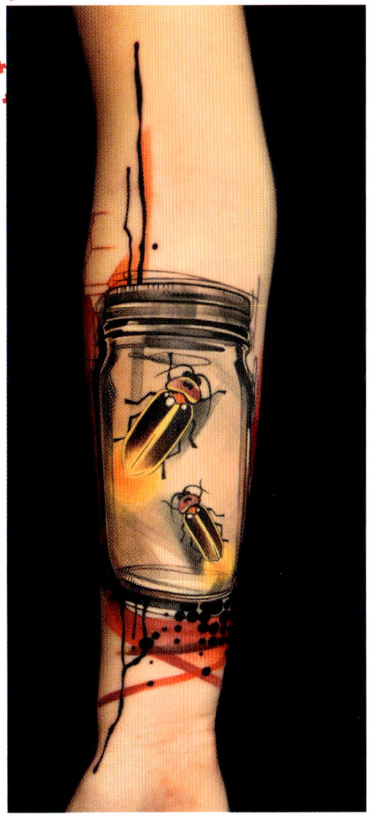

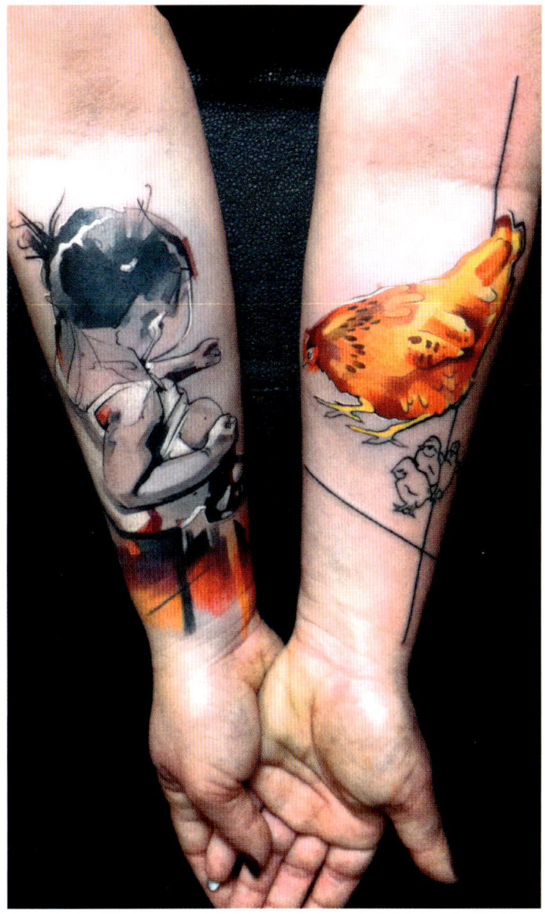

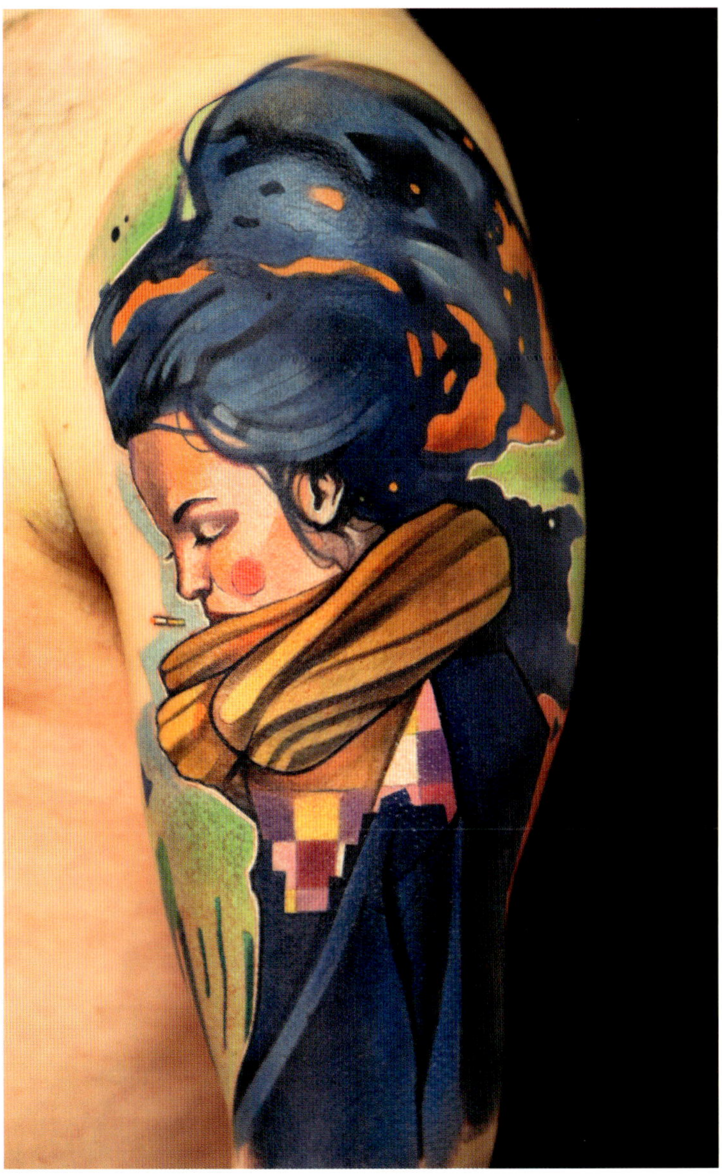

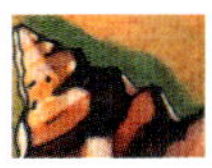

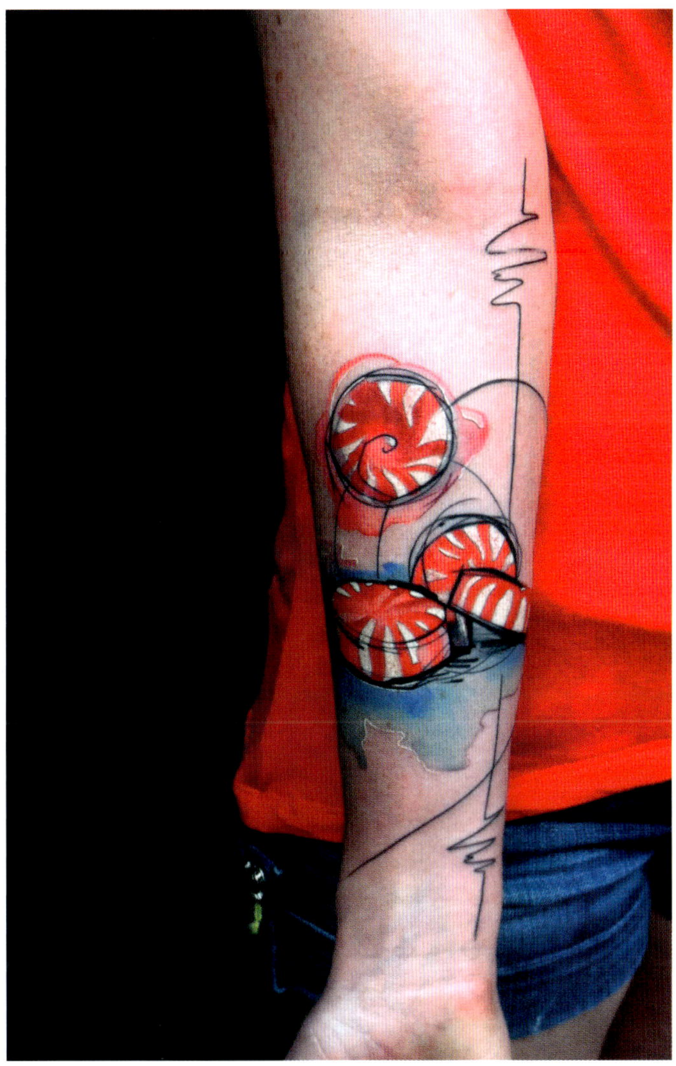

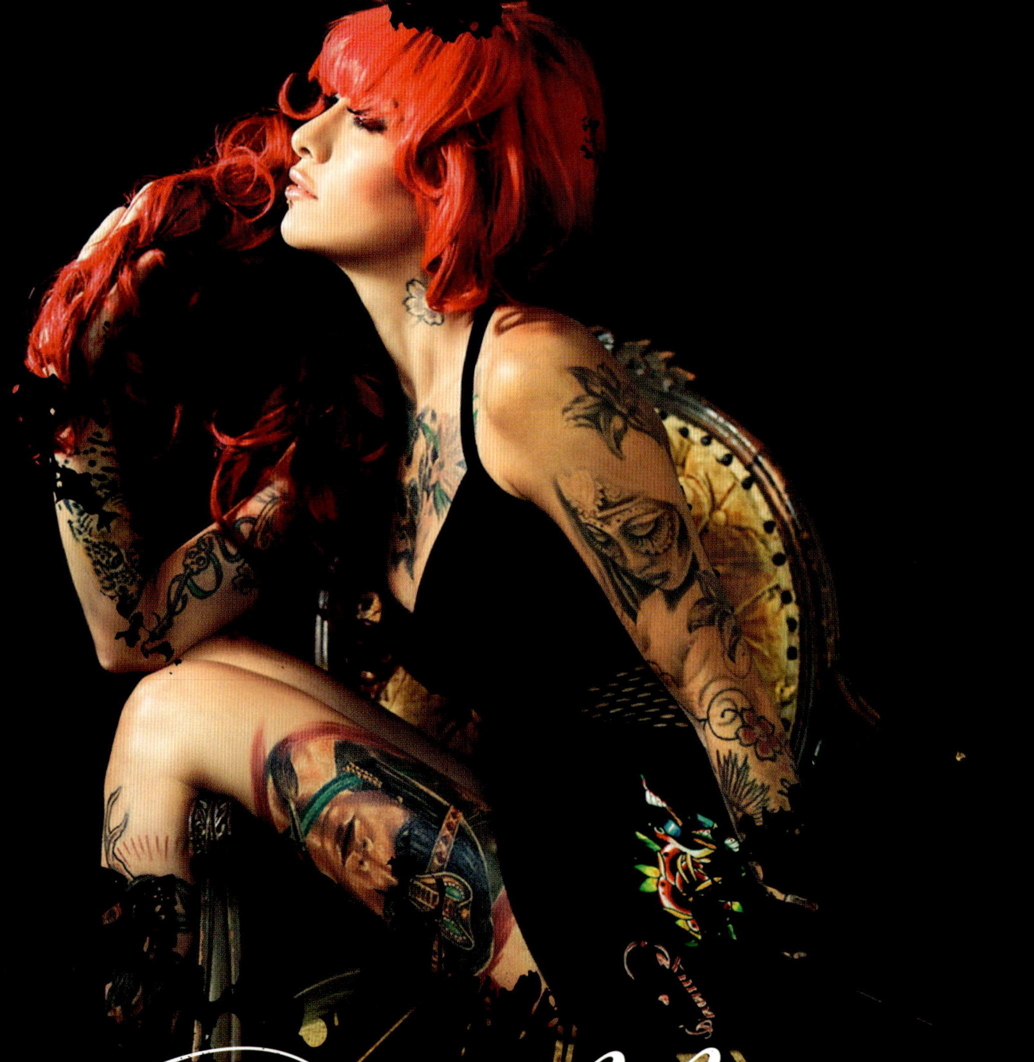

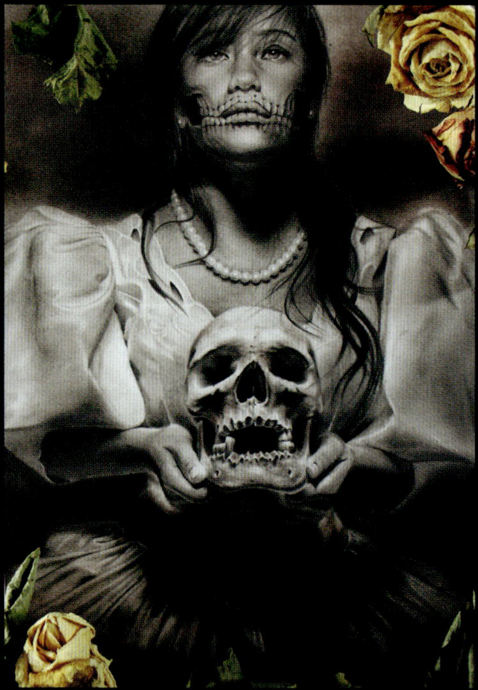

Moni MARINO

An Austrian tattoo artist with Italian and Sicilian roots, **MONI MARINO** has been tattooing for twenty years. She's the daughter of a painter and a seamstress. As a child Moni was constantly smeared with oil paints, she drew and painted with her hands and feet, and sometimes also licked tubes of paint.

"You must have the art in your blood, you can't just learn it at school"

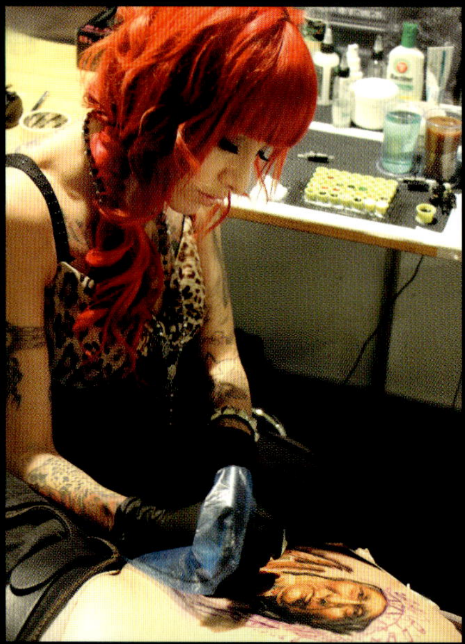

www.monimarino.com
www.facebook.com/pages/MONI-MARI-NO-TATTOOARTIST/140946925977945
colorhaut@hotmail.de
monimarinoart@hotmail.com
instagram @moni_marino_artist

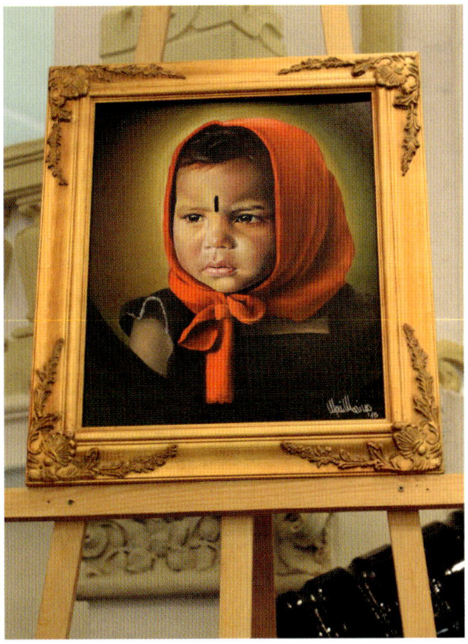

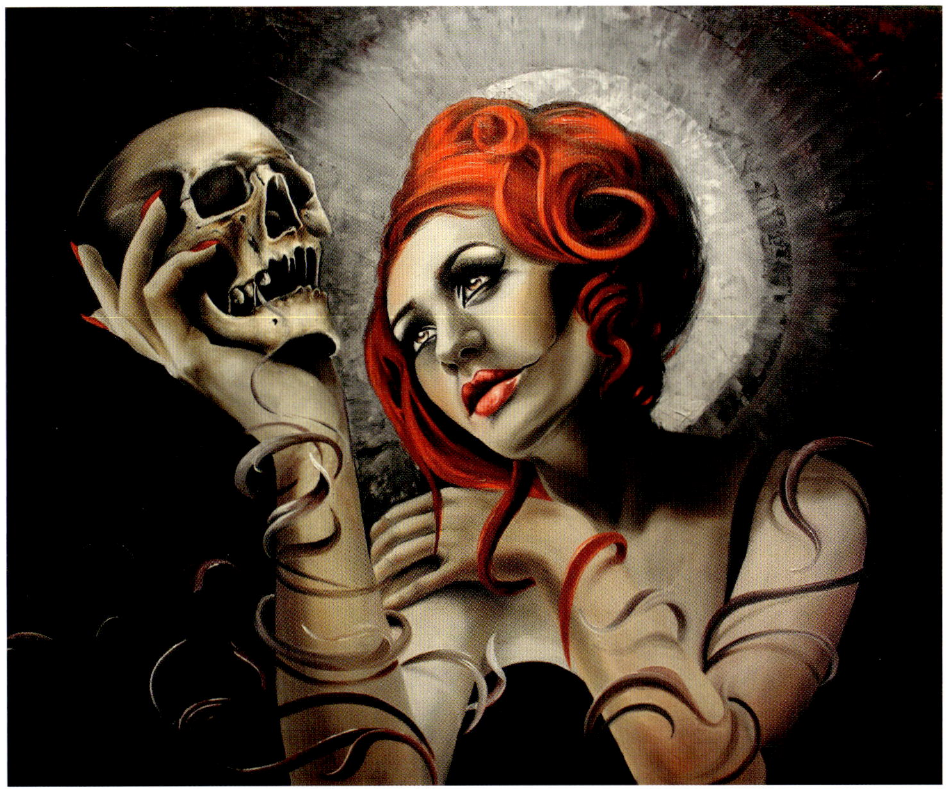

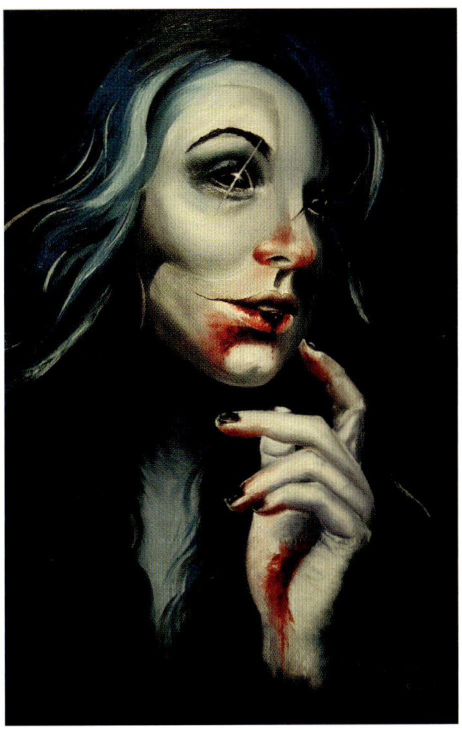

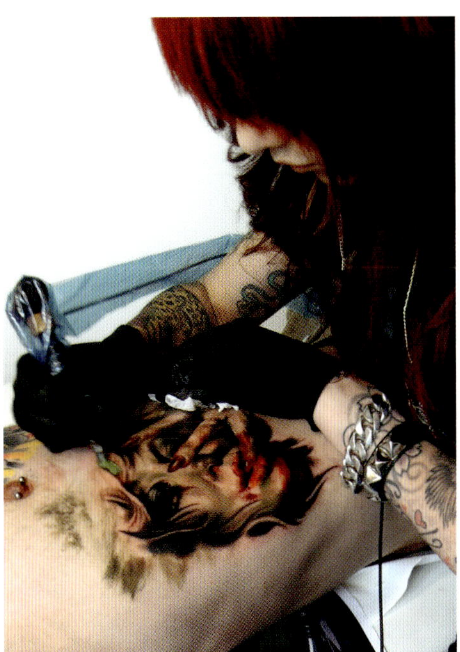

What was your initial exposure to the tattoo world?

I admired my father's painting; I'd watch him for hours, totally fascinated and in love with the brushes. At the age of fourteen, I saw a tattoo magazine for the first time and something in my brain and in my heart clicked. At that moment I knew what I wanted: to become a tattoo artist. At fifteen, I started tattooing my first boyfriend, then all his friends, and kids in the small town where I lived. The word spread quickly, many people stopped speaking to me, and I was really sad about that. So after I finished school, I left Italy and my family. I went to the station, and without any money and without a destination I got on a train, running away from all the people with prejudices and from the separation of my parents.

After fourteen hours of traveling I found myself in Berlin, Germany. Then came a week of survival on the streets, without money and without knowing a word of German, until an Italian family led me to the other side of Germany and I began to work in a pizzeria and learn German. It took me five years to save enough money to buy a new machine, colors, and needles for tattooing…and to begin to be happy again.

Being a tattoo artist is a unique job; can you tell me why you chose tattooing as a form of artistic expression?

Yes it is, but to be honest I didn't decide—this art chose me. I believe that's because I'm the daughter of a painter-poet and a seamstress. I come from the union of those genes…

What was the most inspiring thing or person for you in the very beginning?

Definitely it was my father.

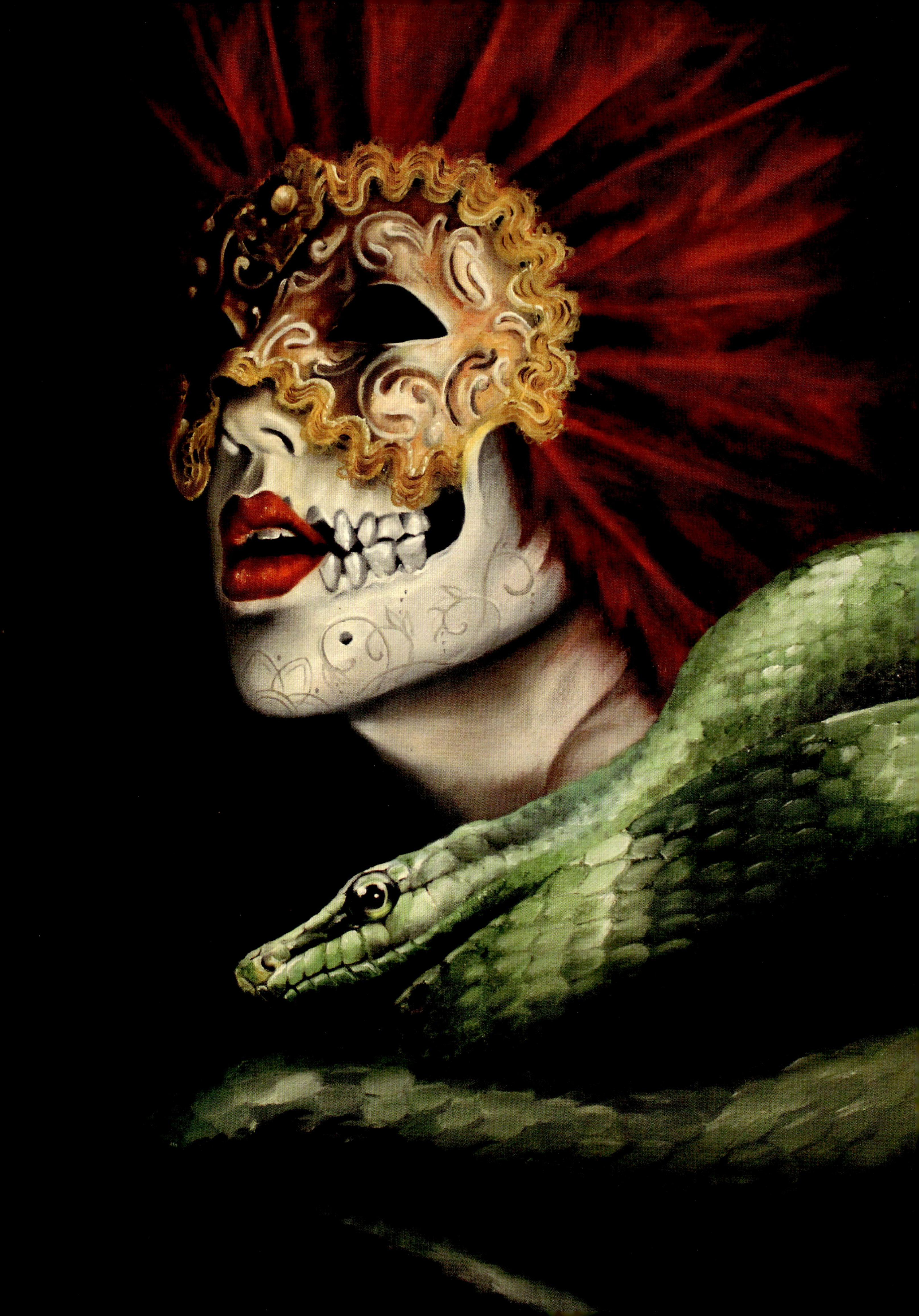

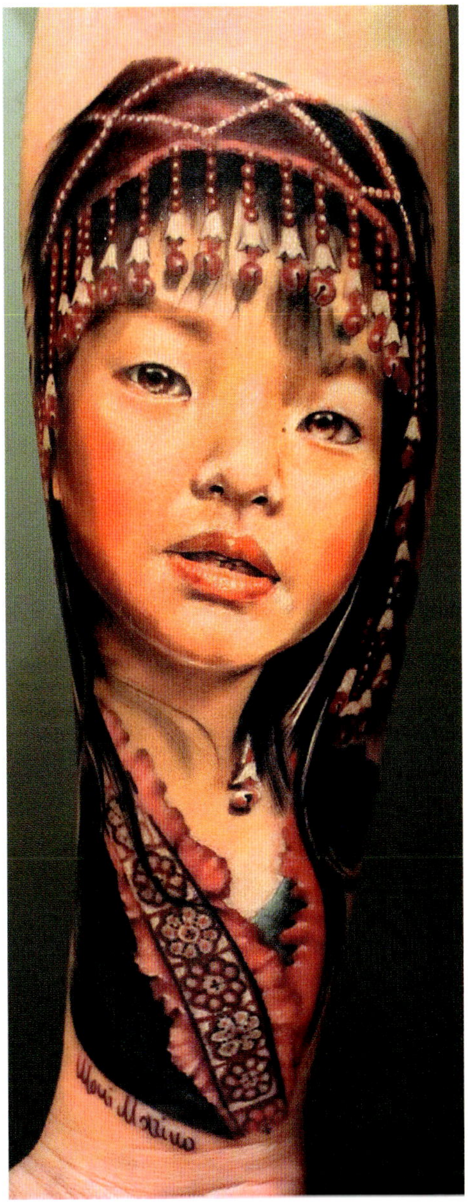

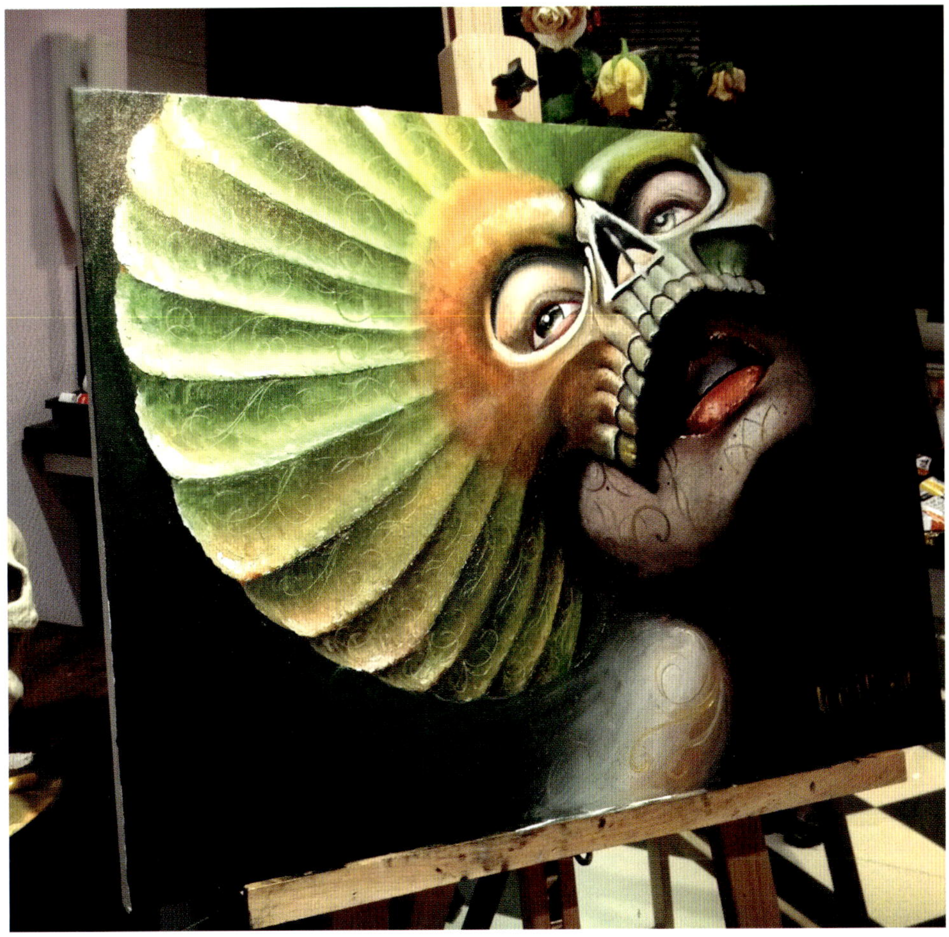

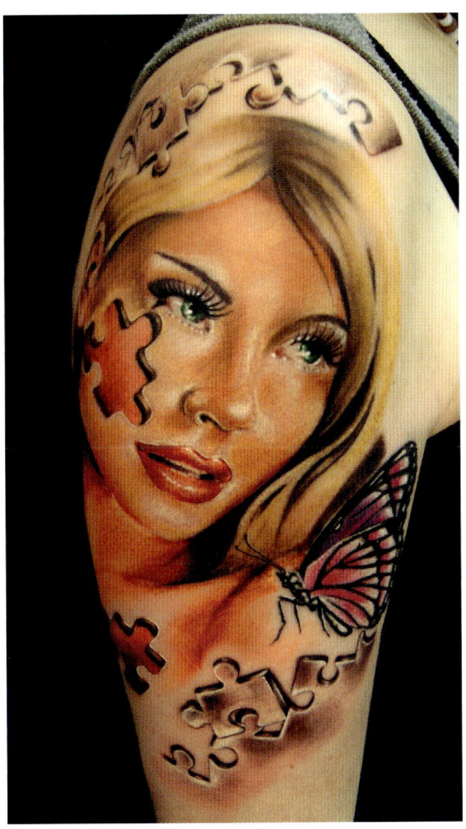

What would your job be if you weren't a tattoo artist?

I can't imagine my life any other way, but I think I would become a veterinarian.

There are many tat styles now on the tat scene. What is your specialty?

I love the Chicano style, but my speciality is photorealism in full color.

Do you remember where and when your love and fascination with that style first began?

Twenty years ago I didn't have a computer or Internet. I bought tattoo magazines, and that was enough for me to see the work of Jose Lopez and Steve Soto. They were my inspirations.

Are there any other famous artists who have influenced you down the path of your career?

I admire many tattoo artists…for example, Nikko Hurtado, Carlos Torres, and Randy Engelhard.

You create custom works. Do you have full creative freedom?

My clients usually give me some input, tell me why they want this tattoo, or tell me the story of the design if there is one, and then I have full creative freedom.

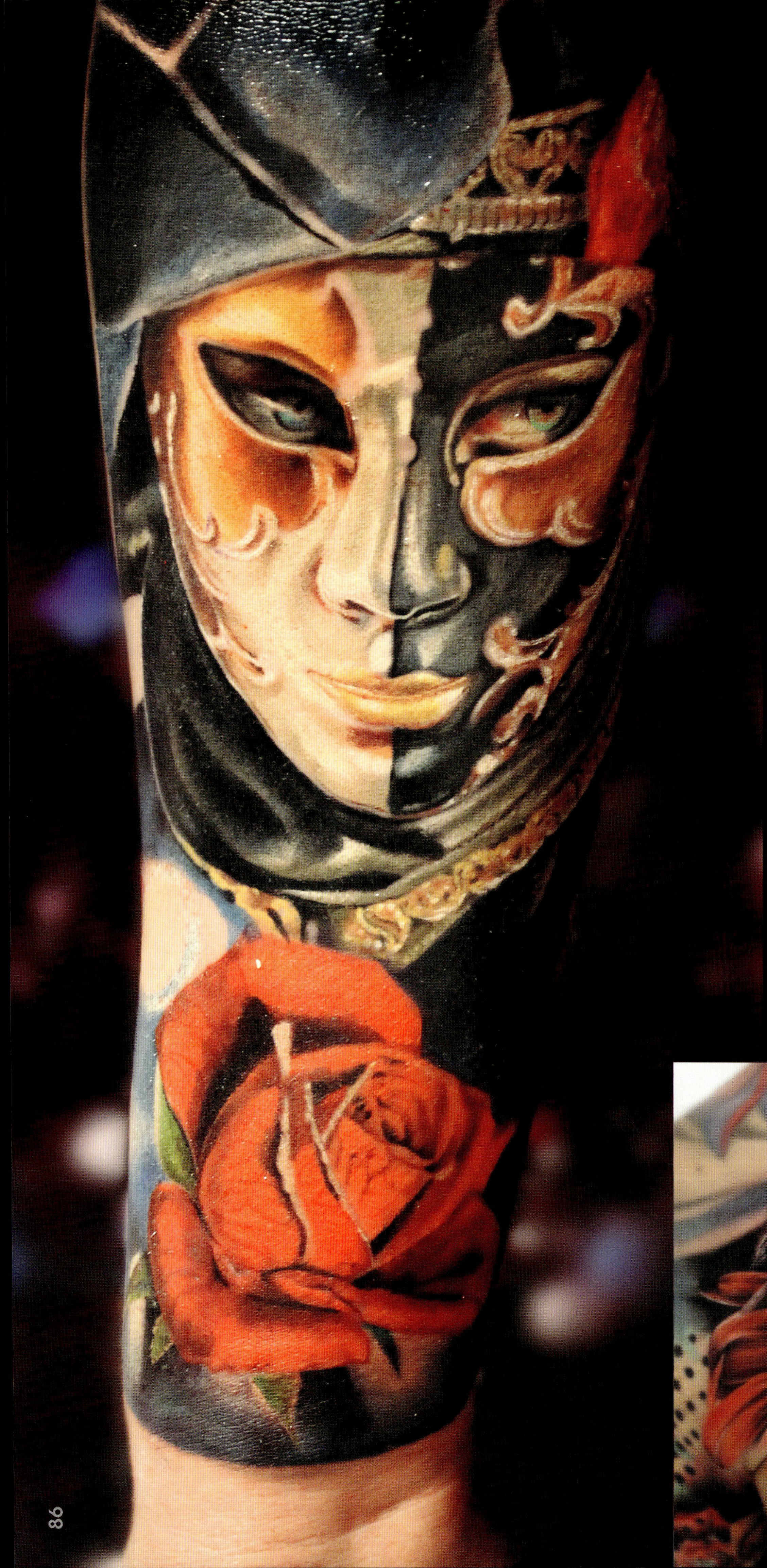
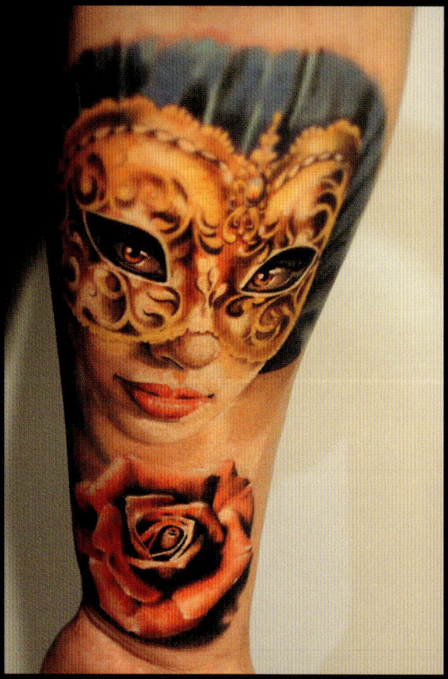
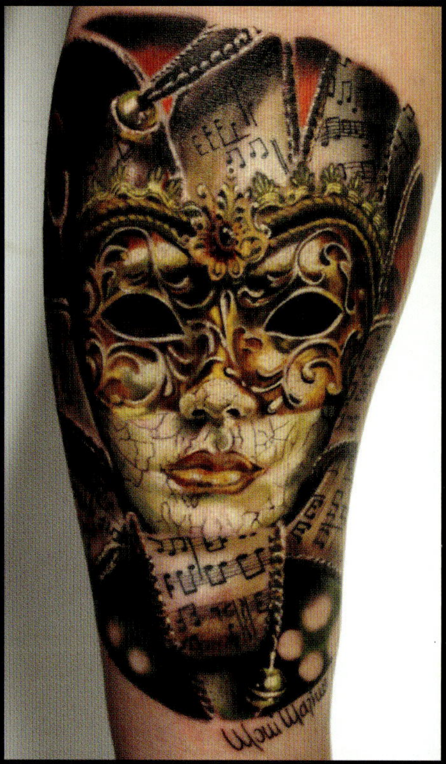
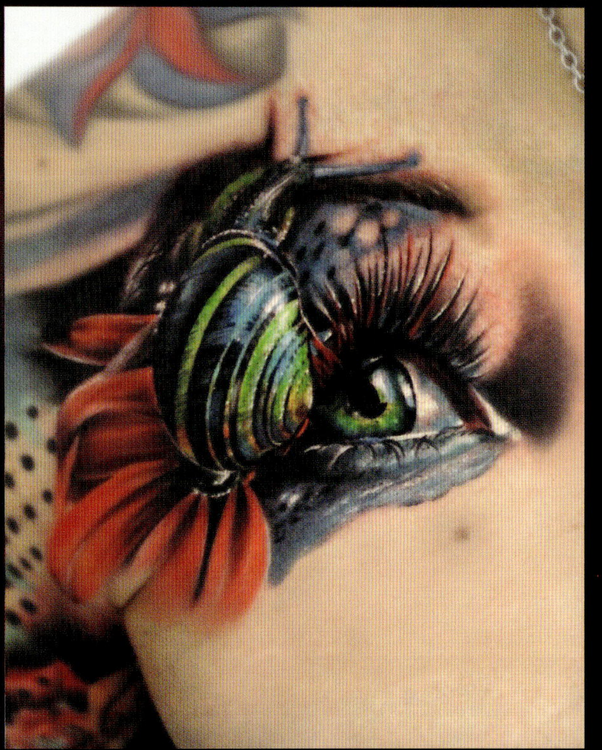

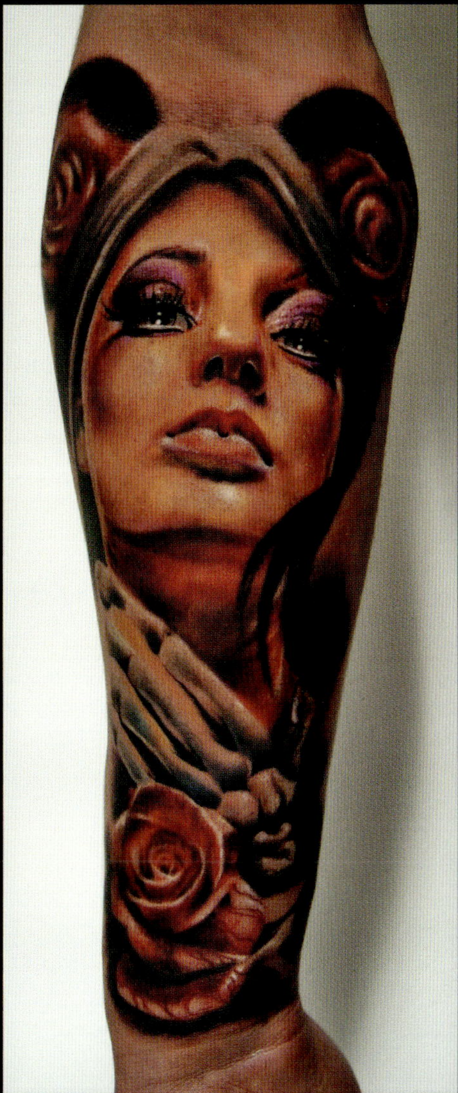

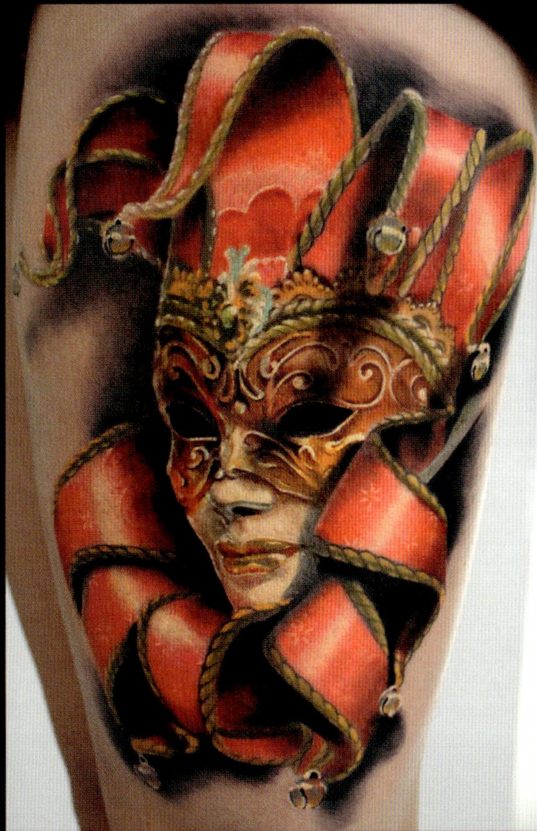

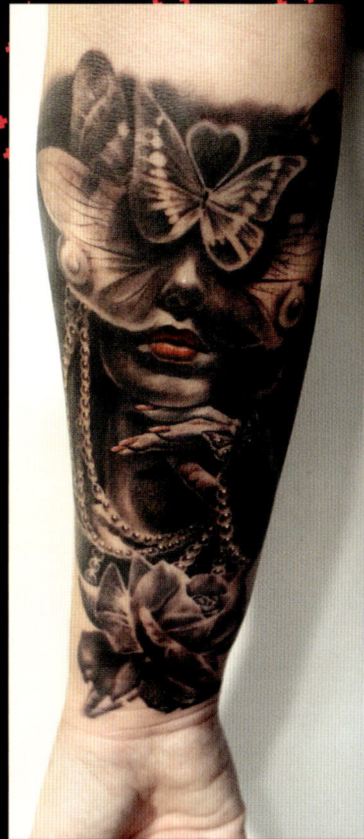

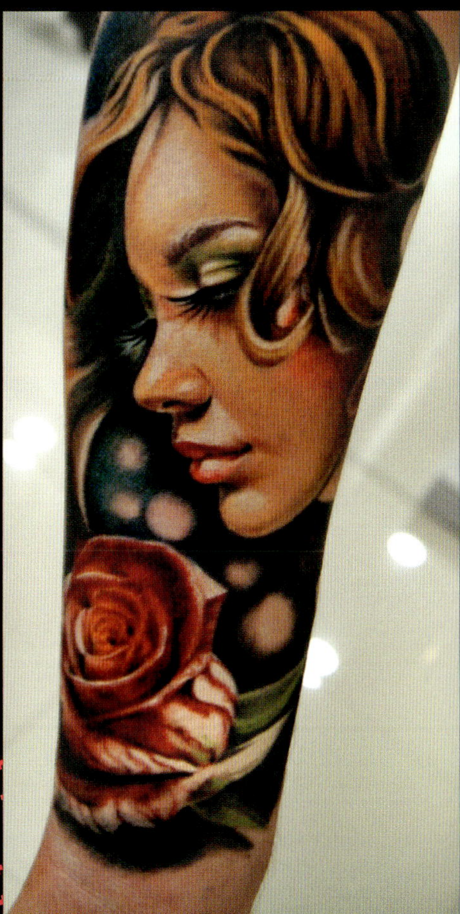

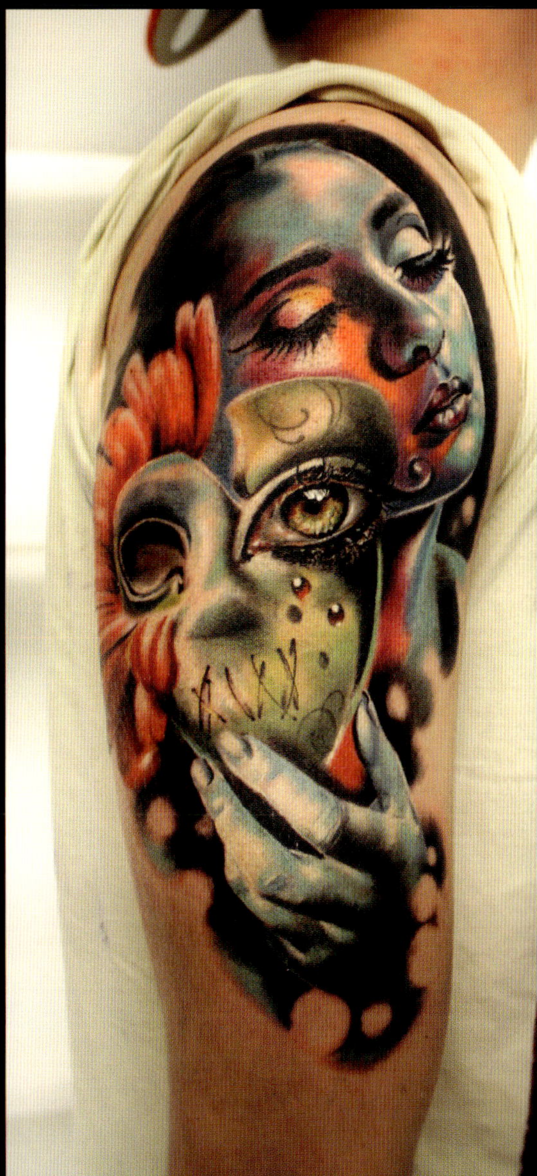

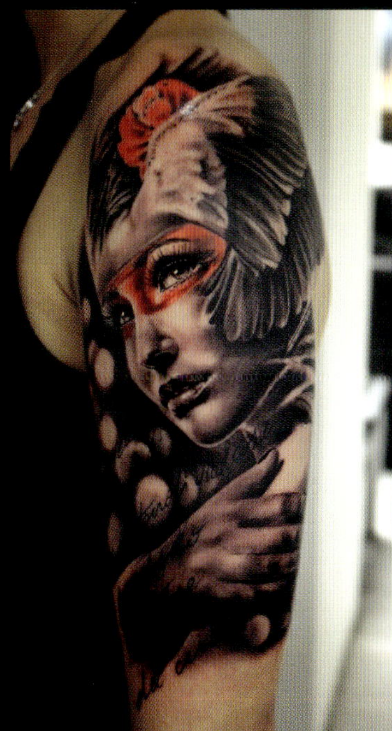

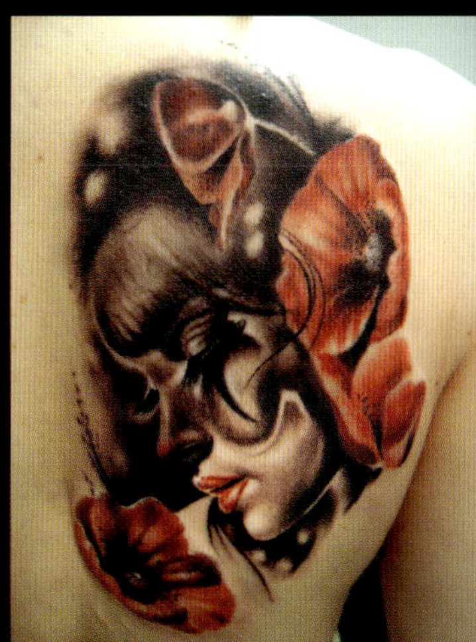

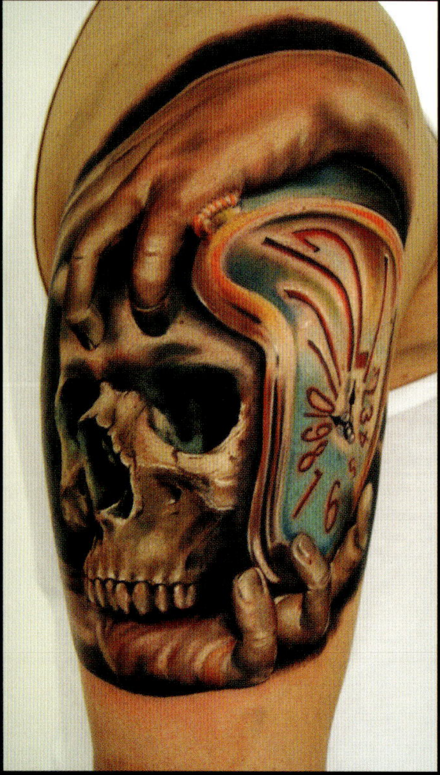
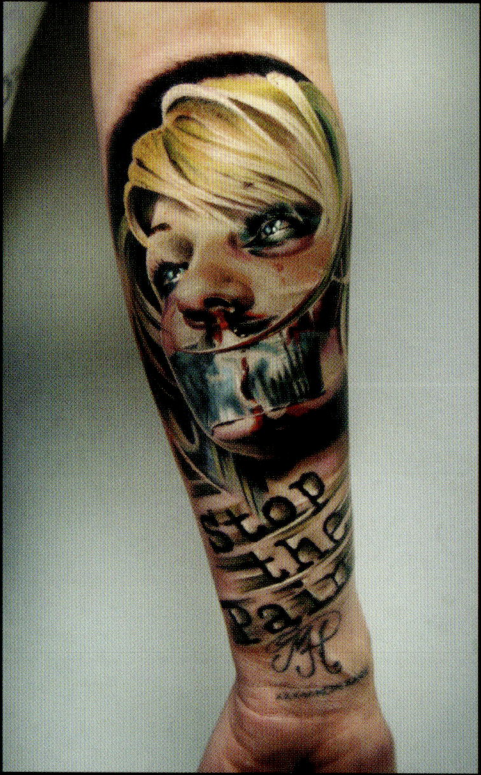
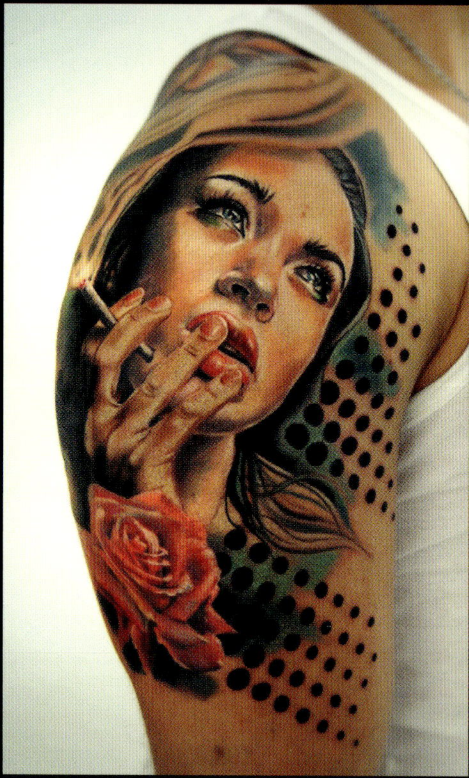
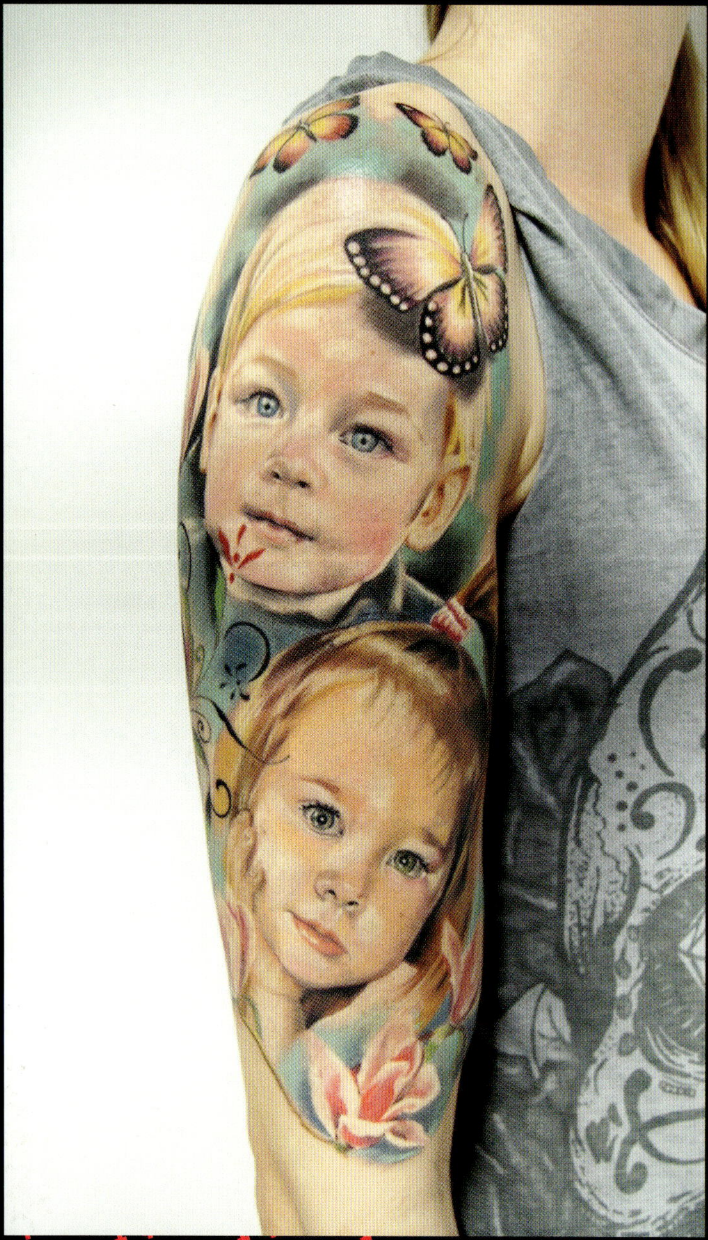
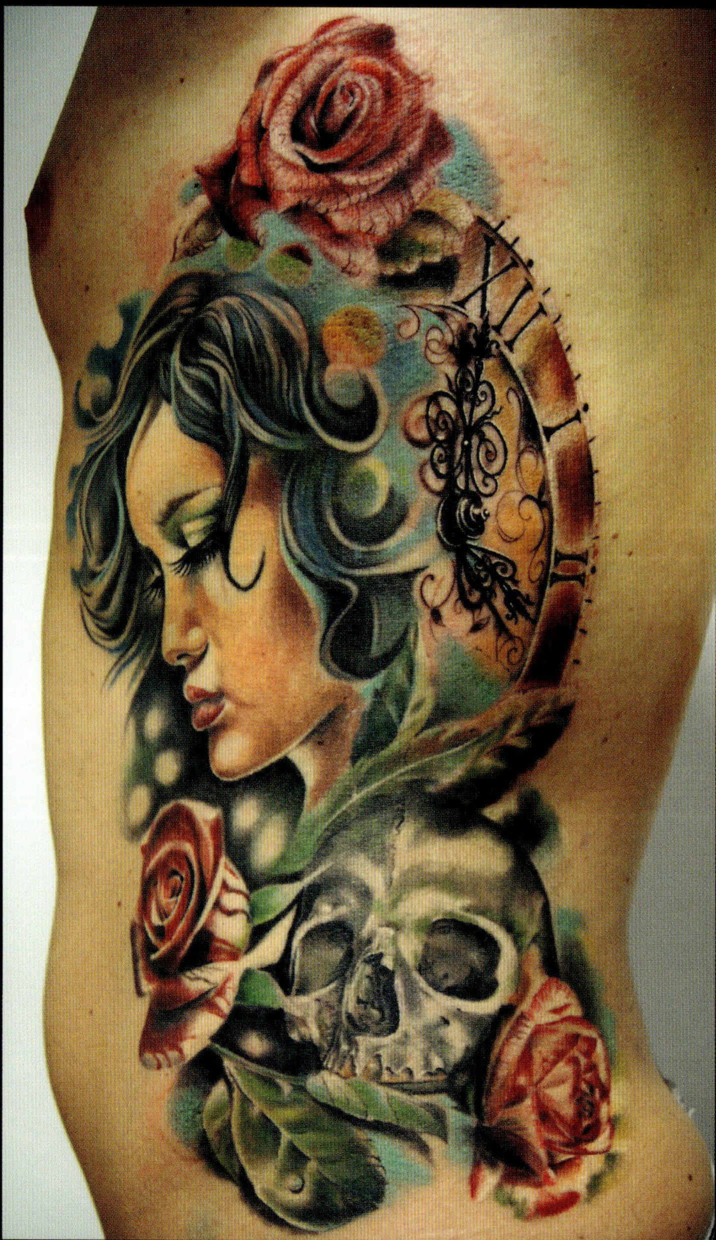

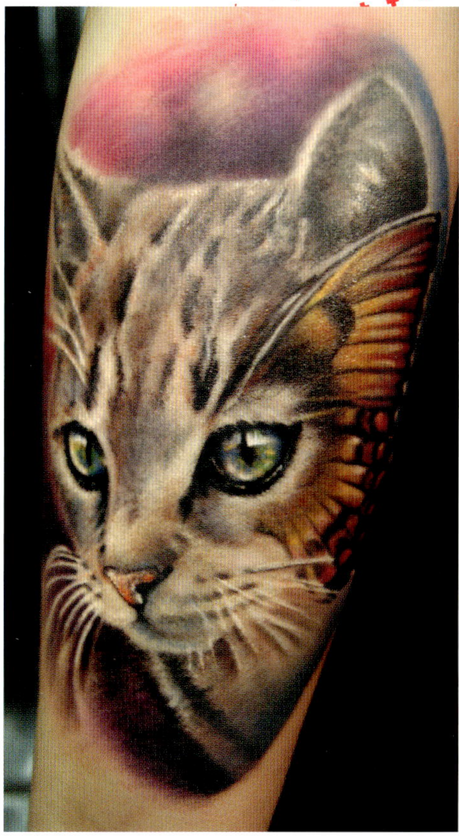

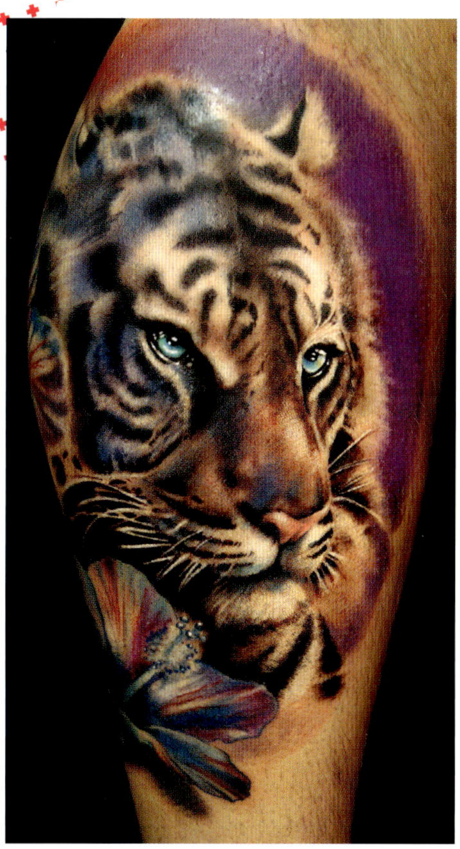

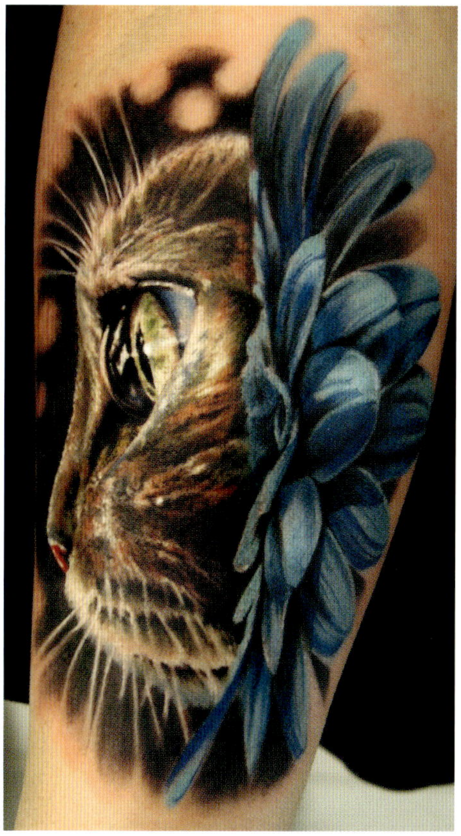

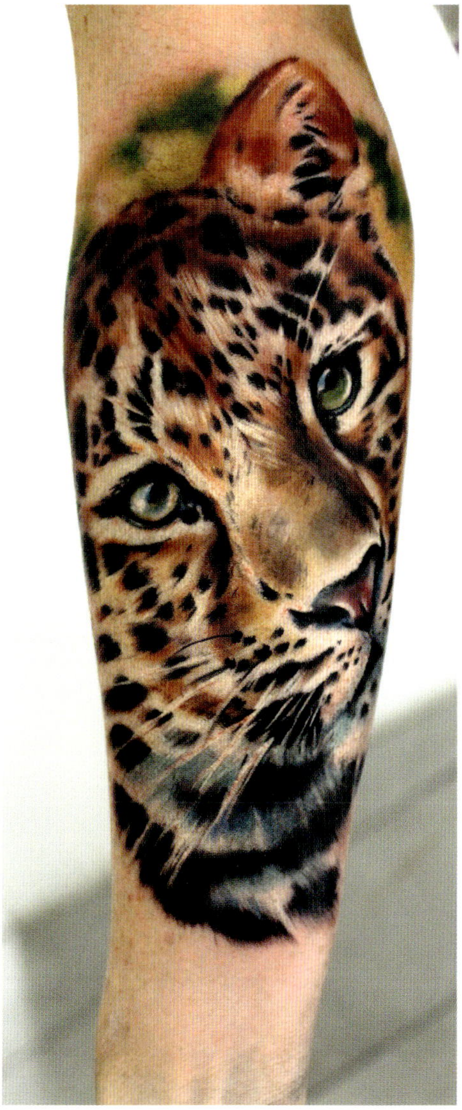

Can you tell me about a memorable moment you had while doing someone's tattoo?

One day a twenty-seven-year-old guy appeared at the shop. He looked tired, destroyed, and he told me he couldn't sleep anymore. He wasn't going to go back to work anymore either, because his baby died after just seven months of life. He wanted a portrait of his baby on his arm, a black-and-gray tattoo with the text "Daddy's little hero." It took me eight hours to do it, I gave it my best, and while I was working, my tears flowed. When this guy looked at the tattoo in the mirror, his face lit up like a withered flower that you give water to again. He was infinitely grateful, and he started to sleep well again and to go back to work. I'll never forget that experience!

What would your dream piece be to work on?

I wish I could tattoo someone completely freehand on the skin without any stencils, and just see what happens.

What is your favorite thing about being a tattoo artist?

Traveling around the world to make people happy.

What's the strangest request you ever had for a tattoo?

Once I received an e-mail from a person who wanted a Virgin Mary with the face of Atatürk. I didn't even know who Atatürk was, and when I looked on Google, I just laughed. I replied that it was not my style. *(Laughs.)*

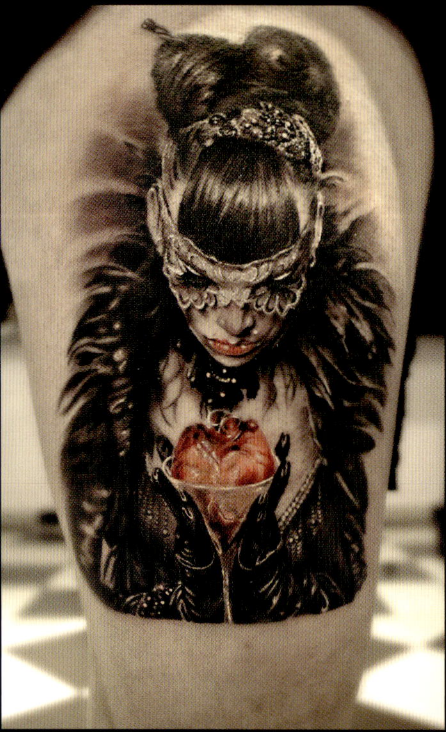
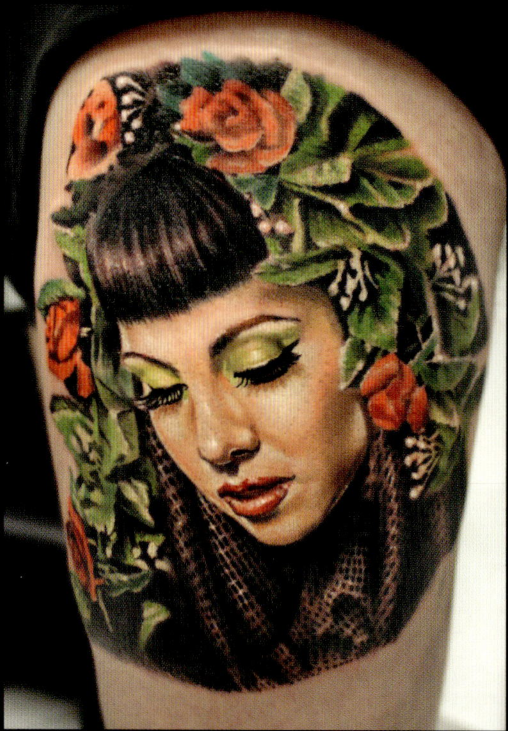
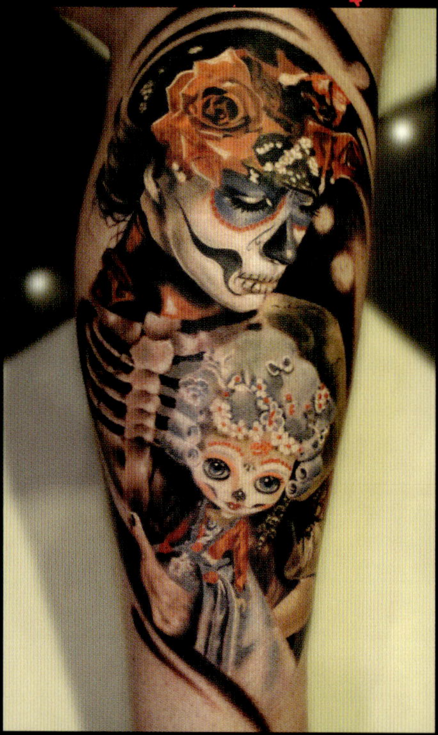
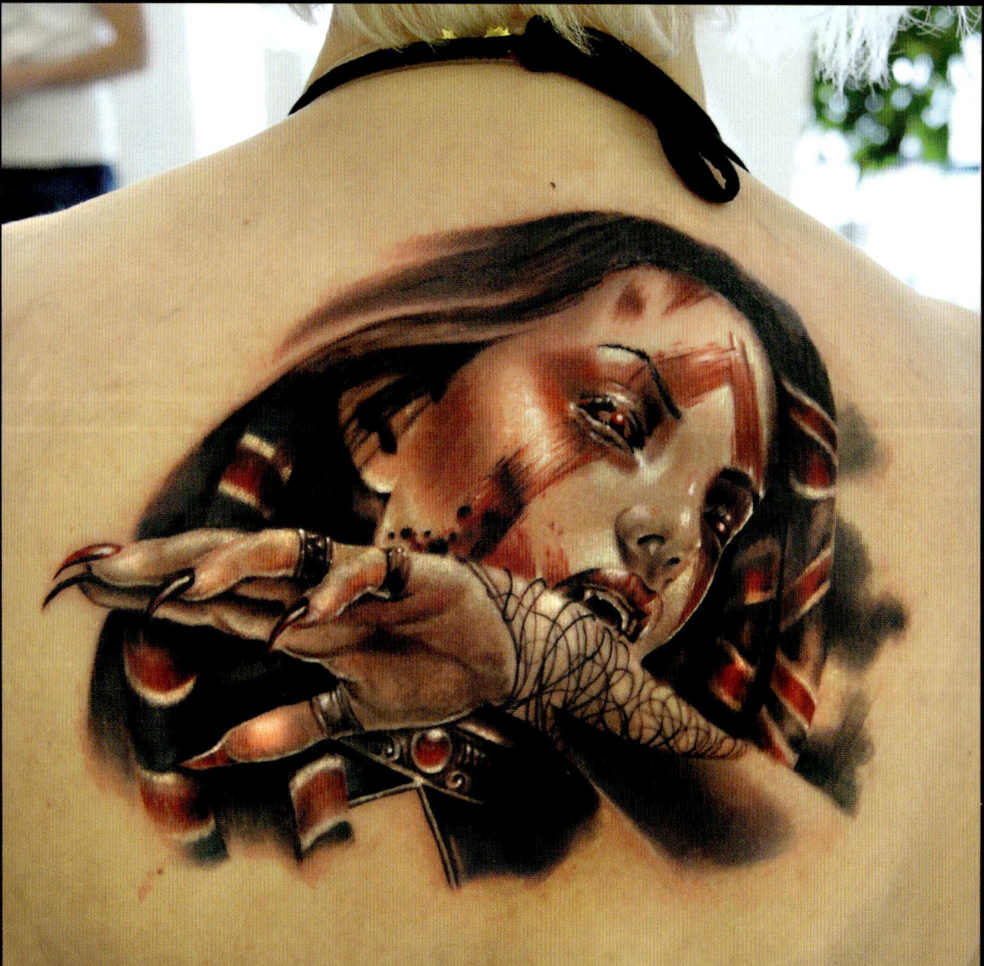
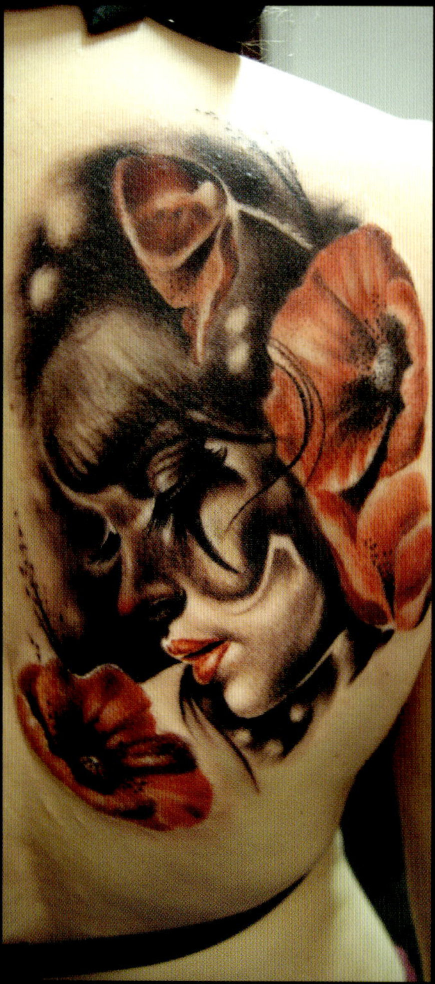

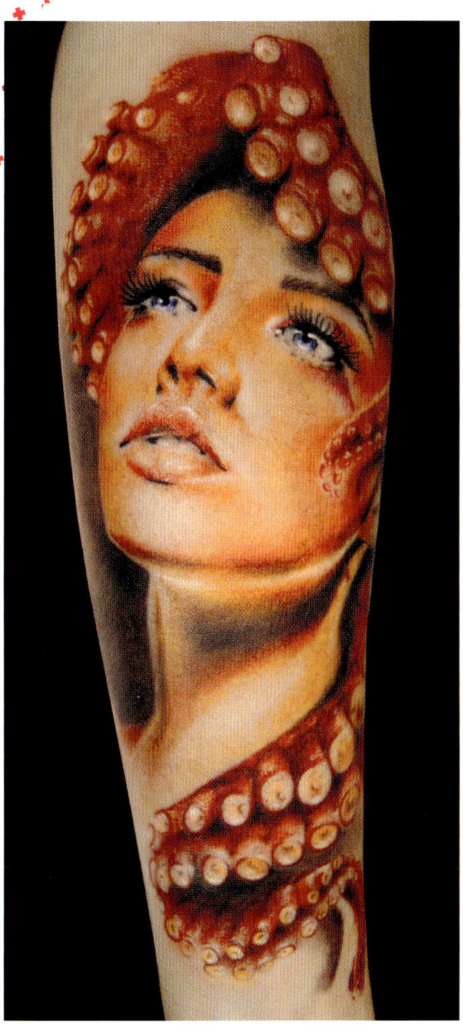

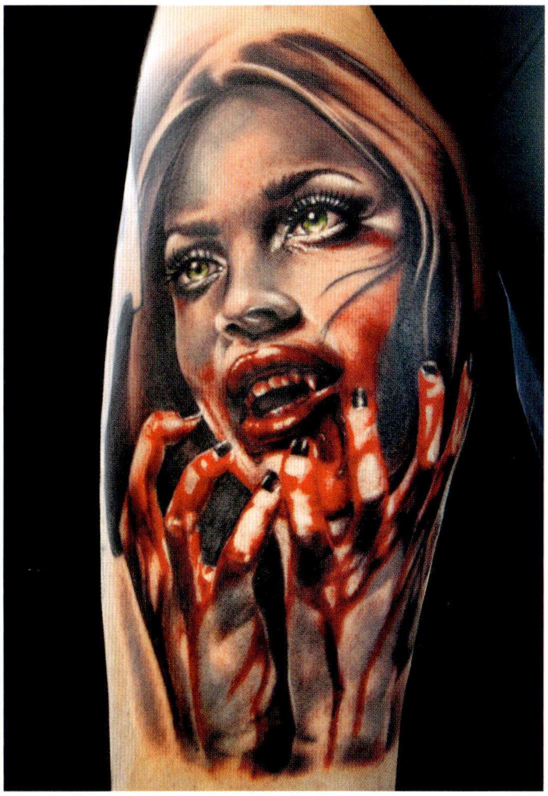

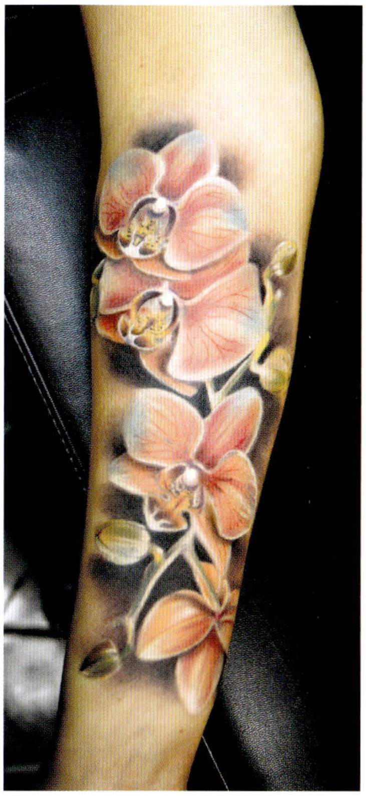

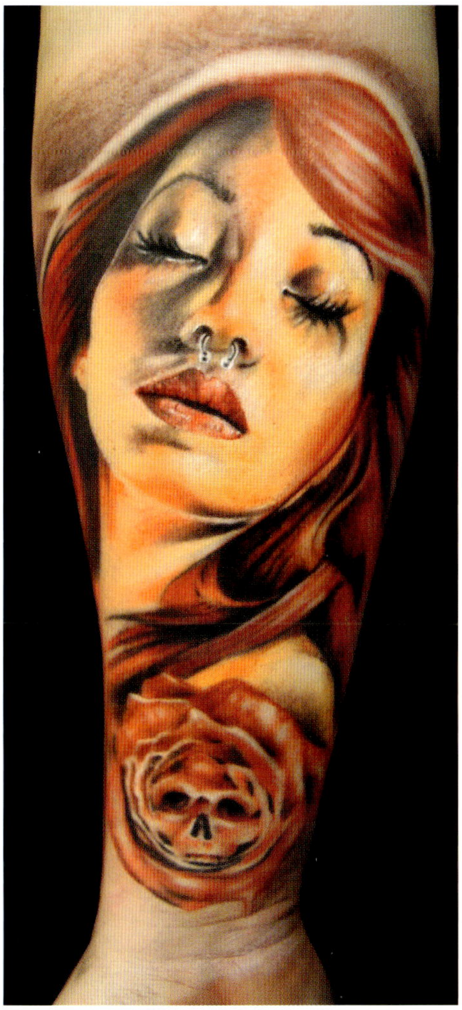

It seems to me a lot of younger tat artists have college degrees in the fine arts. The things they can do on the skin are outstanding. Do you think it is necessary for a tattooer to have a background in fine arts, or any formal training?

That's great, but I think that it isn't absolutely necessary. You must have the art in your blood, you can't just learn it at school.

Nowadays the tattoo industry is booming with more new products—inks, machines, etcetera. Do you think that is good progress?

That is definitely great progress! I'm really proud to see how hard people are working for tattoo art. The tattoo world is advancing ever more rapidly in the right direction.

Tattoos have been treated as a deviation etc. Do you think it will ever become fully accepted as an art?

Unfortunately there are some countries that are fighting against this form of art, in a part of France it is forbidden to have a tattoo, and in Spain seems to be banned tattooing the hands and neck to protect the natural image of the human race.

I believe that these attempts are futile and will arrive the day when the children will read our names in the books at the school.

Is there anything else you'd like to say?

Let me just remind you of a Moni Marino quote: "You never stop, you always have to continue, to improve, to go forward." And no employer will give you a second life after death. You have one life, and each day is a precious gift and should be lived as we want, fighting for our dreams and ideals, never giving up.

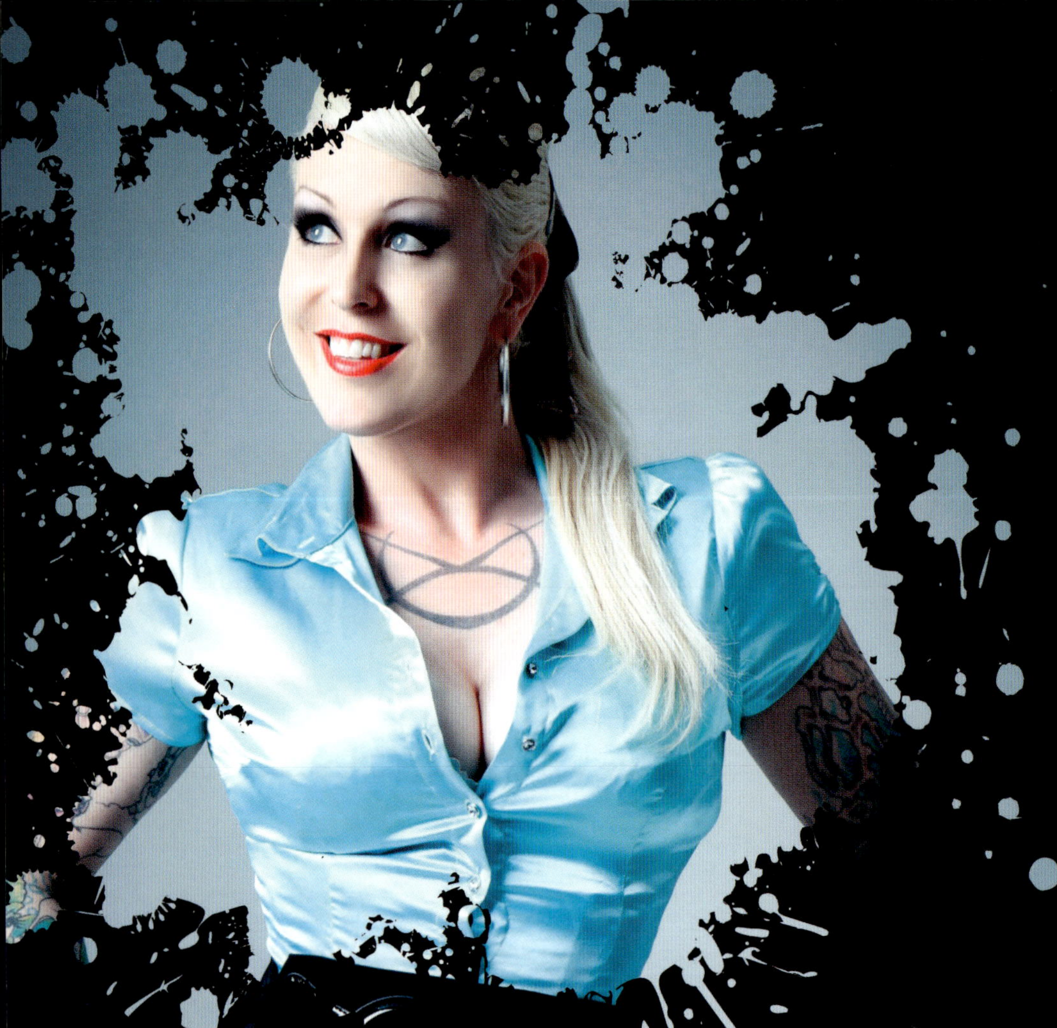

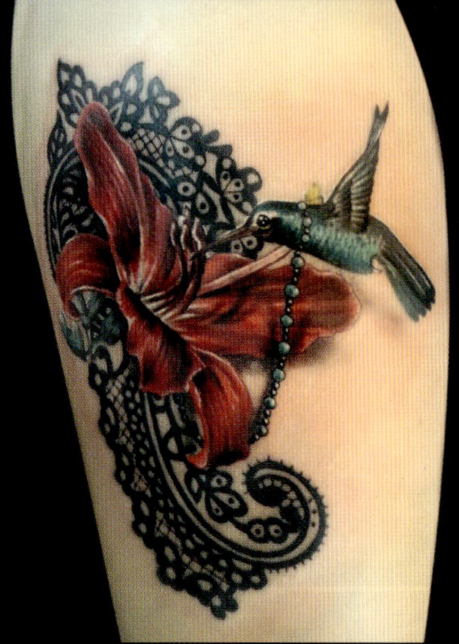

NADINE BRYANT MARRIOTT was born in the south of England and grew up loving art. She studied art and art history at college, and left school wondering how she was going to use her art to make a living. She got a job sorting mail at the post office and in her spare time did art for friends and clubs. Nadine was asked several times to design tattoos, and approached a local tattoo artist who eventually took her on as an apprentice. At that time it was rare to get a chance to tattoo ,and even rarer for a girl, so she made sure she took that position seriously and quickly realized she loved it.

Nadine MARRIOTT

> "I'm really enjoying the feminine style I'm doing a lot of at the moment, with beads and lace"

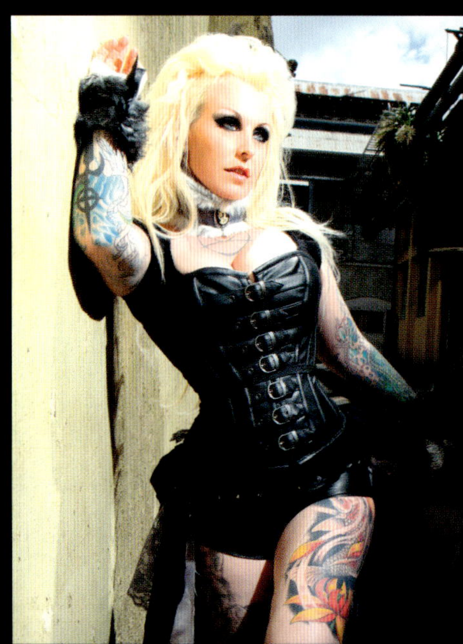

www.facebook.com/nadinebryanttattooartistnz
www.facebook.com/pages/Nadine-Bryant-Black-Pearl-Studios/391804170889887
www.facebook.com/nadine.bryant.5
twitter.com/NadineBryantnz

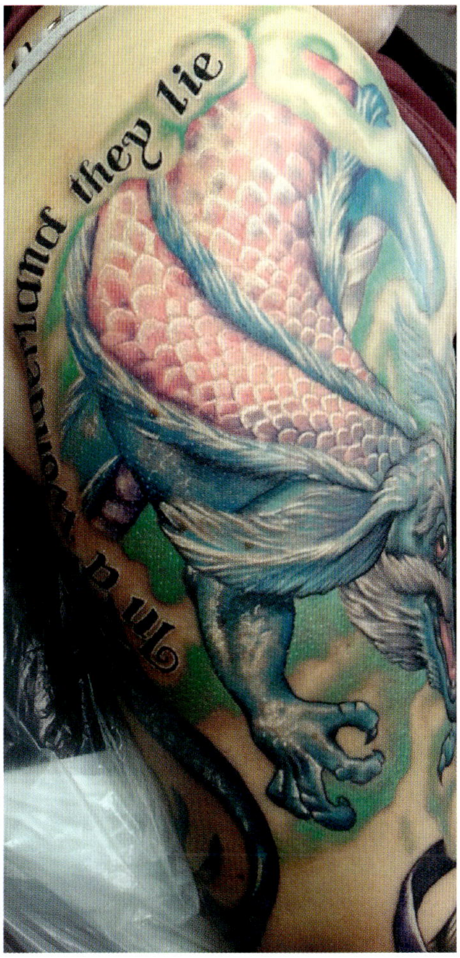

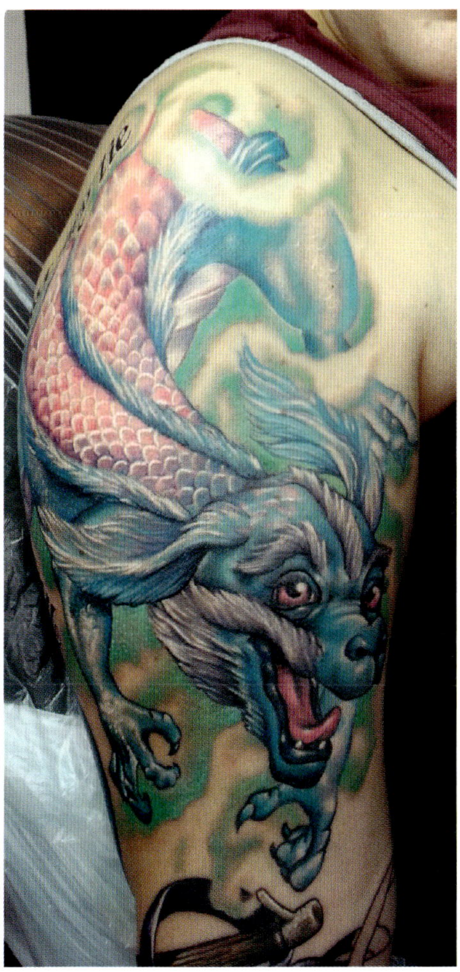

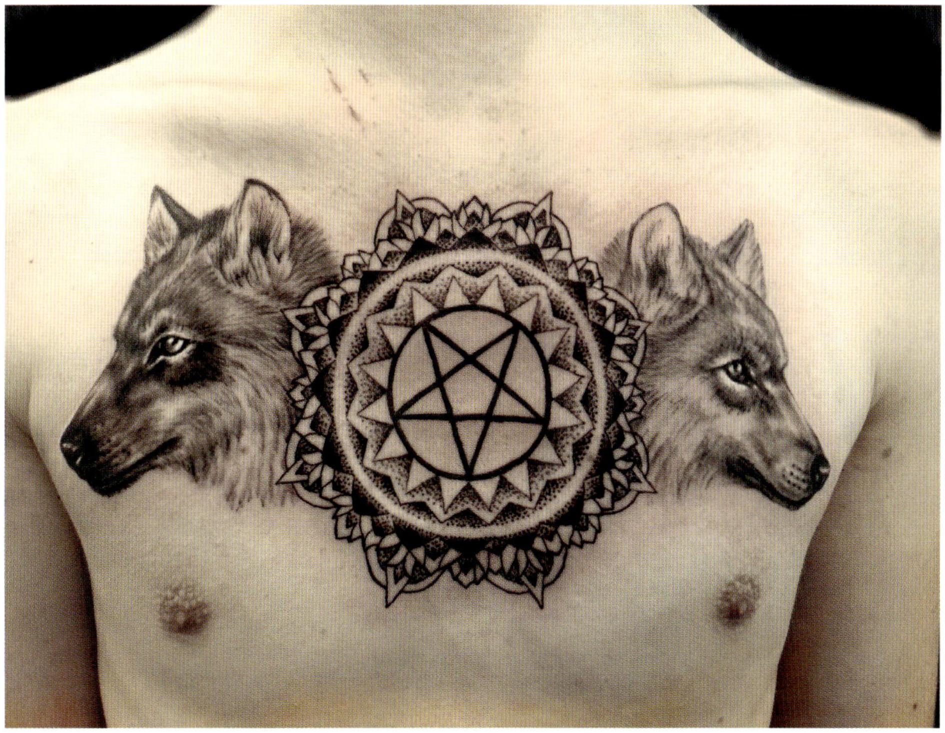

When you were a child, did you think you would grow up to become an artist, or work in the artistic field? Do you remember drawing and creating a lot as a child?

I remember my mum saying she found a little picture of a bird drawn on the bathroom wallpaper, when I was three years old. I pretty much have always drawn, and would sit for hours drawing even as a small child. I entered every art competition at school and always seemed to do pretty well. I only ever wanted drawing stuff for Christmas; I would get new felt-tip pens and nice paper. I don't think I thought at school that I could become an artist for a career; I got told I could be a nurse or a secretary. I thought, bugger, I hate poo and vomit and I can't type. *(Laughs.)*

What was your initial exposure to the tattoo world, and when did you first add your own piece of ink to your skin? Was that a transformative time in your life?

I've always been into heavy metal bands and have ridden bikes, so tattoos have been around me for always. I went to get one when I was sixteen but the local parlor was closed, so I waited 'til I was eighteen. My boss did my first one after I had started my apprenticeship. I'm pretty much covered now so only get work done here and there.

What's it like being a female artist in a primarily male workplace?

It was pretty scary at first, always treated like you can't be very good 'cause you're a girl. But I have big balls and a big personality so I didn't let that stop me. It wasn't long before the likes of Kari Barba came along and made female tattoo artists more high profile.

In some ways being a girl made it easier as you weren't taken too seriously so there was less pressure. I was fortunate that at a lot of the competitions I did early on, I had a lot of

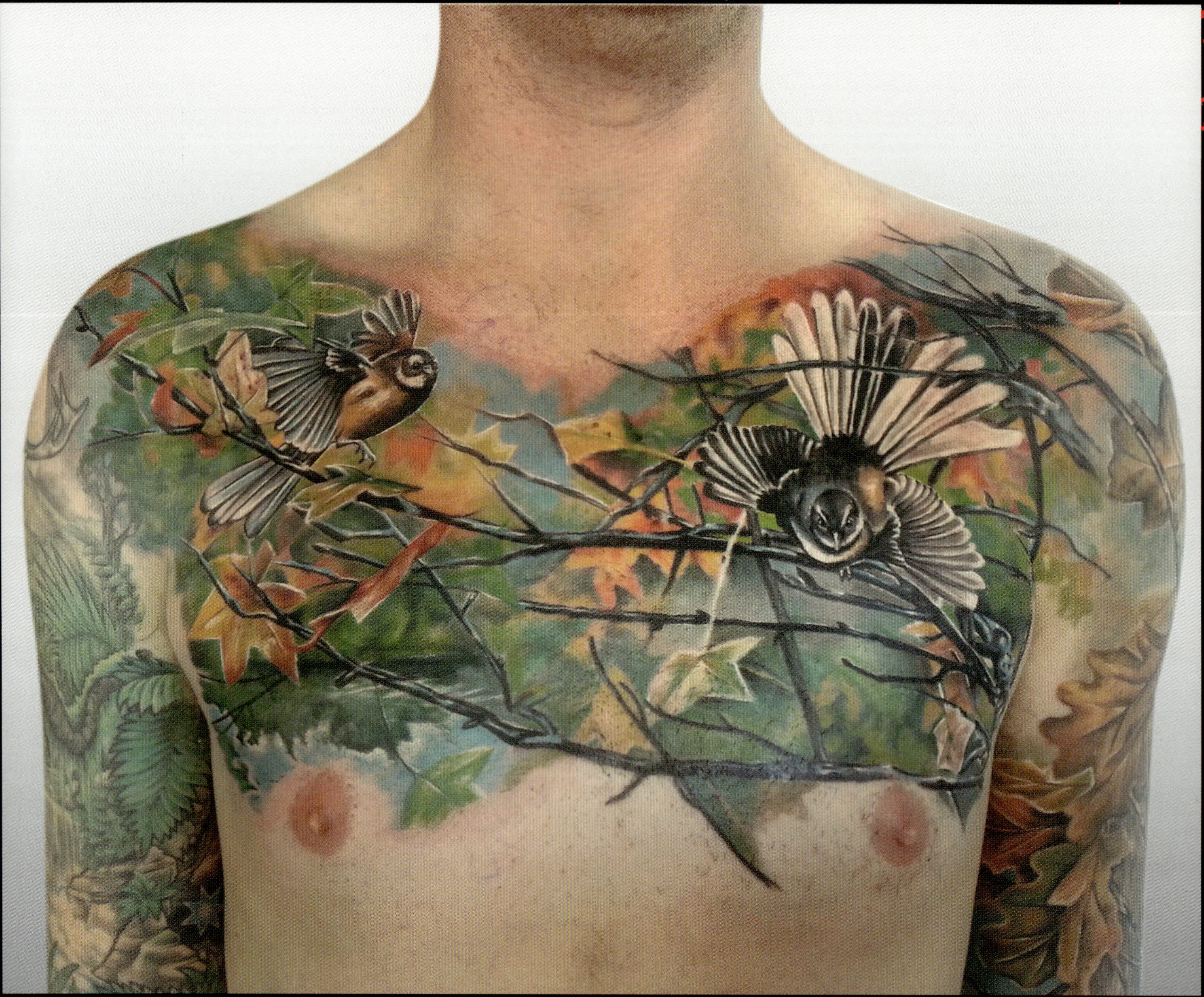

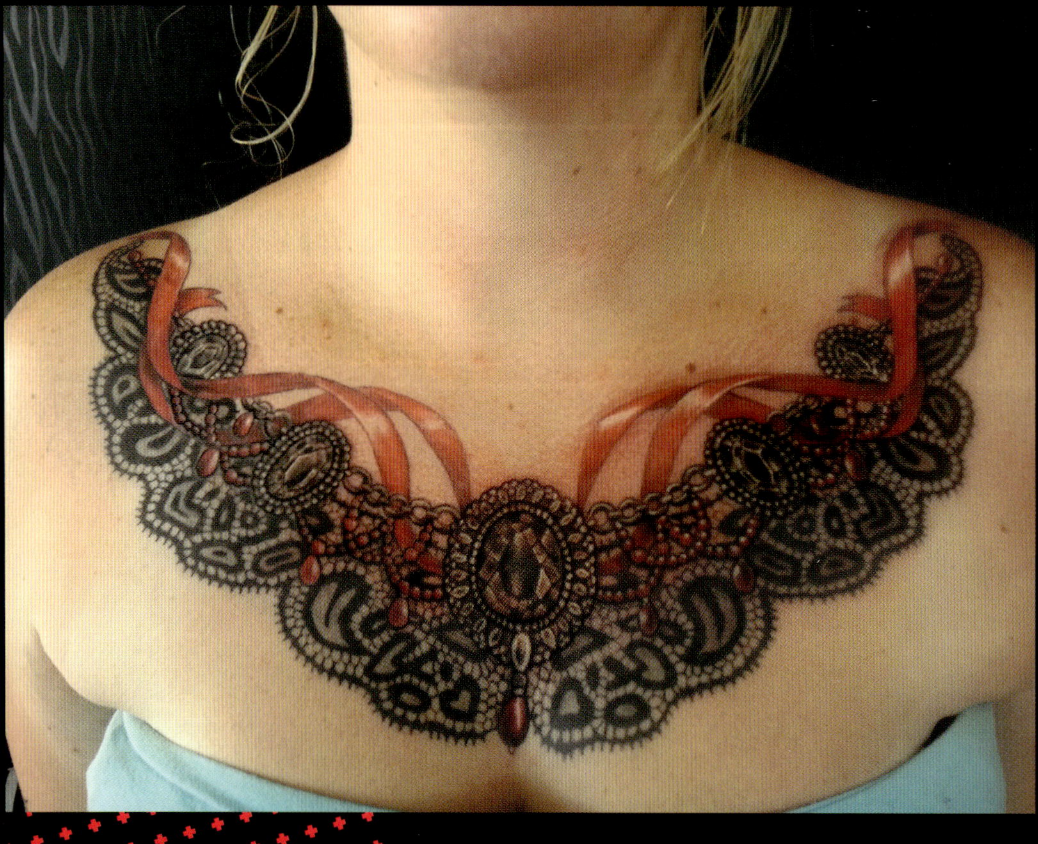

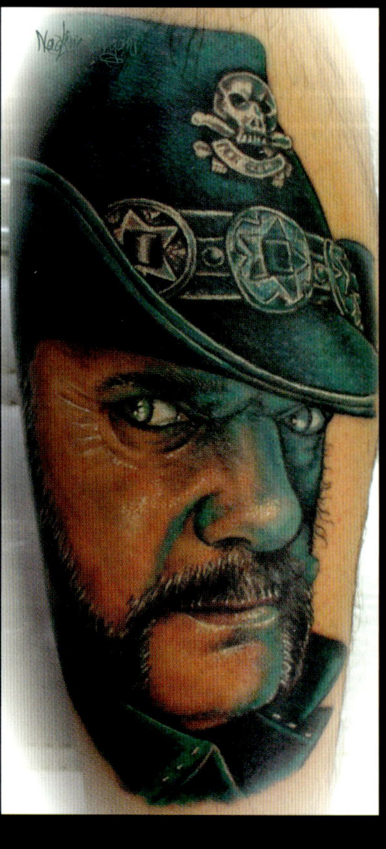

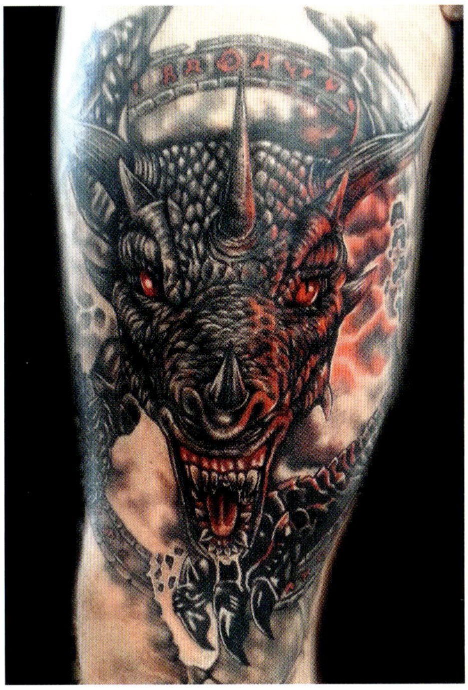

great clients who came along and competed for me. You soon get taken more seriously when you win a few things. And hey, we look better on the covers of mags. *(Laughs.)* Joke. I still think it's about quality of work. It has taken a turn for the ridiculous with some female tattoo artists being more about the rock-star attitude and look, and their work isn't really that good, but they are pretty so get on TV and in magazines. That sucks for ugly dudes who are great tattooists.

Do you feel that male customers treat you differently?

I think years ago some did; now I don't think it's a big deal. Sometimes I think guys prefer girl artists as they seem gentler. All tattoos hurt but sometimes I guess ladies have a gentler manner. Personally I don't think it matters as long as you pick your artist for the work.

What did your family and friends think about you getting into the business?

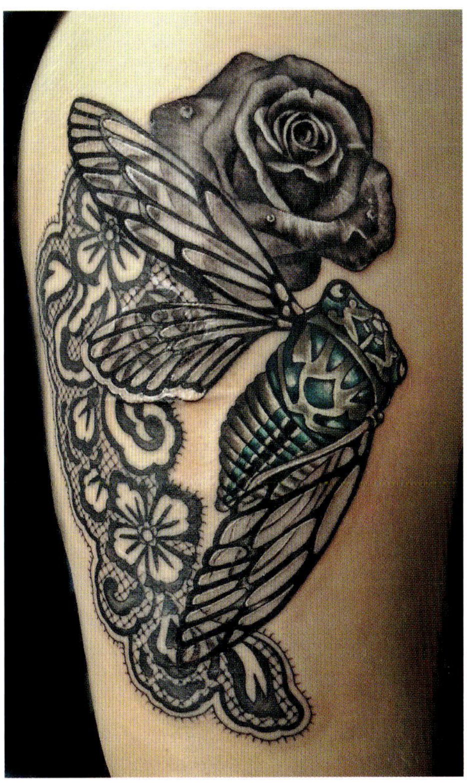

My mum was shocked, but after a while she could see that it's another art form, no different from painting. My friends love it as they are all musicians, etcetera. I think all my mates thought they would get tons of free tattoos. *(Laughs.)*

Tell me more about the shop you work at; what it's like working there?

I used to own a shop called Skinks in Hamilton, New Zealand. I owned that for twenty years, but the scene was getting more and more crazy, shops opening up everywhere every week. I was having my new son and my biological dad died, so I had a moment where I thought, what do I want to do. The shop was a lot of work and I wasn't getting to pick my work and was working six days a week with no holidays. So I sold the shop and put up a purpose-built studio on my three-acre block of heaven. So now I have my private studio right outside my home. I book appointments, usually only one or, at the most, two a day. I focus on a very intimate private service where the focus is the client and great quality tattoos. It's so much more relaxed, I see my family all day, and my clients get uninterrupted time. It's great.

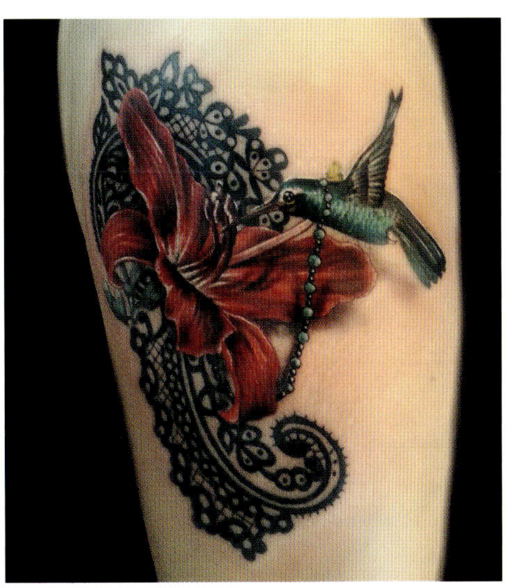

Describe how you go about creating a tattoo from concept to finished design. How do you try to put your own unique touch on your tattoos?

I usually get key points from the client, and talk about what we can get rid of if it's getting too busy with ideas, less is more, we talk about placement and flow. I then go away and get some basic research done, and then do a rough concept in pencil. I usually work the rest out on my Cintiq tablet so I don't have a hundred bits of paper.

What was the first tattoo you ever did? Can you tell me about it?

I redid a li'l logo on my ex; it was a little waiter who was the logo for a beer company, I was shaking so much I nearly cried. *(Laughs.)*

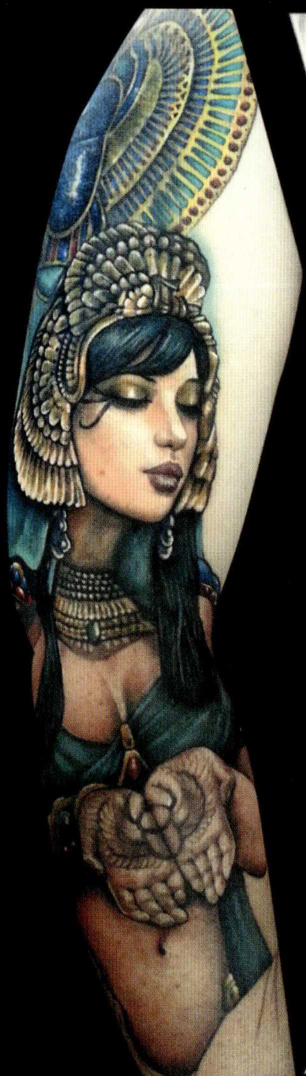
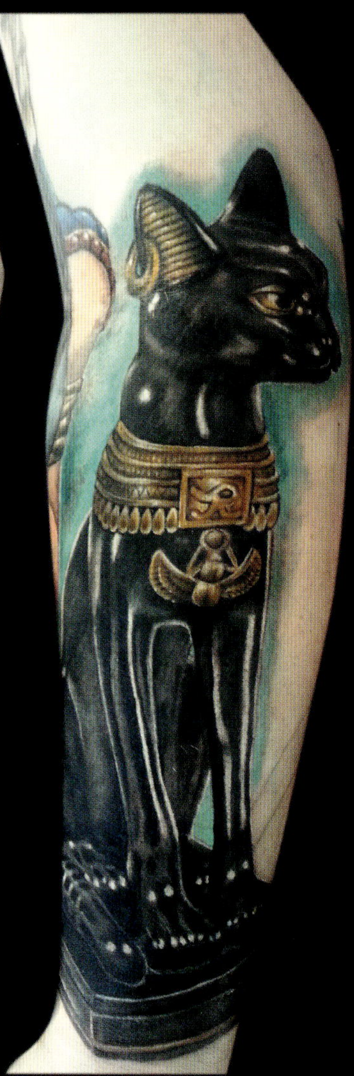
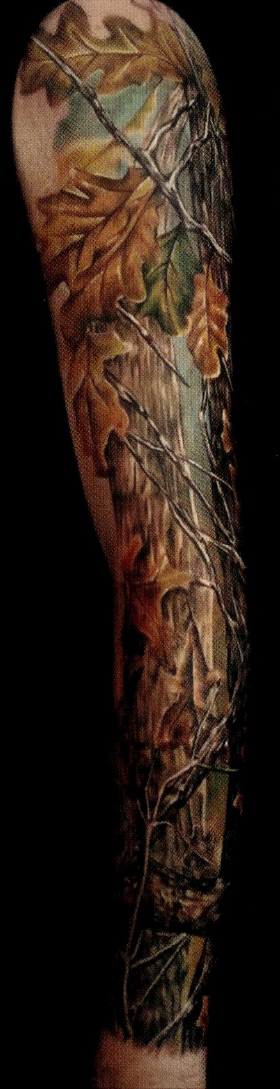
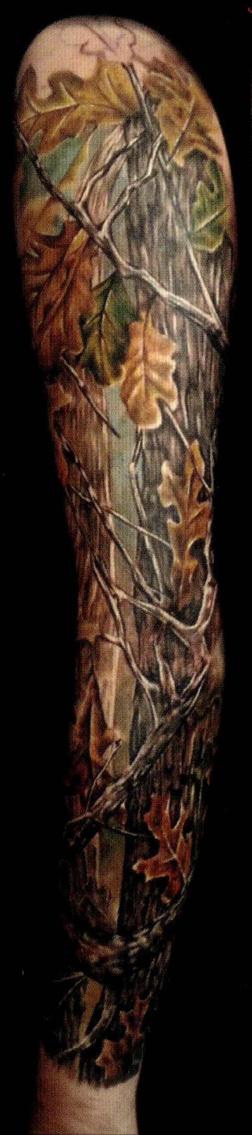
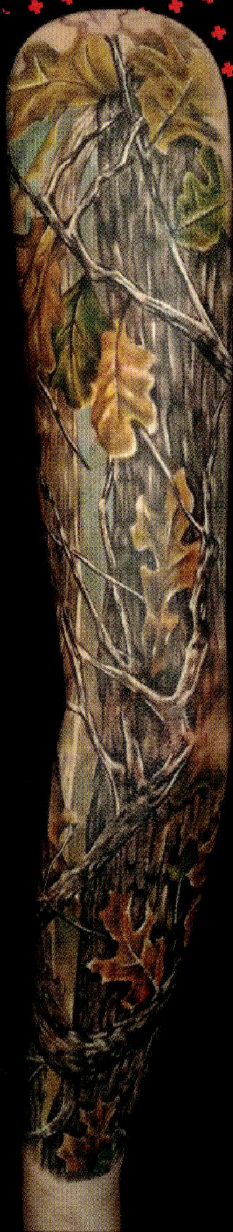
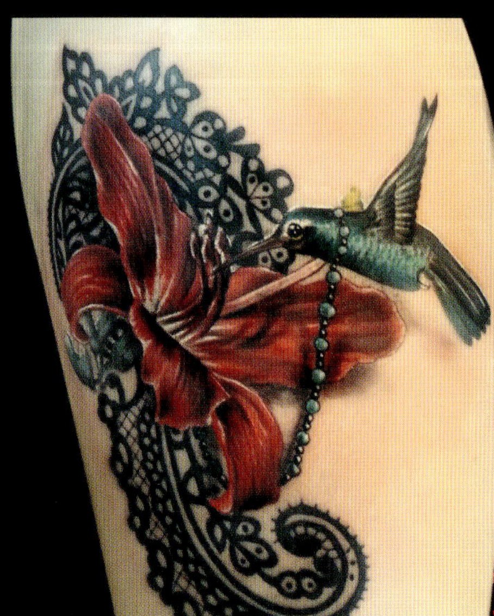
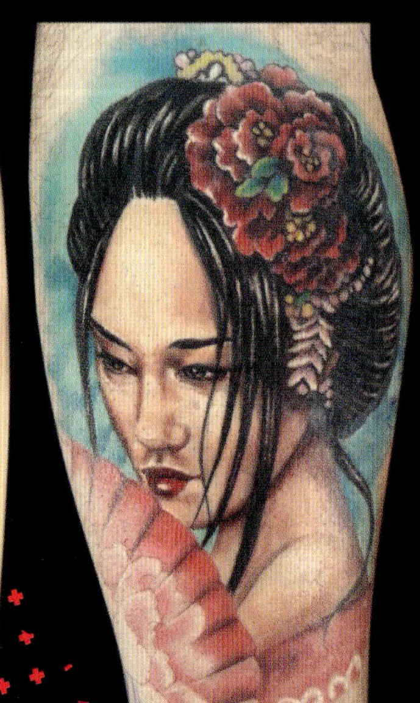
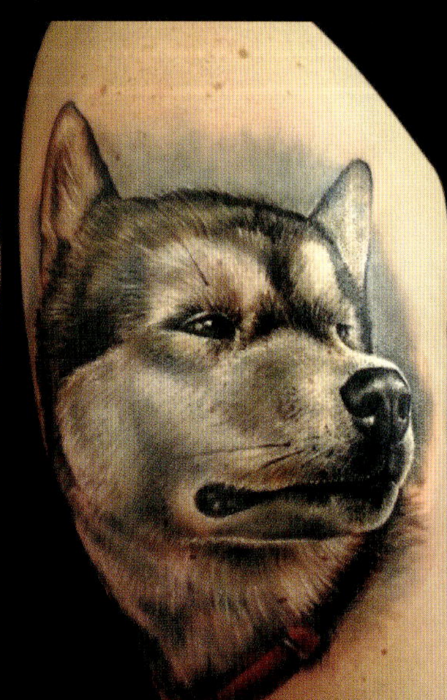

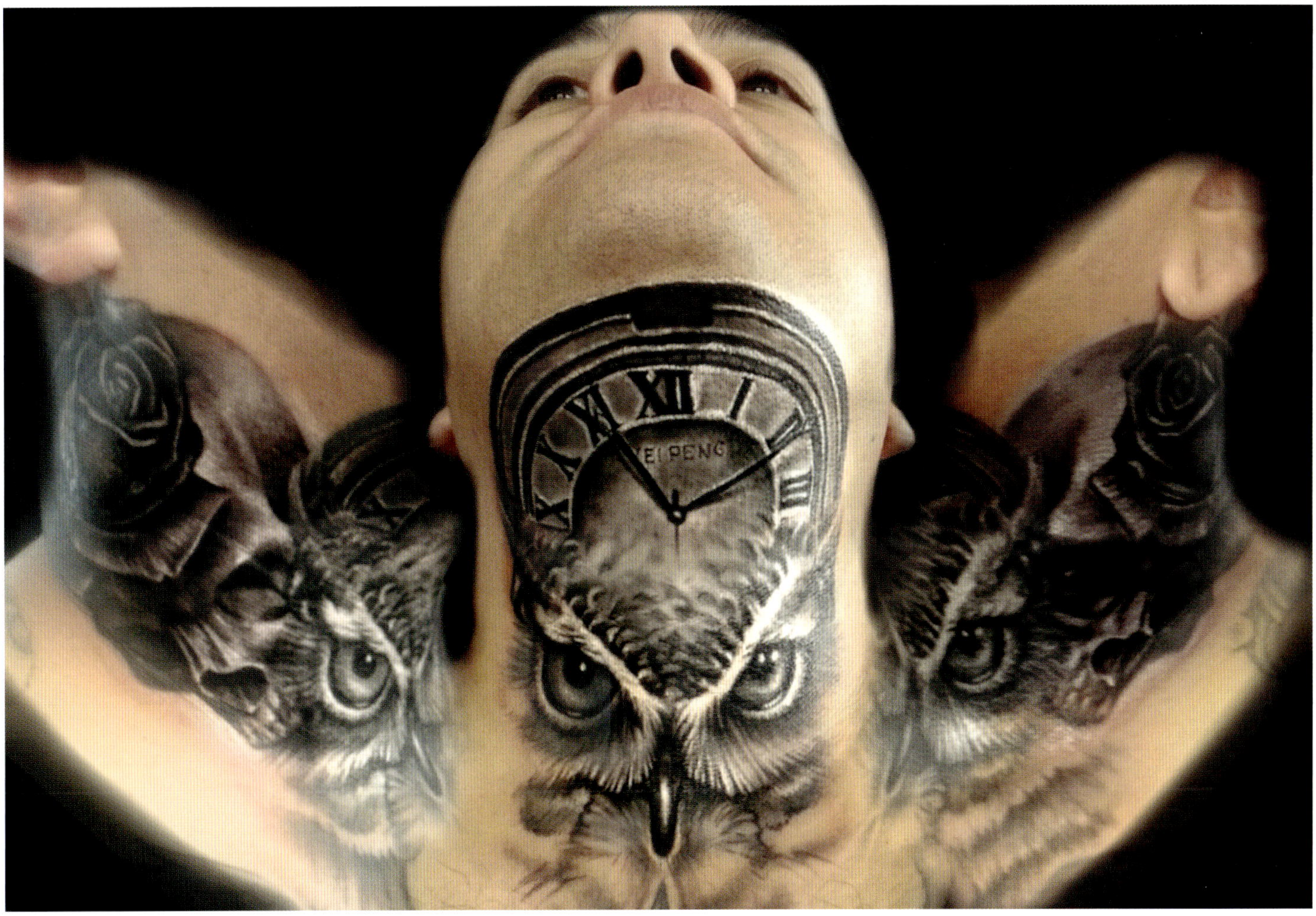

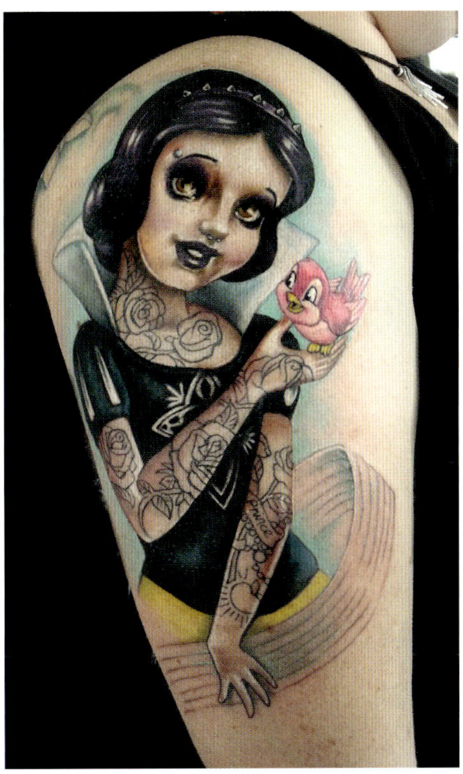

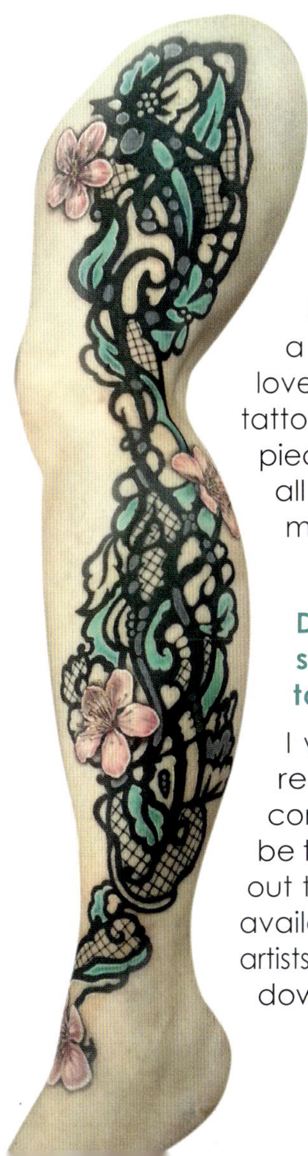

It came out okay but I realized then that it wasn't as easy as it looked. Thankfully I have a few years under my belt since then.

What is your favorite style of work to tattoo? What would your dream piece be to work on?

I'm really enjoying the feminine style I'm doing a lot of at the moment, with beads and lace. I love doing portrait work also, but realistically, I love tattooing anything. I don't know if I have a dream piece at the moment. Hmm, I do my dream tattoos all the time. I am always thinking, "Damn I need more arms." *(Laughs.)*

Describe how your role models and any other sources of inspiration have affected your tattoo style.

I was tattooing way before all these fantastic realistic artists came along. I would go to conventions and think, "Wow, one day I'm gonna be that good if I work hard." So many great artists out there before we had the amazing references available via the Internet. I really appreciate the artists that actually do their own thing, not just copying downloaded pictures. They are great too, but too

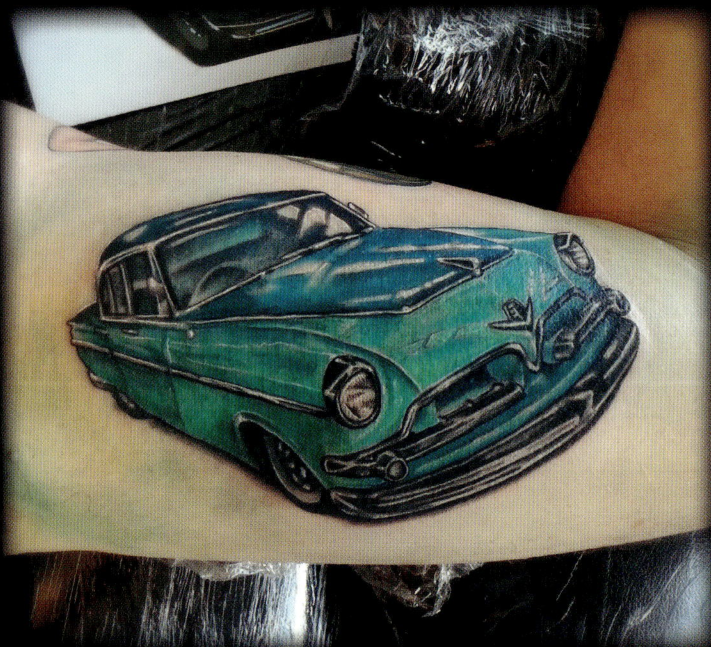

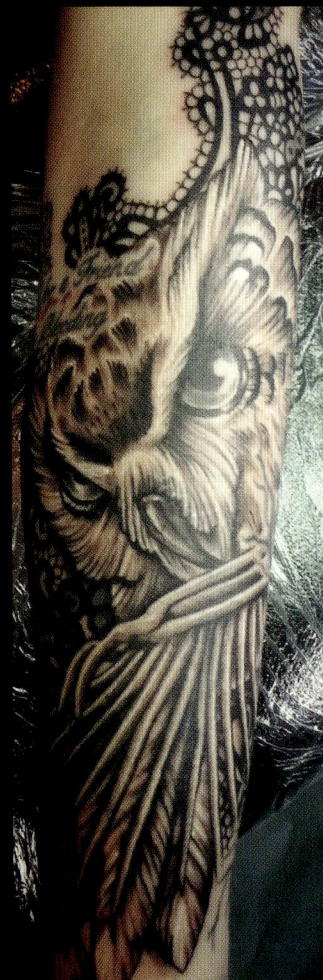

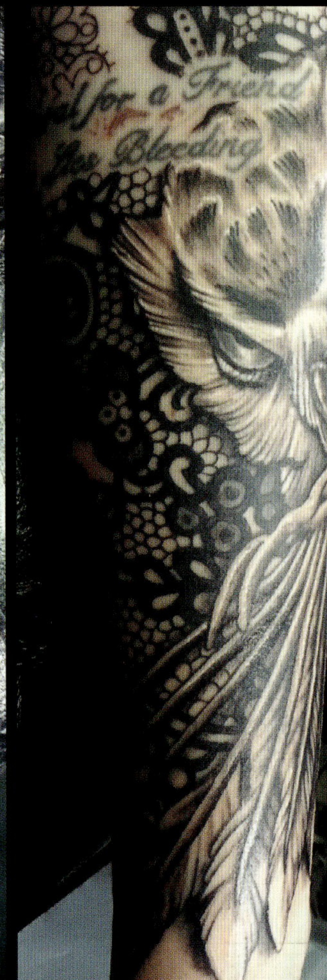

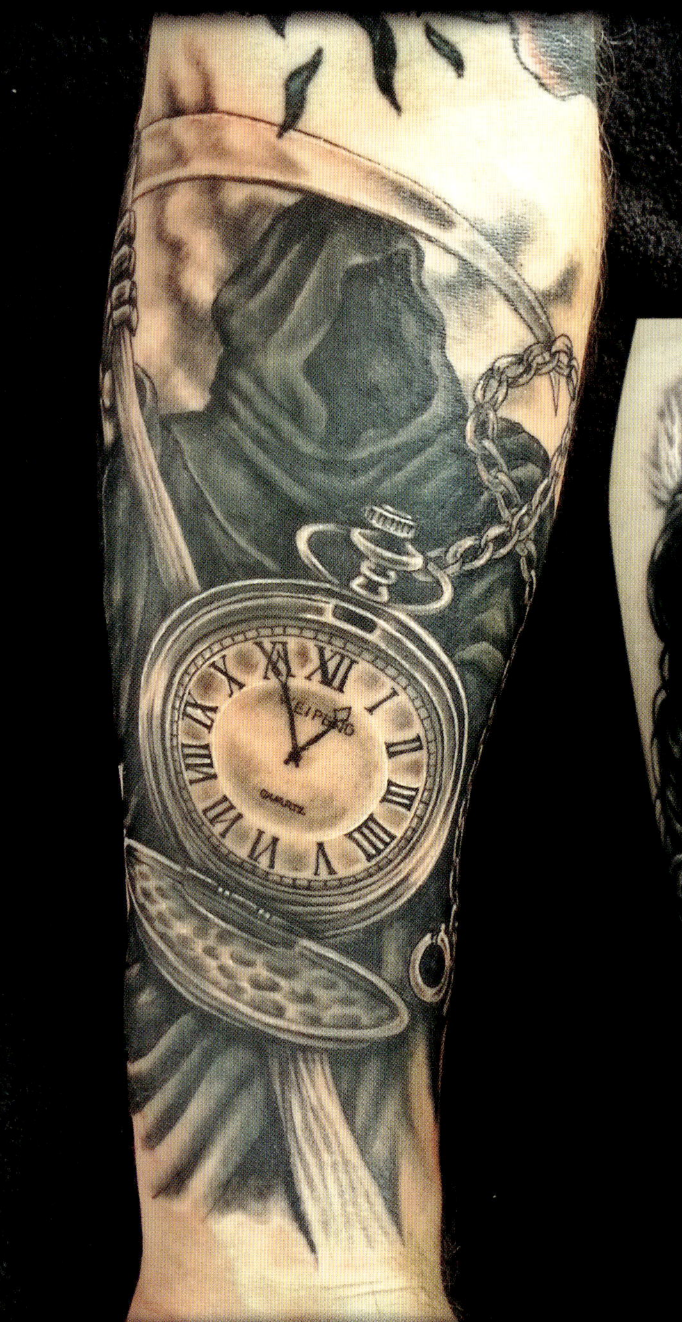

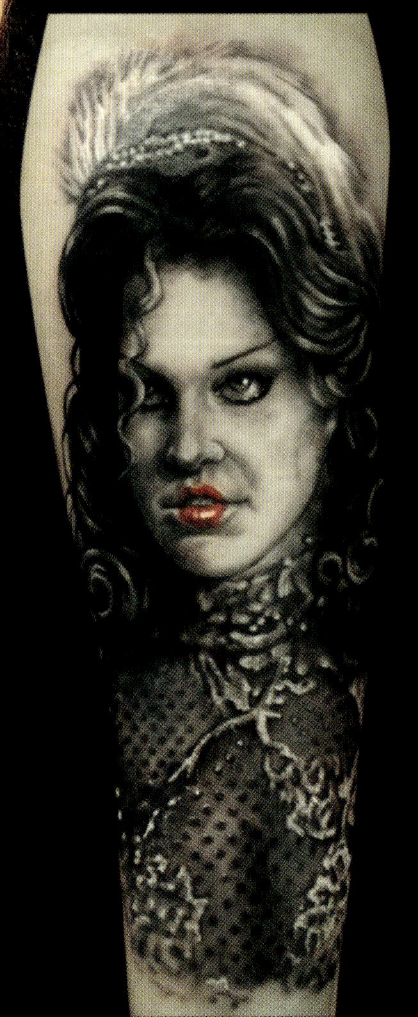

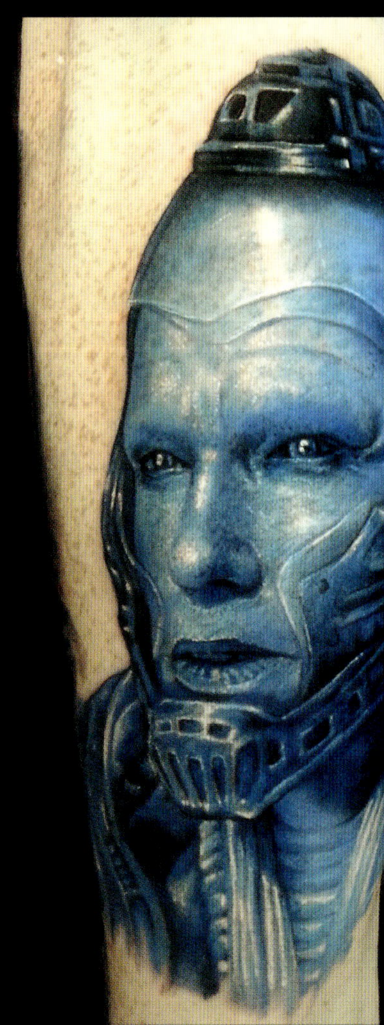

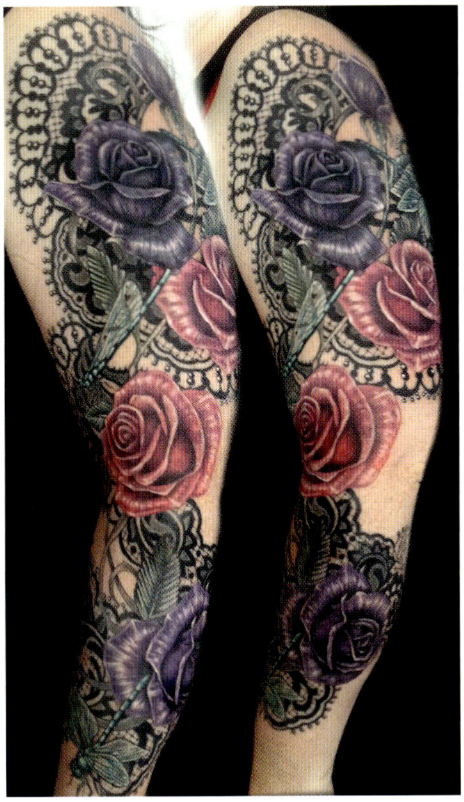

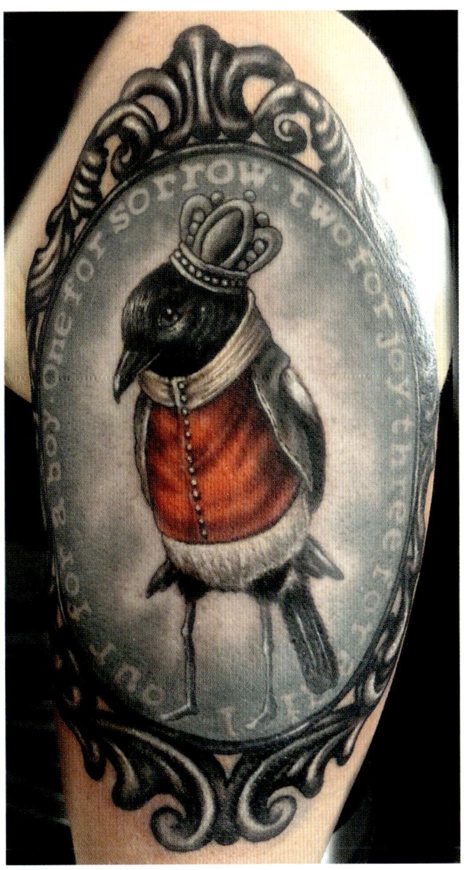

many artists get praised for literally just copying a picture. Nuthin' wrong with that but I think the creative process is more fun if you have done most of the work yourself.

What's one of your favorite pieces that you've tattooed on someone else?

I did a Black Label Society back job on my friend Craig who got Zakk Wylde to sign it, we tattooed that on as well, I love that band so that was rad. I tattooed Mr. Freeze the other day too, and heaps of people gave me shit about Arnold Schwarzenegger being a terrible Mr. Freeze. *(Laughs.)* I love that tattoo.

What's one of your favorite pieces on your own body, and who did it?

My daughter is on my hand, I did that one. She is my inspiration, she is such a wonderful human, she keeps me humble and is one of my best friends. Hopefully she will follow in my footsteps.

What is your favorite thing about being a tattoo artist?

The rippin' and tearing and the wild wild women. *(Laughs.)* No, seriously, I've made some of the coolest friendships through my job. I am so privileged and blessed to be able to use my art every day to make others happy and get paid.

Do you have a funny tattoo story?

I have a penis tattooed under my arm…I enjoy asking people if they want to see it.

You have built up such a loyal clientele. What is your waiting list like right now and what is the best way for a collector to make an appointment with you?

I am usually booked solid for a minimum of six months ahead. It would probably be worse but I usually cut off bookings when it gets that far, so I can plan ahead for time off. The best way to reach my booking agent is nadinebryant666@gmail.com. At the moment I'm working six days a week so I do my best to keep up with demand.

How would you describe the current status of tattoos among the general public in New Zealand?

Tattoos are popular in New Zealand. Unfortunately it's difficult to educate the public in seeking out quality tattoo artists that are good and safe. A lot of the time the Kiwi way is "the cheaper the better and if you can swap anything for beer even better." I'm glad I don't drink beer. *(Laughs.)* I really don't understand when someone shows you a patchy blowout back-to-front map of New Zealand and says, "Yeah it only cost me ten dollars." *(Laughs.)* Well, good.

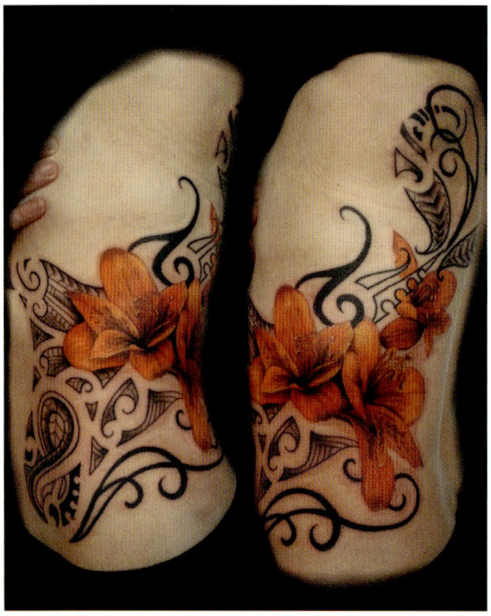
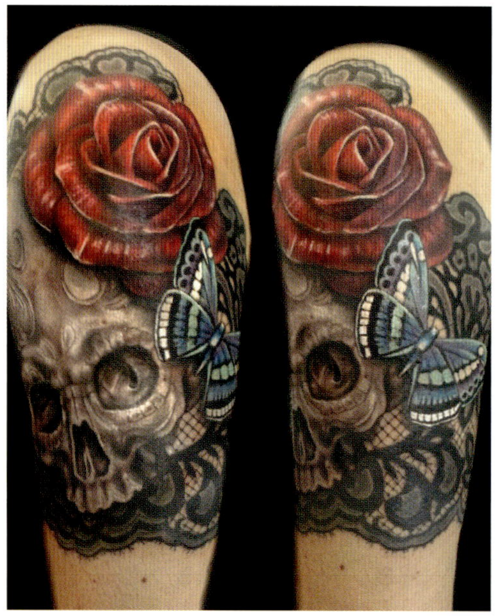
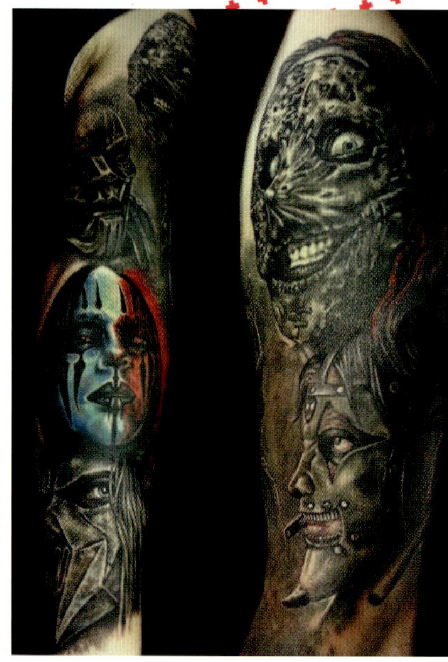
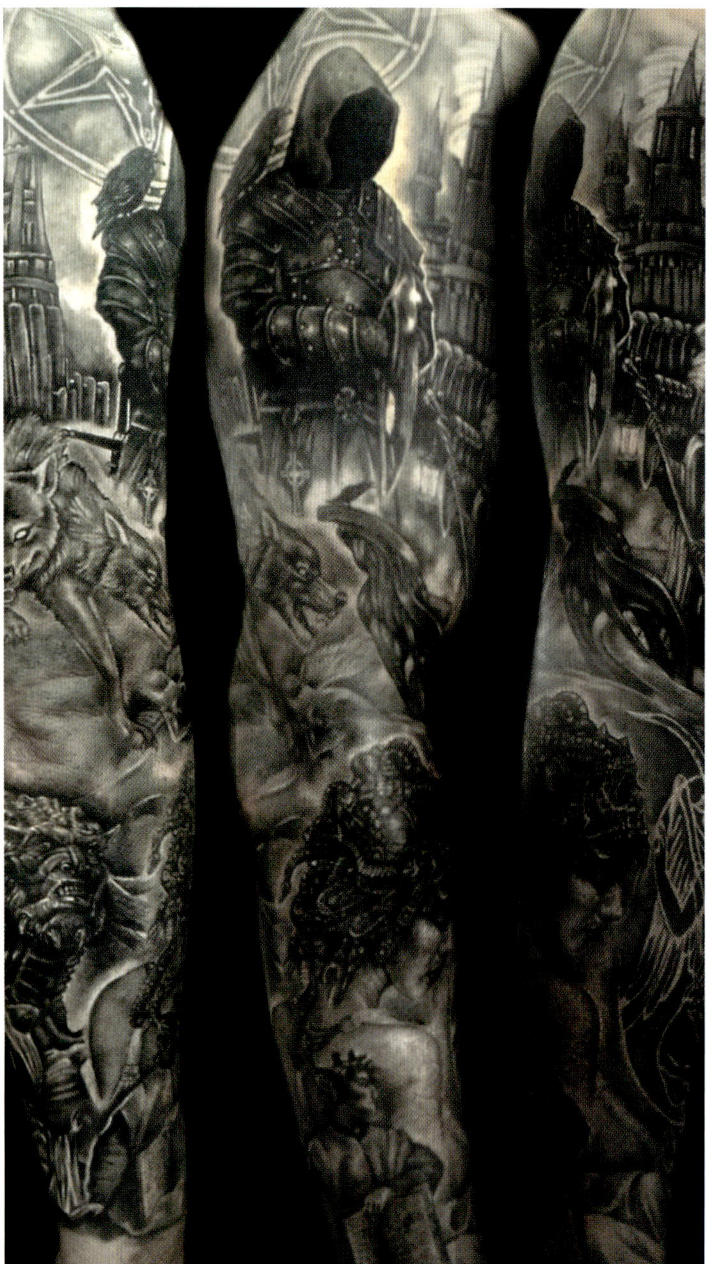
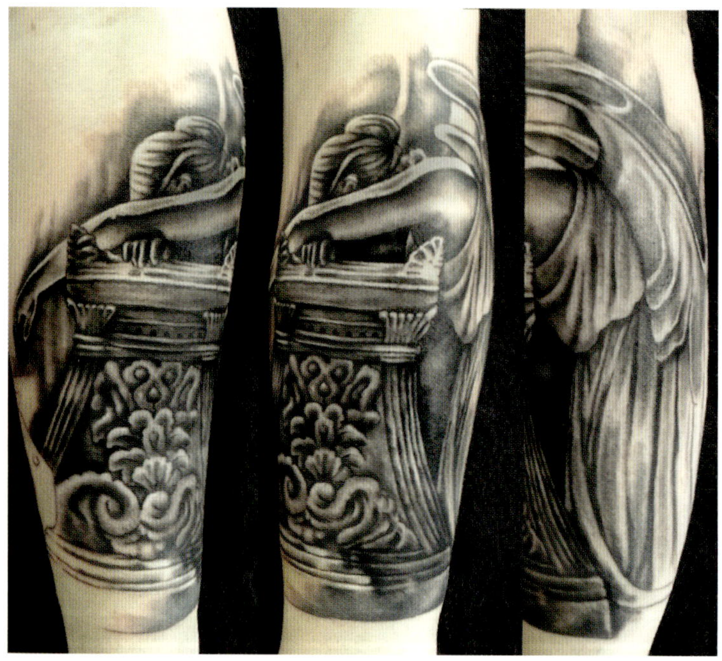
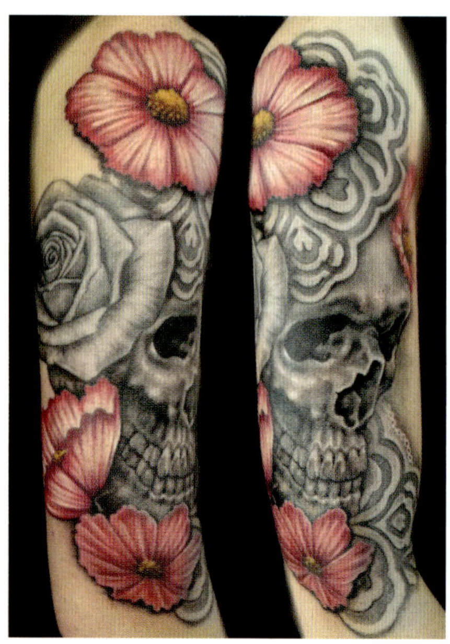
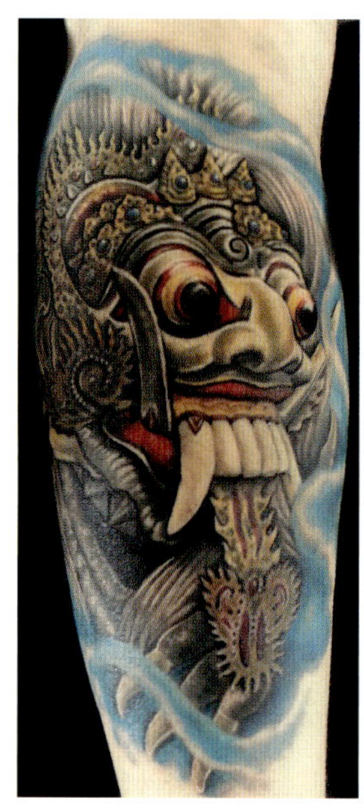

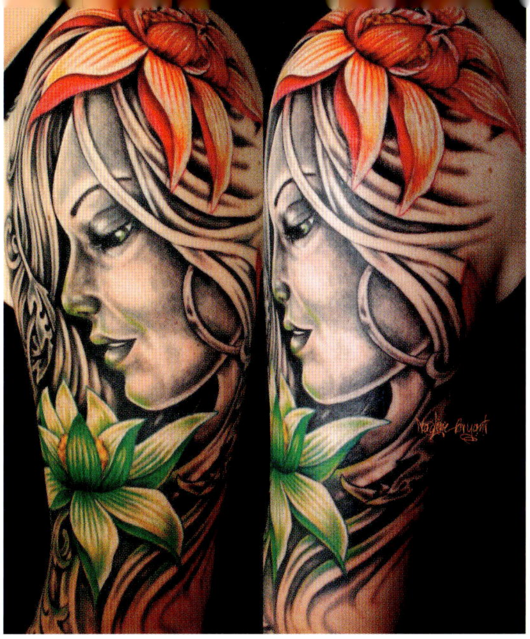

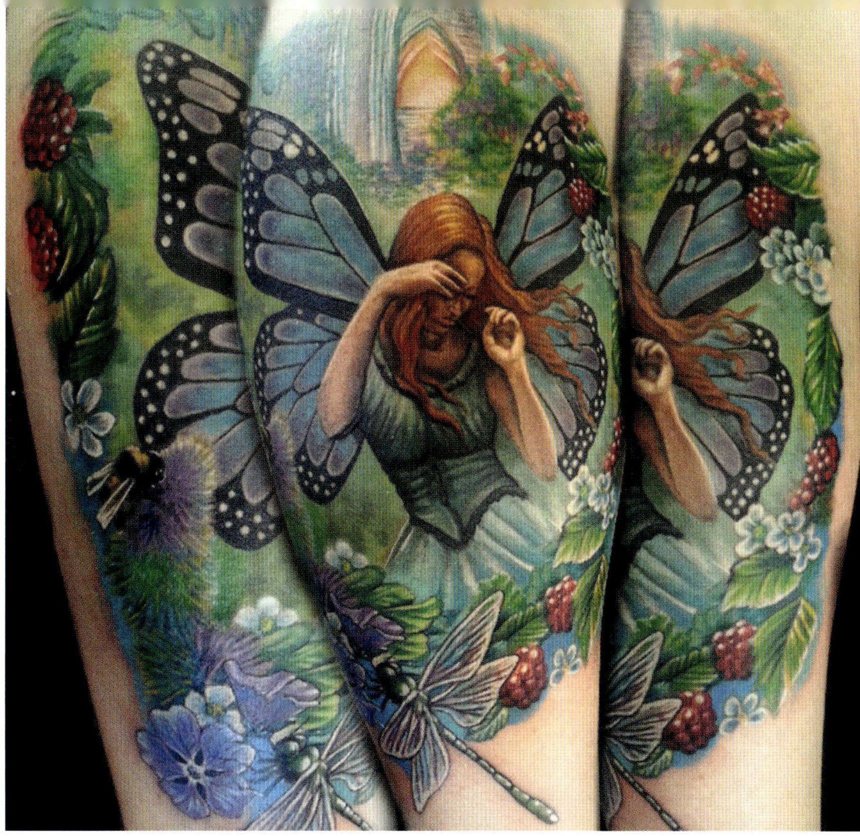

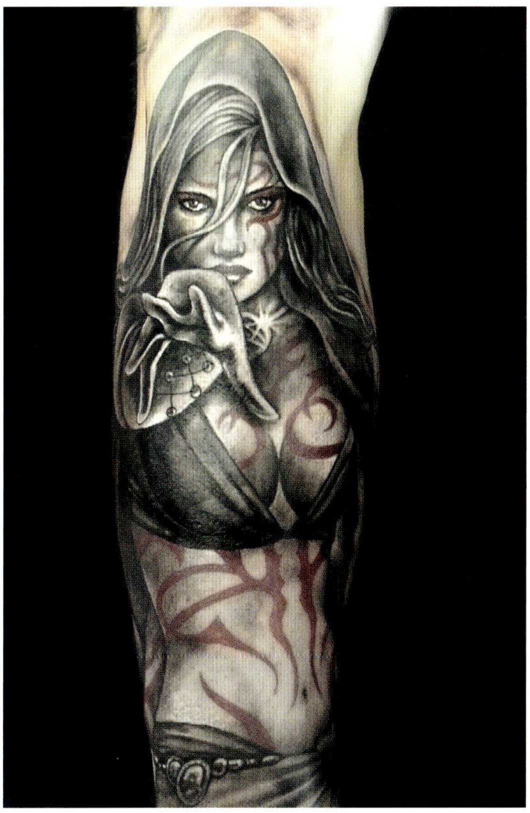

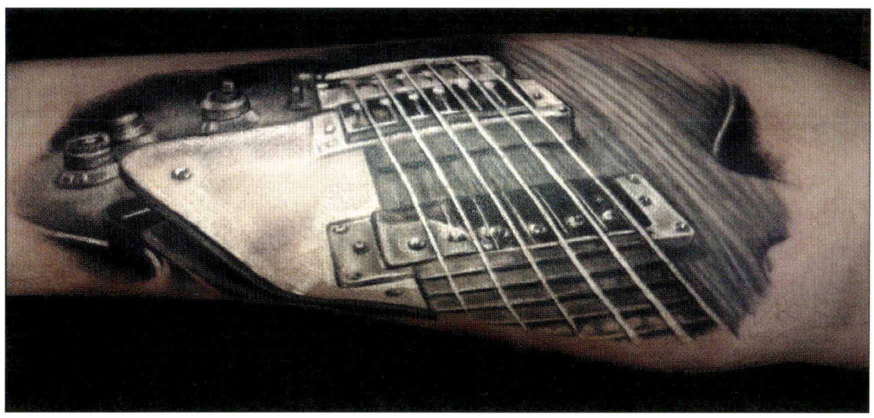

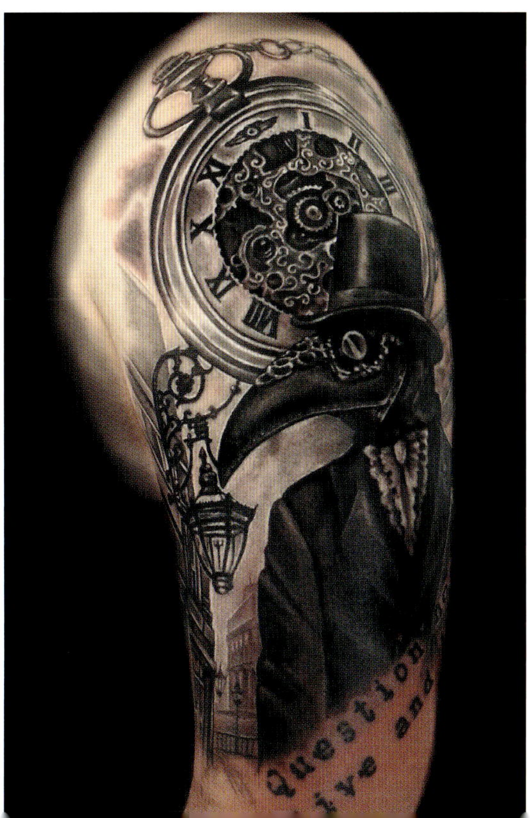

TV shows, Internet, and especially social networks like Facebook and Twitter have come to have an extremely wide influence in recent years. What positive and negative impacts do you think it has for the future development of the tattoo industry?

Everyone is or wants to be or knows a tattooist now. Equipment is easy to get, though it's usually substandard. Everyone thinks they know better than a professional.

I saw a post on Facebook recently asking for someone to go and tattoo a girl at her house. She said she didn't want to go to a studio but asked for anyone who was good to contact her. She had posted up before that that her dog was back from the vet's after suffering from parvovirus. An artist commented, saying she was crazy asking for someone to put her at risk by tattooing her at her house, and no quality artist would accept. She left abusive comments after. That pretty much sums up what TV and social media have done to the tattoo world, though people are equally quick to blame a tattoo artist for problems after. I had so many people wander into the shop after *Miami Ink* started and get angry because you couldn't draw them a sleeve while they waited, or tattoo it in two hours. I would love to see a show based on the actual reality of tattooing.

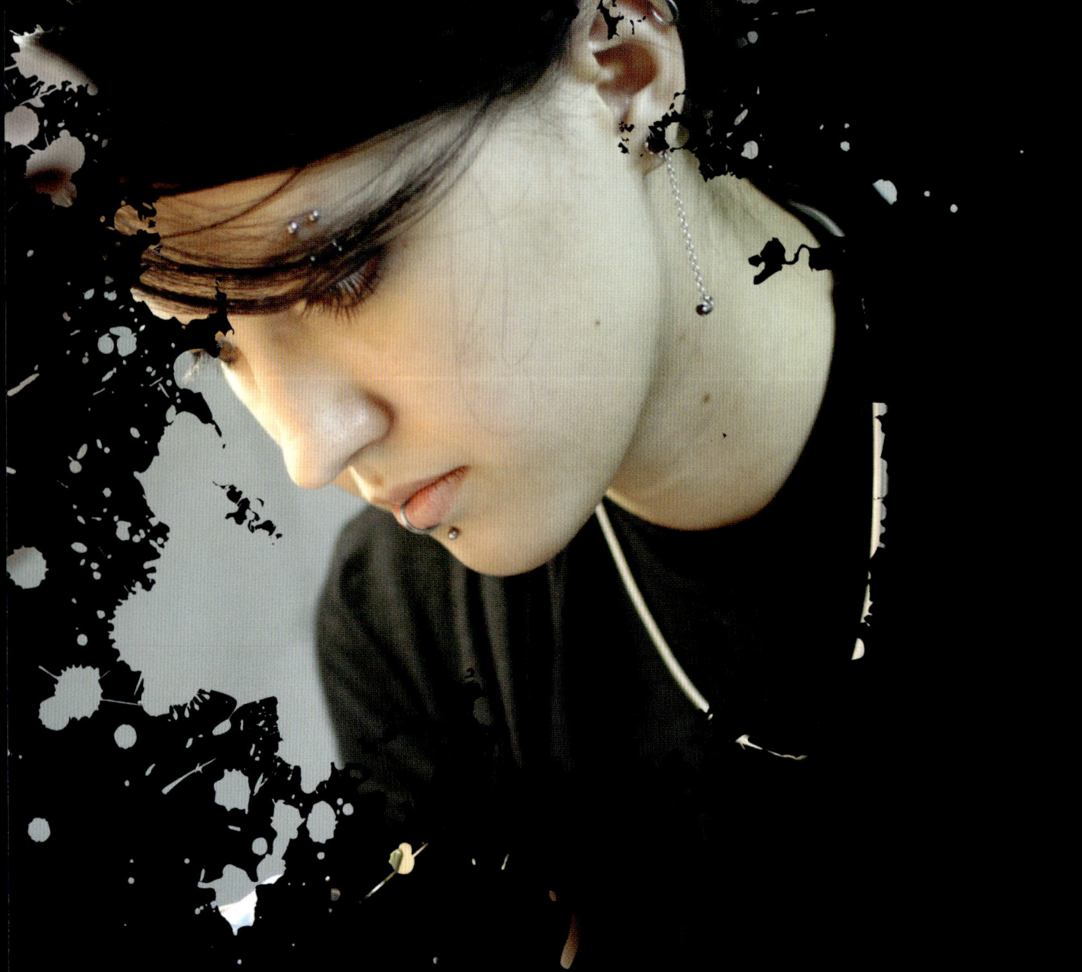

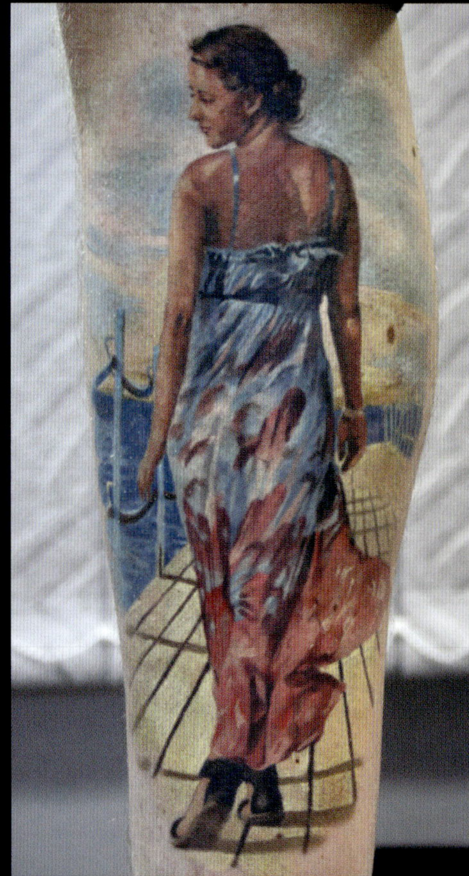

Katerina MIKKY

KATERINA MIKKY VOLKOVA, a tattoo artist from Moscow, Russia, started tattooing when she was sixteen. And only a few years later she became one of the most talented female realistic tattoo artists of her country.

"I didn't have a particular dream of becoming a tattoo artist"

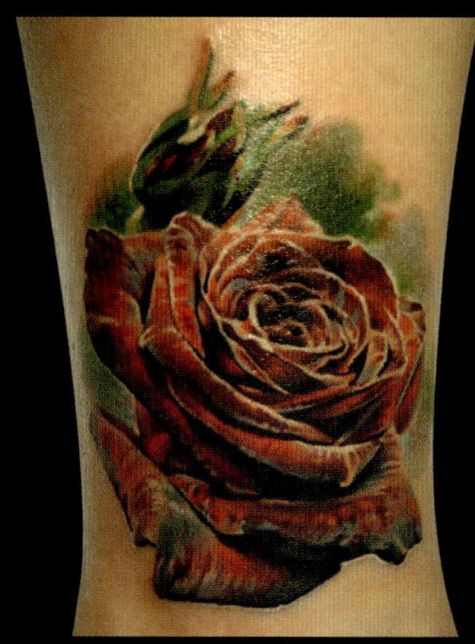

mikky-tattoo.ru
www.facebook.com/tattoo.mikky

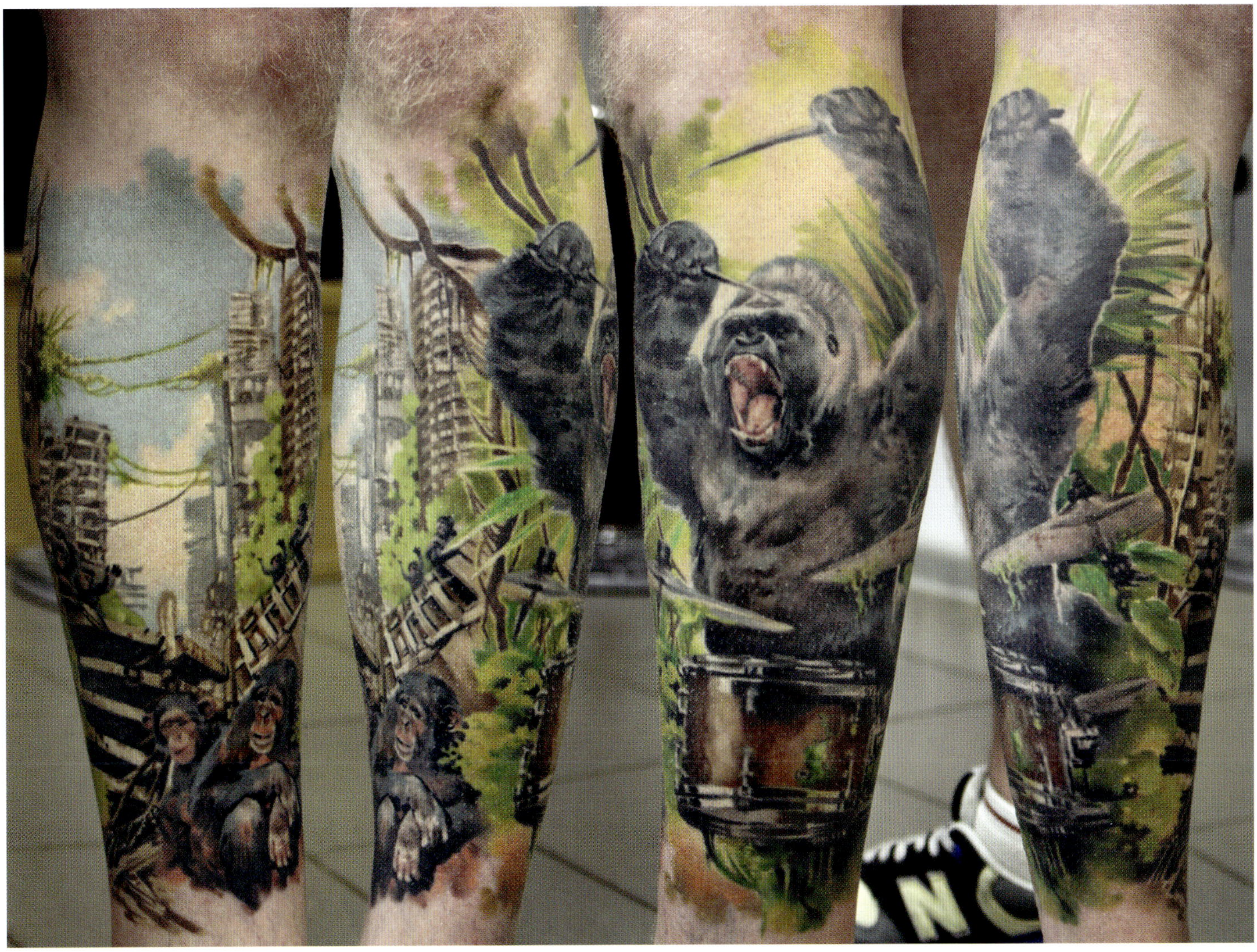

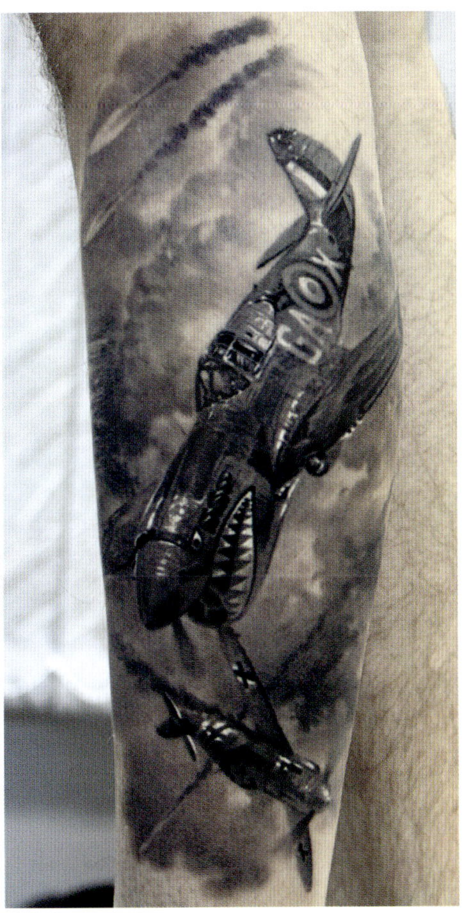

What made you want to become a tattoo artist and how long have you been tattooing?

I've been doing tattoos since the autumn of 2005. I didn't have a particular dream of becoming a tattoo artist. What I'm doing, tattooing—it's just coincidence.

Where did you learn to tattoo? Did you have a formal apprenticeship? If so, can you tell me about this time in your life and how it prepared you for all that you do now?

There was a tattoo studio that opened next to the college where I studied. I decided to go and find out whether they'd accept me for training. Of course it was not a tattoo "course," there was no formal training with a diploma or certificate. They just let me be an apprentice there, with the proviso that I buy my equipment myself. So in the autumn of 2005 I went to study there, and I worked there for six years.

What's it like being a female artist in a primarily male workplace?

It was only hard at the beginning. Very few of the customers were willing to get a tattoo from a young girl, especially when there was a tattoo master in the same studio. But once there is a

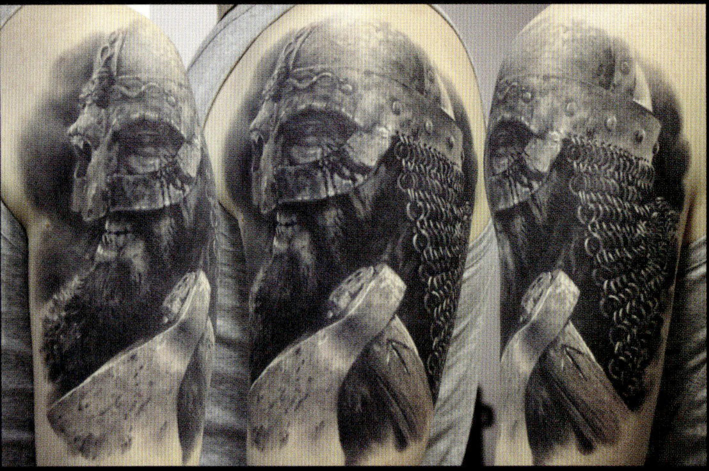

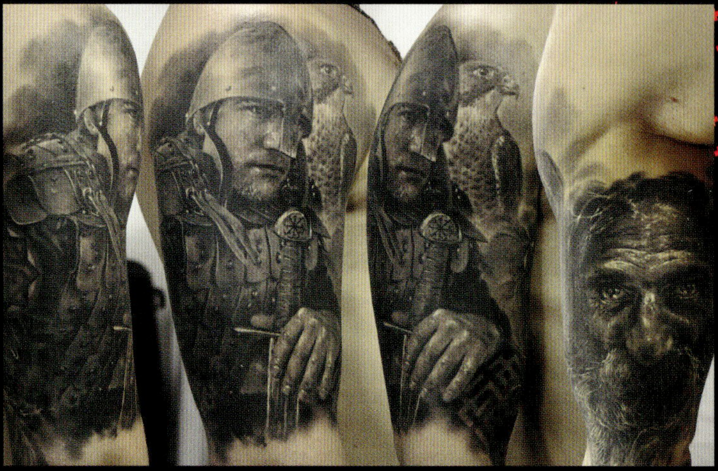

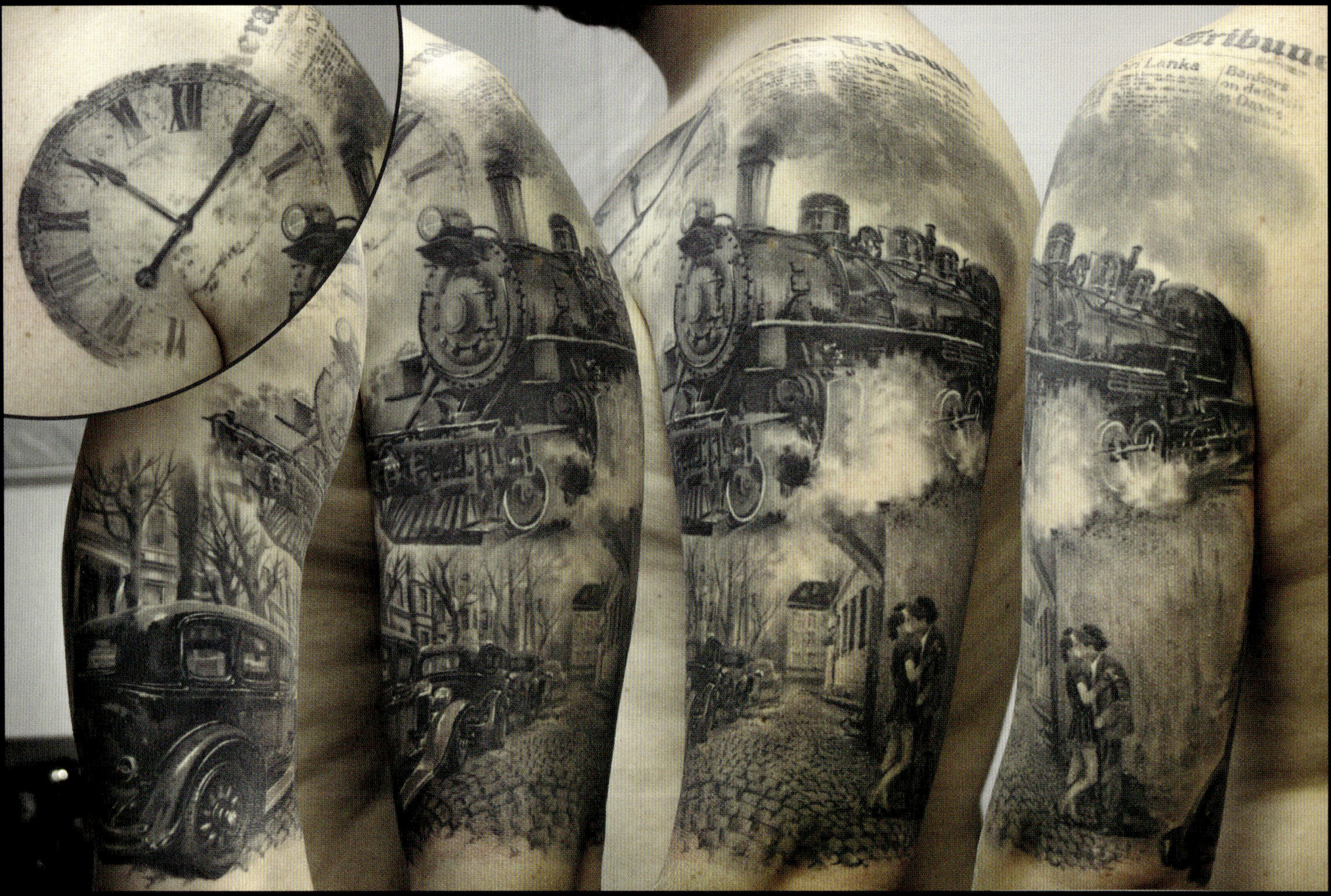

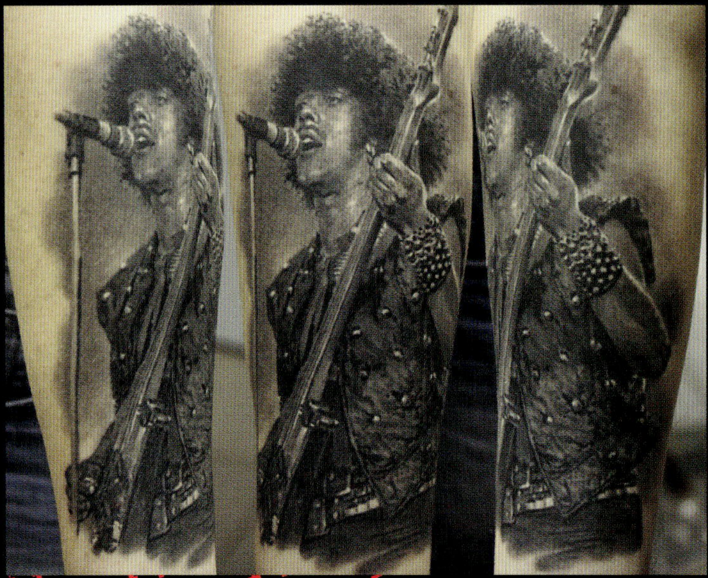

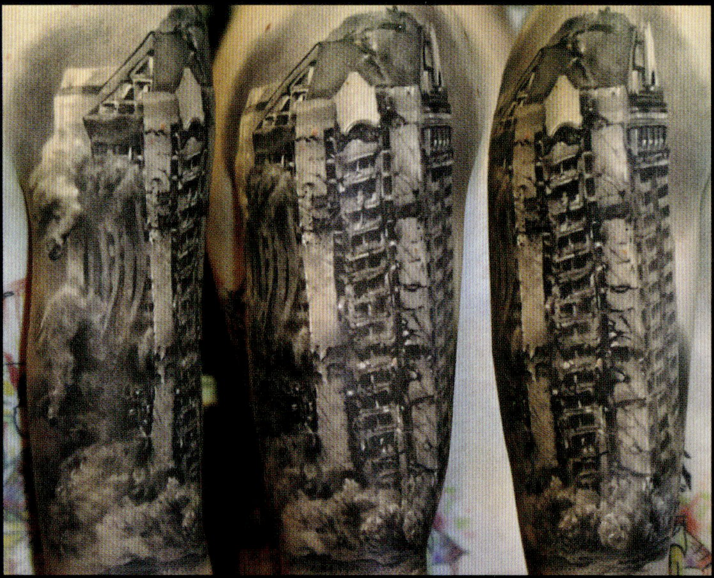

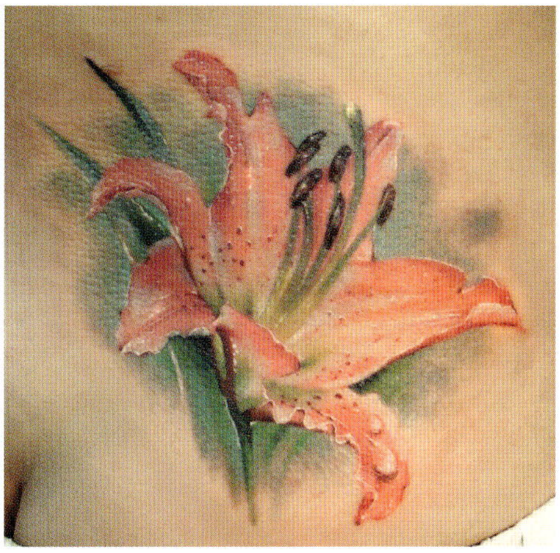

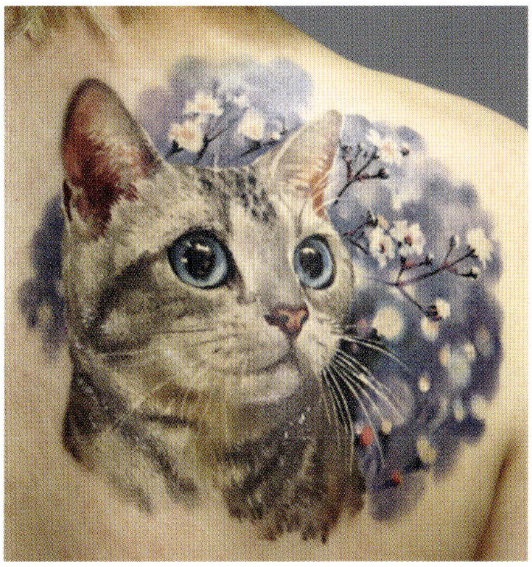

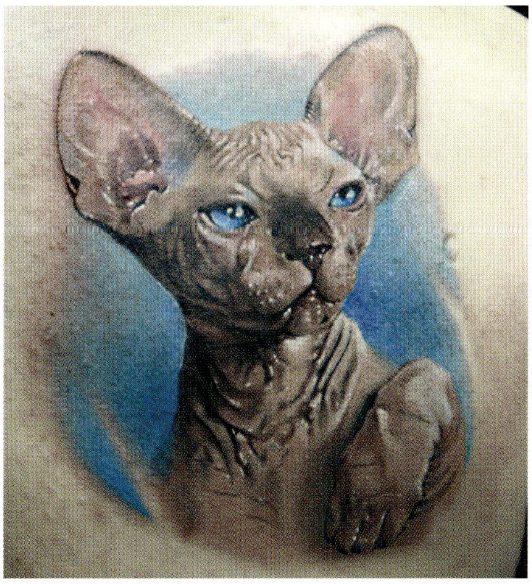

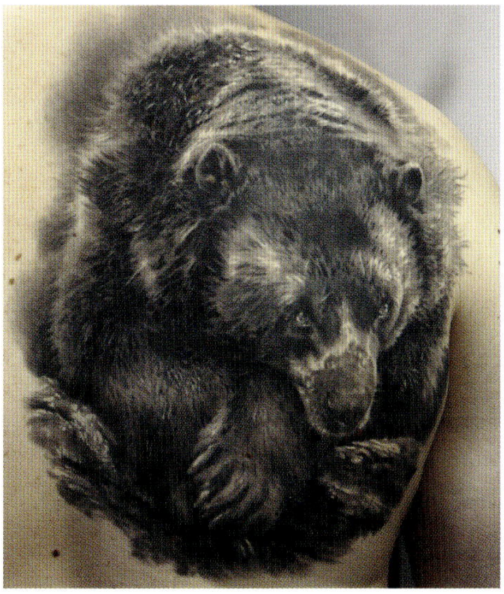

portfolio, being a girl starts to be a plus—it adds interest to the master himself. Also, many female customers are just very shy about undressing in front of a male tattooist.

Do you feel that male customers treat you differently?

I'm pretty selective about my customers so I didn't have any problems with that. If they think of me in a different way, they don't show it.

What did your family and friends think about you getting into the business?

At first they thought it was just a hobby, not serious, and something that's impossible to make a living at. Of course now the situation is different, but there's still the view out there that the work of a tattoo artist is very easy. Let me just clarify something that is still a big problem in Russia for tattoo artists. Only about ten or fifteen years ago, tattoos were distributed only in prisons and the criminal world. Tattooing as a form of art didn't exist back then. And despite the fact that the situation in our country today has changed a lot, the older generation does not view the tattooing profession seriously, and some even openly disapprove of it.

Do you have your own shop?

I only worked in a tattoo studio for six years. Then I decided to work for myself, as a private tattoo artist. I don't have my own shop. In Russia it's very difficult to open a tattoo studio—a huge number of problems with documents, permits, and authorities—so only a few artists decide to open their own shops. So I have my own space in a beautiful shop, because this way is much easier for me.

Describe how you go about creating a tattoo from concept to finished design. How do you try to put your own unique touch on your tattoos? How would you describe your style? And which tattoo style do you like best?

I think that I can relate all my works to one style: realism. The basic idea of realism is moving a photographic image onto the body in a way that's as close as possible to the original, or at least to use a photo as the foundation. So I can't say that I have my own style of tattooing. The concept and composition is designed only for large tattoos—usually it's a collage of different photos, collected with the participation of the client.

What was the first tattoo you ever did? Can you tell me about it?

I did my first tattoo for a friend. It was a black-and-gray fly. It was very ugly. A few years later I covered it with a bat.

Describe how your role models and any other sources of inspiration have affected your tattoo style.

I don't want to say that I only like realism, but for me, the most interesting thing is to do exactly realistic works. I like to look at tattoos in different styles, but it doesn't interest me to draw them.

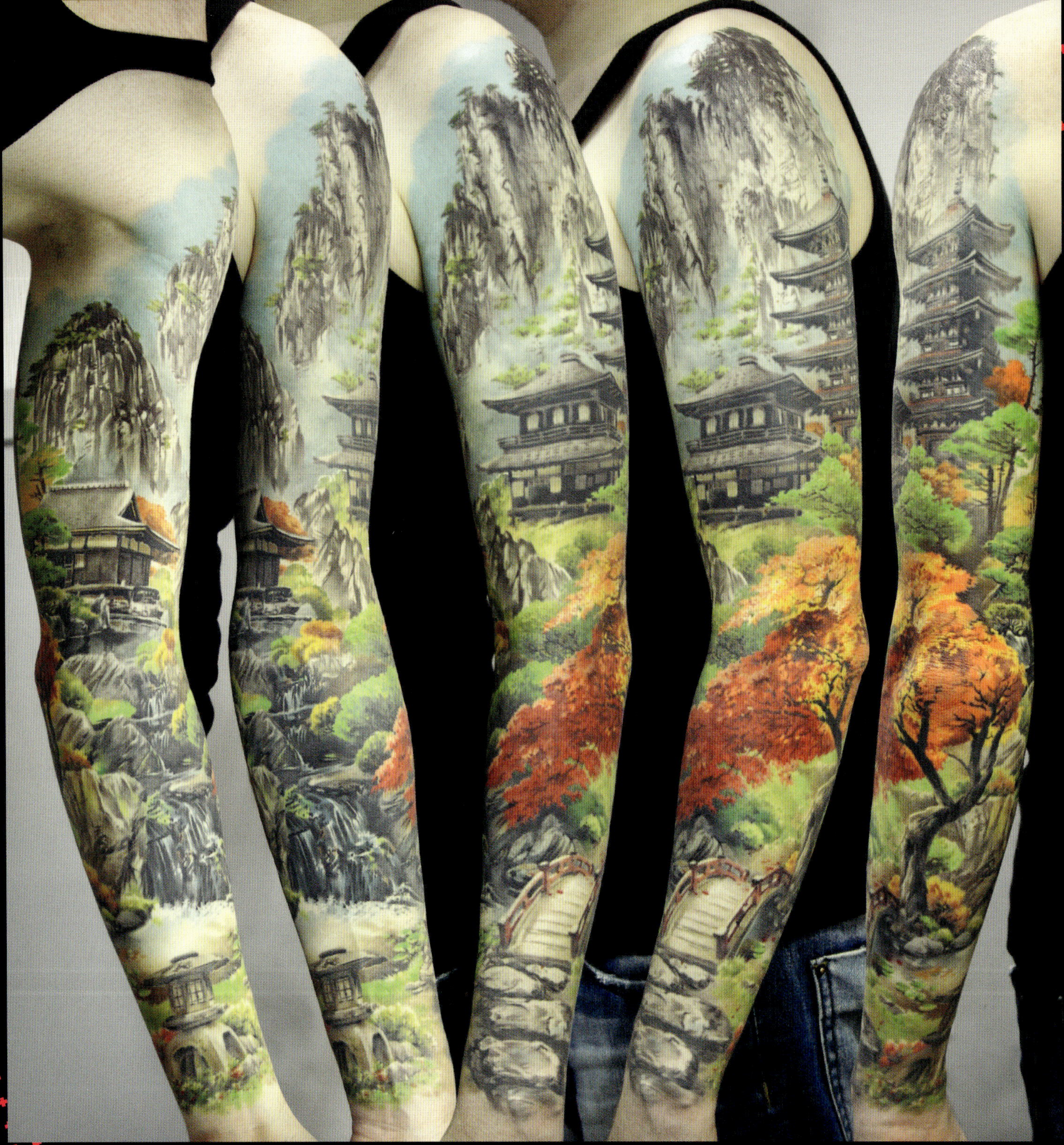

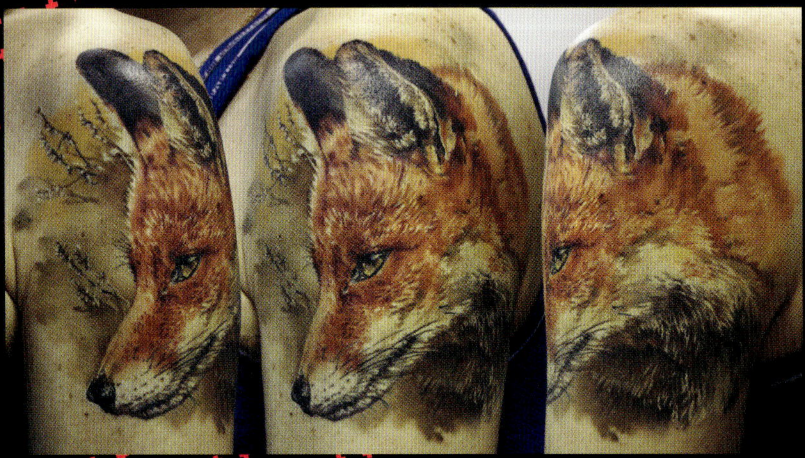

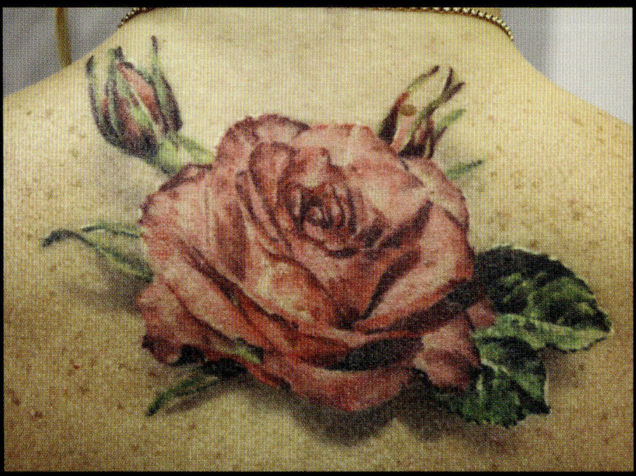

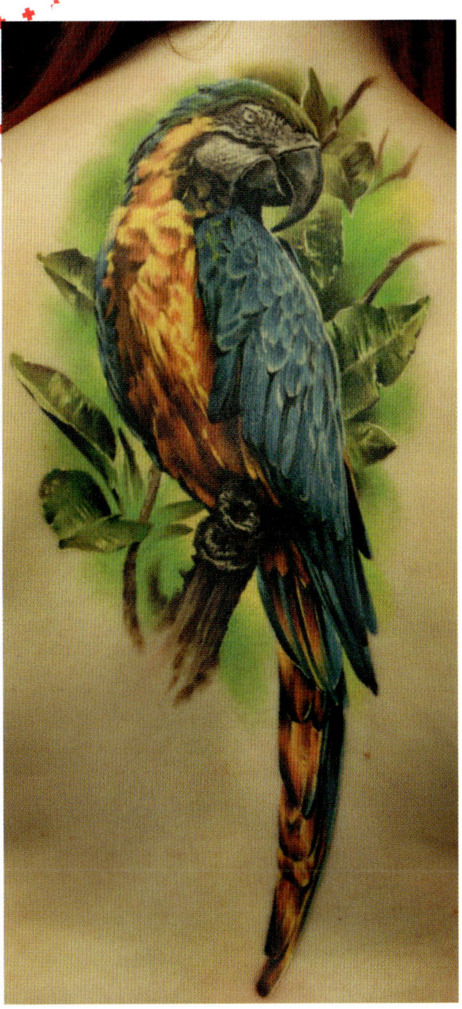

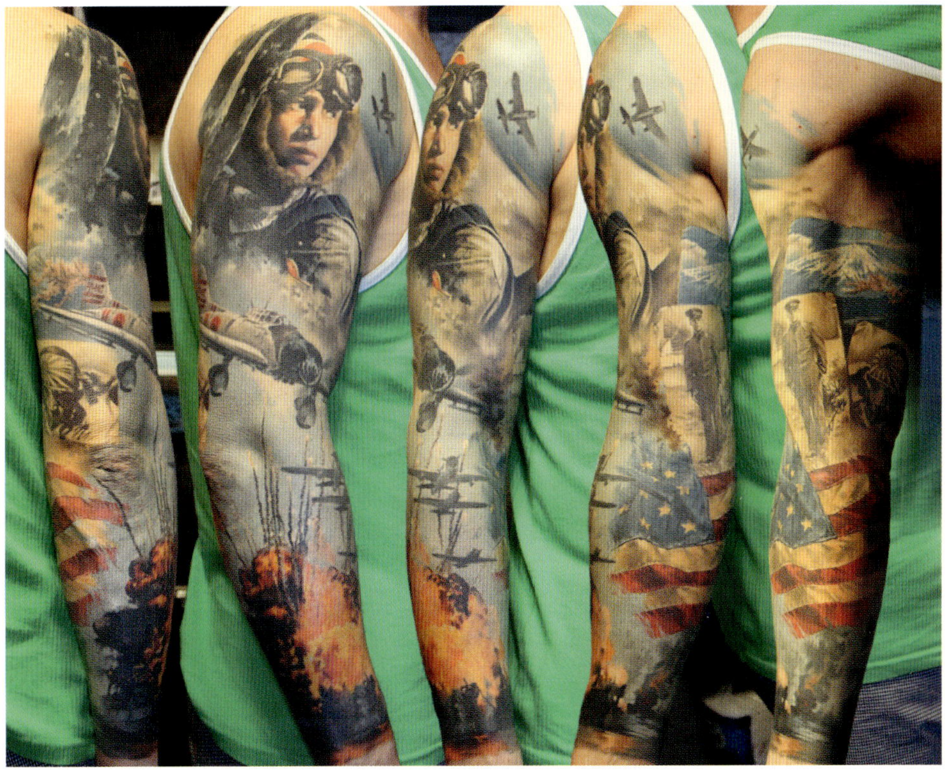

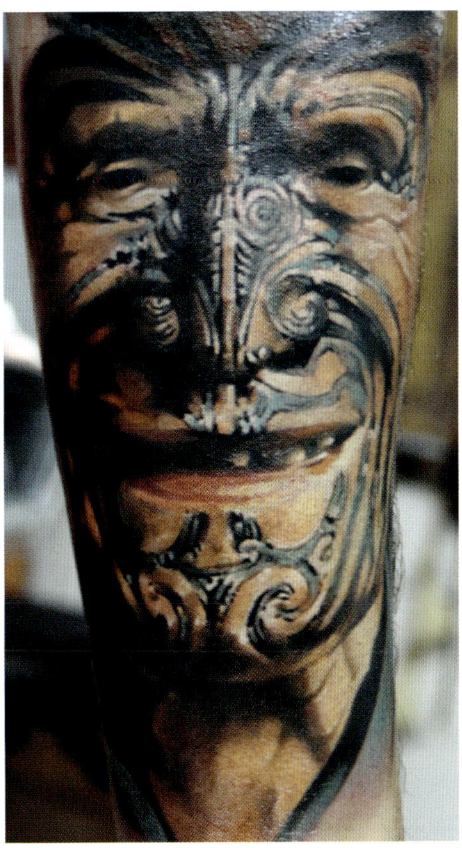

What's the hardest part about being a tattoo artist?

For me it's the communication with the customers.

What's the most rewarding part about being a tattoo artist?

When I see the finished tattoo.

What do you think a client should expect from you as a tattoo artist, and what do you, on the other hand, expect from a client to make a successful tattoo and a good collaboration?

The client should have a clear idea of what he or she wants, when we discuss the basis for the work—the main source (photo). For everything else, the client must trust the tattooer. Of course, a tattoo doesn't always turn out exactly as it was designed. Russian customers often take a very active part in the planning of a future tattoo. They try not to give the tattooist any opportunity to do something on his or her own. They're not able to compromise, when it comes to their tattoo.

What criteria do you think that a tattoo convention should have to be really successful, both for you as a tattoo artist, but also for the visitors? Can you give some examples of conventions that meet these criteria well?

I am a very lazy person and I like to work in a comfortable environment, so I participate in tattoo conventions very rarely.

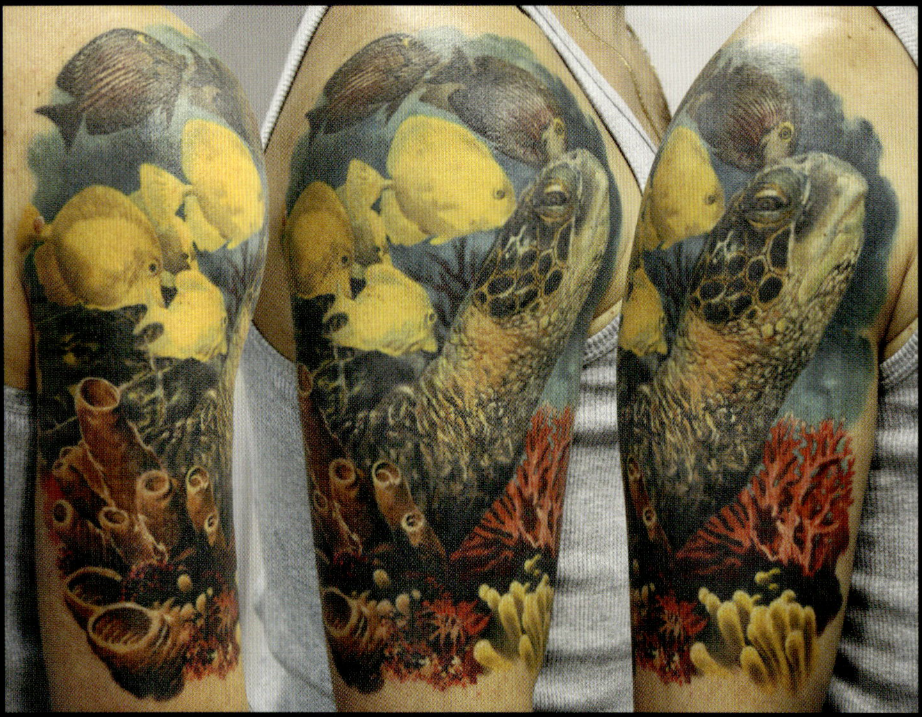
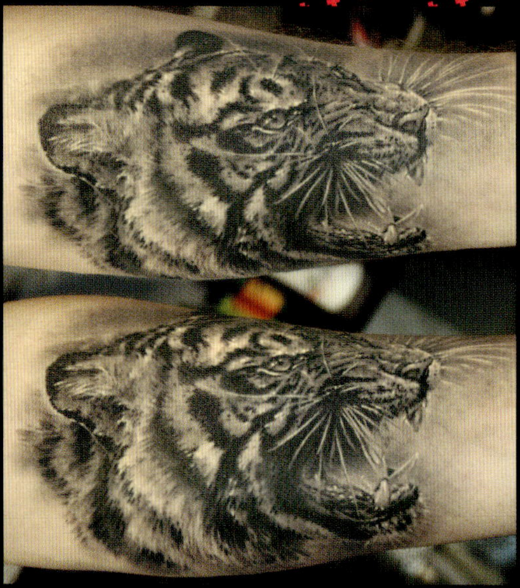
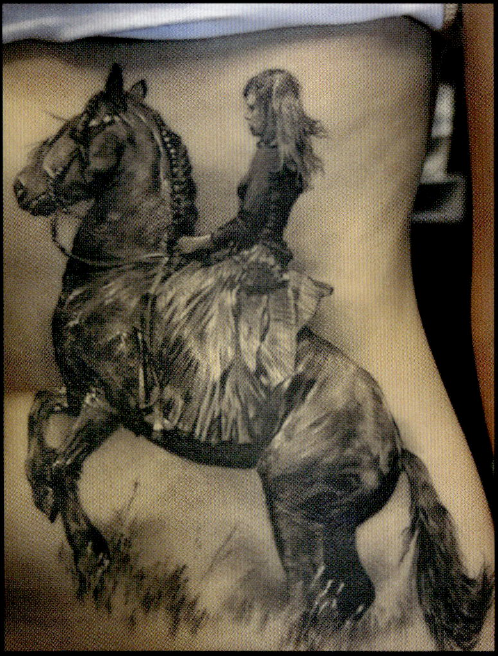
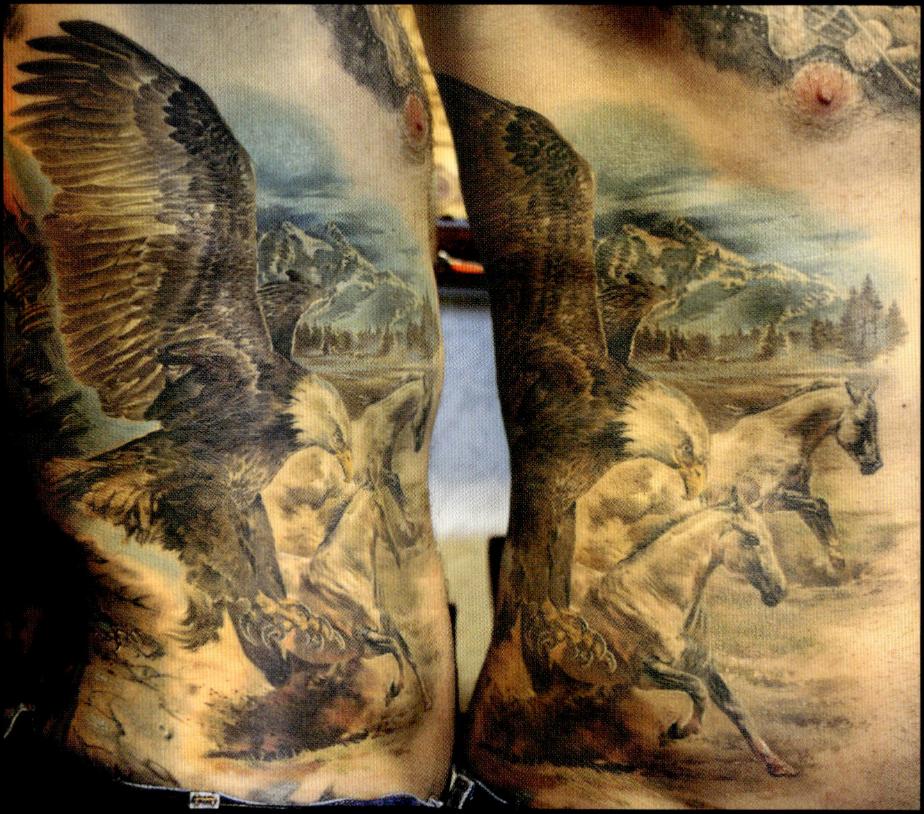
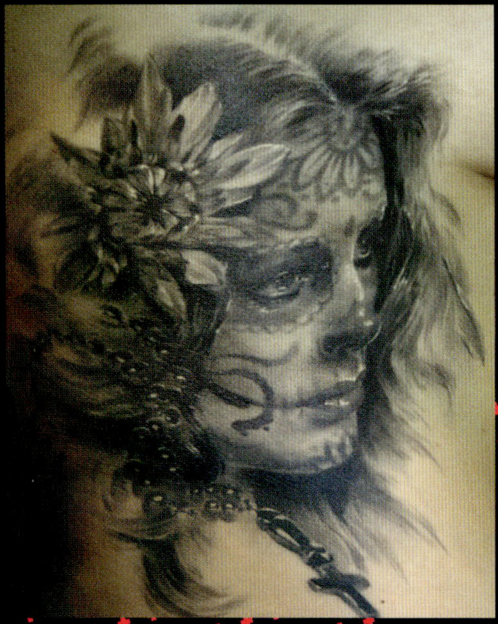
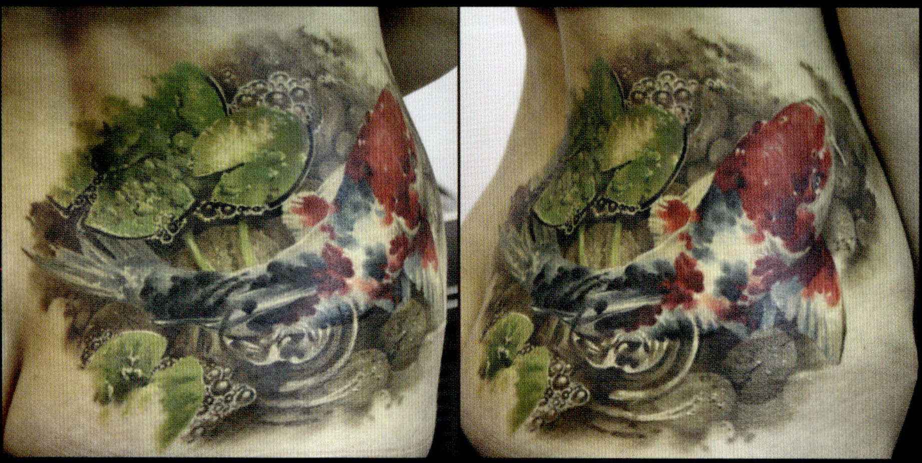

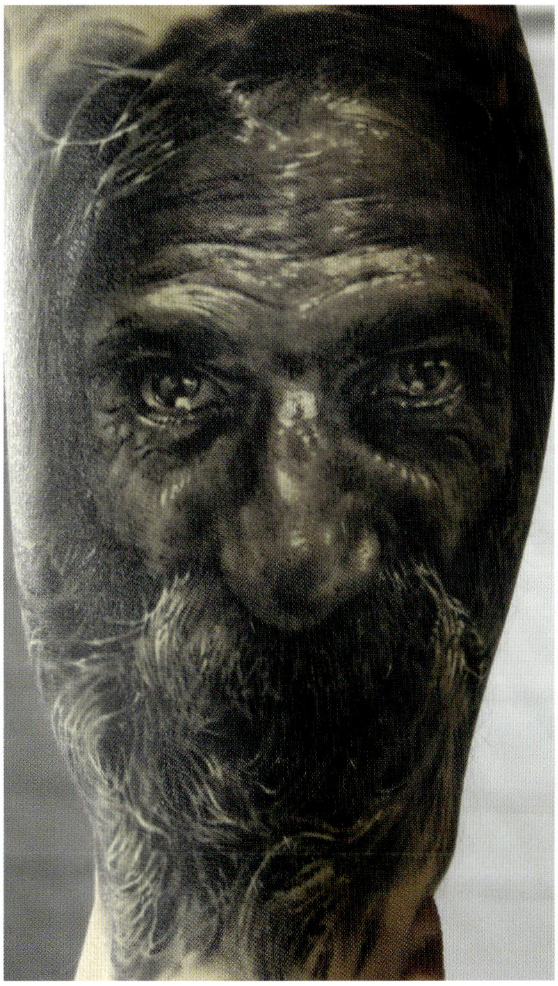

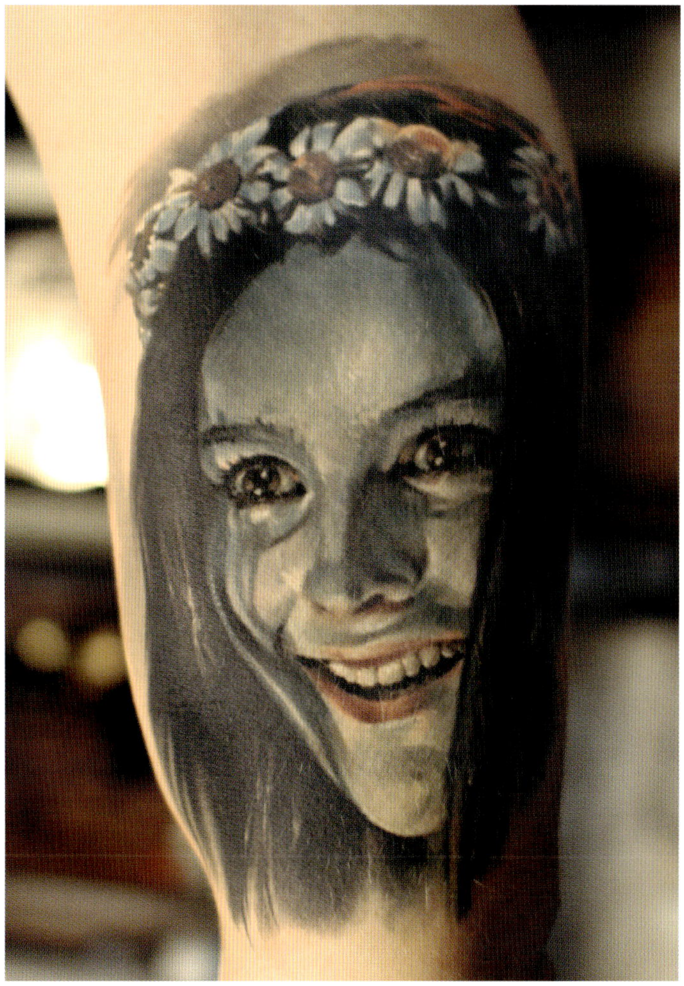

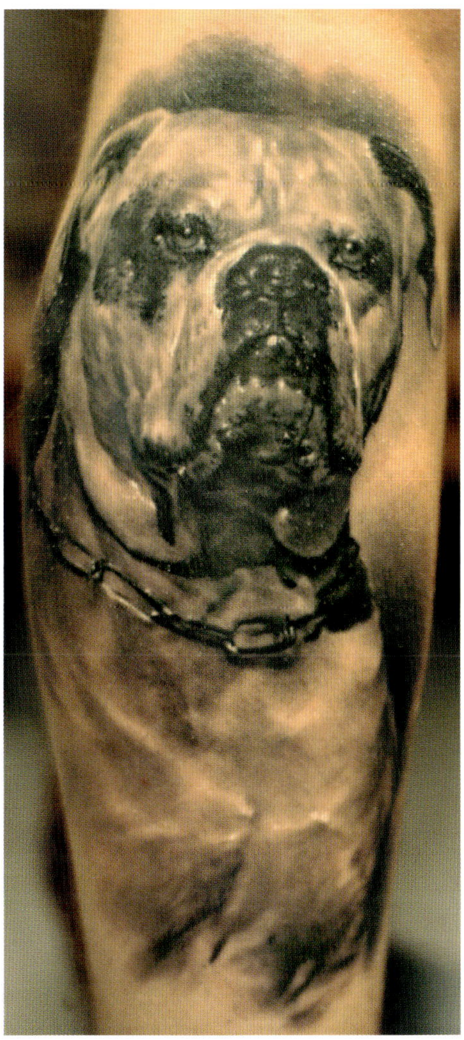

How would you describe the current status of tattoos among the general public in Russia?

Russia now has a lot of good artists. Many people come into this profession with an art education. We have a demand for tattoos in all styles, but I think that the most popular are realism and old school.

TV shows, Internet, and especially social networks like Facebook and Twitter have come to have an extremely wide influence in recent years. What positive and negative impacts do you think it has for the future development of the tattoo industry?

I do not see anything wrong with that. Ten years ago in Russia, when the tattoo culture just started to evolve, customers couldn't find information about tattoos anywhere, so the tattoo artist had to explain every simple thing. It got to the point of absurdity—even five or ten years ago, there were people who didn't know about the existence of colored tattoos. And now with the desire and ability to use the Internet, you can find all the necessary information… it is perfect.

Is there anything else you'd like to say?

I'd like to wish all the tattoo artists lots of good work and obedient customers. And I hope all the customers will find their perfect tattoo artist.

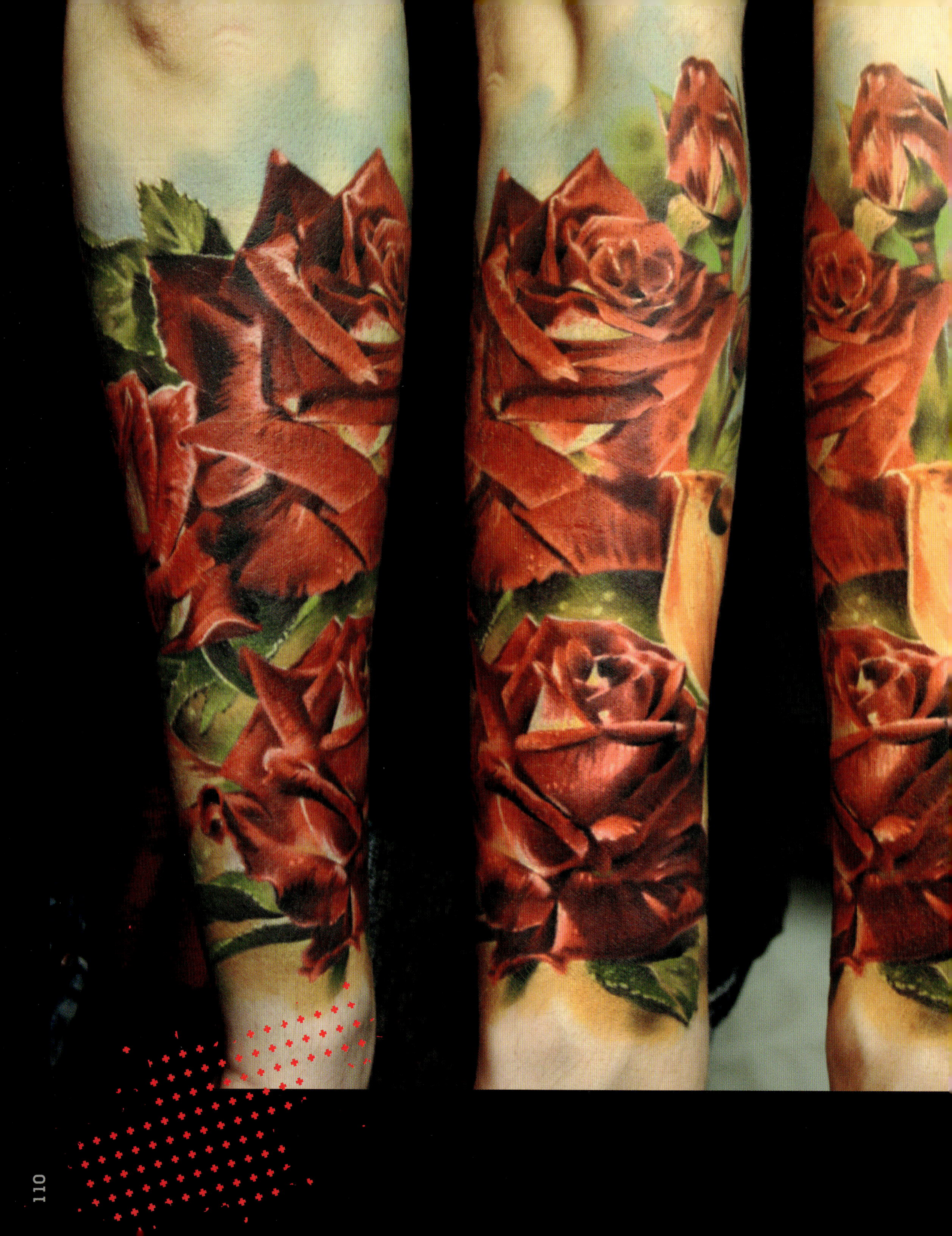

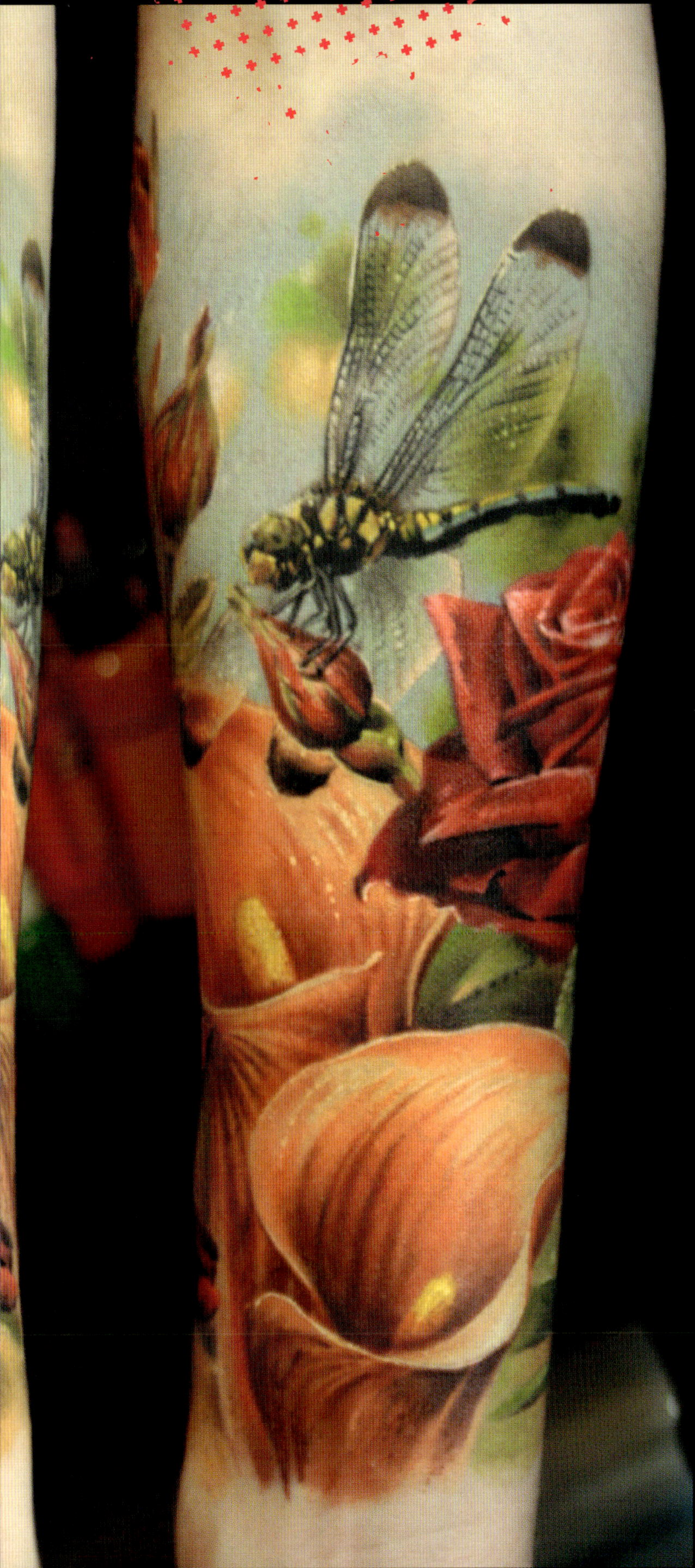

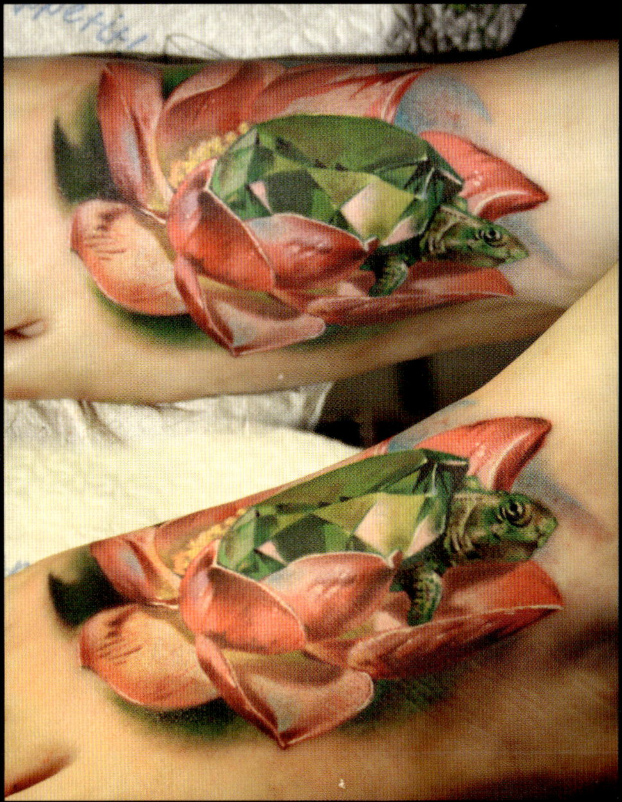

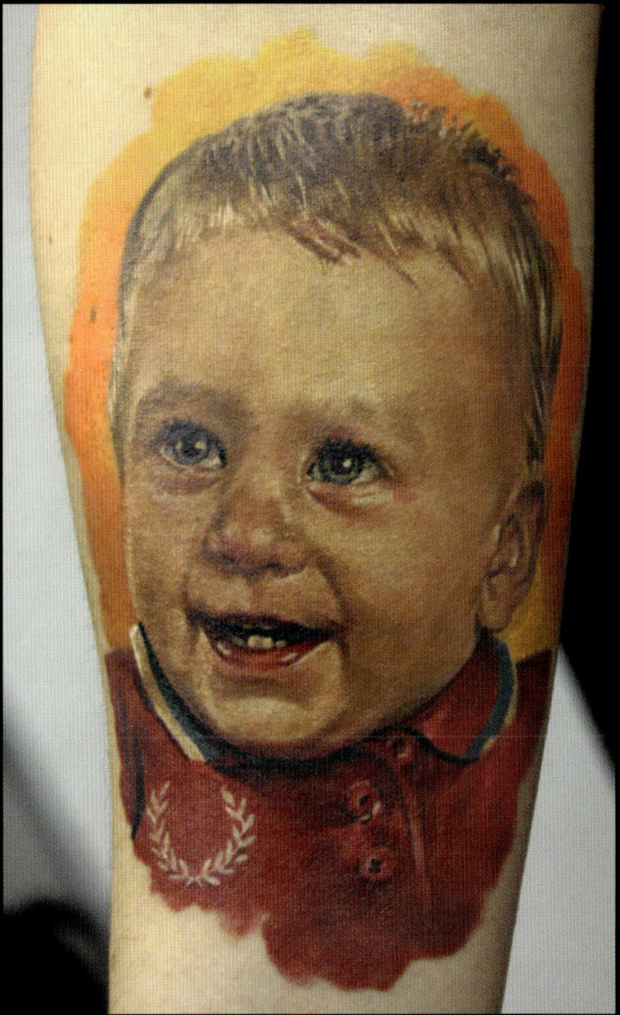

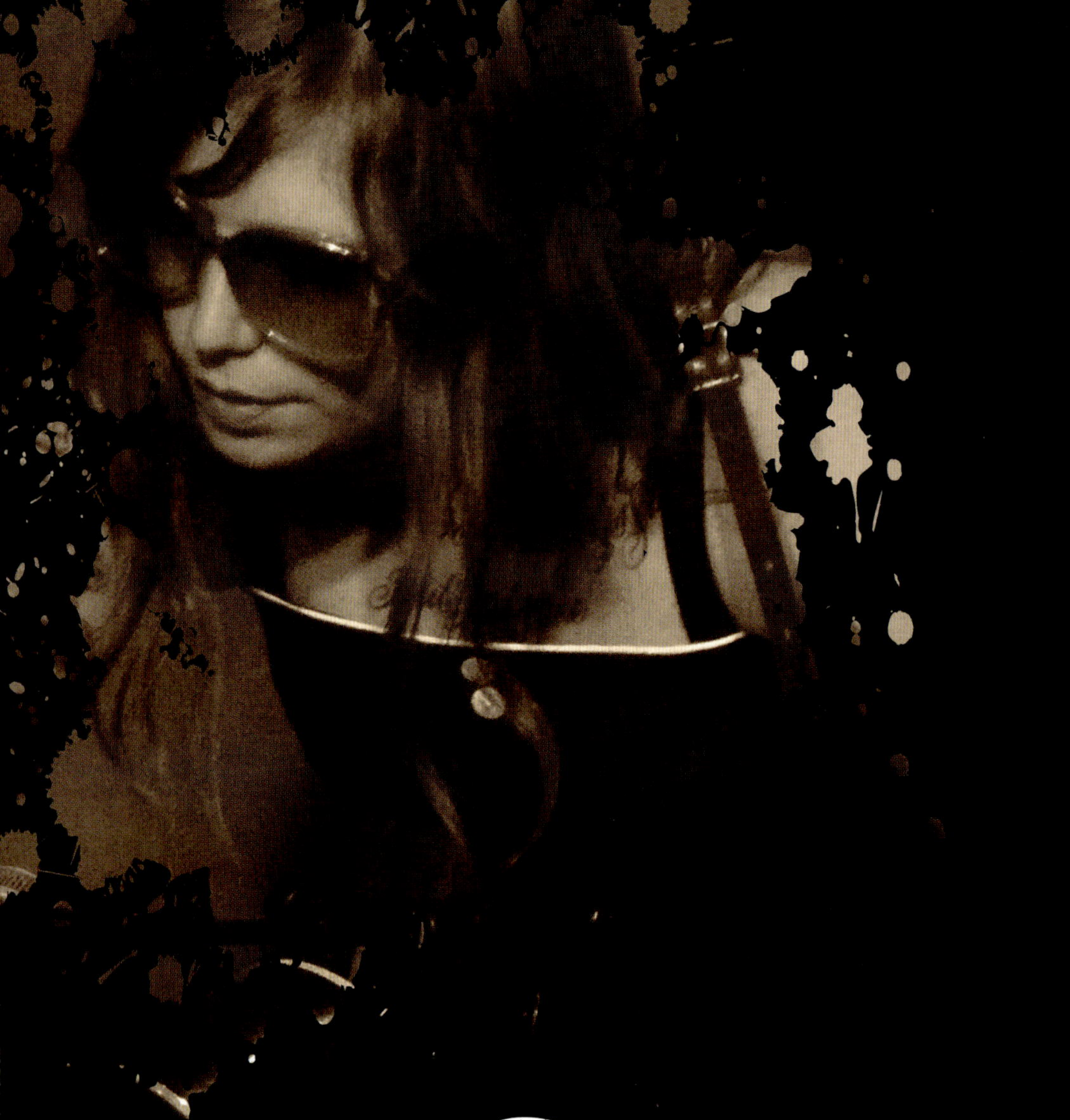

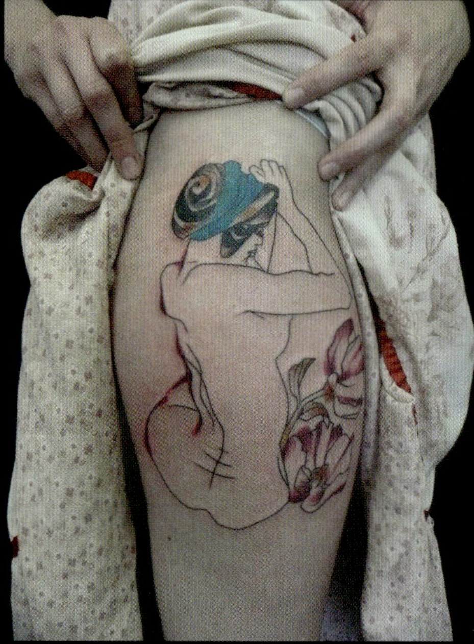

LÉA NAHON was born and raised in Paris. Now she lives in Brussels, Belgium, and works at La Boucherie Moderne. She finished art school, then worked for a sex messaging service on Minitel (the grandfather of the Internet) to pay for film because she was taking a lot of photos. Meanwhile, she was working on movie scripts with a friend of hers, and was studying to become a contemporary dance teacher, but she put these things aside when she started tattooing.

Léa NAHON

"I love tattooing my sketches because when I draw them they always come from a personal experience"

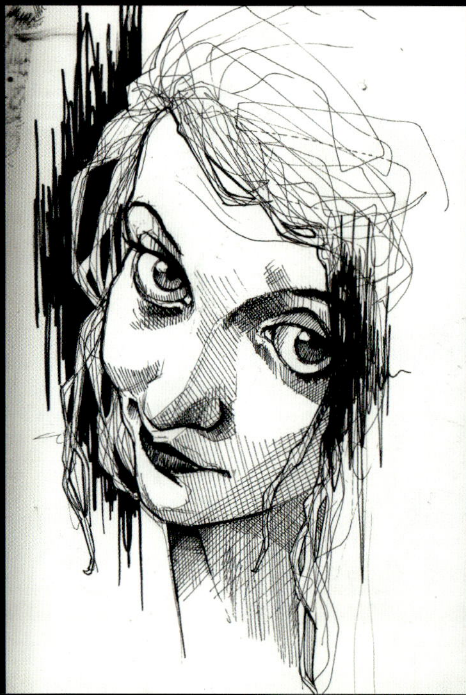

www.leanahon.com
www.facebook.com/laboucheriemoderne
www.boucheriemoderne.be

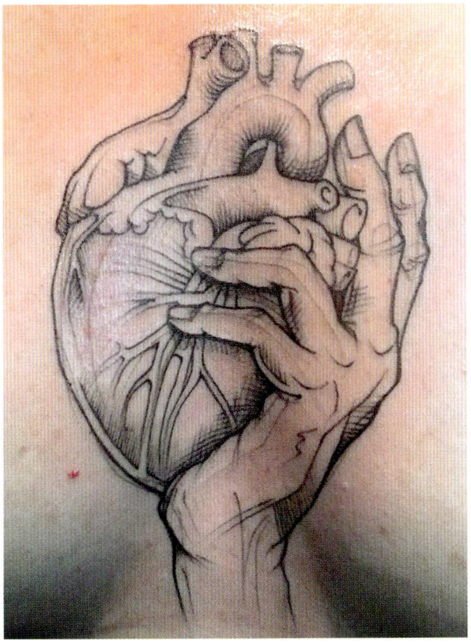

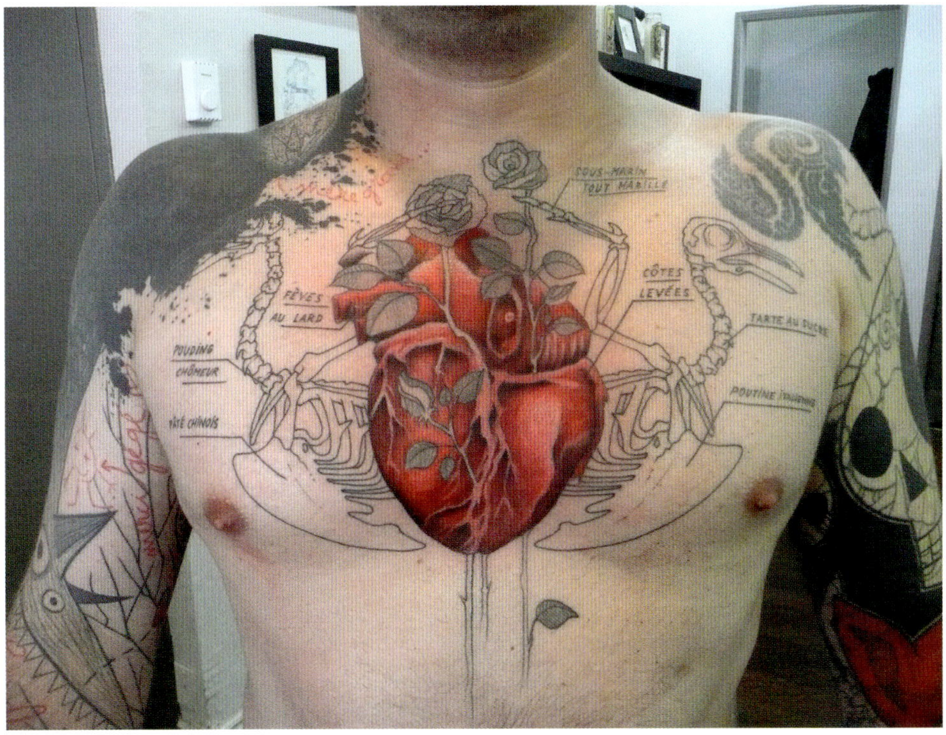

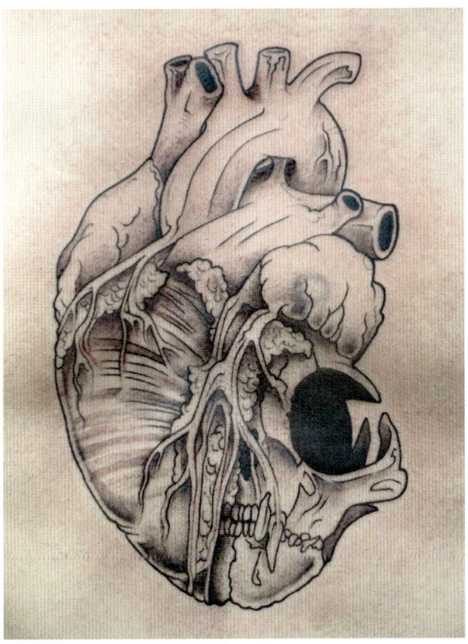

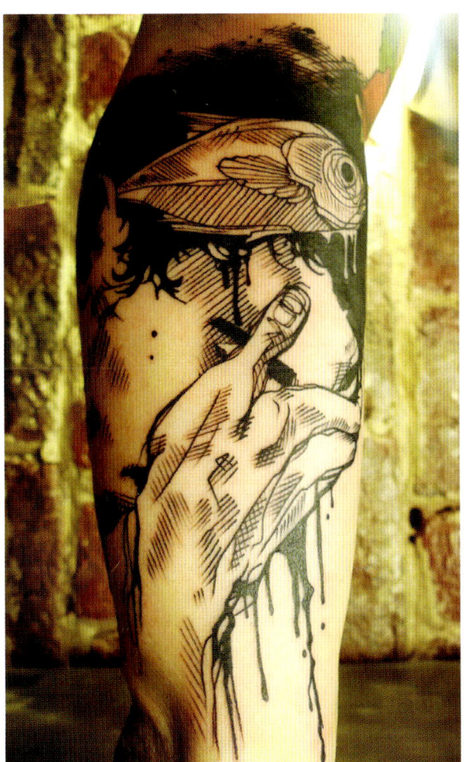

At what point in life did you decide to become a professional tattoo artist?

It wasn't an actual decision. I was interested, and I tattooed already, but I'd never thought seriously about it. I was an art student at the École Boulle and after my graduation, I was looking for a part-time job and walked into a tattoo parlor. The owner was looking for an apprentice, he asked for some drawings, I brought some stuff in, and it started right away.

What did your family and friends think about you getting into the business?

Well, my mom didn't really understand at first how seriously I was into tattooing. She was always asking me when I would find a real job, but after a while she kind of got used to it. I tattooed her and I guess now she understands it a lot better. As for my friends, of course they thought it was great, free tattoos and a cool job...My teachers, on the other hand, thought it was a step down from the architect or stylist career that was kinda traced for me, but I realize now that I must be one of the rare ones among my classmates who's holding a pen and drawing every day, so I couldn't have dreamed of a better job!

What is your earliest memory of someone close to you being tattooed?

I don't remember having anybody around me with tattoos... or maybe I didn't notice it because I didn't think it was strange. My parents are tattooed now, by me. My earliest memory of tattoos is from a movie. In *Cry Baby*, Johnny Depp gets a tear drop tattooed under the eye while doing time in prison. The tattoo itself, I didn't care about, but how to do it...that was cool! So I did one on myself with a needle and some ink. I got it touched up pretty fast, because half the ink came off after healing. I was fifteen.

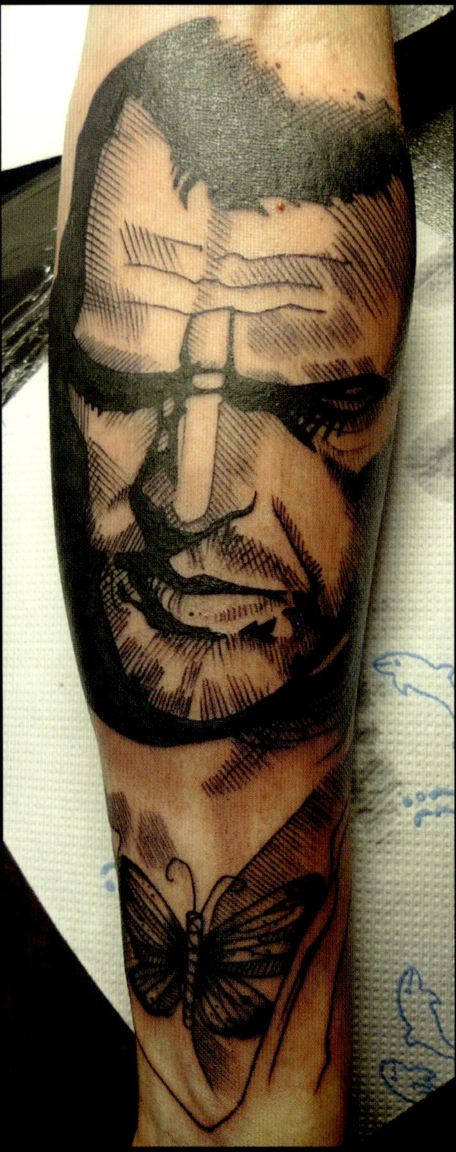
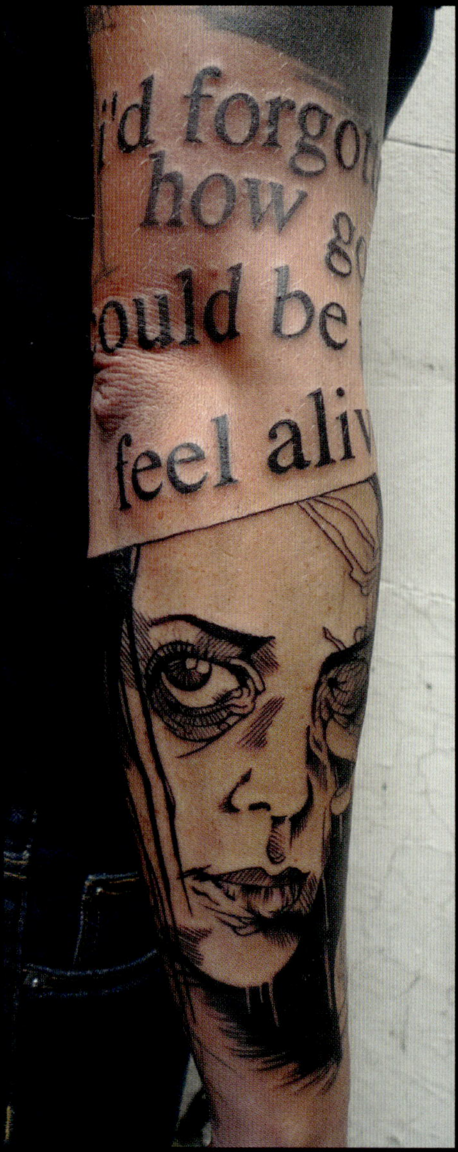
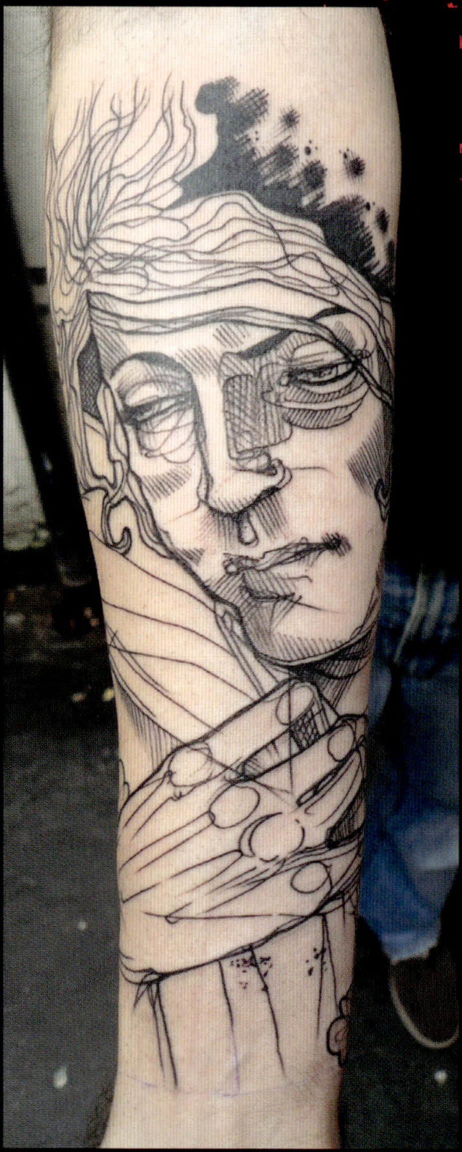
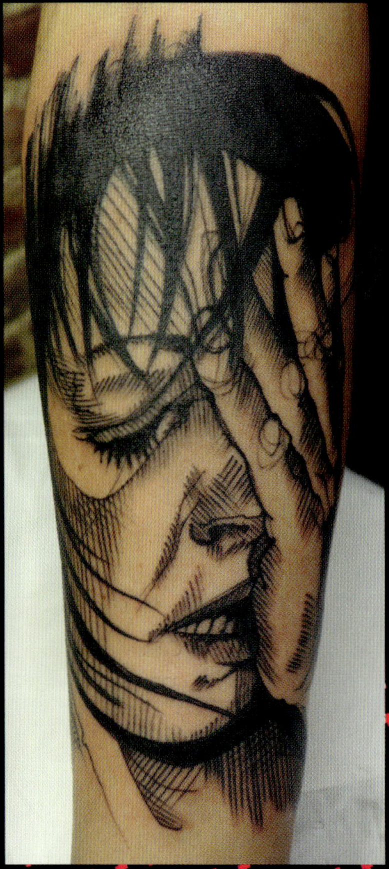
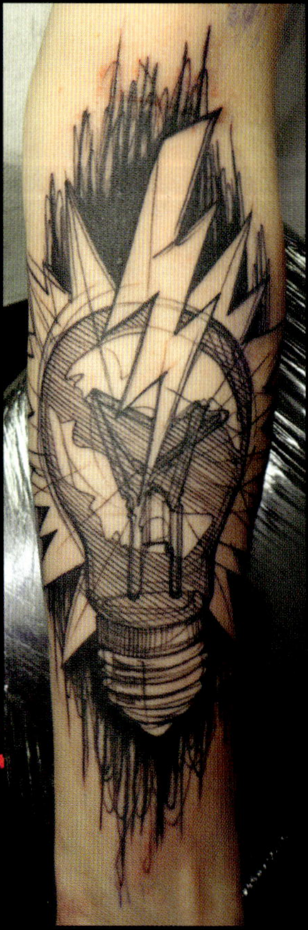
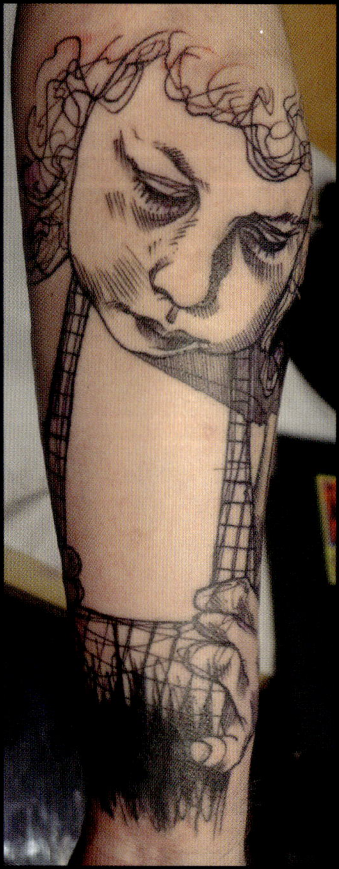
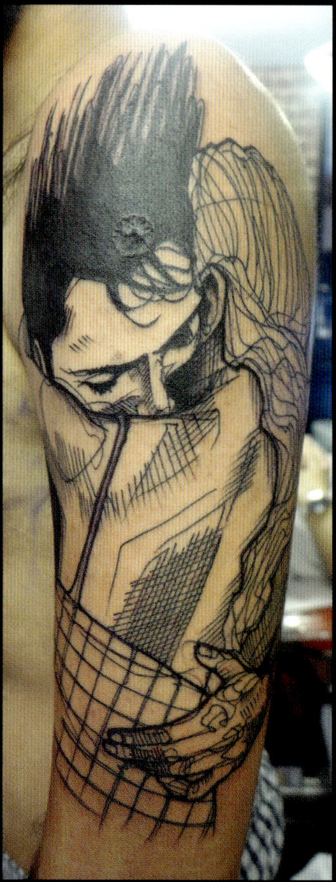

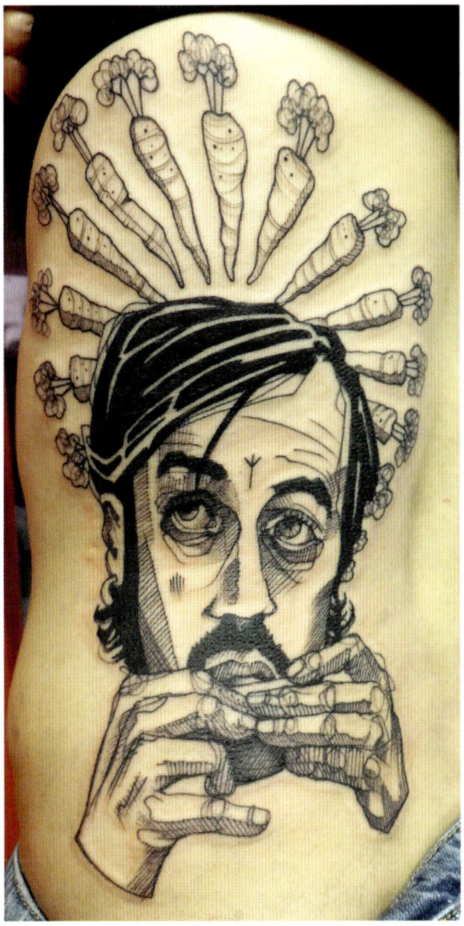

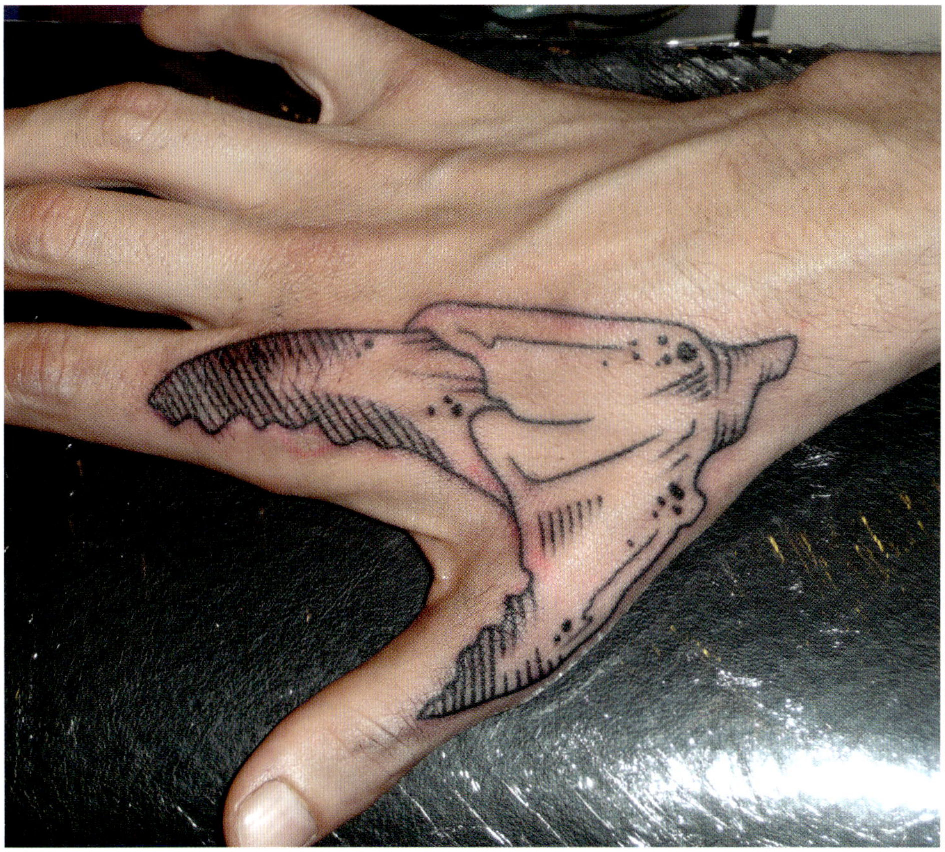

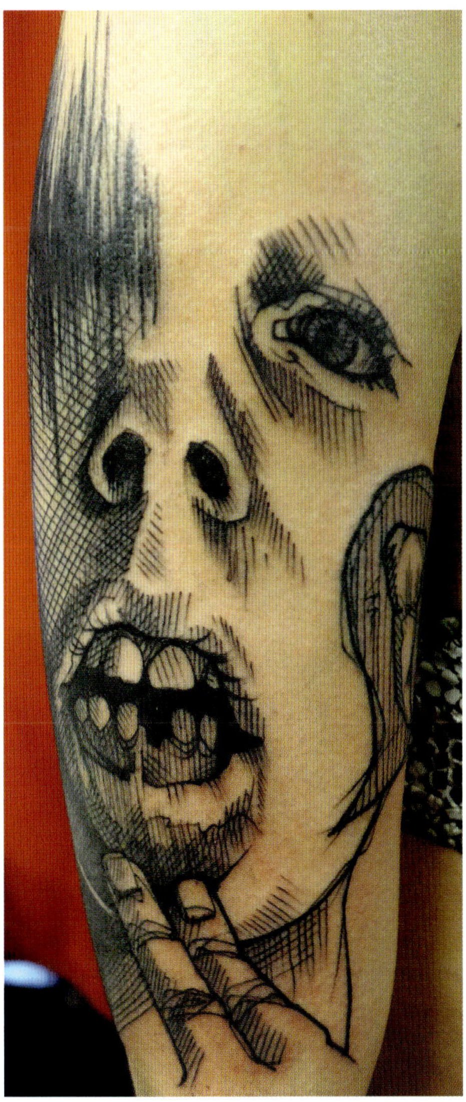

What was the first tattoo you ever did?

It was a tribal, onto the lower back of a friend of mine. She said she trusted me no matter what. I spent two and a half hours on a ten-centimeter tribal. It was quite clean, after so much working time…

What's your favorite style of tattooing?

I love tattooing my sketches because when I draw them they always come from a personal experience. People pick them from my sketchbook. I guess some drawings make them feel something about their own experiences, so the drawing changes meaning and then it goes onto the skin. The best tattoos I've done came from drawings that were really important to me, where there are a lot of feelings put into it. Whether it's funny or not, people feel something about it. I like that.

Please tell me about the most important or meaningful tattoos you ever did.

I guess that would be Marcus's arm. I met him in San Francisco. It was his first tattoo and had no idea what he wanted so he picked a drawing from my sketchbook. There are very often sentences in my drawings. He wanted the sentence as well 'cause for some reason, it made sense to him. Then he came to Paris on holiday and picked some more drawings with other sentences. Then he visited me in Los Angeles while I was working there and we continued his tattoo. Finally we finished his arm in Brussels with a last drawing and sentence. So his arm is full of drawings in frames, kinda like a comic book with sentences that have nothing to do with one

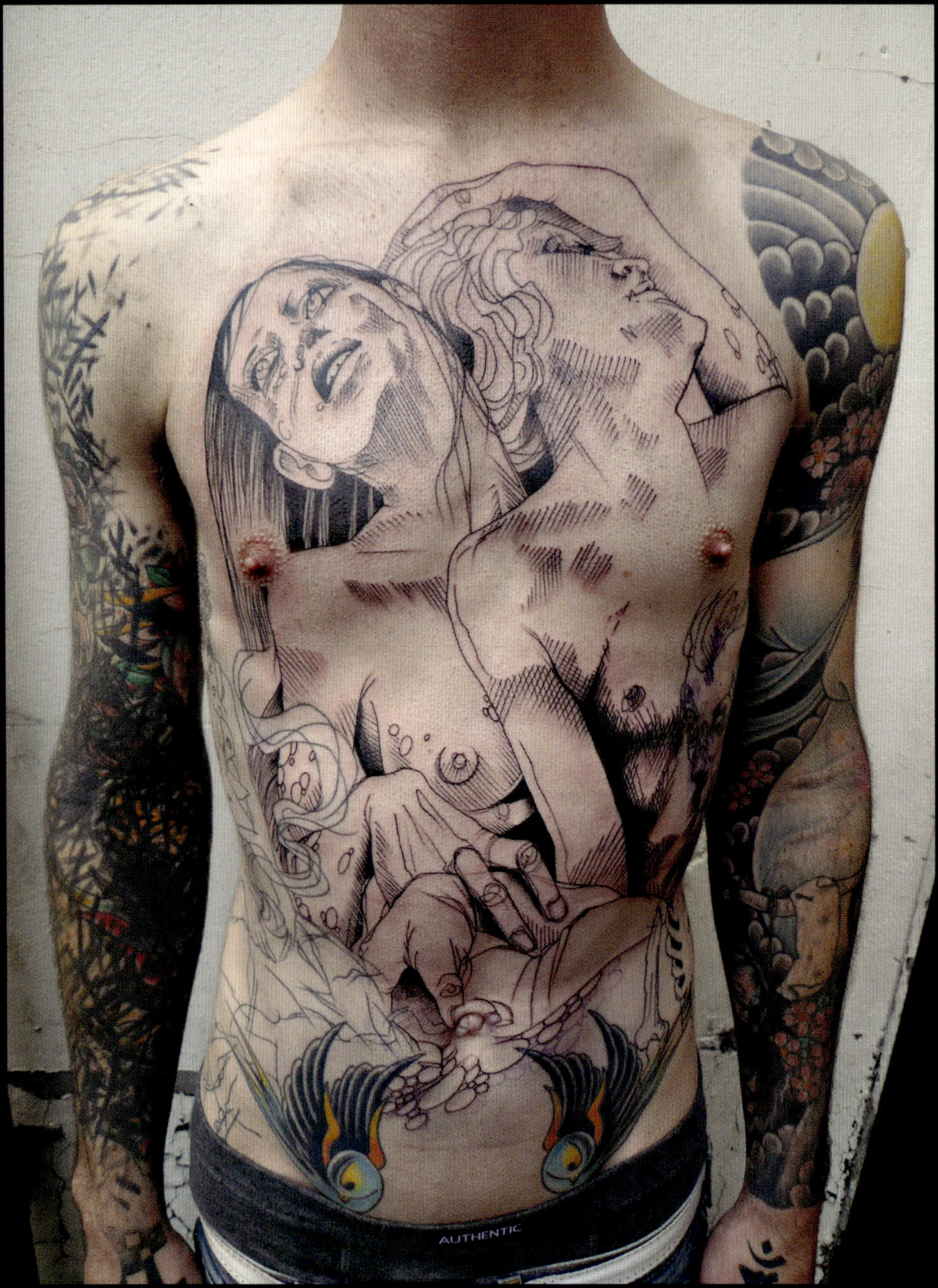
AUTHENTIC

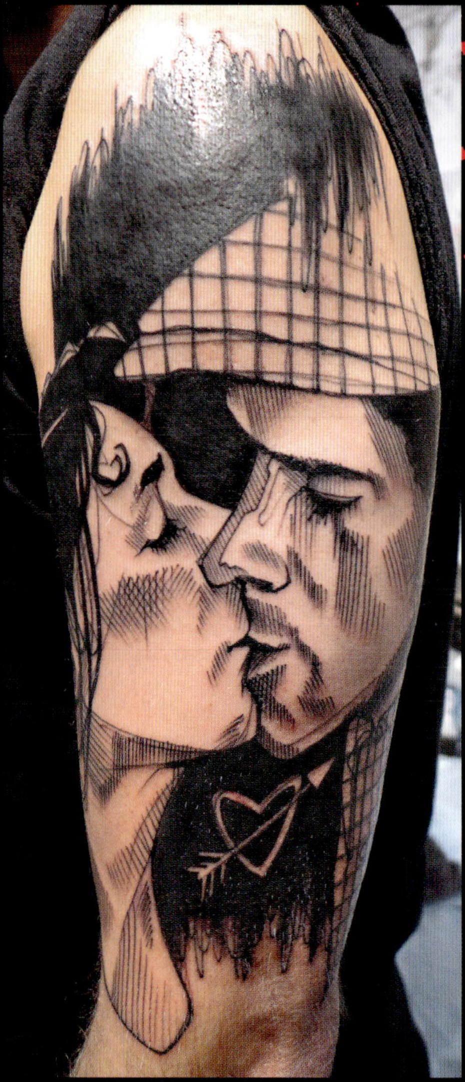

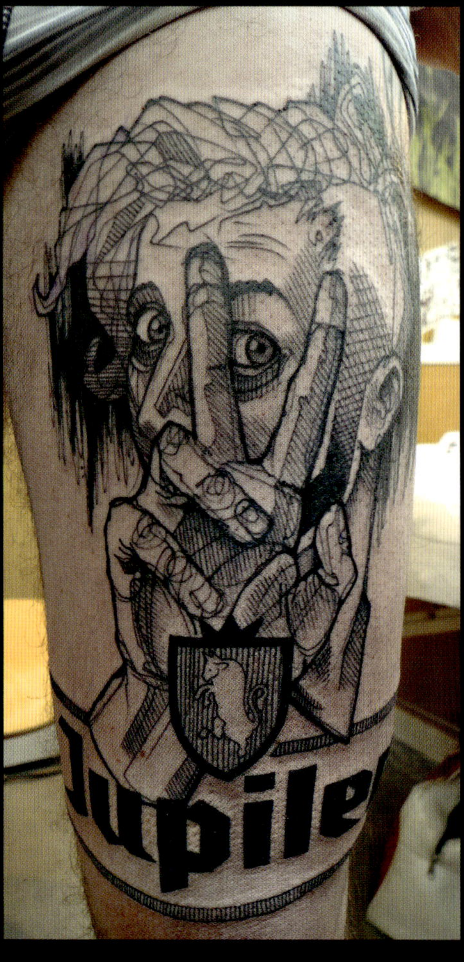

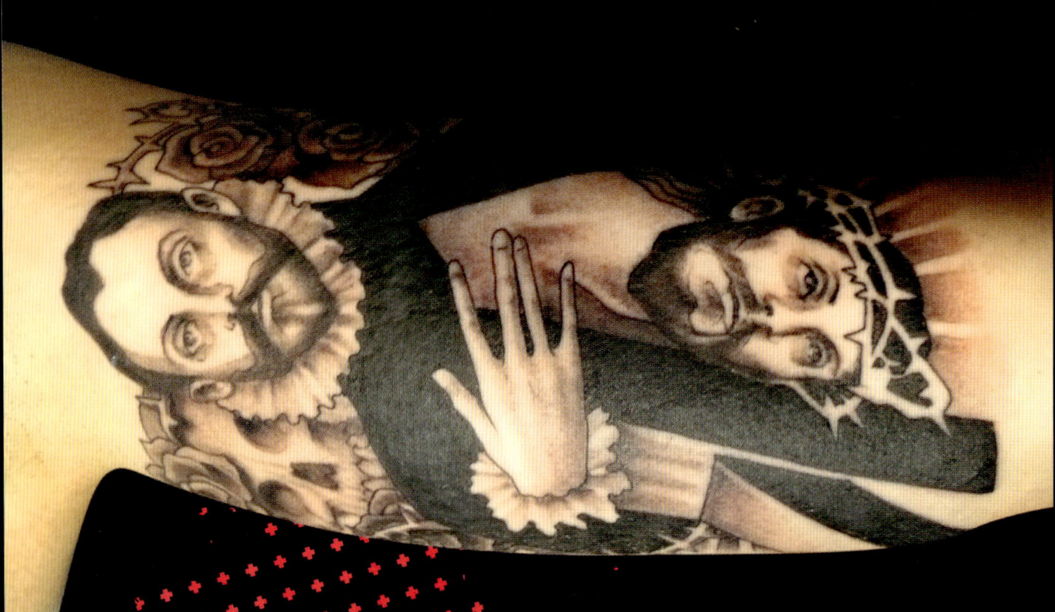

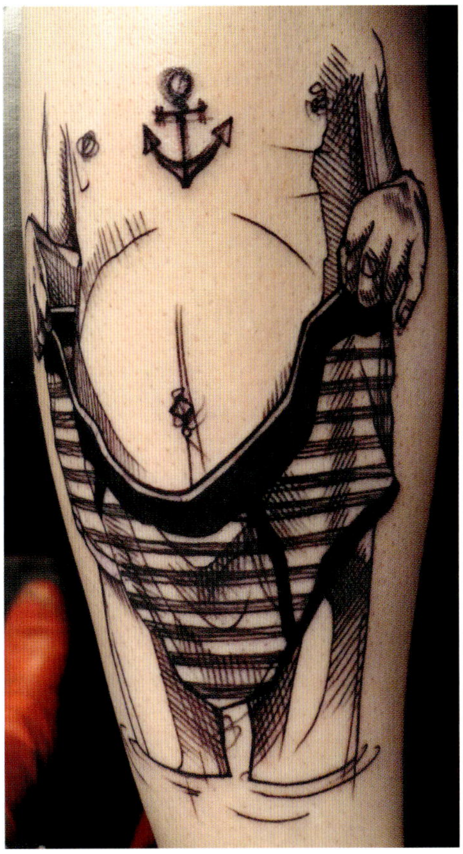

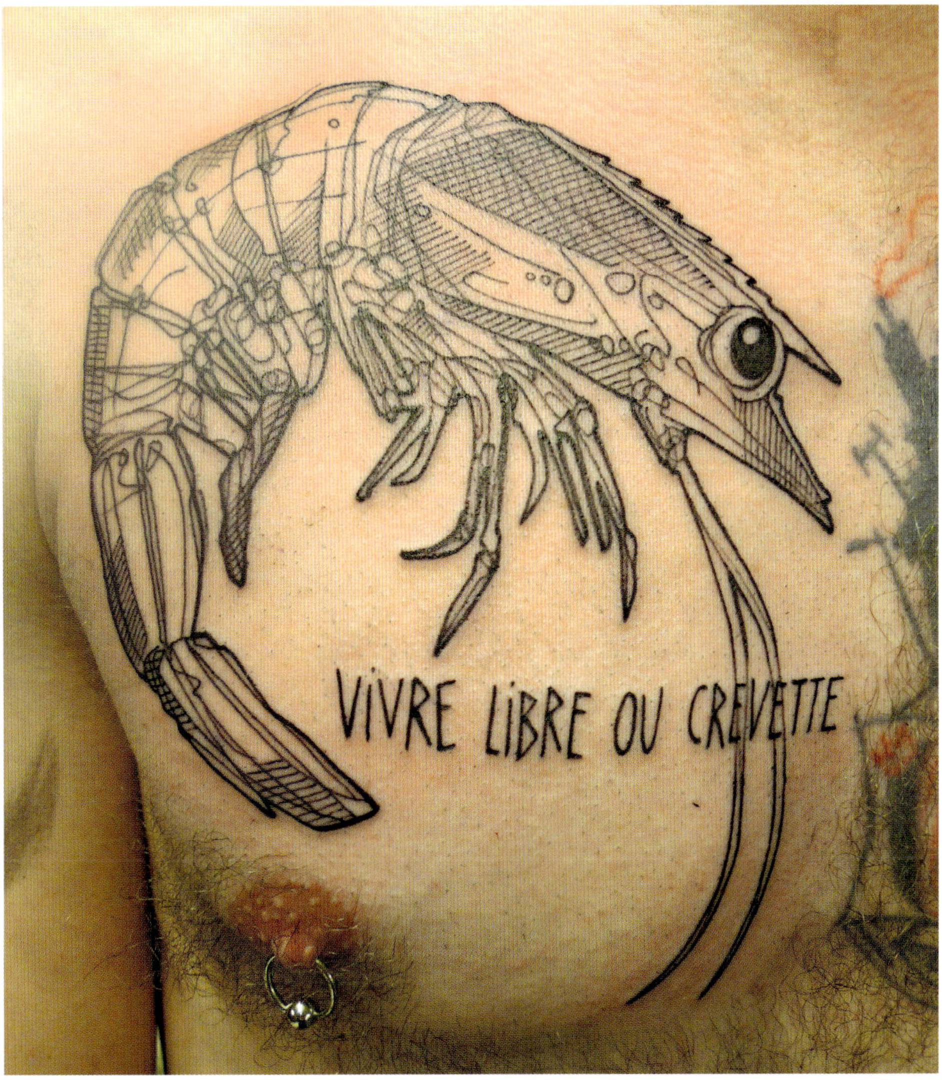
VIVRE LIBRE OU CREVETTE

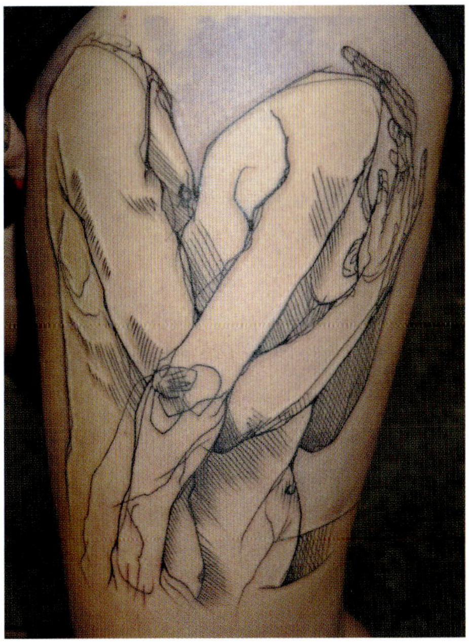

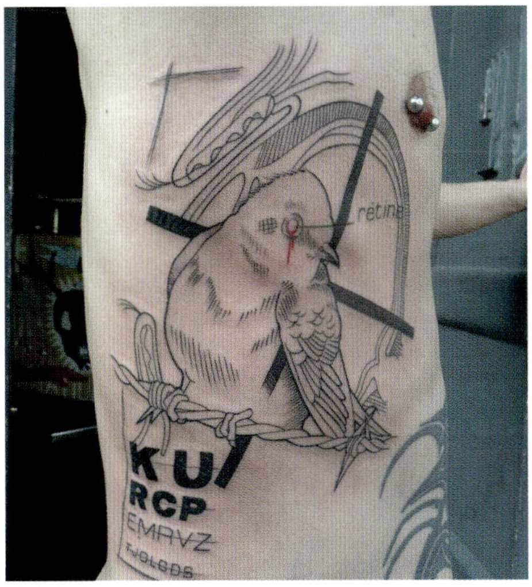
retine
RCP

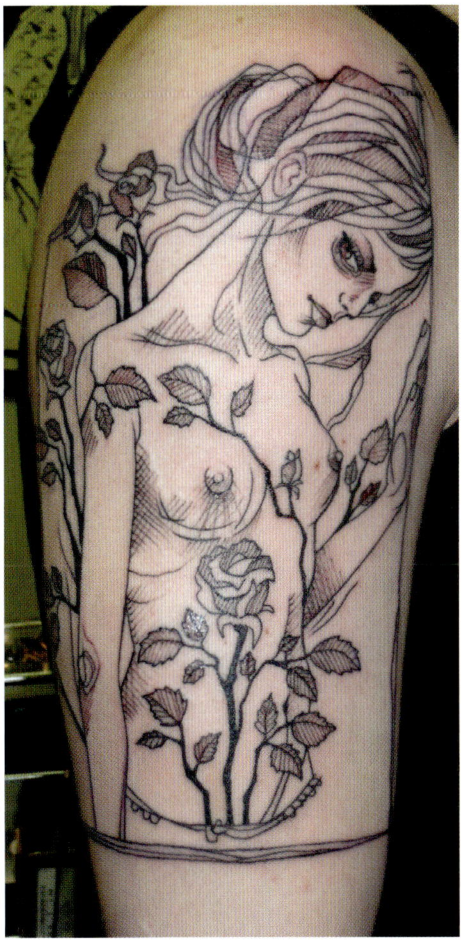

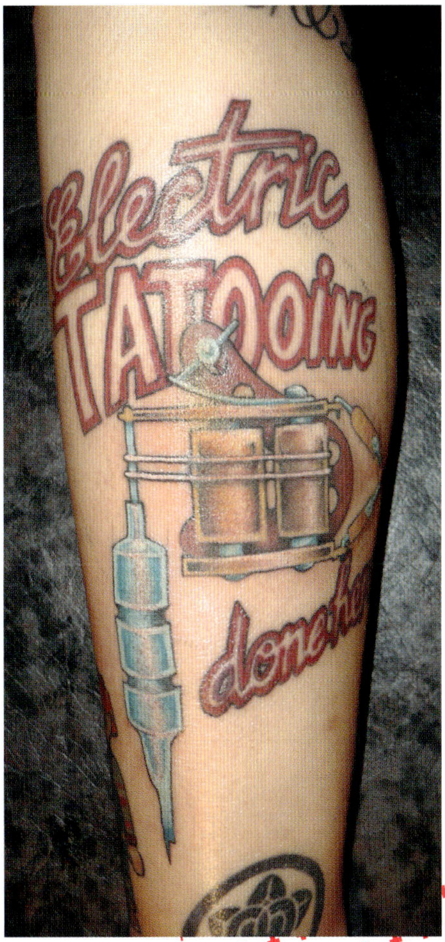
Electric
TATOOING

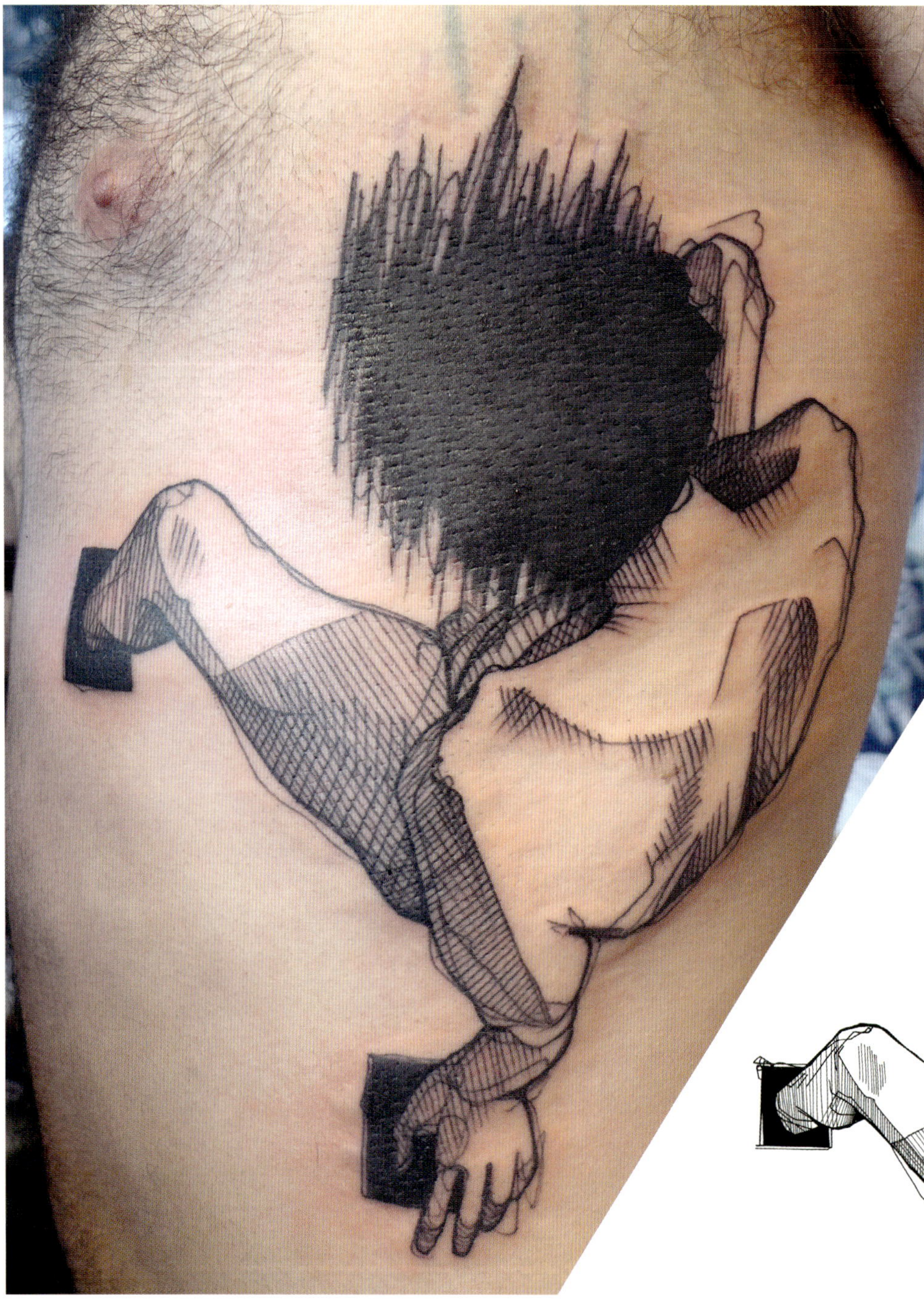

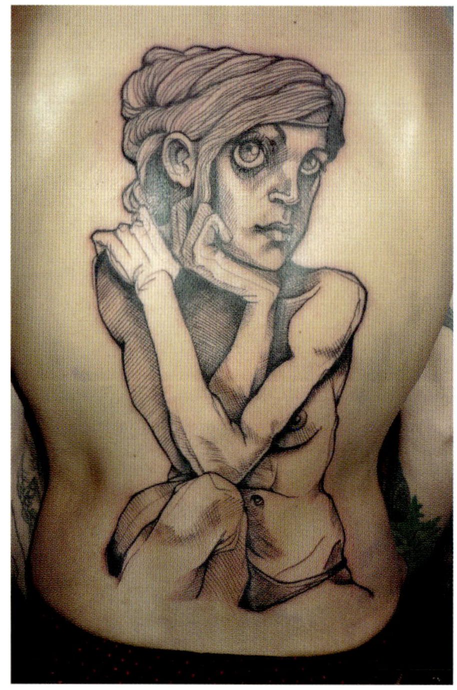

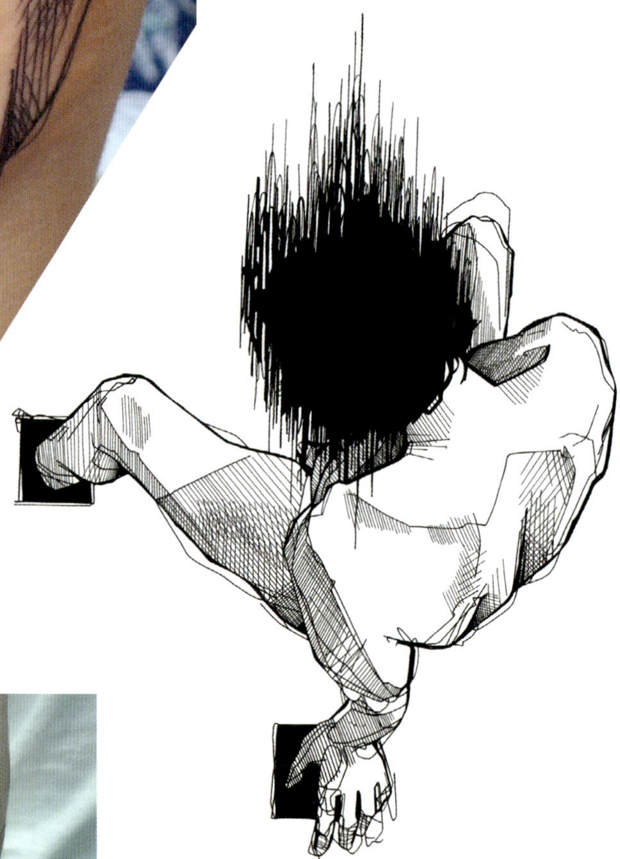

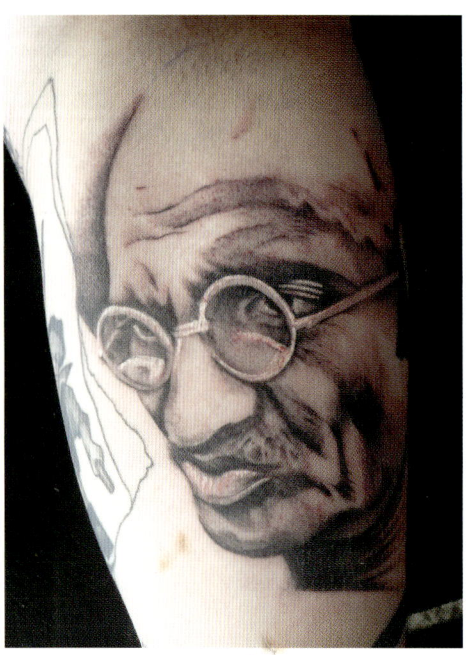

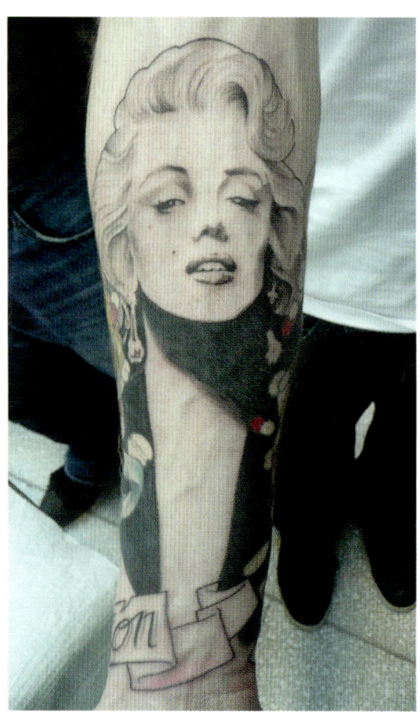

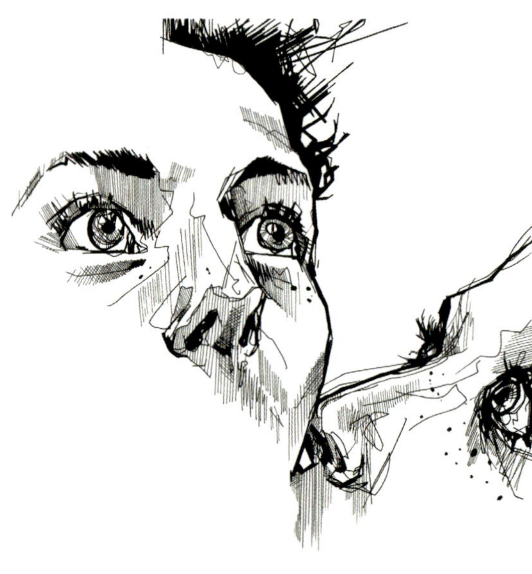

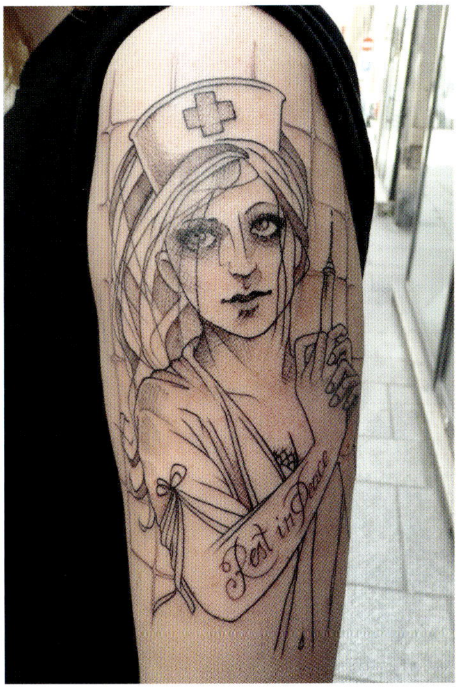

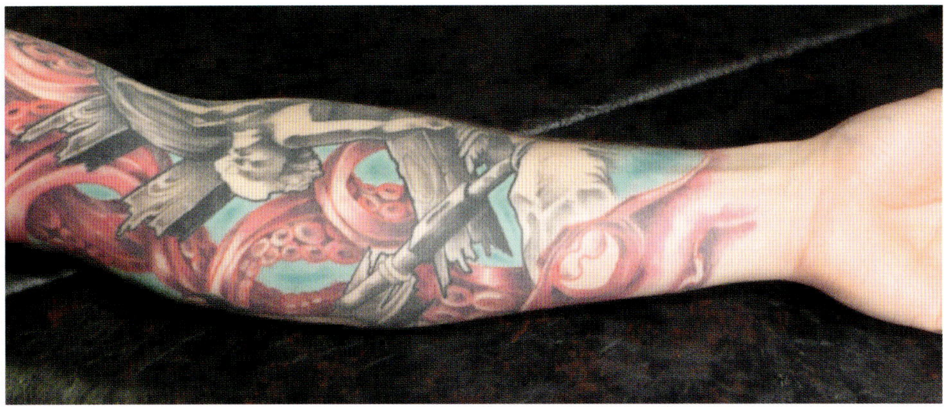

another but somehow make a nice little story. I love working like that and personally; you get to know the person really well, just like the person gets to know you. And that tattoo has no deep meaning at first, it's only the events and opportunities that follow it that make it meaningful, and make good friends as well.

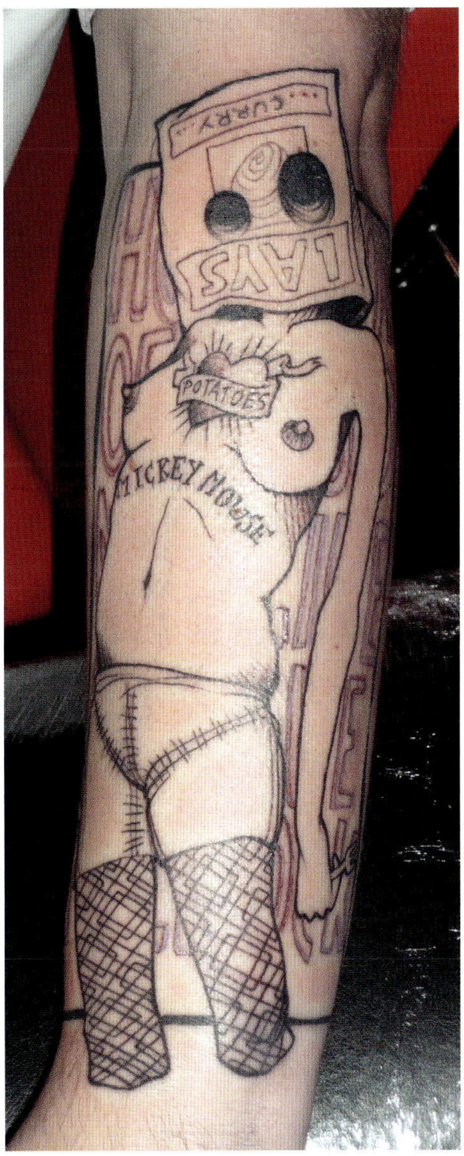

Is there anything you would not tattoo?

Barcodes, 'cause they never really look good. Hard core political stuff and such. I'm not too much into birds, wings make me nervous for some reason, or realistic animals. You know, I don't like tattooing fur, 'cause I just don't know how to do it. Then it's just logical stuff; if someone asks me for traditional Japanese, I tell them I can do it, but that I know enough very good tattooers who do it a thousand times better than me.

Do you have a funny tattoo story?

I guess that happenend in Montreal. I was working with Yann Black there and Dave—Yann's very good friend that I just met—came to me asking for a tattoo on his hand. He said I could do whatever I wanted. So the next day I was having a smoke outside the shop with Yann and was wondering what I could tattoo on Dave. Yann said: "Well, you like doing portraits, do a portrait on his hand." "A portrait of who?" I asked. "A portrait of someone he likes." "But he likes *you*!" So I decided to do the portrait of Yann Black on Dave's hand. I found the worst picture of Yann I had (drunk in a bar in Brussels, posing with a transvestite dressed up with feathers, pretty funny), drew it my way, and tattooed it on Dave's hand. Since then, he's been telling everybody that Yann Black opens doors for him, beer cans, and whatever nasty things he finds for him to do...

Given all that you have achieved so far, what are you especially proud of?

Being able to take a plane without anti-anxiety pills...by myself! It took me a while!

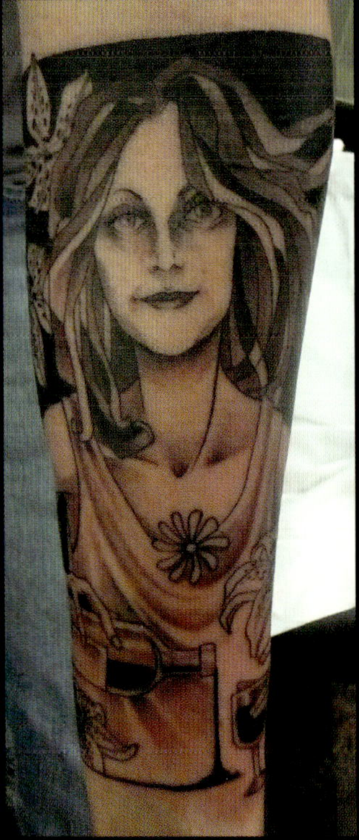
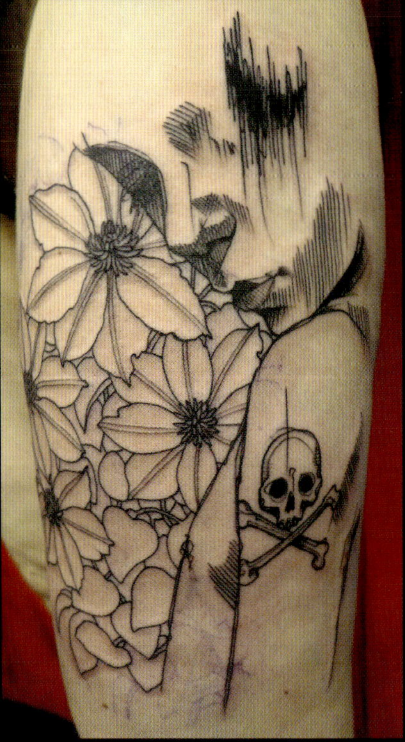
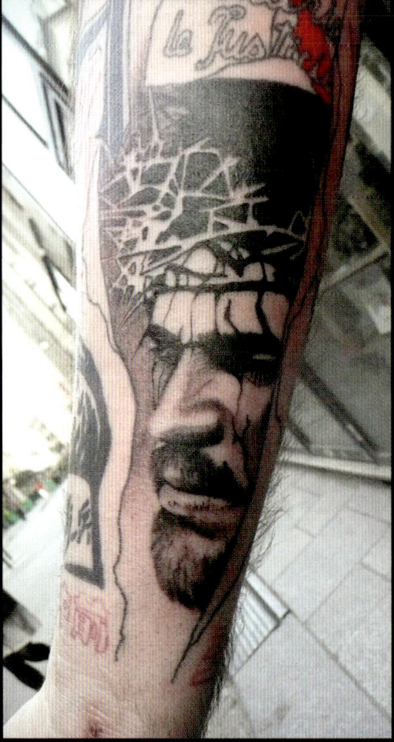
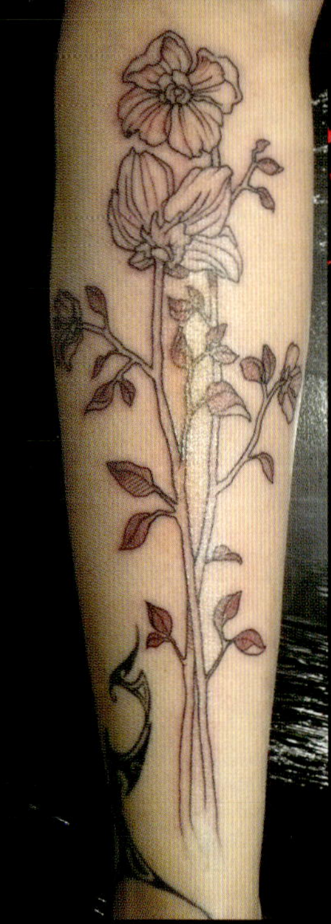
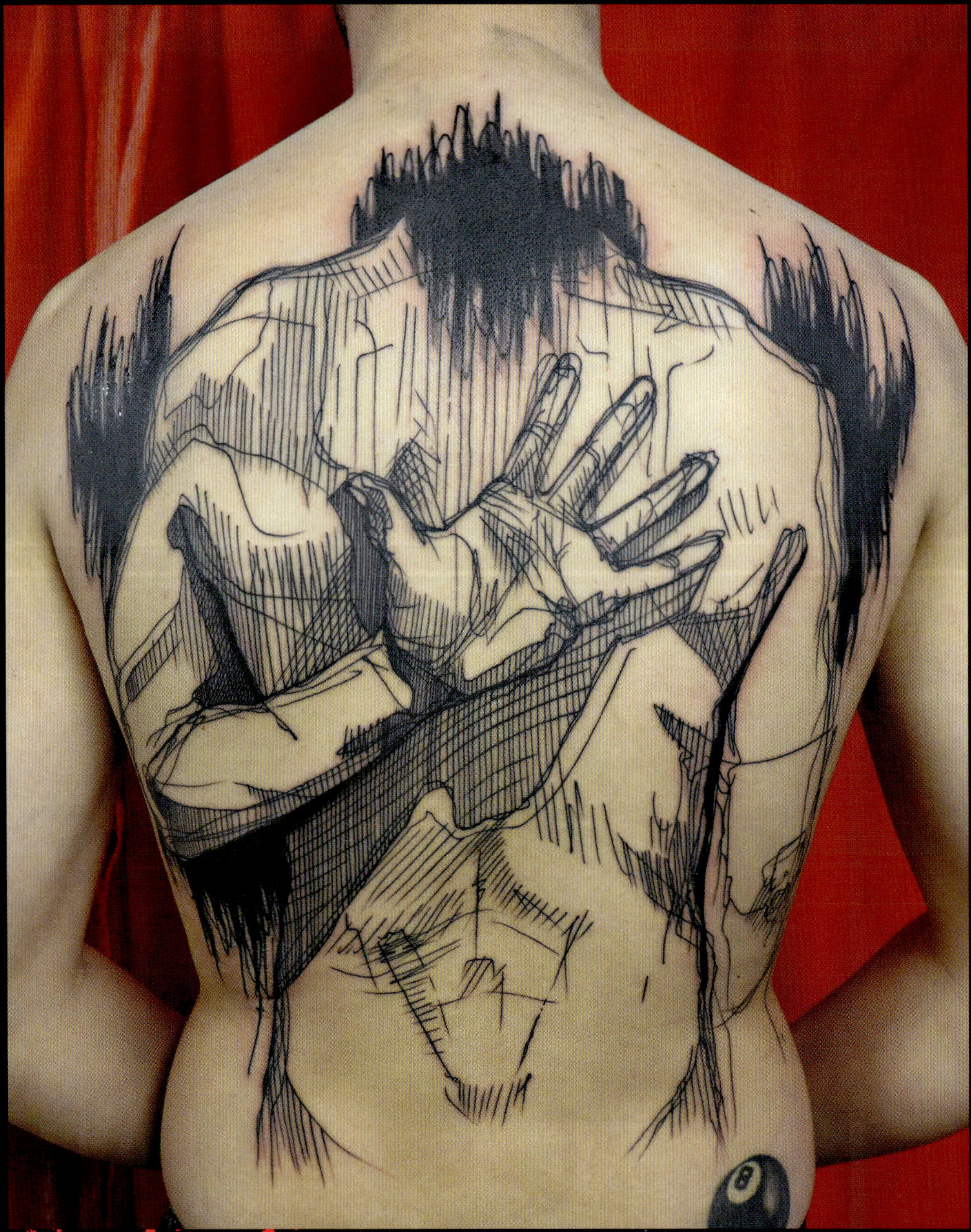
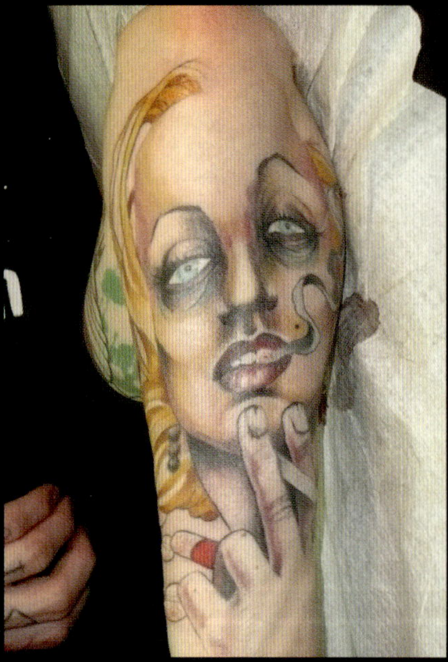
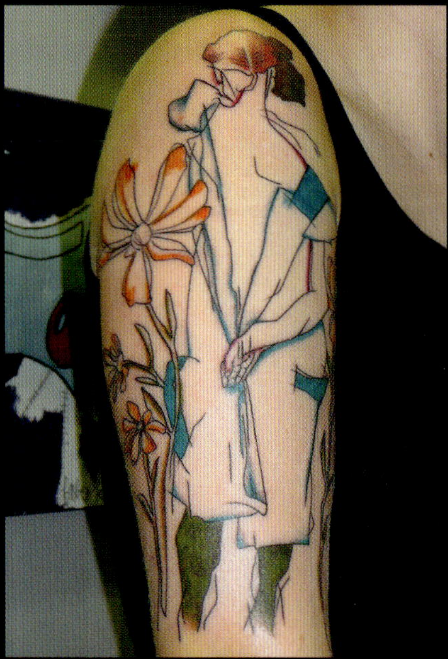

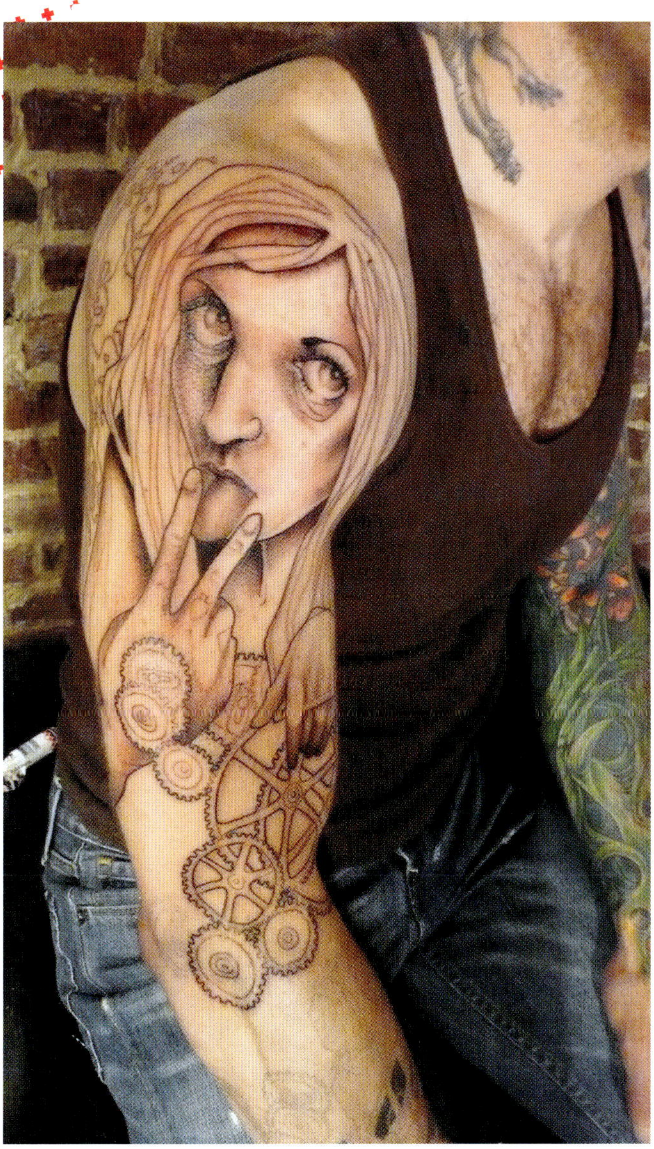

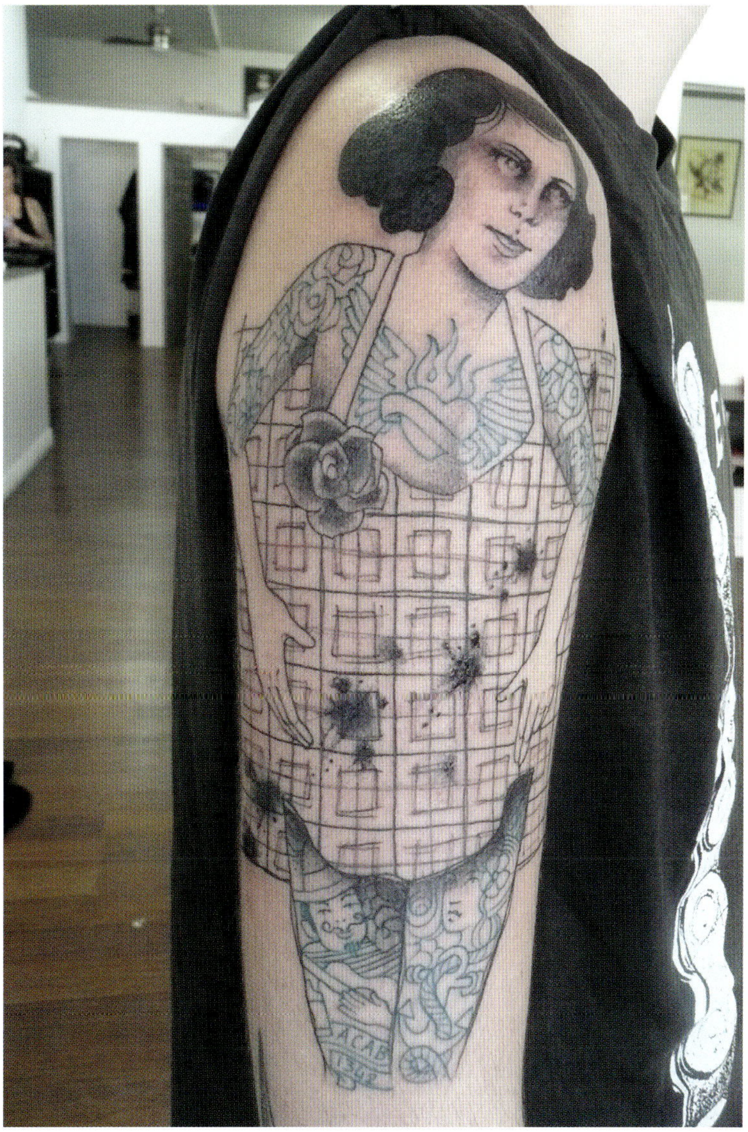

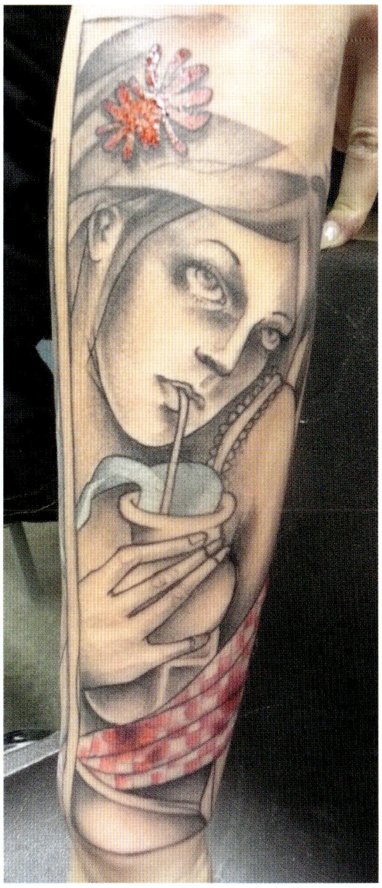

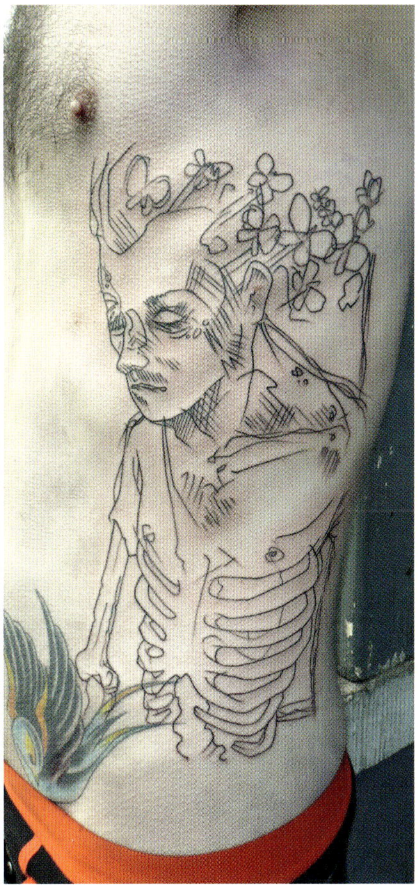

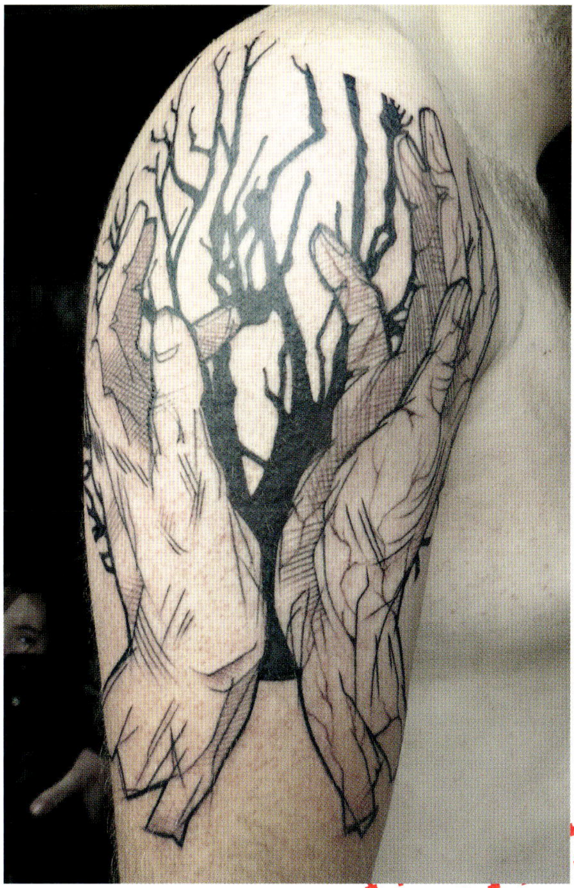

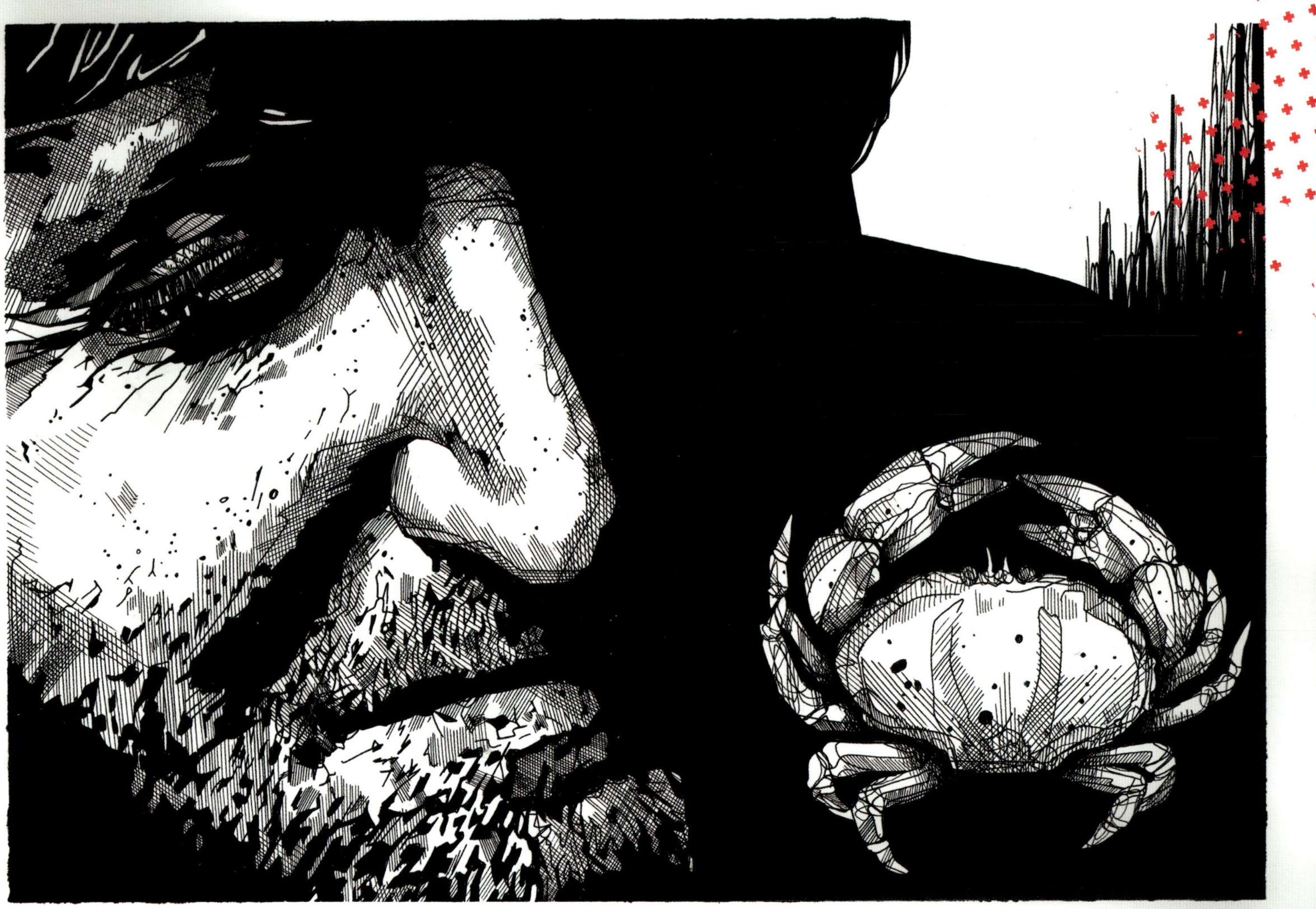

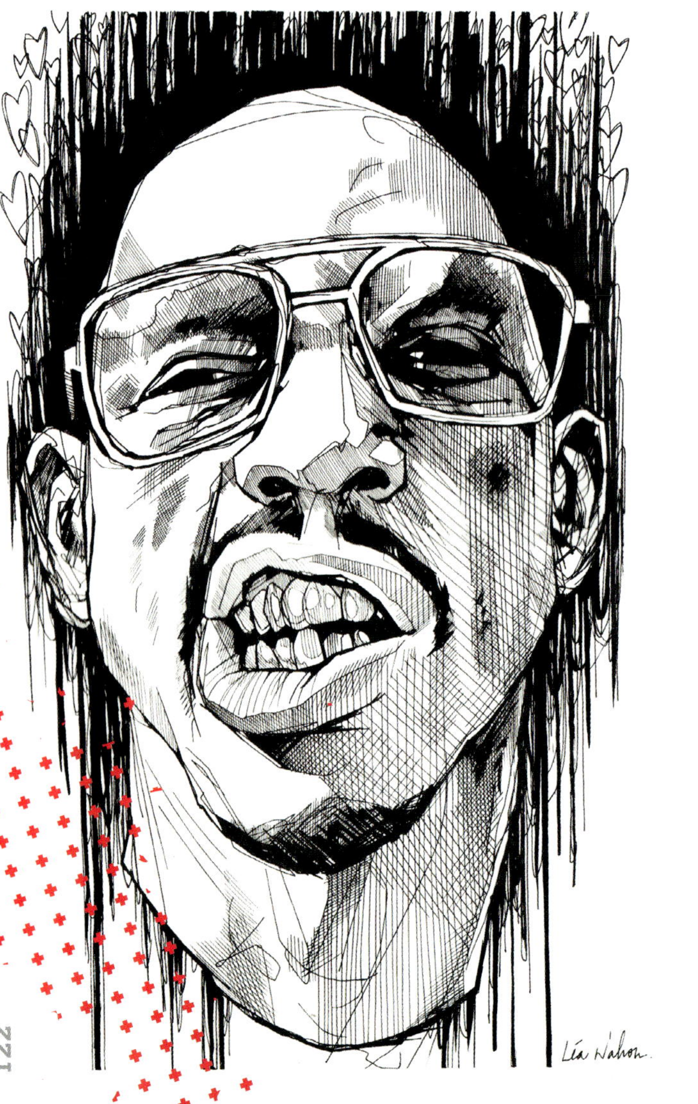
Léa Nahon

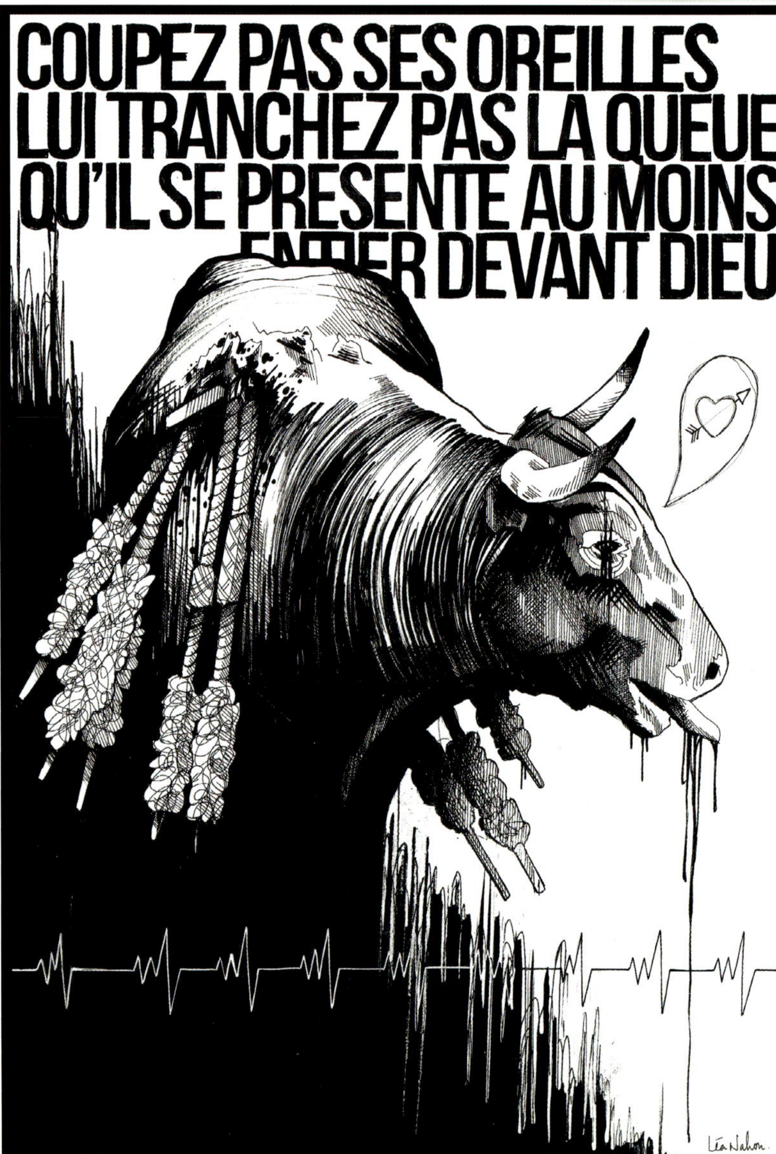
COUPEZ PAS SES OREILLES
LUI TRANCHEZ PAS LA QUEUE
QU'IL SE PRESENTE AU MOINS
ENTIER DEVANT DIEU
Léa Nahon

LÉA NAHON

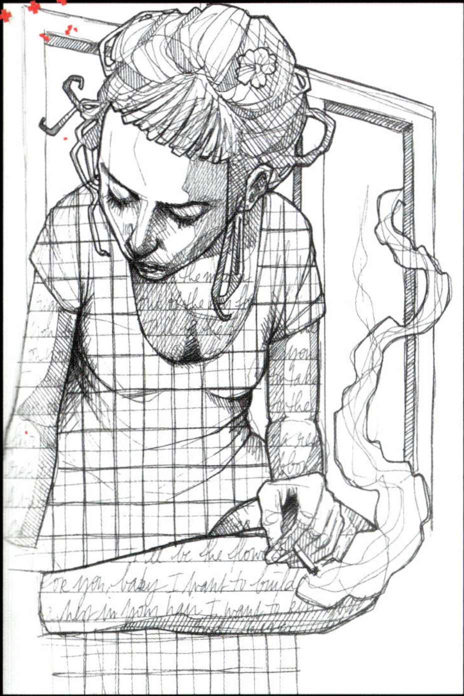

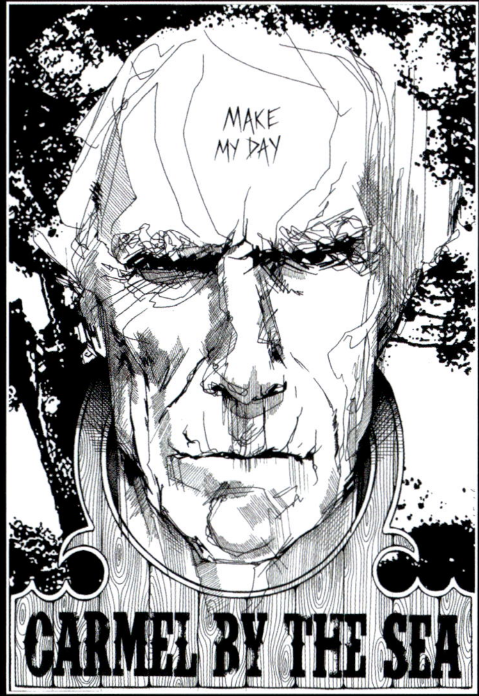

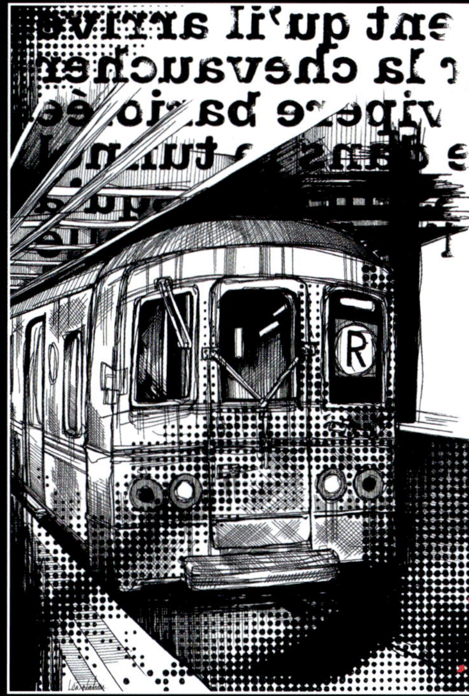

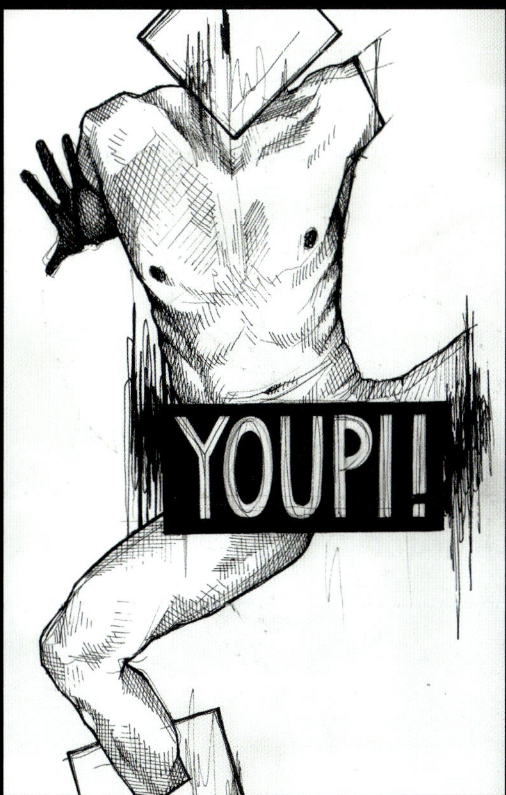

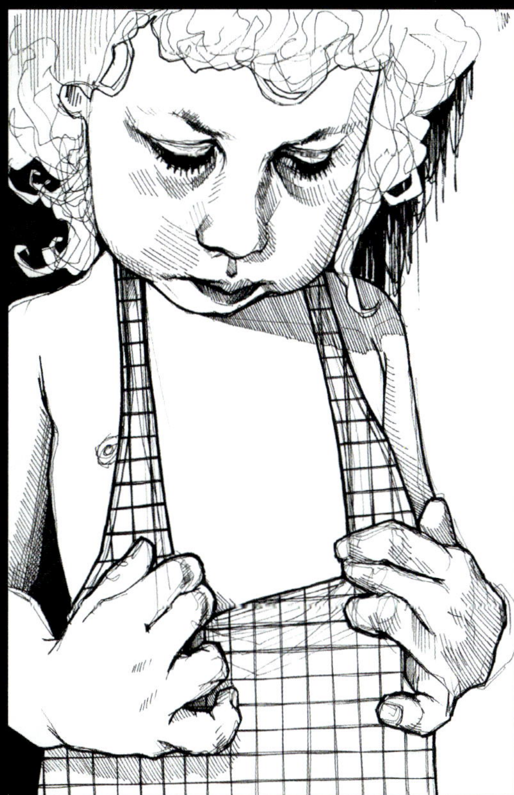

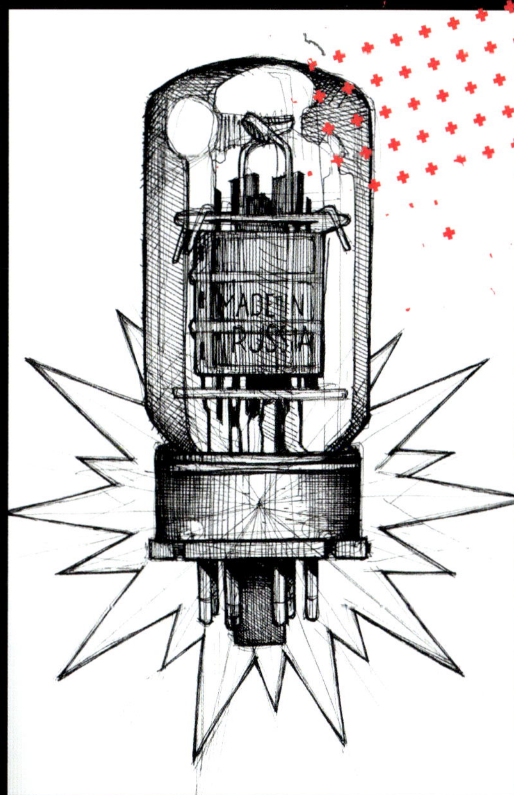

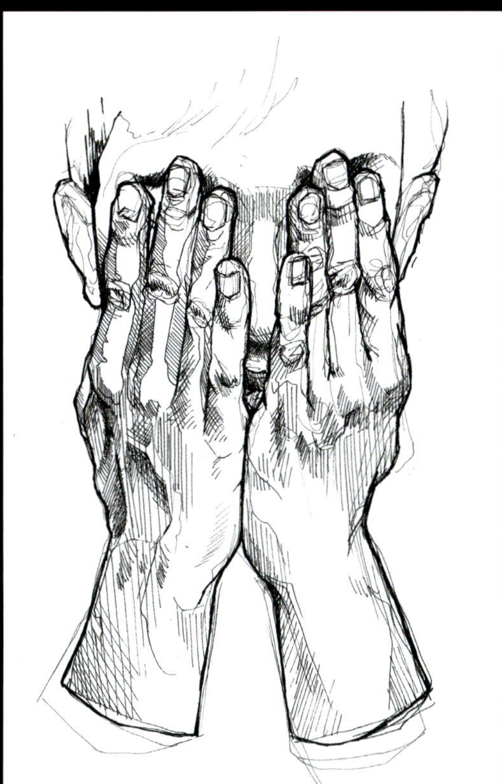

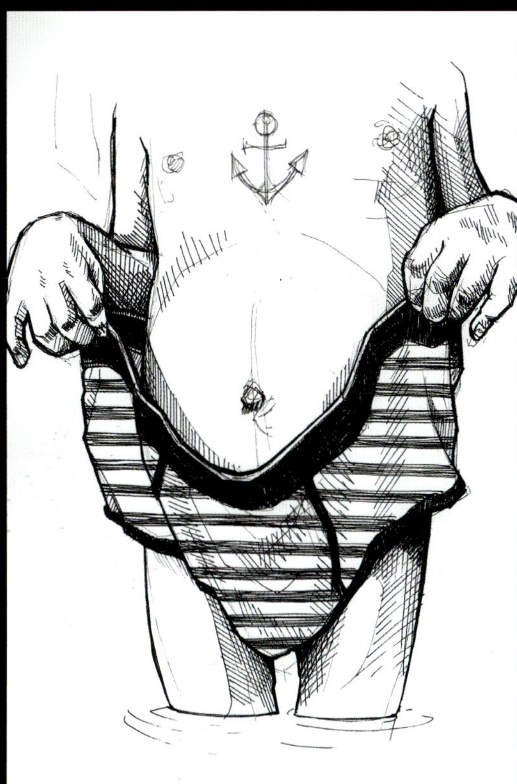

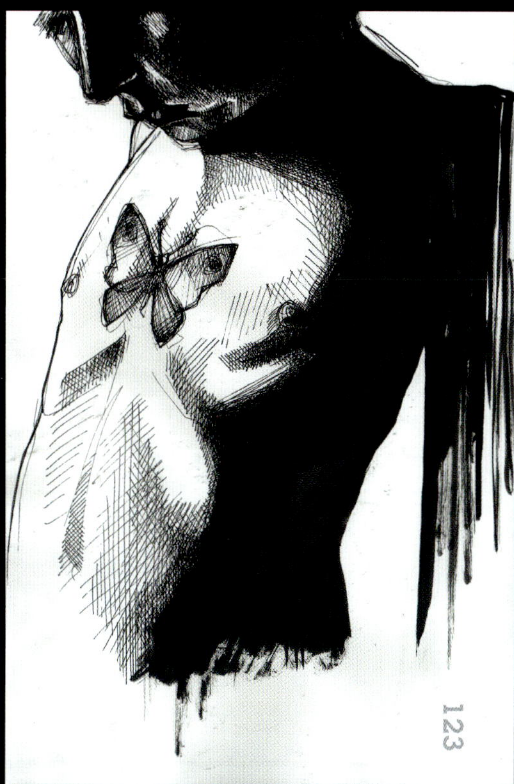

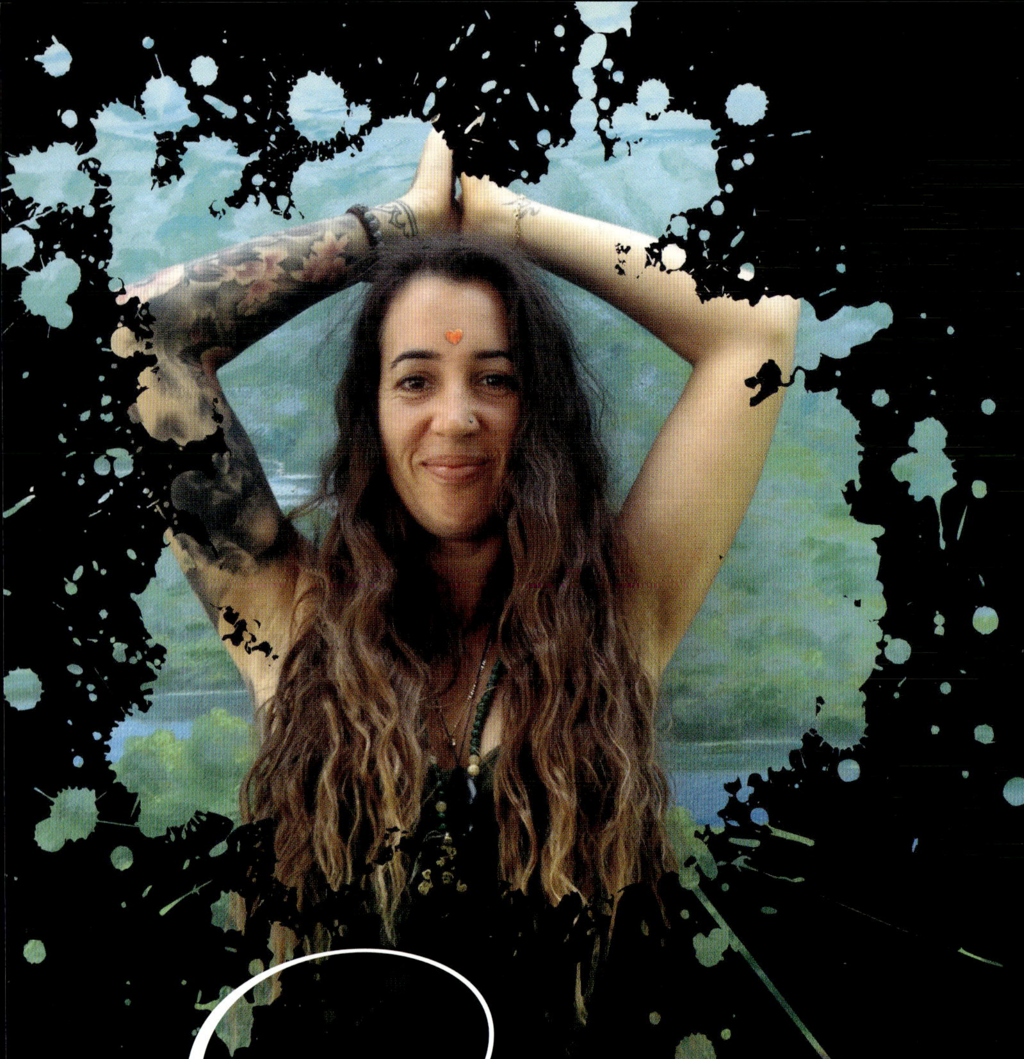

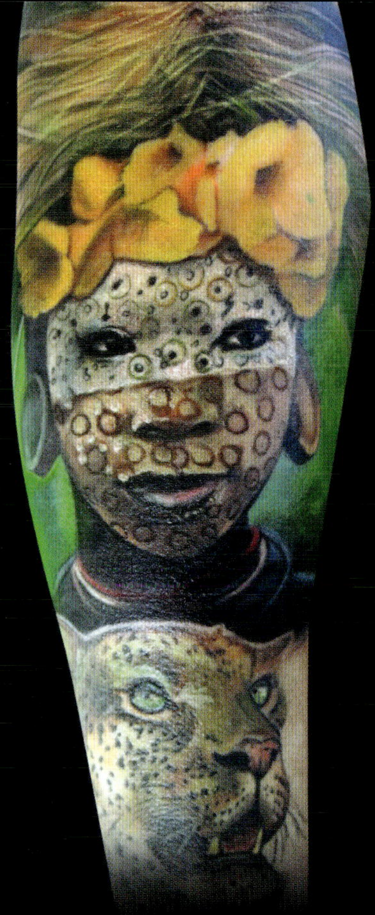

Claire REID

CLAIRE REID was born in England in 1982 and has always had an obsession with art. As a child she was constantly drawing, or in nature. She loves all forms of art and self expression, and over the years Claire delved into many different mediums that enabled her to express her voice.

"Tattooing is a way of life for me, I live it and breathe it"

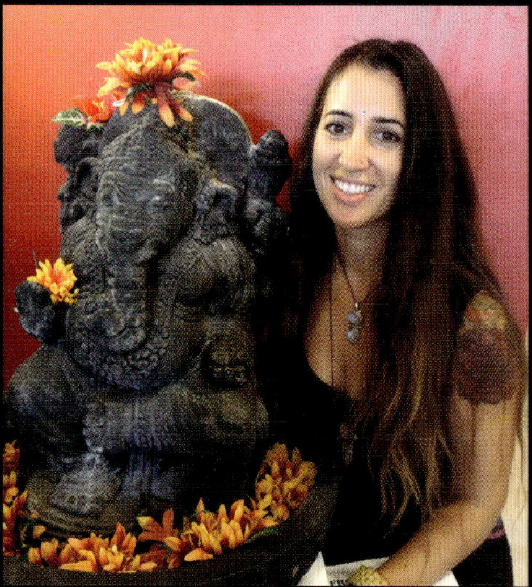

www.clairereid.net
ajnatattoo.com
www.facebook.com/claire.reid.9400
www.facebook.com/pages/Claire-Re-

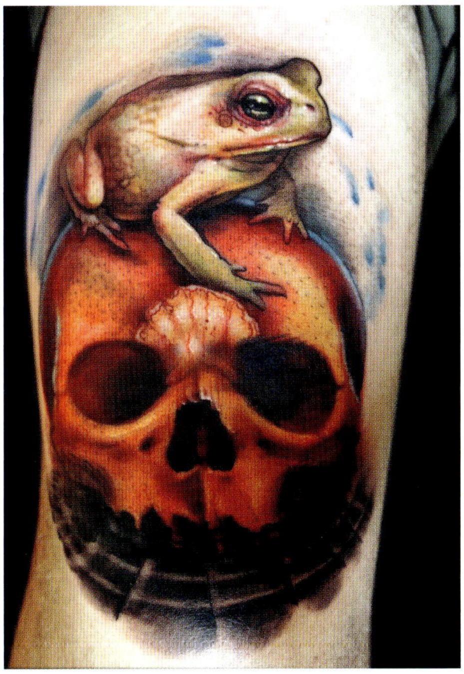

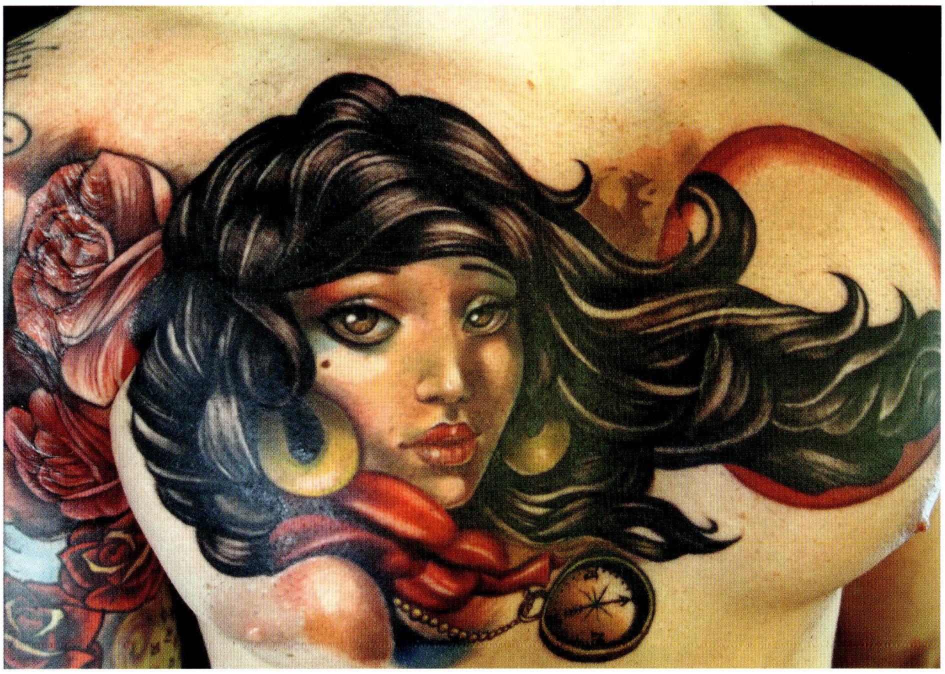

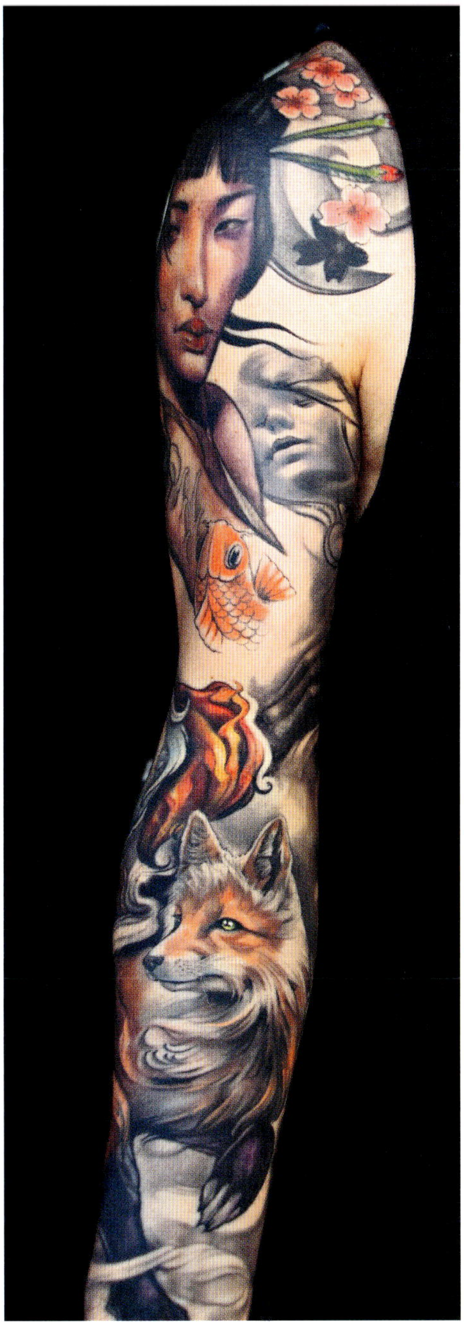

How long have you been a tattoo artist? Did you have a formal apprenticeship?

I first became interested in tattooing when I was sixteen since I loved art, anything alternative, and body modification. I went to university and studied sociology, because I was told that art would not get me a job, and I didn't follow up with tattooing until I finished university in 2004 and I became a piercer. I started tattooing in 2005 and had a six-week apprenticeship that gave me the basics of what I needed to know. From there I started on a journey to study with some of the most incredible tattoo artists around the world. I have been really lucky and worked alongside many famous tattoo artists and they've all taught me everything that I know. After nine years of tattooing, I still feel that I am an apprentice just scratching the surface of tattooing and all that I could know about the profession.

What's it like being a female artist in a primarily male workplace?

I love working in a predominantly male industry with male tattoo artists and have always been treated with the upmost respect. There is always so much laughter in the studios, and I think that tattoo artists are a whole different breed from others in normal society. Many of us do not fit into the box or society, and it takes a certain person to be drawn to this lifestyle. We have the freedom to travel all over the world with our art and experience so many incredible cultures. It takes courage to live a form of self-expression that many hide from the rest of the world, and because of this we are free. I love the family that I have found through tattooing.

Do you feel that male customers treat you differently?

I have the most incredible customers, the vast majority being male. All of my customers have had amazing journeys and I feel honored to be a part of this. My customers generally know that I believe tattoos to be a rite of passage, and they want their

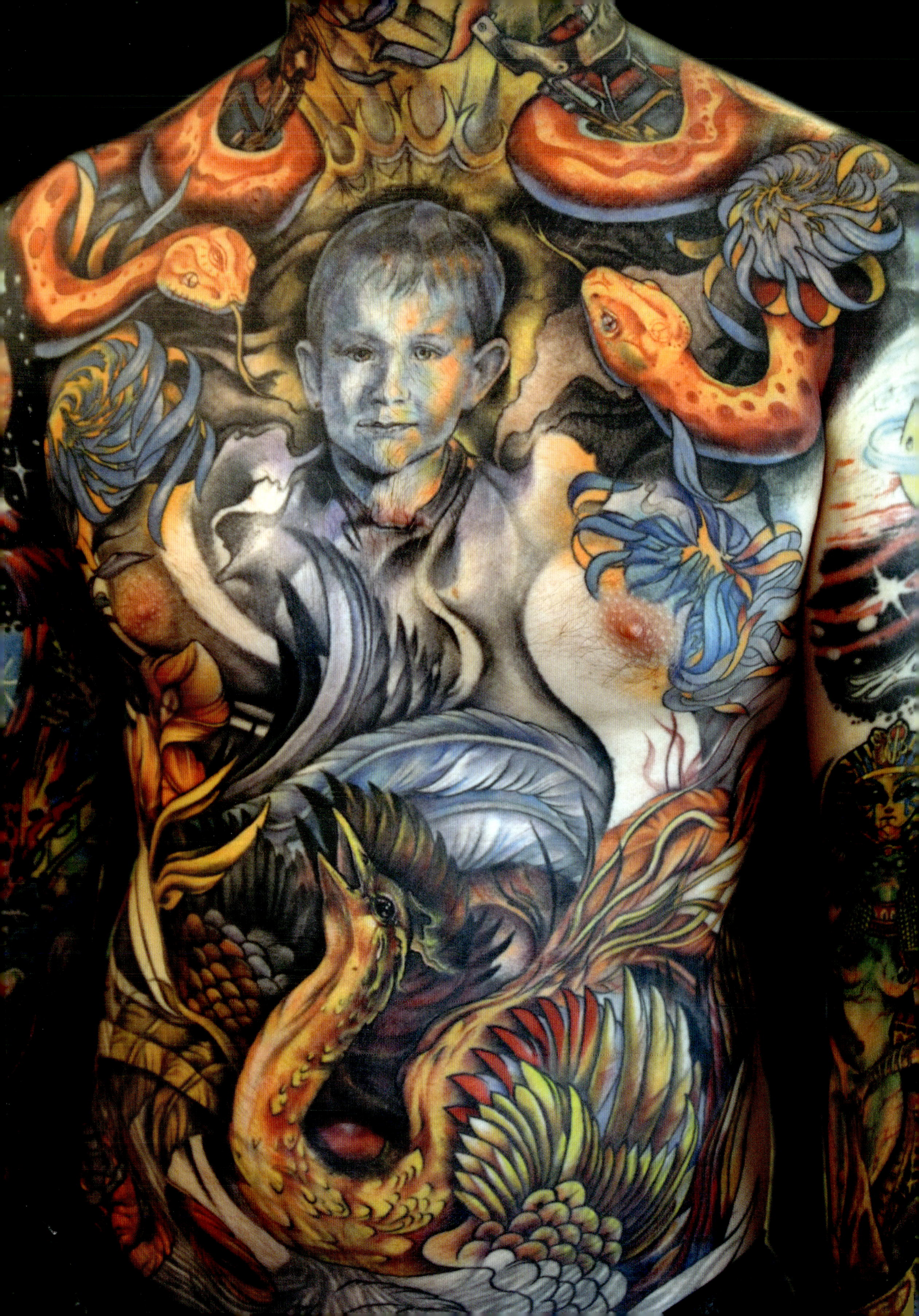

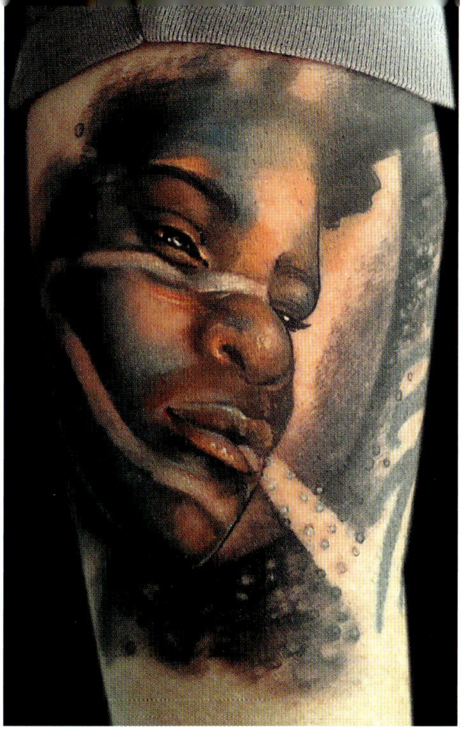

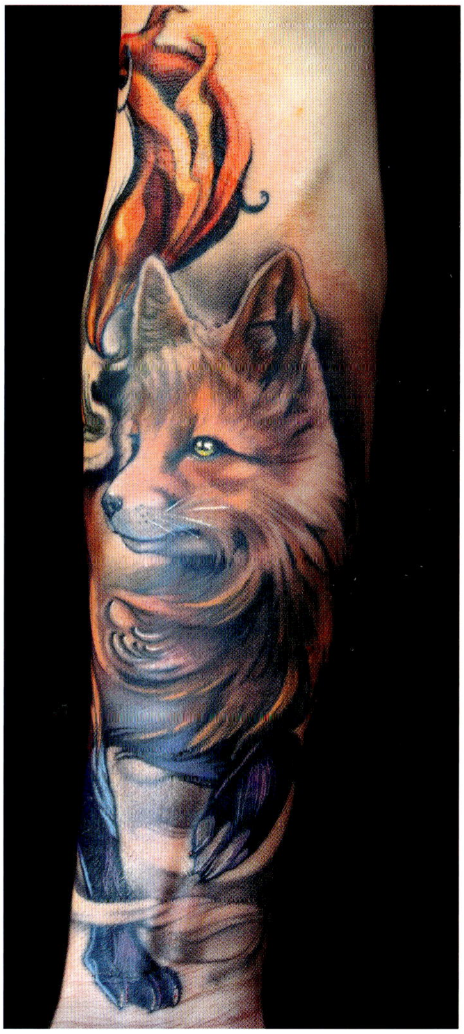

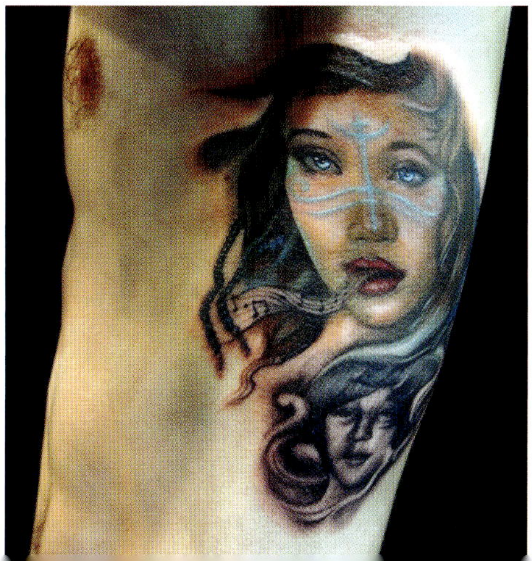

tattoos to have that deeper meaning too. I love talking over the metaphysical aspects of their journeys, and delving under events for greater understanding. By marking the skin people are transformed, and wear their journey and transitions that took them from where they were to who they are now. It is important to express who we are, with tattoos being a window to the soul, and it is important to find the right tattoo that can portray what the person is wanting to express. I love to try and connect with what my customers want to get tattooed, and understand who they are and what they are trying to express.

Though the dynamics are constantly changing, there are obviously many fewer women tattoo artists in the industry than men. Has being a female ever presented challenges to you along the way? Do you feel you have had to work even harder to achieve the success you have than might have been necessary for a man?

I have found that my success has come from the standard of my work. I have only experienced equality as a tattoo artist in a male industry. My main observation about what's not equal would be the constant portrayal of women as sex symbols in tattoo culture—on websites, in magazines, at tattoo conventions. Tattoo magazines are filled with beautiful women wearing nothing and showing their bodies as if that is all that they are. As a tattoo artist I am respected as equal, but in tattoo magazines tattooed women are encouraged to be boxed into a stereotype; it's as if this is their identity and all they are, this is what is revered. The power of a woman is within.

Tell me more about the shop you work at; what's it like working there, and what makes up a typical day?

When I'm not traveling and doing guest spots, I work from my private studio in the rainforest on the east coast of Australia. The studio is twenty-five minutes from a shop and has incredible nature and wildlife all around it. There is an eighty-foot waterfall up the road, and the ocean is forty minutes away; I often take customers out to beautiful places in the area before they get tattooed. I also have pet peacocks roaming around the studio. My customers all love the experience, as many of them fly in from the city to get work done.

I tattoo using solar power, and use as many earth-friendly products as possible. I've planted an orchard, and veggie patches, I keep chickens, and I have a nice creek down the hill where we can swim. I work with another tattoo artist who is one of my best friends. His name is Jacob Gwynn and he tattoos beautiful realism and paints like a Renaissance painter. We bounce off each other all the time with ideas, and I'm constantly inspired by him and his work.

I love to come home to this environment after being on the road, because I can reconnect with the earth and clear my mind. The forest helps me to become more intuitive and relax. I only tattoo one person per day so that I can take time to design and understand what that person wants. I love tattooing in this way.

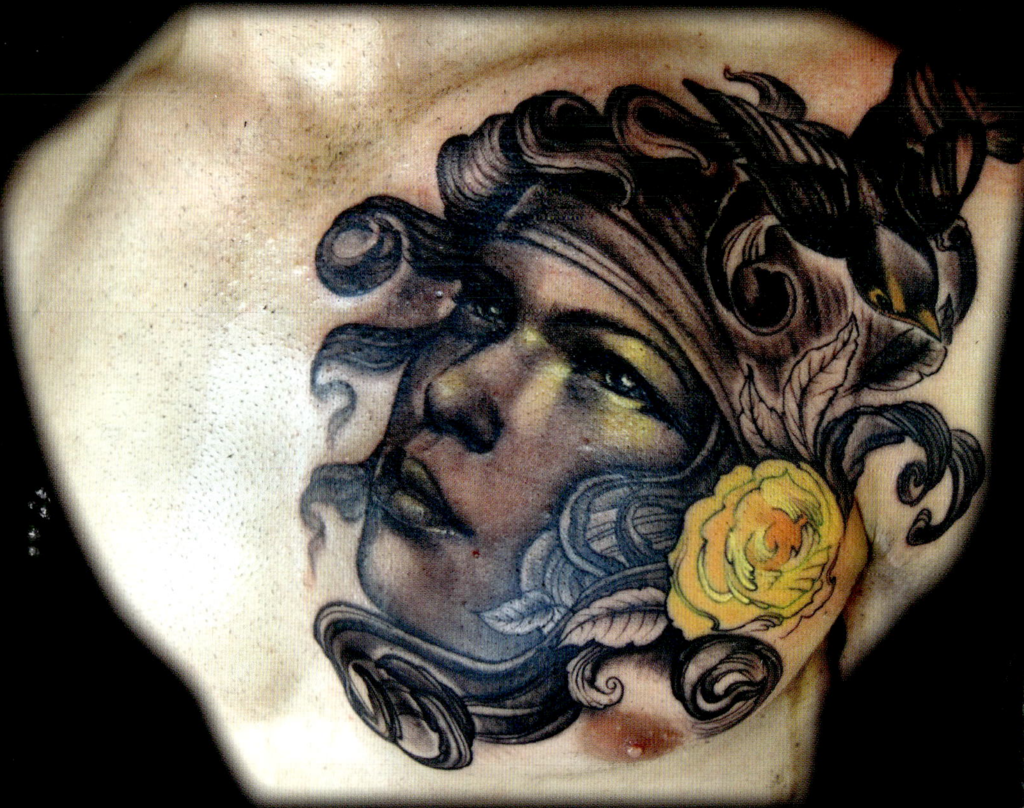
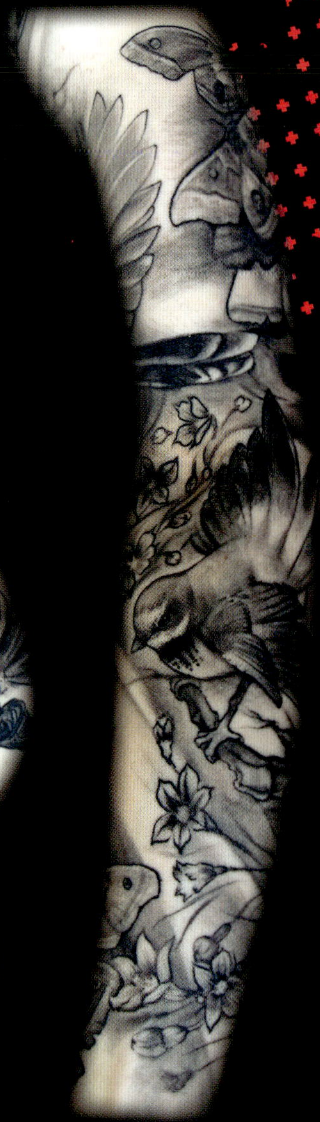
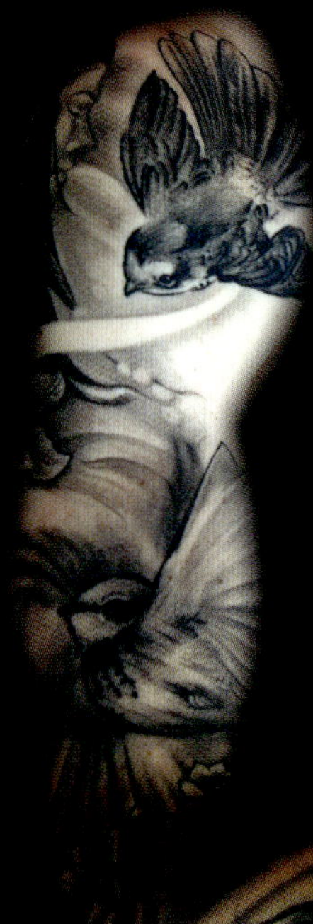
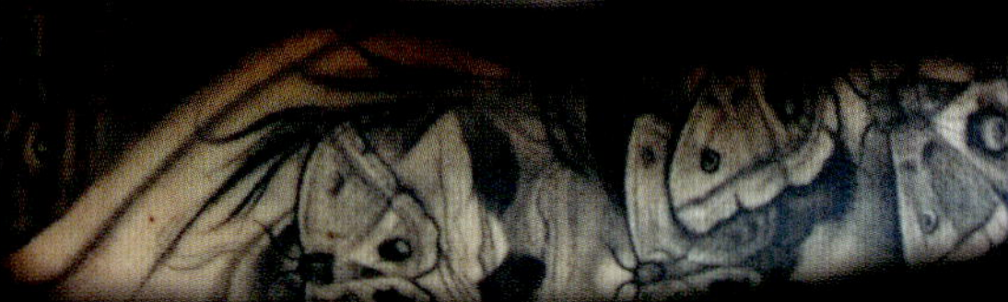
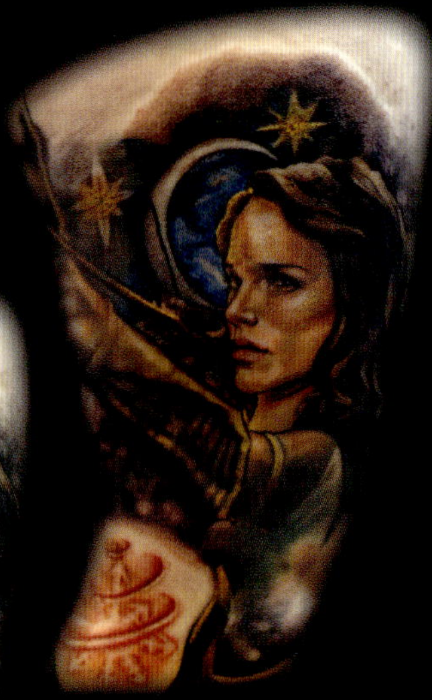
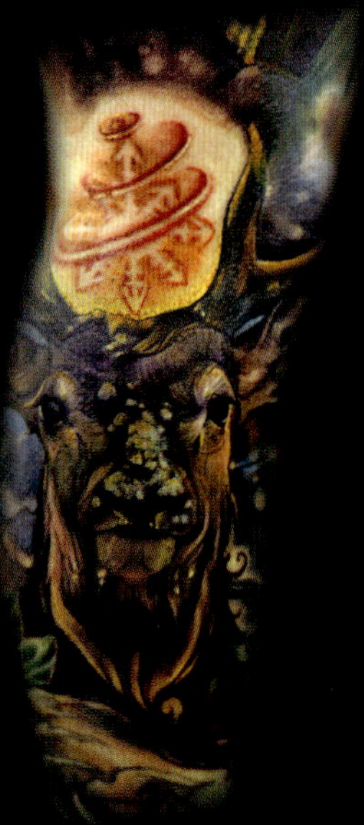
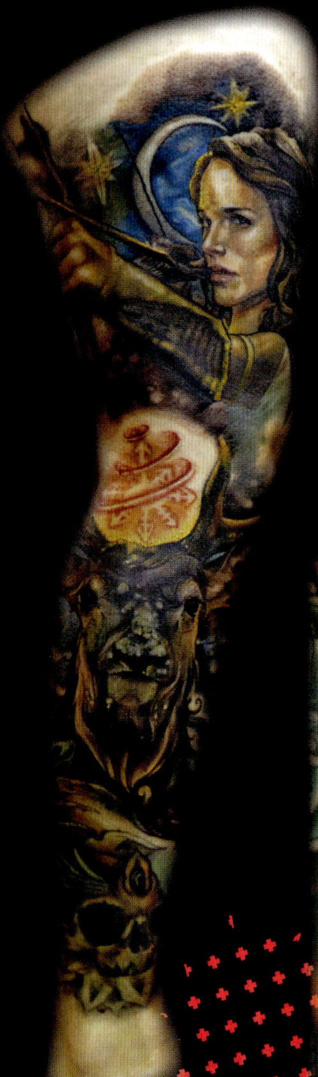
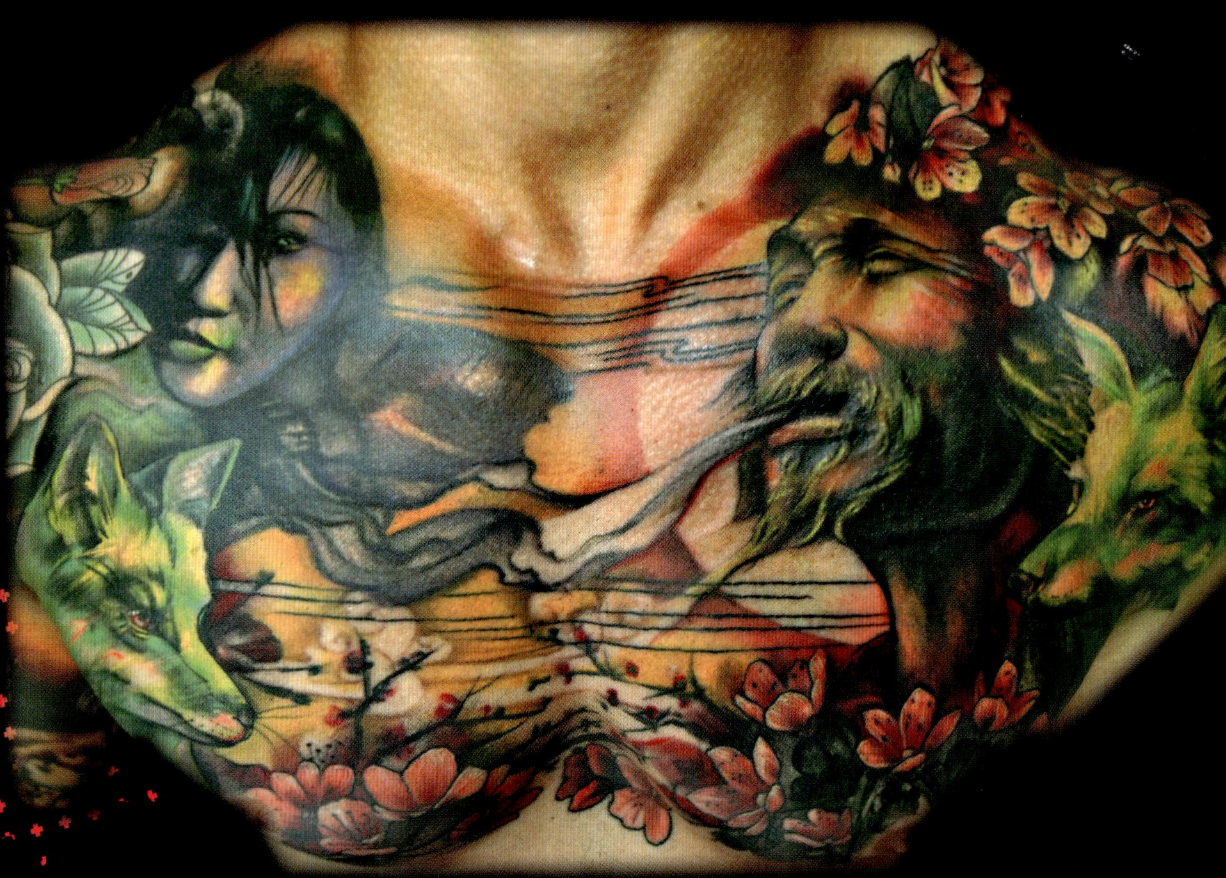

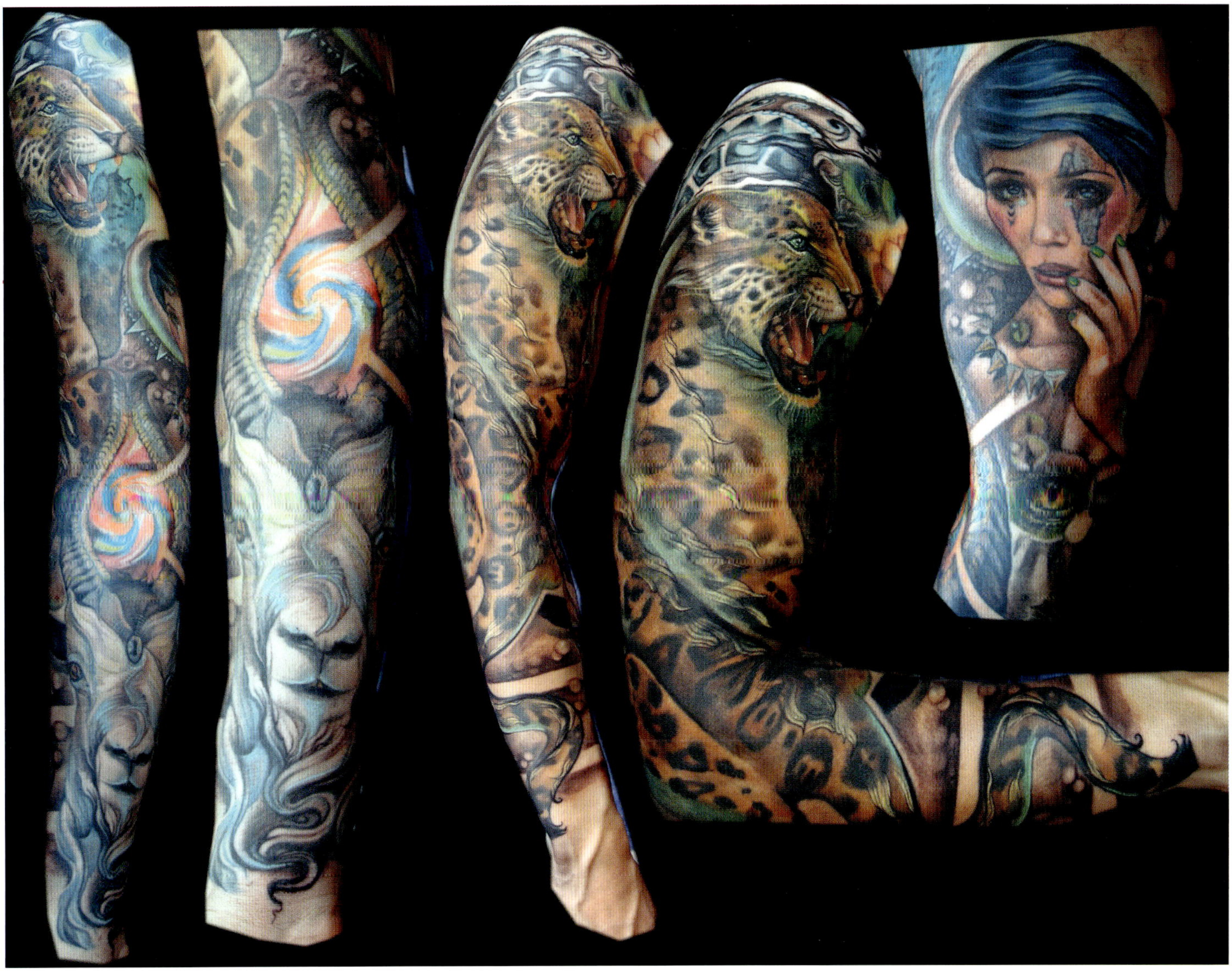

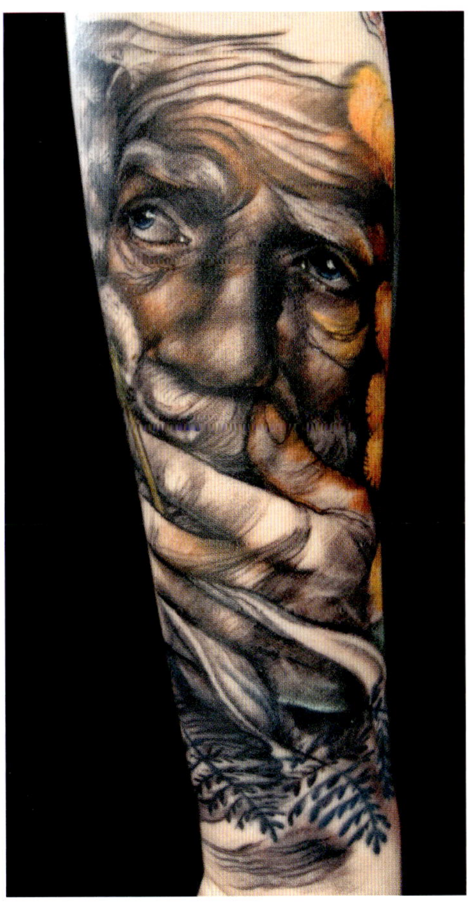

Do you see tattooing as a job or as a way to express your creative side?

Tattooing is a way of life for me, I live it and breathe it. I am serious about what I do and have a great respect for my customers. I feel that since I started tattooing I have never worked a day in my life as it is such a great passion for me. I feel that there are unlimited avenues to explore with tattooing that extend me constantly.

For the past five years I have been greatly interested in indigenous cultures and the practice of shamism and healing through tattoos. This is an ancient practice that I see playing out in the present day with people going through incredible transformation and healing when getting tattooed. Many of my friends who are tattoo artists are also interested in shamanism, and I love to hang out with them to expand my knowledge further. I especially love to spend time in New Zealand with shamanic tattoo artists, who have taught me a great deal about their spiritual practices behind tattooing. I have great respect for all indigenous cultures, especially in Australia since the Aboriginal culture is so ancient and holding vast knowledge about the land and the universe. I only hope to gain a fraction of this knowledge in my lifetime and use it to help those around me.

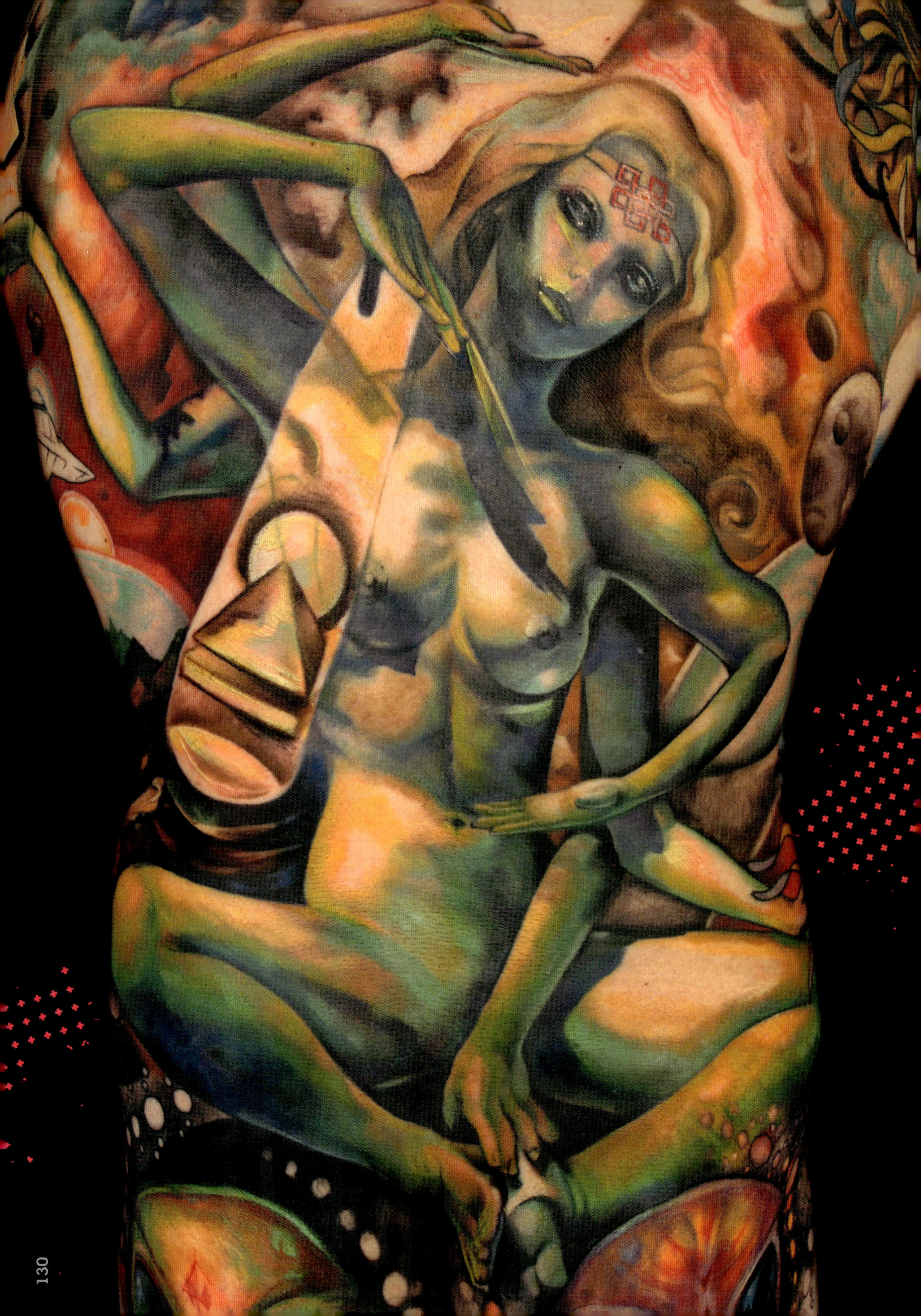

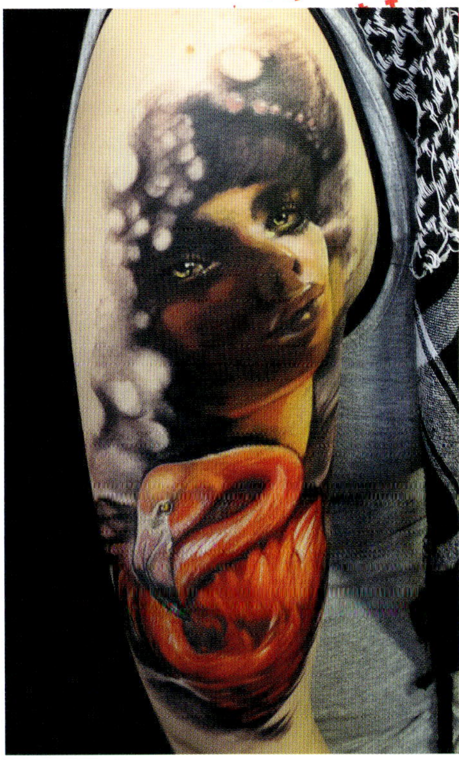

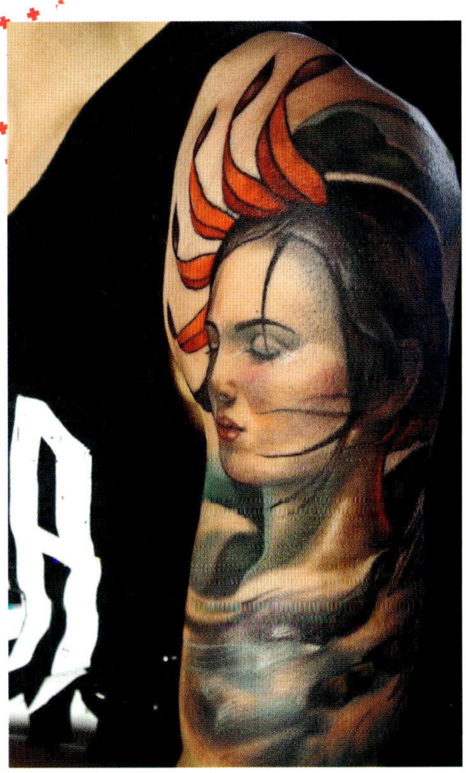

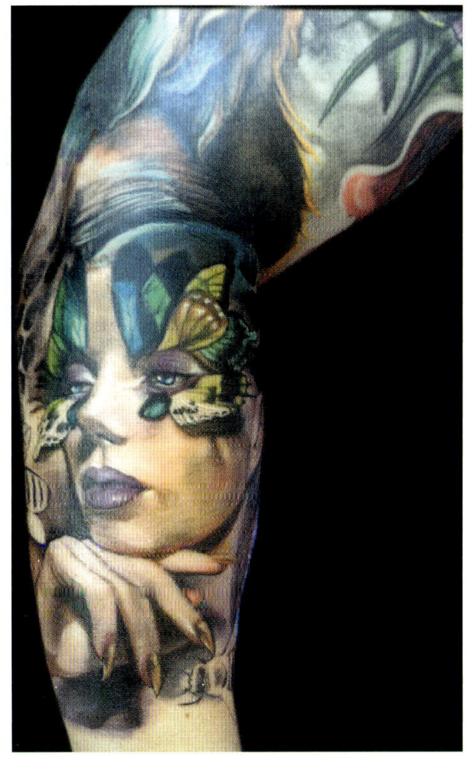

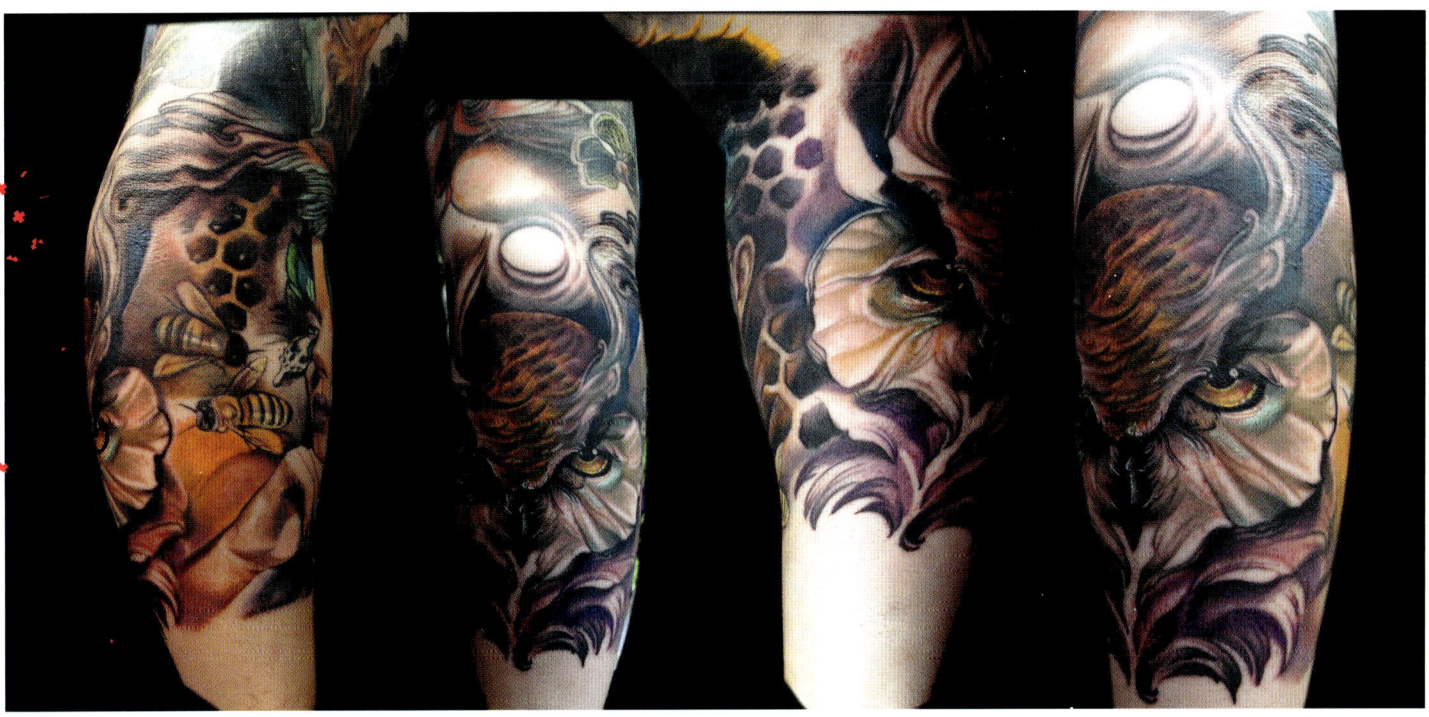

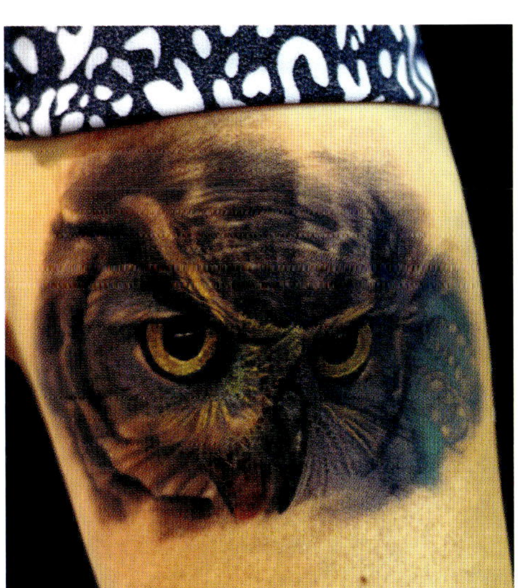

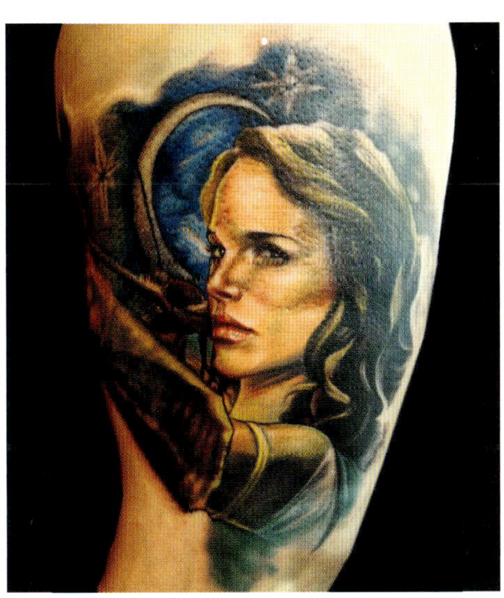

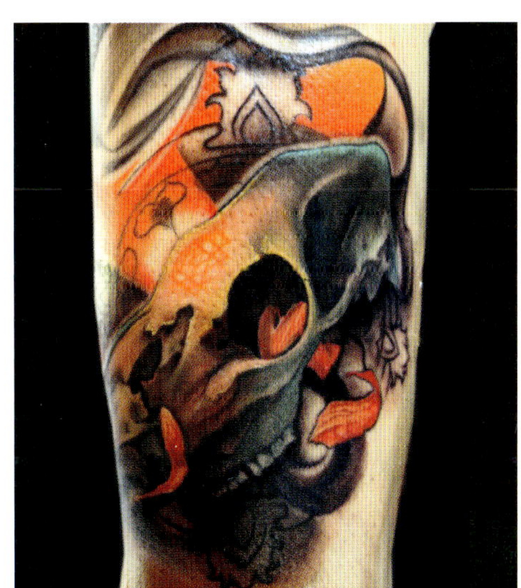

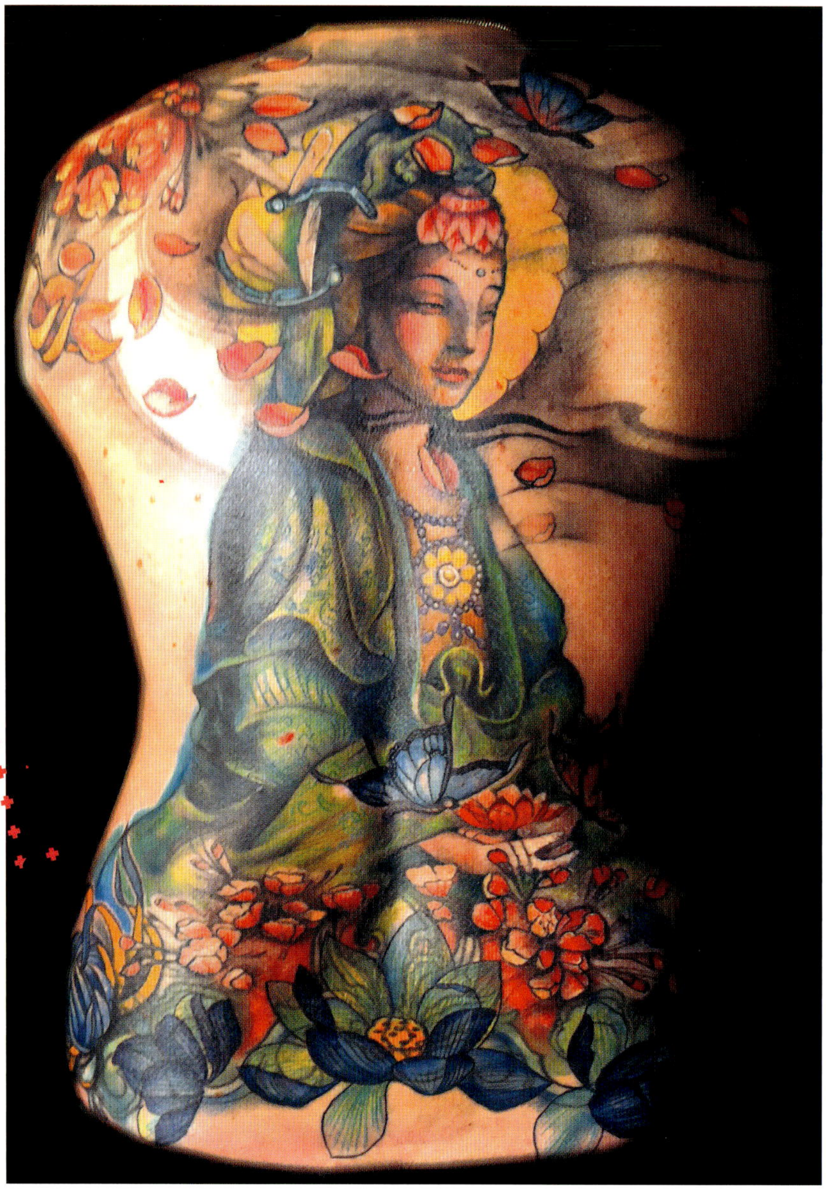

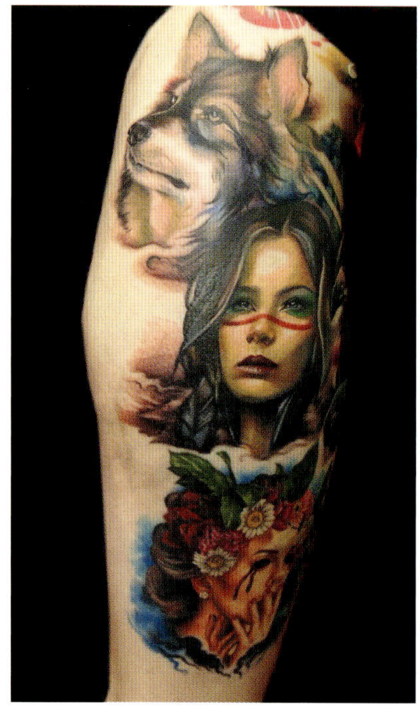

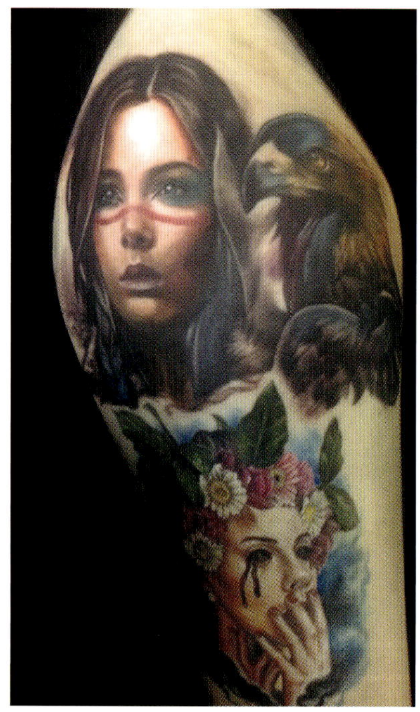

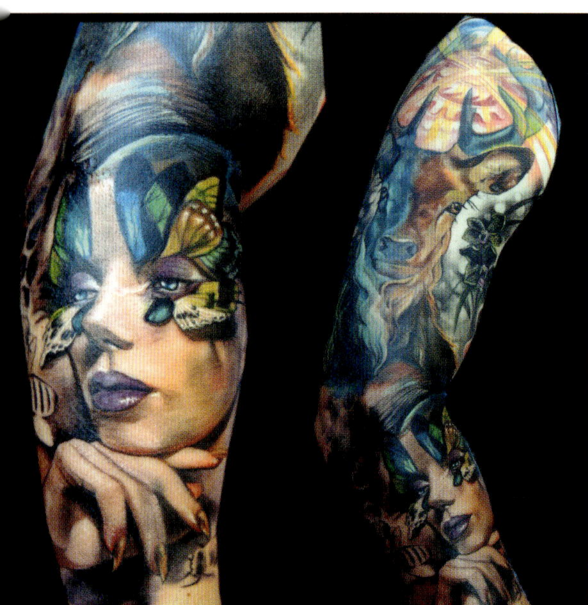

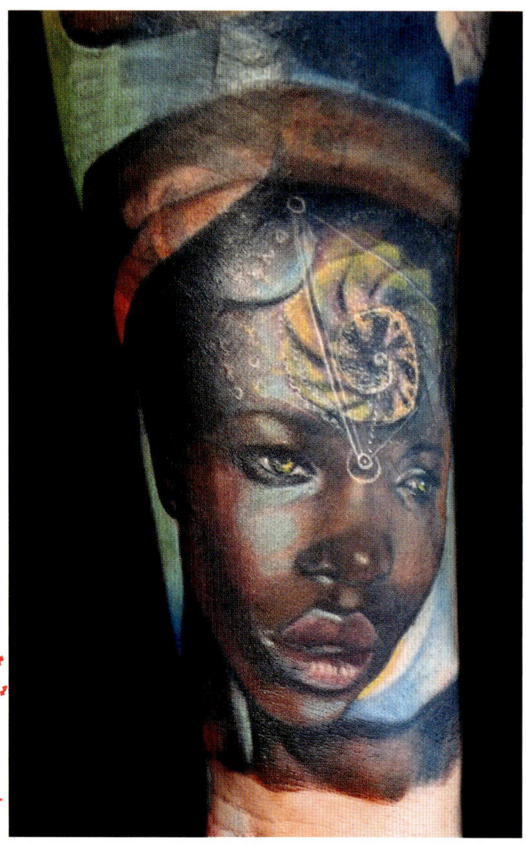

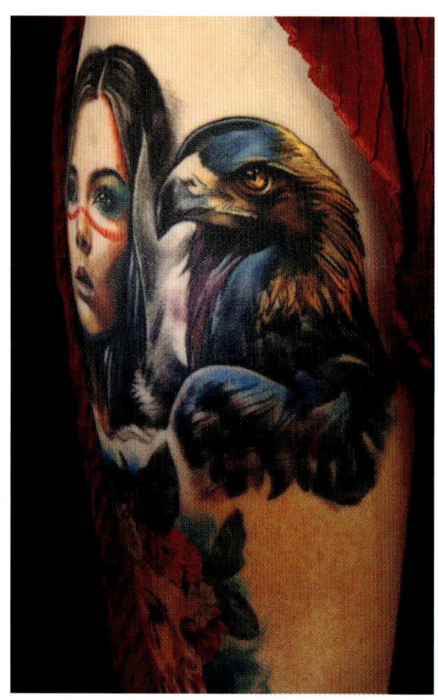

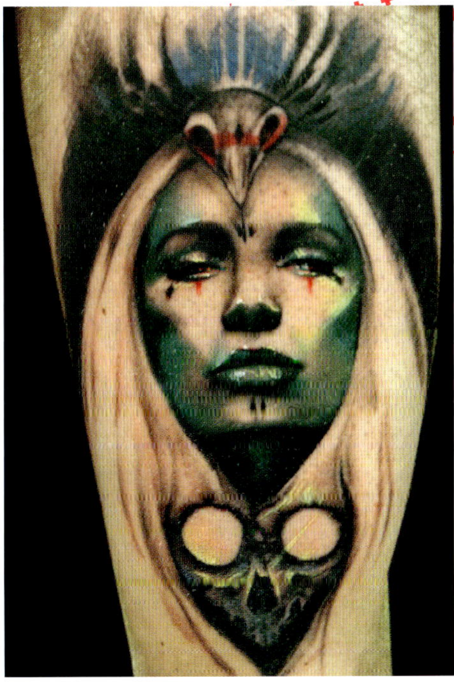

What inspires you when you create?

I am inspired to create and portray my view of the world; I dream of world peace and of a time when everyone becomes one realizing that we are all the same. A lot of my artwork comes from this place, and a lot of my customers are attracted to my art, wanting designs that represent similar things, such as their own spirituality.

What do you enjoy most about tattooing, and what are some of the challenges?

I love everything about tattooing—I love interacting with my customers for so long, I love being creative and artistic all day, I love traveling, I love the depth and spirituality behind tattooing, I love the inks and the technical side, the actual art of putting ink under the skin, the colors, playing music all day…I love the whole process.

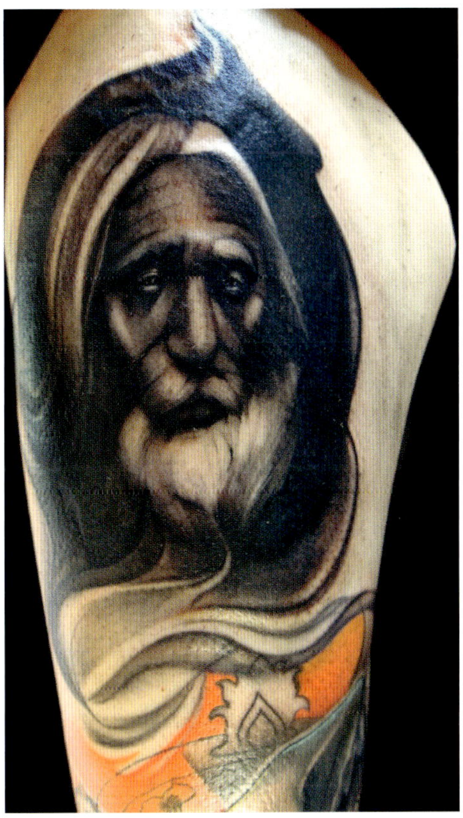

Art can be a great influence on someone's personality. What is the best lesson that you've learned from your art journey?

Art has taught me to connect with my soul. When I am painting and tattooing I am in that place and feel like the creation comes from there. Art has carried me through all of my life's journeys, and I am grateful to have had that there as a means of expression and consistency through all situations.

How did your style progress and develop to the point you are at now?

I am constantly developing the way I tattoo and paint through technique, subject matter, and finding ways to communicate clearly. I try not to think too much when I am creating. My style has progressed from the influences around me; I notice that my art is always changing and reflecting my environment. I've had many incredible teachers along the way, and enjoy learning.

Describe how your role models and any other sources of inspiration have affected your tattoo style.

My main role models inspire me to live life to the full and put my all into every moment, to live in a space of love and not fear, to be completely present and attentive toward what I am doing. They inspire me to live truth and be free, to express who I am, and live with compassion. I have been deeply affected by some incredible people in my life, and I will carry their effect on me throughout my life. I am lucky and honored to have shared their time in such a profound way.

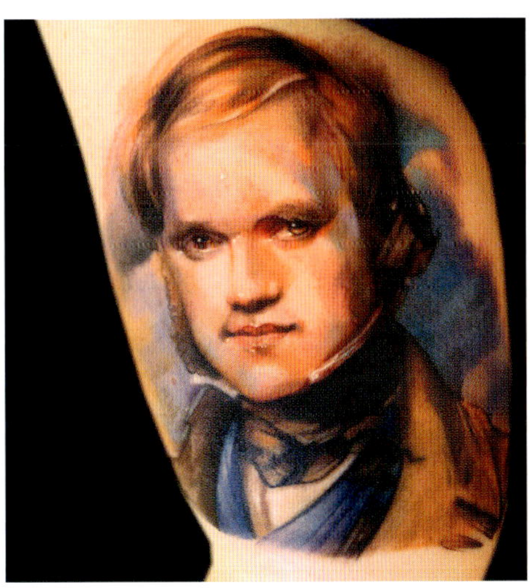

What's one of your favorite pieces that you've tattooed on someone else?

My favorite piece is on my friend Brad—it's a sleeve of cycles from creation, to birth, to death, and so on. There's an eye in there, a hand with a seed, nebulae, a skull with orbs, a portal, and a man creating energy. With each session, we did ceremonies

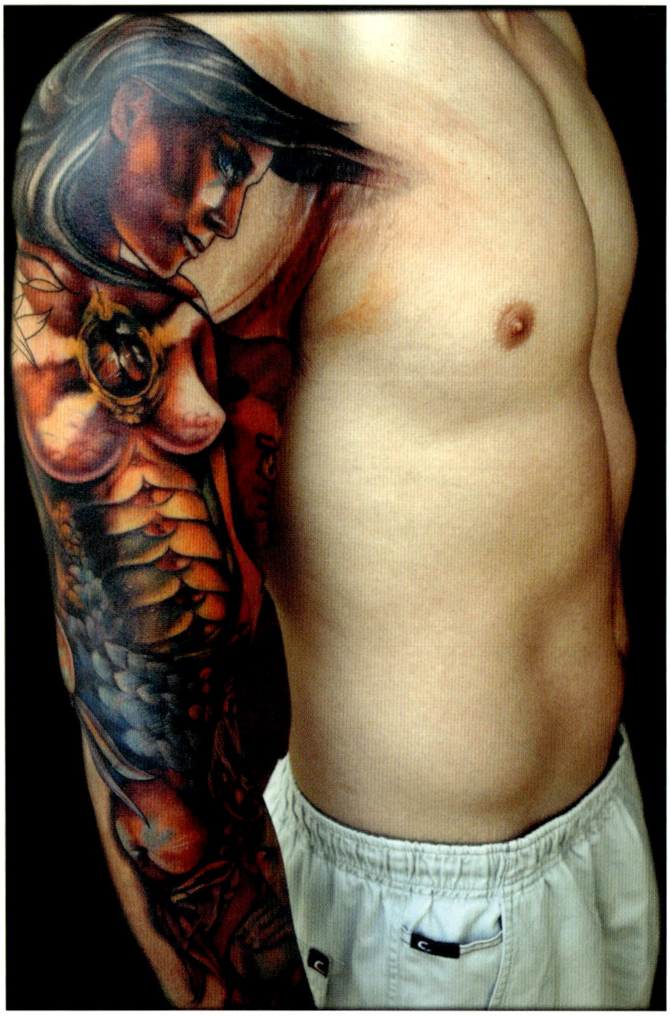

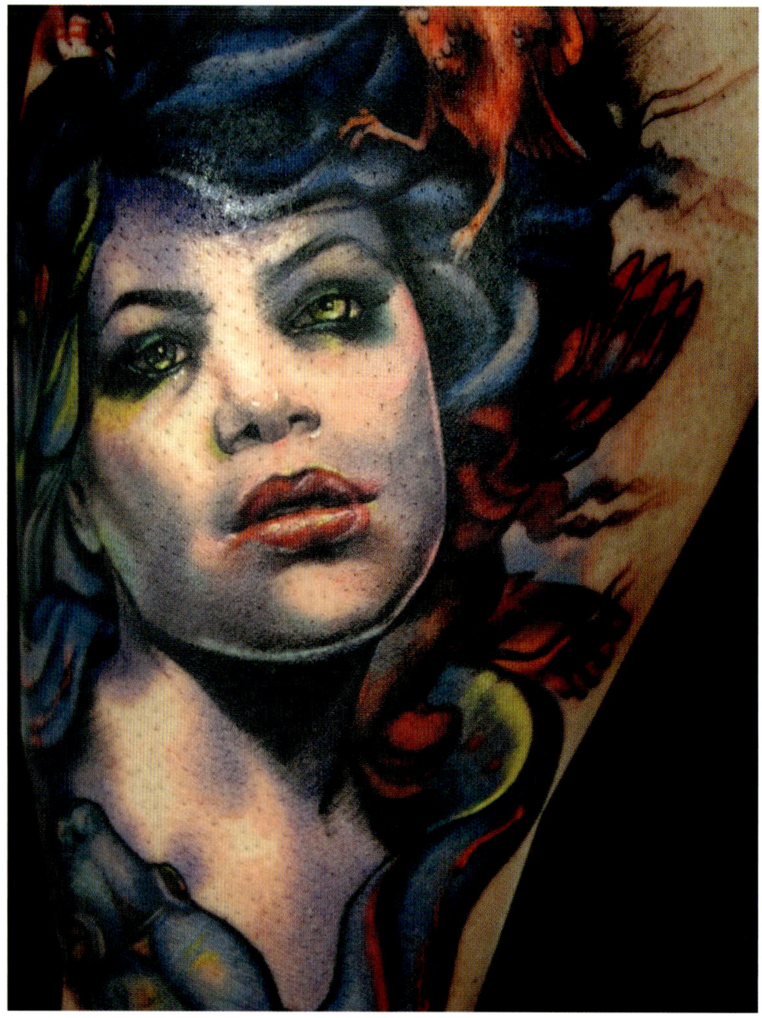

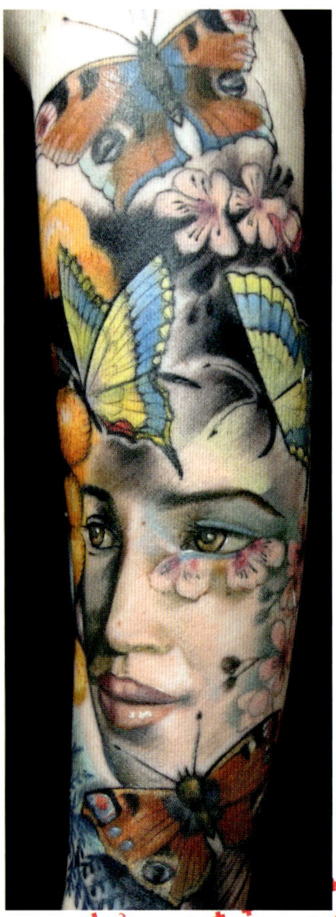

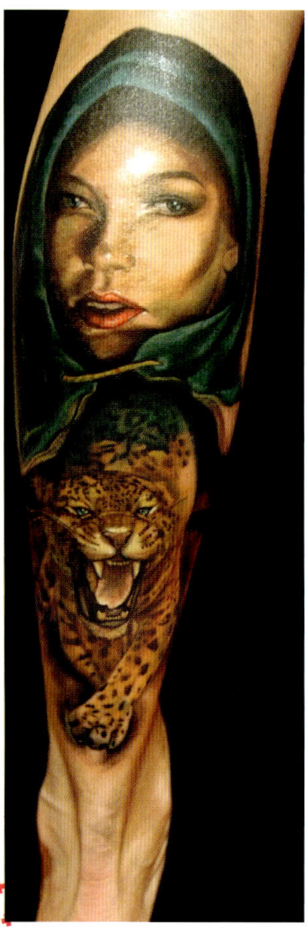

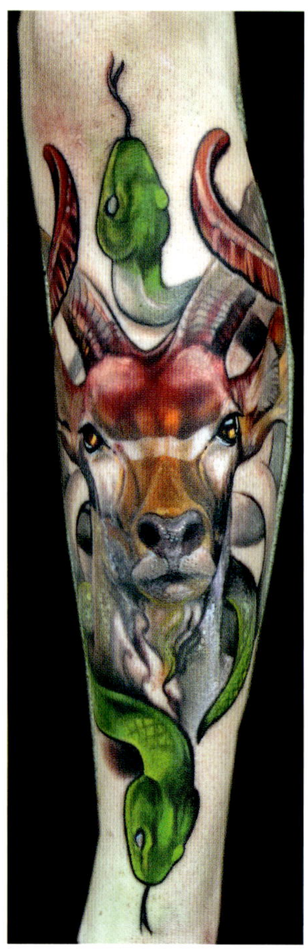

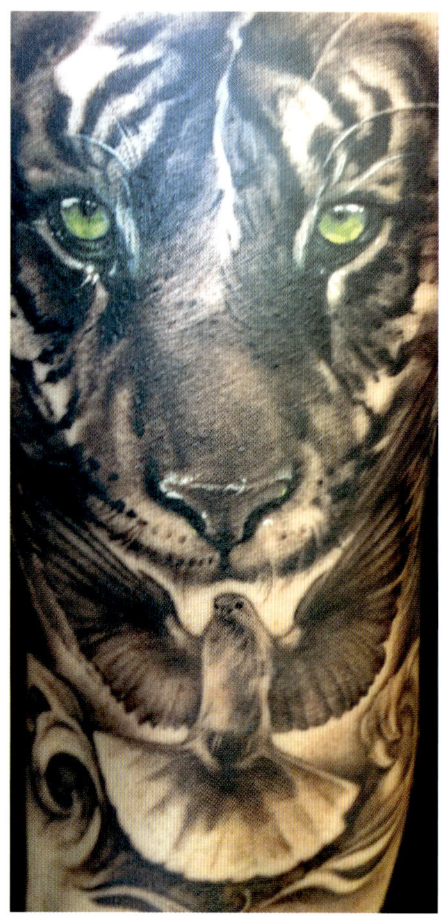

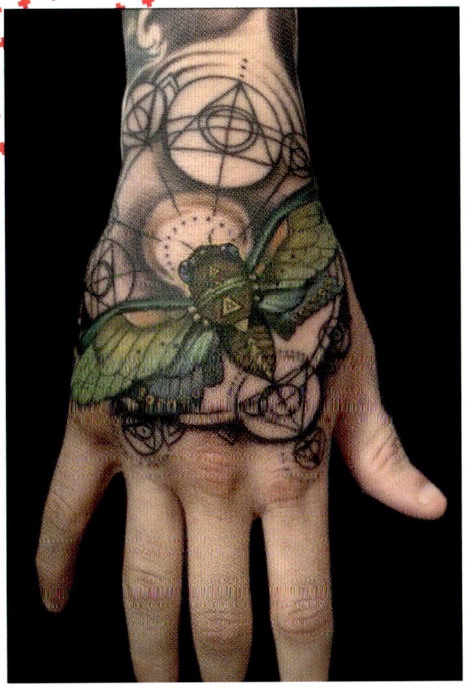

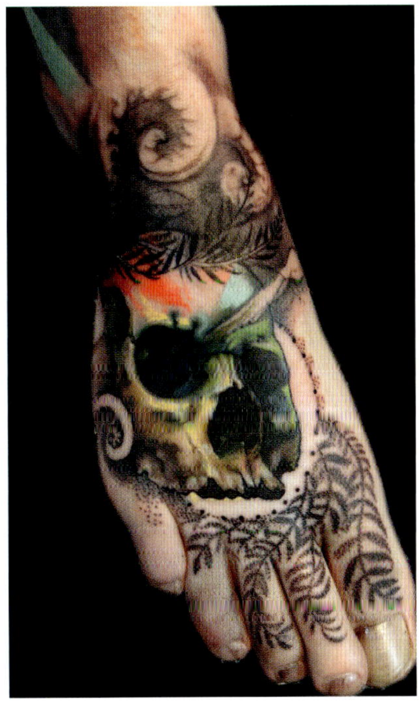

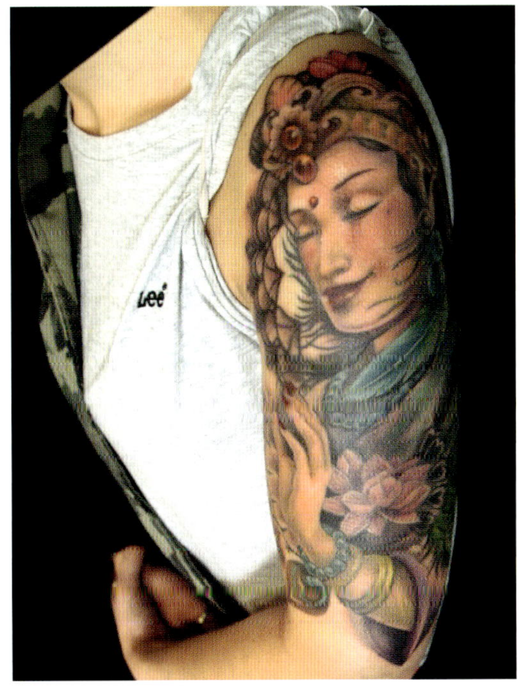

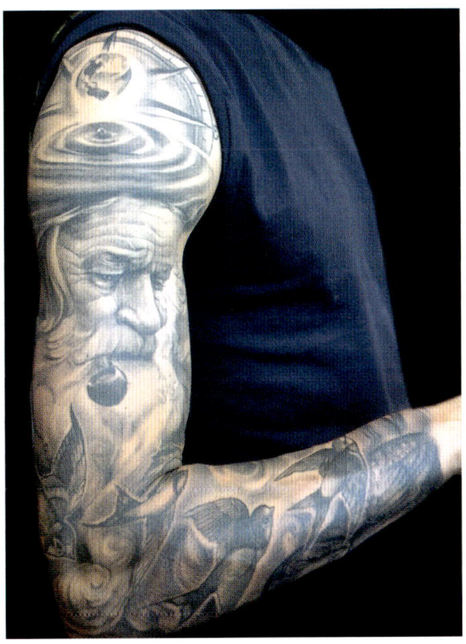

taught to me by my Maori friends, with Brad experiencing big shifts in his life each time. After finishing the tattoo we got the opportunity to travel across Australia together from east to west, on a journey with many other people to help protect the land from mining. The journey was incredible, and the protests were successful as the land is now protected.

What's one of your favorite pieces on your own body, and who did it?

I have many. I love my full back piece by Paolo Acuna; I have a full leg by Jeff Gogue, and a sleeve by Robert Hernandez and Chris Nieves; thank you guys!

What is your favorite thing about being a tattoo artist?

There're too many things…being free.

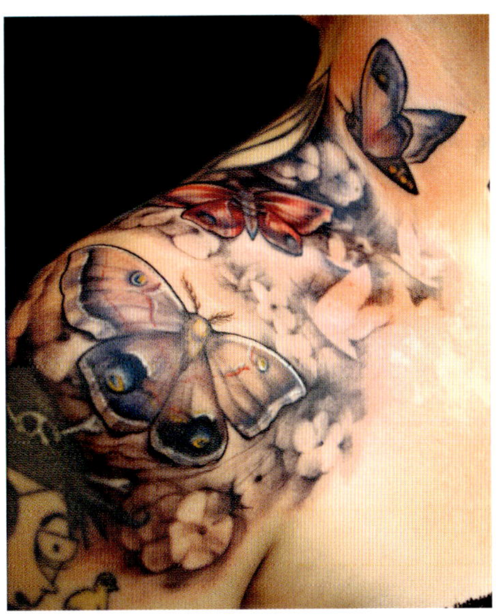

Have you noticed a change in the types of images people have asked for over the years you've been tattooing?

I think I get asked to tattoo a certain type of imagery, but I have noticed that people are wanting more supernatural tattoos that represent the universe now.

Tattoos seem very mainstream now. Do you think that's good or bad?

I think that things will change and it is really positive that people are expressing themselves, and that tattooing is a positive thing now.

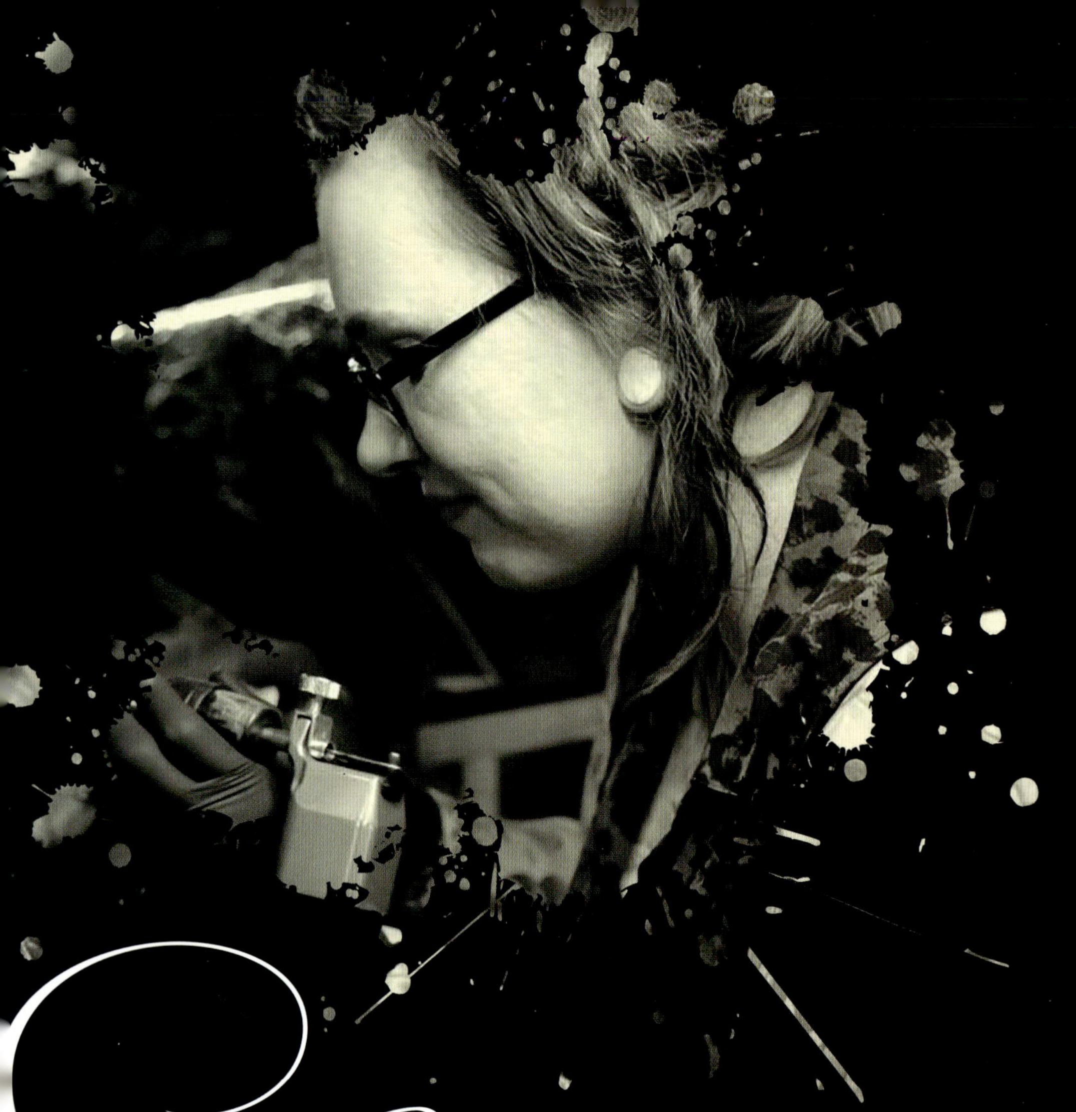

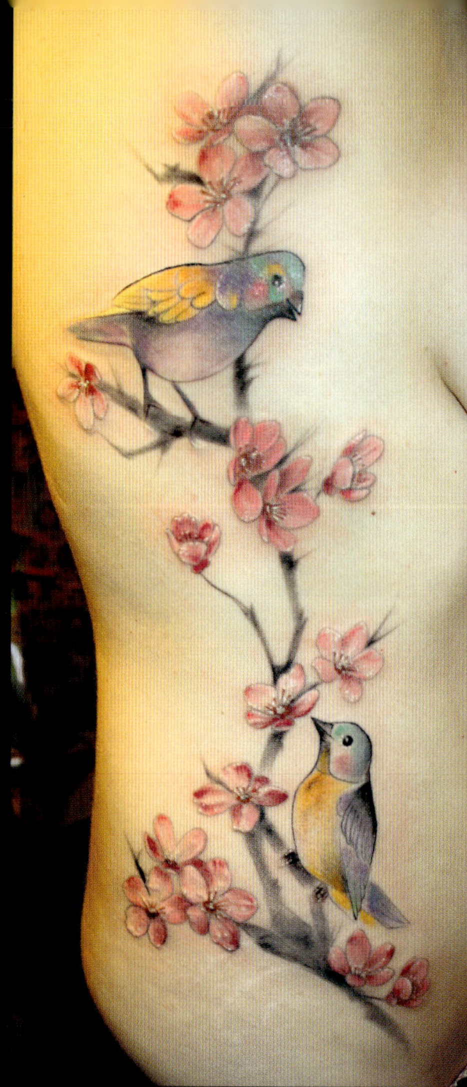

Charlotte ROSS

CHARLOTTE ROSS was brought up in Fife, Scotland. Before she tattooed, she worked on her BA honours degree in fine art, while working in a cinema at night.

"If you're a good tattooist it doesn't matter what sex you are"

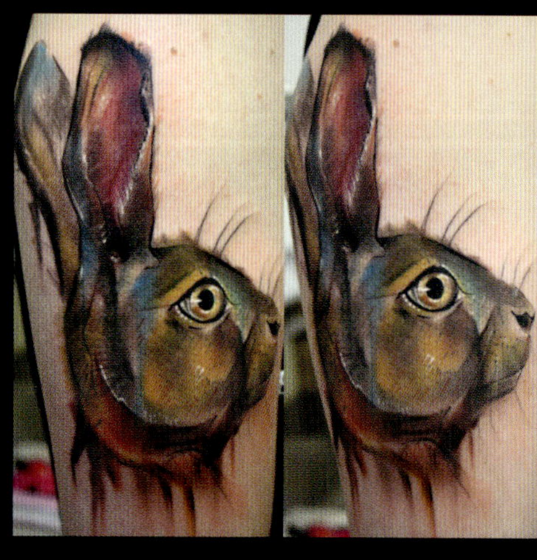

charlotte-ross-tattoos.tumblr.com
instagram.com/charlotteross_tattoos
charlotterosstattoos.wordpress.com
www.facebook.com/charlotte.ross.35

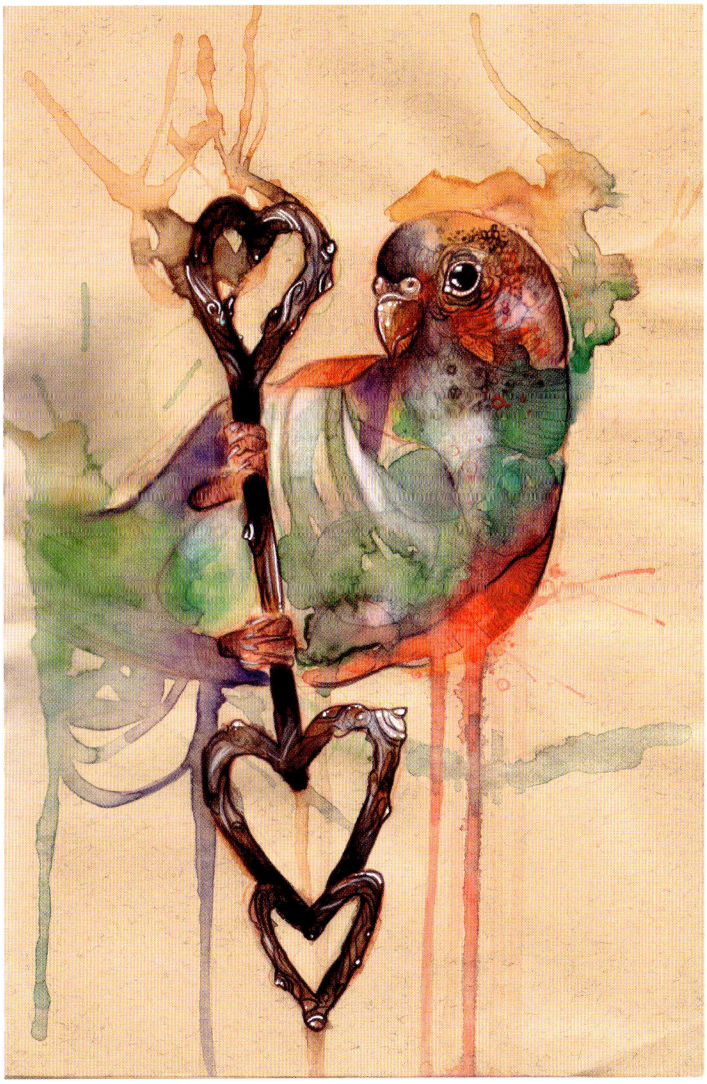

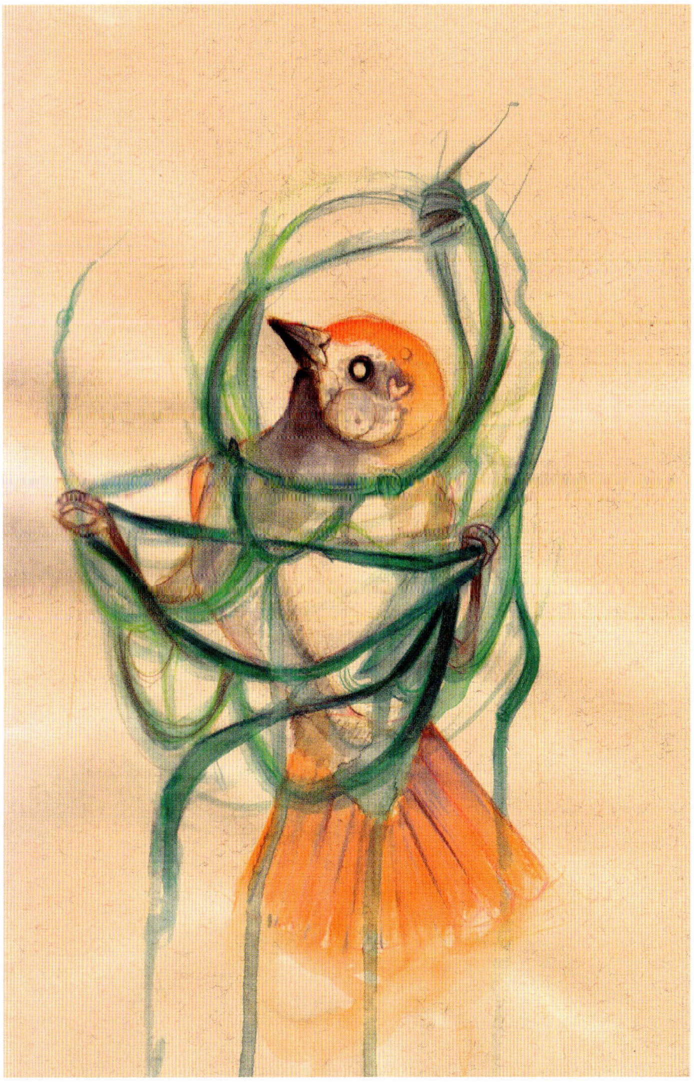

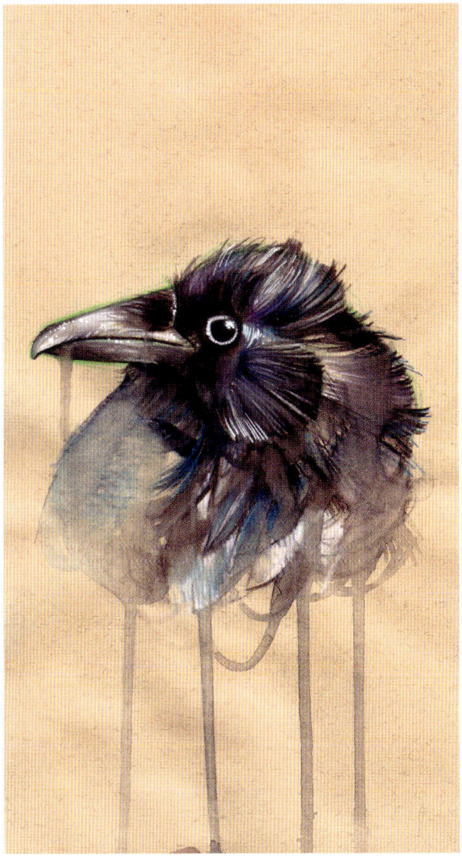

What made you want to become a tattoo artist and how long have you been tattooing?

I have always drawn and painted and have always wanted to have an art-based job. Once I started at university, tattooing became something I was more and more interested in. Especially through looking at work by Robert Hernandez, Angelique Houtcamp, Sean Herman, and Paul Booth. I have now been tattooing for six years.

Where did you learn to tattoo? Did you have a formal apprenticeship? If so, can you tell me about this time in your life and how it prepared you for all that you do now?

I had a formal apprenticeship in a street shop in Dundee, Scotland. I was doing my apprenticeship at the same time as my final year in university and working two jobs. It was a tough time, but my determination and love for tattooing kept me enthusiastic and eager to learn and do everything I was told. I did a good year of helping out without pay, before picking up a machine; then once I was tattooing, I did it at every opportunity I could. Being a painter, I found it hard to go back to basics, learning to put in a straight line and block color before I could experiment with it.

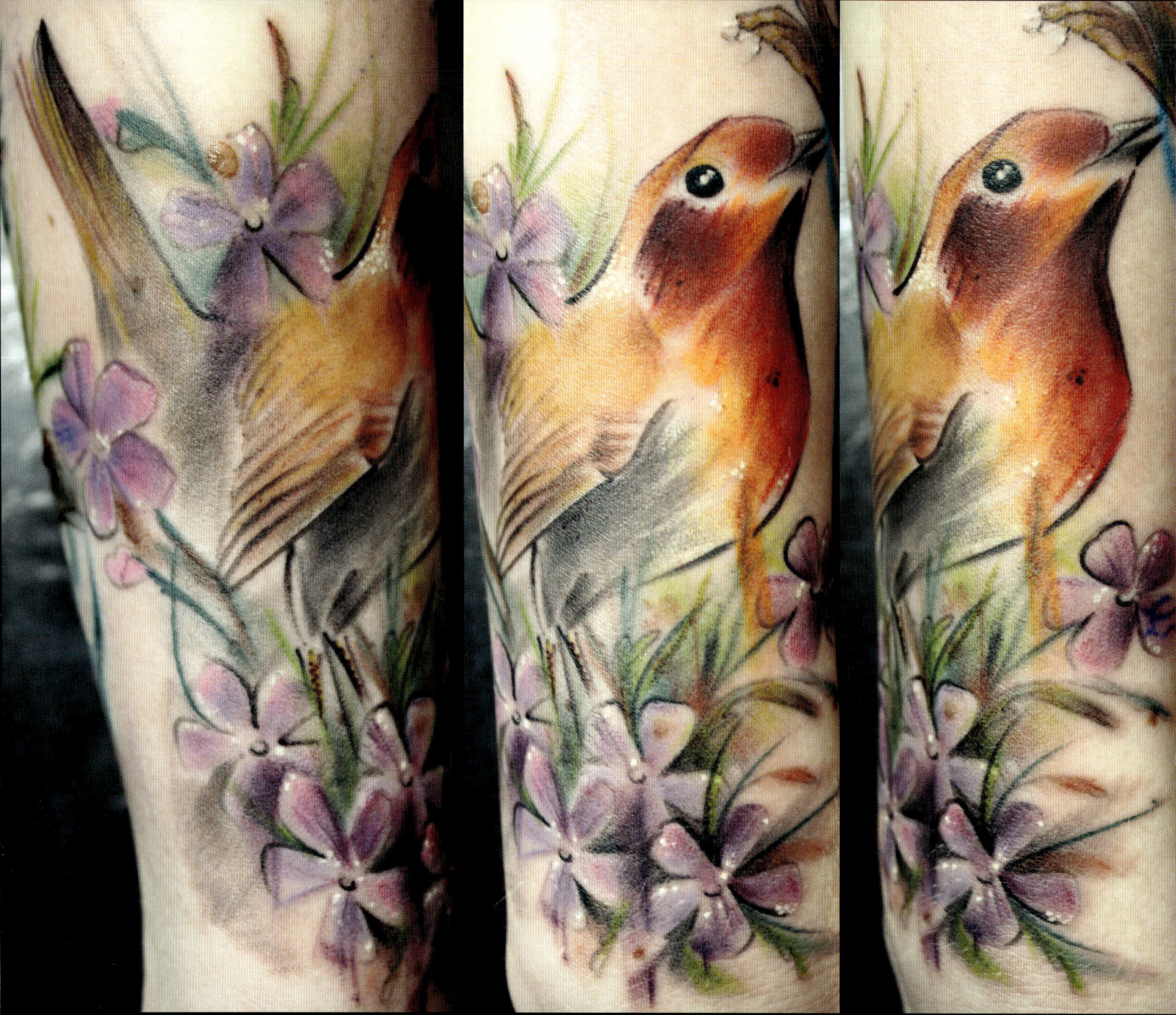

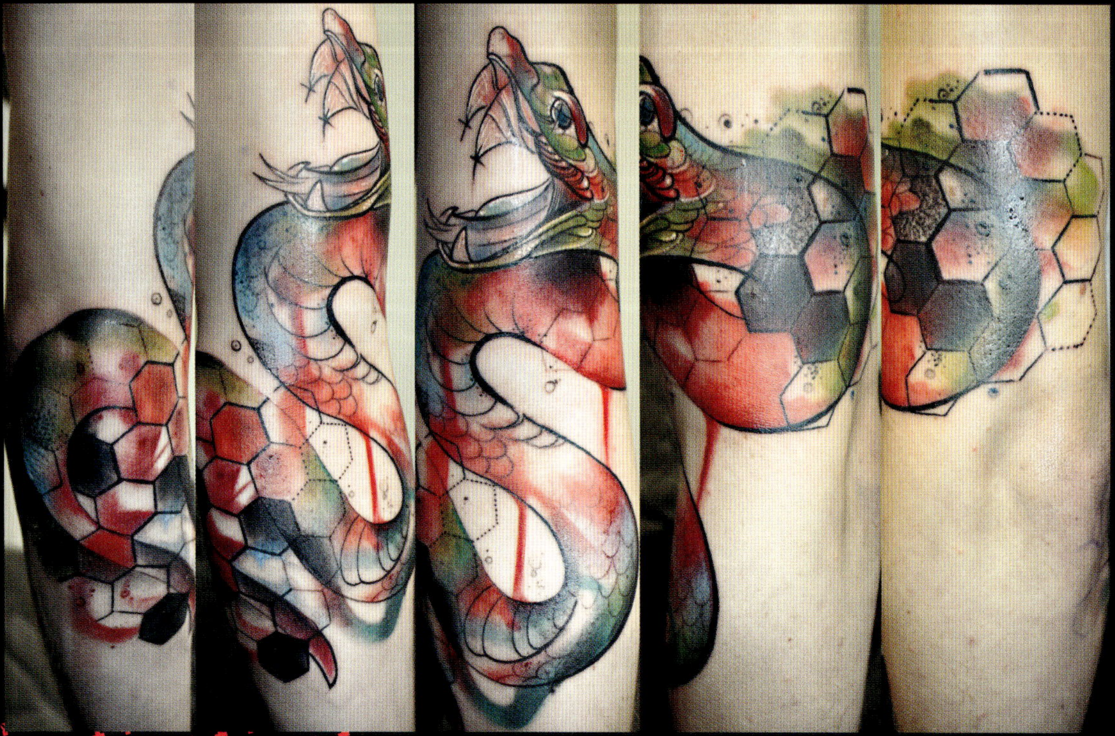

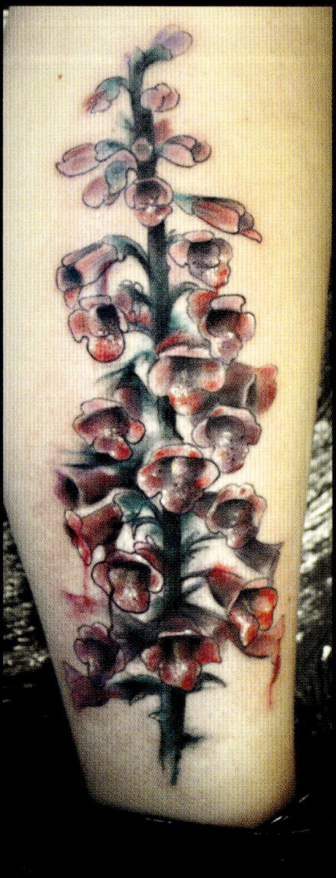

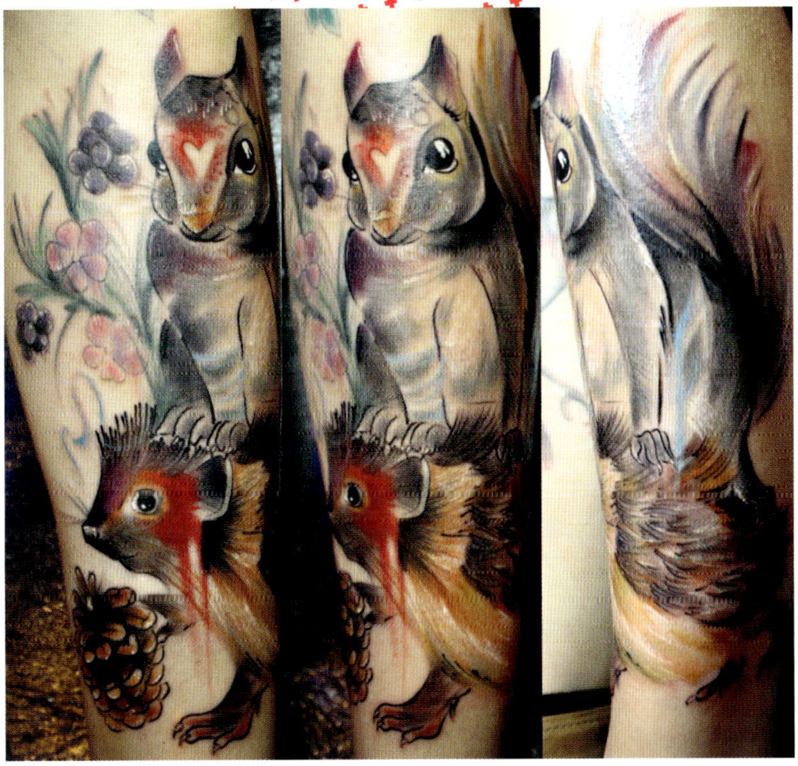

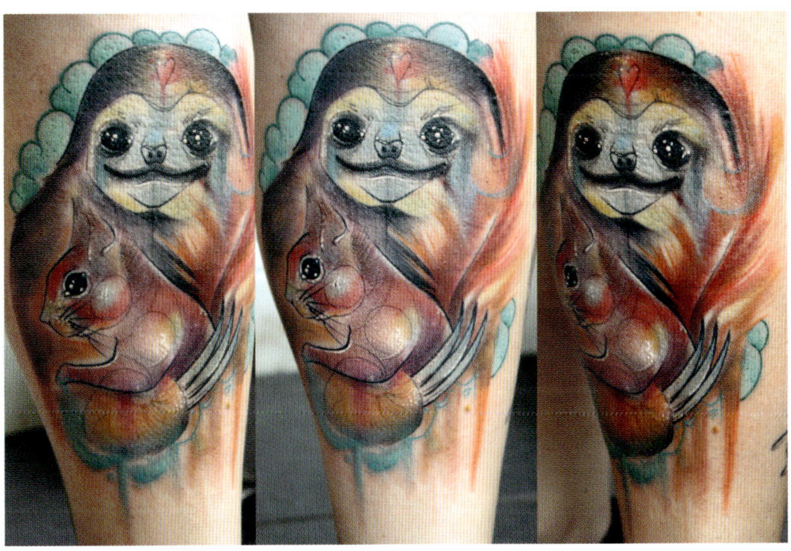

My time at university prepared me for dealing with tough criticism. Tattooing is a tough job and people can be very opinionated. Especially when you begin. I just had to remember that everyone has to start somewhere, and to listen to everything I was being taught.

What's it like being a female artist in a primarily male workplace?

I don't really notice that I work in a male dominated industry and it doesn't bother me. There's more and more female tattooists popping up, so I don't really notice that there's more guys. I'm a strong believer in everyone being equal… if you're a good tattooist it doesn't matter what sex you are.

Do you feel that male customers treat you differently?

I've never had any problems or felt any client has treated me differently because I'm a woman. I do, however, have some female clients who tell me they feel more comfortable being tattooed by a girl; but I treat all my clients the same which in return means I'm treated well.

What did your family and friends think about you getting into the business?

My family were very supportive. They all knew from a young age that I would go into an artistic career, so it didn't really come as much of a surprise! My family don't have a lot of tattoos so it is lovely how accepting and supportive they are, and how interested they have become in my career and the industry. I love it.

Can you tell me about the shop you work at?

I work at Aurora Tattoo in Lancaster, North England. I love where I work; it's a very hard-working studio owned by my extremely talented boss Emma Kierzek. It's a creative environment that encourages me in all aspects of my life. It's nice to be able to bounce ideas off of each other, and I feel I'm always learning. It really is a great place.

Describe how you go about creating a tattoo from concept to finished design. How do you try to put your own unique touch on your tattoos?

I always like to speak personally to my clients, even if it means grabbing five minutes while I'm tattooing. That way no wires get crossed and we can discuss properly what they want. Then I go away and draw. I do have references in front of me for structure and proportions. I start all sketches in my earthtone sketchbook with color pencils, to start mapping out the piece. Then, working with water, I flatten down areas, to then build up with watercolors. I stencil a copy of the painting and have the original beside me

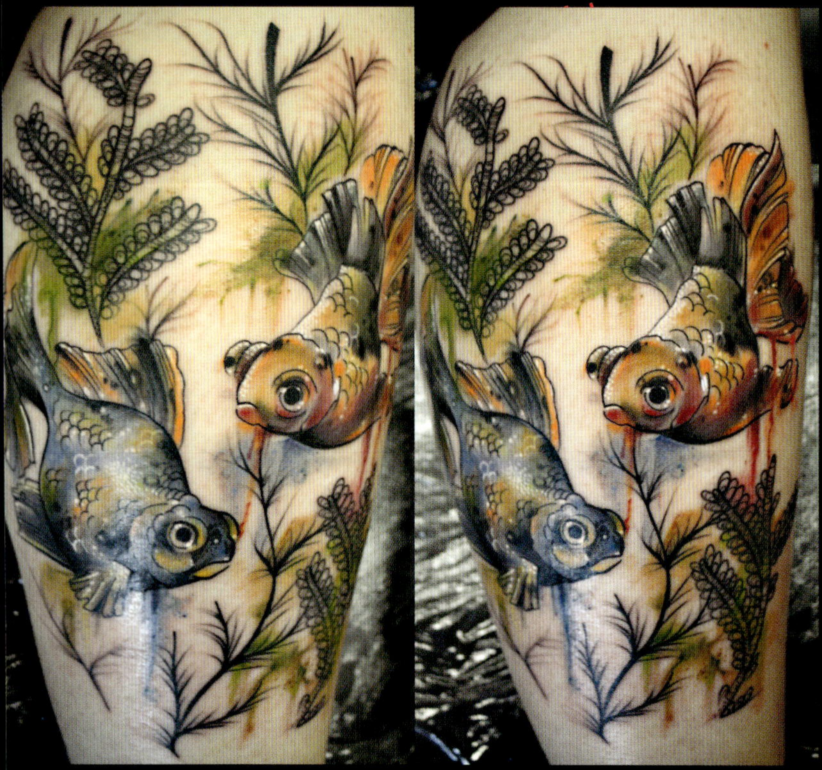
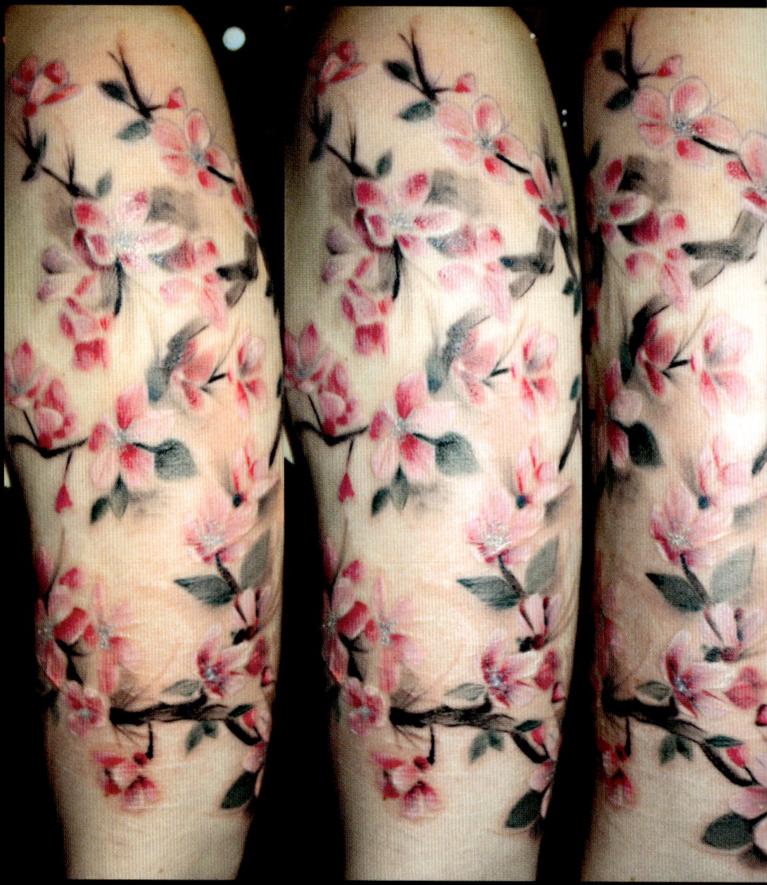
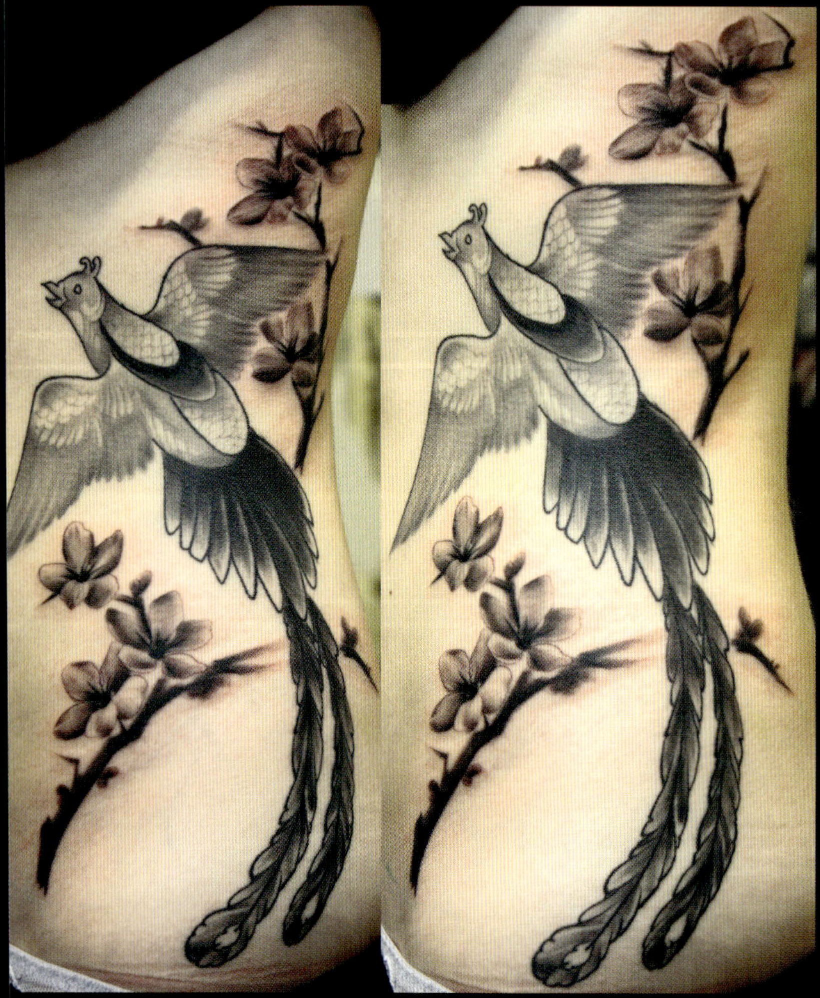
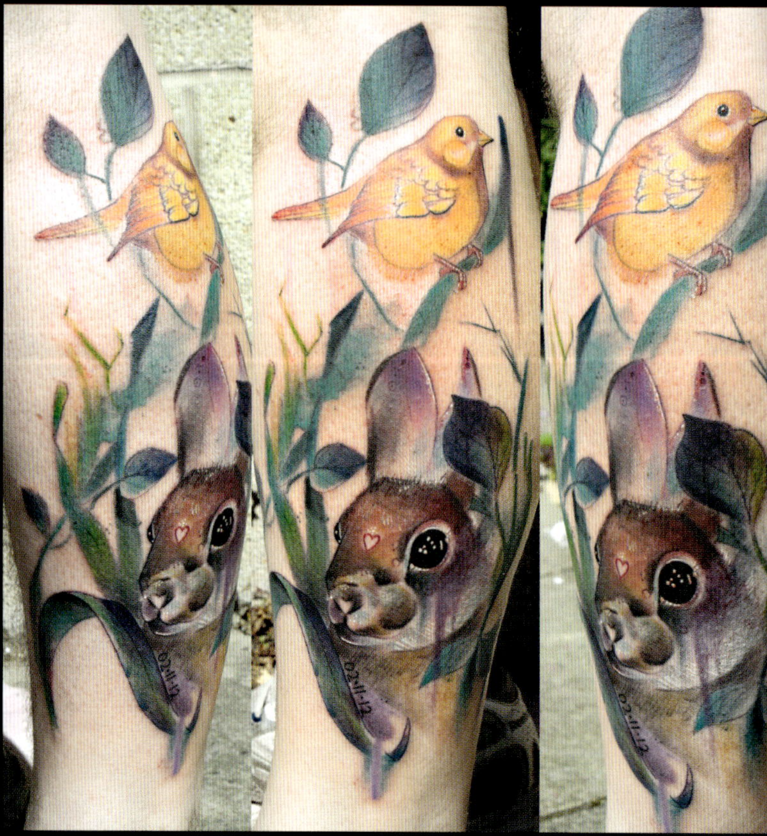

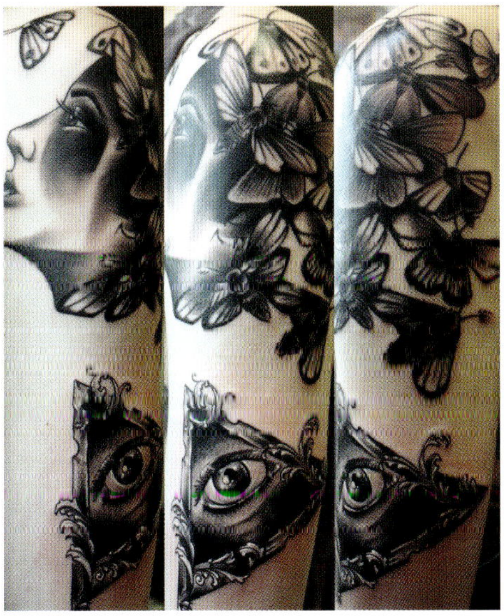

to work off of while I tattoo. My preparation paintings take a few hours to do. I love painting them up, and I feel I always get a better finished tattoo because I paint them rather than doing only a basic line drawing.

What was the first tattoo you ever did? Can you tell me about it?

My first tattoo was on myself, on my inner ankle, and it was terrifying! That one tattoo was going to decide whether I was to be a tattooist or not! I put a lot of pressure on myself, because I know if it sucked really badly I wouldn't be able to continue and go on to put shit tattoos on my friends. I had nerves like I did when getting my first tattoo!

I sorted myself out, and lined a wave and a few blossoms, which took forever. And it wasn't so bad! So in a couple of weeks

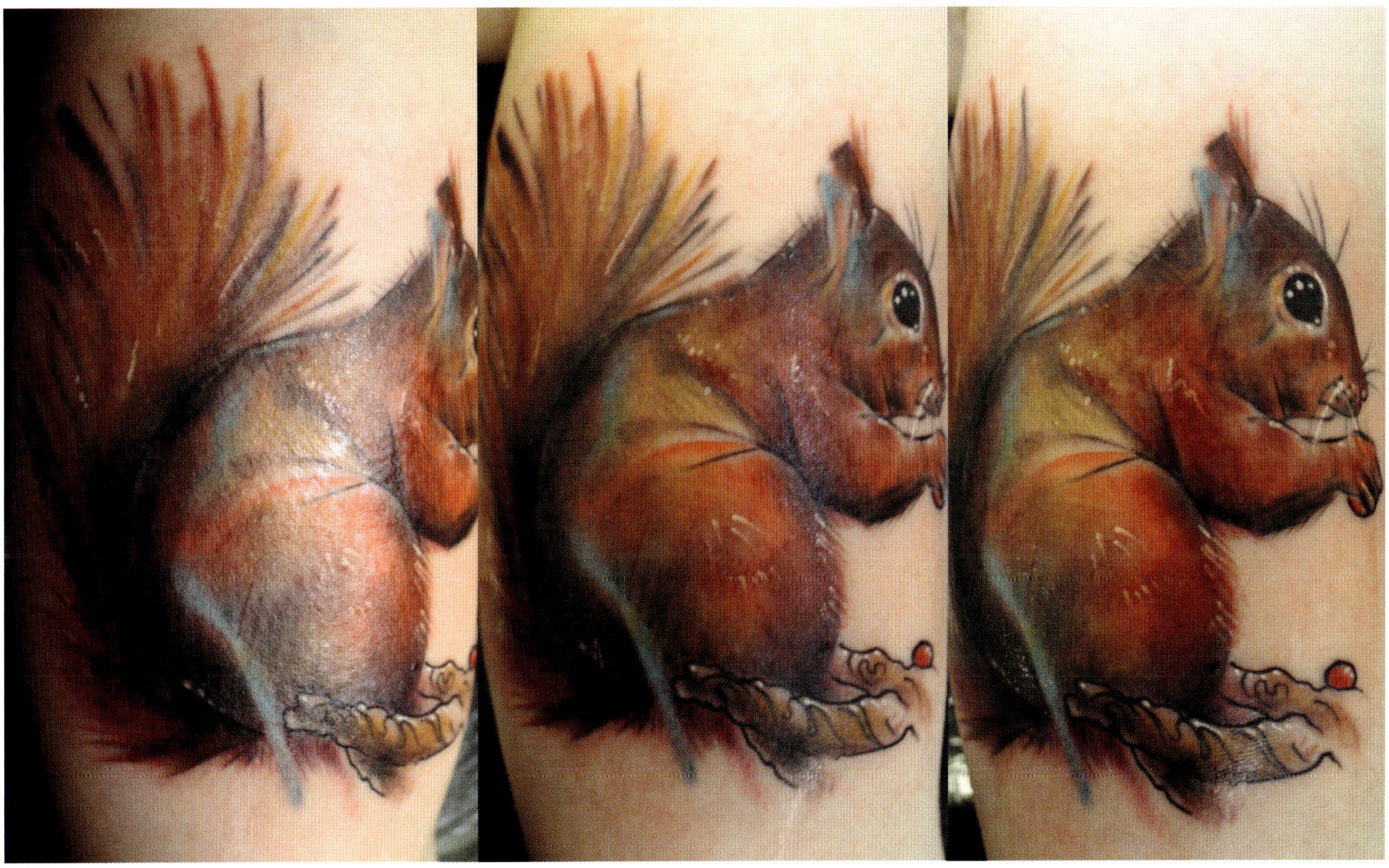

I then colored the blossoms in and did a little shading on the wave. I took my time and did okay, so after that I got some friends in to tattoo.

How would you describe your style? And which tattoo style do you like best?

I get bracketed with watercolor tattoos. But I class my work as simply painterly. Sometimes my work is very soft like watercolor, and other times it's solid, more of a heavier painted piece. Just depends on what suits the piece. I like all sorts of tattooing, and collect all different kinds of tattoos. But I am drawn to creative tattoos, pieces that push the boundaries and take more of a painterly approach.

Describe how your role models and any other sources of inspiration have affected your tattoo style.

Whenever I see a tattoo that I adore, it always pushes me to do better. I get inspiration from a lot of different places now. I take a lot of photos when I'm back home in my parents' garden, which is filled

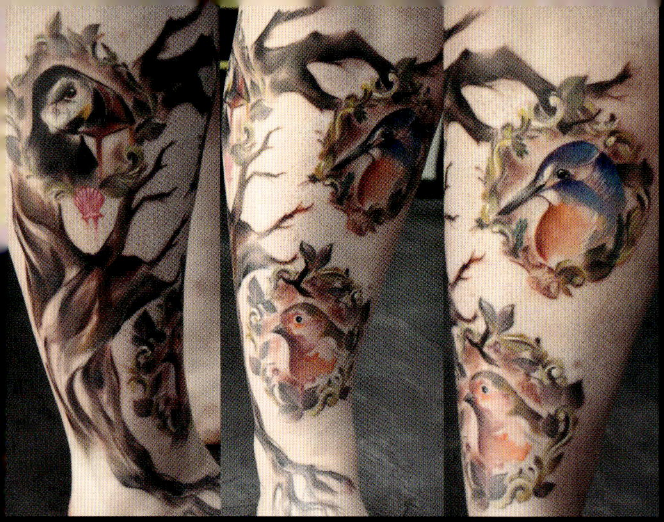
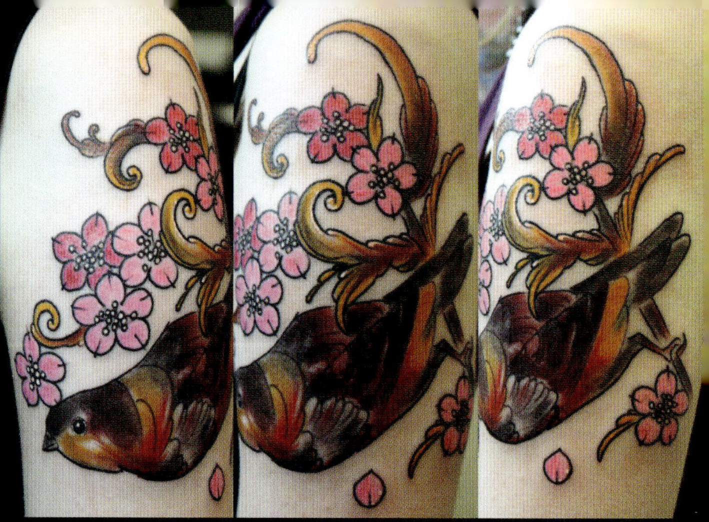
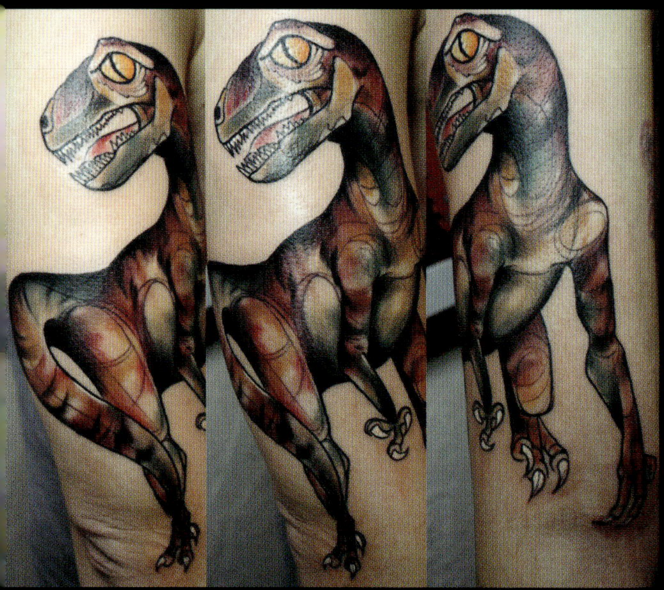
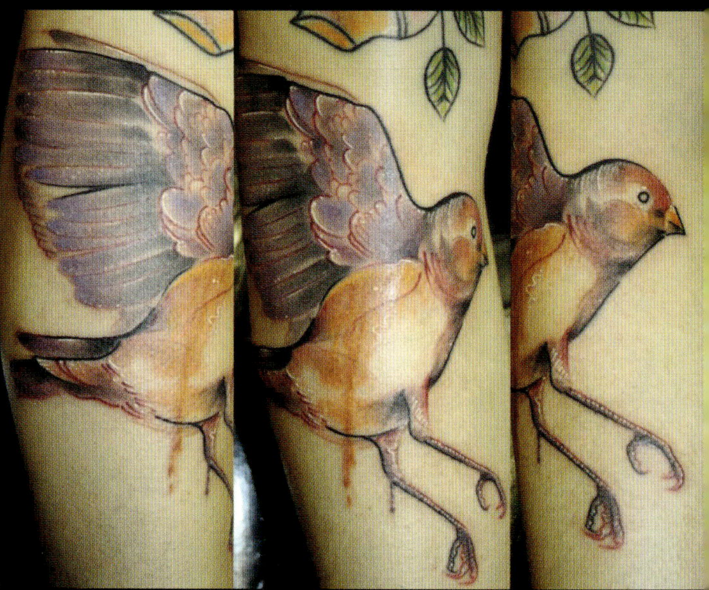
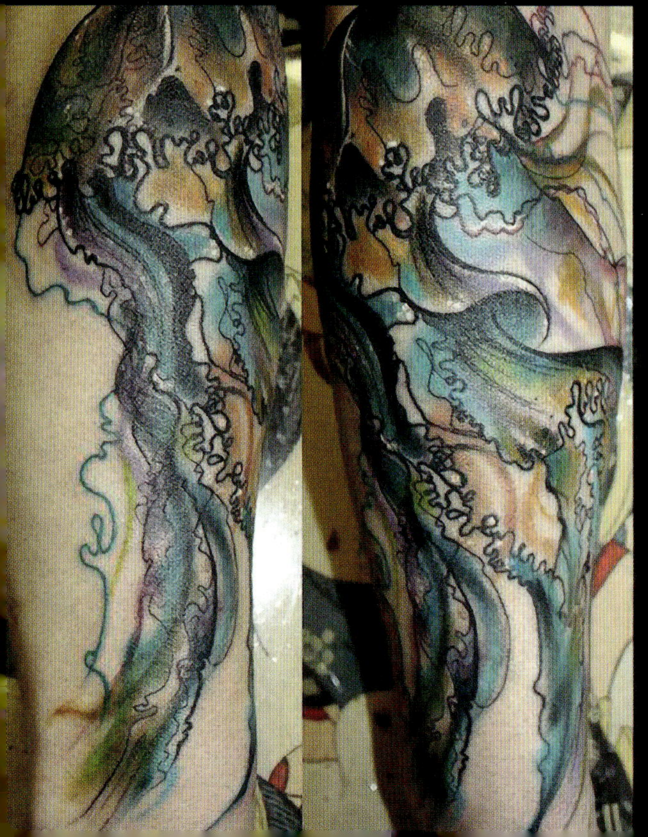
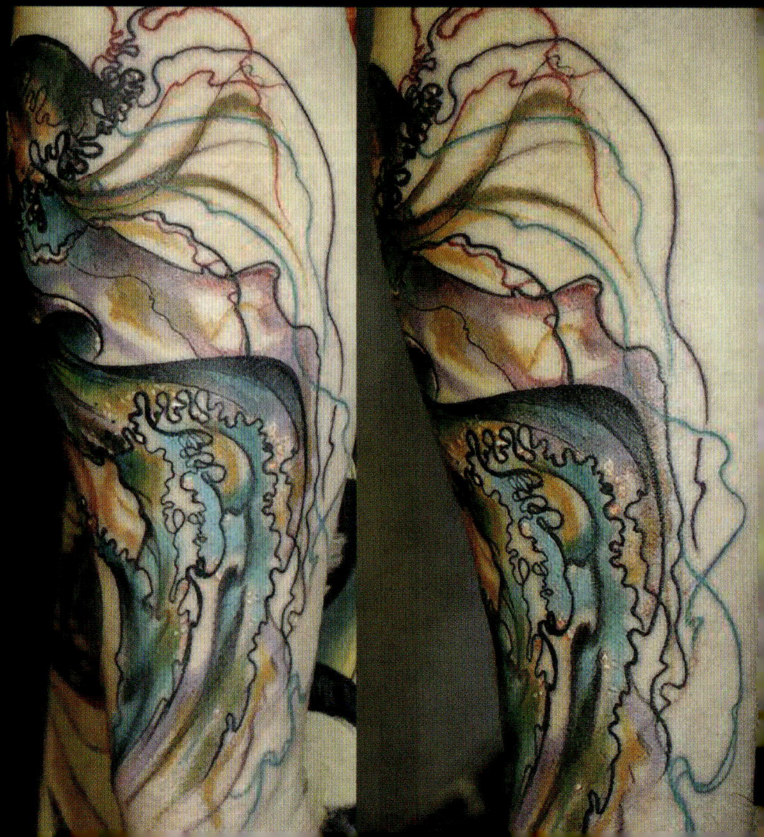

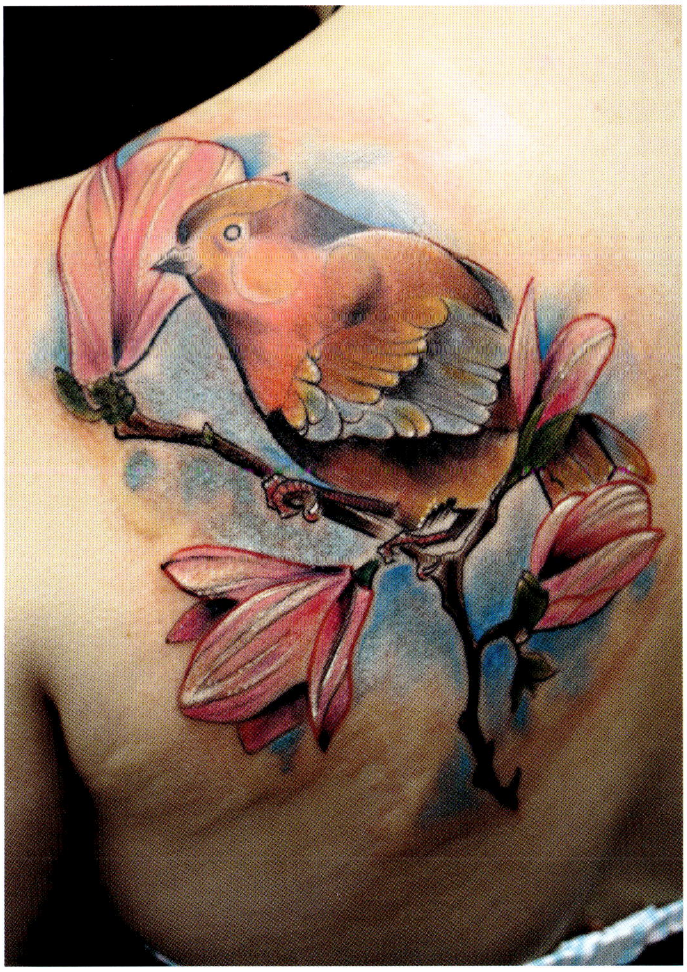

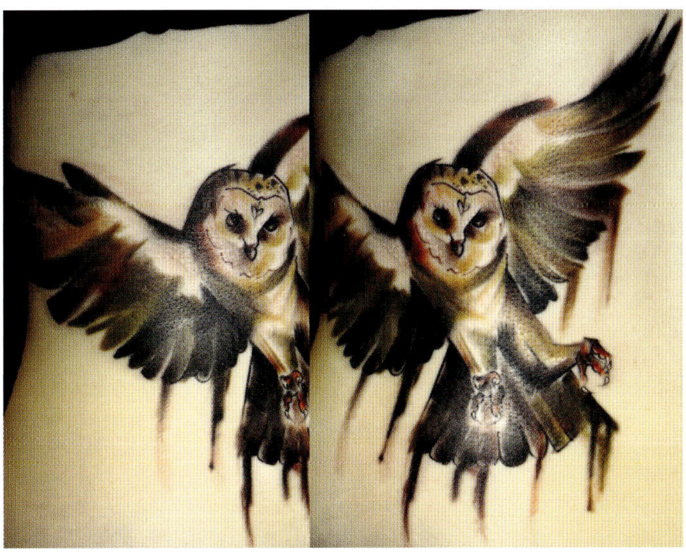

with lovely bright flowers. Local wildlife, and trips to zoos…Online the best place for me is the social media site Pinterest where I see so much artwork, old and new, of all kinds of styles. Nature photography too, and it all gets me excited to start a new painting!

My work naturally progresses with every piece I do. I never force change on it. The times I have tried to make my work take a drastic change, it has always ended in me feeling frustrated and upset. It's important to be patient and let my work grow organically to get the best result, and one I'm happy with.

What's the hardest part about being a tattoo artist?

I find the toughest part of being a tattooist is having time away from the job. I really struggle to switch off, and even when I do take a little time for myself I'm still thinking about work! This job consumes me and most other tattooists. And I allow it to do so because I love my job, being an artist is everything. However, it is very important to take time away from it to reflect and grow as an artist, and most importantly spend time with the people I love.

What's the most rewarding part about being a tattoo artist?

I love when I get a client willing to travel for my work, who gives me a vague idea of what they want, and who trusts me to run with it and do what I want. Knowing a stranger has that trust in me is amazing.

What do you think a client should expect from you as a tattoo artist, and what do you, on the other hand, expect from a client to make a successful tattoo and a good collaboration?

I think what any client expects from any tattooist is professionalism. I make sure that every client is treated the same and dealt with in a professional manner, being as helpful as possible. Getting all their artwork to them before their appointment, and most importantly getting it to them when I say I will. I expect every client to be polite and patient; to research their tattooist, and make sure they are going to the right person. As artists we all have our strengths and it is important to recognize that. And when the client is being tattooed, it's nice if they sit still!

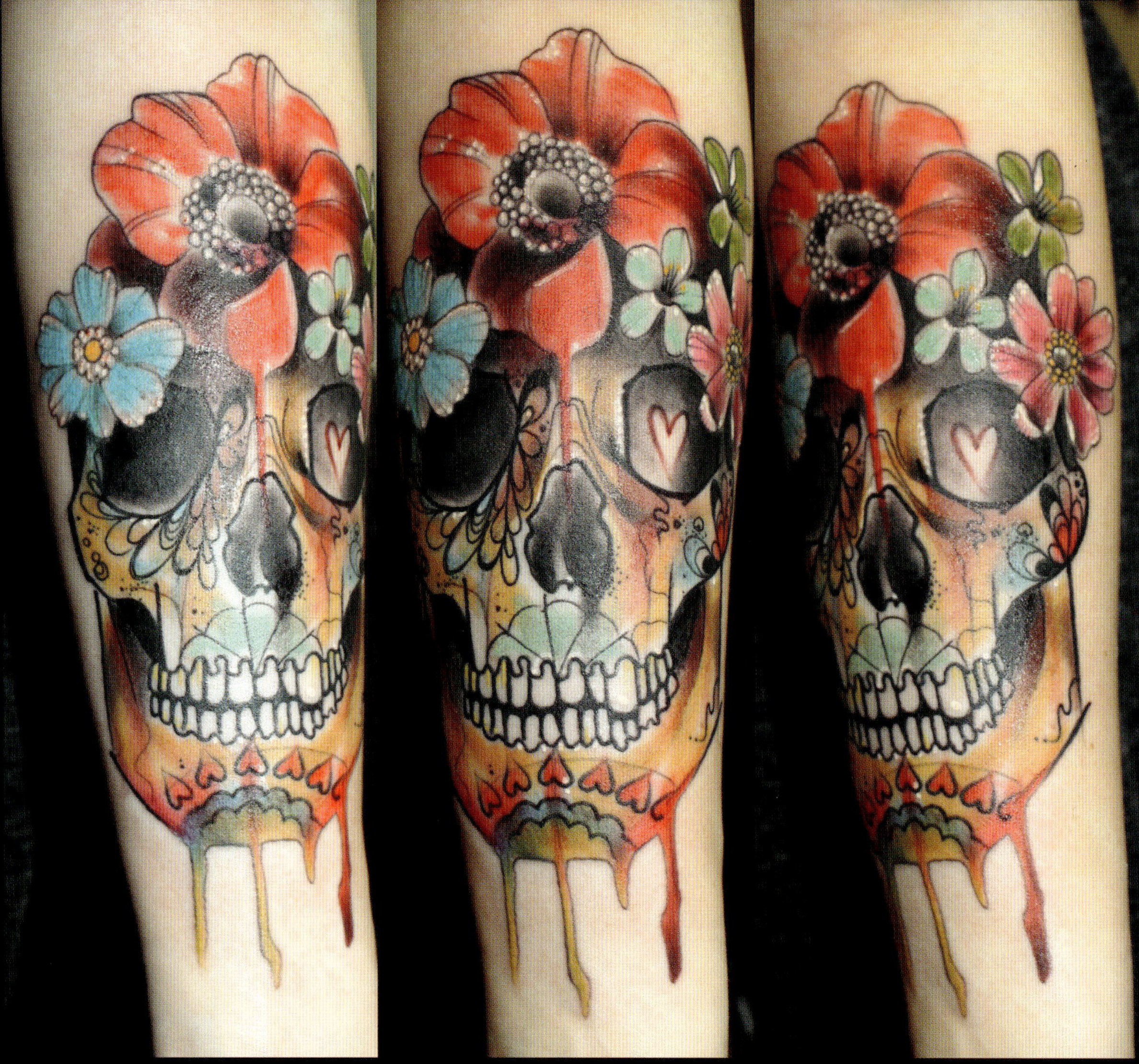

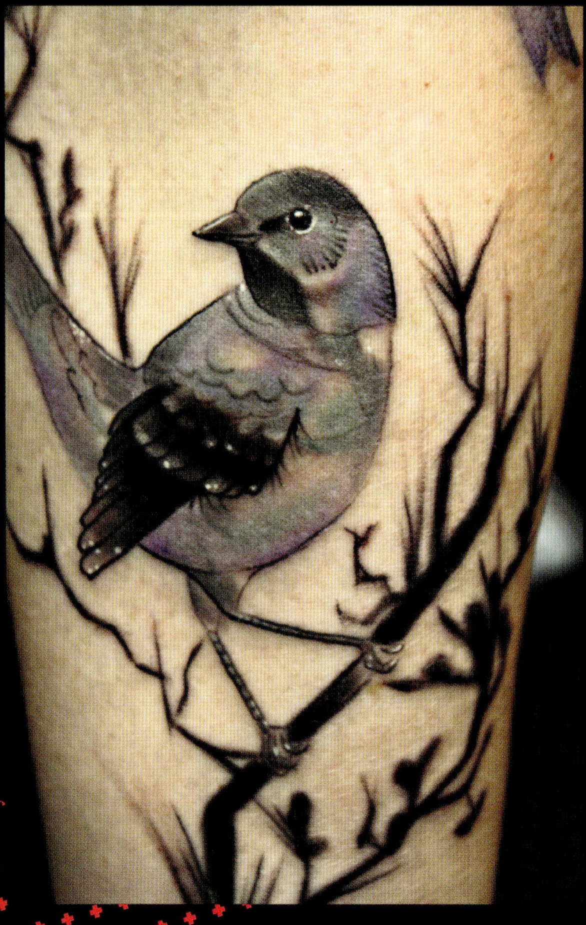

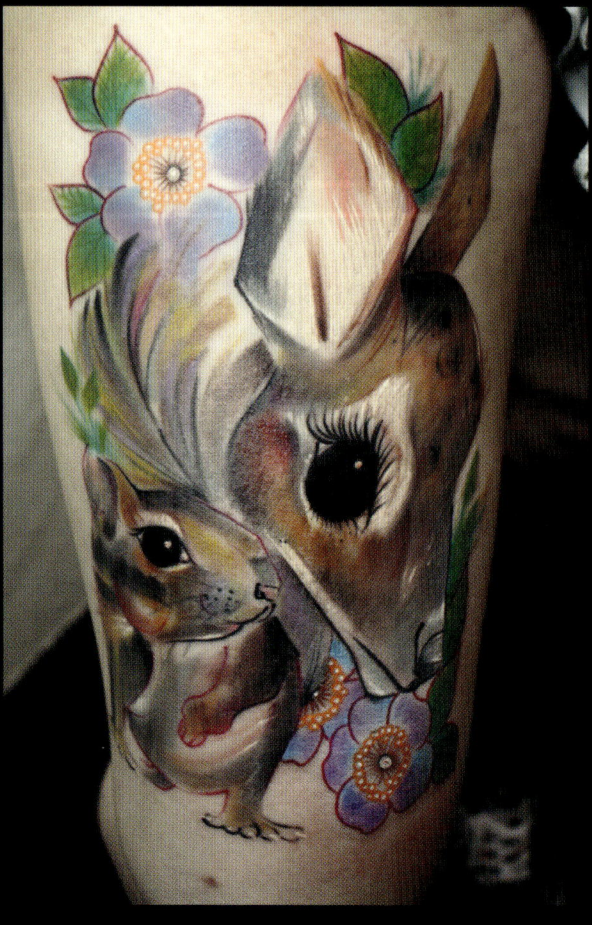

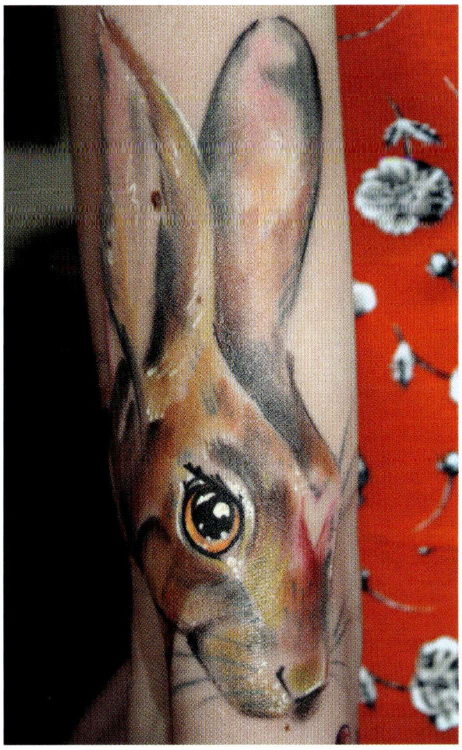

What criteria do you think that a tattoo convention should have to be really successful, both for you as a tattoo artist, but also for the visitors? Can you give some examples of conventions that meet these criteria well?

I like working shows that add a little extra to it. Like a best-dressed booth prize or a themed show. The tattooists get right into the show and get a bit more excited about working it. It's important to use a venue that is easy to get to because the public just won't go if it's a hassle to find.

How would you describe the current status of tattoos among the general public in the UK?

Everyone has tattoos these days in Britain, it's far more accepted now. But heads do still turn if you are heavily tattooed.

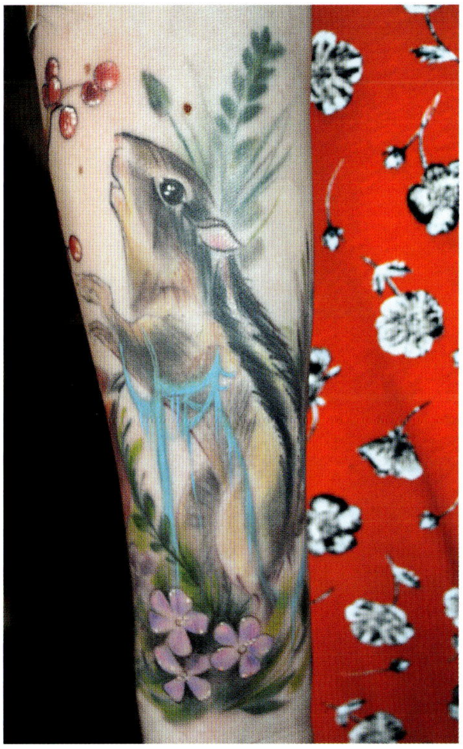

TV shows, Internet, and especially social networks like Facebook and Twitter have come to have an extremely wide influence in recent years. What positive and negative impacts do you think it has for the future development of the tattoo industry?

I think social media is great for promotion in tattooing. I get a lot of clients through people stumbling across my work or researching my work on Facebook, Instagram, Pinterest. However, it also allows people to print your work off and copy it, or even worse, pass it off as their own. That's the risk you take in putting your work on the Internet, but it's a risk for a tool that can be incredibly useful. The TV shows are the same, some positives and some negative elements. I like that they can give people without tattoos a little insight to the process and the quality of work that can be done. However, a lot of these shows imply that every tattoo needs a reason behind it rather than being just a nice tattoo, and also with the show editing it can be deceiving on how long tattoos can take to do. But I don't mind the shows.

Is there anything else you'd like to say?

I really do love my job and I appreciate every client I've had in these seven years of tattooing, and everyone who has bought my paintings. I work really hard and it's nice to know that it doesn't go unnoticed.

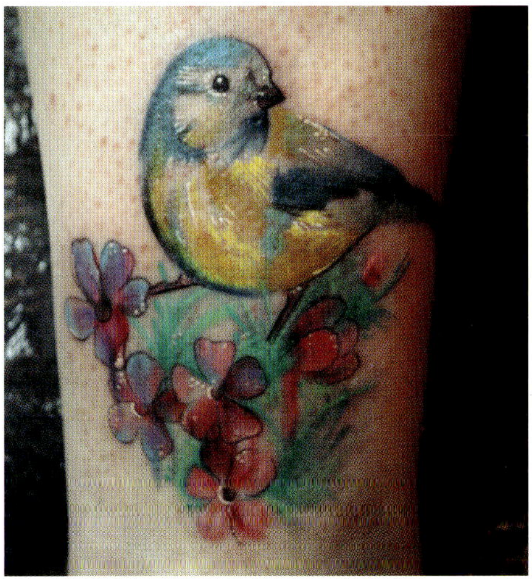

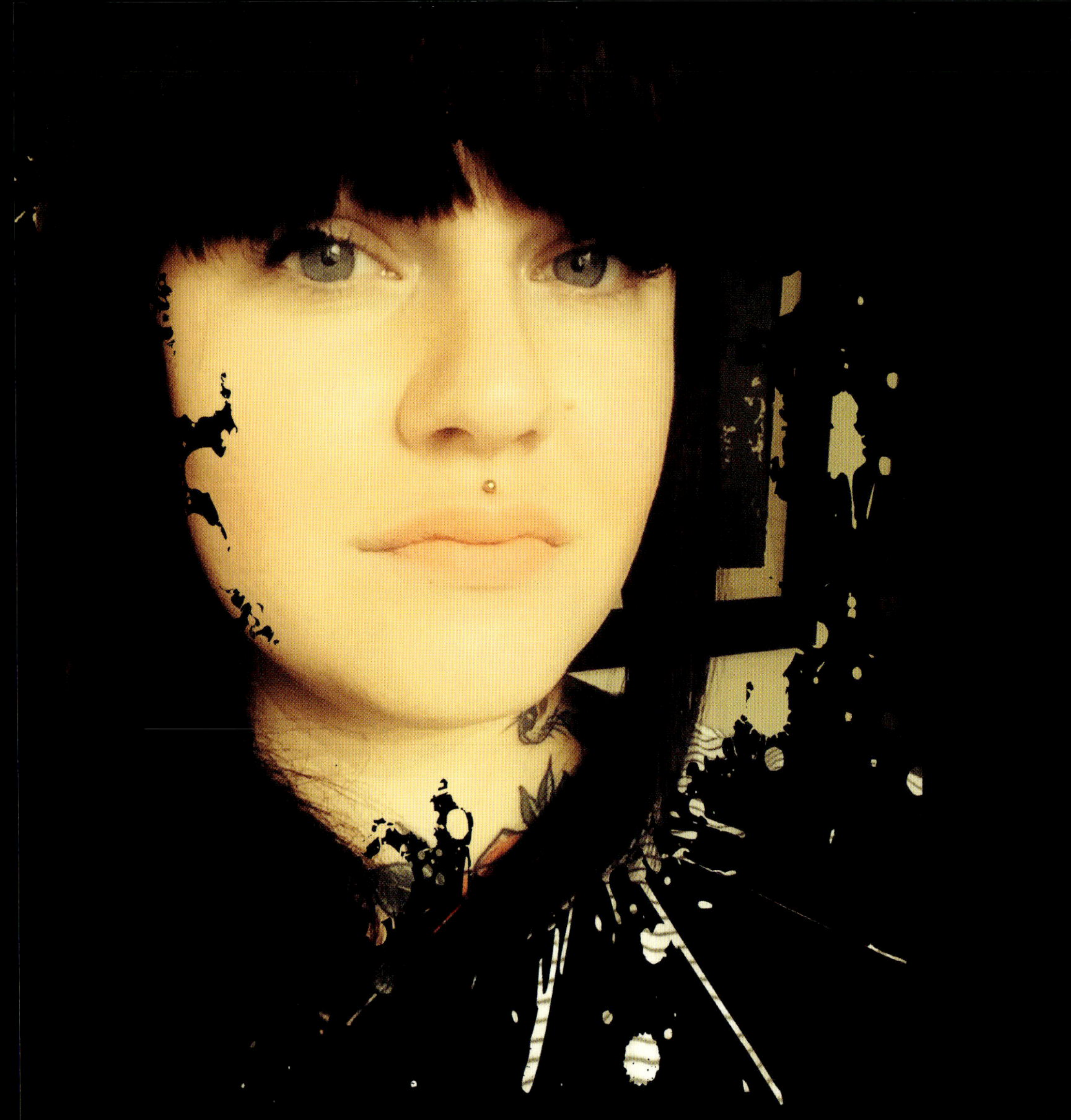

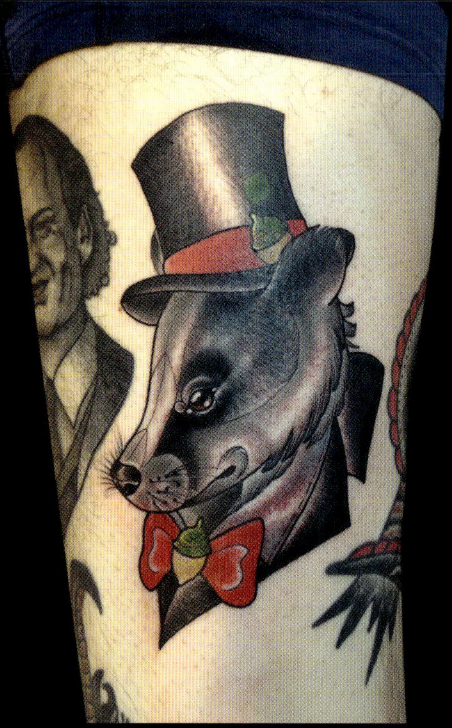

English tattoo artist **AMY VICTORIA SAVAGE** has always had a huge love affair with both animals and art, and this caused her to be torn between the two when she was trying to decide on a career path. Amy's love for animals led to years of voluntary work and a degree in Behaviour Science of Animals. However, now she just tattoos images of them!

Amy Victoria SAVAGE

"Art is a cruel mistress"

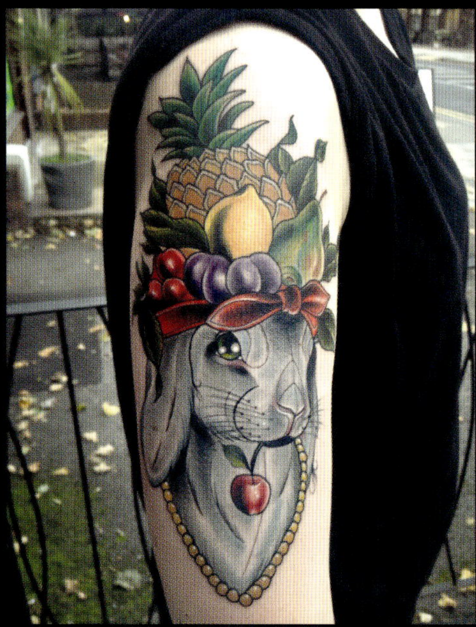

www.sweethearttattoo.bigcartel.com
www.facebook.com/amyvictoriasavage
instagram.com/amyvsavage
amyvsavage.tumblr.com

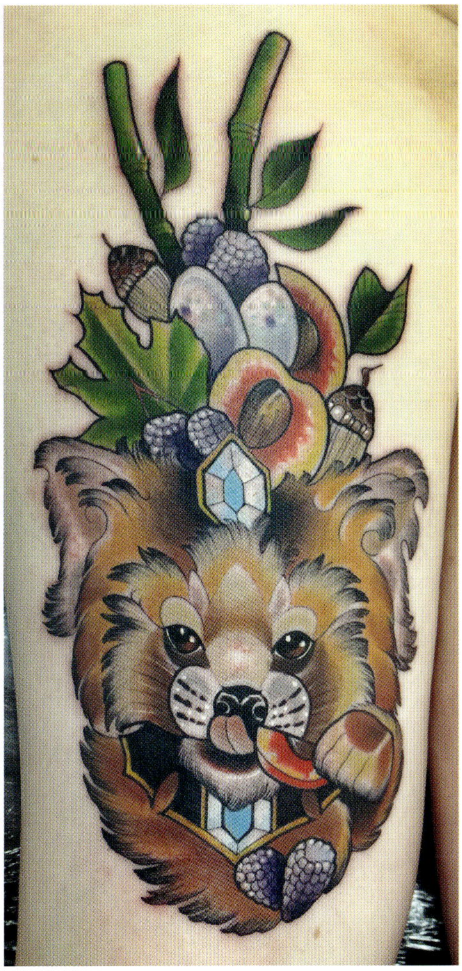

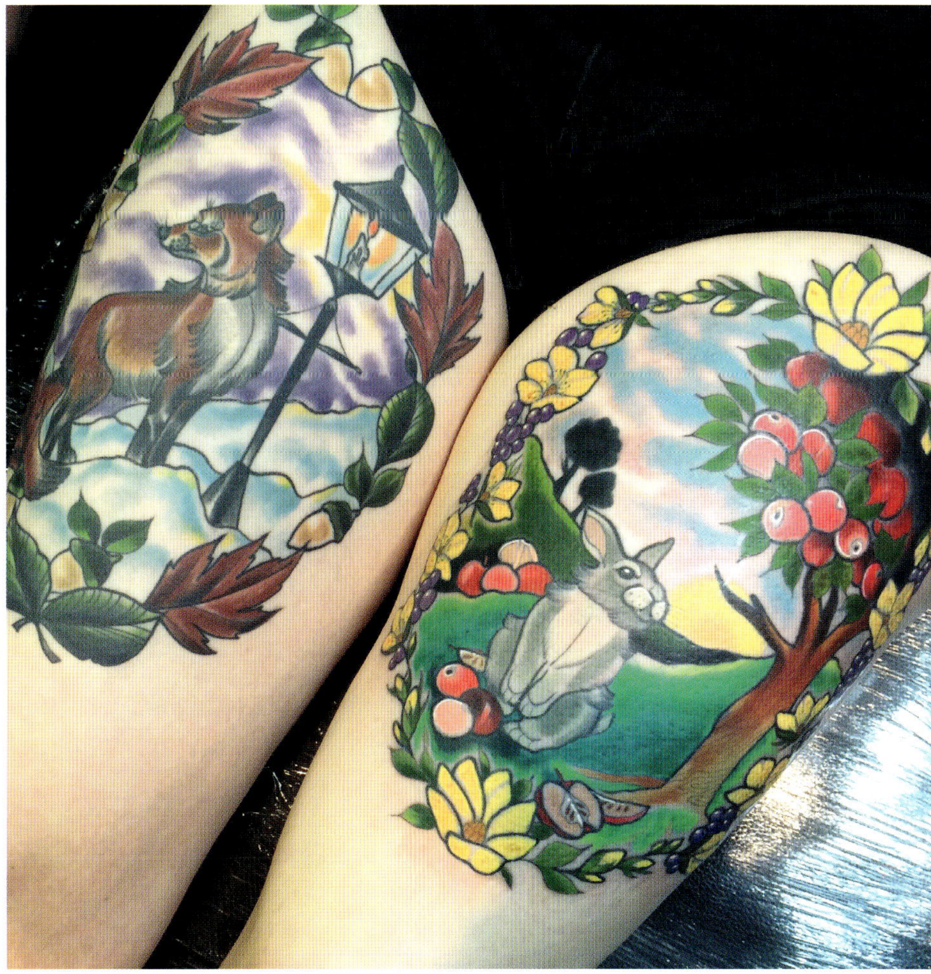

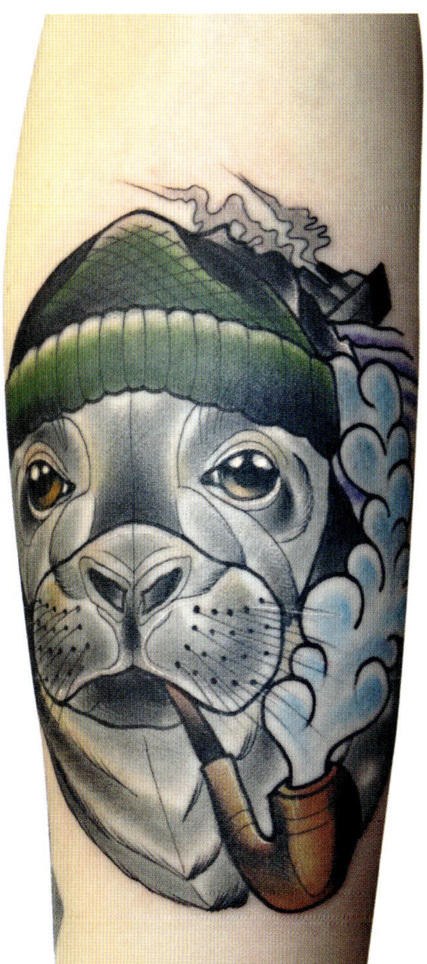

When you were a child, did you think you would grow up to become an artist, or work in the artistic field? Do you remember drawing and creating a lot as a child?

My family are very artistic and inspired me to be creative as I was growing up. I had a particular interest in portraits and realism, and was always clutching a pencil and doodling away.

When did you know that you wanted to be a tattoo artist, and what were the first steps you took to learn the craft?

I surrounded myself with tattoo literature and imagery in my teens. I was always fascinated by the controversial medium. My initial interest was in realism, which I guess went hand in hand with the imagery I was drawing at the time. It wasn't until I started studying biology at university that I realized I actually wanted to tattoo...I spent a lot of my spare time watching and helping out at shops, and once I finished my degree, I obtained an apprenticeship and began to learn! Although it was not the smoothest of rides.

Do you feel that male customers treat you differently?

Not at all. The majority of my clientele are ladies; I wouldn't mind a few more male clients...I like skulls and blood too!

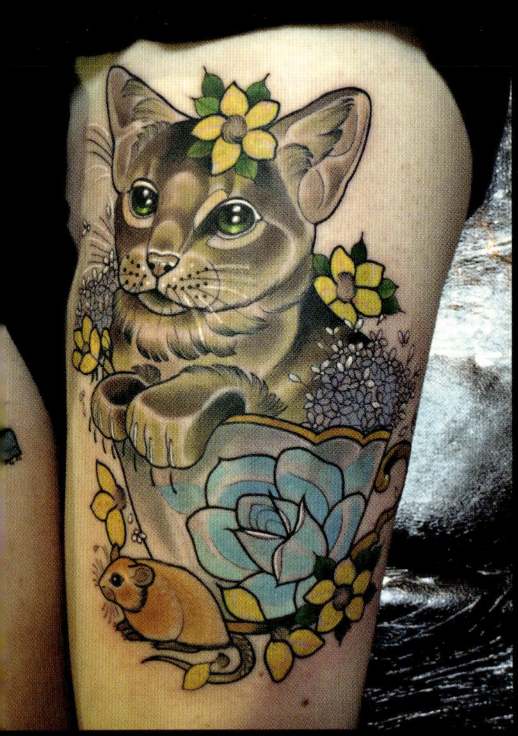
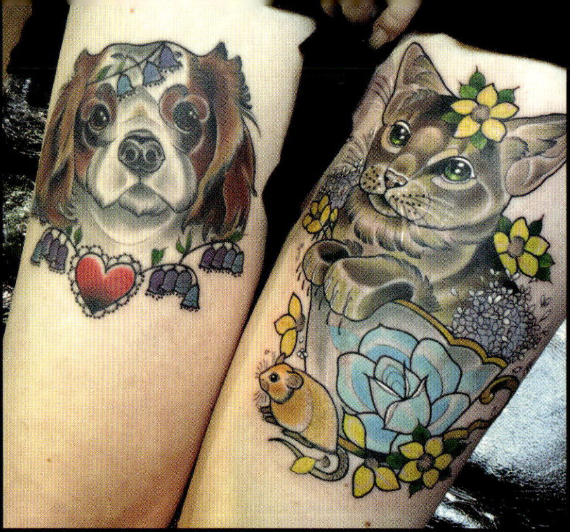
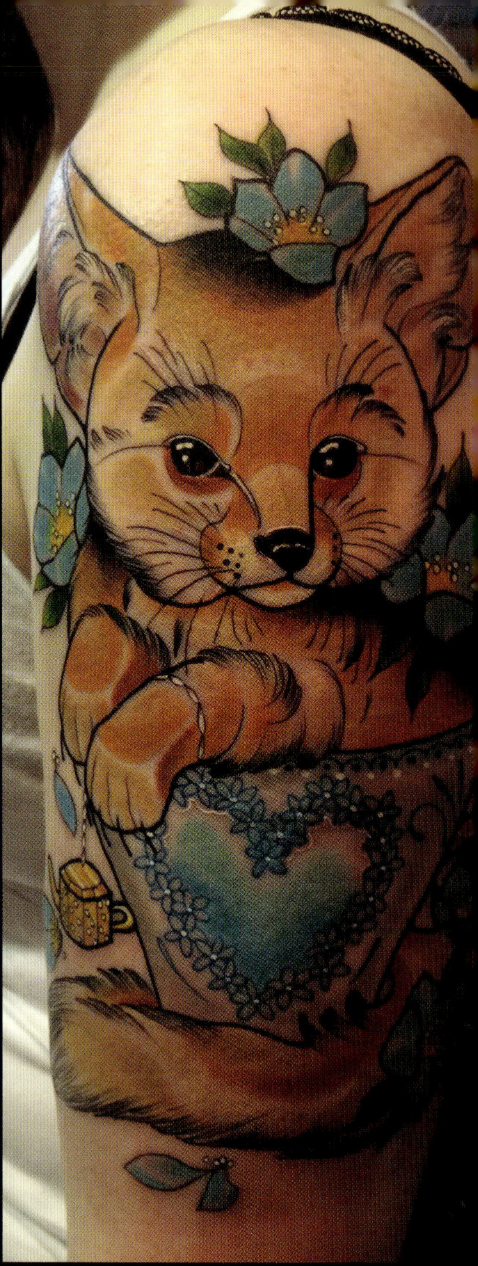
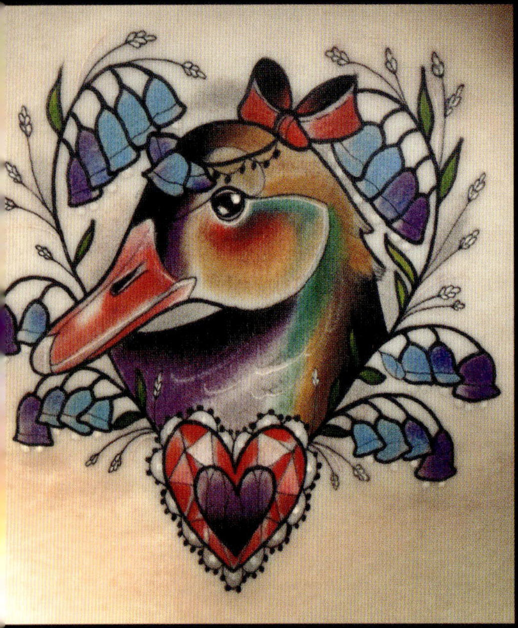
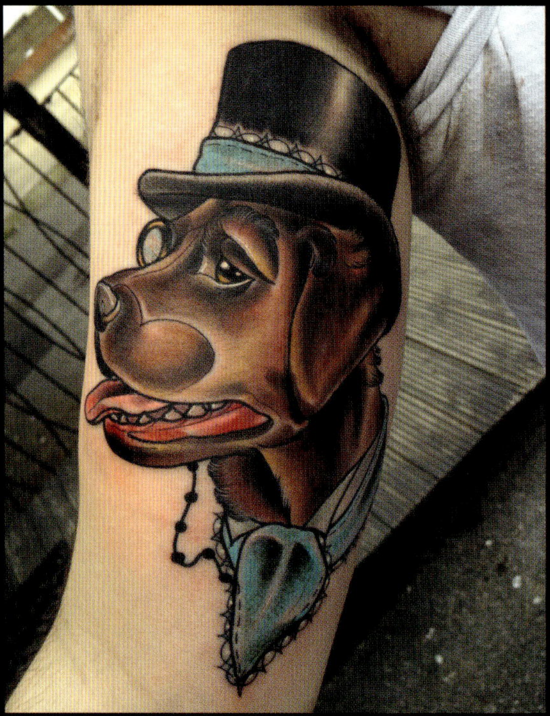
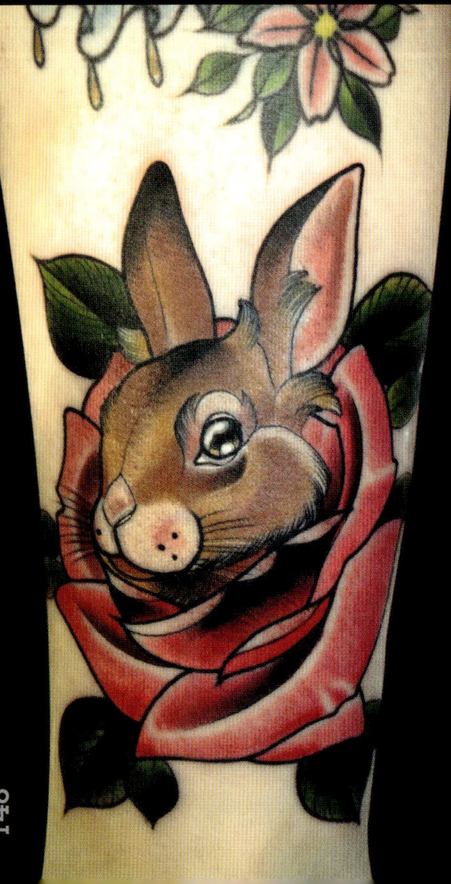
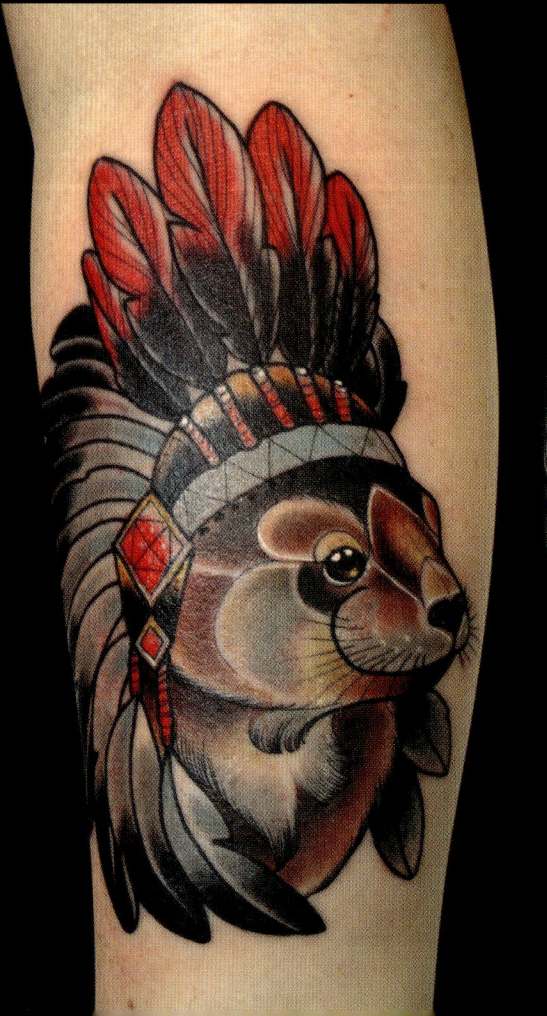
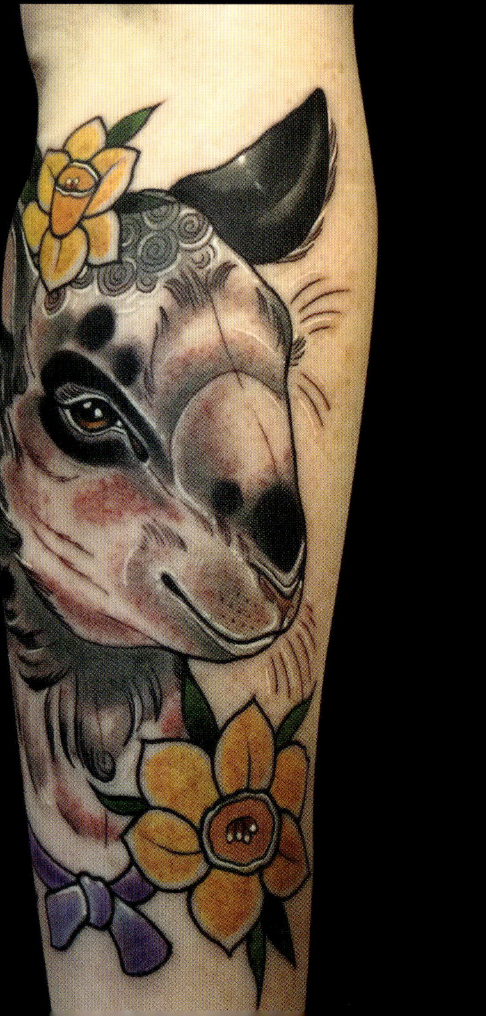

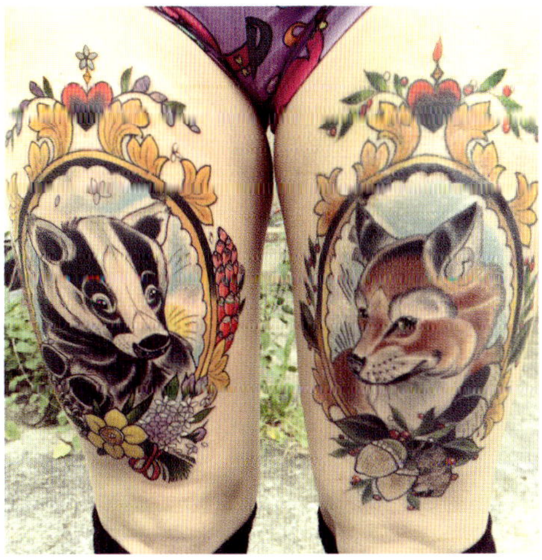

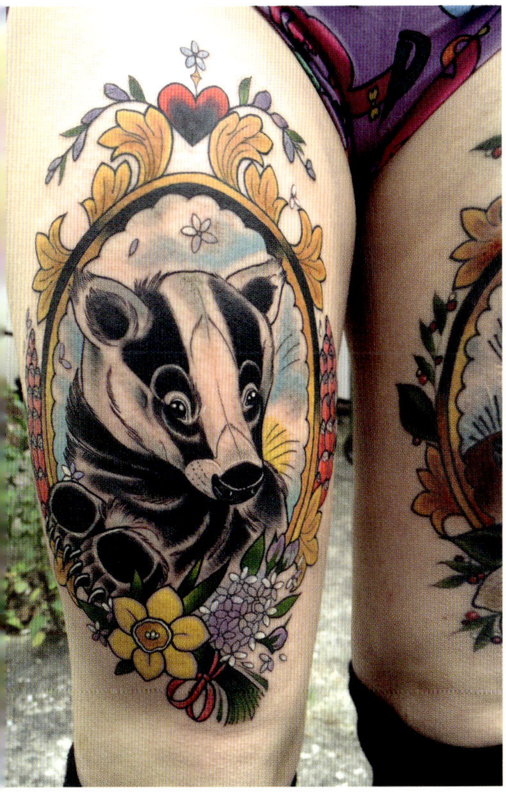

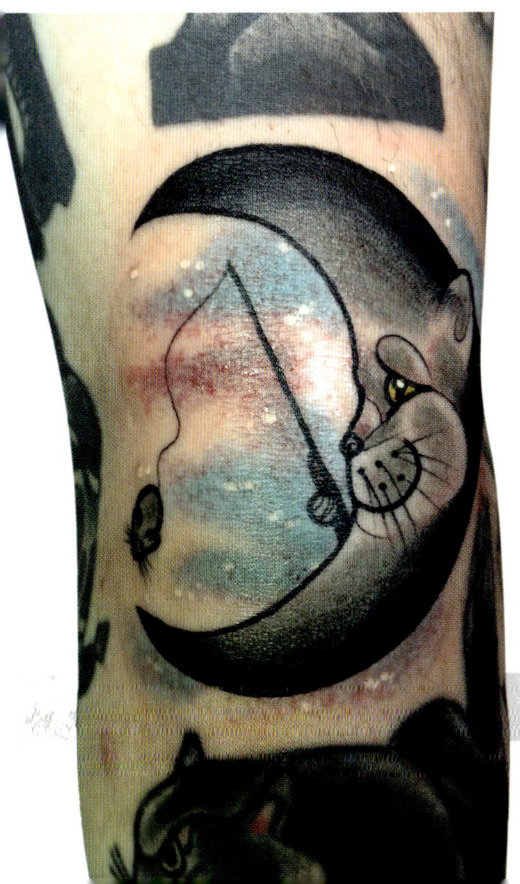

Do you feel that female tattoo artists are treated fairly in the business? How do you feel things have changed for women in tattooing, as well as for yourself from when you started out?

I personally do not feel like I am treated differently at all. I've only been tattooing for about five years and in that short amount of time, I have not experienced any change but I have not experienced any negativity either. With all the pro-female tattoo Instagrams and conventions, it may be the men who are starting to feel left out!

Tell me more about the shop you work at; what's it like working there, and what makes up a typical day?

I work at Jayne Doe in Essex, near London. I have been here for almost three and a half years and it's the second shop I've worked in. It's a pretty laid-back shop. We are very busy, but the atmosphere is pretty chilled, so clients are made to feel like it's a home from home.

Describe how you go about creating a tattoo from concept to finished design. How do you try to put your own unique touch on your tattoos?

The process usually starts with the client sending me an e-mail with their general idea, placement, and sizing. This may include some imagery for reference, but not always. I take the loose measurements and placement into consideration and begin to sketch a composition, altering it until I'm content. At this stage I will plan shading and sometimes the coloring scheme. I sometimes send the sketch to the client, make any necessary adjustments, and draw up the final sketch ready for stenciling.

What was the first tattoo you ever did? Have you always worked in the same general style?

My first tattoo was actually a rose and key on a good friend, and it was in a traditional style. My style has grown and changed since then but still possesses the same thick lines and bold colors.

What's your tattoo style of choice and why?

I guess I do a neo-traditional style, although I think everyone has their own personal take on "traditional" these days. I really enjoy this illustrative style—you can really put your own personal stamp on it.

You are an incredible artist. How did your professional tattoo art journey lead you in this direction?

Thank you, however, I'm always learning, always progressing…I'm definitely not there yet and not sure if I ever will be, in my own opinion. Art is a cruel mistress! But I always strive to improve, and that is never a bad thing!

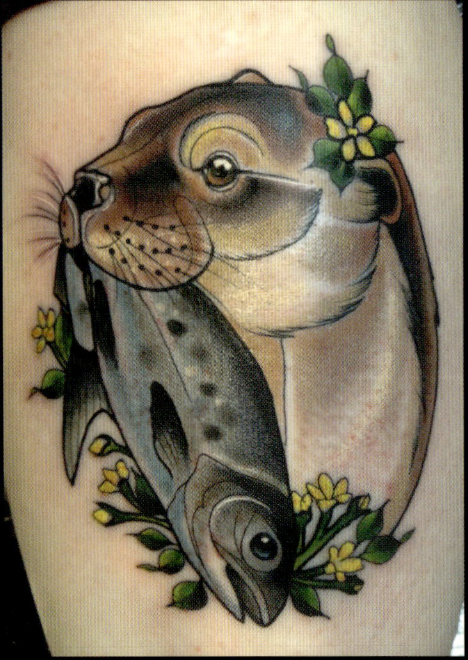
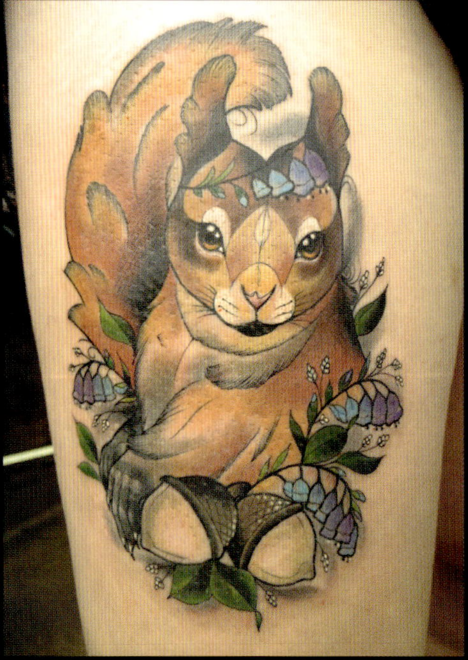
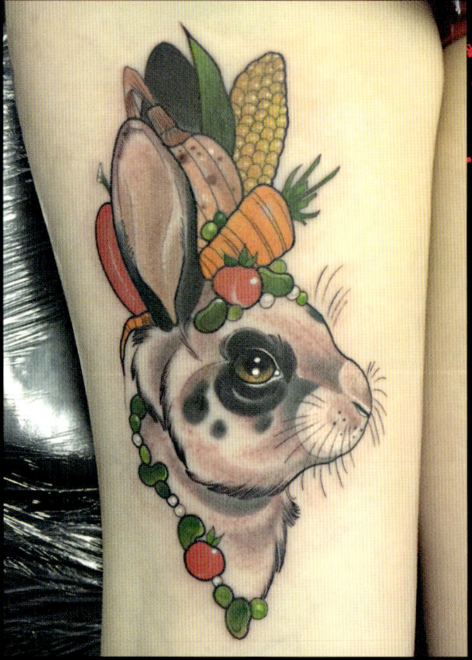
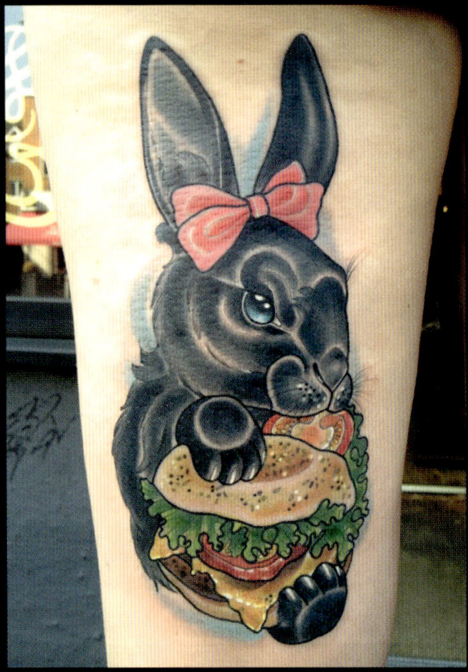
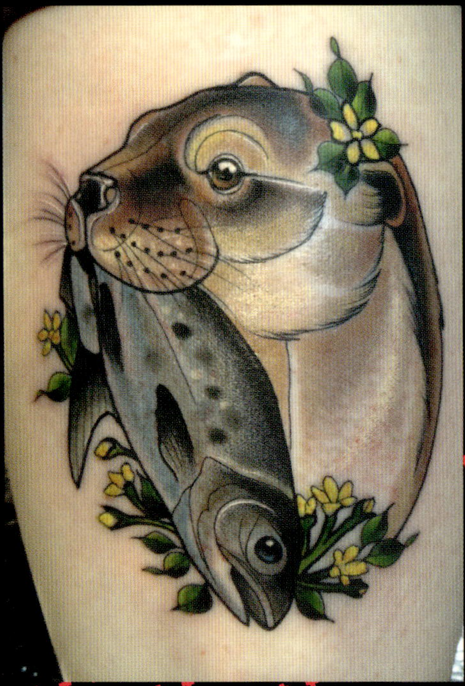
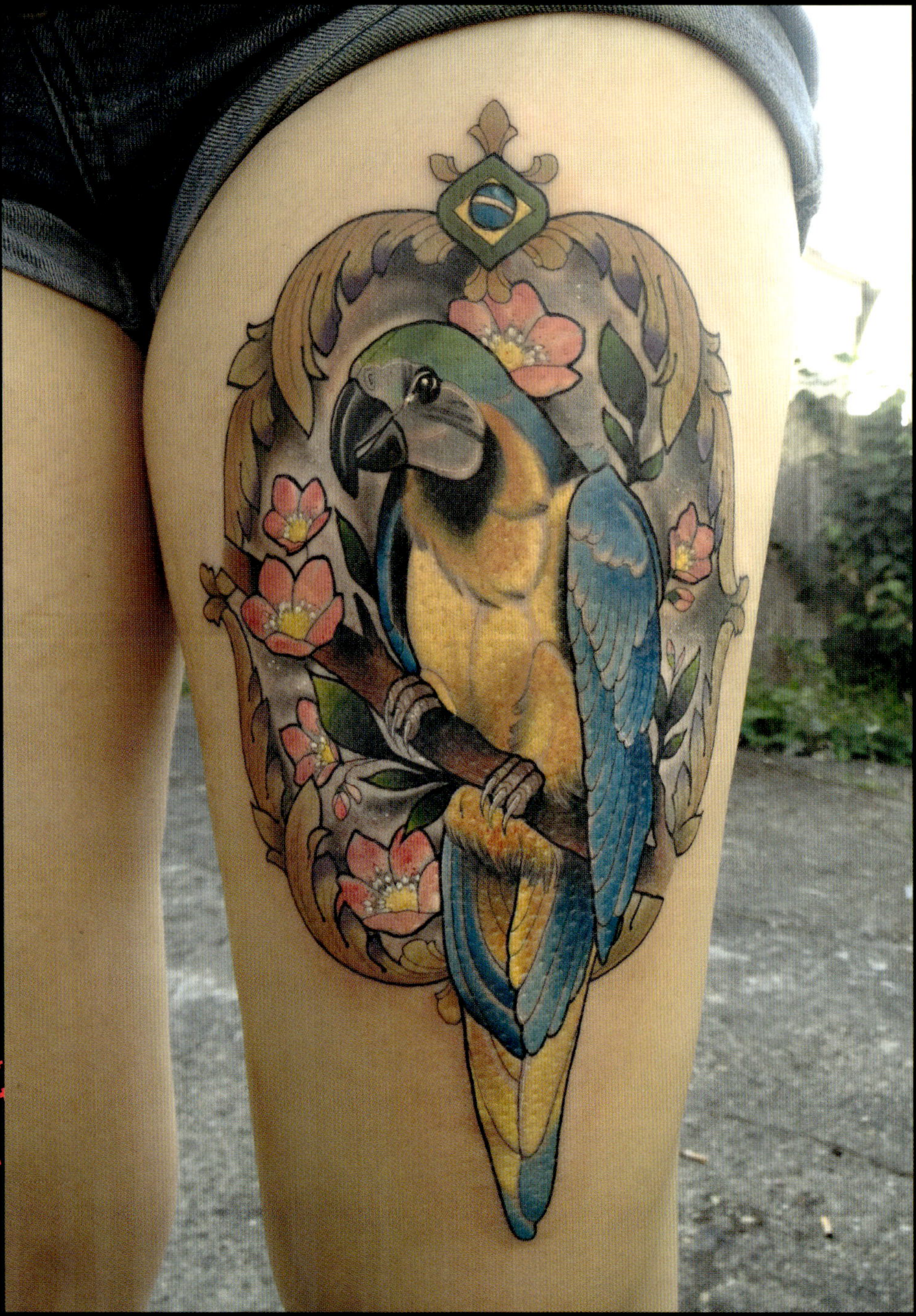

AMY VICTORIA SAVAGE

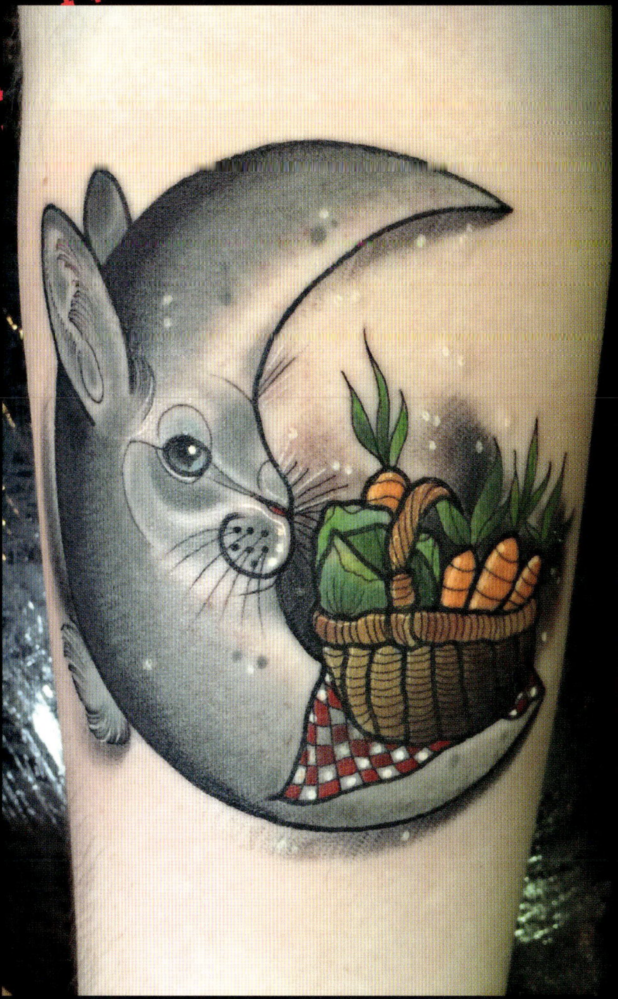

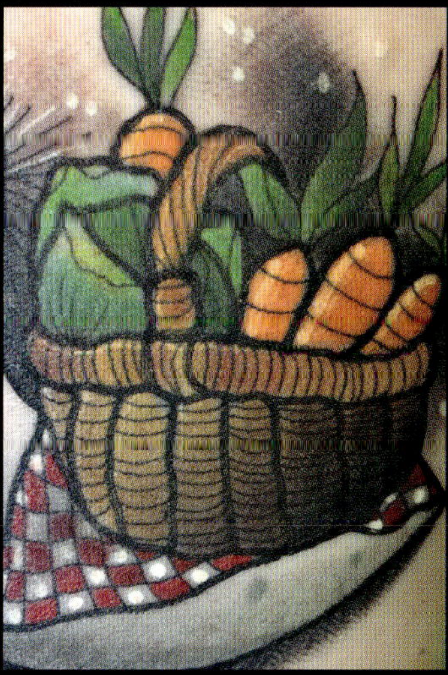

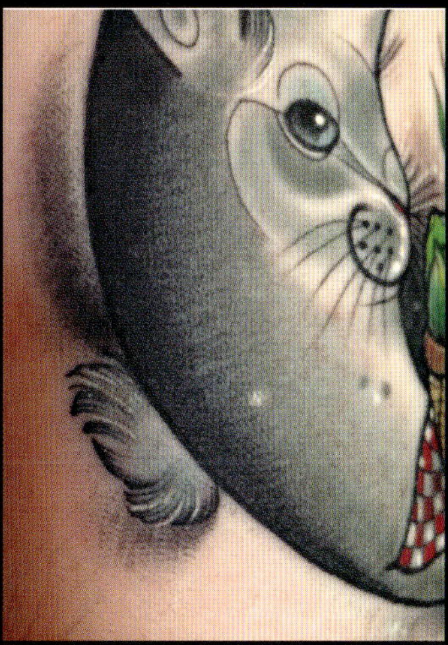

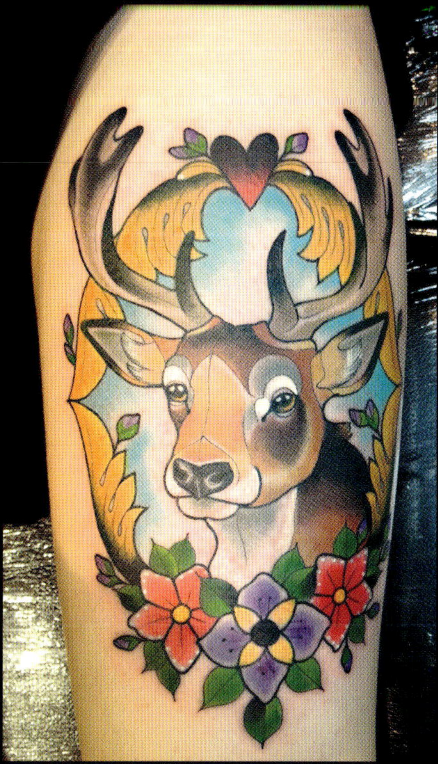

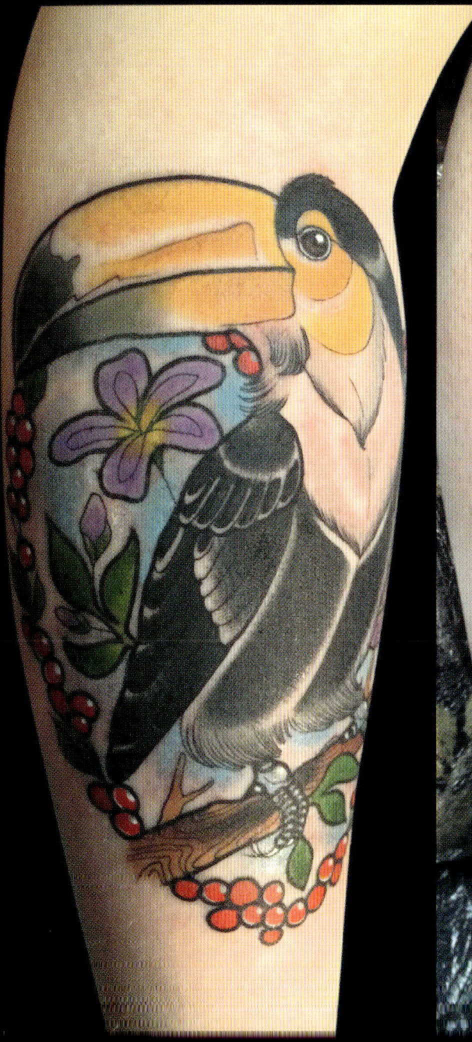

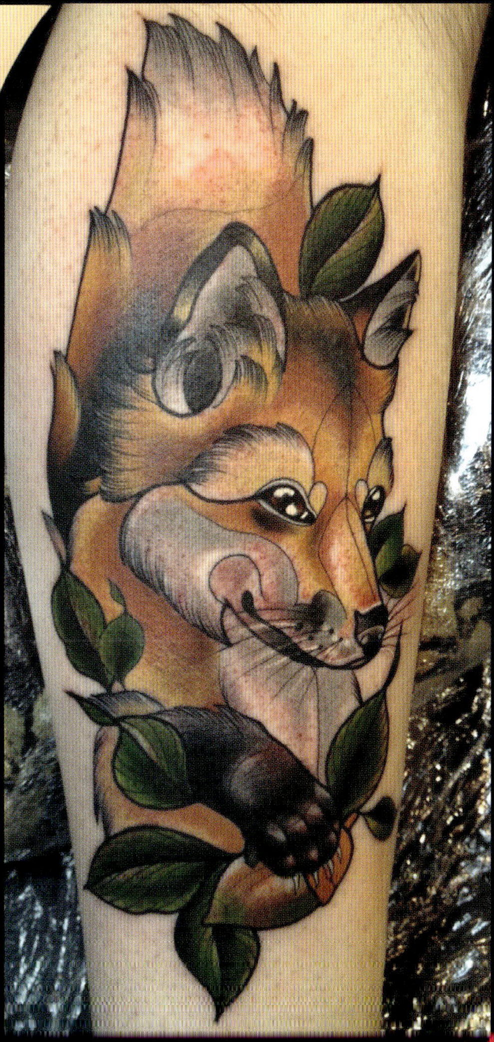

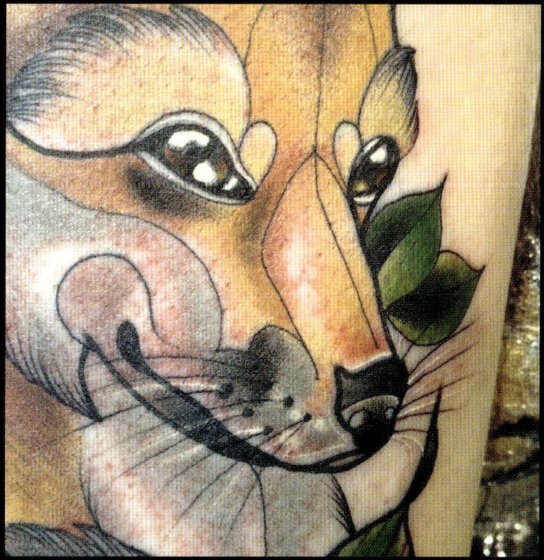

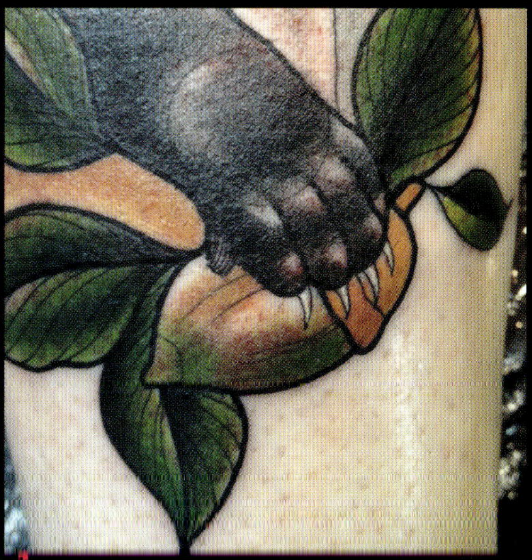

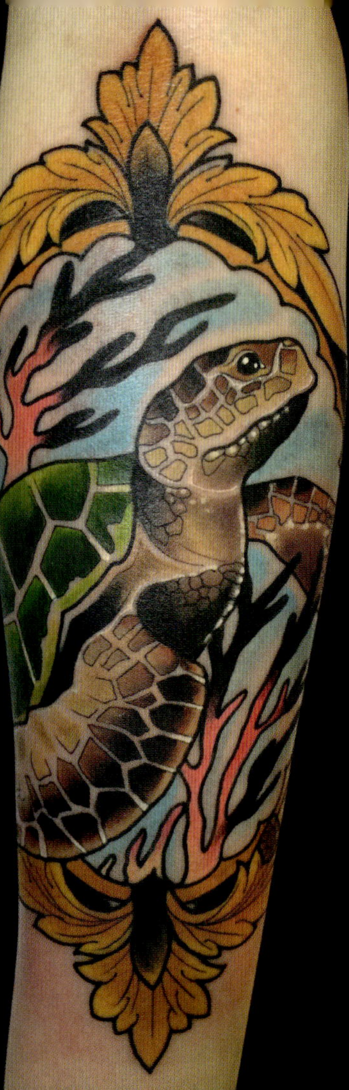

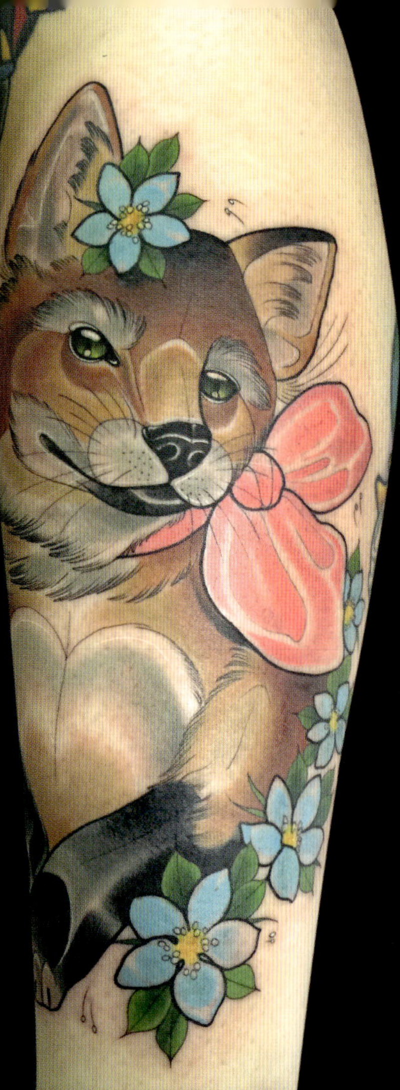

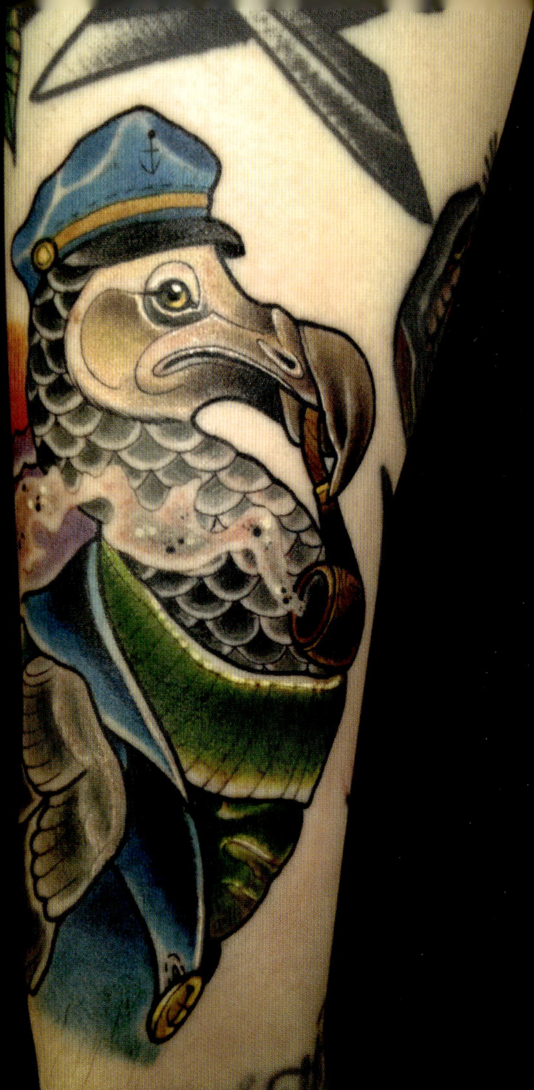

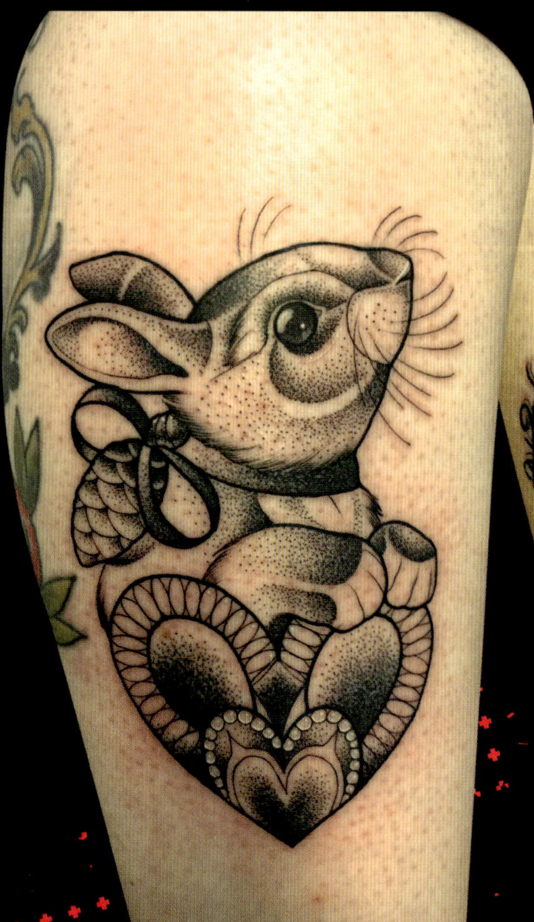

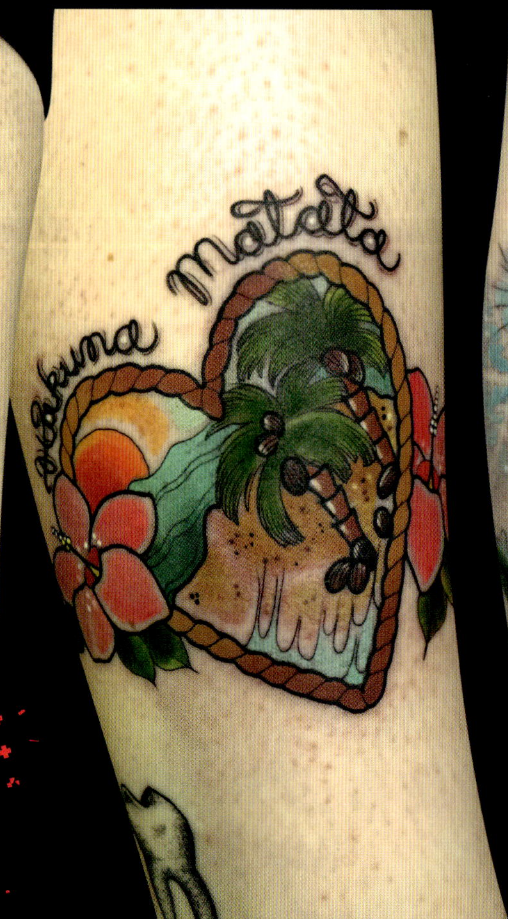
Matata

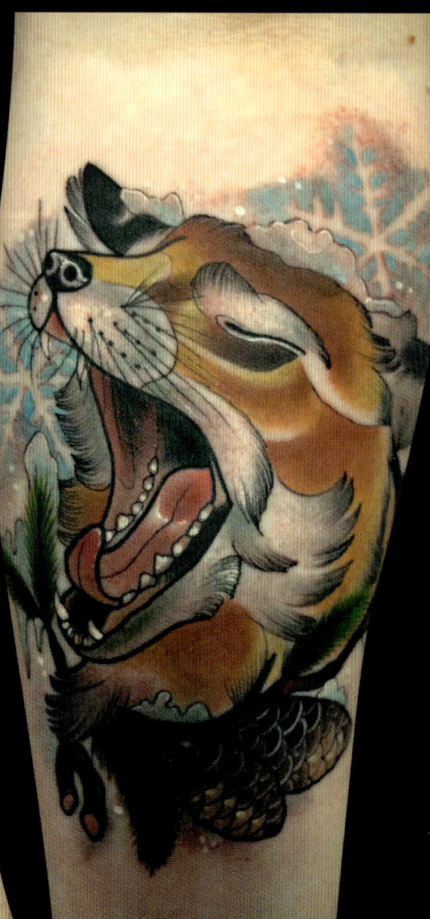

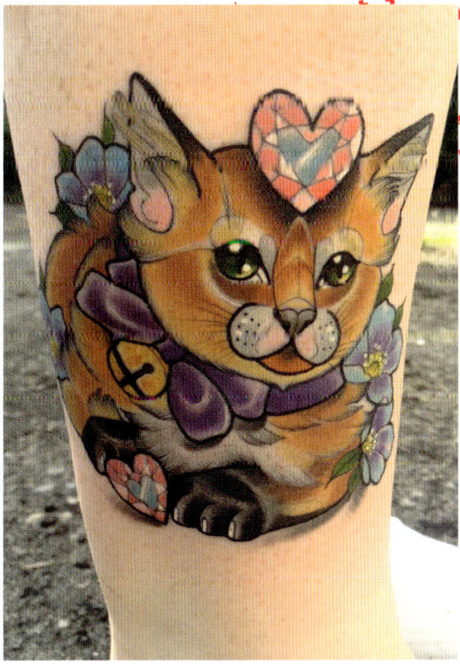

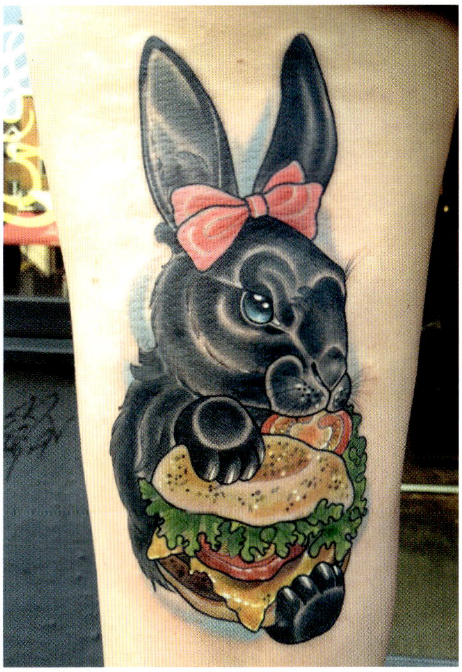

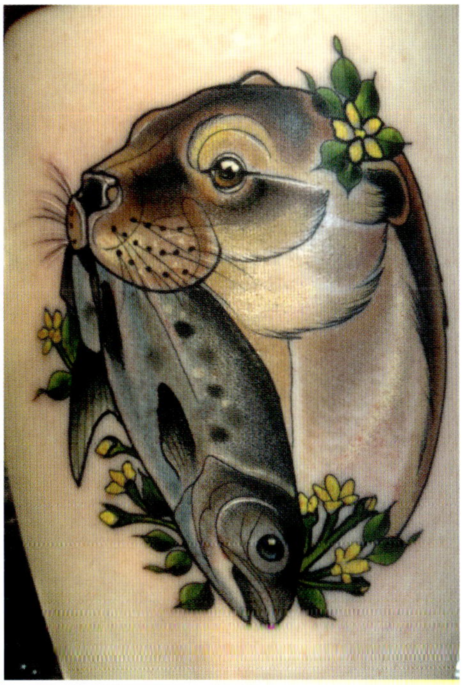

Describe how your role models and any other sources of inspiration have affected your tattoo style.

I have always found inspiration in anything and everything. Whether it be from the impressionists' paintings, Alphonse Mucha's prints, David Bailey's photographs, or some of today's great tattooers. But I think I find my richest inspiration comes from the natural world: animals, the ever-changing seasons, landscapes, natural behaviors. I have always been observant when it comes to the beauty of nature.

What's one of your favorite pieces that you've tattooed on someone else?

I have a few favorite pieces, all for totally different reasons. I recently finished two thighs with a framed fox and badger, each displaying a different season. I had so much fun with these because I could use a more natural color palette and not focus on the jewel and pastel colors that a lot of people tend to ask me for. I also did another badger piece recently, however, this one was stippled using only black ink. I am really getting into stippled critters lately—I love the use of black and how effective it can be.

What's one of your favorite pieces on your own body, and who did it?

I have a lot of great artwork by many great artists. However, I totally love the carousel horse on my leg by Seth Wood; it is flawless!

What is your favorite thing about being a tattoo artist?

I get to create sweet critters on a daily basis, get to indulge my artistic progression, and get to meet a lot of lovely and interesting people.

Do you have any funny tattoo stories? What about horror stories?

Oh there are a few, but that would be telling!

What do you think makes tattoos special?

I think the memories created whilst getting tattooed can make them special, even if the imagery isn't. If someone has a nice experience and is made to feel comfortable, it makes good memories.

Have you noticed a change in the types of images people have asked for over the years you've been tattooing?

I have definitely noticed an increase in animal tattoos…keep them coming! I want to tattoo all the weird and wonderful creatures!

Tattoos seem very mainstream now. Do you think that's good or bad?

I think the "acceptance" of tattoos is positive. People are becoming less judgmental about tattooed men and women, which is great!

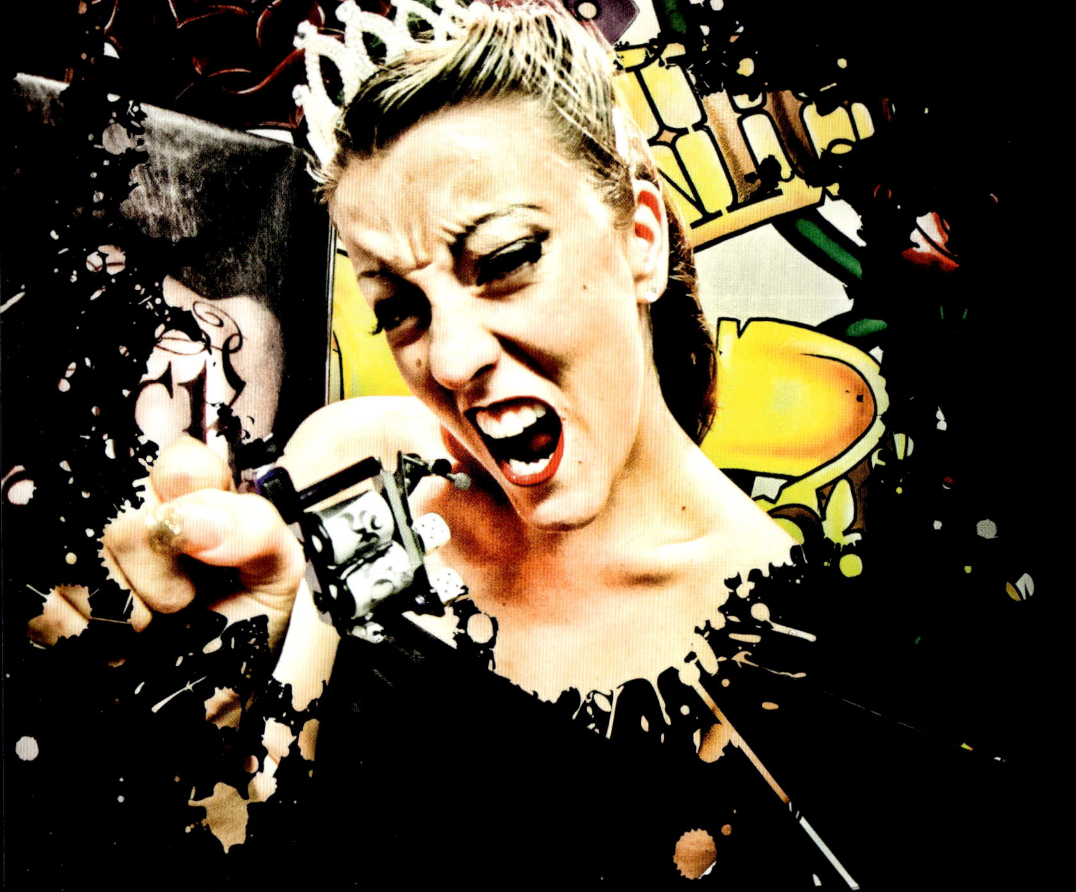

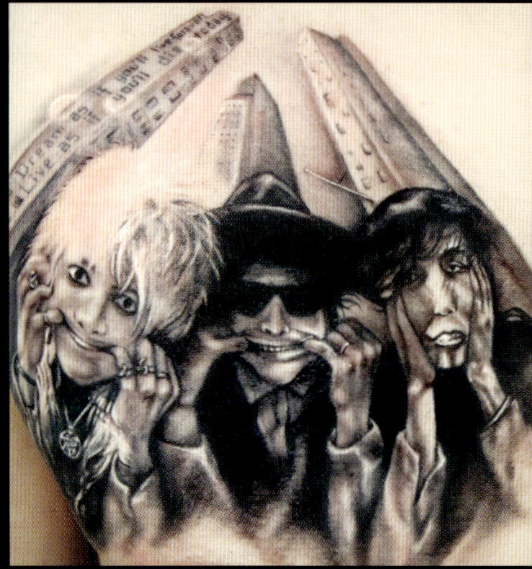

Before starting in tattooing, **SÄDE SONCK** had been living in different countries. In Thailand she spent time diving and doing batik on fabrics. In France she worked as a hostess for companies like Air France and Bosch. In her home country, Finland, she has owned an Italian ice cream café and a dance school (she's a teacher of salsa and reggaeton). Now Säde is a proud owner of the tattoo shop Unique Art.

Säde SONCK

"I feel that if I take myself seriously, everyone else will take me seriously too"

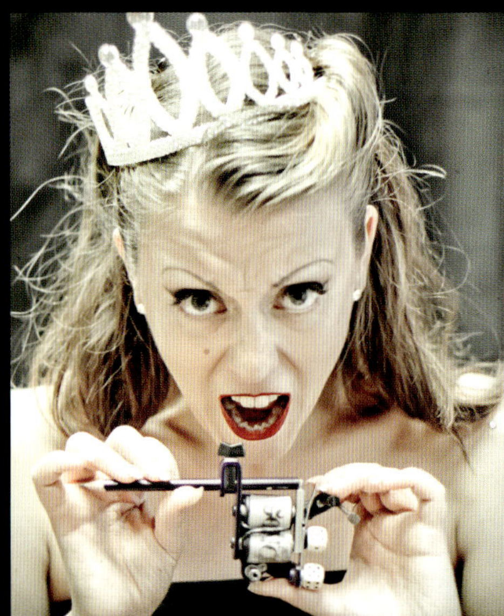

www.sadesonck.com
www.uniqueart.fi
www.facebook.com/SadeSonckTattooArtist
www.facebook.com/sade.sonck

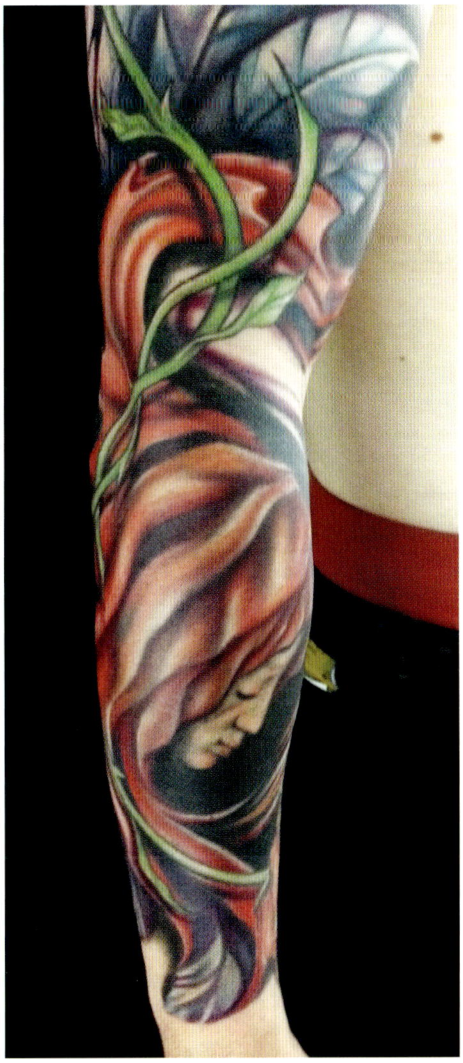

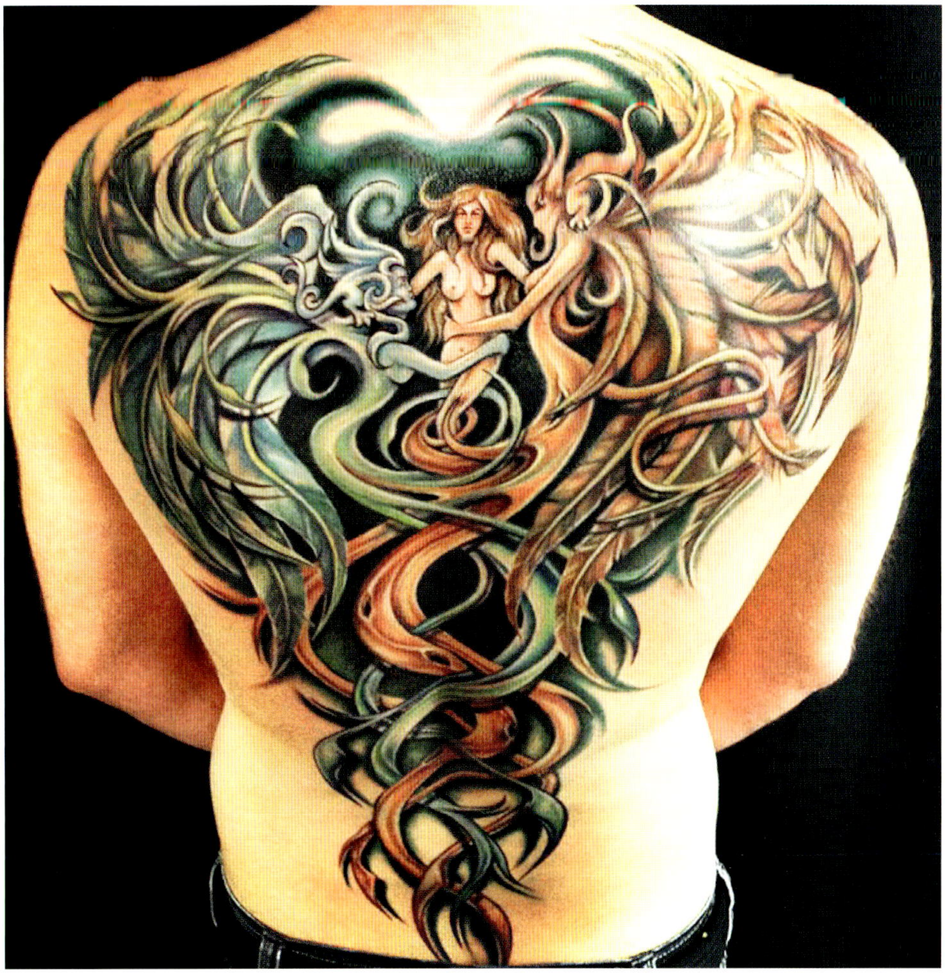

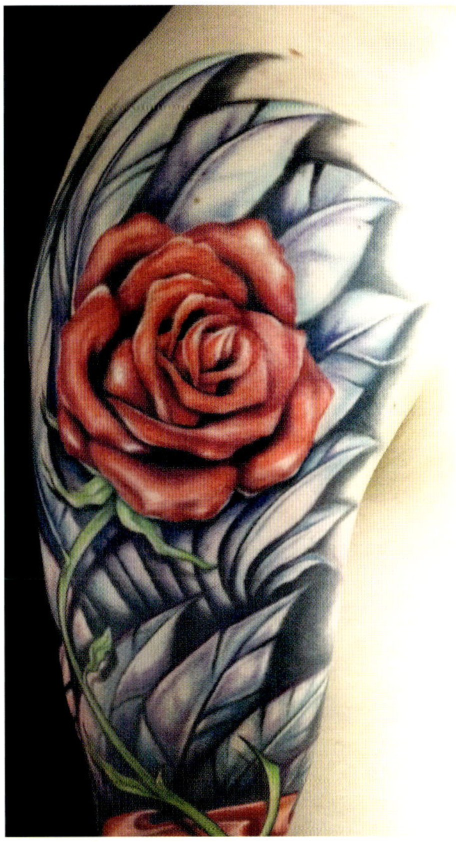

How long have you been a tattoo artist? Did you have a formal apprenticeship?

I found myself in Finland doing an apprenticeship in a local tattoo shop eleven years ago. Soon after that, I founded Unique Art and wanted to develop more of my skills. I contacted Stéphane Chaudesaigues in Paris and he saw the potential in me and welcomed me on as his apprentice. It was a great honor for me, and this was the beginning of our friendship. This is also how doors were opened for American and French tattoo conventions.

What's it like being a female artist in a primarily male workplace?

I consider myself as an artist; for me there isn't any she-artist or he-artist. To create art, it doesn't matter if you are a man or a woman. It's true that when I started tattooing eleven years ago, there weren't so many women in the industry, but now the number is getting bigger all the time. This is great news, the fact that women are getting more of a place in the tattooing world.

Do you feel that male customers treat you differently?

Absolutely not. I think that these days, attitudes have changed so much that art and work speaks for itself. I've never had any problems of any kind by being a female artist.

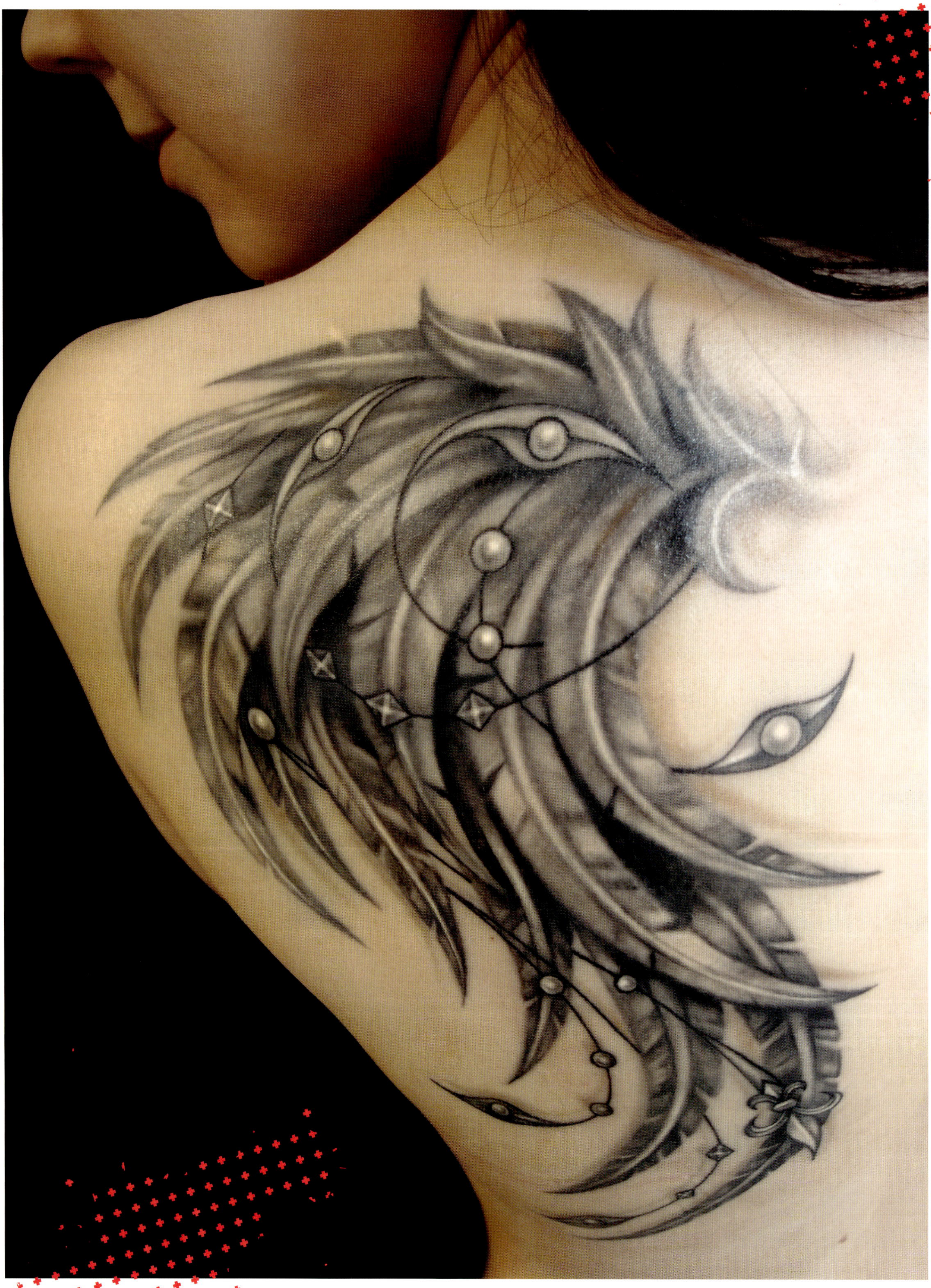

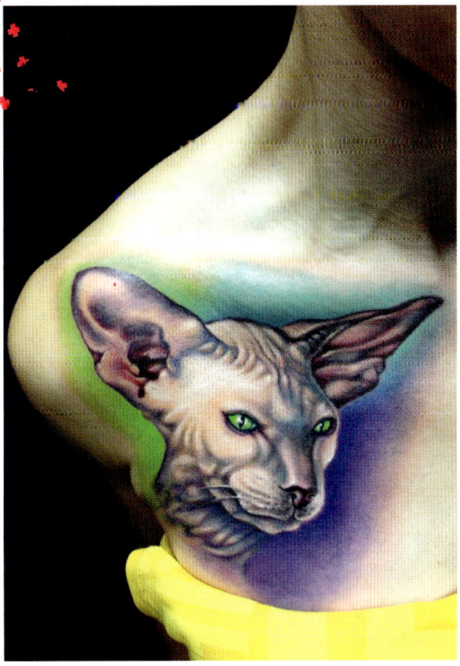

Though the dynamics are constantly changing, there are obviously many fewer women tattoo artists in the industry than men. Has being a female ever presented challenges to you along the way? Do you feel you have had to work even harder to achieve the success you have than might have been necessary for a man?

I come from a country that has had a female president, and where women often work in "manly" professions, so for me it isn't a strange idea to find myself in the tattooing industry. I feel that if I take myself seriously, everyone else will take me seriously too. The only thing where I see a difference is when having a baby, like me in 2014. There you can see a big difference between male and female artists. Men can continue working more easily and building their career than can a mother—the little newborn is fully dependent on me. But this experience as a mom is a whole new world that I wouldn't change for a thing. The next conventions that I'm doing, I'm taking my family with me!

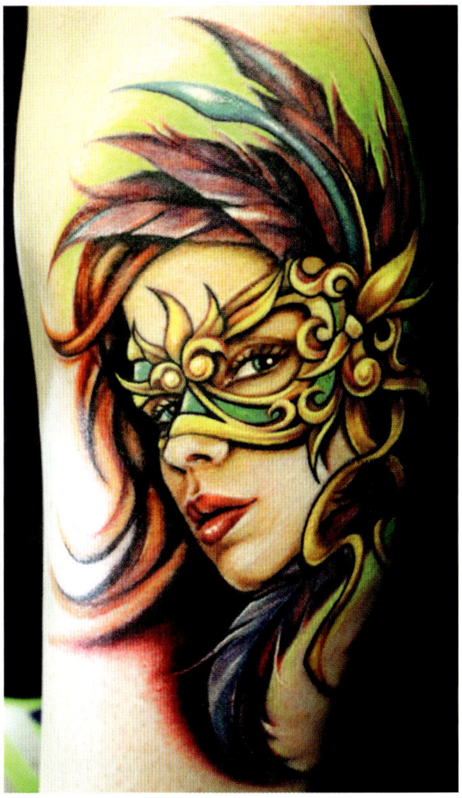

Tell me more about the shop you work at; what's it like working there, and what makes up a typical day?

My shop Unique Art is in Hämeenlinna, Finland, and I'm proud to say that in 2014 my shop received a national certificate of honor from among all the businesses in Finland, for moving the tattooing industry in a positive direction. It's a big thing for a tattoo shop to win this kind of award.

We have a great staff. Every tattoo artist has a different style, and they are some of the nicest people I know. It's more like a family, a way of life, instead of a business. I've always thought that the atmosphere where you work has to be free and open, for good vibes to feed your creativity. Some of us come in early in the morning and others like to work later into the evening. Every day is full of coffee, goofiness, jokes, and some serious tattoo art!

Do you see tattooing as a job or as a way to express your creative side?

It is a way of living, a culture of expressing life.

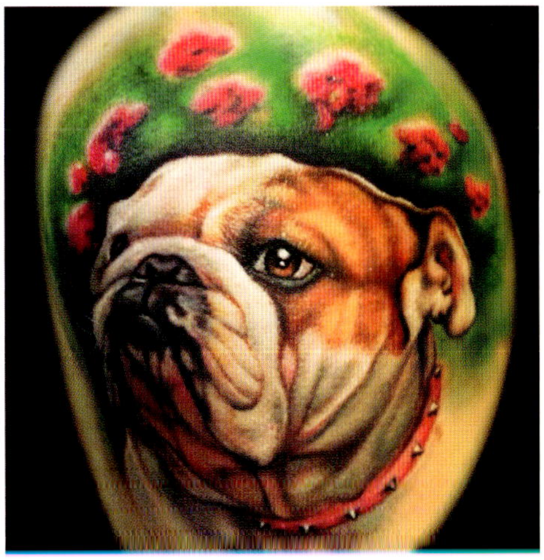

What inspires you when you create your designs?

Definitely nature. I might be soft for a tattoo artist, but that is the thing that inspires me the most.

What do you enjoy most about tattooing, and what are some of the challenges?

Tattooing is hard work; there are so many different aspects you have to handle. You need millions of hours of making lines to understand the right way of creating this art. Tattooing gives you a certain kind of freedom as an artist because it is possible to make a living with your art. I've found that the more you learn

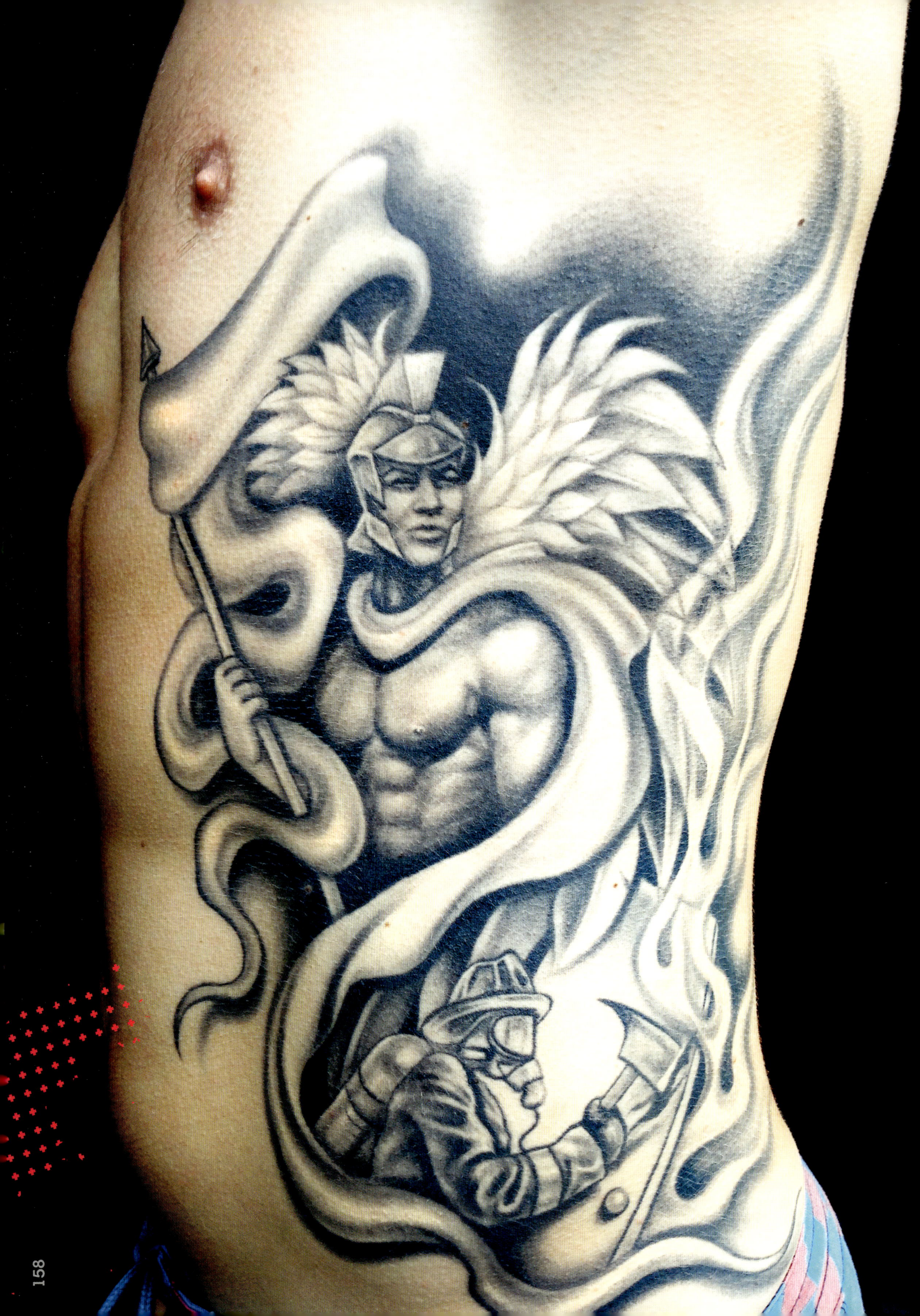

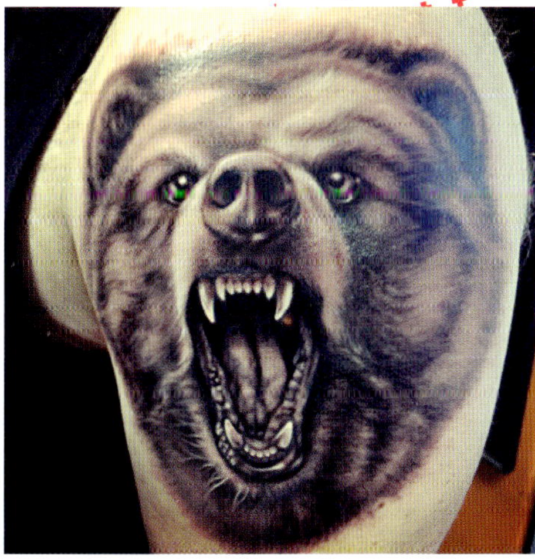

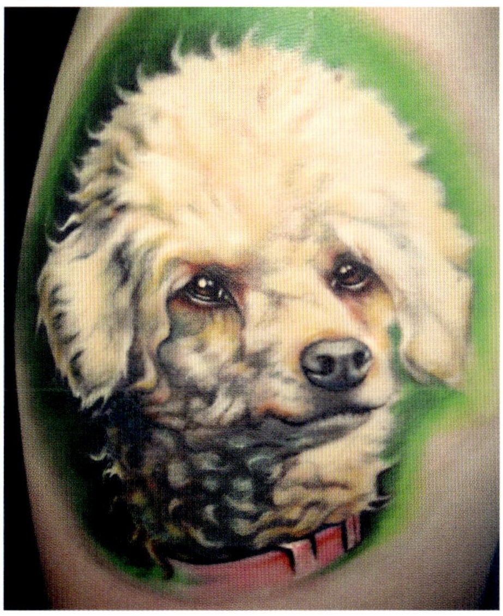

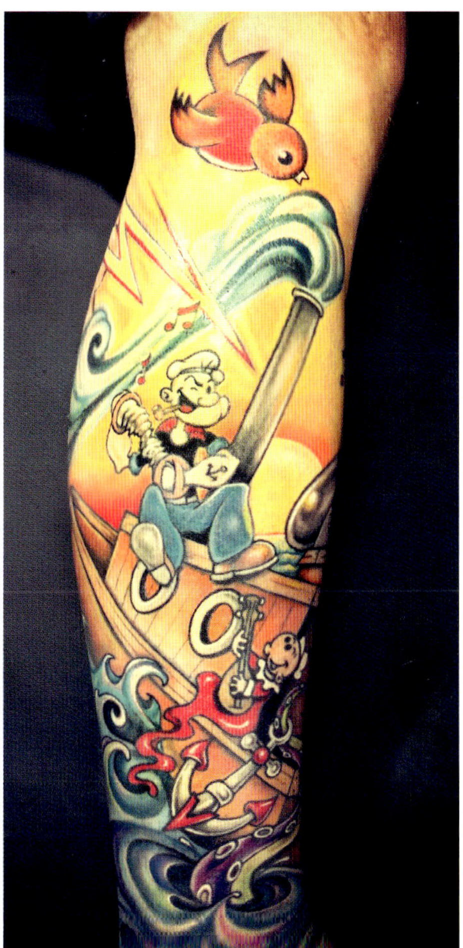

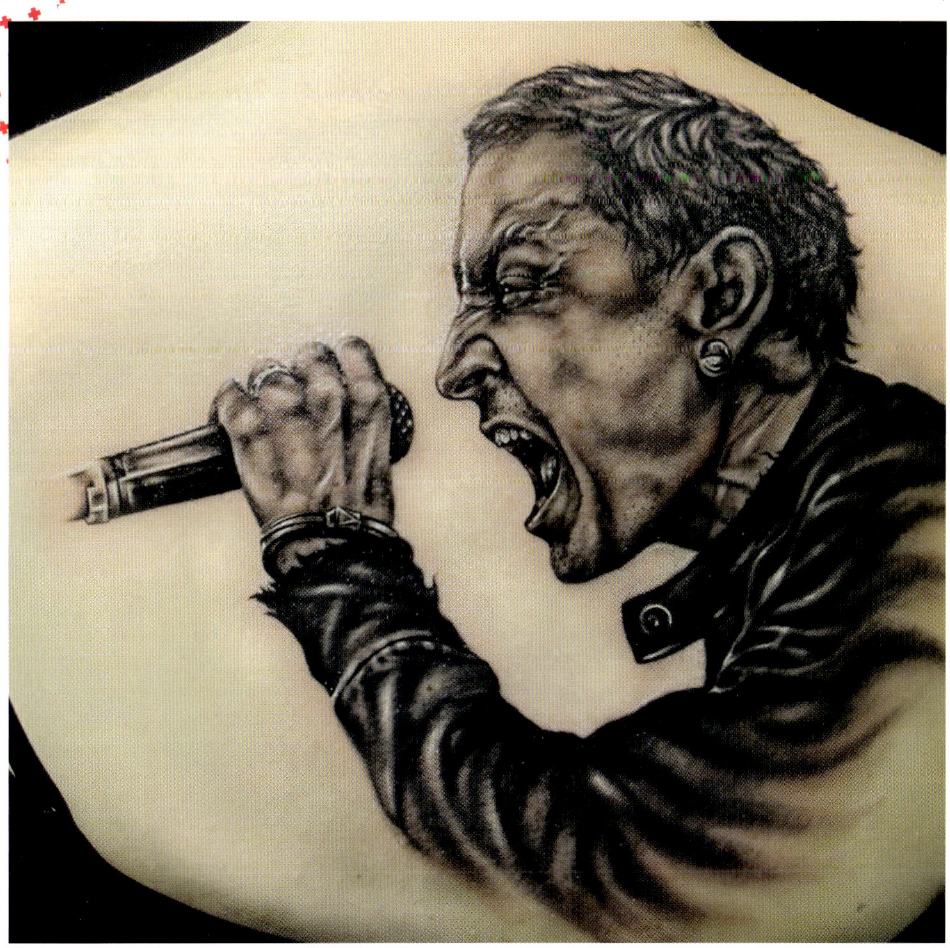

and develop your skills, the more in demand you are. This idea keeps me going: that my art is constantly on exhibit outdoors. When I'm creating a piece, it doesn't end up in someone's closet after a few years. It is a living form of art.

Art can be a great influence on someone's personality. What is the best lesson that you've learned from your art journey?

I think that the best lesson so far is that it doesn't matter if you are an artist yourself or a person experiencing art pieces, the pleasure of enjoying art can be the same. You can find art in your everyday life, and all the things you choose to see modify your personality. So it is better to choose a beautiful environment around you, like Finland! *(Laughs.)*

As an artist you just have to accept that the journey of an artist is the constant suffering of creating the new. No matter what your level, you are never finished or "ready" as an artist; you grow all the time. You just love it and hate it at the same time.

How did your style progress and develop to the point you are at now?

When starting a career you have to take the projects that clients propose to you, and tattoo by tattoo, you start to understand what type of style you enjoy doing most. My eye has always loved realism, and that is the aspect I've chosen to develop. I had been admiring Stéphane Chaudesaigue's style and was lucky to have him as my mentor, to give me tools to improve and grow my own style.

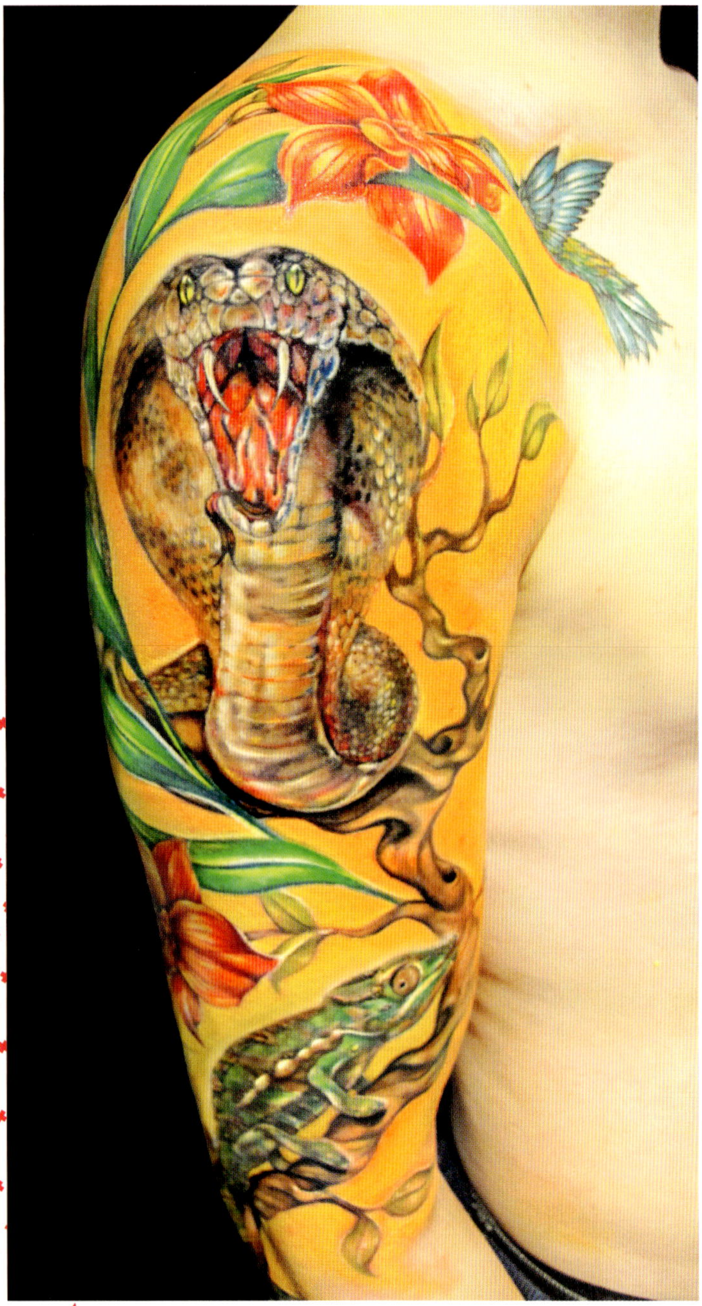
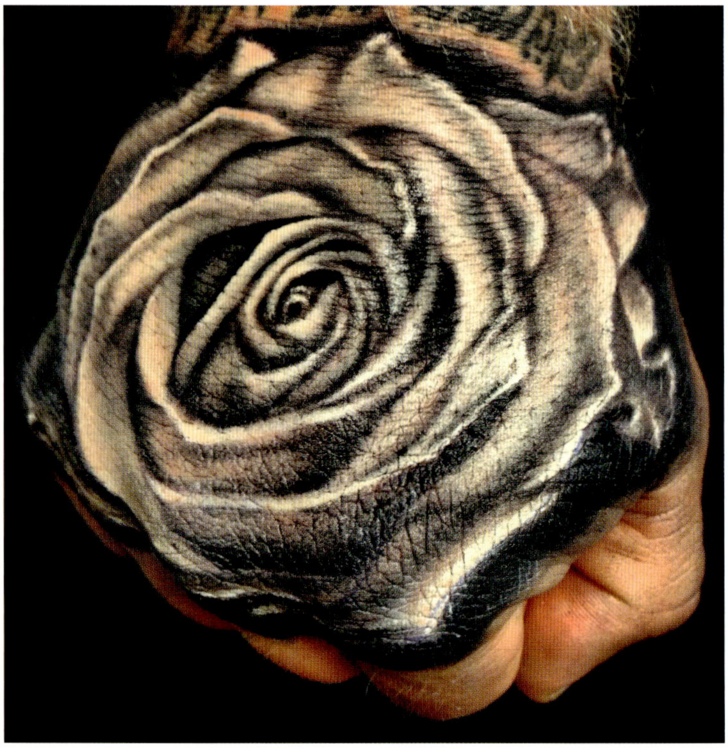
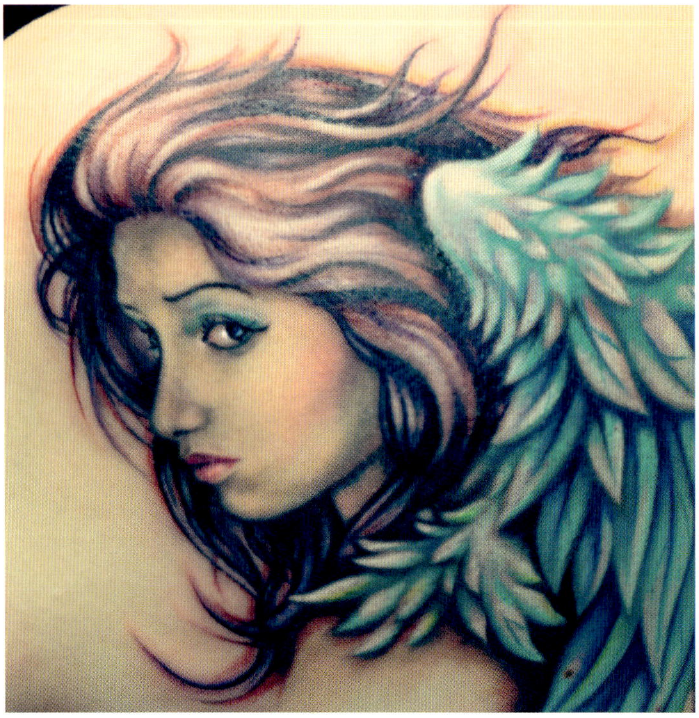
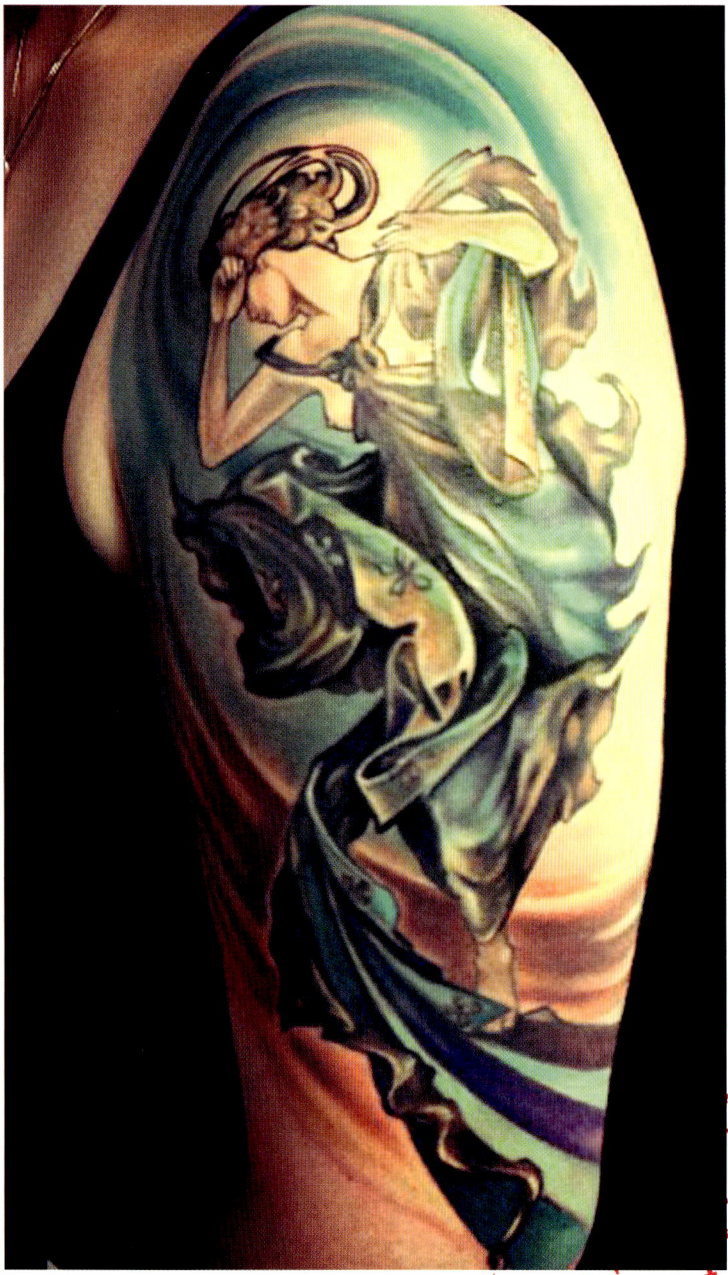

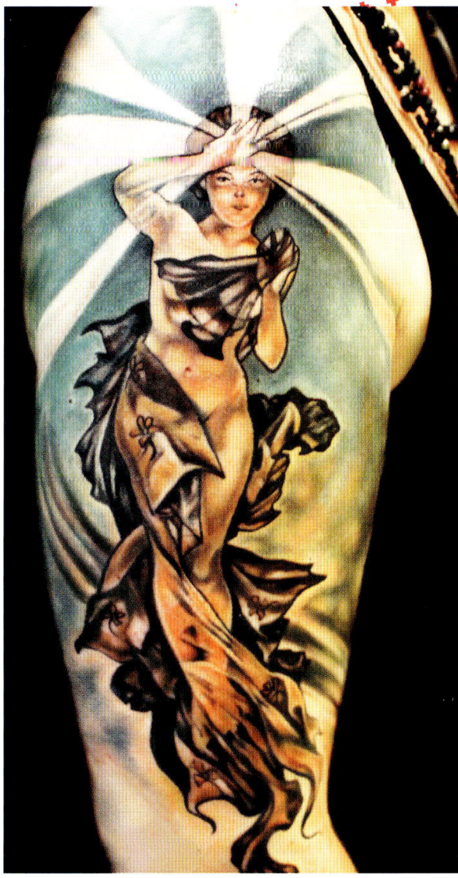

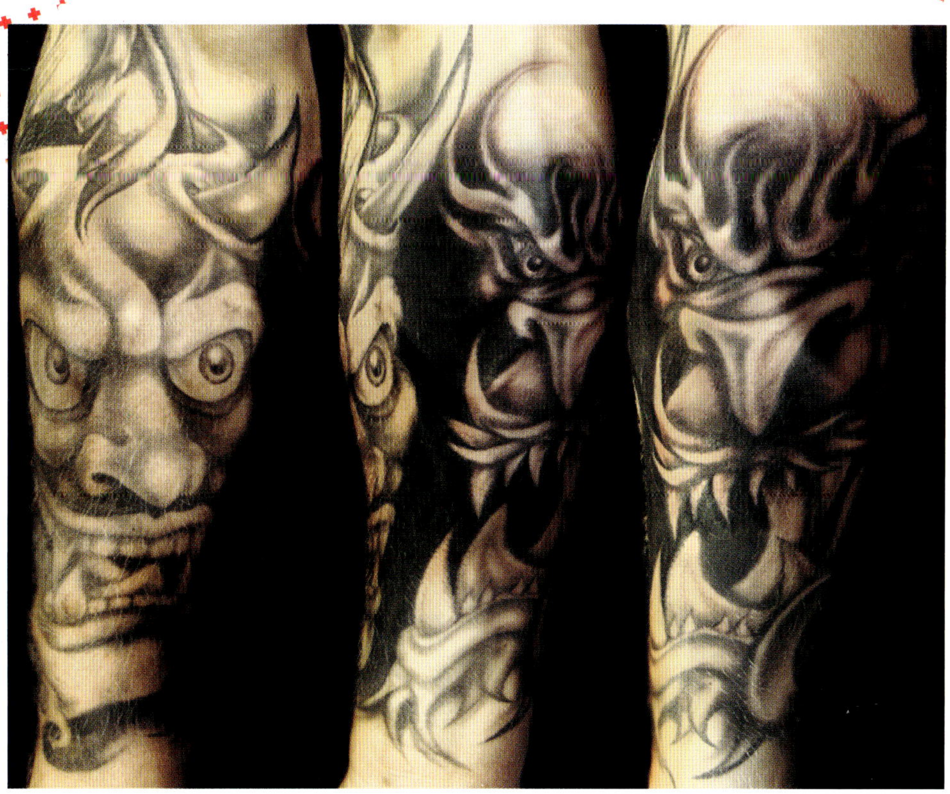

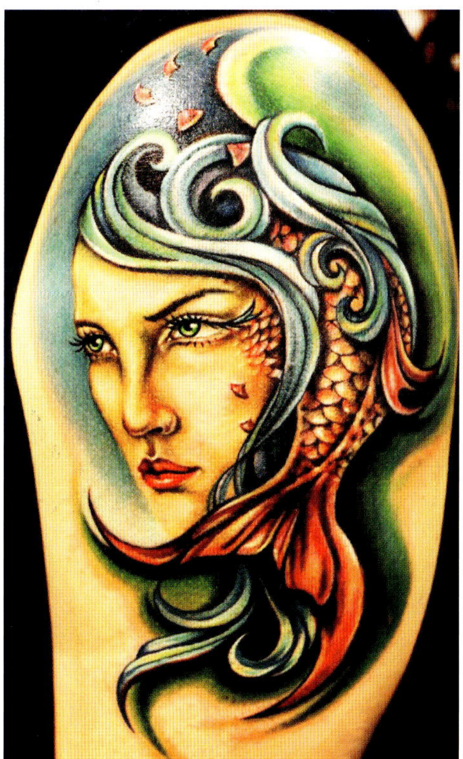

Describe how your role models and any other sources of inspiration have affected your tattoo style.

One of my role models in the tattooing industry is Nikko Hurtado. I went to his seminar organized by Tatouage & Partage in Avignon, France, in 2012. It was a great pleasure to see what a nice person is there behind his masterpieces. His style of coloring has had an influence on my work. Also I love Shawn Barber's art in painting; I enjoyed going to his painting course in Colorado in 2013. It's good to follow what fellow artists are doing, and it always has an impact on your own work when you see beautiful pieces.

What's one of your favorite pieces that you've tattooed on someone else?

One of my favorite tattoos is a Mardi Gras themed woman with a mask that I tattooed at the Best in the MidWest convention in Iowa, in 2013. I designed it in Finland and tried hard to find out what Mardi Gras really is about. Finally, after my research, it turned out nice and was in keeping with Mardi Gras coloring and themes. It was great fun doing this piece. My client and I laughed for eight hours, and finished up by winning best of the day and best small color.

What's one of your favorite pieces on your own body, and who did it?

I'm kind of a weird tattoo artist, not having any tattoos...yet! I know myself, and I know that after getting the first one, I'm going to be full soon after. So I have to put some brakes on my desires, and try to think though what kind of art I would like to wear for the rest of my life. I guess I take it too seriously!

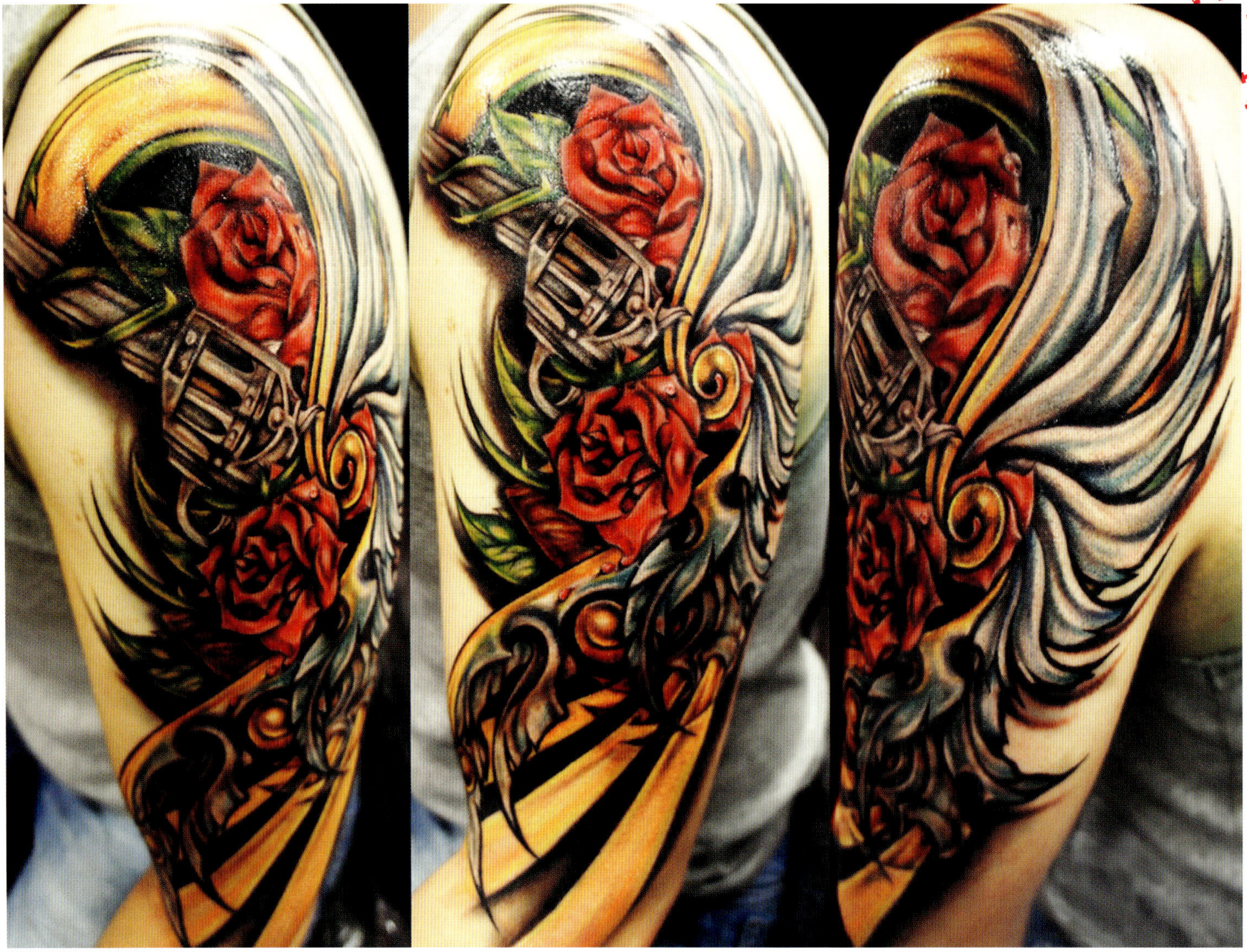

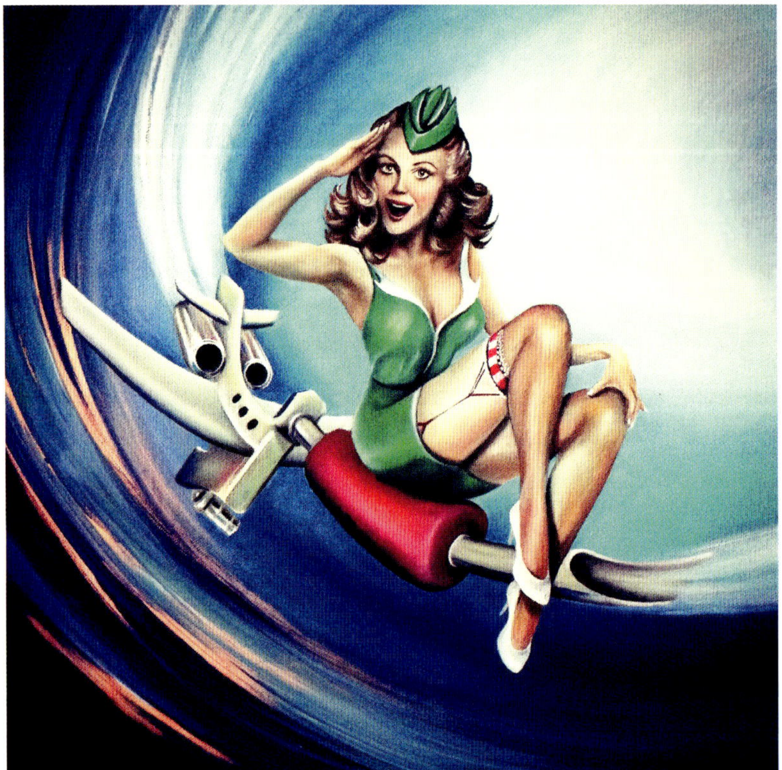

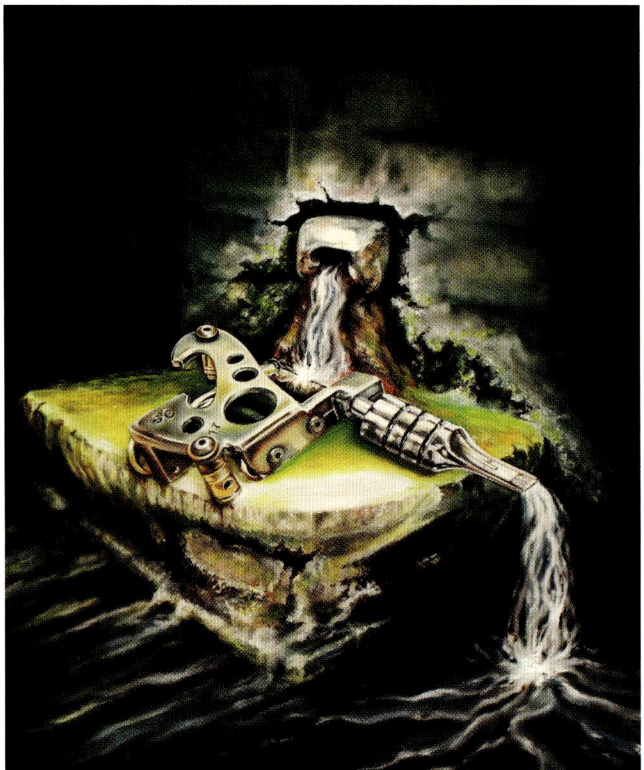

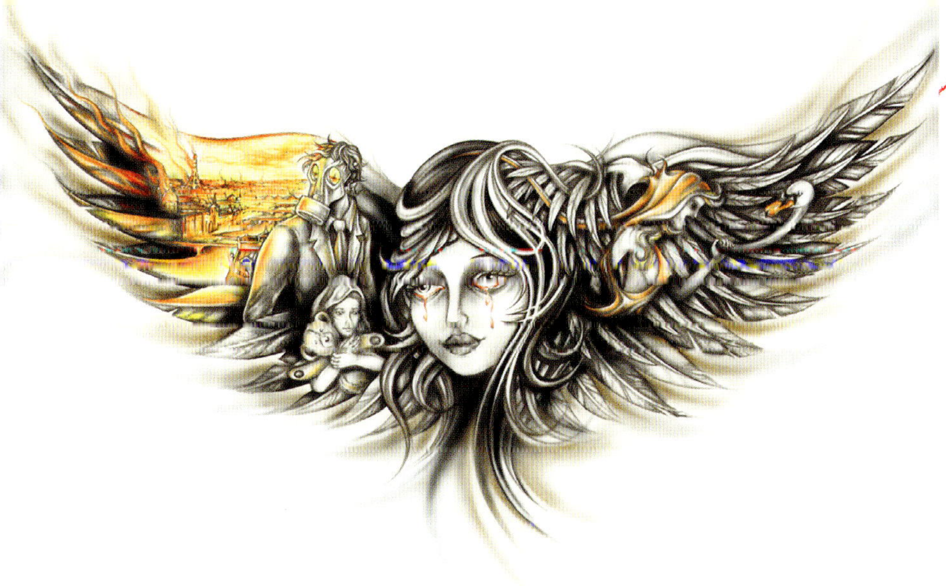

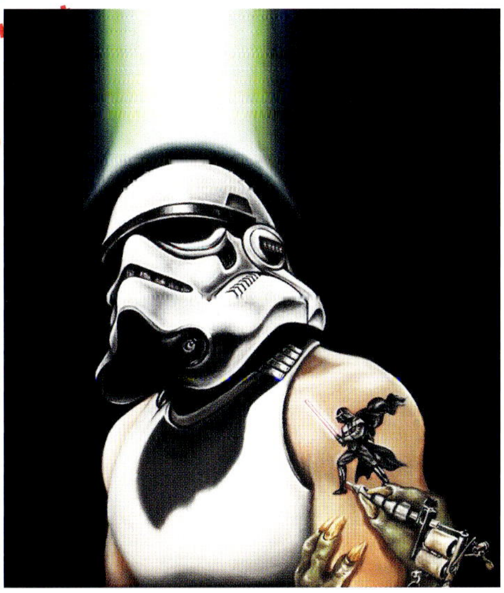

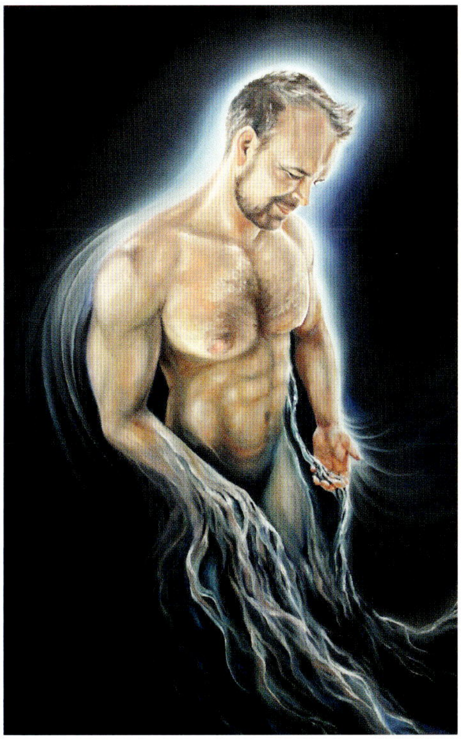

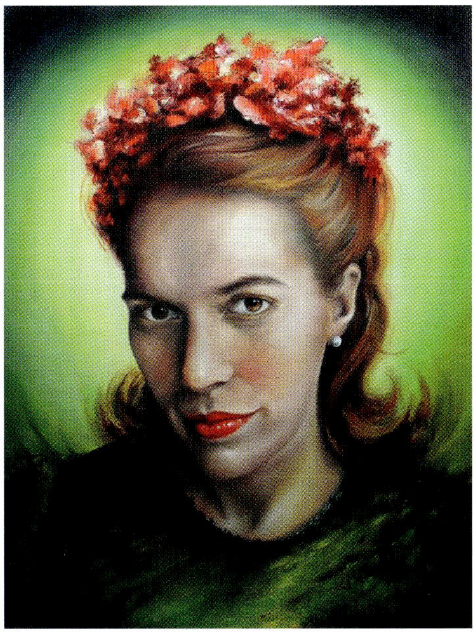

What is your favorite thing about being a tattoo artist?

I love my work and the fact that I can do art for living. I feel lucky that I have been able to make my passion into my work. Every tattoo is made by hand, and the journey of turning the client's personality into an image on skin is the thing that I love. Every piece is unique.

What is the most interesting tattoo you have been asked to do?

There are so many interesting ones that it is hard to choose. But some that I really enjoyed doing were Alphonse Mucha's pieces *Morning Star* and *Evening Star*, which won an award in Cantal In'k the Skin in 2013. It was a great journey to dive into Mucha's world of all the smart details he has in his style, and modify everything into a tattoo. I just love those tattoos!

Is there any subject or taboo you wouldn't ink on someone, even if it was their request or design?

I haven't had this kind of problem in my career. The people who come to ask me for an art piece have had the same kind of ideology as I do.

Have you noticed a change in the types of images people have asked for over the years you've been tattooing?

I've earned my steady tattooing hand from the tribals and simple black-and-gray tattoos I did when starting. Now people dare to get a lot more colorful, bigger tattoos and collections.

Tattoos seem very mainstream now. Do you think that's good or bad?

It is a good thing of course. But the bad side of this is that so many people are doing tattoos at home with poor equipment and education. I think this is something that should be restricted. This growth of the tattooing industry now will be fun to see after fifty years, when every granny and grandpa is full of skin art!

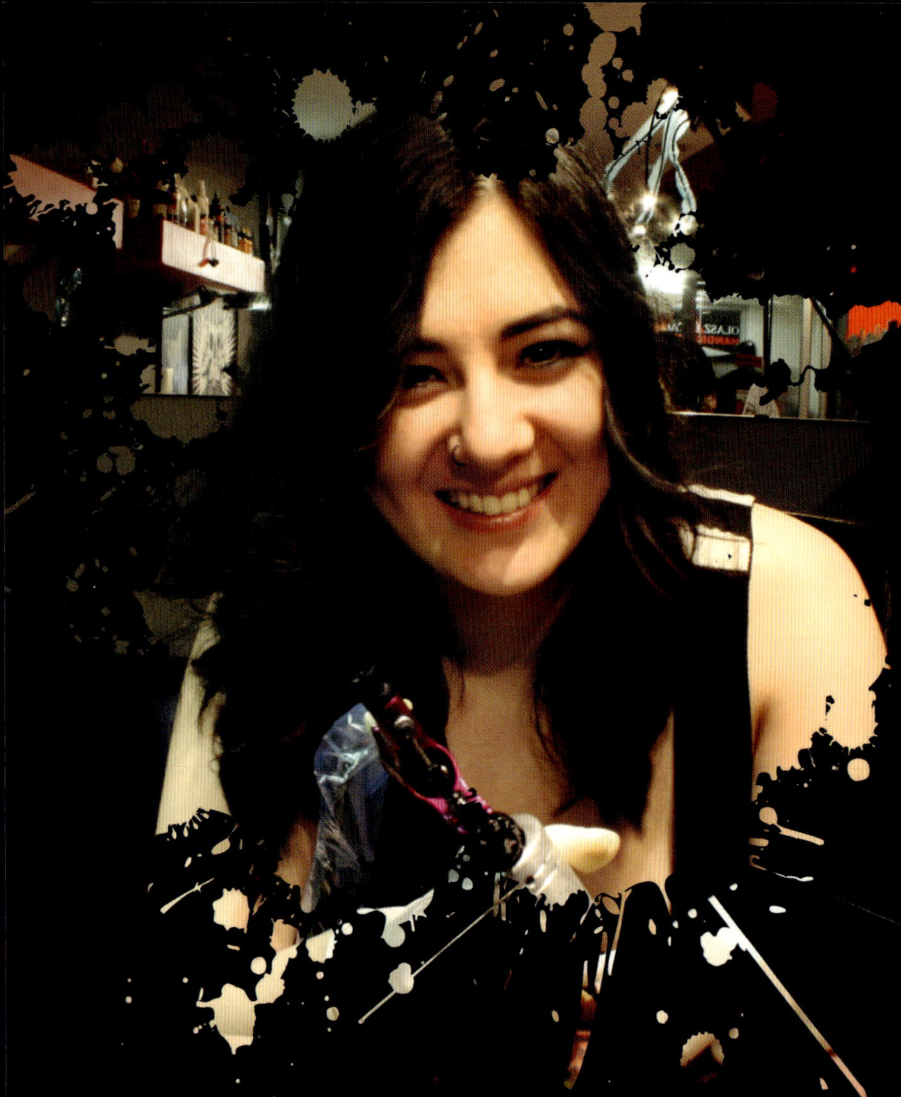

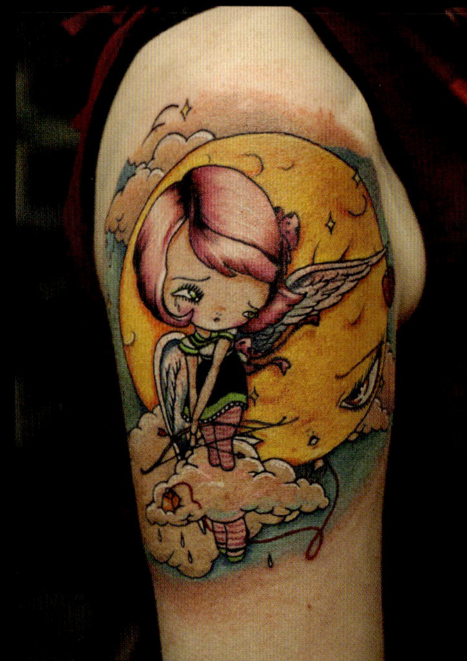

Hungarian tattoo artist **XU YI LILI** was born in the city of Miskolc in 1992. She has been drawing since elementary school, and took part in drawing courses and competitions. After finishing art high school she started to learn animation, and wanted to be an animator. But her growing interest in tattooing led Lili to leave her animation courses, because she couldn't study and tattoo at the same time.

Xu Yi LILI

"I am too young to have my own style"

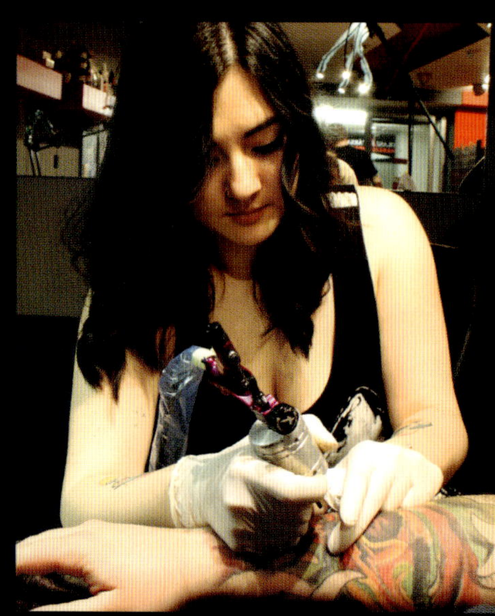

www.facebook.com/xuyiLee
www.facebook.com/swtattoo
xu-yi-lili.tumblr.com

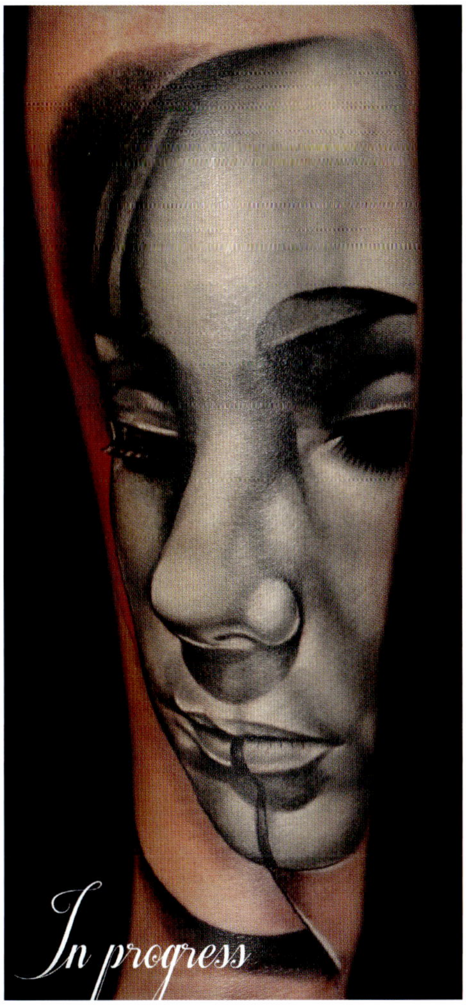

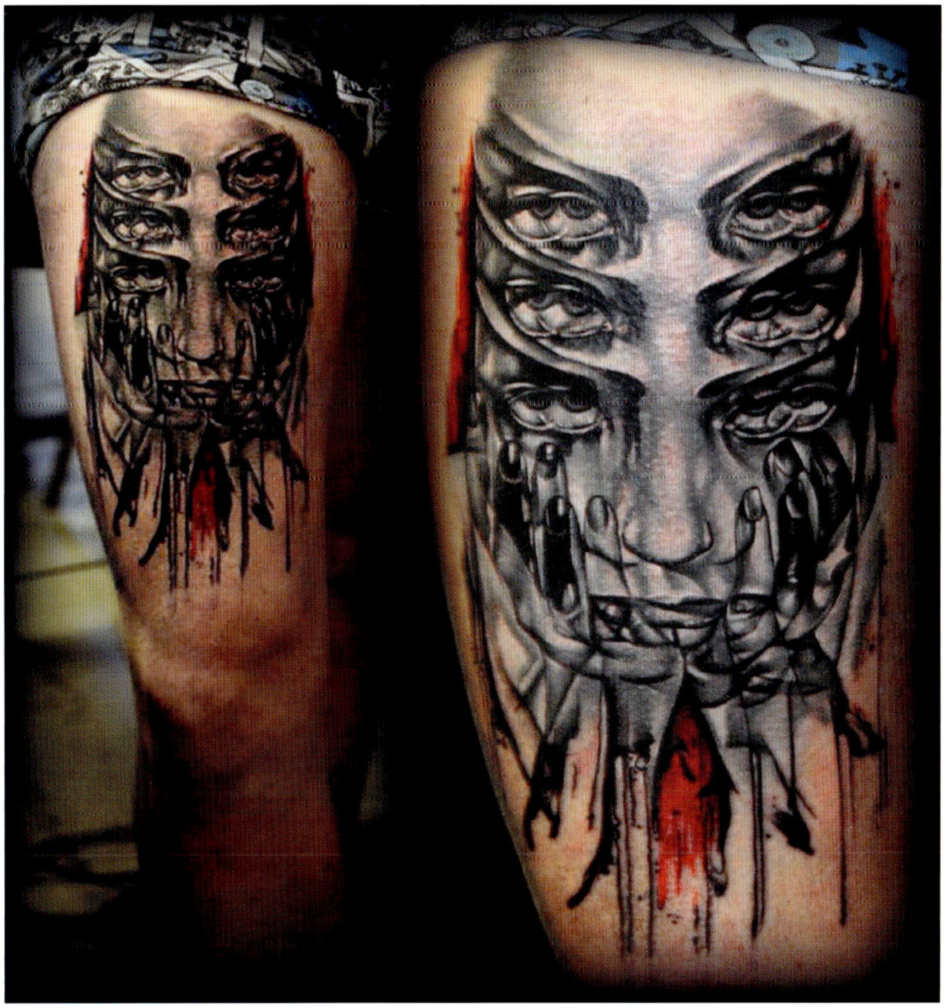

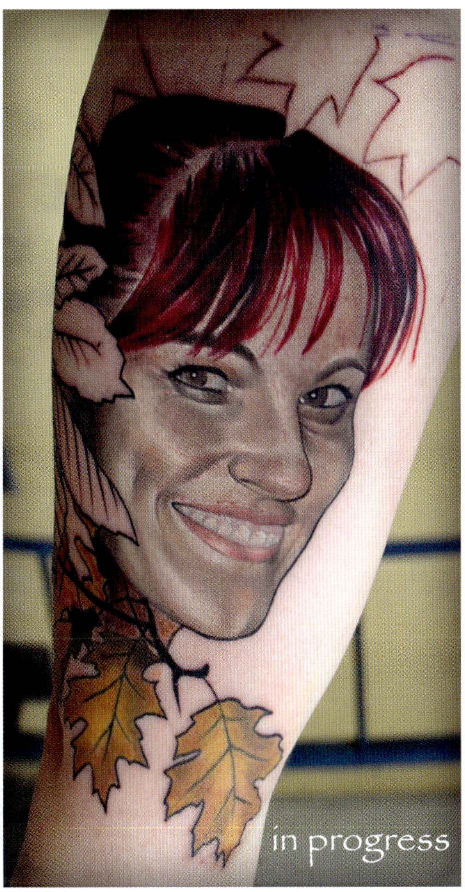

When you were a child, did you think you would grow up to become an artist, or work in the artistic field? Do you remember drawing and creating a lot as a child?

I never once thought that I'd tattoo, but I was always sure that I wanted to deal with drawing in some way; I wanted drawing to be an important part of my life.

What was your initial exposure to the tattoo world and when did you first add your own piece of ink to your skin? Was that a transformative time in your life?

I got acquainted with the world of tattooing through my uncle Norbert Pók. He has some tattoos on his body and I liked those designs. I had gone with him several times to the Orion, the tattoo studio he went to. I heard there that the Skin Workshop Tattoo Studio was looking for a new tattoo apprentice. I rushed into the shop with my drawings immediately, but I was afraid they wouldn't want a disorganized teenager. But in spite of that I was called back, and I've been here ever since. And I'd like to say thank you here, for the teaching and help, to Norbert Halász! Anyway, my first tattoo was made here in this studio too, by Lehel Nyeste, on my left arm.

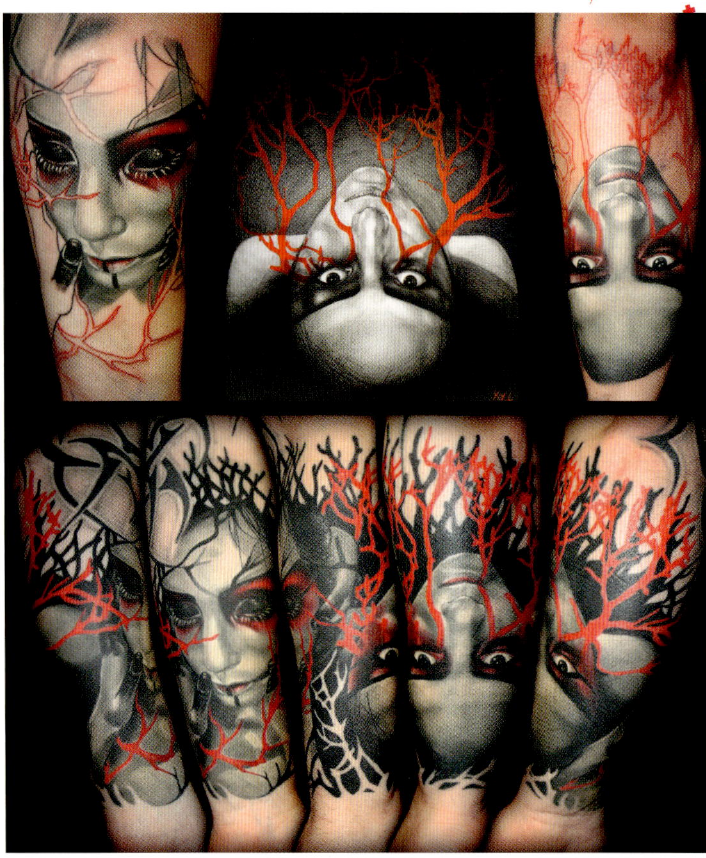
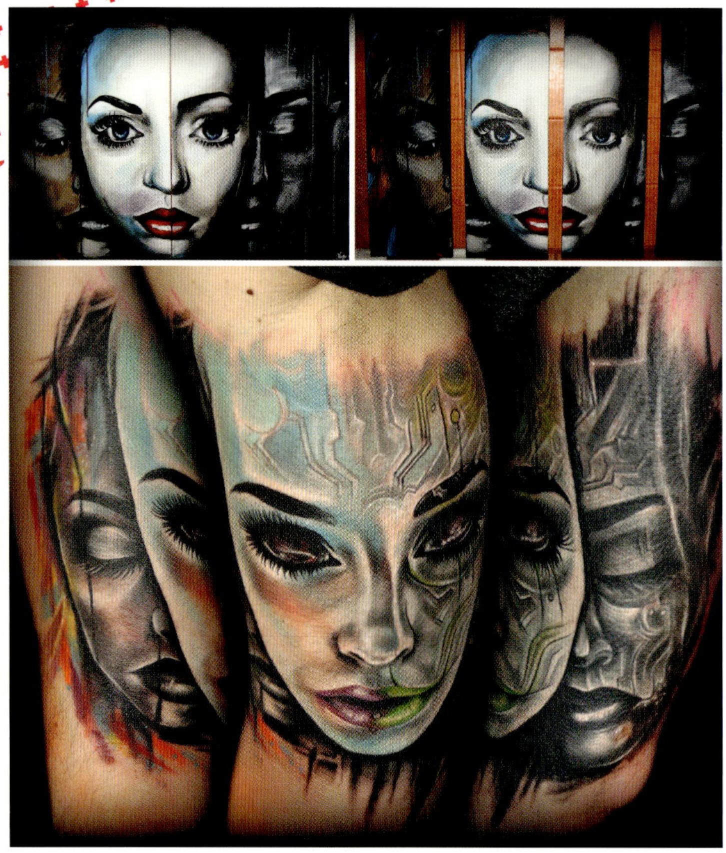
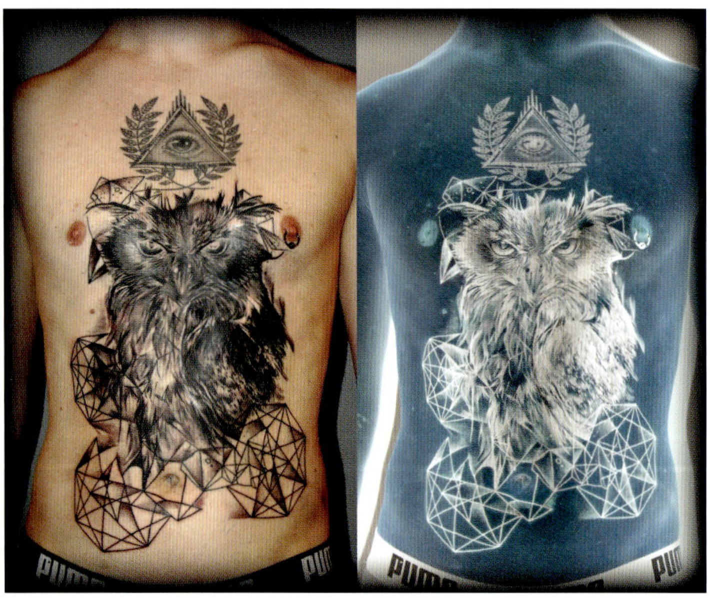
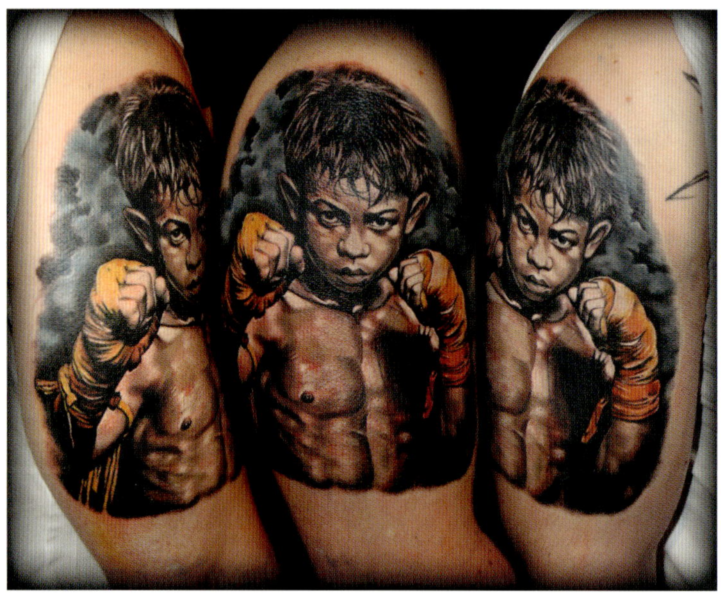
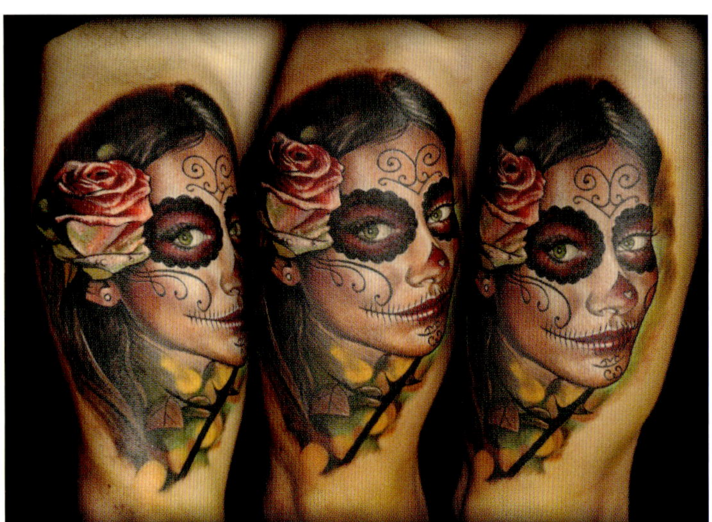
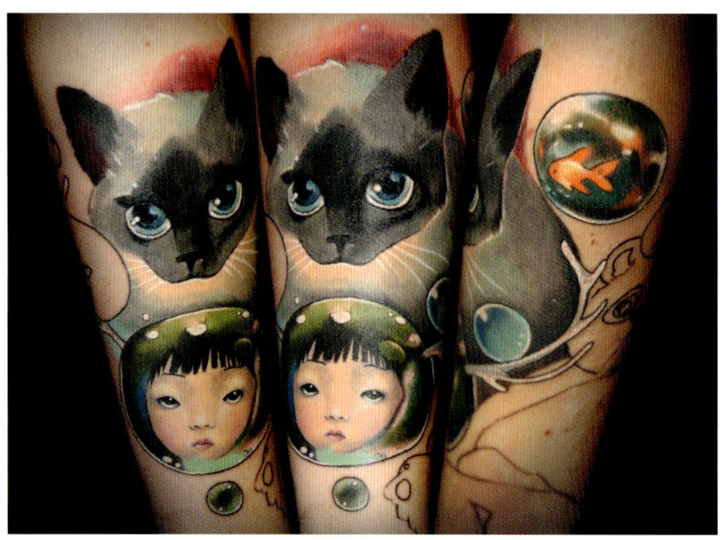

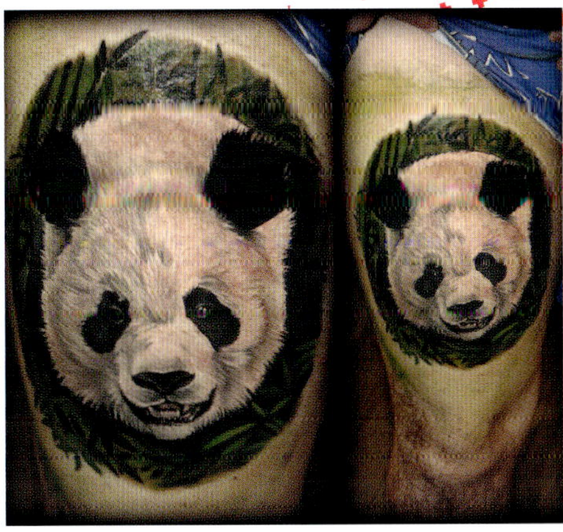

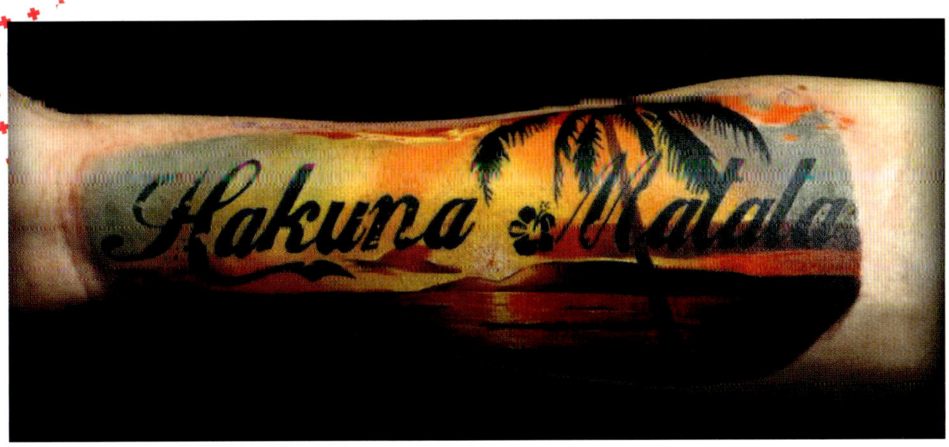

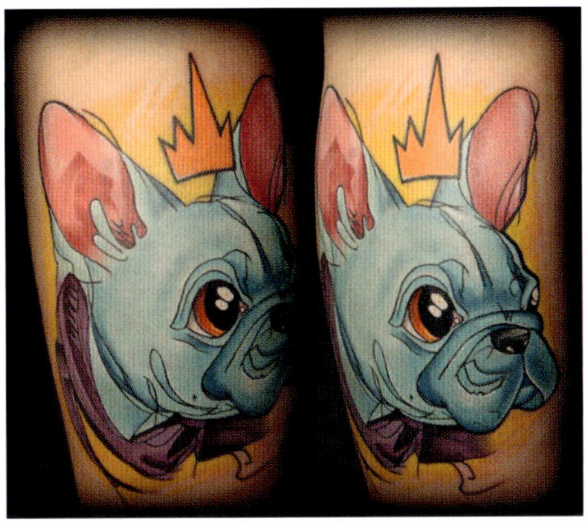

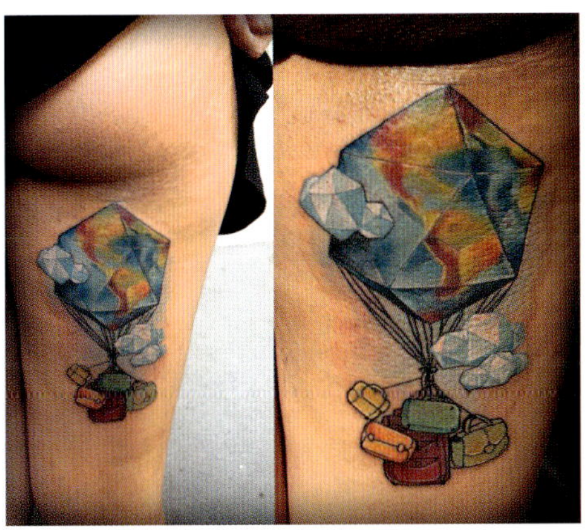

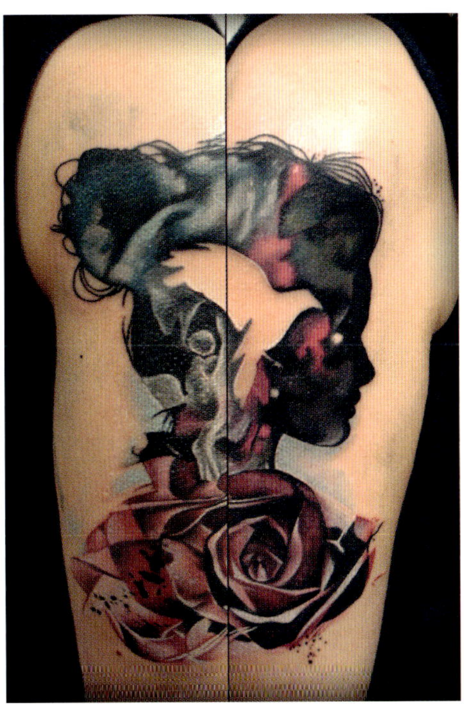

What is it like being a female artist in a primarily male workplace?

When I started to work as a tattooist there were already more women in this profession, so I didn't experience that era when only men did this sort of work. In my workplace, as a female artist, I don't feel any discrimination.

Do you feel that male customers treat you differently?

I am sure that there are people who think differently about me, but most of the people don't treat me differently, because they care about my work and not about me.

What did your family and friends think about you getting into the business?

My friends were happy and they got in line because they wanted to be the models for my practicing. *(Laughs.)* I can't say the same about my parents, they were not happy about my decision... Unfortunately my father didn't like that I was interested in drawing, because he thought it wasn't possible to earn money with it. Maybe that was the reason I really wanted to be successful and show him what I can do. My mother was a little more sympathetic, but both of them wanted me to work in a different profession, so it was really difficult to persuade them. But in the end I did it, and now I feel that they are proud of me.

What was the first tattoo you ever did?

I made my first tattoo, a diamond, on my colleague Peti Kovács's thigh. Originally I'd planned it for one of my customers, but Peti really liked the drawing and he asked me to do it. My first portrait and my first cover up were done on him too. *(Laughs.)*

Can you tell me more about the shop you work at, Skin Workshop, and what it is like working there?

I owe a big thanks to the studio because they gave me the chance to be a professional artist so that I didn't have to work at home without enough knowledge. And with the help of my colleagues—who unfortunately have since moved to other countries or to the capital, Budapest—I could develop. During

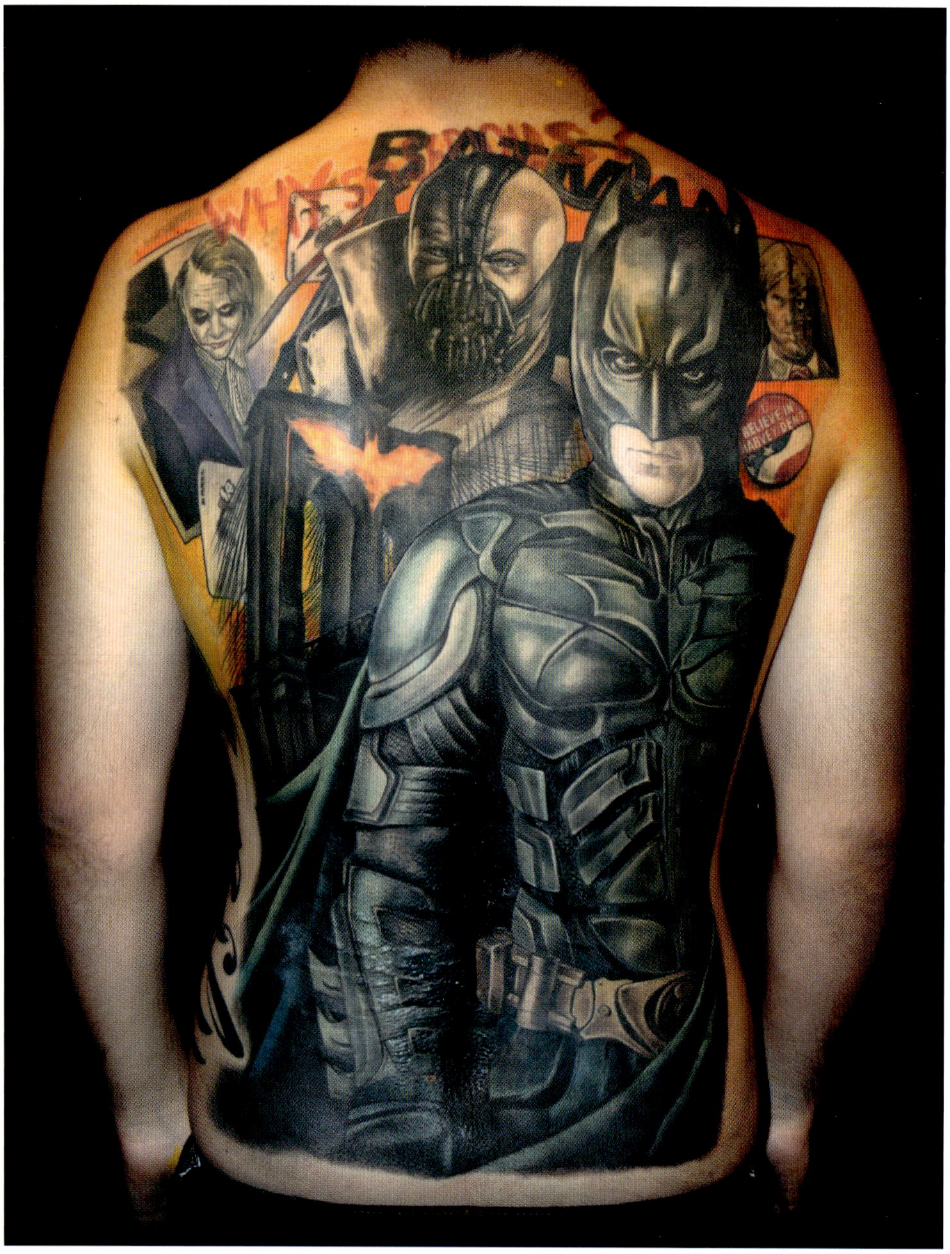

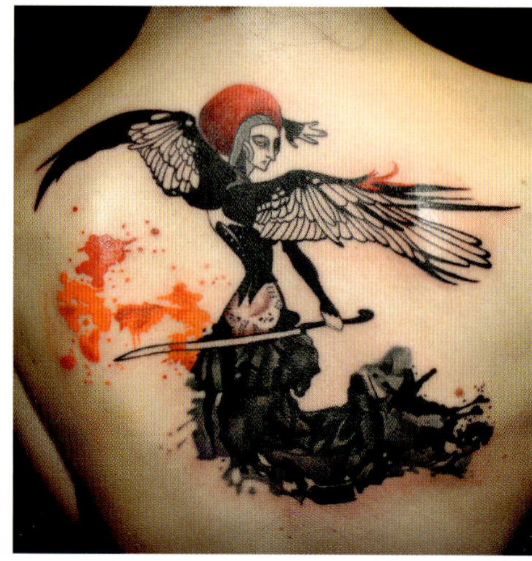

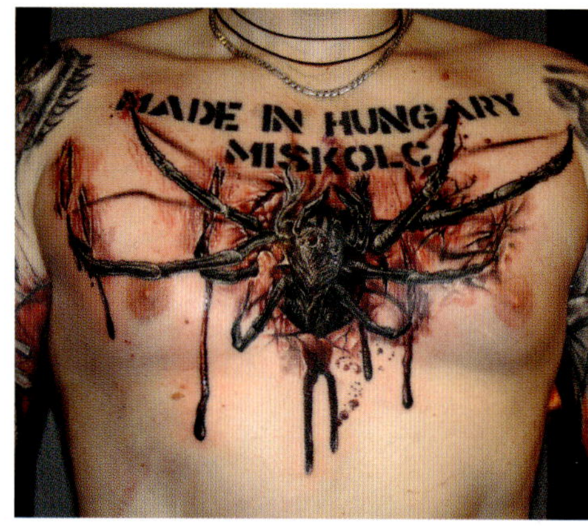
MADE IN HUNGARY
MISKOLC

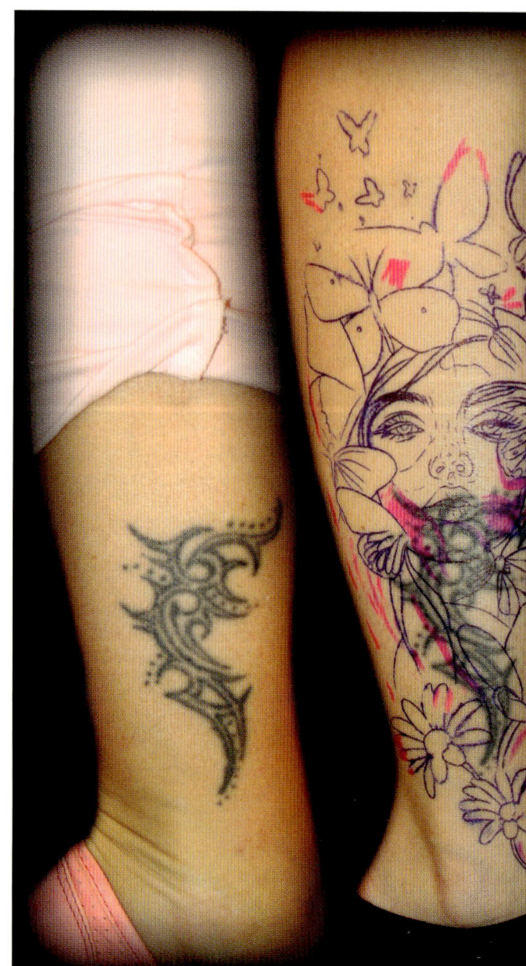

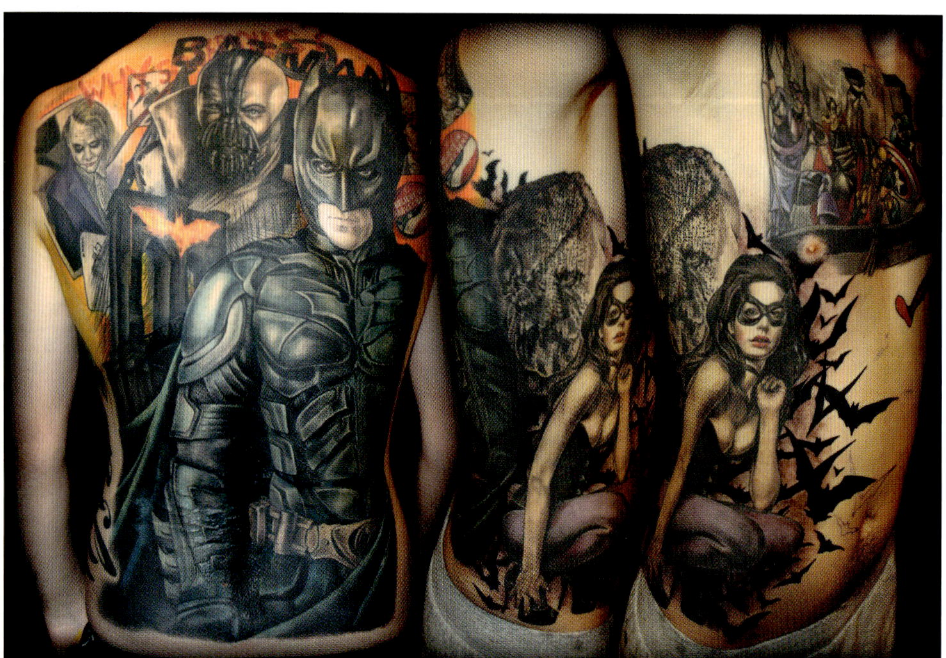

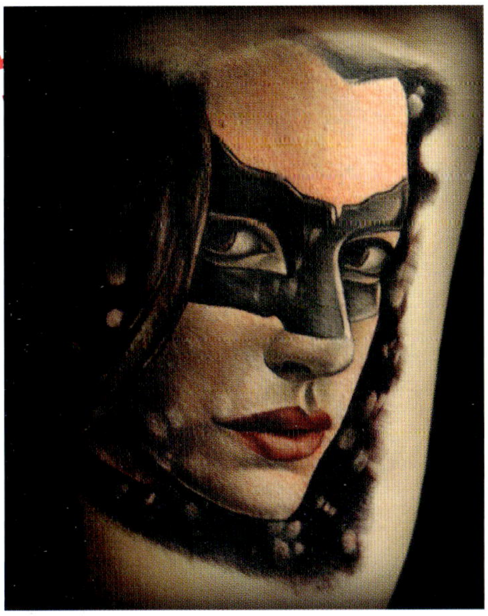

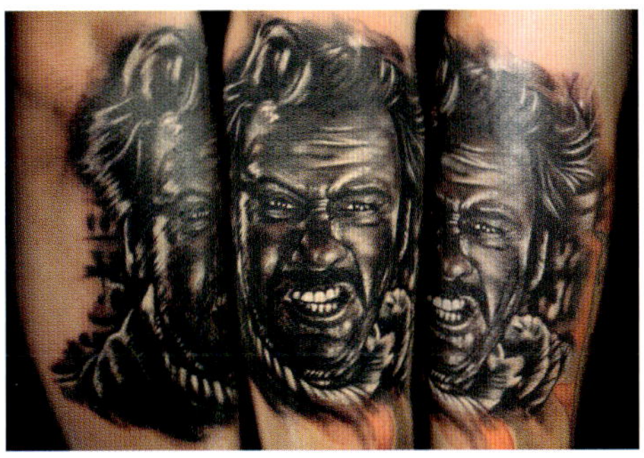

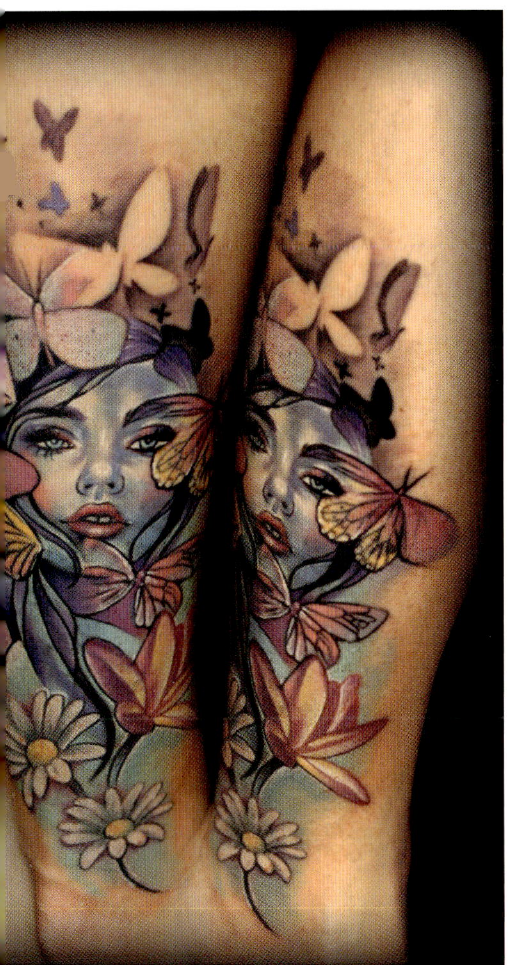

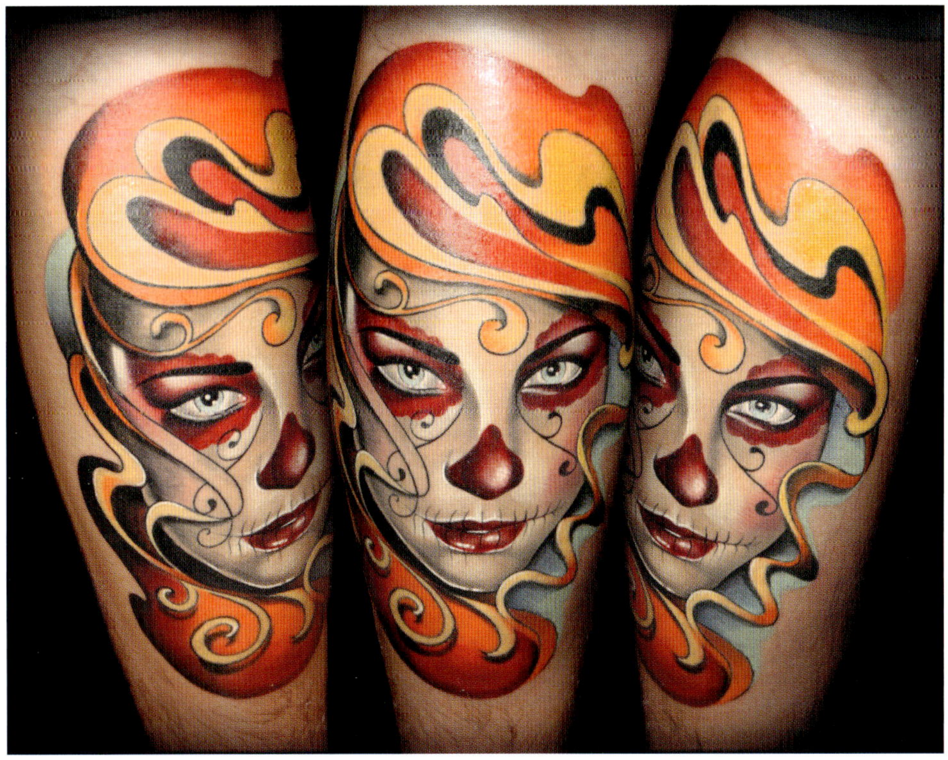

these last years I've met a lot of famous artists, too. And above all I like working here.

Describe how you go about creating a tattoo from concept to finished design. How do you try to put your own unique touch on your tattoos?

I make a special personalized design for each of my customers. I usually draw up three plans and they can choose from them. Before that, we have a consultation together to talk about the ideas. Fortunately my customers give me freedom, so this part of the process goes fluidly. I don't want to constrain my ideas and style—I want both of us to be satisfied with the upshot. Other than that, in terms of a unique style…I don't know how to describe my tattooing style, so I also don't know whether it appears in my works or not. I like realistic designs with a lot of colors. I think I am too young to have my own style.

What is your favorite style of work to tattoo? What would your dream piece be to work on?

This is a really interesting question, because I prefer creating realistic designs, but in spite of that I really love the abstract and surrealistic things. The dream tattoo for me would be to tattoo my drawing without any changes.

Describe how your role models and any other sources of inspiration have affected your tattoo style.

I would like to be equal to every other style, without anybody influencing me too much. But subconsciously, my major role models obviously affect me: the works of Marcell Jankovics, Salvador Dalí, and Kuba Kujawa.

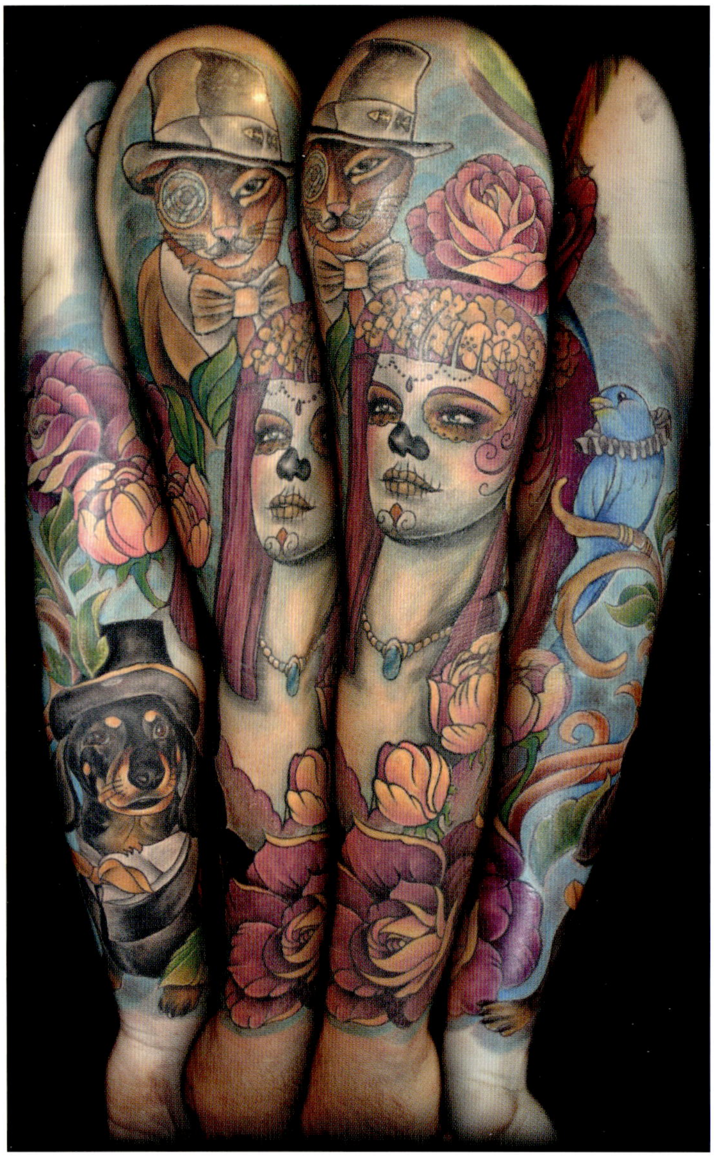

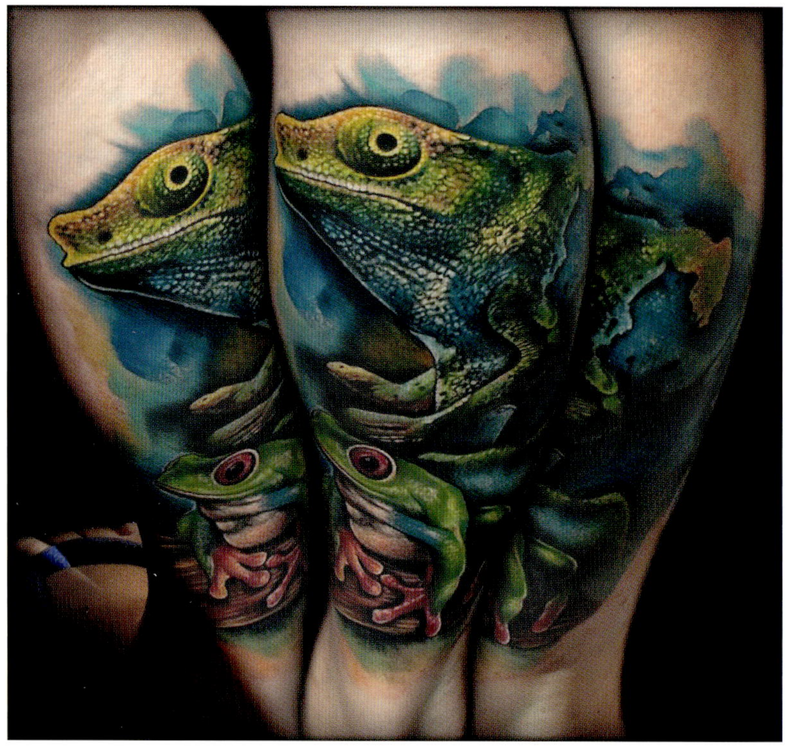

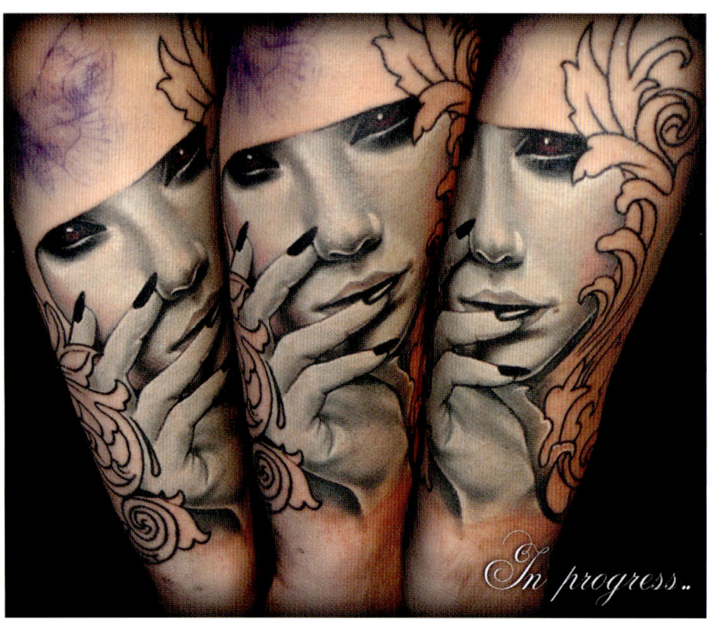
In progress..

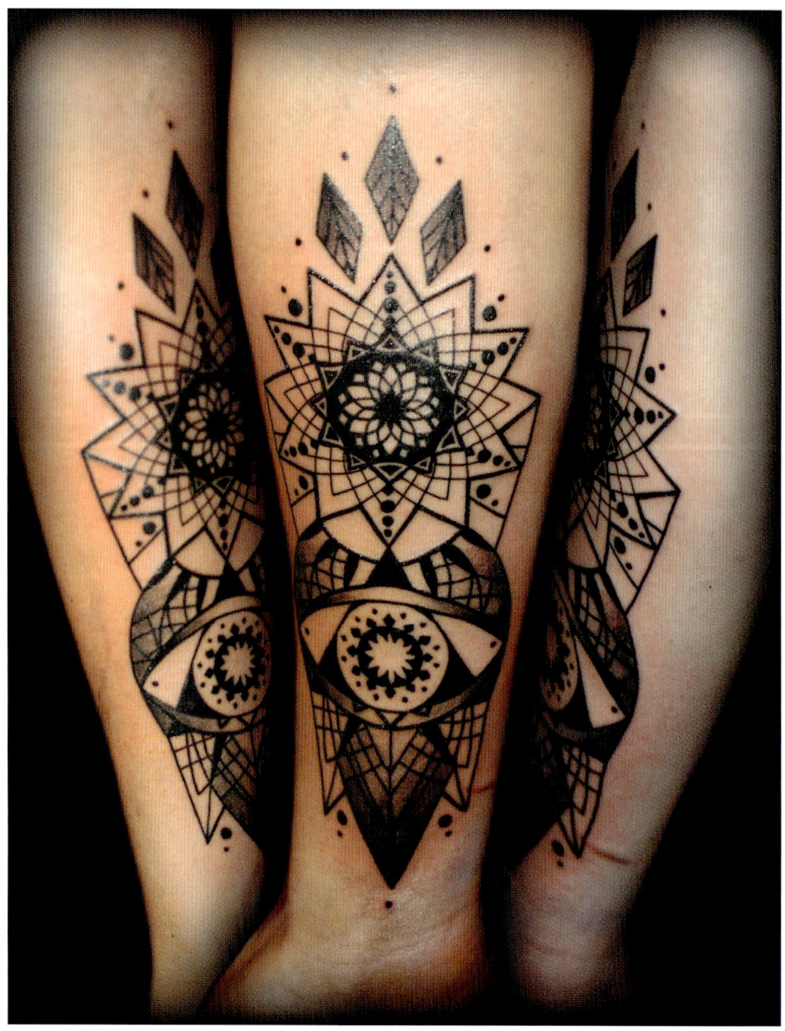

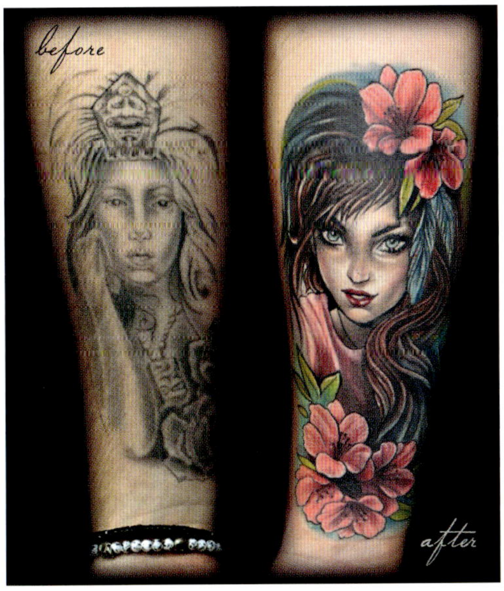

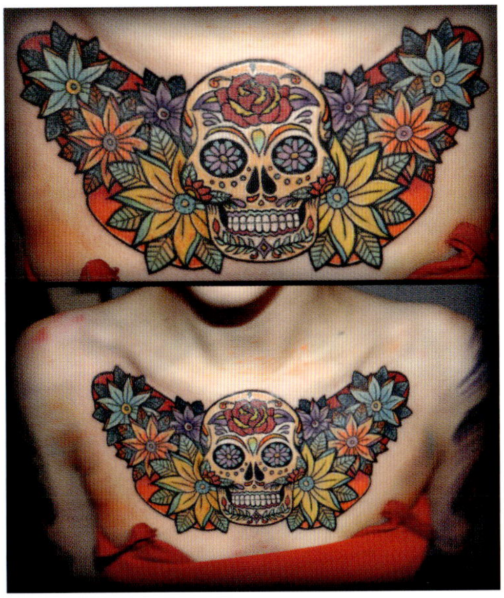

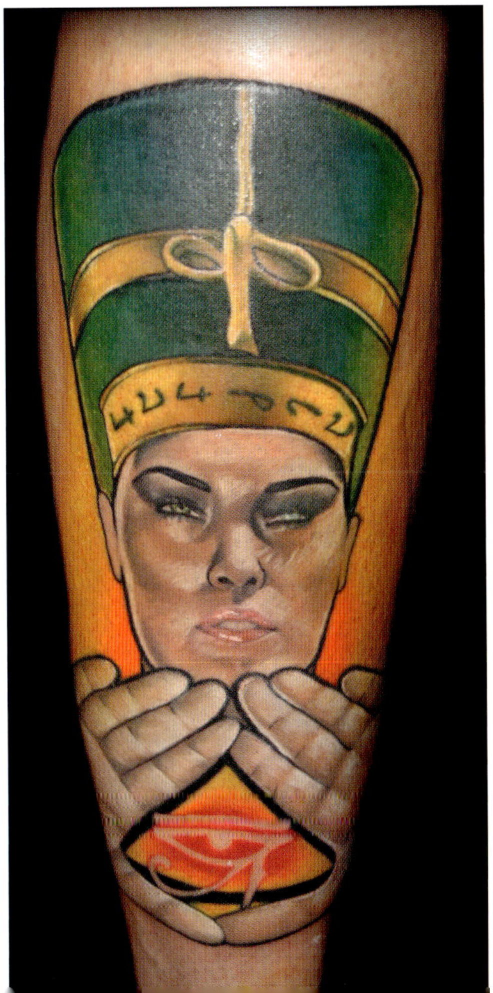

What is one of your favorite pieces that you've tattooed on someone else?

I made a four-piece black-white-red drawing series which was based on my sister's face, but changed a little bit...I tattooed three different pieces from those pictures.

What's one of your favorite pieces on your own body and who did it?

I love all of my tattoos but I would like to stress the one on my left thigh, because it was made recently, by my big role model Kuba Kujawa.

What is your favorite thing about being a tattoo artist?

Fortunately I belong to that group of people who can do what they like without any money problems. And I can travel a lot too.

Do you have a funny tattoo story?

A lot of them! *(Laughs.)* Because our studio is in the Plaza [one of the largest shopping malls in Miskolc] you can find a lot of different kinds of people here. One of my favorite stories is when a man brought a picture to us. A gladiator and a lion were fighting in front of the Colosseum. He said that he wanted the fight on his body but without that big fence in the background.

And I was really surprised too when somebody asked me to tattoo the Hungarian flag in black and white...*(Laughs.)*

You have built up such a loyal clientele. What is your waiting list like right now and what is the best way for a collector to make an appointment with you?

My schedule is full for almost a year in advance...and I have a waiting list too. The best way is for me to talk with my customers privately and face-to-face about the planned appointment, because I can get the right measurements and I can see what I should do. It makes the process smoother.

How would you describe the current status of tattoos among the general public in Hungary?

The Hungarian tattoo community is strong; everybody knows everybody, we can share our opinions and experiences, and I like that. And I think the public has started to realize that we don't do "prison tattoos" and that tattooing is a separate art.

TV shows, Internet, and especially social networks like Facebook and Twitter have come to have an extremely wide influence in recent years. What positive and negative impacts do you think it has for the future development of the tattoo industry?

On the one hand it can be positive because tattooing can spread to a lot of people, but on the other hand I don't like that TV shows change the facts and reality. This is why I haven't got a TV. I really like that with the social networks we can advertise ourselves for free, but I'm not a like hunter. *(Laughs.)*

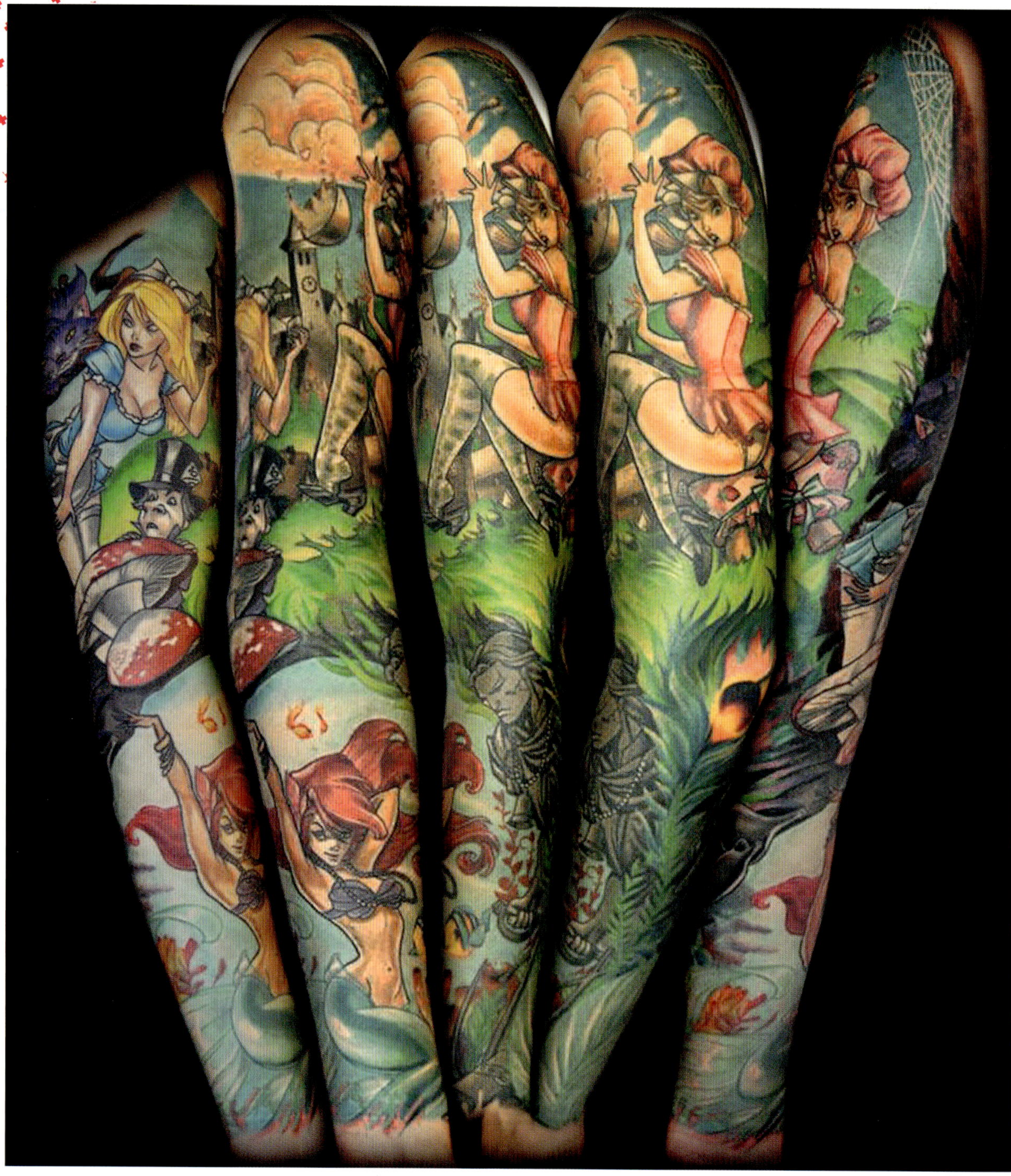

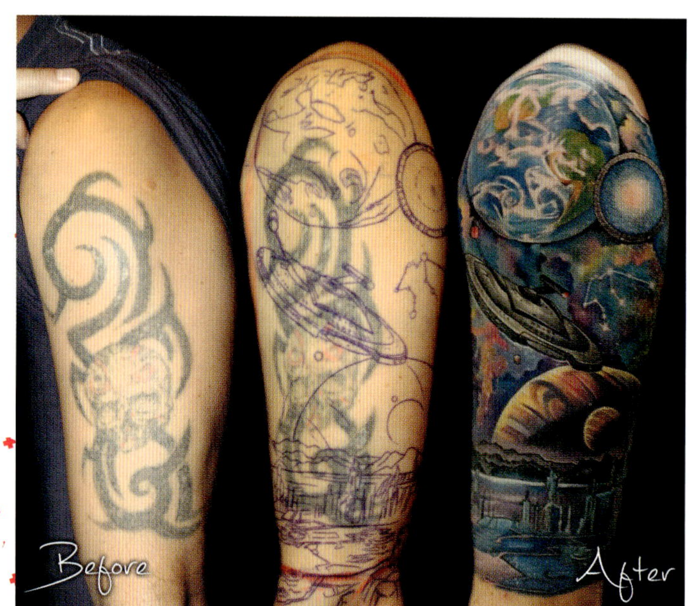
Before
After

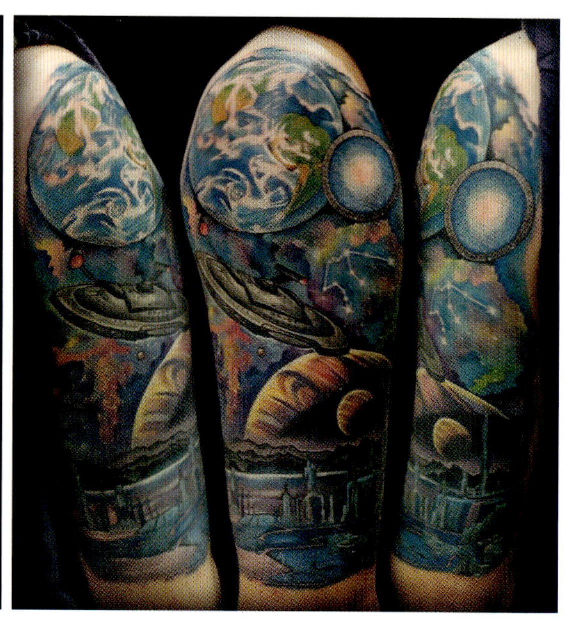

XU YI LILI

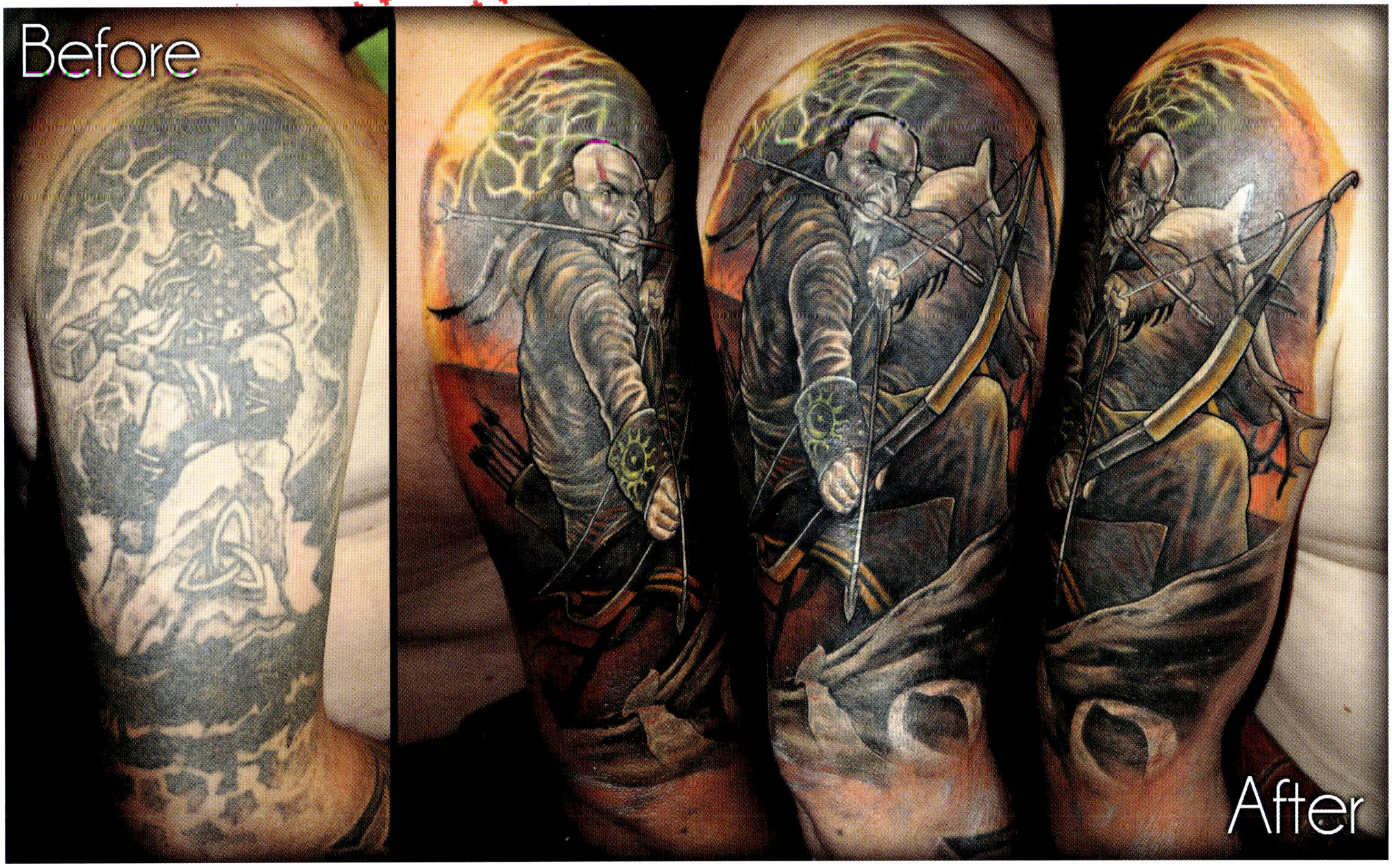

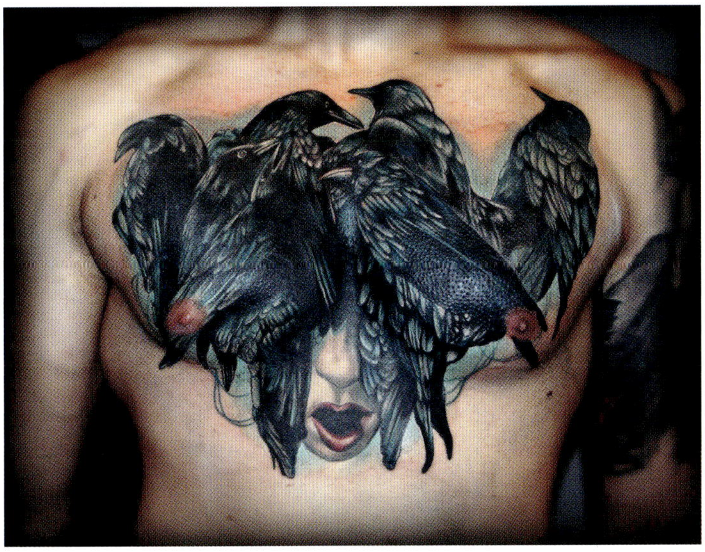

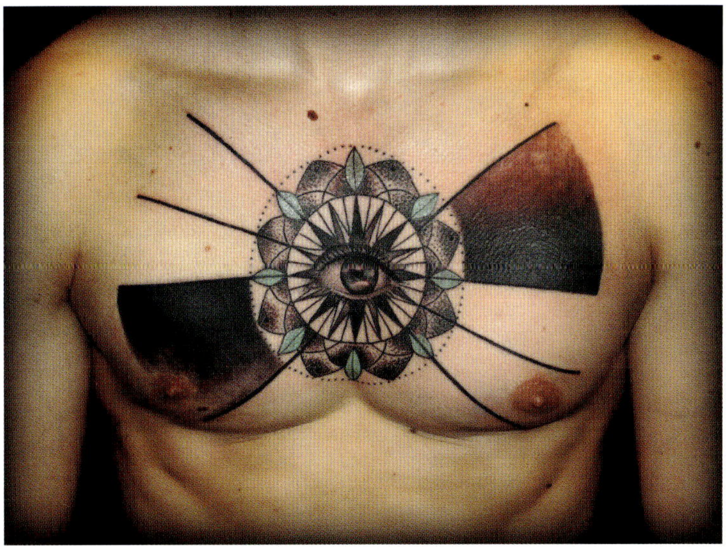

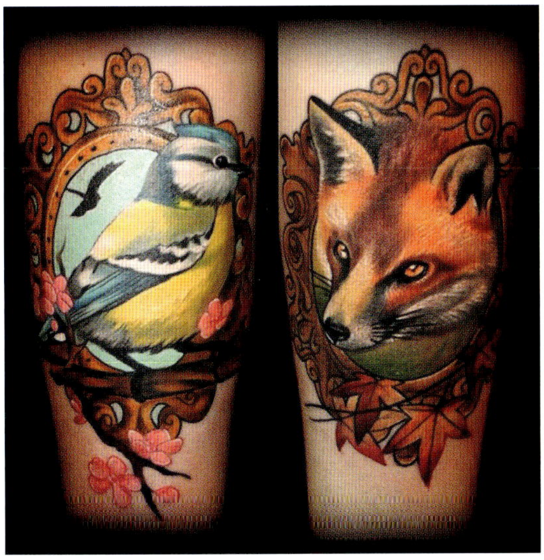

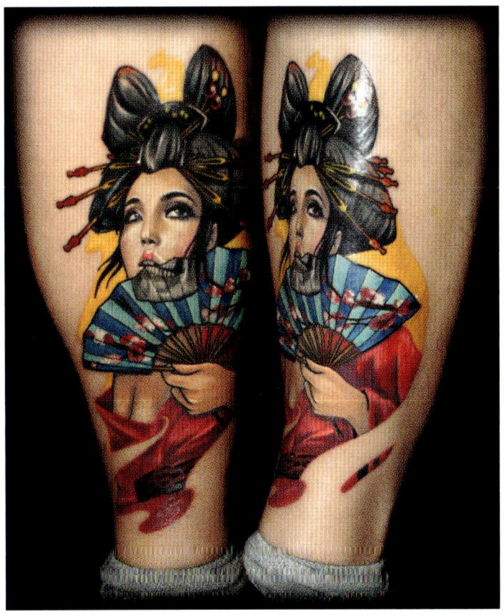

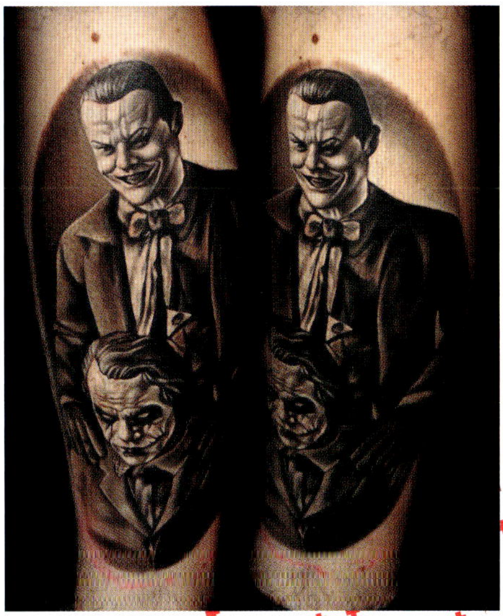

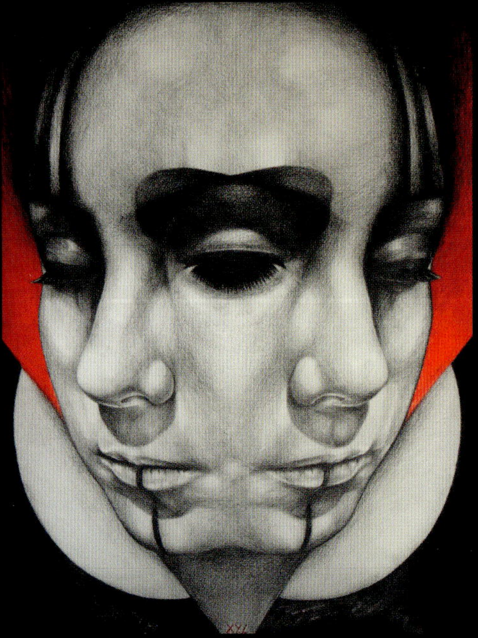
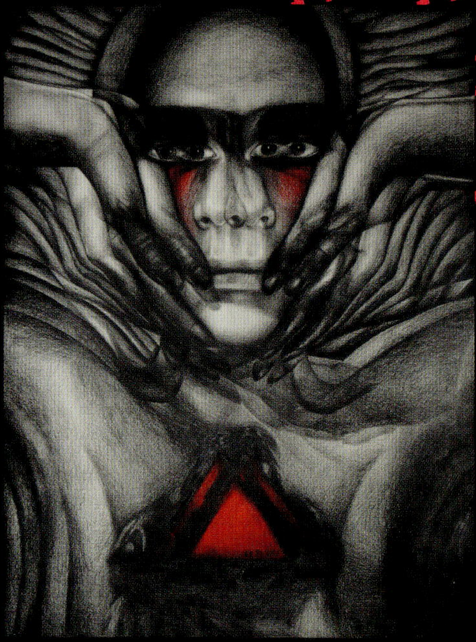
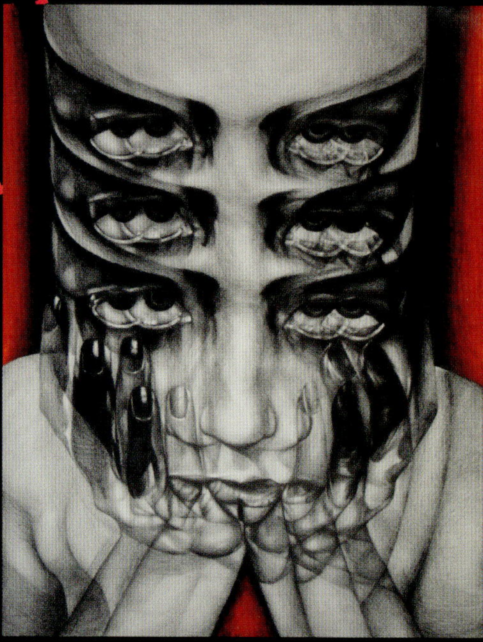
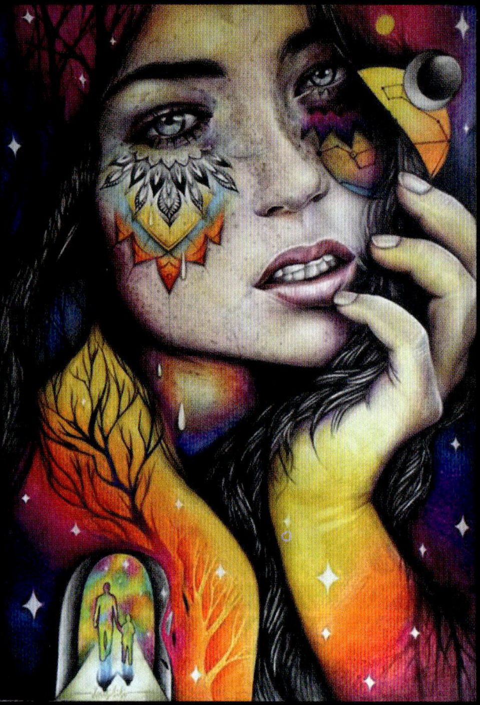
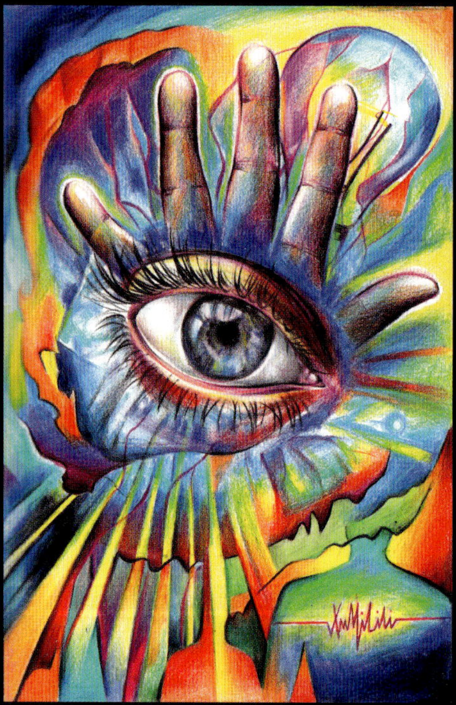
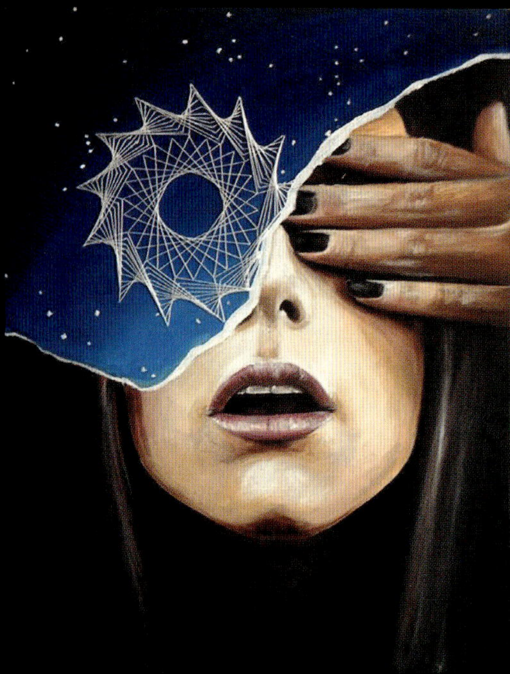
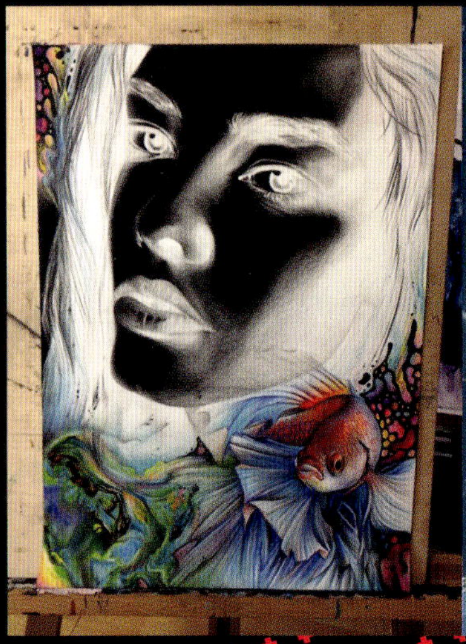
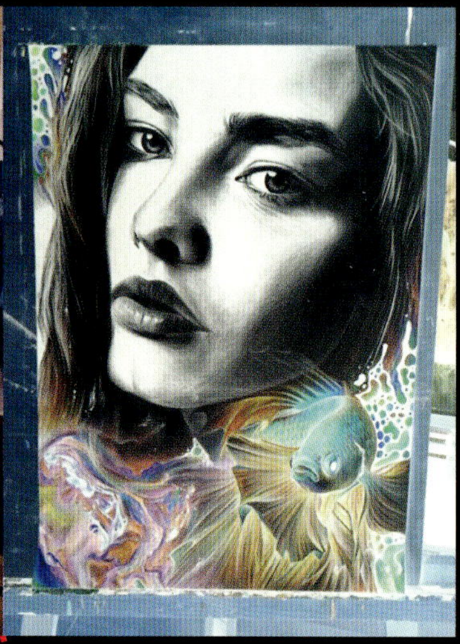
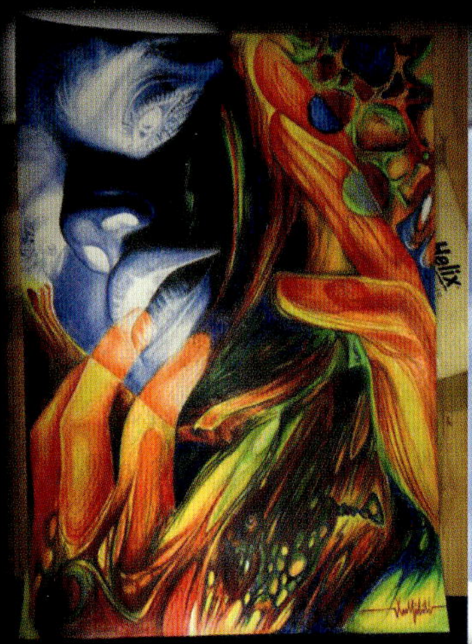
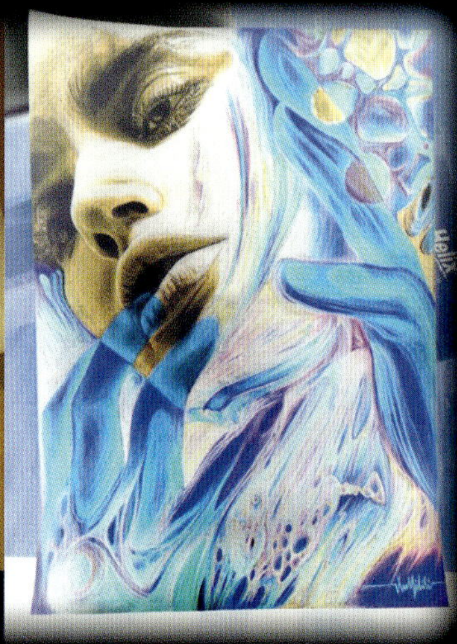

XU YI LILI

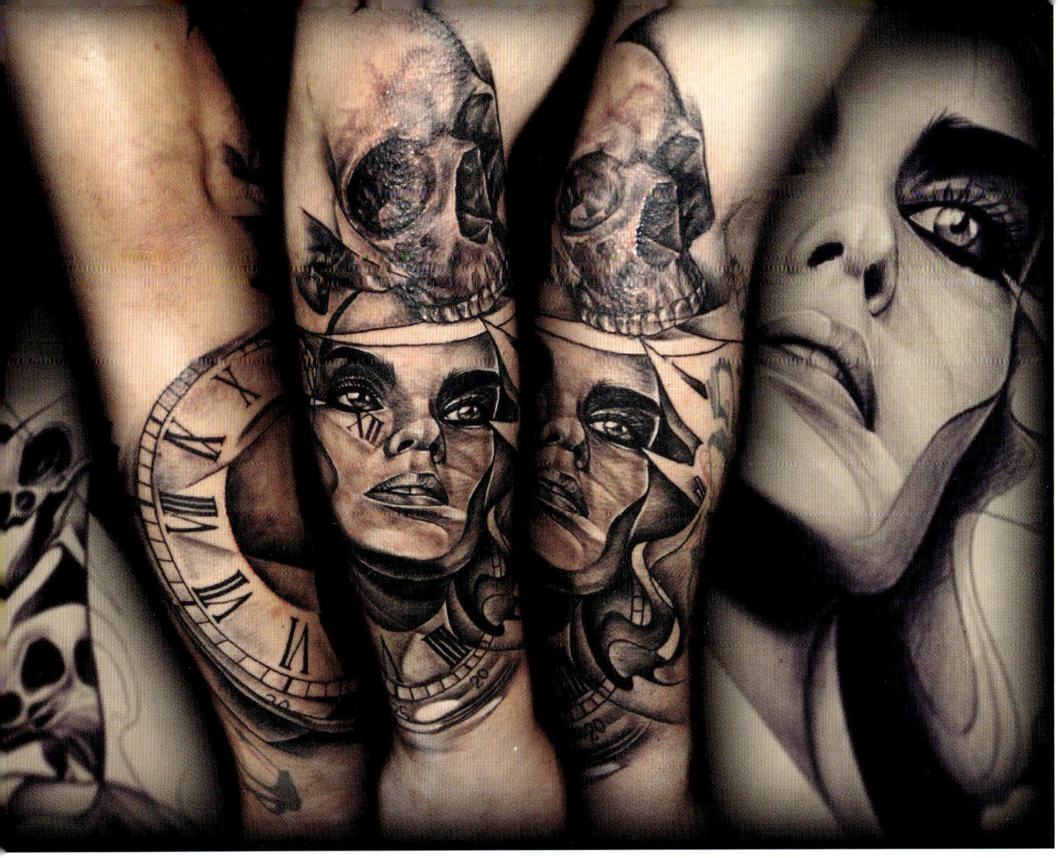

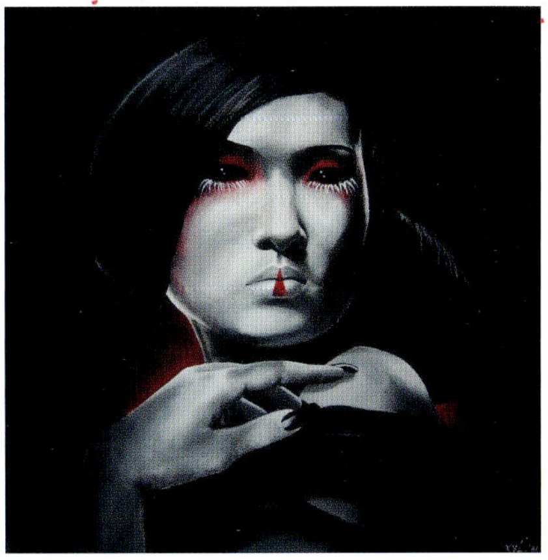

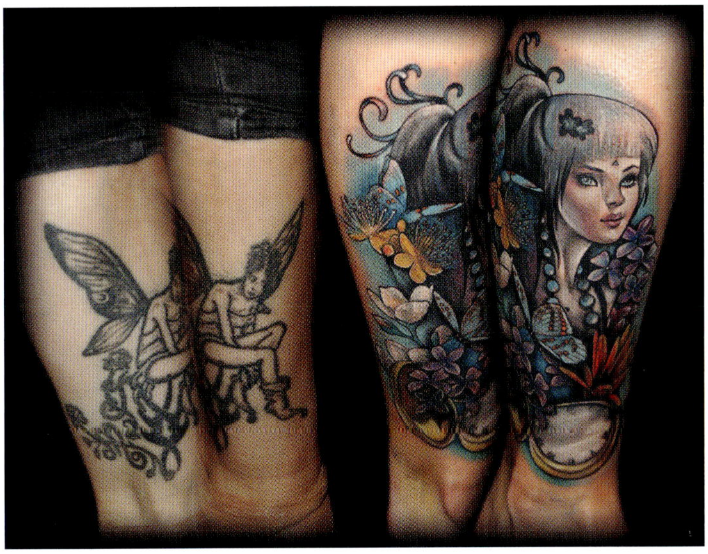

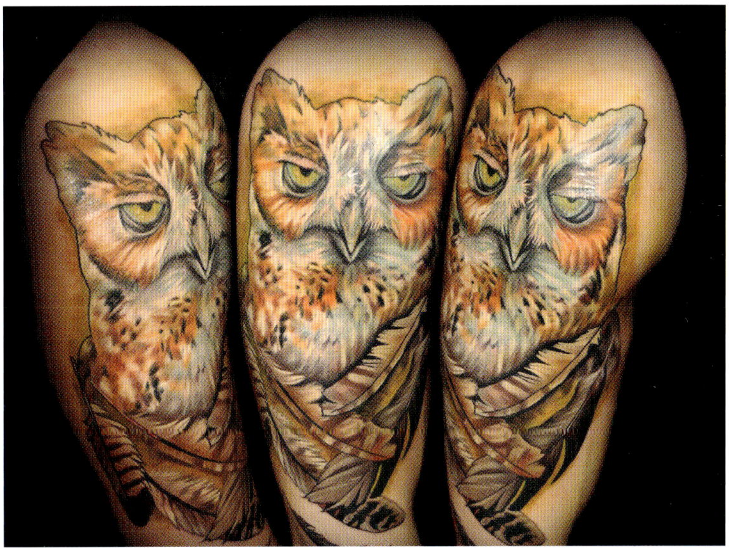

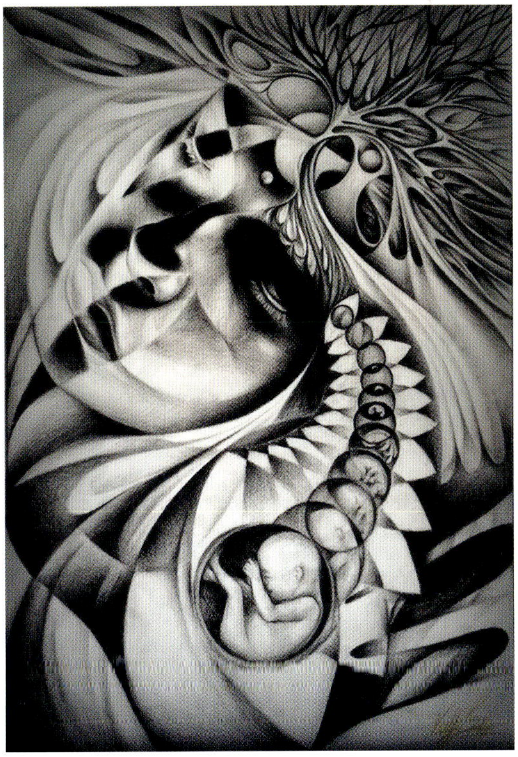

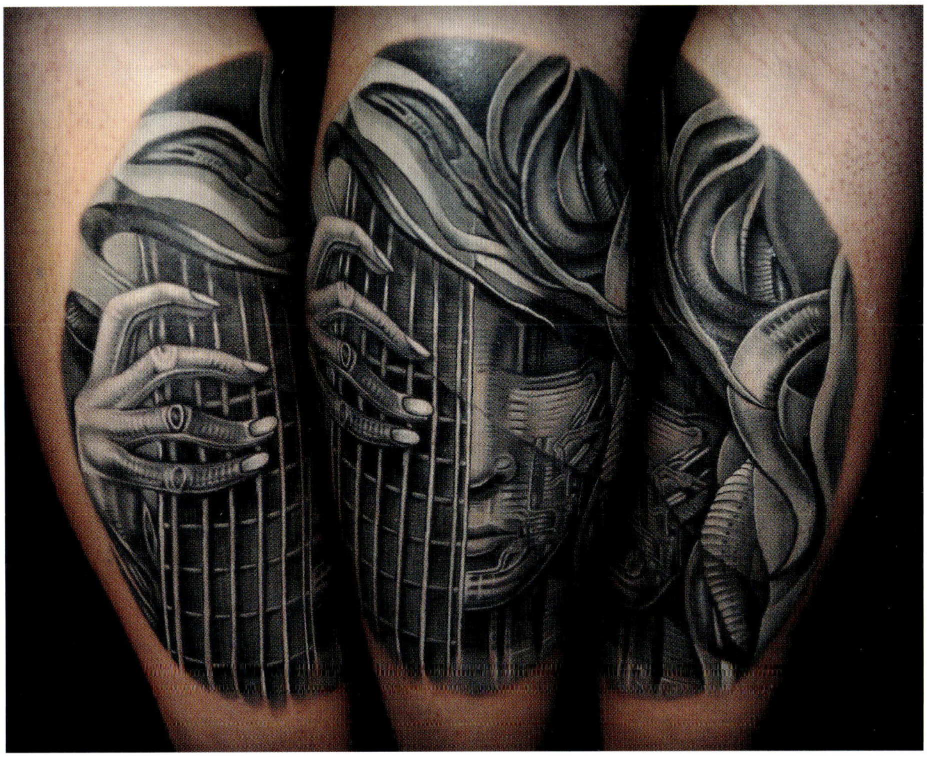

ACKNOWLEDGMENTS

I would like to say thank you to the following people for their help:

Angelika Bánfalviné Szőke, Zalán Bánfalvi, Sándor Bánfalvi, Éva Bánfalviné Kokovai, Éda Bánfalvi, Csenge Bánfalvi, Bulcsú Bánfalvi, Zsolt Bánfalvi, Diána Bánfalviné Patik, Olivér Zilahy of Troll Tattoo Studio Hungary, Alex Tyler of Black Market Art Company and Lowbrow Art Company, Candies Deezy Liu and InkSpired Magazine, Sean Hartgrove, Boldizsár Laki-Lukács of www.diffikult.com, Juan Patino, Pete Schiffer, Alex Potter, Catherine Mallette, Jesse Marth, Sandra Korinchak, Barna Bartha and the Hungarian Tattoo Magazine, Jarkko Viitasaari, Zoltán György, Viktor Szilágyi, Ferenc Mida, Gábor Mélypataki, Péter Ágoston, Krisztian Szász, Zoltán Szutor, Attila Rozsák, Csaba Krajnyák, and:

Julie Becker, Chantale Coady, Liz Cook, Petra Hlavácková, Eva Huber, Megan Hoogland, Ivana Tattoo Art, Moni Marino, Nadine Marriott, Léa Nahon, Claire Reid, Charlotte Ross, Amy Victoria Savage, Säde Sonck, Katerina Mikky Volkova, and Xu Yi Lili.